"An asset for instructors of American Indian studies."

—APRIL M. BOND, *American Indian Culture and Research Journal*

"Drawing on the activist-intellectual's personal papers and less well-known writings from the period, *Life of the Indigenous Mind* is more than mere commentary. Moreover, the book's critical edge distinguishes it from prior scholarship that erred toward hagiography. Overall, it is a long-overdue addition to the existing literature on Vine Deloria, Jr., and on Red Power more generally."

—JOHN H. CABLE, *American Indian Quarterly*

"As David Martínez observes, the Indigenous mind is the Indigenous community's most potent weapon against colonialism. This powerful statement triggers a challenging responsibility: to identify the types of ideas that should inform the efforts of Indigenous intellectuals. Martínez charts a framework for future intersectional analysis, providing an important contribution to the growth of American Indian intellectualism. This book offers a magnificent appraisal of Vine Deloria Jr.'s legacy and the power of critical thought."

—REBECCA TSOSIE, Regents Professor of Law at the University of Arizona and faculty co-chair of the Indigenous Peoples Law and Policy Program at the James E. Rogers College of Law

"David Martínez transcends hagiography in this complex analysis of four key early works by Vine Deloria Jr. This fascinating book takes a deep dive into Deloria's thinking. Martínez does an admirable job of both placing these works in the historical context of turbulent changes in Indian affairs in the United States and illuminating Deloria's intellectual acumen as he challenged federal bureaucrats, academia, the public at large, and, perhaps most significantly, Indian Country to rethink the place of American Indians in the United States."

—DAVID R. M. BECK, professor of Native American studies at the University of Montana

LIFE OF THE INDIGENOUS MIND

**New Visions in Native American
and Indigenous Studies**

SERIES EDITORS

Margaret D. Jacobs
Robert J. Miller

Life of the Indigenous Mind

Vine Deloria Jr. and the Birth of the Red Power Movement

DAVID MARTÍNEZ

CO-PUBLISHED BY THE UNIVERSITY OF NEBRASKA PRESS

AND THE AMERICAN PHILOSOPHICAL SOCIETY

The University of Nebraska Press is part of a land-grant institution
with campuses and programs on the past, present, and future
homelands of the Pawnee, Ponca, Otoe-Missouria, Omaha, Dakota,
Lakota, Kaw, Cheyenne, and Arapaho Peoples, as well as those
of the relocated Ho-Chunk, Sac and Fox, and Iowa Peoples.

First Nebraska paperback printing: 2022

Library of Congress Cataloging-in-Publication Data

Names: Martinez, David, 1963–, author.
Title: Life of the indigenous mind: Vine Deloria Jr. and the
birth of the Red Power movement / David Martinez.
Other titles: New visions in Native American and indigenous studies.
Description: Lincoln: Co-published by the University of
Nebraska Press and the American Philosophical Society, [2019] |
Series: New visions in Native American and indigenous
studies | Includes bibliographical references and index.
Identifiers: LCCN 2018045053
ISBN 9781496211903 (cloth)
ISBN 9781496232618 (paperback)
ISBN 9781496213563 (epub)
ISBN 9781496213570 (mobi)
ISBN 9781496213587 (pdf)
Subjects: LCSH: Deloria, Vine. | Indian authors—United States
—Biography. | Indian activists—United States—Biography. |
LCGFT: Biographies.
Classification: LCC E90.D45 M37 2019 | DDC 810.8/0897—dc23
LC record available at https://lccn.loc.gov/2018045053

Set in Charis by Mikala R. Kolander.
Designed by N. Putens.

CONTENTS

ACKNOWLEDGMENTS

Similar to John Donne's proverbial island, the writing of this book only occurred because of its deep connection to a world of friends and colleagues, all of whom played roles, great and small, in the development of the present volume. Indeed, the first thank you goes to Vine Deloria Jr. (Standing Rock Sioux), whom I fondly remember for his support of my work as an undergraduate philosophy student, even sending me a much-needed letter of encouragement when I was looking for guidance while far from home. "If you can get thoroughly grounded in western philosophy without losing your confidence that the tribal traditions contain a good many sophisticated ideas that need proper elaboration in western terminology, you could do an invaluable service to Indians." Although my scholarly career moved from philosophy to American Indian studies, thanks to Deloria's influence, I never lost my confidence that tribal traditions were a source of profound ideas and wisdom.

The next word of gratitude goes to David E. Wilkins (Lumbee), who at one time taught a seminar on federal Indian law and policy for the American Indian studies master's program at the University of Arizona, where Dave and I met. He later became one of my most valued colleagues at the University of Minnesota's Twin Cities Campus. In fact, it was thanks to Dave that I had the opportunity to spend nearly two decades as an American Indian studies scholar and teacher. During our seven years working together, more specifically, my former professor shared countless anecdotes about his revered mentor, whom he always referred to as "Vine," which over time informed my perception of his work. In fact, Dave and I were colleagues when Vine passed away in November 2005.

As my work in American Indian intellectual history grew, one of the first times I ever spoke about my plans to do a book on Vine was at the 2012 Indigenous Book Festival at the University of New Mexico, where I had the honor of seeing Vine's younger brother Sam Deloria (Standing Rock Sioux) in the audience. Sam and I had known each other for a while at that point, thanks to social media. However, upon hearing of my intentions to write a book about Vine, Sam sent me a very thoughtful and illuminating email containing his feelings and opinions about his brother's work and legacy. In fact, Sam displayed great candor, sharing tales and critiques about his brother's writings, especially *Custer*. While Sam did not dispute Vine's rightful place in the history of American Indian/Native American studies, he was also aware that much of what had been written about Vine was largely limited to laudatory essays, which were short on critical analysis. With that in mind, Sam encouraged me to resist the temptation to simply produce a "hagiography" and to "hold him [Vine] to the highest critical standards." Indeed, some of the criticisms to which Vine's work is subjected to below were initiated by Sam's perceptive and thought-provoking message. With respect to the above event, thank-yous are in order to Beverly Singer (Santa Clara Pueblo) for inviting me and to Amanda Cobb-Greetham (Chickasaw) for being such a wonderful copanelist.

As the present work began to mature into what it is today, I was fortunate to share my research with friends and colleagues at the 2013 Great Plains Writers' Conference at South Dakota State University, which held a two-day meeting dedicated to Deloria's work and legacy. Thank you to Steven Wingate for organizing this splendid event. Needless to say, I appreciated the opportunity to present on the same program as Elizabeth Cook-Lynn (Crow Creek Sioux) and Philip J. Deloria. Then, at the 2013 Western Social Sciences Association annual conference held in Denver, Colorado, I had another remarkable experience. Thank you to Leo Killsback (Northern Cheyenne) and Cheryl Bennett (Navajo) for organizing the American Indian Studies panels and allowing me to present on the same program with David Wilkins. Finally, at the 2016 Organization of American Historians annual conference held at Providence, Rhode Island, I enjoyed a robust discussion about Deloria's historical impact on archeology and the social sciences. Thank you to Gregory Smithers for organizing our panel and to Daniel Cobb and Sherry Smith for joining us.

At the point when this project matured to a level where I was actually producing chapter drafts, a number of people appeared in my scholarly life at just the right time. Among those who deserve a word of sincere thanks is Ranjit Arab, who was the acquisitions editor for another press, who gave me the idea of focusing on Vine's Red Power–era writings, as opposed to "trying to do it all." At this phase of my project, I was fortunate to get some insightful and immensely helpful feedback from Tsianina Lomawaima, which went a long way at enabling me to refine my scholarly vision. Of course, what my readers hold in their hands today would not have been possible without the copious and brilliant feedback that I received from two anonymous peer reviewers, arranged for by my outstanding editor at the University of Nebraska Press, Matthew Bokovoy. Their respective comments were invaluable at helping me shape this epic discourse into the work that bears Vine Deloria Jr.'s name.

Also, I want to thank the graduate students that, since 2013, took my seminar on Vine Deloria Jr.'s work and legacy at Arizona State University. Their energy and enthusiasm for reading, discussing, and debating Vine's opinions and ideas buoyed my spirit, giving me the impetus to create a work that not only honored the generation about which Vine wrote and influenced, but also the generation of young scholars and activists who still need Vine's intellectual leadership as much as their elders. With that in mind, thank you to Lorena Yaiva (Havasupai), Laura Medina (Ojibwe), Cliff Kaye (Hopi), Eric Hardy (Navajo), Waquin Preston (Navajo), Janel Striped-Wolf (Lakota), Naomi Tom (Tohono O'odham), Justin Hongeva (Hopi), Emery Tahy (Navajo), Stephanie Honeycutt (Salt River Pima), Marlena Robbins (Navajo), Ona Austin (Lakota), Taylor Strelevitz, Delphina Thomas (Navajo), and Dorothy Rhodes (Gila River Pima). Speaking of my Arizona State University family, I cannot thank enough my program director, James Riding In (Pawnee), and my dean,

Libby Wentz, for allowing me to take a semester sabbatical. While relatively brief, the time away from teaching and committee work enabled me to devote hundreds of hours to this project that I would not have otherwise been able to find.

Speaking of my research, I want to thank Cal Vornberger, director of digital media, Daphne Productions, dickcavettshow.com, for his assistance about a pressing question regarding Vine's activist career and the media. Also, a sincere thank you to Joyce Martin, librarian and curator of the Labriola National American Indian Data Center, Hayden Library, Arizona State University, for her much-appreciated assistance at helping me amass copies of the *NCAI Sentinel Bulletin*. Also, a sincere word of gratitude to Dolores Colon, Beinecke Rare Book and Manuscript Library, Yale University, for the superb job she did at assisting me with accessing vital material in the Vine Deloria Jr. Papers.

As with any life-changing journey, there are always an array of unexpected people who help you to get further along to your destination, providing advice and information that turn out to be keys that open doors in your mind that you did not even know were there. In light of which, I want to thank Imani Perry, African American studies, Princeton University; Bryan Brayboy (Lumbee), Arizona State University; and Thomas Cowger (Chickasaw), East Central University. Lastly, the most heartfelt thank you goes to my wife, Sharon, who not only tolerated me obsessing over my work day and night, seven days a week, but also was my muse and confidante. Thank you, Sharon. You make me feel like I can do anything!

LIFE OF THE INDIGENOUS MIND

Prologue

Fanfare for the American Indian

Appearing in 1967, Stan Steiner's *The New Indians* showed its readers a
Vine Deloria Jr. who was articulate, wry, and insightful about the world
of Indian politics. More specifically, Deloria emerged as a major Indian
thinker in *The New Indians* through a series of anecdotes, which Steiner
had assembled from traveling the country and speaking with the key
players in an Indian protest movement that Steiner referred to as "Red
Power." Whenever Deloria appeared, he was typically sharing his opinion
about the generation of young Indians that had surfaced since the end
of World War II that Deloria characterized as "thinking for themselves,"
which in itself sounded trite, yet signified a growing awareness that the
reservations were actually home to Indigenous nations in which sovereign
peoples endured, not "wards" of the Bureau of Indian Affairs. Deloria also
expressed enthusiasm for the Indian students who were conscientiously
learning their culture and history, for the ability that reservation Indians
had for adapting small businesses to the local economy, and for how
the "Indian has a free spirit," for which "his tribe is his source."[1] As an
initial contribution to the study of Deloria's life and work, Steiner did
the most to present to readers the integral relationship between Deloria's
developing political agenda of tribal self-determination, his critique
of Western politics and religion, and the forge that was his leadership
position in the National Congress of American Indians.

Two years later, when Vine Deloria Jr.'s first major publication appeared in 1969, it marked a sea change in American Indian political activism as well as a turning point in American Indian intellectual history. Charles Wilkinson would later describe *Custer Died for Your Sins: An Indian Manifesto* as "widely read and influential," with an impact that "altered the political landscape."[2] Indeed, when Dee Brown, author of *Bury My Heart at Wounded Knee*, reviewed Deloria's *Behind the Trail of Broken Treaties* for the *New York Times*, he stated at the outset: "Among his people Vine Deloria Jr. has achieved a status somewhat similar to that of Sitting Bull's leadership of the Sioux tribes a century ago," not as a warrior but as a "strategist," a "thinker," and a "planner."[3] As for *Custer*, upon its release during the fall publishing season—just a few months after N. Scott Momaday won the Pulitzer for *House Made of Dawn*—it catapulted its author into celebrity status; and as Rep. Lloyd Meeds (D-MT) said, he became a national spokesman for Indian people, complete with two reviews in the *New York Times* (Edward Abbey[4] and John Leonard[5]), features in major trade publications (*Playboy Magazine*[6] and the *New York Times*[7]), and appearances on nationally televised talk shows (*The Dick Cavett Show* and *The Merv Griffin Show*).[8] However, it was Deloria's influence on his Indian readers that mattered more than his appeal to the American public. For it was his recognition from Indian readers that was his greatest sense of accomplishment. At the same time, some Indian readers expressed the most poignant criticisms, such as W. Roger Buffalohead (Ponca),[9] who raised questions about Deloria's opposition to "militant action," and Alfonso Ortiz (San Juan Pueblo), who focused on Deloria's predilection for Plains-oriented references.[10] As for non-Indian critics, of course they were plentiful among anthropologists. However, one of the more perceptive critics of Deloria's political agenda was Francis Paul Prucha, author of *The Great Father*, who challenged the foundation of Deloria's treaty-based notion of tribal sovereignty.[11] There are also the critiques that have yet to be made—many of which are beyond the scope of the present work—such as an Indigenous feminist analysis of both the portrayal of women in Deloria's writings and their obvious absence from much of his work, not to mention his tenuous relationship with the hemispheric Indigenous movements, most notably in Mexico, Peru, and Brazil. Like any other historically important figure, the luster of the legend was complicated by the shadows of the legend's shortcomings. Deloria, in this regard, is no less of an historic figure.

As part of the late-1960s counterculture, *Custer*'s ascent into bestseller status was due in large part to riding a nearly decade-long wave of headline-generating activism created by the Chicago American Indian Conference (1961),[12] the formation of the National Indian Youth Council (1961),[13] the Pacific Northwest fish-ins (1964),[14] and the more recent occupation of Alcatraz Island by a group calling itself the Indians of All Tribes (1969–71).[15] Indeed, *Custer*'s appearance and sudden ascension was instigated in part by the occupation of a former federal prison in the middle of San Francisco Bay:

> The Alcatraz news stories are somewhat shocking to non-Indians. It is difficult for most Americans to comprehend that there still exists a living community of nearly one million Indians in this country. For many people, Indians have become a species of movie actor periodically dispatched to the Happy Hunting Grounds by John Wayne on the "Late, Late Show." Yet there are some 315 tribal groups in 26 states still functioning as quasi-sovereign nations under treaty status.[16]

In this context, the University of Colorado law student and former executive director of the National Congress of American Indians stipulated a political agenda complete with an emotional impetus for a generation of Indians agitating for an end to the termination policy that was devastating reservations, which sought an end to the federal government's fiduciary, legal, and moral obligations to tribes. Tribal leaders, tribal elders, and young Indian college students wanted a change in Indian affairs that profoundly respected the tribal sovereignty that they saw affirmed in hundreds of ratified treaties. Although American Indian writer-activists had long been a part of the American political landscape—beginning with Samson Occom, an eighteenth-century Mohegan minister—for many *Custer* was the first time they had ever seen a book about the "Indian experience," written by someone from a contemporary Indigenous community as opposed to historic speeches or as-told-to autobiographies, all of which referred their numerous readers to the lives and times of people in the distant past. Theodora Kroeber, for example, published two highly regarded and popular books about "the last Yahi": *Ishi in Two Worlds; A Biography of the Last Wild Indian in North America* (1961) and *Ishi, Last of His Tribe* (1964).[17] Additionally, there were the popular books on Indian history that Alvin Josephy Jr. wrote during the 1960s, namely *The Patriot Chiefs* (1961),[18] *Chief Joseph's People and Their War* (1964), and *The Indian Heritage of America* (1968).[19] In contrast, for many Indian readers, *Custer* was more than a manifesto, it was a revelation. Indeed, other than *Custer*, there was very little that was available that spoke about the contemporary Indian experience, excepting rare titles like *Indians and Other Americans: Two Ways of Life Meet* (1959) by Harold E. Fey and D'Arcy McNickle and *The New Indians* (1967) by Stan Steiner. Appearing at a time when American Indian/ Native American studies were being established as an academic program at various universities, starting with the University of Minnesota and San Francisco State, *Custer* played an immediate role at influencing the curricula and scholarly projects at developing Indigenous institutions. Minnesota, of course, was where Buffalohead, noted above, served as the first chair of the Department of American Indian Studies.

The origin of *Custer Died for Your Sins*, however, as an idea whose time had come was much more down to earth. As Deloria recounted, the infamous leader of the U.S. 7th Cavalry was the butt of numerous jokes. Even among tribes far away from the Plains, belittling George Armstrong Custer was greatly appreciated. As for the enigmatic phrase "Custer died for your sins," Deloria remembered it as part of the Indian humor tradition:

> Some years ago we put out a bumper sticker which read "Custer Died for Your Sins." It was originally meant as a dig at the National Council of Churches.[20] But as it spread around the nation it took on additional meaning until everyone claimed to understand it and each interpretation was different.
>
> Originally, the Custer bumper sticker referred to the Sioux Treaty of 1868 signed at Fort Laramie in which the United States pledged to give free and undisturbed use of the lands claimed by Red Cloud in

return for peace. Under the covenants of the Old Testament, breaking a covenant called for a blood sacrifice for the United States breaking the Sioux treaty. That, at least originally, was the meaning of the slogan.[21]

Although it was unclear whom Deloria meant by "we" in the above passage, he did make clear the practical intent of the slogan.[22] The anecdote also shed light on the purpose of Deloria's book bearing the same declaration. More to the point, *Custer* was an intense and focused response to the broken covenants that defined United States–Indian treaty relations, replete with stolen lands, forced removals, and an oppressive reservation system.[23] Moreover, *Custer* was a caustic critique of the racist stereotypes that had from the earliest days besotted Indian affairs, the federal policies and statutes that arose from these, and the series of perfidious Supreme Court decisions that have continued to hamstring Indigenous sovereignty and self-determination. In light of which, Deloria states as the objective of *Custer*:

> In this book we will discuss the other side—the unrealities that face *us* as Indian people. It is this unreal feeling that has been welling up inside us and threatens to make this decade [the 1970s] the most decisive in history for Indian people. In so many ways, Indian people are re-examining themselves in an effort to redefine a new social structure for their people [emphasis in original].[24]

From the outset, Deloria unapologetically referred to "us," meaning other Indians like him, like you and I, as his primary audience. Indeed, even at the end of his discourse, Deloria underscored that Indian readers, especially young readers, were his primary concern: "One reason I wanted to write [this book] was to raise some issues for younger Indians which they have not been raising for themselves." Toward that objective, Deloria sought to goad these young Indian readers into "bringing to the surface the greatness that is in them," instead of milling "around like so many cattle."[25] Yet, despite Deloria's audacity *Custer* almost did not see the light of publication.

When *Custer* was but merely a manuscript, the author, like many with a first book, ran into the kind of obstacles that one encounters when one has created something unheard of in the publishing world. In a word, he ran into rejection. Recollecting his travails as a writer in the thirtieth anniversary edition of *God Is Red*, Deloria pointed out the intransigence he and his friend, Stan Steiner, encountered when striving to find a publisher interested in a book on contemporary Indian affairs. In spite of the headlines the Indian protest movement[26] was grabbing, as more events occurred from one end of the United States to the other, when it came to the publishing world, Indians were irretrievably stuck in the past. "It was disconcerting," as Deloria recalled, "to realize that many people felt that the old books on Indians [such as *Sun Chief*[27] and *The Son of Old Man Hat*[28]] were sufficient to inform the modern American public about the nature of Indian life and to give sufficient information about Indians to make an intelligent choice as to how best to support Indian goals and aspirations."[29] The story was an important example of the institutional bulwarks preventing the Indigenous perspective from being seen or heard. It was in the nature of institutions, of course, to become conservative and resistant to change, usually under the pretense of "maintaining standards," not to mention protecting the interests of those benefiting from the status quo. However, institutions can and do change, though not without a great deal of perseverance on the part of those seeking to make a difference, be it in terms of reform or revolution. In Deloria's case, his diligence paid off when Macmillan Publishers, long known for supporting unorthodox new ideas and trends such as the work of Immanuel Velikovsky, best known for *Worlds in Collision (1950)*, which outraged the mainstream western scientific and religious communities,[30] and Michael Harrington, whose *The Other America* (1962), revealed a subculture of endemic poverty, which shocked Americans who thought such destitution was a thing of the pre–World War II Depression past, took on *Custer* as their latest subversive title.[31] One can easily imagine that Deloria felt pleased about such company.

As for *Custer*, the plan guiding Deloria's manifesto consisted of twelve parts, beginning with an introduction to the "Indian plight" of stereotypes and other historical misconceptions and an afterword in which the author accounted for his confrontational discussion of the topics covered in his book, as well as the hopes he had for where the dialog on Indian affairs may lead. In between were ten chapters that can be divided evenly between two major themes. Chapters 2 to 6 were historical and political analyses of colonial institutions[32] that had egregiously oppressed the interests of tribal nations, specifically government, religion and education: government, most notably in the form of the Bureau of Indian Affairs; religion, in the form of Protestant Christian missionaries; and, education, in the form of university-trained social scientists, most notoriously, anthropologists. Chapters 7 through 11 are a demonstration of the different types of agency that Indigenous people had used for resisting, adjusting to, and understanding their colonization at the hands of the American empire. Of particular significance in *Custer* were the chapters on Indian humor as a way of coping and as a way of teaching; Indian-Black relations and the significance of learning from other race-based power movements, especially the civil rights movement and the emergence of Black Power; and Indian leadership, in particular the need for tribal leaders, political and nonpolitical, to begin setting their own goals instead of waiting for non-Indians to offer direction. Deloria also included an array of examples in which tribal leadership had developed self-defeating customs, which were a product of federal Indian policy. Waiting for America to realize on its own the error of its ways with respect to Indians was like waiting for an abusive person to recognize him- or herself as an abuser. One would likely be dead long before that happened. Such was the dilemma that tribes faced during the termination era. On the contrary, one must engage in intervention, disruption, and liberation from the status quo directly and unequivocally. Toward that end, Deloria presented an account of contemporary American Indians whose only predecessors were *The Indian To-Day: The Past and Future of the First American* (1915) by Charles A. Eastman and *The Problem of Indian Administration* (1928) by Lewis Meriam.

As for what role *Custer* played in Deloria's Red Power Tetralogy, it laid the discursive foundation on self-determination that he expanded upon in his subsequent works, which one can argue played an indirect, albeit meaningful, role in the passage of the 1975 Indian Self-Determination and Education Assistance Act. Furthermore, Deloria's critical analysis of federal Indian laws and treaties, which were covered in chapter 2, and their implications for tribal sovereignty, would be further explored in chapters 5, 6, 7, and 9 of *Behind the Trail of Broken Treaties*. In turn, the chapter on termination policy and its role in the instigation of the Indian protest movement continued in chapter 1 of *God Is Red* and chapters 1 through 4 of *Broken Treaties*. In the case of the infamous critique of anthropology in *Custer*'s chapter 4, except for a brief reference to the archeological profession in *God Is Red*, Deloria instead maintained a more substantial analysis of the discourses he initiated on the Christianity and the Bureau of Indian Affairs in chapters 5 and 6 of *Custer*, respectively. More specifically, Deloria's critical examination of the relationship between Christian churches and tribes dominated much of *God Is Red*, while his reflections on the federal trust relation, as mediated by the Bureau of Indian Affairs, returned in various parts of *We Talk, You Listen* and *Broken Treaties*. Also, while Deloria continued to display an abundance of humor, complete with witty anecdotes, in his accounts of Indian affairs, he did not write about Indian humor as he did in *Custer*'s chapter 7. However, he deepened his understanding of Indian-Black relations in *We Talk, You Listen*, in particular chapter 6, which was about Black Power, then again in chapter 12, which covered the controversial Forman Manifesto. Speaking of power, Deloria's comments about the significance of power movements, the emergence of tribalism, and the opportunity for Indian leadership on issues regarding sovereignty, modern society, and the political awakening of urban Indian populations, all of which defined the latter chapters of *Custer*, also reappeared in the ensuing works of Deloria's Red Power Tetralogy, which collectively shattered the assumptions of the American master narrative on Indian people, which limited them to the roles of enemies, wards, and vanishing tribes, and supplant this with an assertion of self-determination.

The above developments in Deloria's writings were paralleled in his professional career, as he went from the University of Colorado law school (1967–70) to the Ethnic Studies Department at Western Washington University (1970–79). More specifically, Deloria stated "I am coming to be a visiting lecturer in Bellingham this coming year [fall 1970]. Since the national scene has gone completely to hell . . . I decided to take off for the year and spend it doing research on a series of booklets on Indian law to be used by tribal councils."[33] In addition, Deloria maintained his ties to the National Congress of American Indians, complete with the connections he had acquired during his years as executive director. From 1967 to 1974, more specifically, Deloria appeared before Congress on behalf of the Tiwa Indians of Texas (1967), at the Senate hearings on the examination on the War on Poverty (1967), the Senate hearing on the American Folklife Foundation (1971), the Senate California Indian oversight hearings (1973), the Senate hearings on the Menominee Restoration Act (1973), the Senate hearings on the establishment of the American Indian Policy Review Commission (1973), and the Senate hearings on the Indian Self-Determination and Education Assistance Act (1974). Developing concurrently in federal Indian affairs during this same time period was the Indian Civil Rights Act (1968), Nixon's "Special Message on Indians" (1970), the return of Blue Lake to Taos Pueblo (1970), the Alaska Native Claims Settlement Act (1971), the Menominee Restoration Act (1973), and *United States v. State of Washington* (1974). Equally important, within the American Indian community the American Indian Movement was founded (1968), the Indians of All Tribes occupied Alcatraz Island (1969–71), Navajo Community College began admitting students (1969), the Department of American Indian Studies was established at the University of Minnesota, Twin Cities Campus (1969), the Native American Rights Fund was founded (1970), the Little Earth of United Tribes was established in South Minneapolis (1973), and the International Indian Treaty Council was organized (1974). Lastly, the literature that appeared during this critical epoch included *House Made of Dawn* (1968) and *The Way to Rainy Mountain* (1969) by N. Scott Momaday; *The Everlasting Sky: New Voices from the People Named the Chippewa* (1972) by Gerald Vizenor; *Ascending Red Cedar Moon* (1974) by Duane Niatum; *The New Indians* (1968) by Stan Steiner; *Bury My Heart at Wounded Knee* (1970) by Dee Brown; *Touch the Earth: A Self-Portrait of Indian Existence* (1971) by T. C. McLuhan; and, *Native American Tribalism* by D'Arcy McNickle (1973). It was within this dynamic environment of events and ideas that Deloria launched one of the most significant discourses in American Indian intellectual history, which began with the statement: "Indians are like the weather. Everyone knows all about the weather, but none can change it."

CHAPTER 1

Vine Deloria Jr. and the Discourse on Tribal Self-Determination

Independence beyond the Reservation System

Legacies

In his much-overlooked afterword to *Custer Died for Your Sins*, Deloria stated at the end of a tour de force covering a plethora of issues confronting contemporary American Indian society: "I make no claim that this book represents what *all* Indian people are *really* thinking. Or that Indian people should follow the ideas presented in this book" [emphasis in original].[1] Yet, contrary to Deloria's proclamation, this is exactly how *Custer* has been remembered by generations of Indian readers. Like many before me, my initial encounter with the phenomenon of Vine Deloria Jr. (Standing Rock Sioux, 1933–2005) consisted of a fortuitous reading of *Custer Died for Your Sins*. I am uncertain of how I first heard of Deloria. He is one of these figures who seems to have always been a part of my life as an Indigenous person. Whereas other Indian writers were more capable at deepening my cultural and historical understanding of Indigenous peoples—such as his contemporaries Gerald Vizenor, Paula Gunn-Allen, and James Welch—Deloria compelled me to reckon with my political existence as an American Indian. Indeed, a common reaction among first-time readers of Deloria, *Custer* in particular, includes some form of reexamination of themselves, be they Indian, anthropologist, missionary, or Bureau of Indian Affairs employee. At the same time, while *Custer* was most assuredly a seminal text, it was far from being the sum of Deloria's contribution to the modern discourse on American

Indians. For the greater part of the next three decades after *Custer*'s appearance in 1969, Deloria produced some seventeen books, most of which he authored alone, while a smaller portion were coauthored or edited volumes. This was in addition to two hundred or so articles and a surfeit of book forewords, chapters, and afterwords, and an array of editorials, keynote addresses, and congressional testimonies. At the same time, while Deloria's body of work is prodigious in terms of output, numbers of topics, and years of contribution, his legacy largely rests on a corpus of early works published over a short span of time, 1969–74, the first of which was *Custer*, an influential text that is still being read, not to mention inspiring a new generation of thinkers and activists.

Because several works that followed *Custer* became canonized in their respective fields and Deloria's advocacy for tribal political rights has resulted in positive reforms, Deloria's writings have long held a prominent place in American Indian intellectual history. In fact, Deloria's reputation had risen so quickly in the aftermath of *Custer* it even reached the halls of Congress. In 1973 when Rep. Lloyd Meeds (D-WA) introduced Deloria to the House Subcommittee on Indian Affairs, he stated matter-of-factly but with great admiration: "Our next witness is Vine Deloria, who is a noted author, an Indian philosopher, spokesman for [the] progressive Indian movement—probably mostly noted for his authorship of 'Custer Died for Your Sins'—and I think [is] a spokesman for Indian people everywhere."[2] How Deloria may have felt about being designated "a spokesman for Indian people everywhere" was not recorded. After asking Deloria if he were still a Washington state resident, where he was a lecturer at Western Washington University, Meeds proceeded with the business of asking for Deloria's testimony on behalf of the Menominee, whose federal services were formally terminated in 1961. More to the point, Deloria was asked why the Menominee deserved to be reinstated as a federally recognized tribe. As an example of Deloria's status, the Menominee Restoration Act hearing spoke volumes, both in terms of the reach of his writings and the respect with which his opinion was accorded by Indian and non-Indian alike.

With regard to the legacy that Deloria's writings and advocacy work created, while it was accurate that he influenced a variety of audiences, upon closer examination there were two very different but complementary legacies, Indian and non-Indian, that emerged. For Indians, Deloria's most meaningful contribution to the needs of tribes was his discourse on self-determination as an integral part of tribal political existence. Self-determination, as the collective expression of sovereignty, is essential to each tribe's sense of nationhood and all of the rights that that entails. Moreover, Deloria asserted that knowing one's rights as Indigenous nations was especially important in response to ongoing developments in U.S. federal Indian law and policy, which were recurrently seeking to undermine tribes' powers of self-governance, as indicated by the Menominee example above. As a result of Deloria's lifelong defense of tribal self-determination, on January 12, 2005, *Indian Country Today* ran a number of articles in recognition of the editorial committee's decision to bestow the 2005 American Indian Visionary Award on him. In an editorial explaining the committee's selection, the Indian Country Media Network staff wrote: "Deloria served as executive director of the National Congress of American Indians from 1964 to 1967. He was a young contemporary of the generation that confronted termination, active and brilliant. So that when the rallying cry of sovereignty and self-determination sounded loud and clear in Indian country, Deloria was readiest of all to make sense of it, to fortify it, to lead the discourse."[3] The other contributors praising Deloria's distinction were Norbert Hill (Oneida), Daniel Wildcat (Muscogee Creek), John C. Mohawk (Seneca), and Hank Adams (Sioux-Assiniboine).

For non-Indians, Deloria's most lasting legacy was the paradigm shift he created in the anthropological profile of tribes, from vanishing relics of the past to contemporary and dynamic nations, complete with societies actively adapting to the modern world. In fact, when one assesses the status of the scholarly response to Deloria's writings, which is provided below, the most vigorous comments were from non-Indian readers in reaction to *Custer*'s "Anthropologists and Other Friends." The American Anthropological Association (AAA), in fact, devoted two major symposia to Deloria's caustic critique. First, on November 20, 1970, the Symposium on Anthropology and the American Indian was held during the AAA annual meeting in San Diego, California. Omer C. Stewart and Margaret

Mead, among others, defended their science as best they could from Deloria's accusations.[4] Second, in 1997, the 1989 AAA meeting papers on Deloria's ongoing influence in anthropology were collected into an edited volume, titled *Indians and Anthropologists: Vine Deloria, Jr. and the Critique of Anthropology*.[5] Consequently, social scientists have been compelled to acknowledge not only the colonial roots of their scholarly discourse—white researchers amassing studies of tribes supposedly vanishing under the wheels of progress and civilization—but also the disappointing extent to which anthropological studies have assisted tribes in redressing current issues.

Of course, the demarcation between Indian and non-Indian readers is not as clear-cut as the preceding summary may make it appear, as there were exceptions on each side. For example, Puebloan anthropologist, Alfonso Ortiz, had much to say as both a social scientist and as a member of San Juan Pueblo about Deloria's excoriation of the anthropological profession; while Sen. Ted Kennedy once did an excellent job at summarizing for his peers in the Senate many of the political arguments articulated in *Custer*. Both of these examples will return for closer analysis at the appropriate points in the ensuing discourse. In the meantime, suffice it to say, these exceptions emphasize the rule, which was that each type of reader, Indian and non-Indian, taken as a group, exhibited the tendencies described above. As such, it is the argument of this book that these two legacies ultimately arose from what I refer to as Deloria's Red Power Tetralogy: *Custer Died for Your Sins* (1969), *We Talk, You Listen* (1970), *God Is Red* (1973), and *Behind the Trail of Broken Treaties* (1974). The Red Power Tetralogy was the product of a unique time in American Indian history, when, because of a decade of termination policy in which the federal government sought to end its trust relationship with tribes, a political awakening erupted, which not only led to an organized campaign against termination, but also a growing demand for the recognition of treaty rights as well as a host of grievances against the federal government. Motivated by his work as executive director of the National Congress of American Indians (NCAI), which began in 1964, Deloria initiated a discourse on tribal self-determination as being the most important objective for making a viable future for tribes. While certainly not the only one who advocated a protribal sovereignty agenda, Deloria none-theless demonstrated a gift for combining sharp political analysis with a cutting sense of humor, which rattled his adversaries such as those in the Department of Interior and the Bureau of Indian Affairs, as much as it delighted his growing readership, particularly young Indians going to college and looking for ways to raise their political consciousness.

With the foregoing in mind, *Custer Died for Your Sins,* which is sub-titled *An Indian Manifesto* and which laid the foundation for the three major works that followed, was more of a manifestation, or perhaps the better word is "epiphany," whose eleven chapters laid to waste the American colonial mythology that claimed that Europeans "discovered" America and were "destined" to settle the land, leaving Indians to either "assimilate" or "vanish." Deloria, to the contrary, recounted an Indian-white history besotted with misunderstandings, racial stereotypes, political malfeasance, and institutional indifference. In responding to this history, Deloria advocated for an American Indian agenda based on self-determination, cultural revitalization, and political resistance, all of which was based on a critical analysis of the statutes, case law, and policies that defined the Indian-federal relationship. Noteworthy is the fact that the works composing the Red Power Tetralogy were written and published at a critical juncture in Deloria's life, namely going from NCAI executive director to law student at the University of Colorado at Boulder to ethnic studies faculty at Western Washington University. In other words, his most influential writings arose before Deloria fully defined himself as an academic. In this sense, he was a part of a long line of Indian intellectuals who served their nations outside of academia. Throughout it all, Deloria never relented on his conviction that tribes should think of themselves as nations and demand that others, from the average person on the street to the president of the United States, respect them as sovereign powers. Deloria consistently kept faith that American Indians had a great deal to teach the white immigrants who came to these shores centuries ago looking for a better life, only for their descendants to find themselves, as of the early 1970s, in the ravages of political, spir-itual, and environmental upheaval. In other words, one of the reasons Deloria wrote the things he did was because he believed that America was in desperate need of Indian knowledge and wisdom. This faith in Indian knowledge and wisdom was reinforced by the realization that tribes know a great deal more about this land than do their non-Indian counterparts by virtue of having lived *here* for countless generations. Similar to his predecessors, Charles A. Eastman and Luther Standing Bear, Deloria thought that America could resolve many of its problems if it took the time to listen to the native voices of this continent. What follows is a critical historical analysis of how these ideas developed across four influential works, which collectively defined a generation of American Indians in the heady process of reaffirming their nationhood.

Origins

"As long as any member of my family can remember, we have been involved in the affairs of the Sioux tribe."[6] On March 8, 1970, Deloria recounted his humble origins in an editorial published in the *New York Times*, titled "This Country Was A Lot Better Off When the Indians Were Running It," which was about the ongoing occupation of Alcatraz Island. Deloria explained this event in light of American history, the Indian protest movement, reservation history, and personal experience:

> I was born in Martin, a border town on the Pine Ridge Indian Reservation in South Dakota, in the midst of the Depression. My father was an Indian missionary who served 18 chapels on the eastern half of the reservation. In 1934, when I was 1, the Indian Reorganization Act was passed, allowing Indian tribes full rights of self-governance for the first time since the late eighteen-sixties.[7]

Born on March 26, 1933, a mere forty-five miles from Pine Ridge, along State Highway 18, Vine Victor Deloria Jr. was the eldest son of Vine Sr. and his wife Barbara (née Sloat Eastburn). As such, the future author of *Custer Died for Your Sins* was the descendant of generations of illustrious Deloria men, not to mention a paternal aunt of remarkable distinction. More specifically, the younger Vine was the grandson of Philip Joseph Deloria and the great-grandson of Françoise des Lauriers, whom the Dakota called "Saswe." The latter, as his great-grandson recounted in *Singing for a Spirit: A Portrait of the Dakota Sioux* (1999), was the child of a French fur trader and his Yankton wife.[8] Saswe, more importantly, would become a respected medicine man and a leader of the White Swan community on the Yankton Reservation, where, during the 1860s, he welcomed Presbyterian and Episcopal missionaries, which precipitated, not only changes in the Yankton community, but also personal changes for Saswe and his descendants. Among Saswe's children was a son he named "Tipi Sapa," "Black Lodge," who grew to take a profound interest in the new religion that arrived with the missionaries. Upon his baptism, Tipi Sapa accepted the name Philip Joseph Deloria. Among Philip's accomplishments as a proponent for his new-found faith, and as an advocate for his community, was cofounding the Planting Society, Wojo Okolakiciye, in 1873, which was an ecumenical association. Philip also "served as a lay reader and was an ordained deacon in 1883 and as a priest in 1892." He was then "appointed to supervise all Episcopal mission work on the Standing Rock Reservation," a position he held until his retirement in 1925.[9] Equally significant, Philip named his son Vine Victor Deloria, raising him in the family's adopted religion, in which he too distinguished himself. When the latter died on February 26, 1990, the obituary that appeared in the *New York Times* noted that Vine Victor Deloria Sr. had been ordained as an Episcopalian deacon in 1931. "In 1954 he was appointed national executive secretary for the Episcopal Church's work among Indians, the first Indian named to a top executive position by a major Protestant denomination." As for Vine Sr.'s survivors, the obituary acknowledged his wife "Barbara, in addition to two sons, Vine Deloria Jr., an author, of Tucson, and Sam, of Albuquerque, NM; a daughter, Barbara Sanchez of Puerto Rico, nine grandchildren and three great-grandchildren."[10] Not mentioned, because she had passed away in 1971, was an elder sister, Ella.

Ella Deloria had achieved, comparable to her brother's, a life of accolades, which must have had an untold influence on her nephew, Vine Jr. Perhaps her most important work was *Dakota Texts* (1932), which rendered translations of Dakota myths and oral histories, complete with the original stories in Dakota, all of which was complemented with linguistic analysis. In *Speaking of Indians*, which appeared in 1944, Deloria assembled the public lectures she gave in New York City at the behest of the Missionary Education Movement,[11] in which she spoke about traditional Dakota and Lakota culture that demonstrated how Indians were also a part of the modern world, including participating in the ongoing war effort.

About his aunt's impressive qualities, Vine Jr. shared two anecdotes in his preface to the 1998 reissue of *Speaking of Indians* that said as much about Vine as they did about Ella. First, with respect to the number of elders Ella spoke with from a young age and the traditional knowledge they passed on to her:

> I tried one time to get her to talk about these things, but she got very angry and told me that these things were so precious to the old people that my generation would not appreciate them and should not know them. They should not be talked about by people who cannot understand, she argued, and when she died an immense body of knowledge went with her.

It is worth noting, before proceeding, that the author of *Custer* had his own memories of Lakota elders and the knowledge they possessed, which suggested that, while not as knowledgeable as his aunt, Deloria nonetheless possessed some meaningful connection to the old ways:

> Many times I stood silently watching while old men talked to the buffalo about the old days. They would conclude by singing a song before respectfully departing, their eyes filled with tears and their minds occupied with the memories of other times and places.[12]

On another occasion, as Ella visited her nephew in Quantico, Virginia, where the work she had done on the Lumbee came up:

> Ella deeply believed that she could have reconstructed the original Indian language spoken by these people. . . . Tracing back from the colloquial expressions of these women and then comparing their slang words with words in other Indian tongues, she was preparing a sophisticated [Lumbee] dictionary that she believed was very close to their original language before English words and phrases were added.[13]

Taken together, the two anecdotes signified a relationship to traditional knowledge and community-related research that informed Deloria's concept of research, particularly his critique of anthropology.

As for how Deloria made the transition from following his father and grandfather's path into the ministry to serving the secular needs of the American Indian community, Deloria recalls an opportunity to work in the field of Indian education:

> I left the reservation in 1951 when my family moved to Iowa. I went back only once for an extended stay, in the summer of 1955, while on a furlough, and after that I visited only occasionally during summer vacations. . . . After I graduated from the seminary, I took a job with the United Scholarship Service. . . . I had spent my last two years of high school in an Eastern preparatory school and so was probably the only Indian my age who knew what an independent Eastern school was like.[14]

In spite of going to Lutheran Seminary in Rock Island, Illinois, where he earned a bachelor of divinity in 1963, Deloria forsook his calling to become a minister like his father and grandfather. Instead, as noted above, the younger Deloria worked with the United Scholarship Service, which, although sponsored by the Episcopal Church and the United Church of Christ,[15] set him on a path that led him to becoming the executive director of the National Congress of American Indians.[16] Moreover, Deloria saw his nomination as the consequence of an organization going through some less than impressive times while the world around it was in a paradigm shift. In the midst of these tumultuous times, Deloria recalled his life altering appointment as almost accidental:

> In August of 1964 I went to Sheridan, Wyoming to meet a teacher from Exeter to show him around the All American Indian Days celebration there. Meeting in conjunction with that celebration was the annual convention of the National Congress of the American Indians. I wandered around the convention naively, trying to get introductions for my teacher friend with some of the tribal chairmen attending the convention.

The NCAI was undergoing one of its periodic purges and was looking for a new Executive Director. More of a pawn than an active candidate, I ended the week as the new director.[17]

With regard to the political climate into which Deloria found himself at the NCAI, Imelda N. Schreiner, who was serving as the underpaid office manager, stated in a letter to Red Lake chairman, Roger Jourdain, on September 2, 1964: "Is it worth the worry, suffering, and heartbreak Roger or is it the fate of persons who are dedicated to the Indian cause to be so crucified? I wish I knew." Schreiner also confided about the pillorying of Robert Burnett (Rosebud Sioux), the executive director whom Deloria had replaced in October 1964. The NCAI was undergoing a serious financial crisis stemming from issues with poorly kept financial records: "Bob took a terrible beating at Sheridan and to me it was all uncalled for."[18] Nevertheless, Deloria obliquely saw his ascent into the NCAI leadership as something that was induced by the rising tide of activism occurring around Indian Country. On this point, Deloria said in Jennings C. Wise's *The Red Man in the New World Drama*: "By late 1964 [the National Indian Youth Council (NIYC)] was conducting activist programs in the northwest in defense of Indian treaty fishing rights and had become an influence in national Indian affairs politically." Furthermore, "The NIYC worked behind the scenes at the NCAI conventions and put two of its members into the position of Executive Director of the NCAI during the 1960s."[19] Although the relation between Deloria and Clyde Warrior, the principal leader of the NIYC, turned from rivalry to a tolerable acquaintance during a fleeting five-year period, until Warrior's death in 1968, there was a time, when they "met at the 1963 Boulder [Colorado, NIYC] workshops" where they "became fast friends for a short, fortuitous time." According to Paul R. McKenzie-Jones: "Warrior was impressed enough with Deloria to invite him to join the NIYC but quickly developed other ideas about how the young Sioux could be a useful ally."[20]

Because Deloria's tenure as NCAI executive director began as the Indian protest movement was getting underway in 1964 with the much-publicized fish-ins up at Frank's Landing in Washington state, the greenhorn leader "learned more about life in the NCAI in three years than [he] did in the previous 30."[21] With respect to Deloria's leadership role in the NCAI, it should be noted that the executive director was selected by the executive committee, "which consists of the president, the first vice president, the recording secretary, the treasurer, and the twelve regional vice presidents."[22] When the committee is assembled, the president serves as chairperson. Deloria's three year-tenure thus overlapped with three presidents, namely Walter Wetzel (Blackfeet), Clarence Wesley (San Carlos Apache), and Wendell Chino (Mescalero Apache). Although, Deloria's role was largely administrative, as a representative of the NCAI to tribes, federal and state governments, not to mention the American public, the executive director indubitably required intellectual leadership. Speaking of which, in an NCAI editorial ostensibly about NCAI membership, it stated in spring 1965: "Now, as NCAI comes of age"—it had just reached twenty-one years of operation—"it faces some basic organizational problems. New forms of Indian participation in [the] NCAI must be found in order to serve the interests of the people more fully."[23] In other words, the NCAI was suffering a severe membership problem: "The NCAI was deeply in debt. Tribal and individual membership was at an all-time low."[24] Incredibly, the NCAI even "considered closing and declaring bankruptcy," but for the generosity of "a few devoted tribes," among which were the Coeur d'Alene, which "raised over $1,000 during the summer [of 1965] to keep us in business." On this matter, Deloria sang the praises of "Mrs. Leona Garry, the [Coeur d'Alene] chairman's wife."[25] While the NCAI was not out of the proverbial woods, it did manage to slowly recover from its imminent demise. After another lean but solvent year in 1966, Deloria began law school during the fall semester 1967. "By that time," Deloria recalled, "the NCAI was doing well financially, had managed to bring together nearly a hundred tribes nationally, and fought and beaten the Interior Department in a number of skirmishes."[26] Among the more significant skirmishes was a confrontation that tribes had with Stewart Udall, President Johnson's secretary of interior, over a proposed omnibus bill (H.R. 10560) that Udall attempted to get passed into law without any of the promised consultation with tribes.

In the case of Deloria's developing profile as an Indian leader, when one looked at Stan Steiner's portrayal in *The New Indians*—which was the earliest description of Deloria—it was apparent that many of the young Lakota's political ideas and opinions developed during this era. Furthermore, Deloria's experiences as NCAI executive director provided his first book several of its anecdotal references. In the case of Steiner's account of the Indian protest movement—or Red Power, as it became more commonly known during the mid 1960s—Deloria's name came up more than three dozen times in its nineteen chapters, beginning with a recounting in the book's foreword of the new executive director's meeting with a prominent, though unnamed civil rights leader, who tried to convince Deloria to take up the struggle for equality. Deloria's response took the "gray-haired Negro leader" aback when he argued that Indians possessed "a superior way of life," which had much to teach American society. Thus, began a tribally based political agenda that, in reference to civil rights, set Indians apart politically from all other ethnic groups. Steiner, for his part, went on to describe Deloria as "the Rousseau of the new Indians" for his work at raising the political awareness of Indians across the country.[27] At the same time, Deloria was having his own political consciousness raised as he learned through his NCAI experience about the scope of the problems facing tribes, which recurrently arose from their political status as "domestic dependent nations," a legal ambiguity that was first articulated by Chief Justice John Marshall in *Cherokee Nation v. Georgia* (1831). Indeed, Deloria argued in *Custer*, then again in *Broken Treaties*, that the termination policy that was afflicting tribes across the country was the logical result of the equation many made between "dependent" and "wardship."

Speaking of the status of tribes within the federal system, what Steiner did not mention, which was pertinent to understanding Deloria's development as a political leader and activist-intellectual, were the appearances before Congress that he engaged in regularly on behalf of tribes. By "appearances" this meant a range of examples, from testifying before a Senate or House committee to letters and essays read into the record, along with occasions when senators and representatives quoted or summarized Deloria's work during a hearing. The most important of these, of course, were the in-person testimonies. Within the time frame of the book at hand (1964–74), there were seventeen separate documents in which Deloria's opinions, observations, and recommendations were integral to the dialog on different facets of Indian affairs.

A letter, for example, was entered into the record during the 1965 hearings before the House Subcommittee of the Committee on Appropriations. Dated February 10, 1965, the statement was addressed to Rep. Winfield K. Denton (D-ID) about the issue of Indian health and the need for "additional appropriations."[28] About two months later, Deloria sat before the Senate Subcommittee on Indian Affairs regarding S. 1413, which was for the purpose of terminating federal supervision over the property of the Confederated Tribes of Colville Indians. In his testimony before the committee, chaired by Sen. Lee Metcalf (D-MT), Deloria argued that the Colville Tribes were not ready for termination due to the preponderance of evidence documenting their low level of educational achievement. The latter clearly implied that tribal members, although voting to accept termination, nonetheless did not understand the content of the bill then before the Senate. Instead, Deloria proposed that Congress support improving the quality of Colville schools, which community leaders were on record as stating was a major concern of theirs. Perhaps, once "the educational level is sufficiently high to insure success in the competitive world of today that they [the Colville Indians] then [and only then] consider the question of termination of Federal services if they so desire."[29]

Subsequent congressional appearances included a statement before the House Subcommittee on Indian Affairs about making "more credit facilities become available" so that tribes can "increasingly pick up the small loans to their own members," which in turn will aid in establishing small reservation-based businesses.[30] Deloria also provided comments on an amendment to the Indian Revolving Loan Fund (S. 2196) and a law to guaranty and insure loans to Indians and Indian organizations (S. 2197).[31] Equally important, if not more so, was a four-day hearing in June 1965, during which Deloria presented testimony on the constitutional rights of American Indians. The impetus for the hearings before the Senate Subcommittee on Constitutional Rights was complaints that tribal constitutions did not adequately protect tribal citizens' civil rights, as defined by American constitutional law. In Deloria's 1965 testimony, he also commented on a number of pending bills, ranging from an early version of the Indian Civil Rights Act to the further extension of state jurisdiction over crimes involving non-Indians, which included a provision for providing tribal members the option of taking appeals over cases in which the plaintive claimed that his or her civil rights had been violated into the federal appellate system. While Deloria willingly acknowledged needed developments in tribal governance and litigation, he was wary of endorsing increased federal interference into matters over which tribes should have jurisdiction. Toward that end, Deloria explained the differences between tribal customs that were based on kinship, which constituted a tribal tradition of what non-Indian scholars call "the rule of law," and the individual-based rights of the Anglo-Saxon tradition, which often regarded the state as seeking to impinge upon individual rights. Given the vast cultural differences between Indian and non-Indian, Deloria advocated supporting the development of the tribal court system, including additional training for judges who were more acquainted with the communities in which tribal cases originated than were federal judges and attorneys. As stated in a memorandum that Deloria sent to John Belindo, dated August 22, 1968: "Tribal judges right now are beginning to keep adequate records of proceedings in their courts. These records can be used to create a unique '*Indian Common Law*' in much the same manner as English Common Law was created after William the Conqueror."[32]

Indicative of his ideas regarding tribal financial reform, which was key to self-determination, Deloria appeared before the Senate Subcommittee on Employment, Manpower, and Poverty in Albuquerque, New Mexico. During the April 1967 hearing, Deloria testified on the effectiveness of the Economic Opportunity Act (EOA) and the opportunities it created for tribes through the Office of Economic Opportunity (OEO). Deloria thought the EOA was good for tribes in general, which he illustrated with special emphasis on Navajo Nation and the Pueblo Indians.[33] In fact, Deloria's remarks about the OEO were effusive enough that Senator Metcalf had Deloria's remarks, as documented in a *New York Times* article by Joseph A. Loftus, read into the Congressional Record: "No longer would an Indian be required to wait, hat in hand, outside an office of the Bureau of Indian Affairs or Public Health Service waiting for a few crumbs to fall his way. Instead he could form his own programs and get funding through the OEO and begin to make real plans for progress for his people."[34] Later, of course, Deloria, along with a chorus of tribal leaders bemoaned the limitations of this project-based approach to addressing job creation, per capita income, and poverty.

Two things were apparent in what these congressional duties meant to the development of Deloria as a political leader. One, working within the federal system as a tribal advocate, not to mention critic of the system, was vital to the ongoing tribal interests in compelling the federal government to acknowledge tribes' inherent rights as sovereign nations, not the least of which was expecting the federal government to uphold its trust obligations. In other words, Indians could not afford to limit their struggle for sovereignty to direct action alone, such as occupations and marches, although these were often crucial at turning systemic problems into political issues. Second, tribes needed a long-term plan for changing the federal system, be it in terms of policy or statutory fixes, which they should not leave to Congress to devise on its own— input from Indian leaders was indispensable. In light of which, Deloria realized, while still with the NCAI, that it behooved tribes to increase their proficiency at working with and on the federal legal system, not as a way of assimilating tribes into the system but as a means for resisting federal impulses to overreach its jurisdiction.

In 1967, following his own advice, Deloria resigned from his NCAI post to earn his JD, which he acquired in 1970 from the University of Colorado at Boulder. As Deloria recalled his decision, which was as significant as when he abandoned his religious vocation: "It was apparent to me that the Indian revolution was well under way and that someone had better get a legal education so that we could have our own legal program for defense of Indian treaty rights."[35] What may have also influenced Deloria's decision were two intertwining factors. First was the high turnover rate in NCAI leadership due to overwork and burnout. Second was the ongoing sectarianism that percolated during the 1950s, as the NCAI organized a massive response to federal termination policy, which resulted in a substantial increase in membership. "But with increasing membership," Deloria observed, "came unanticipated problems within the Indian community. The group split into two political factions which spent almost as much time fighting each other [as] they did fighting the government policy."[36] The source of the factionalism grew out of the fishing rights controversy embroiling the Pacific Northwest: "Tribal councils were rather reluctant to engage in the struggle to protect treaty rights. The National Congress of American Indians came to be dominated by a few larger tribes that lived rather comfortably while their brethren from the smaller tribes were pushed around."[37] At the same time, as McKenzie-Jones documents, Deloria was hardly neutral in the factionalism that occurred. Contrary to Clyde Warrior's ambition for an NIYC-NCAI partnership,

> By 1966 the relationship between the NIYC and the NCAI was strained. This was primarily due to the breakdown in relations between Warrior and Vine Deloria, Jr. Neither saw value in the other's singular approach to Indian affairs. Warrior and the NIYC viewed the NCAI's methodical lobbying process as too slow and ineffective, while Deloria and the NCAI felt that Warrior and the NIYC were too brash and abrasive.[38]

As Deloria pursued his law degree (1967–70), he published his first two books, *Custer Died for Your Sins* and *We Talk, You Listen*, thus initiating one of the more prolific careers in American Indian thought. In turn, Deloria transitioned into an academic career, when he accepted an appointment at Western Washington University that combined his original interest in contemporary Indian political issues with a more scholarly approach to his critique of the Western traditions affecting the discourse on tribal self-determination as a cultural value. Among these topics of critique were mass media, race and the law, tribalism as a form of nation-building, and the relation between corporate entities, such as tribes, and the U.S. Constitution. As 1970 witnessed his transition from the heady days of representing an array of tribes as the NCAI executive director against the U.S. Department of Interior to the staid halls of academia, perhaps as an indication of his awareness of the emerging new era of tribal self-determination, Deloria disclosed in a letter to Hank Adams, dated June 22, 1970: "I will probably be in Denver with the exception of the July 4th weekend, until, July 22 at which time the Bar Exam will be over and I will be taking two weeks off in the Black Hills hidden from the outside world."[39] Equally enlightening was what Deloria stated a mere three years earlier to Leslie Dunbar, executive director of the Field Foundation, regarding what he thought was the purpose of focusing on the law and how it can inform the NCAI mission:

> I hope to use the next 3 years as a period of isolation and contemplation and to lay the ideological foundations for later work in legal affairs for the NCAI. As I see the problem it is very tricky, we have to get the tribes mad enough to defend their rights and then offer responsible means of doing so. Too many splinter groups are now working merely for headlines and do not have a plan for action and accomplishment after they do get the people when they do get aroused.[40]

That plan of "action and accomplishment" was what Deloria articulated in the pages of *Custer* and the subsequent volumes of his Red Power Tetralogy.

Uncle Vine

In addition to a *New York Times* obituary, in which Deloria was proclaimed a "Champion of Indian Rights," not to mention the *Washington Post*'s labelling him as "The Indian Who Overturned the Stereotypes," the Indigenous news site Indianz.com announced Deloria's death in more dramatic terms: "Vine Deloria Jr., giant in Indian Country, dies at 72." In its obituary, Indianz.com quoted the heartfelt reactions to Deloria's death from Richard West Jr., then director of the National Museum of the American Indian; Wilma Mankiller, former principal chief of Cherokee Nation; as well as comments about Deloria's intellectual legacy from Susan Shown Harjo (Cheyenne/Hodulgee Muscogee), an *Indian Country Today* columnist and director of the Morning Star Institute. Among the mourners quoted was Faith Spotted Eagle (Yankton Sioux), identified as Vine's niece, who shared these words of remembrance: "In Indian country the name Vine Deloria Jr. is a household word. His quotes are on walls and often roll off the tongues of young Natives doing reports and speeches. Most importantly, he writes what we all would like to say. I read somewhere that someone said that an act of genius 'is saying what we are all thinking.'"[41]

Out of the pall that had descended upon the American Indian community after Deloria's death, a special 2006 issue of the *Wicazo Sa Review* appeared. Edited by James Riding In (Pawnee), the issue featured several prominent figures in American Indian/Native American studies, who eulogized their fallen friend, teacher, and hero. David E. Wilkins (Lumbee), Elizabeth Cook-Lynn (Crow Creek Sioux), George E. Tinker (Osage), Edward Valandra (Rosebud Sioux), and Sidner Larson (Gros Ventre) took turns recalling personal anecdotes that complemented their praises and appreciation for the example Deloria set. As is typical of eulogies, their remarks were long on admiration and heart-warming tales and short on critical analysis and insight. At the same time, the valedictory essays assembled were not without their value, especially at illustrating the lofty status that Deloria held in the hearts and minds of the Indigenous scholarly community. In this regard, Cook-Lynn, Wilkins, and Tinker had the most insightful remarks about Deloria's life and contributions to share, which was largely due to the number of years they each knew him, a quality that added substance to their respective portrayals of his work and his status.

Cook-Lynn, for her part, stated: "Deloria's work tied together the depth of the white man's psychology and political theory and gave Indian writers and thinkers the language to defend ourselves against the merciless 'Westward Ho!' mentality we faced in the past and continue to face today."[42] Wilkins, in turn, was the most expansive in his adoration for his friend and mentor, in which he mixed personal remembrances of the man that he and his cohort at the University of Arizona affectionately called "'the Godfather' of Indian politics, law, and policy" with a systematic summary of Deloria's political itinerary. For Wilkins itinerary consisted of "the Delorian trilogy," "his powerful articulation of *tribal sovereignty*, his distinctive conceptualization and defense of the essential doctrine of tribal *self-determination*, and his cogent discussion and analysis of the importance and sacredness of *space and place* for Indigenous nations" [emphasis in original].[43] Because Deloria was frequently in opposition to the values and beliefs, not to mention policies, of the dominant American society, Wilkins likened Deloria to "the *exilic* intellectual" of which Edward Said spoke of in *Representations of the Intellectual* (1994). At the same time, Wilkins noted: "Vine was never taken with the notion of being identified as an 'intellectual.'"[44] Deloria's aversion to the label may have had as much to do, as will be explained below, with Margaret Mead's use of the term to characterize Indians who served as "informants," as it did with the intellectual's ivory-tower stereotype.

Perhaps the better sobriquet for Deloria was "Coyote Old Man," which George "Tink" Tinker called him after watching his friend deliver comments at "a small church conference on religious diversity." According to Tinker, Deloria responded to his teasing with "a wry smile."[45] Kidding aside, Tinker continued with a generous account of a man he respected as much for his inspiration and guidance to young Indian scholars as his perspicacious intellect, which expounded on a variety of topics, replete with a boundless sense of humor. Certainly, it was on the basis of Deloria's capacity to connect with younger Indian scholars that Tinker turned his sympathetic remarks from the past to the future of his friend's legacy: "Indeed, Deloria's greatest contribution may be the theoretical and philosophical foundation for Indian intellectual resistance that became the starting point for a whole generation of Indian scholars who followed him and the extent to which he served as a role model." As such, in Tinker's estimation, Deloria's "writings will be a starting point for young Indian students for another hundred years as they begin their own intellectual journeys."[46]

In 1995 Robert Allen Warrior's (Osage) *Tribal Secrets: Recovering American Indian Traditions* was the first of three short but meaningful treatments of Deloria's impact as a writer and thinker that emerged during the 1990s. The additional two were by Jace Weaver and James Treat. In Warrior's work, Osage writer John Joseph Mathews and Deloria represented two very different generations of Indigenous intellectual culture. In the case of Mathews, he emerged in an era Warrior labeled "a Generation of Free Agents" (1925–60), which was situated in-between the Progressive Era (1890–1916) and the Red Power movement (1960–73). Consequently, whereas Mathews's generation was defined by the 1934 Indian Reorganization Act and World War II, Deloria's was energized by termination, the civil rights movement, and Vietnam. Warrior, more specifically, focused his attention on Deloria's historic impact of the climactic stage of the Red Power movement, in which *Custer* and *God Is Red* made their appearances. Of particular interest to Warrior was the philosophical work that Deloria embarked on in *God Is Red*. Contrary to Christianity's dependence on a linear timeline defined by biblical events, which climaxed with the apocalyptic return of Jesus, the Indigenous cosmos was based on a nonlinear relationship to space, which was defined for each tribal group in terms of its homeland and the landmarks therein that they regarded as sacred, customary, and historically significant. More specifically, Warrior underscored Deloria's intervention into the Christian timeline, as he disrupted its temporal paradigm and asserted the place of nonlinear, which is to say kinship relationships with the land. As such, Indigenous practices, which were contingent on maintaining balance with the environment, were oriented toward collective well-being. On this premise, Warrior observed, reasserting tribal peoplehood was key to comprehending tribal rights as collective, as opposed to a conglomerate of individuals. "The return to tradition," however, as Warrior explained in his succinct examination of *We Talk, You Listen*, "cannot in Deloria's analysis be an unchanging and unchangeable set of activities, but must be part of the life of a community as it struggles to exercise its sovereignty."[47] Deloria, in fact, was an example of his own notion of innovation within a traditional framework. In light of which, Warrior argued:

> In comparing Deloria and Mathews I maintain that Native critical studies and literature have come to a point where Native critics can and should engage one another with more vigor and energy than in the past. The explosion of American Indian writing that has followed the ground-breaking reception of N. Scott Momaday and Deloria now demands sincere engagement and a willingness to ask tough questions. . . . [Indeed,] critical interpretation of those writings can proceed primarily from Indian sources.[48]

Appearing on the heels of Warrior's inaugural work was Jace Weaver's 1997 *That the People Might Live: Native American Literatures and Native*

American Community. Similar to Warrior, Weaver focused on Deloria as a religious thinker. In fact, he cites *Tribal Secrets* multiple times throughout his survey of Deloria's major ideas. In a slight departure, though, from Warrior's discourse on the primacy of place in *God Is Red*, Weaver was more interested in Deloria's notions of personhood and humanity. More to the point, Weaver referred to Deloria's comprehensive critique of North American paleontology in *Red Earth, White Lies (1995)*, which at the time was creating as much of a shockwave in archeological circles as did *Custer*'s treatment of anthropology. Moreover, Deloria's dispute with Darwinian evolutionary theory, as Weaver observed, which was aggressively confronted in *Red Earth, White Lies*, was actually an old argument that had begun in *The Metaphysics of Modern Existence* (1979). In Weaver's reading of Deloria's critique of contemporary evolutionary theory, Deloria continued his deconstruction of human evolution in the thirtieth-anniversary edition of *God Is Red*, in which Deloria's version of the "ancient astronaut theory" was presented. According to Weaver, Deloria added a twist to Erich Von Däniken's notion of ancient extraterrestrial visits to earth, as recounted in *Chariots of the Gods* (1968): "It is not indigenous peoples, but Westerners, who were influenced by these intergalactic intruders."[49] Consequently, Weaver saw Deloria's handling of Däniken's theory as a "novel way" of addressing "the humanity of Native peoples," though it was not entirely clear in Weaver's discourse what exactly he thought the reader learned about Native peoples' humanity. However, the resulting ambiguity may be less Weaver's fault at interpreting Deloria's text and more Deloria's confused and perplexing use of the ancient-astronaut theory in the first place.

Speaking of theories of human origins, also appearing in 1997 was Thomas Biolsi and Larry Zimmerman's *Indians and Anthropologists: Vine Deloria, Jr. and the Critique of Anthropology*. While Deloria was still very much alive and argumentative, Biolsi and Zimmerman, two respected anthropologists and academics, coordinated probably the most thought-provoking book dedicated to Deloria's influence on the discourse on American Indians. The papers assembled were written for the purpose of responding to the criticisms Deloria enumerated in *Custer*'s "Anthropologists and Other Friends." *Indians and Anthropologists* brought together ten papers by ten different contributors. Most were anthropologists, some were not; some were American Indian and Canadian First Nations, most were not. The results of *Custer*'s effect, according to Herbert T. Hoover, Elizabeth S. Grobsmith, and Murray L. Wax, were existential in the sense that social scientists working in American Indian communities had become more self-conscious about making their work relevant to those communities and that one could see the changes in the policies—in some cases, laws—governing the implementation of field research. Randall H. McGuire and Larry J. Zimmerman, in turn, analyzed how archeologists proclaimed themselves as stewards of the American Indian past, which positioned them as the authoritative voice in how that past was recalled in the annals of American prehistory.

What was also pertinent were the ethical issues generated by the act of excavation itself, which archeologists regarded as good science, but which American Indians regarded as an ethical violation. Biolsi and Zimmerman's papers provided an account of how Deloria's critique of archeology influenced the development of the Native American Graves Protection and Repatriation Act, which Congress passed into law on November 16, 1990.[50] The five papers by Cecil King, Marilyn Bentz, Thomas Biolsi, Gail Landsman, and Peter Whitely discussed the various ways in which anthropology had invaded American Indian communities. Biolsi and Landsman's papers, in particular, gave the reader concrete examples of how anthropologists had shaped and dominated the narrative on specific tribal groups, each reflecting the issues that Deloria had raised in his original 1969 critique.

Although it was unfortunate that Deloria's controversial *Red Earth, White Lies: Native Americans and the Myth of Scientific Fact* did not appear in time to be included, Biolsi and Zimmerman's edited volume was nevertheless one of the more engaging works on Deloria's ideas.[51] More to the point, the introduction and the opening three papers by Hoover, Grobsmith, and Wax were the most significant contribution to Deloria studies out of all the works analyzed in this assessment of Deloria's legacy. With respect, more specifically, to the discourse on Deloria's intellectual development and influence, the papers recounting Deloria's personal effect on working anthropologists and how their change of heart—or rather, how Deloria changed how they saw what they were doing—was testament to the importance of Deloria's work as an activist-intellectual:

> The publication of Deloria's book [*Custer Died for Your Sins*] in 1969 can be seen as representative of a new period in relations between American Indian people and anthropologists in particular, between Indians and non-Indians in America generally, and between colonized peoples and the metropolis globally.[52]

In 1999 James Treat, in a return to the theme of Deloria as religious thinker, edited a collection essays titled *For This Land: Writings on Religion in America*, which brought together Deloria's commentaries on the historic and contemporary relations that tribes have maintained with Christianity, be it in the form of missionaries, churches, or theologies. Of particular interest to Treat was examining how Deloria, in spite of vehemently rejecting Christianity, still emerged as one of the more important religious thinkers of the late twentieth century. In a September 9, 1974, issue of *Time*, for example, the weekly news magazine ran a story highlighting eleven prominent "shapers and shakers of the Christian faith," in which Deloria was a featured figure.[53] In light of this recognition, Treat regarded Deloria as more of a passionate reformer than an archenemy of Christianity. Rather than "getting even," *God Is Red* was motivated by a profound concern "about the institutional churches' 'credibility gap,' a symptom of 'religious breakdown' and the 'spiritual desperation' it has generated in the contemporary situation."[54]

In response to this credibility gap and other concerns, Treat's anthology presented Deloria's theological explanation for why he left his calling to serve the church in "It Is a Good Day to Die" (1971), as well as the current struggle for Indian rights in "The Theological Dimension of the Indian Protest Movement" (1973), not to mention the lessons learned from the 1973 conflict at Wounded Knee in "Religion and Revolution among American Indians" (1974). In sum, *For This Land* argued that the civil unrest, corrupt presidential politics, an unpopular and unwinnable war, along with a looming environmental crisis that were sending early 1970s America into upheaval stemmed from a nation born from the illegal occupation of Indian lands, which included the gross violation of the rights of Indian peoples. In Treat's analysis of Deloria's religious writings, such calamities had been perpetrated by a settler-colonial government that found justification for its heinous acts in the tenants of its Christian religion, which regarded—and perhaps still does—the whole earth as its dominion to dispose of, i.e., waste, in any way it sees fit.

Adding to the complexity of Deloria's historical legacy, a mere four years after Treat's anthology appeared, *Native Voices: American Indian Identity and Resistance*, edited by George Tinker, David E. Wilkins, and Richard A. Grounds was released in 2003. More than paying homage to Deloria, several essays made contributions to what had grown into a sophisticated academic field, namely American Indian/Native American studies. Furthermore, in comparison to Warrior, Weaver, and Treat, *Native Voices* was a step forward in the burgeoning field of Deloria studies:

> With his remarkable achievements as a legal theorist, theologian, historian, and political scientist, Deloria has influenced a whole generation of younger Indian scholars to be self-consciously indigenous thinkers—to reclaim an American Indian intellectual tradition, along with a political activism rooted in the oral traditions of our peoples and the wisdom of our elders and ancestors. Out of polemical and apologetic necessity, he has been a true polymathic educator.[55]

Motivating a generation of people to be more "self-consciously Indigenous thinkers," by the way, should not be undervalued. The alternative, after all, when speaking about a colonized people, is to turn them into assimilated automatons, unquestioningly fitting into the status quo. Although, Deloria did not accomplish this feat single-handedly, he nevertheless is regarded as a major voice awakening young Indigenous minds to their political identities. As for *Native Voices*, while the editors were emphatic that their volume was not simply "intended to glorify the work or life of Deloria," but rather "to honor him by presenting the original work of a variety of young (and middle-aged) scholars who have been deeply influenced by him," there were nonetheless four contributors whose papers pay specific homage to Deloria's intellectual legacy, which are pertinent to the discourse at hand.

Glenn T. Morris, Cecil Corbett, Ward Churchill, and Inés Talamantez

focused their respective essays on Deloria's contributions to the Indigenous intellectual community. Morris (Shawnee), for his part, took up the
topic of decolonizing Indigenous peoples' international relations. Toward
that end, he reflected on the ideas presented in Deloria's *Behind the Trail
of Broken Treaties*, which argued that Indigenous nations ought to be perceived within the context of international law as Marshall suggested in
Cherokee Nation v. Georgia (1831). Moreover, as Morris read *Broken Treaties*,
Deloria's argument must be further considered within the context of early
1970s national and international affairs, as not merely a local issue. On the
one hand were the power movements driven by disenfranchised minorities, namely the Black and Chicano communities, which wanted "greater
inclusiveness" in the American political structure. The power movements
did eventually include the Red Power phenomenon, as embodied by the
National Indian Youth Council and the American Indian Movement (AIM).
On the other hand was the disarray of global politics affected by the Cold
War, Vietnam, and the decolonization efforts across the so-called Third
World, most notably in Africa and Southeast Asia. Melding the local and
the global, Deloria inaugurated according to Morris an argument for self-
determination based on tribalism (a concept that came up in both *Custer*
and *We Talk, You Listen*) as a coherent and viable political philosophy, in
which tribes were reinstated as members of the community of nations,
complete with restarting the treaty-making tradition.[56]

Cecil Corbett (Nez Percés), in turn, offered a short but insightful
account of Deloria's transformation from seminary student to social and
political activist advocating for Indian rights. Corbett was particularly
instructive about Deloria's changing relationship to the church he once
sought to serve as a young minister. Long before Deloria wrote *God Is
Red*, according to Corbett, "Deloria expected much from the church in
terms of righting the wrongs that had been perpetrated on American
Indians in the course of the European conquest of North America."[57] In
this sense, Corbett is paralleling an interpretation of Deloria's criticisms
of Christianity that came up earlier in Treat's *For This Land*. Corbett,
however, emphasized the spirit of spiritual reform, arguing that Deloria was hardest on those from whom he expected the most, specifically
"Congress, the anthropologists, and the Churches."[58]

Unlike the eulogies in the special issue of *Wicazo Sa*, Ward Churchill underscored in his contribution the repercussions that Deloria faced when he continued advocating for working within the system rather than eliminating it altogether, as was evident in his two coauthored books with Clifford Lytle, *American Indians, American Justice* (1983) and *The Nations Within: The Past and Future of American Indian Sovereignty* (1984). In spite of many equating his name with Indian radicalism, Deloria was a strong proponent of understanding and working within, though certainly not on behalf, of the federal system. In fact, from early in Deloria's intellectual career, he showed himself as both advocate and critic of the Indian protest movement. More specifically, in his essay, Churchill covered the permutations of Deloria's thoughts on Indigenous nations as members of the international community, and how his thinking changed in light of how Indigenous people were treated in the aftermath of decolonizing revolutions (e.g., the Sandinista oppression of the Miskito in Nicaragua).[59]

Inés Talamantez (Apache/Chicana), in "Transforming American Conceptions about Native America," paid homage to the influence that Deloria had on disrupting colonial theories of Indigenous peoples. In particular, Talamantez evoked *Custer*'s innovative ideas, underscoring the stifling effect that "anthropologists, historians, linguists, folklorists, and literary critics," complete with their "trendy theories," had on Indigenous perspectives. Omitting Indigenous voices from contemporary scholarship, especially when conducted by non-Indians, was supposedly justified on the misguided assumption that "there are no 'real' Indians anymore, but only Indians that have been assimilated," which was a constant concern for generations of ethnographers worried about the cultural purity of their fieldwork. Deloria's critical analysis of anthropology in *Custer* consequently pushed the dialog on Indigenous cultures away from social-science theory and more toward the realization that tribes were a part of the modern world, complete with the ability to speak, not to mention write, for themselves.[60]

As the field of Deloria studies slowly emerged, it was clearly limited by an impulse to honor a revered elder, as opposed to critically engaging his work. While Deloria's writings have been criticized, often caustically, those reproaches have typically come from representatives of the colonial institutions Deloria's work sought to reform. In this regard, anthropology was the obvious example of a spirited response from Deloria's critics. Within the field of American Indian studies, however, one encounters mostly a climate of gratitude for a life and career dedicated to Indigenous nations. While the sentiment was understandable, there was nevertheless a lingering question as to whether or not American Indian studies can advance as an intellectual field if it was incapable of criticizing its most distinguished figure.

In 2006 a mere year after Deloria's passing, Steve Pavlik and Daniel R. Wildcat (Muscogee Creek) edited *Destroying Dogma: Vine Deloria Jr. and His Influence on American Society*. More specifically, the volume was led by Deloria's keynote address at the 2002 Western Social Sciences Association meeting in Albuquerque, New Mexico, titled "Where Is the Academy Going?" As was typical of Deloria's presentations, he spoke ex tempore about the issues that were bothering him the most, in this case, academic culture. In turn, seven of Deloria's longtime followers, Thomas J. Hoffman, Tom Holm (Creek/Cherokee), Steve Pavlik, Nicholas C. Peroff, Richard M. Wheelock (Oneida), Daniel R. Wildcat (Yuchi/Muscogee Creek Nation), and David E. Wilkins, contributed papers documenting their friend and mentor's impact on a variety of institutions, from law to anthropology. Taken together, their papers were meant to demonstrate how Deloria shaped the intellectual analysis of American Indians, be it in terms of religious freedom (Hoffman), tribal leadership (Holm), human evolution and origins (Pavlik), human society (Peroff), mythmaking and nation building (Wheelock), sacred space (Wildcat), or the interconnection of sovereignty, self-determination, and place (Wilkins). The three most noteworthy contributions to Deloria scholarship came from Holm, Wildcat, and Wilkins. The others, although they covered topics that were important to Deloria's analysis of Western jurisprudence, science, history, and politics, they nonetheless referenced Deloria's ideas and opinions only fleetingly, doing little to deepen the reader's understanding of how Deloria's work developed over time, let alone how it influenced the work of mainstream, i.e., non-Indian, researchers and scholars. As for Holm, Wildcat, and Wilkins, they led their readers into a more thorough interrogation of Deloria's writings, interviews, and speeches.

In "Decolonizing Native American Leaders: Vine's Call for Traditional Leadership," Tom Holm addressed Deloria's examination of contemporary Western notions of leadership and governance, their implementation in the form of tribal governments—which were established according to the 1934 Indian Reorganization Act—and the negative effect they had on Indigenous nations. Holm observed, furthermore, that Deloria and Lytle covered the process of organizing tribes into constitutional governments in *The Nations Within*,[61] which Holm interpreted as creating a problem of legitimate authority:

> Legitimate authority, to use Max Weber's terminology, has fallen into the hands of bureaucrats, who place emphasis on management rather than on the ability to solve problems through peaceful persuasion, to reach consensus, to inspire others to virtuous behavior, or to correct past wrongs. With constitutionalism, a number of Native American nations have more or less reached this same level of impersonal and visionless governance.[62]

Because of the dissonance between modern tribal governments and pre-1934 traditional governance customs and values, many in the Indigenous population tended to regard tribal government as inherently corrupt. Consequently, while constitutionally based tribal governments may have provided Indigenous nations a footing on which to assert, or rather reassert, a nation-to-nation relationship with the United States, they also produced a separate class of politicians and functionaries, which typically viewed issues and problems in terms of serving the interests of government and its agencies, rather than the interests of the people. As Holm noted: "Leaders no longer have to be leaders. All they need do is administer policy, manage funds, and maintain an impersonal, objective approach to problem solving."[63] What Holm saw as critical in Deloria's work was for tribes to reaffirm their governance customs as the basis for institutional reform, as opposed to limiting themselves to adapting American legal thinking to otherwise non-Indigenous tribal governments.

Wildcat, in turn, in "Indigenizing the Future: Why We Must Think Spatially in the Twenty-First Century" analyzed Deloria's more philosophical ideas about history and space as explained in *God Is Red*. Wildcat's essay was divided into four sections covering the status of human beings in modern times, the value of privileging Indigenous knowledge traditions as a way of understanding the world in which we live today, the significance of thinking spatially (as opposed to linearly), then concluding with the "Big Picture." More specifically, Wildcat considered the manner in which Deloria deconstructed the concepts that underpinned much of the western religious tradition, concepts that in turn influenced the West's secular institutions, such as politics and government. Moreover, insofar as these fundamental Western concepts were antithetical to Indigenous beliefs and values, according to Wildcat's interpretation of Deloria's work, they were at the root of the recurring conflict that Indigenous people faced with Western, i.e., American institutions. As the title of Wildcat's essay implied, the concept of space was of utmost importance in the spiritual battle between Indigenous and non-Indigenous people in America. As a purveyor of Indigenous ideas and an advocate for the relevance of Indigenous values to contemporary issues, Wildcat argued, in yet another invocation of *God Is Red*, that Deloria's critique of western notions of time and space were ultimately grounded in the same knowledge traditions that distinguished his ancestors' relationship to and connection with the world. That Indigenous worldview—Standing Rock Sioux, in Deloria's case—informs not only his understanding of Western history and civilization but also his ideas and opinions about Indigenous and non-Indigenous issues.

According to David E. Wilkins, in "Forging a Political, Educational, and Cultural Agenda for Indian Country: Common Sense Recommendations Gleaned from Deloria's Prose," the author of *Custer Died for Your Sins* made his greatest contribution to Indigenous nations in the form of practical suggestions for reforming a multitude of institutions affecting Indigenous lives. After humbly admitting that his intellect was less capacious than his mentor's, which covered an impressive spectrum of topics and interests, Wilkins stated that his analysis of Deloria's career as a problem solver was limited to two areas: "(1) [the] federal government in its unique political, legal, economic, and historical relationship to First Nations and (2) tribal nations and their citizens in the same areas, with culture and education factored in."[64] Wilkins then proceeded to present his exposition in two parts. Part one was titled "Challenges, Ideas, and Admonitions for the US Government," which was about Deloria's suggestions for making federal Indian policy more effective at fulfilling the federal government's trust relation, in addition to being more amenable and respectful of Indigenous nations' inherent sovereign status. Part two was titled simply "Deloria to First Nations," which, as the title suggested, was about Deloria's numerous, typically scolding, recommendations for tribal leaders, especially political leaders. The value of Wilkins's essay was the way in which it systematized Deloria's various treatises on Indian law and politics that were articulated in works ranging from *Custer* to *Tribes, Treaties, and Constitutional Tribulations* (2000). In the final analysis, Wilkins's essay was more of an exposition of Deloria's ideas as categorized above than a critical assessment. In fact, nowhere in any of Wilkins's writings on Deloria will one find any criticism of the work under analysis. The same was true for Wildcat and many others.

Interestingly, the most substantial single-authored piece on Deloria's work and legacy appeared outside of American Indian/Native American studies. In 2011 Michael A Lawrence, a professor of law at Michigan State University, published *Radicals in Their Own Time: Four Hundred Years of Struggle for Liberty and Equal Justice in America* in which Deloria was discussed in the last of five chapters. The additional chapters were devoted to Roger Williams, Thomas Paine, Elizabeth Cady Stanton, and W. E. B. DuBois. The format of the book was a series of biographies in the *Profiles in Courage* tradition, in which a biographical portrait was provided for each personage, highlighting their respective career in the struggle for religious, political, gender, race, and tribal rights. While the chapter on Deloria did not add much to the works examined above, Deloria's appearance in Lawrence's book was significant nonetheless for the reason that it symbolized the extent to which Deloria's legend as a proponent for tribal self-determination had become a part of the larger dialog on American politics and minority rights. With respect to Deloria's historic status:

Deloria . . . sought to educate people that under the terms of their historically unique political arrangement with the United States, Indian tribes are entirely separate (albeit dependent) sovereigns. As such, they are entitled, under well-established principles of international law, to the respect given any other such sovereign.[65]

Speaking of portraits, Frederick E. Hoxie observed in *This Indian Country: American Indian Political Activists and the Place They Made* (2012) that when Deloria assumed the role of executive director of the National Congress of American Indians, he appeared to be the antithesis of the 1960s Red Power activist that became the dominant stereotype.[66] "With his thick glasses and biting wit," Hoxie wrote, "the NCAI's new executive director seemed far better prepared for an academic symposium than for legislative hearings or courtroom confrontations."[67] Throughout Hoxie's account of Deloria's career as an activist and writer, anecdotes and analyses were provided from his major publications and his legal and political work, which were presented to the reader as examples of Deloria's visionary perspective on the most salient issues facing American Indian communities. Indeed, Hoxie portrayed Deloria as going from an "unlikely leader" of the NCAI to becoming, less than a decade later, the foremost intellectual among a generation seeking to radically reconfigure the political status of Indigenous nations. At the same time, Hoxie makes clear that Deloria immediately demonstrated an aptitude for leadership when he argued that instead of resigning itself to being reactive to proposed legislation coming out of Congress, the NCAI should take its own initiative at developing a legislative agenda. As a contribution to the still underdeveloped field of Deloria studies, Hoxie's chapter, "Indian American or American Indian?" was largely laudatory, as were several of the previous items that had appeared. If anything, when Hoxie juxtaposed Deloria to the activist-intellectual work of Sarah Winnemucca Hopkins, Thomas Sloan, and D'Arcy McNickle, among others, he made it clear that Deloria had irrefutably metamorphosed from active member of the Indian community to historical figure, which was to say he was now among the ancestors.

With respect, then, to the foregoing highlights in the nascent field of Deloria studies, it is apparent that the most energetic criticism of Deloria's work has come, as noted, from the anthropological community.[68]

In turn, the discourse that began with Warrior, Weaver, and Treat was focused on Deloria as a religious thinker who created a paradigm shift through his comparative study of Christianity and Indigenous sacred traditions. Warrior and Treat, in particular, regarded *God Is Red* as critical to understanding Deloria's notion of tribalism as both a political and religious philosophy, thereby forming the basis of tribal self-determination, not only as a form of political self-governance, but also as a means for Indigenous cultural liberation. In the case of *Native Voices*, Morris, Corbett, Churchill, and Talamantez highlighted Deloria's ideas about tribal sovereignty as a component of international law, Indian-based Christian reform, as well as his insightful but controversial ideas about working within the federal system, a proposition that was tempered by his criticism of anthropology and its ethnocentric research agenda. Continuing the tradition of honoring Deloria's legacy was *Destroying Dogma*, in which Holm, Wildcat, and Wilkins demonstrated Deloria's influential discourse on tribal leadership as a means for restoring traditional governance values within contemporary tribal government; his articulation of the Indigenous, nonlinear, non-Christian worldview; and his explication of tribal sovereignty as an extension of tribal land relations, and how the connection to place informed Deloria's notion of self-determination. As for the other works analyzed above, such as the book chapters by Hoxie and Lawrence, while they are examples of Deloria's stature as an historically important figure, they may be nonetheless characterized as similar in tone to the array of other essays and book chapters, in which Deloria's intellectual output is honored and explained, but spared any criticism.

So, then, what does the book in hand have to offer purveyors of Deloria's work and legacy? A word now about the objectives of this book. First and foremost, this work fills in a major gap in the existing literature, specifically the need for a monograph devoted to Deloria's contributions to the American Indian intellectual tradition. In fact, Warrior commented in *Tribal Secrets*: "Few scholarly studies have been written about Deloria, though he is mentioned in passing in a number of theological, anthropological, and political works." At the time (1994), Warrior thought this had to do with the fact that Deloria was an active member of the scholarly community, unlike historic figures like D'Arcy

McNickle (Salish Kootenai) or Charles A. Eastman (Dakota), who were frequently the subject of work in literary studies.[69] Unfortunately, more than two decades after Warrior's observation, not much has changed. At the same time, because of the magnitude of Deloria's publications, which cross numerous topics, genres, and disciplines, any attempt to systematize the work that Deloria produced between *Custer* (1969) and *Singing for a Spirit* (1999), not counting his posthumous works, would be an enormous undertaking that would result in either a superficial analysis, if limited to a single work, or a multivolume work of encyclopedic proportions. What I have opted to do is focus my analysis on Deloria's Red Power Tetralogy, which, as noted, consisted of *Custer Died for Your Sins* (1969), *We Talk, You Listen* (1970), *God Is Red* (1973), and *Behind the Trail of Broken Treaties* (1974).[70]

As for why I chose these four books, they correspond to an important epoch in American Indian history, specifically the climactic period of the Indian protest movement, which stretched from the occupation of Alcatraz Island, San Francisco Bay, in late 1969 to the 1973 conflict between the American Indian Movement and U.S. federal forces at Wounded Knee, South Dakota. In light of this, because of the correlation between these books and the times in which they appeared, it is accurate to say that Deloria's Red Power Tetralogy, when compared to his subsequent works, had a disproportionate influence in the fields of American Indian law, politics, history, and religious studies, which was in addition to the droves of ordinary men and women in various American Indian communities who felt that they heard their own voices in Deloria's words, especially when reading *Custer*. Indeed, many of those ordinary men and women were college students during the early 1970s and were a part of the burgeoning discipline of American Indian/Native American studies, in which Deloria's work, *Custer* above all else, quickly became required reading. Consequently, one can expect to see in the following pages an appreciable level of recognition for Deloria as a distinguished elder.

As an Akimel O'odham, who is an enrolled member of the Gila River Indian Community, located in southern Arizona, and as an Indigenous scholar, respecting one's elders is a value that I believe is essential to understanding the significance of Deloria's work as a Standing Rock

Sioux. Having said that, according Deloria's work its due respect does not mean that his work is thereby beyond criticism. On the contrary, as will be demonstrated, Deloria's ideas and opinions were often challenged by other American Indian scholars and community members, be it because of Plains Indian–centered view of Indian affairs—which Alfonso Ortiz saw as largely omitting Southwestern tribes—or because certain Indian activists, such as Mel Thom (Walker River Paiute), did not think Deloria was radical enough in his confrontation with federal authorities. Then, there is the question of how well formed were Deloria's arguments, as his writing was frequently regarded as lacking proper revision. *Custer*, in particular, upon multiple readings, starts to look hastily written, as well as carelessly documented. One of the most frustrating characteristics of *Custer* is its numerous uncited references to important government documents, namely congressional hearings, statutes, case law, and policy statements. For anyone trying to utilize *Custer* as a resource for addressing law and policy issues, they were soon confronted with having to track down these references at their nearest law library or, as occurs today, in a variety of databases, such as ProQuest Congressional or HeinOnline.

As influential as Deloria's Red Power tetralogy may have been, these four works tended to be long on rhetoric and personal anecdote and short on scholarly precision, even as they displayed a vast amount of learnedness. For example, Joseph G. Jorgensen faulted Deloria for his less than adequately substantiated criticisms of acculturation research, which was where much of the focus was being placed in the post-1945 anthropological studies that were castigated in *Custer*. More specifically, Jorgensen stated: "Recently the clichés and erroneous concepts of acculturation research have been challenged by Vine Deloria, Jr. (1969), an Indian author. Although Deloria's criticisms are sound, he does not adequately explain why Indians are as they are. It is clear, however, that the political, economic, and social conditions of American Indians are not improving, and this is the nub of the issue."[71] In turn, Jean K. Boek complained in her review of *We Talk, You Listen*: "As he [Deloria] hops from one topic to the next under the rubrics of the communications gap, stereotyping, black power, and the artificial universe, among others, he provides few clues as to the basics of who, when, where and what. Because of this, it is difficult to learn much from the examples cited, or, indeed, to be very certain of the accuracy of their reporting."[72]

A word now about methodology. With the above criticisms in mind, I engage in a critical historical analysis of Deloria's ideas, arguments, and observations of the topics and issues raised in *Custer*. These are explicated with an eye for how these were developed in his subsequent works, namely *We Talk, You Listen, God Is Red,* and *Behind the Trail of Broken Treaties.* Consideration for the writings that Deloria published concurrently with his first four books will be included as a way of broadening the reader's comprehension of Deloria's activist-intellectual agenda, as he strove to reshape his readers' understanding of tribes as sovereign nations, and what that implies for federal Indian affairs. Consequently, because Deloria's analyses of politics (federal Indian affairs), religion (Christian missionaries and mainstream churches), and academia (social-science research) are premised on regarding these as colonial institutions in which each has played a role in the suppression of tribes' political, religious, and cultural sovereignty, one cannot analyze his discourses on these topics without looking at the critical, often vehement reaction to his criticisms. Out of this dynamic emerges the political and historical context in which Deloria generated his argument for tribal self-determination.

More often than not, Deloria wrote in response to developments in ongoing issues within the American Indian community, be it the relationship to the federal government, social scientists, or national church bodies, not to mention the activists and organizations purporting to represent the interests of tribes. Through an examination of Deloria's primary works, plus the pertinent government documents and archival material, what takes shape is an intellectual history of a body of work, namely the Red Power Tetralogy, in which the name "Vine Deloria Jr." signified a political discourse that occurred during a specific time, 1964 to 1974, which advocated for tribal rights and sovereignty by means of criticizing those colonial institutions that did the most to negatively affect American Indians as tribes, as people, and as nations. Equally important is an examination of Deloria's ideas, opinions, recommendations, and suggestions for reforming Indian–United States relations, tribal governments, as well as enhancing American Indian religious freedom and cultural revitalization.

In light of the above, the chapters are organized topically to parallel the organization of *Custer Died for Your Sins,* which, it should be noted, was how Deloria organized his subsequent books. In spite of being identified as a historian—along with legal and religious scholar—Deloria was anything but a linear thinker. When Deloria does invoke a linear historical narrative, it was typically when he was criticizing some aspect of the history of federal Indian law and policy, which is an aggressively linear Manifest Destiny–based agenda—not to mention non-Indigenous. Otherwise, Deloria's method of expounding on a topic was to examine how Indians related to particular ideas, issues, or events impacting their world. One need only look at *Custer*'s chapters on anthropology, Christian missionaries, or the Bureau of Indian Affairs; *We Talk, You Listen*'s chapters on communication, stereotyping, and othering; *God Is Red*'s chapters on time, space, and history; or, *Behind the Trail of Broken Treaties*' chapters on the major doctrines governing Indian law and policy. To put it succinctly, Deloria's books are books about ideas and how these ideas have historically, politically, and culturally affected the American Indian community.

Insofar then as *Custer* set the stage for what became Deloria's Red Power Tetralogy, the book in hand is organized into chapters on Indian-white relations and how this historic relation has been based on misperceptions and biased assumptions (chapter 2), which informed negatively the discourse on federal Indian law and policy, including one of the most egregious chapters in American Indian history—termination (chapters 3 and 4). Out of this background, an agenda for Indian liberation was set, beginning with disabusing the American public and its federal representatives from conceiving of Indians as just another "minority group" and more as nations (chapter 5). Equally important to affirming Indians' nationhood is freeing them from the shackles of an anthropological enterprise that regards them as cultural relics, which is to say, when Indians are not demeaned as uncivilized heathens in need of salvation (chapters 6 and 7). Only when Indians assert their right to speak on their own behalf, as opposed to being treated as wards of the government, will

Indians not only be respected as equals in contemporary society, but also be thought capable of establishing their own political agenda, complete with addressing their leadership needs, in addition to the major trends that will impact the political future of the American Indian community, such as the movement among federally unrecognized tribes and a growing urban Indian population (chapters 8, 9, and 10).

Given that the book in hand is a work in American Indian intellectual history, for those seeking to know the man behind the writings, the ensuing discourse may not satisfy the urge to learn about Deloria's private life, be it his life growing up Martin, South Dakota; the alliances and rivalries he created during his tenure with the NCAI; or, his relationship with his colleagues at the various institutions of higher learning where he taught and served. Having said that, although the book thus written is more formalist in orientation—if I may hazard the language of literary studies—it is not without its humanitarian aspects. What comes through loud and clear in any reading of Deloria's work is his sincere concern for Indian people and his impassioned desire to assert their rights as both human beings and as sovereign nations. Toward that end, Deloria emerges in the following chapters as a brilliant and influential thinker who was respected even by his detractors. Although recurrently abrasive, particularly with those who could and should have done more for Indian liberation—he was unforgiving of Stewart Udall—Deloria was by equal measure a strong proponent of Indian rights, be it for Indian people on and off the reservation, recognized or unrecognized tribes, virtually everywhere, living and dead. In the end, it is the works that have to speak for themselves if Deloria is to have any meaningful legacy in the American Indian community. So, now it is to those works we shall turn, as the Indian revolution has begun.

CHAPTER 2

Coyote Old Man Tells a Story

History, Plight, and Indian-White Relations

The reality of Indigenous lives in America, according to *Custer Died for Your Sins*, was hidden underneath layers of non-Indian ethnocentric distortions, which non-Indians treated as historical fact, mostly because they often have not directly experienced many Indians in their lives. In light of this inexperience, what may seem like harmless caricatures or literary conventions to non-Indians were actually disrespectful and problematic racial stereotypes for Indians, the density and intransigence of which precluded Indigenous communities from being heard in their own voices, even when they were appealing for justice and fairness.[1] At the top of Deloria's list of misconceptions was our so-called plight, which every non-Indian supposedly saw and, more importantly, knew the answer to its resolution. Indeed, when Kenneth M. Roemer reviewed *Custer* in a 1970 issue of the *American Quarterly*, he identified the supposed "transparency" of Indians as their foremost "plight": "Most non-Indians see Indians as they want to see them: they are 'folk' people and 'bi-cultural' beings to anthropologists, 'pagans' to the missionary, a 'subcategory of black' to civil rights leaders, and savages or Tontos to mass media audiences."[2] In fact, one did not even need to ask any Indians about the "Indian plight" because it was just that obvious. How the Indian plight was defined depended on who was asked, excepting Indians, of course, who need not be asked a thing. Accordingly, "experts paint us as they would like us to be." Experts, in turn, came from all walks of life, yet they were all knowledgeable, i.e., presumptuous, about what they thought was a "real Indian." Consequently, "the more we try to be ourselves the more we are forced to defend what we have never been."[3] Even during pre-Contact times, not all Indians went on "vision quests" or "counted coup" on an enemy. Nevertheless, it was an unfortunate part of the Indian experience to be held unfairly accountable for not living up to the expectations of other people's images.[4]

Before proceeding, it is worth noting that in addition to setting the agenda for one of the defining issues in American Indian/Native American studies, namely stereotypes and popular images, Deloria also established a key component to his methodology with *Custer*'s chapter 1 "Indians Today, the Real and the Unreal." More to the point, it was commonplace for Deloria to initiate the discourse in his books with an examination of the prevailing stereotypes about Indians that were pertinent to his topic and that he felt compelled to dispel before embarking on his analyses. For example, in *We Talk, You Listen*, chapters 1 and 2 were about how mass media generated widely distributed and instantaneously consumed images, of which movies and television were a part, a phenomenon, moreover, that produced and reinforced through repetition an array of false images. Then, in *God Is Red*, Deloria expanded upon his discourse in *Custer* with a chapter titled "The Indians of the American Imagination," which was about how the eruption of the Indian protest movement shattered the romanticized images of historic Indians, such as became popular in Dee Brown's *Bury My Heart at Wounded Knee*. Speaking of the Indian protest movement, in *Behind the Trail of Broken Treaties*, Deloria began with a preamble and an opening chapter in which he portrayed an Indian protest movement that was about Indians being neither a minority group nor wards of the government, but sovereign nations instead. Deloria went on in other works to employ this pattern of criticizing stereotypes and other misconceptions about Indians, which was typically followed by an historical analysis of the events, issues, laws, and policies that created a given problem that tribes were struggling to overcome, which in turn set the stage for a philosophical analysis of the major ideas at the root of the problem (in which there was often a profound difference between the Western and Indian way of thinking), concluding with thought-provoking and original ideas for future action, which were frequently aimed at furthering tribal self-determination.

Unique among the bevy of "Indian experts"—getting back to *Custer*—was the descendant of the "Indian princess." The storied ancestor was typically Cherokee and most often female,[5] hence the gender bias, which in Deloria's experience, as occurred while he was the NCAI's executive director, enabled the alleged descendant to claim not only a connection to "royalty," but also a benign connection to the land that was occupied at the expense of actual Indians.[6] However spurious, claiming an Indian "grandmother," or great to great-great-great-grandmother, in the family tree permitted one to make a genteel affirmation of entitlement to the Indigenous estate, which was typically seized under the "Doctrine of Discovery," an actual historical phenomenon that Deloria covered in *Custer* chapter 2, then again in *Broken Treaties* chapter 5, which predated American independence by several centuries. At the same time, with regard to Deloria's NCAI experience, the influx of "Cherokee" descendants may have at least in part been induced by the racialized politics occurring during the civil rights era. Denise Bates explained this phenomenon in her study of the southern Indian movement: "Southern identity is malleable. Despite decades of marginalization and discrimination against Indian people within a biracial system, many southerners began to reimagine their own identities as 'Indians.'"[7] With respect then to the claims of Cherokee descent, Bates cited *The New Encyclopedia of Southern Culture*: "Southerners are more likely to assert American Indian ancestry than Europeans and African Americans in other regions . . . [and] the most common genealogical lore entails a mythic 'Cherokee Princess in the family tree.'"[8] With respect to the African American population, Deloria did not mention in *Custer* if any of the "Cherokees" he encountered, in spite of working in Washington DC, were Black.[9] Deloria, it should be noted, exhibited a tendency to think of race relations in binary sets, namely Indian-White and Indian-Black, without much allowance for interracial relations, such as intermarriage, be it between whites, Blacks, and Indians or other racial groups, namely Asian or Latino.

Be that as it may, the next layer of delusion was people who "*understand* Indians." Such understanding was not only thorough but also indisputable, even Indians could not contravene this level of expertise, which characterized not only tourists and summer camp children, but also explorers from Columbus to the American pioneers, not to mention missionaries who were certain that Indians were the "lost tribes of Israel" and archeologists postulating an equally unlikely connection to wandering Siberian migrants.[10] Truly, as Deloria observed: "Anyone and everyone who knows an Indian or who is *interested,* immediately and thoroughly understands them" [emphasis in original]. In fact, as noted above, actually meeting Indians and taking their knowledge and opinions seriously has never been required.[11] Such attitudes, as Deloria demonstrated in his historical criticisms of federal Indian doctrines, had devastating effects on tribal communities whose opinions were systematically ignored by treaty commissions, Indian agents, congressmen, and various Indian Bureau and Department of Interior bureaucrats, all of whom categorically presumed to know what lay at the root of the "Indian problem," as well as what to do about it.[12] In an application to the Council on Indian Affairs for a joint leadership project, the so-called Indian problem was described in a way that paralleled much of the critical comparative work that Deloria engaged in both *Custer* and *God Is Red*:

> Historically the problem has been that of conflict between a literate and non-literate people, a technical and non-technical economics, an objective and a subjective society, and a moral system of guilt and shame. . . . Because there has been such a gulf of cultural attitudes Indians have been more susceptible to conquest and more handicapped in effectively maintaining themselves and their rights, property, and society than would ordinarily occur between two different groups of diverse people.[13]

Whether one sympathized with their suffering, admired their rugged resourcefulness, or feared their incomprehensible savagery, one ineluctably knew how to "help" America's Indians. Most often, the answer to the Indian problem, i.e., plight, involved some form of assimilation, which was premised on the belief that Indians were a "primitive" and "child-like" people. Even before Deloria published *Custer*, American Indian activist-intellectuals had long observed the hypocrisies underpinning federal Indian policy, particularly with its efforts at bringing so-called civilization to the "frontier." Whether it was William Apess decrying the incessant and unjustified land seizures instigated by the 1830 Indian Removal Act in his "Eulogy on King Philip,"[14] Sarah Winnemucca Hopkins excoriating the insensitivity of the Indian Bureau in its handling of settler encroachments on Paiute lands in *Life among the Piutes*,[15] or Charles Eastman mourning the slaughtered innocents at Wounded Knee in *From the Deep Woods to Civilization*,[16] Indigenous intellectuals have been repeatedly frustrated and perplexed by federal policies that seemed more effective at creating mass suffering than at spreading peace and civilization. Deloria thus added his name to this tradition when he covered in *Custer* the "disastrous policy of termination," not to mention in *Broken Treaties* the government's failings during the 1972 occupation of the Bureau of Indian Affairs building in Washington DC and the subsequent 1973 confrontation at Wounded Knee.

Recurrent throughout the late nineteenth century and early twentieth century, particularly between the Civil War and the 1930s, was a pseudoscientific hypothesis that if Indians can be regarded as human, as opposed to subhuman—or more blatantly as animals—then they must possess an aptitude for learning and enjoying the trappings of civilized, i.e., modern agrarian, Christian life. In which case, the most civilized life, if it was measured in terms of technology and power, rather than spiritual or artistic sophistication, was clearly the sovereign distinction of the United States. Assuming, of course, that one was willing to allow Indians to become a part of American civilization, then it went without saying—according to the logic of ethnocentrism—that Indians would need to become as Americans, who—in spite of their rapidly growing diversity—regarded themselves as a white Anglo-Saxon Protestant nation. In spite of the doubtful veracity of the premises, as Deloria observed, Indians were treated diametrically opposite to their counterparts in the African American community, which was categorically denied access to mainstream American society:

Law after law was passed requiring him [the Indian] to conform to white institutions. Indian children were kidnapped and forced into boarding schools thousands of miles from their homes to learn the white man's ways. Reservations were turned over to different Christian denominations for governing. Reservations were for a long time church operated. Everything possible was done to ensure that Indians were forced into American life. The wild animal was made into a household pet whether or not he wanted to be one.[17]

As a result of nineteenth-century federal policy initiatives that dogmatically asserted white American superiority over Indigenous nations, two major developments happened concurrently with respect to Indigenous cultural integrity and political self-determination. First, because of the constantly growing bureaucracy governing Indian affairs, which was based on the firm belief that Indians were incompetent "wards" of the federal government—which Deloria regarded as a heinous misreading of *Cherokee Nation v. Georgia* (1831)—much of what happened on the reservation was hidden within a dense forest of Indian Bureau reports, which applauded the steady "progress" that "their Indians" were making at adapting to white social standards.[18] Most prominent in this bureaucratic tradition were the annual reports of the commissioners of Indian affairs, who were always anxious to cast the Indian Bureau in a good light, no matter how much Indians on the reservations, along with their white allies, belied the falsehoods of "Indian progress" with evidence of poor health conditions, endemic poverty, and Indian Service corruption.[19] When word of the humanitarian crises impacting the reservation system did make it to the general public, the more philanthropic elements, such as church-run charities, temperance unions, and Indian rights organizations, typically responded with ways to enhance Indian progress into civilization.[20] The latter brings up another perennial problem in Indian affairs, namely the conflict between what Indians' white allies think is best for Indians and what Indians themselves say that they want for their communities.

In other words, although most problems on the reservation stemmed from the government's efforts at forcing Indians to assimilate into white society, instead of renouncing that objective, the philanthropic community sought to somehow make the process "better." "People were horrified," for example, "that Indians continued to dress in their traditional garb." Consequently, "do-gooders in the East held fantastic clothing drives to supply the Indians with civilized clothes."[21] Anyone who has ever had to rely on a ramshackle assortment of hand-me-downs can imagine how this turned out.[22] Even more infamous was the effort at providing irreproachable Christian leadership for the Indian Bureau in response to the numerous accusations of corruption in the reservation system, which, ironically, led to an increase in government malfeasance.[23] Second, Indigenous nations witnessed a steady downfall in their status as politically distinct entities, as their confederacies, nationhood, and kinship ties were slowly decimated by westward expansion, leaving individual survivors in legal and political limbo—neither citizen nor alien.[24] Yet, as Deloria noted with admiration, Indian people had endured through it all, which was less a vindication of federal policy and more of a testament to Indigenous resiliency:

> Conforming their absolute freedom to fit rigid European political forms has been very difficult for most tribes, but on the whole they have managed extremely well. Under the [1934] Indian Reorganization Act Indian people have generally created a modern version of the old tribal political structure and yet have been able to develop comprehensive reservation programs which compare favorably with governmental structures anywhere.[25]

Deloria revisited the topic of tribal governments and their contentious relationship with the federal system on multiple occasions, most notably in *Behind the Trail of Broken Treaties* and, coauthored with Clifford Lytle, *The Nations Within* (1984). And while his analyses in these subsequent works were less idealistic and more critical in their assessment of the effectiveness of modern tribal governing institutions, one point that Deloria remained emphatic about was that *Indians can think for themselves!*

Nevertheless, Indigenous people were constantly the victims of "racial erasure," in which the arrogance of non-Indians—typically those representing political, religious, and academic institutions—led to the subsuming of the Indian experience into the dominant discourses on "Indian progress" and the "vanishing Indian." Consequently, "Indians are probably invisible because of the tremendous amount of misinformation about them," and much of this misinformation arose from the misguided notion that there was an "Indian problem," which was a government fiction that informed federal Indian policy until the 1960s.[26] There was no Indian problem, there was only *a white problem with Indians*. Unfortunately, the myth of the Indian problem not only persisted but also generated additional myths that further blurred the line between fantasy and reality. As Deloria noted after observing that American Indians were completely omitted from Michael Harrington's seminal study of poverty *The Other America (1962)*: "Mythological theories about the three sectors [government, business, and tribe] are as follows: paternalism exists in the governmental area, assistance is always available in the private sector, and the tribes dwell in primitive splendor. All three myths are false."[27] Moreover, these myths were the premises on which federal Indian policy had been based, most notoriously in the post-1945 drive toward termination, which purported to be a resolution to the problem of federal paternalism.

As Deloria made abundantly clear, paternalism was a congressional task force concoction, which was repeatedly identified in reports as the source of the problem of Indian affairs. In turn, House and Senate leaders hoped to settle the Indian problem through "a consistent policy of self-help with adequate loan funds for reservation development." While such a plan may sound acceptably "pro-active," as one says today, the ulterior motive unfortunately was utterly unacceptable to tribes: "Congress always wants to do away with paternalism. So it has a policy designed to do away with Indians. If there are no Indians, there cannot be any paternalism."[28] As of 1969 the most recent and devastating example of this approach to the "Indian problem" was the dual effect of 1953's House Current Resolution 108 (HCR 108) and Public Law 280 (P.L. 280), which defined the federal Indian policy infamously called "termination," in which dozens of tribes and thousands of Indians were forced to struggle through government-induced poverty, unemployment, and inadequate health care.

Complementing government policy was the private sector, which consisted of churches, universities, and private firms. Supposedly, in the absence of government support of tribal programs, Indians could turn to them for their health, education, and social welfare needs. Each entity, as Deloria portrayed them, invaded America's reservations with their own definition of paternalism that they sought to address "IN THEIR OWN INIMITABLE WAY. No one asks them to come out [to the reservations]. It is very difficult, therefore, to get them to leave." Missionaries and anthropologists—each of which had a chapter in *Custer* devoted to their unique relation to Indians—stood as examples of uninvited do-gooders pushing their way into Indigenous peoples' private lives, the former to presumably "save" their pagan souls, the latter to "salvage" their dying culture. Meanwhile, private sector entities often maintained "Indian advisory" boards, which typically commended the organizations they represented.[29] Ultimately, the product of the private sector's notions of paternalism, be they missionaries or academics, was a range or irreconcilable contradictions, which perpetuated the alleged need for saving and salvaging Indians, while never doing anything constructive to either alleviate their suffering or support their ambitions.

In light of the foregoing remarks about Congress and the private sector, it is fair to point out that Deloria had a habit of making sweeping generalizations about the major mainstream institutions he scorned, be it the federal government, Christian churches, or social science. Indeed, Indian and non-Indian readers alike have observed Deloria's tendency to, at best, hint at the real target of his reproaches and, at worst, simply to lash out without so much as a citation. For example, Merle W. Wells observed about Deloria's attitude toward whites in his 1970 review for the *Pacific Northwest Quarterly*:

> Deloria neither understands nor appreciates some important aspects of white theoretical science, but at this point he reflects a lot of white confusion for which he is hardly responsible. Indians, like everyone else, differ in experience and outlook, but a great many of them agree in rejecting attitudes that seem to be typically white. In presenting such an Indian position, he resorts to some overdone generalizations

about whites, in an all too faithful imitation of an excessive number of overdone (and usually false) white generalizations about Indians.[30]

In turn, Alfonso Ortiz, in his perceptive 1971 review of *Custer* for *American Anthropologist*, took Deloria to task, as mentioned earlier, for his own biases, in particular his conspicuously Plains-centric notion of being Indian:

> Deloria . . . talks of anthropologists of creating a kind of mythical super Indian in their writings, one which does not conform to Indian realities. But in his turn he also creates his own mythical Indian, a member of a High Plains tribes. Consider the following facts. The Navajo are mentioned only three times in the whole book, and then only in passing, while the Apaches, the most Plains-like of the Southwestern tribes, are given extended and favorable mention.[31]

Deloria did refer to Puebloan groups in *Custer*, though obviously not to Ortiz's satisfaction. Insofar then as Deloria was Standing Rock Sioux one might argue that his ethnocentrism was understandable. Deloria, after all, was hardly the first Indian writer to be biased toward his own tribe and tribal worldview. Eastman, for example, was unabashedly Dakota-centric in his writings about "the Indian" who barely acknowledged his Lakota and Nakota cousins, let alone other tribes, although he did express much admiration and respect for the Ojibwe. Nonetheless, given that Deloria was recently the executive director of the National Congress of American Indians one might have expected him to demonstrate more awareness about the diversity, culturally and politically, among tribal nations.

As a manifesto, though—returning to *Custer*'s nonacademic attributes—the book was not about accumulating citations for the sake of contributing to the scholarly discourse on Indian affairs, but rather it was about completely shaking up the status quo and motivating Indians to take action against their oppressors. So, yes, not all politicians, Christians, and academics were guilty of the offenses that Deloria enumerated in *Custer*, but that was not the point. The point was that these institutions and the people who were a part of them were guilty of condoning attitudes and behaviors that had subjugated Indian people with the policies, credos, and theories that had violated their freedom and integrity as sovereign nations. As such, *Custer* was not a comprehensive appraisal of developments in the works of government, church, and academia. Rather than being about colonial institutions, *Custer* was about how Indians experienced these institutions when they imposed themselves onto Indian lives. At the same time, Deloria's sparse citations—which ranged from adequately documented to nonexistent—made it difficult for activists in the field to utilize Deloria's legal analyses. Of course, Deloria later learned the importance of documentation as his career moved from NCAI executive director to university professor.

To focus now on how Indians experienced the private sector, Deloria noted: "To hear some people talk, Indians are simultaneously rich from oil royalties and poor as church mice." He then added the sarcastic observation that Indians were also "underprivileged" because they did not enjoy "the pleasures of the mainstream, like riots, air pollution, snipers, ulcers, and traffic."[32] Americans, of course, had long believed in the inherent supremacy of the "American dream," particularly when trying to convince other nations to buy into their economic system in which social problems were presumably a small price to pay for the opportunity of wealth and power. Complementing the supposition that all U.S. citizens aspired toward the American dream was the notion that class distinctions transcended racial and cultural differences, as if members of the same socio-economic class exhibited similar traits, such as denoted by references to "the poor" or "the wealthy." Such a notion was what drove Martin Luther King Jr.'s organization of the Poor People's Campaign, which was based on the Christian belief in the inherent blessedness of the poor. Unfortunately, while the "kingdom of heaven" may belong to "the poor in spirit," the political rights that Indian and non-Indian poor wanted were fundamentally different.

As for the state of Indian cultures, Deloria tritely observed, "primitive purity is sometimes attributed to tribes. Some tribes keep their rituals and others don't." The source of Deloria's cynicism toward those who perpetuated a myth of a pre-Contact utopia was, as he explained, the military, political, and religious assault that tribes confronted as a consequence of westward expansion. This expansion compelled tribes to adjust as best they could to the cultural oppression that was integral to federal Indian policy, such as the assault on Indian spiritual and healing traditions instigated by the 1883 Courts of Indian Offenses, which condemned the Sun Dance as barbaric, or the efforts by missionaries and Indian agents to suppress Indian dancing and the right of medicine men to practice. In the final analysis, as argued, Indians defied any attempt at categorization—surviving genocide does that to a people, they defy assumptions—implying that the transparencies outlined above are nothing more than political, religious, and academic fictions.

> The best characterization of tribes is that they stubbornly hold on to what they feel is important to them and discard what they feel is irrelevant to their current needs. Traditions die hard and innovation comes hard. Indians have survived for thousands of years in all kinds of conditions. They do not fly from fad to fad seeking novelty. That is what makes them Indian.[33]

What Deloria compelled his reader to do, contrary to any fads, was to learn about how Indian society and politics were organized "today," meaning the post–World War II generation, not the mythical times of a romanticized pioneer past. Instead, Deloria drew attention to the much less fantastic era initiated by the 1934 Indian Reorganization Act, which enabled tribes to form constitution-based governments. Indeed, one of the more interesting facets to Deloria's discourse on tribal self-determination was the conundrum of tribal government, which Deloria criticized as a source of problems and as the best available option for reaffirming tribal nationhood:

> I have been a strong supporter of tribal governments and have always preferred to support the elected tribal officials rather than the activists because I have felt that only by official tribal action with Congress can we get real reform. Thus it comes as a great sadness to me to realize where our problems are generating. I believe it is in the failure of our elected tribal officials, specifically in the tribal chairmen, that we are losing the battle. They have miserably failed to bring out the

conditions on the reservations. They have refused to bring any news to Washington except good news—and the news on the reservations is not all good. Most of it is bad.[34]

Rather than primitive splendor, each one of these constitutional governments, whose political and social status was defined by the historical and contemporary forces of federal Indian policy, not the least of which was the reservation system, constantly straddled the line between self-determination and accommodation. Because of historical circumstances, a given reservation may be made up of a single tribe or a combination of some kind, such as the Pima-Maricopa reservations in Arizona or the Mandan-Hidatsa-Arikara of North Dakota. A reservation may, moreover, include distinct bands or clans speaking a common language; or, they may represent mutually exclusive groups, which maintains very different languages and cultures. Since the reservation system was created by nineteenth-century federal Indian policy, which sought political and often military control over Indigenous populations, reservation boundaries and their respective memberships typically reflected the needs of the Indian Bureau, the U.S. Army, and the settlers for whom Indian lands were seized. Among the many historical examples, the most infamous was the Indian Territory created by the 1830 Indian Removal Act, which was little more than a massive refugee camp for unwanted southeastern tribes, such as the Cherokee, Choctaw, Chickasaw, Creek, and Seminole.[35]

Nonetheless, it was within the confines of this politically repressive system where Indigenous sovereignty has been on the long road to recovery. Augmenting this process were various national and local organizations, such as the National Congress of American Indians, the National Indian Youth Council, and various Indian centers in major metropolitan areas, such as "Los Angeles, Oakland, Chicago, and Minneapolis," not to mention groups organized around a particular issue (e.g., Survivors of American Indians, Inc., which was focused on fishing rights, and the Original Cherokee Community Organization,[36] which was dedicated to Cherokee hunting and treaty rights). Of the groups that Deloria enumerated, the one he mislabeled "Survivors of American Indians" was the most important to him at a personal level. Deloria was referring of course to the

Survival of American Indians Association (SAIA), of which Hank Adams was executive director from 1968 to 1972, and whose mission was the protection of Indian fishing rights. In his correspondence with Adams, Deloria frequently spelled out the group's name incorrectly, in addition to getting it wrong in *Custer*. He made the mistake in spite of the fact that Adams regularly copied Deloria on his correspondence advocating on behalf of the tribes SAIA represented.[37] In a project proposal to the Episcopal Church's executive council, SAIA described its historic mission:

> The SAIA is an independent organization of Indian people that came into being in late 1963 in direct response to efforts by the State of Washington to extinguish certain Treaty Rights in relation to commercial salmon fishing by Indian people. . . . Past activities have involved continuous confrontation with the State and in some cases the federal government and opposing Tribal Councils . . . We have assisted families of arrested fishermen and secured subsistence for many; and helped alleviate the excessive burden of replacing confiscated fishing gear and equipment.[38]

According to Deloria, the phenomenon of urban Indians would see the most growth, both in terms of numbers and political influence, a prediction that reached its climax in 1972–73, as noted in chapter 11 of *Custer*, then documented in the first four chapters of *Broken Treaties*.[39] With respect to the latter, Deloria led his reader across an Indian world that was contemporaneous with the turbulent society in which America's Indigenous communities—on and off the reservation—were struggling to adapt, survive, and succeed. "Indian tribes are rapidly becoming accustomed to the manner in which the modern world works," Deloria observed. In fact, it was commonplace for Indigenous nations to send delegations to Washington DC, embark on federally funded programs, and keep up with national and international news. "Few events of much importance pass the eyes of watchful tribal groups without comment."[40] Certainly, Deloria had the NCAI in mind when he made this observation.

Indigenous nations, as Deloria portrayed them, belied the myths and stereotypes that have informed, or rather misinformed, the American imagination for generations, from the Plymouth colony to the Space Age and beyond. More to the point, they were not only diverse— "Individual tribes show incredible differences"—but also they were resilient in ways that mundane words like "tradition" and "modern" cannot adequately describe. For example, the Pueblo communities, who "have a solid community life," undertaking major development projects at the same time they were seeing an "influx of college-educated Pueblos."[41] Then, there were the Apache communities inhabiting northeastern Arizona and adjacent areas in New Mexico, which had "probably less than a dozen college graduates among them," yet, as of the late 1960s, had managed to develop impressive ski and tourism businesses "without the benefit of the white man's vaunted education."[42] If anything, education had only generated a brain drain, such as occurred among the Ojibwe communities. In these cases, "migration to the cities has meant an emphasis on land sales, little development of existing resources, and abandonment of tribal traditions." The exception among the Great Lakes Ojibwe nations was Red Lake, which was "probably the most traditional of the Chippewa [Ojibwe] tribes."[43] In fact, with the Red Lake Ojibwe and the Apache reservations in mind, Deloria argued that the more grounded a given community was in its traditional ways, the more likely they were to succeed at their nation-building endeavors.

As Indigenous nations have adapted to the prevailing political order, first, by the reservation system and, secondly, by the 1934 Indian Reorganization Act (IRA), modern traditions, if you will, have also emerged. Deloria referred to, for example, the "great tradition of conflict" among the Lakota, going back to their historic battles with U.S. forces, and extending forward to today, in which political contentiousness was a commonplace part of governance. "Fortunately strong chairmen have come to have a long tenure on several [Lakota] Sioux reservations and some of the tribes have made a great deal of progress," in spite of a tendency "to slug it out at a moment's notice."[44] Speaking of political contentiousness, Deloria detailed the disputes over fishing rights in the Pacific Northwest, which was not just a battle between tribal and nontribal fishermen, but also between smaller Indigenous nations, which were fighting for their treaty-based rights, and larger Indigenous nations, which had been reluctant to support the treaty-rights movement. In addition to "fish-ins," these smaller nations took their grievances into the court system, which, as these cases were decided, established a body of common law that would be as influential as the Cherokee cases decided during the nineteenth century.[45] Deloria's estimation in *Custer* turned out to be prescient, as the latter dispute formed the basis of the 1974 Boldt Decision.[46] To put things, succinctly, Deloria's examples above are evidence of a modern American Indian community in which individual Indians and tribes have grown accustomed to the battle that is modern life, and even succeeding under the rules of engagement be it on the front lines of a protest event, at a tribal council meeting, or in the hallowed halls of the American judicial system. Indians have learned not be docile about their politics.

Similar to the Cherokee during the 1820s and 1830s, the Indigenous nations—from the Pacific Northwest to the Great Lakes, and down to the Southwest—were becoming more aware of themselves as nations, complete with greater awareness of their inherent rights and powers. In light of which, as "Congressional policy [moves] away from termination toward support of tribal self-sufficiency, it is conceivable that Indian tribes will be able to become economically independent of the federal government in the next generation." Tribal governments were rapidly growing, after all, due to the War on Poverty programs proliferating across the reservation system. While it was true that these programs were under federal regulations, which the tribes were obliged to honor lest they risk losing their funding, a turning point had occurred nonetheless where tribal governments were seeing their self-governance begin to grow. Still, what exactly Deloria meant by "independence," of course, was open to some discussion. Did he mean something merely administrative in scope, Indians running federally mandated Indian programs, or did he have in mind something more dramatic? While Deloria did have practical suggestions for tribes being more effective under existing late-1960s policy guidelines, as demonstrated in the chapter on the Bureau of Indian Affairs in *Custer*, he was also aware that Indian communities wanted more than a more efficient bureaucracy—they wanted national independence.

Deloria thought deeply about the question of national independence in *Broken Treaties*, in which he surveyed in his 1974 analysis the various "sizes and status" of smaller nations that practiced sovereignty, complete with setting the agenda for their own economies without having to go to the extremes of isolating themselves from the international community. What may yet impede this movement toward economic liberation is the legacy of paternalism that still dwells in the hearts of well-intentioned but uninformed non-Indian political, religious, and academic leaders who firmly believe that Indigenous people were in need of their help at saving their culture or guiding them into civilization. Referring back to *Custer* on this point, Deloria shared a revelation:

> Some years ago at a Congressional hearing someone asked Alex Chasing Hawk, a council member of the Cheyenne River Sioux for thirty years, "Just what do you Indians want?" Alex replied, "A leave-us-alone law!!" The primary goal and need of Indians today is not for someone to feel sorry for us and claim descent from Pocahontas to make us feel better. Nor do we need to be classified as semi-white and have programs and policies made to bleach us further. Nor do we need further studies to see if we are feasible. We need a new policy by Congress acknowledging our right to live in peace, free from arbitrary harassment. We need the public at large to drop the myths in which it has clothed us for so long. We need fewer and fewer "experts" on Indians. What we need is a cultural leave-us-alone agreement, in spirit and in fact.[47]

One can say that what Councilman Chasing Hawk was really demanding was a form of decolonization.[48] Leave us alone meant at the political level for federal agencies to quit impeding tribal nation progress as Indians defined it with non-Indigenous and archaic legal concepts, not to mention misinformed policy initiatives.[49] Obviously, when one took into consideration the size and breadth of the institutions mentioned above, which had been hampering Indigenous peoples, then it went without saying that "leave-us-alone" required some explanation. Hence, the need for *Custer*, not to mention Deloria's subsequent work. More specifically, Deloria addressed the topics of laws, treaties, and the deleterious effects of the post-1945 termination policy, which stemmed, as Deloria argued in *Broken Treaties*, from the doctrines of discovery, dependent domestic nation, and plenary power. The purpose of Deloria's critical historical analysis was to clear a legal space for self-determination as defined by his concept of tribalism. In fact, Deloria demonstrated across a number of writings that one could not talk about Indians or Indian affairs without understanding how both were impacted by federal Indian policies, statutes, and case law. Even the definition of "Indian" and "Indian Country" was defined by federal law, as opposed to Indigenous language and kinship customs.

CHAPTER 3

The Law of the Land

Tribes as Higher than States, Indians as Lower than Human

In his all but forgotten 1971 anthology, *Of Utmost Good Faith*, Deloria argued with respect to the government documents that he assembled for the purpose of indicting the U.S. federal government of multiple treaty and trust violations that Americans have been the victim of a grave historical hoax. More specifically, they have been led to believe by generations of historians that the march toward nationhood and status as a global power was the result of triumphant moments of conquest and progress in which a more perfect nation ultimately was created for all. In the case of the American Indian's role in this narrative, when it was acknowledged at all, it was typically recounted in "unbiased," "neutral" tones. "It is not so," Deloria asserted. "Each and every incident, every treaty, statute and case is loaded with values, viewpoints and biases." As such, the history of federal Indian law and policy, and the documents they generated, was overflowing with wisdom, courage, and justice, as much as they were with greed, selfishness, and cruelty. To focus, then, on the American Indian perspective on these legal and political documents, as opposed to marginalizing that view point vis-à-vis the non-Indian conquest narrative, is to engage directly with the innumerable violations of federal and international law, not to mention human rights violations. With respect to what Deloria thought he was doing in *Of Utmost Good Faith*: "It makes, for example, provocative efforts to call attention to the unresolved liabilities of the United States government for massacres of Indians at Wounded Knee and Sand Creek."[1] Before proceeding with Deloria's critique of federal Indian law and policy, it may be worth noting that *Of Utmost Good Faith* appeared the same year as his revised edition of Jennings C. Wise's *The Red Man in the New World Drama*, which took an unforgiving view of European and American colonialism in North America. Interestingly, Wise's original publication occurred in 1931, just after the outrage generated by the 1928 Meriam Report and not long before the passage of the 1934 Indian Reorganization Act. Perhaps with the publication of these two volumes Deloria hoped to signal that American Indians were once again at the cusp of a major new era of reform. Only this time, Indian thinkers like Deloria would play more of an active intellectual role at articulating the objectives and agenda.

As noted in chapter 1, Deloria's most significant contribution to the American Indian community was his passionate argument for tribal self-determination. Much more than a critical analysis of federal Indian law and policy, Deloria's articulation of sovereignty originated in the peoplehood that bound each tribe together, which federal forces sought to eliminate, but which nevertheless endured until they were revalidated by the 1934 Indian Reorganization Act. Indian Commissioner John Collier's reforms not only enabled tribes to form their own governments, but also to begin revitalizing their cultural values as tribal peoples. "The Act," as D'Arcy McNickle summarized in a 1938 issue of *Indians at Work*, "made possible the granting of specific powers to tribal governments. These powers were written into the constitutions or charters which the tribes are adopting." As intended, tribes began to reawaken to their former powers of self-governance. "A tribal government which successfully performs the duties assumed by it will find itself taking over more and more of the authority which in the past was exercised by the Commissioner of Indian Affairs and his agents."[2] Termination policy notwithstanding, the self-determination genie had been let out of the bottle. On this basis, Deloria argued for reasserting tribes' nationhood status by pursuing their political agenda on the premise that they had historically engaged foreign nations, including the United States, as nation to nation. This historic relationship was documented on the nearly century-long tradition of treaty making, which occurred between 1778 and 1871. With respect, then, to the objective of reestablishing the treaty-making custom of Indian-white relations, complete with the sovereign nationhood that that entailed, like all of Deloria's most important ideas, it began with *Custer*.

More to the point, Deloria, in *Custer* chapter 2, "Laws and Treaties," did more than bemoan the colonization of Indigenous nations, he also offered suggestions for turning these unprecedented historical events into constructive legal strategies. More exactly, Deloria argued that the basis of federal Indian policy, which was subsequently turned into public laws, was a triad of perfidy, theft, and exploitation. At the root of Indian colonization was the infamous Doctrine of Discovery, a legal concept that went back to the Spanish and English invasions of the Western Hemisphere. Because the Age of Discovery was so long ago, when men sailed in wooden boats, one may think that the doctrine is a mere relic of the past, like the crossbow and musket. Yet, however archaic and reactionary, the effectiveness of this sixteenth-century doctrine at justifying the seizure and occupation of Indian lands was so thorough, as evidenced in the complete aggrandizement of the Western Hemisphere, that colonial Americans did not think twice about assuming its power of expropriation.

At the onset of Deloria's explication, the Doctrine of Discovery was not merely an historical artifact, but a prominent part of contemporary Indian affairs, a point he illustrated with references to Presidents Lyndon Johnson and Richard Nixon. The former was portrayed as affirming America's need to honor its commitment to Vietnam,[3] while the latter was quoted reviling the Soviet Union's broken treaty promises.[4] Deloria was unsurprisingly sarcastic about the American presidents' moralizing about commitments and promises, given their nation's shameful record at absolving itself from its treaty promises to Indigenous nations. Indeed, the assertion that the United States had frequently and unilaterally violated its hundreds of treaties with tribes was so pervasive that it had become an unquestioned truism among proponents of Indian rights. In fact, the double indignity of being a primitive people tragically robbed of their land by a superior race of men became the stuff of legend powerful enough to influence the legal minds of the Supreme Court, as displayed in *Tee-Hit-ton Indians v. United States* (1955).[5] Francis Paul Prucha, however, who expressed the antinomy of the Delorian worldview, argued many years later, in his monumental *American Indian Treaties: The History of a Political Anomaly*, that the historical record was much more nuanced than Deloria's unsparing accusation of American perfidy made it appear. After quoting *Custer* on the point of the legislative violations of treaties perpetrated by Congress, Prucha observed:

> The matter is not that simple. . . . There certainly are well-confirmed cases in which the federal government failed to live up to the stipulations of the treaties, just as there are cases in which the Indian signatories "broke" the treaties. Neither the United States nor the Indian tribes were able to control the actions of their subjects, as aggressive white settlers moved illegally into lands reserved for the Indians and as young Indian warriors continued their raids on white settlements after the chiefs had agreed to permanent peace. On the side of the whites the governmental system contributed to the problem, for treaties negotiated and signed in good faith by the executive branch were delayed, amended, or rejected by the Senate, and Congress was often slow or negligent in appropriating the funds needed to implement the treaties. But it is not proper to maintain, as some Indian groups have done, that an initial treaty is absolute and that any subsequent treaty, agreement, or statute that changes its provisions is an illegal abrogation of the original treaty.[6]

While one ought to be more cognizant of the historical circumstances in which treaties were made, maintained, and violated, there was no question that the United States exploited the treaty-making function for its own purposes, namely to extinguish Indian land title while concurrently pressuring tribes into accepting the status of nonthreatening dependents, whose political rights would be in question for generations to come. Or, as Deloria rebutted Prucha's argument in his 1995 review:

> Prucha seems to accept the idea of Manifest Destiny as a proven fact and aligns his discussion to suggest that these treaties were no longer

the bargains made by two sovereign entities. Missing, of course, is the admission that a good many of these treaties were made necessary by the failure of the United States, indeed its refusal in many instances, to keep its word. One cannot fault a smaller nation for trying to negotiate in good faith with a larger one whose word is generally worthless.[7]

As of 1969, Deloria observed in *Custer* that at the same time America was presumably defending the free world from communism, it violated one of its oldest treaties with an Indigenous nation. Article 3 of the 1794 Pickering Treaty, which was a product of President Washington's effort at acquiring the Iroquois confederacy's much-needed friendship against the British, clearly affirmed "Seneka" land rights, which would remain theirs, undisturbed by the United States, until the Seneca chose to sell them to the United States. Nearly two centuries later, when the United States determined that it needed to build a dam in Seneca territory it did not wait for the Seneca to choose to sell—it forced them. This was hardly the first time, it should be noted, that the United States violated its treaty with the Seneca, merely the latest in an American tradition of duplicity. The dam, which flooded much of the land protected by the Pickering Treaty, was allegedly "the price of keeping Pennsylvania in line for John F. Kennedy at the 1960 Democratic convention."[8] Stealing Indian land for political or economic gain, alas, is a longstanding American political custom, which, as Deloria observed sardonically, was regularly sanctioned by federal laws that exonerated the United States from its fiduciary and humanitarian obligations to Indigenous people whenever they determined that there was a greater interest at stake, most obviously the non-Indian settlers who supposedly would "improve" the lands they occupied with their "civilization."

As indicated above, the notion that one nation could claim rights to a given area by virtue of "discovery," even if the land was already occupied by Indigenous people, was a legal non sequitur inherited from the Spanish and British empires. Moreover, as these lands were "discovered," whereas the claims of any other Christian nation would be recognized, those of non-Christians would not be accepted as valid. In other words, Indigenous people did not possess a right to say "no" to invasion precisely because they were non-Christian primitive peoples who neither possessed souls nor the rights of Christian men.[9] Consequently, Christianity "endorsed and advocated the rape[10] of the North American continent, and her representatives have done their utmost to contribute to this process ever since."[11] The United States in turn retained in the founding of its own republic the fundamental prejudice that non-Christian, not to mention nonwhite, people were incapable of legally possessing land. Holding land title, after all, is contingent upon a people's ability at maintaining a recognizably Western, preferably Anglo-Saxon, legal system, in addition to the intellectual maturity, which is to say educated in the finest Western-style schools, to comprehend legal principles. Once discovered—or, more precisely, when the British right of discovery was assumed after the 1787 Treaty of Paris—the United States embarked on a treaty-making campaign, the purpose of which was to ostensibly establish peace between Indians and settlers, but which also carried ulterior motives, ones that were nothing if not heinous acts of extortion.[12]

As pointed out earlier, Deloria went on to expand upon his historical analysis of the Doctrine of Discovery in *Behind the Trail of Broken Treaties*, which Delta Books published in 1974. In between, Deloria published, among other works, his sequel to *Custer, We Talk, You Listen* (1970) and *God Is Red*. In the case of *We Talk, You Listen*, Deloria argued that tribalism, which, more than the customary practices of Indigenous people, was the only viable way in which the various power movements, including Red Power, could organize the demand for the political rights into a coherent policy treating groups as corporate entities under U.S. constitutional law. Indians, after all, are designated as such in the Commerce Clause, alongside states and foreign nations. With respect to *God Is Red*, it was not just that Indian religious customs and beliefs were fundamentally related to a given place, a homeland, whereas Christianity was based on a particular notion of time expressed in the New Testament; rather, it was that tribes possessed a relationship with their environment, which, as an integral part of their religious lives, required legal protections that were not covered by the First Amendment, such as access to sacred places on public land. According to the principles stipulated in the Doctrine of Discovery, public lands were the product of a superior civilization, i.e., the United States, affirming its rightful place as the true owner of the continent, including the right to set an agenda for stewarding the land, an approach that was more about regarding the land as a natural resource in the economic sense as opposed to being a place in which spirits dwelled. Equally noteworthy is the fact that in addition to Nixon's 1970 message to Congress on Indian affairs, in which the president asserted: "Self-determination among the Indian people can and must be encouraged without the threat of eventual termination," the 1972 Trail of Broken Treaties occupation of the Bureau of Indian Affairs building had produced its "Twenty-Point Position Paper," in which was proposed that the 1871 House rider that unilaterally ended treaty making be legislatively overturned and the president's treaty-making power with tribes be reenacted. All of the foregoing, one can argue, informed Deloria's discourse on the Doctrine of Discovery in *Broken Treaties*. For what mattered more than the dissolution of the occupation of Alcatraz Island or the disappointing end to the Trail of Broken Treaties occupation was the realization among Indigenous peoples everywhere that they were nations and that, even when the headlines have ended and Americans have moved on to other things, tribes still have a way of understanding their self-determination.

Because of the treaty-based notion of independence that Deloria advocated, which was inspired by the Trail of Broken Treaties' "Twenty-Point Position Paper"—a drastic departure from the customary dependent domestic nation definition of tribes—many balked at the idea of reinstituting treaty making and according tribes international status, even if Deloria meant that in the "protectorate" sense, as articulated in a bevy of treaty articles. In his 1974 review of *Broken Treaties*, Robert A. Fairbanks found Deloria's and his coauthors', Kirke Kickingbird and Fred Ragsdale,[13] argument to be flawed:

> Apparently, the text was written by American Indians to be read by American Indians. Undoubtedly, the text reflects the state of confusion and conflict which pervades the American Indian community. *Behind the Trail of Broken Treaties: An Indian Declaration of Independence,*

"written to demonstrate that the proposal to reopen the treaty-making procedure is far from a stupid or ill-considered proposal," will accomplish little in the way of convincing adverse parties to implement its suggestions regardless of its merits.[14]

In spite of the lackluster impression that *Broken Treaties* obviously made on some readers, Frederick E. Hoxie acknowledged the book as "foundational," equaled only by *God Is Red*. As Hoxie observed: "*Behind the Trail of Broken Treaties*, which appeared ten months [after *God Is Red*], summarized Deloria's views of the Red Power phenomenon and outlined the principal political adjustments that could ensure the long-term viability of the nation's tribes."[15] Indeed, in a 1973 editorial that Deloria published in *Akwesasne Notes*, which more than likely Fairbanks did not read, the "Twenty-Point Position Paper" was presented as a rallying point around which those seeking meaningful reform in Indian affairs could focus their efforts: "While I did not become involved in the Trail of Broken Treaties, it has seemed to me that the Twenty Points which the people of the caravan drew up and were to have presented to the federal government were the most comprehensive and inclusive list of reforms that I have seen presented to any government officials for quite a while." Furthermore, Deloria argued to his readers that the twenty points should form the basis of how tribes, be it in the form of tribal governments or urban Indian organizations, should develop a unified agenda focused on "a new federal relationship which we need and which we must have to bring any sense out of the present state of Indian Affairs [*sic*]."[16]

Deloria, more specifically, after recounting the Indian protest movement from its emergence in the early 1960s with the Pacific Northwest fish-ins to the occupation of the Bureau of Indian Affairs building in Washington DC and the armed confrontation at Wounded Knee during the early 1970s, Deloria segued back into the colonial history of the Western Hemisphere. Not only were the early European exploration and settlement of the "New World," and the competition for resources that that entailed, the origin of the Doctrine of Discovery, but also the context in which Deloria formed the basis of his claim that Indian affairs needed to be regarded as a facet of international relations.[17] Although Anglo-Saxon legal thinking reduced Indigenous peoples' centuries-long inhabitation of their lands to mere "Aboriginal title," as affirmed in *Johnson v. M'Intosh* (1823), Deloria argued that the implicit recognition that the Indians possessed rights—however diminutive in the minds of the English and Americans—formed the basis of his rebuttal of the claim that white settlers possessed a superior right to the land because of their presumed superior civilization. The latter is no more than the right of the stronger and not the superior. For if in fact the Indians possessed a civilization and a humanity at least comparable to the European invaders, then the claims of superiority were invalid. Certainly, the reversal of the Indian Bureau's historic efforts at suppressing Indigenous cultures enacted by President Franklin D. Roosevelt's commissioner of Indian affairs John Collier and the 1934 Indian Reorganization Act, which acknowledged the Indians' capacity for self-rule, not to mention direct support for the maintenance of traditional culture articulated in the 1935 Indian Arts and Crafts Act, were unequivocal evidence that the U.S. federal government recognized that Indians possessed cultures and societies that had as much of a right to exist as their own. All of which would be reinforced by the 1975 Indian Self-Determination and Education Assistance Act and the 1978 American Indian Religious Freedom Act.

With the above objective in mind, Deloria did not hesitate, in *Broken Treaties*, to point out that some early settlers emphatically rejected the egregious claims of conquest against the Indians' rights as nations and as human beings. In other words, one did not need to wait for modern times to find persons who were well aware of the injustices being visited upon Indigenous peoples. More specifically, Deloria observed in his historical analysis the subversives who laid the groundwork for an Indigenous confutation of the Doctrine of Discovery's principles. Deloria cites in this regard the work of the Spanish humanist Franciscus de Vitoria; the English theologian and founder of Rhode Island Colony, Roger Williams; not to mention the American legal scholar, Roger Cohen. Of course, subversives notwithstanding, most of what Deloria recounted in his treatment of the Doctrine of Discovery was the plundering of Indian lands, which was done under the color of law. At the same time, Deloria made clear that, in the aftermath of the 1787 Treaty of Paris, the Americans did not encounter tribes that were either weakened or chastened by their unsuccessful alliances with Britain. On the contrary, the tribes west of the Appalachians were still very much in control of their domains, which was further evidence against the American claim about superiority.

> In all of this [post-Revolution] confusion, the articulation of the status of the Indian tribes and the nature of their land titles lagged behind the development of the national political identity. During colonial times, the eastern lands were quite often acquired from the Indians by purchase, despite any grants from the King that colonists possessed. When the settlers began to encounter the larger and more and more powerful tribes in the Mississippi Valley and Illinois country, they discovered that all lands had to be purchased. As the controversies swirled around the development of the policy of removing the Indians from the lands east of the Mississippi—which came to fruition in the 1830s—the nation was forced to examine its treaties with the Cherokees, Creeks, and Choctaws of the south and the powerful Miami confederacy of the Indians' Illinois country, and the question of the full nature of Indian title arose.[18]

Consequently, as the United States assumed political control over the territory ceded to it by Britain, which was augmented by the 1804 Louisiana Purchase from France, according to the principles of the Doctrine of Discovery, the United States acquired the exclusive right to extinguish Indian title to the lands within its territorial boundaries. Complicating the situation were some of the individual states, most significantly Georgia, which wanted jurisdiction over Indian affairs, insofar as any pertinent Indian lands lay within state boundaries.[19]

Prior to the Georgia crisis, there was of course the situation that arose in Piankashaw Indian country, where Thomas Johnson purchased land from the tribe during the 1770s, which his descendants inherited. In the intervening years, however, William M'Intosh obtained a land grant from the United States for the same real estate, which created a dispute that went all the way to the Supreme Court. Ultimately, the court decided in favor of M'Intosh on the basis that the Piankashaw only possessed "aboriginal title" to their land, while Britain, which at the time held political control of this land, possessed the superior right to extinguish the title. Consequently, because the Piankashaw only possessed usufructuary rights, as opposed to property-owner rights, they could not sell their own land to Johnson. While the attitude toward the Piankashaw could have been substantially worse—they could have been dismissed altogether as possessing no more rights than the deer inhabiting the forest—it was still the case that the Court's decision in *M'Intosh* was premised on a blatantly racist preconception of Indians. The *M'Intosh* decision in *Broken Treaties* was juxtaposed to Marshall's subsequent opinion in *Worcester v. Georgia* (1832), in which the Cherokee were designated as a "sovereign nation." More important, Deloria's—and his co-authors'—analysis of these two opinions led to the conclusion that the limits of the Doctrine of Discovery were defined by the limits of what the "feeble settlements made on the seacoast" were capable of controlling, which was no more than the actual lands occupied by these settlements—as opposed to the wrongful presumption that such settlements entailed a much more expansive land claim. This, then, went against the popular image of discovery as symbolized by numerous images of Columbus, surrounded by his men, ceremoniously claiming the "New World," all of it, on behalf of the Christian God and the King of Spain. The historical reality was much different. Indigenous nations were, in spite of Spanish arrogance, still very much in control of all of their lands. Furthermore, given that the United States, its victory over Britain notwithstanding, was still a feeble nation at the time it inherited British territory west of the Appalachians, it stood to reason, as Deloria argued, "It would be pure folly to assert that in 1832 (and even more in 1788) the United States had conquered the Indian nations."[20]

Even during the darkest days of the Indian Removal Era, which occurred during the 1830s to 1850s, Indian title endured as a legal right, even as the United States continued to assume—as seen in the Georgia-Cherokee controversy—that it had a superior right and a more compelling need for Indian land. Remarkably—some might say, paradoxically—the United States maintained treaty making as a vehicle for its removal policy, most notably with a range of southern tribes. As Prucha summed up this astounding era of federal Indian affairs:

The southern Indians had been forced into treaties they did not want, treaties whose validity they denied but which were adamantly enforced by the federal government. The hardships of removal were extreme. Yet these Indian nations were not destroyed. . . . The removal was accomplished by means of formal treaties (which [President Andrew] Jackson had earlier called farces), which in their recognition of the Indians' nationhood and the fee simply[sic] ownership of land formed a foundation for continuing political existence that even tribal factionalism did not crush. With regard to the southern Indians, the treaty system had a new lease on life.[21]

Nevertheless, the American judicial system remained reticent at affirming Indigenous rights as the rights of sovereigns equal to itself. However, because of the tradition of legal precedent, the notion of Indian title proved difficult to topple, as seen in two cases: *Holden v. Joy* (1872)[22] and *United States v. Shoshone Tribe* (1938).[23] These were significant not only for how they maintained Indian title against the intense pressures of westward expansion, but also for how they demonstrated the tenacity of this basic principle of tribal sovereignty—and land title—in defiance of an era defined by the 1887 Allotment Act:

> Sovereignty as expressed by the Jamestown colony to the Indians on the James River bears little resemblance to the ideas of sovereignty of the Indian tribes of California in relation to the State of California. But this does not mean that sovereignty is a meaningless concept. *Implicit in the relationship is recognition of a degree of independence by the stronger to the weaker.* This recognition of the residuals of complete freedom and control is the sovereignty which courts seem to discuss in the Indian cases that reach them. Treaties in the formative years of the existence of the United States were a type of sovereign manifestation because they were exercised under the independent wills of the respective contracting parties [emphasis added].[24]

Deloria went on to affirm the enduring principle of sovereignty, namely independence, irrespective of Congress's unilateral 1871 motion to end treaty making, which was less about rejecting the fundamental sovereignty of tribes and more about the House of Representatives not wanting the United States to enter into additional contracts, i.e., treaties, in which the United States would be obliged to appropriate annuities. Congress, because it still dealt with tribes as distinct groups, went on to forge "agreements," which were tantamount to treaties, thereby maintaining the political independence of tribes, entailing, according to Deloria, that "the international theory of treaties still remained a viable operating principle."[25]

In the end, as Deloria, et al., concluded their analysis of the Doctrine of Discovery in *Broken Treaties*, while America's attitude toward treaty making may have been increasingly more cynical and insincere as its imperial ambitions moved farther westward, replete with exploiting the economic and political disadvantages that tribes faced as an overwhelming number of settlers moved in, this did not mean that tribes lost their inherent right as independent sovereigns in the process. Similar to an individual who maintained their free will and the inherent rights of being human, regardless of the oppression and abuse they may be forced to endure, so too does an Indigenous people maintain its sovereignty and the inherent right of all nations for self-governance. As such, just because a tribe agrees to cede, sell, or lease land—even under extreme duress— did not entail that they had surrendered all claims to their dignity. Even prisoners, hostages, and victims retain fundamental human rights. So, too, do nations. For no matter the terms of the treaty, each tribe that signed expected the agreements to be upheld and their status as nations to be respected. As evidenced in the Pacific Northwest in 1964 and at Wounded Knee in 1973, Indians were fed up with feeling disrespected. "Aboriginal title did not extinguish the political rights of the Indian tribes, and they still have the right to be recognized among the nations of the earth, even with the domestic legal doctrines of the United States guaranteeing the validity of their titles as held in a protected status by the United States against the European nations."[26]

In exchange for American protection, as the treaty making proceeded, the United States asserted its exclusive right to any lands that the Indigenous nations entering into a treaty with them may choose to sell. In other words, the United States did not want any Indigenous nations to sell any lands to Britain, France, or Spain. Furthermore, accepting U.S.

protection meant that the signatory nations entered a trust relationship, in which their assumed inferiority became the basis of their treatment as colonial charges of the U.S. federal government, which was to say that Indigenous nations were submitting to American imperial power. Consequently, as Deloria observed: "submission became merely the first step from freedom to classification as incompetents whose every move had to be approved by government bureaucrats," such as the Department of Interior, which assumed control of Indian affairs in 1849.[27] With regard to the antiquity of these preconceptions, the 1785 treaty, for example, between Cherokee Nation and the United States—popularly referred to as the Hopewell Treaty—was at the crux of the 1830 dispute between the Cherokee and the State of Georgia. The dispute then went to the U.S. Supreme Court, where, in its 1831 ruling, Chief Justice John Marshall wrote on behalf of the majority. The 1785 treaty was cited therein as integral to the explanation for defining the Cherokee as a "domestic dependent nation."[28] The Hopewell Treaty also set the stage for the new United States' post-Revolution agenda for treating with tribes.[29] Specifically, article 3 stated, as Marshall quoted: "The said Indians for themselves and their respective tribes and towns do acknowledge all the Cherokees to be under the protection of the United States of America, and of no other sovereign whosoever."[30]

In the spirit of their British—or, more specifically, English—forebears, the United States established a form of feudalism over Indigenous lands and peoples, in which, as noted above, Indigenous nations possessed no more than usufructuary rights to the lands they had inhabited for countless generations.[31] Whatever privileges Indigenous people enjoyed under American occupation they were few, meager, and enforced at the pleasure of the Indian Bureau, which was the federal agency in charge of implementing U.S. federal Indian policy.[32] Under such conditions, Indigenous nations were frequently coerced into relinquishing even more land in hopes of alleviating the suffering they endured under Indian Bureau control. As Deloria further observed:

> Incompetency was a doctrine devised to explain the distinction between people who held their land free from trust restrictions and those who

still had their land in trust. But it soon mushroomed out of proportion. Eventually any decision made by an Indian was casually overlooked because the Indian was, by definition, incompetent.[33]

Yet, as Deloria argued, this trend toward regarding Indians as "wards" or "incompetents" was in contradistinction to the equally important notion that tribes were, not only worthy allies, but necessary ones, capable of fulfilling their obligations as cosigners of the treaties into which they entered with the United States. Beginning with the 1794 Treaty with the Six Nations, more commonly called the Pickering Treaty, in honor of Timothy Pickering (1745–1829), who was George Washington's secretary of state, the United States recurrently offered protection, friendship, plus goods and annuities, in exchange for land. In article 6 of the Pickering Treaty, the United States proclaimed to assembled delegates:

> In consideration of the peace and friendship hereby established, and of the engagements entered into by the Six Nations; and because the United States desire, with humanity and kindness, to contribute to their comfortable support; and to render the peace and friendship hereby established, strong and perpetual; the United States now deliver to the Six Nations, and the Indians of the other nations residing among and united with them, a quantity of goods of the value of ten thousand dollars.[34]

What was initially an agreement between equally sovereign and independent nations turned into an unequal affair between a dominant trustee and its dependent ward. In other words, the protection, friendship, goods, and annuities went from being compensation for land relinquished to a form of dependency as Indigenous nations saw their sovereignty and self-reliance diminish under the pressures of an increasingly expanding settler-colonial power.[35]

With regard to the fundamental traditions of discovery and treaty making, and the powerful tribes that the settlers encountered, Deloria reminded his reader treaties "were originally viewed as contracts."[36] Moreover, the contracting parties were not only equal, as made clear in the language used, but also it was the United States that sent out treaty commissions for the purpose of acquiring much-needed allies against the British. As for Indigenous nations being regarded as dependent, Deloria made quick work at disabusing his reader from assuming that Indigenous nations have always been regarded as dependent inferiors. On the contrary, Deloria referred to articles 5 and 6 of the 1778 treaty with the Delawares, which was the first ratified treaty between the newly independent United States and an Indigenous nation. In fact, the treaty with the Delawares came a mere seven months after the two treaties that the United States signed with France, both on February 6, 1778, which were the first two treaties that the United States signed after declaring its independence from Britain. The implication here was that the United States needed the Delawares more than they needed the United States. It was in this tumultuous context in which the United States acknowledged the Delawares as partners in a "well regulated trade" in which both nations were recognized as "contracting parties" who were forming a "confederation," complete with an opportunity for "other tribes" to join "who have been friends to the interest of the United States."[37] In addition to becoming trade partners, the United States offered the Delawares the possibility of entering the American republic as "states," complete with congressional representation. Indeed, the United States repeated this offer to the Cherokee in the "Hopewell Treaty," in which article 7 stated: "That the Indians may have full confidence in the justice of the United States, respecting their interests, they shall have the right to send a deputy of their choice, whenever they think fit, to Congress."[38]

As for the Delaware treaty, according to Prucha, in contradistinction to Deloria, it "accomplished little, and it left a bad taste in the mouths of the Delawares." More specifically, while the Delaware understood that the treaty acknowledged their "territorial rights," with respect to the rebelling colonials, the Delaware agreed to do no more than allow the colonial army to access a route through their lands to their British enemy. Consequently, it came as a surprise to John Killbuck, one of the Delaware signatories, that he "was looked upon as a Warrior," a status that implied something other than the neutrality that the Delaware acceded to maintaining. In other words, the Delaware wound up feeling duped by the Americans. Moreover, when the colonial trader George

Morgan arranged for a Delaware delegation to bring their grievances to the colonial capital of Philadelphia in 1779, it was to no avail, the "peace and friendship between the United States and the Delawares collapsed." In light of which, Prucha suggested that when the Americans approached the Wyandots with a similar treaty, they adamantly refused to allow the colonial army to march through their lands.[39]

While Deloria did not respond to Prucha's interpretation of the Delaware treaty directly, be it in his 1995 review for the *American Indian Quarterly* or in any of his subsequent books and essays, one could say that Deloria nonetheless had anticipated Prucha's criticism many years before in the pages of *Broken Treaties*. More specifically, in the chapter titled "Dependent Domestic Nations" Deloria added to his argument in *Custer* that tribes were not regarded as incompetent wards, but as nations equal in status to the fledgling American republic. Because the Americans were rebelling against a king and his empire, they sent a delegation to Fort Pitt in western Pennsylvania, where they, as indicated above, requested the Delawares' permission "to travel over its lands in order to attack the British posts in southern Canada." With that objective in mind, Deloria cited article 3 of the treaty, which acknowledged that the Americans undeniably needed the Delawares' assistance with their military ambition to attack the British of southern Canada. However, the article also stated, in spite of what John Killbuck may have thought, that the Delaware nation agreed to "engage to join the troops of the United States aforesaid, with such a number of their best and most expert warriors as they can spare, consistent with their own safety." Whether or not the latter point was made clear to the Delaware was not apparent in either Deloria's or Prucha's comments about this treaty. Obviously, there was a Delaware account of what happened at the treaty council that was missing from both texts. Nevertheless, the agreed upon terms stipulated in article 3, with respect to Deloria's critique of the theory that tribes were dependent domestic nations that were incapable of managing their own affairs, had an opposite meaning:

> Plainly, the colonists were on the ropes in the West, and had the Delawares refused to allow passage, the United States might have been

faced with a violent Indian war in addition to its scrimmage with the British. To have pretended decades later that the American Congress had always asserted its claim to Indian lands under the doctrine of discovery, or that it had always regulated the internal affairs of the Indian tribes in its guardianship capacity, is sheer self-serving rhetoric when the nature of this first treaty is understood. If the Delaware treaty exemplified the way that the United States asserted its plenary power over the Indian tribes, it was certainly a humble way of doing so.[40]

Regardless of how one feels about an Indigenous nation availing itself to becoming a joint member of a colonial power, as was the case in both the Delaware and Cherokee treaties, the implication of Deloria's historical references was clear: the treaty-making tradition was a tradition instituted between sovereign nations—not between trustee and ward—in which the Indians possessed the same power of representation as did their American counterparts. Because the United States–Indian treaty-making custom was one between equally sovereign nations, as documented in the historical record, the assumption that Indigenous nations were "surrendering" to the superior strength of the United States—like Confederate general Robert E. Lee at Appomattox or the Japanese foreign affairs minister Mamoru Shigemitsu onboard the USS *Missouri*—was simply incorrect and an egregious misrepresentation of historical fact. Equally erroneous was the supposition that because of the aforementioned treaty promises enumerated above, e.g., goods and annuities, Indian lands were legally "purchased" and that the Indian descendants of the treaties' signatories, such as those partaking in the 1964 fish-ins, were crying over spilt milk when they demanded that treaties be honored and land restored. On the contrary, while specific lands were ceded to the United States, the agreed-upon compensation often extended into perpetuity. In many cases, unfortunately, the stipulated goods, services, and annuities were either never delivered or, at best, only sporadically. Among the most offensive beliefs among the knowledge-challenged, though, was the belief that treaties "gave" land to Indigenous nations as an expression of American largesse and magnanimity. As Deloria so aptly responded: "The truth is that practically the only thing the white men ever gave the

Indian was disease and poverty. To imply that Indians were given land is to completely reverse the facts of history."[41]

In opposition to the above misconceptions about Indian treaties, Deloria assembled an array of examples in which "Indian rights to lands [were] reserved by them," including treaty articles that became critical to later generations seeking to substantiate the hunting and fishing rights that were legally guaranteed to them when the treaties with their nations were ratified by Congress.[42] In spite of repeated American violations, the treaties were still valid, which, ironically, was confirmed by numerous congressional statutes. In spite of attempts at attrition, tribal leaders consistently did their best to assert their right to self-determination against a growing tide of settlers and imperialistic ambitions. As for the American republic and its promises, Deloria commented in *Custer*:

> The United States pledged over and over again that it would guarantee to the tribes the peaceful enjoyment of their lands. Initially tribes were allowed to punish whites entering their lands in violation of treaty provisions. Then the Army was given the task of punishing the intruders. Finally the government gave up all pretense of enforcing the treaty provisions.[43]

Yet, even at the lowest point in the history of Indian-white relations, which occurred during the 1870s to 1930s, Indigenous nations still made an effort at affirming the covenants between themselves and the United States. The most well-known and historically important example during this epoch was when the Kiowa leader Lone Wolf sought an injunction against the allotment of lands guaranteed to them in the 1867 treaty with the Kiowa and Comanche.[44] In complete disregard to the articles of this lawfully binding agreement, on February 7, 1903, the Committee on Indian Affairs proposed allotting 505,000 acres of Kiowa, Comanche, and Apache lands in the state of Oklahoma. In the proposed rider to H.R. 16280, the lands in question were acknowledged as belonging to the Indians under the provisions of the 1867 treaty; nonetheless, as Sen. John Fletcher Lacey (R-IA) argued on behalf of his committee's decision:

It has been the usual method in opening Indian lands for settlement to first obtain the consent of the Indians by treaty. But in the present case the subject of opening their reservation was fully considered by Congress and by the Indians, and a treaty was agreed upon. The lands in question were included in the original reservation, and the situation is therefore fully understood, and your committee do not deem it necessary that there be future negotiation on the subject. *Congress is the guardian of the Indians and members of the tribes are wards of the nation* [emphasis added].[45]

As far as the tribes, not to mention Lone Wolf, were concerned, those 505,000 acres could not be allotted without their consent. Nevertheless, when Lone Wolf took his case to the U.S. Supreme Court, the tribes not only lost but also the court ruled "that the tribes had no title to the land at all. Rather the land was held by the United States and the tribes had mere occupancy rights. Therefore the [plenary] power of Congress to dictate conditions of life and possession on the reservations was limited only by its own sense of justice."[46] Such was the context in which treaties would be understood thereafter. Supposedly, this plenary power formed the basis of all subsequent treaty violations, including that of the 1794 Pickering Treaty, which justified the Kinzua Dam, not to mention all of the termination acts. What resulted on the part of Congress and the Supreme Court, which successive presidential administrations have perpetuated, was a distorted and biased theory of Indian-white relations, in which land was given to the Indians, who then lived off the government dole and somehow dwelled in the paradoxical existence of primitive splendor (culturally wealthy) and grinding poverty (financially depleted). Such was the Indian condition, if you will, as Deloria wrote about it in *Custer*. In a sense, one can say that much of what Deloria wrote throughout his books and essays was motivated by the never-ending conflict between Indian reality and white fantasy.

As for the theory of plenary power, Deloria confronted this blatant and arrogant violation of tribal sovereignty in *Broken Treaties*. In light of the decision reached in the infamous *Lone Wolf* (1903) case, it was hardly surprising in its contempt for tribal treaty rights. Congress, according to the court's opinion, had power beyond appeal to unilaterally abrogate its treaties with tribes. Consequently, as Deloria pointed out, if tribes could not sue the federal government for violating its treaty agreements, because of its sovereign immunity, then the only option left to tribes was to turn their grievances into political causes, which was a tactic that defined twentieth-century Indian activism. "Indians had come to realize, by 1973," Deloria observed, "that political activism was their only hope. Even assuming the best of intentions by Congress, they could not achieve a modicum of justice." After all, Congress had recently spent more than a decade passing termination bills, which unilaterally ended its trust responsibilities to tribes, treaty or no treaty. Furthermore, the Nixon administration had categorically rejected the Trail of Broken Treaties' "Twenty-Point Position Paper" as a valid approach to reforming Indian affairs. In particular, they were adamant about rejecting the proposal to restart the treaty-making process: "The treaty points were most strenuously rejected by members of the administration task force on the vague grounds that the Indian Citizenship Act of 1924 had precluded the United States from dealing with Indian tribes by treaty because the individual members thereof happened to be United States citizens."[47]

Such discrimination, as exemplified in federal termination policy, was the consequence of Indians having long been vulnerable to congressional fiat due to their poorly defined place in the federal system. In fact, a major concern during much of the allotment era, 1887–1934, was the political status of individual American Indians, as they were being pressured into surrendering their tribal identities. Prior to 1924, for the most part, Indians were only members of tribes, which placed them outside of federal law (see *Ex parte Crow Dog*, 1883). Tribes, as such, were extraconstitutional. Yet, they were simultaneously within American territorial boundaries, thereby placed within the political reach of Congress (the Commerce Clause of the Constitution gave Congress authority over Indian affairs). However, as individuals, Indians were not U.S. citizens during this time. In the parlance of today, Indians were resident aliens, meaning that they had very little access to the justice system, in addition to being denied the right to vote. Deloria emphasized the exceptional denial of Indian voting rights in his explication of *Elk v. Wilkins* (1884), in which John Elk was denied the right to vote in the state of Nebraska, despite having cut off all ties with his tribe and making great effort at assimilating into white society. Insofar as Elk was an Indian, and thereby identified with a group regarded as "alien and dependent," he was judged as still unqualified to practice the right to vote.[48] As a civil rights case, *Elk* was a spectacular display of legal gymnastics in order to arrive at the conclusion that the Indian plaintiff could not become a citizen, let alone vote—even though federal Indian policy told him that this is what he ought to pursue. "The Indians who had followed the directions of the United States and severed their tribal ties thus became men without a country."[49] A mere three years later, the 1887 Allotment Act provided a path to citizenship, however, it was prolonged (twenty-five years), and ultimately depended, after the 1906 Burke Act, on being judged "competent" to manage one's affairs. Only after the 1924 Indian Citizenship Act was passed did Congress clear up the individual status of American Indians. As for the political status of tribes, that was still subject to the conflicting opinions between Indians and the federal government. Whereas tribes saw themselves as sovereign nations (the Iroquois, in fact, famously declined to have the 1924 Indian Citizenship Act applied to them), the federal government maintained its insistence that Indians were wards. As for the Indian attitude toward citizenship, which was at best ambivalent, Deloria explained:

> Unwittingly, the United States was preserving for the Indians of the future a peculiar dimension—a foreignness, if you will—to their political existence which could not be denied. To find, then, at Wounded Knee and other places, the assumption by American Indians that their tribes had international status and that they owed no allegiance to the United States, should not be strange in light of *Elk v. Wilkins*.[50]

Affirming that Indians were ultimately aliens within the American legal system informed the pursuit of citizenship for Indians that defined the Progressive Era, in which Indian disenfranchisement was the source of the deprivations of a reservation system that did not consider Indian voices demanding fundamental reforms. By and large, Indians accepted

U.S. citizenship only under duress and only insofar as they could interpret the attendant rights and privileges as an extension of their rights as sovereign nations.

> The Iroquois have continually maintained that they are not citizens of the United States and that the Indian Citizenship Act was illegally extended over them. Now other tribes are beginning to examine their peculiar status and to consider the advantages of dual citizenship. It may be that the *Elk* case will provide the basis of a new ideology of separatism for the nationalists of all minority groups.[51]

Furthermore, the affirmation of tribal independence was more than a cultural conceit, it was a political status corroborated in federal statutes and case law. *Talton v. Mayes* (1896),[52] for example, as Deloria explored this case in *Broken Treaties*, was about the plaintiff, Bob Talton, who claimed that the Cherokee sheriff who arrested him, the Cherokee grand jury that indicted him, and the Cherokee court that found him guilty of murder as charged, consequently sentencing him to death, were in violation of the U.S. Constitution. Talton's attorney, L. D. Yarrell, argued that the Cherokee Nation must abide as a domestic dependent nation under U.S. law, in which tribes were now covered by the 1885 Major Crimes Act. Upon this premise, Talton petitioned for a writ of habeas corpus against Sheriff Mayes, which was ultimately denied on the basis that the origin of Cherokee Nation self-governance preceded the U.S. Constitution and therefore was not limited by its provision, namely the Fifth Amendment, which stipulated rules for a lawful grand jury and was cited in Talton's appeal. Moreover, in addition to possessing powers of self-governance: "As the court described it, the relationship of the Cherokee Nation to the United States was hardly that of tutelage but rather a protectorate relationship in which the United States had a minimum power to interfere with the self-government of the Cherokee people."[53] Indeed, Deloria went on to point out that, despite the federal government's subsequent actions at dissolving the Cherokee government, including its court system—similar to the supposed end of treaty making—was belied by the ongoing governmental powers that have persisted to today. "The tribe's original rights," Deloria concluded, "as articulated in the *Talton* case would seem to be unimpaired, if presently inoperative, under the theory of the case."[54]

Thus there remains an unanswered question of Constitutional law—can Congress legally extend the Bill of Rights to affect the rights of Indian tribes over their tribal members? Since 1968 it has been assumed by many people that the Civil Rights Bill of that year settled the question forever. *but*, it has not yet been settled and may yet emerge as yet another hot issue of the 1970's in Indian country.[55]

As legal precedent, *Talton* enabled tribes to realize that the self-governing powers of Indigenous nations did not derive from the U.S. Constitution, nor was their power of self-governance given to them in the 1934 Indian Reorganization Act. On the contrary, the Constitution articulated the limits of federal power, namely Congress, as its articles and amendments demarcated the rights of the people that it could not violate. In the case of tribal rights, Deloria brought up two examples. First, a 1954 case in which members of Jemez Pueblo brought suit against Pueblo elders, whom the plaintiffs accused of violating their constitutional rights when they were refused permission to bury their dead in the community cemetery, in addition to not allowing Protestant missionaries into the Pueblo to visit with the plaintiffs. Second, the 1959 Native American Church case against Navajo Nation, in which Navajo church members claimed that their constitutional rights were violated when the Navajo government issued an ordinance forbidding the introduction of peyote onto the reservation. In both cases, the federal government cited *Talton* as precedent in its deferral to tribal jurisdiction, stating in *Native American Church v. Navajo Tribal Council*: "Indian tribes are not states. *They have a status higher than that of states.* They are subordinate and dependent nations possessed of all powers as such only to the extent that they have expressly been required to surrender them by the supreme law of the land, but it is nonetheless a part of the laws of the United States [emphasis in original]."[56] It is worth bearing in mind when looking at the two aforementioned cases that these decisions were handed down during the time of termination, when Congress was ostensibly dissolving its trust relation with tribes. While the court and Congress have frequently been at odds with their respective understanding of the Constitution, it is significant that even under such a politically unfriendly time for tribes, the Supreme Court ruled that there was still some level of nationhood that remained to tribes, even as Congress aggressively sought to abrogate its historic responsibilities to them.[57]

At the same time, as Deloria was compelled to acknowledge that what looked like progress in overcoming *Cherokee Nation v. Georgia*'s assumption that tribes were in a state of tutelage with respect to the United States—as stated in *Talton*, tribes were higher than states—was subsequently offset by the court allowing for habeas corpus in *Colliflower v. Garland* (1965). More specifically, writ was granted for the Fort Belknap Indian Reservation because of the extent to which its court system was under federal control. The significance of *Colliflower* was that it provided Congress justification for its 1968 Indian Civil Rights Act, in which Congress assumed that the conditions found at Fort Belknap were characteristic of the reservation system as a whole.[58] The latter was in addition to the situation that arose at Jemez Pueblo, which was brought up in their 1954 Supreme Court case, noted above. In other words, even though the court made clear in *Colliflower* that the Fort Belknap reservation was a unique situation, this did not stop federal lawmakers from assuming that the inordinate dependence of the Fort Belknap tribal court on federal control was typical of all tribal courts. Indeed, when it comes to the assumptions that federal courts made about the political status of tribes, the most pervasive and problematic one was that the Bureau of Indian Affairs (BIA) was responsible for fulfilling the federal trust relation as a form of "guardianship" over "the property of individual Indians." While there was ample justification for the federal government having a trust responsibility for Indian property, especially land, there was no justification for "regarding the corporate political entity of tribal government as a 'ward' of the executive branch of the [federal] government."[59] This is to say, it was one thing to claim that the U.S. government had a trust responsibility for protecting Indian lands from unlawful expropriation, which it did, for example, when Congress passed the 1934 Indian Reorganization Act, which formally ended the land allotment policy; it was quite another to claim that the Indigenous people living and governing themselves on that land were in need of guardianship. The BIA existed to facilitate the former, not the latter. Because of the ambivalence of the federal understanding of "trust," tribes were often caught in between their definition of trust and the Department of Interior's. The department in particular was quick to assert its role as guardian whenever it deemed fit, while repeatedly reneging on its actual responsibilities to Indians. The Pyramid Lake Paiute's frustrations, for example, over getting their rights to "the Truckee-Carson river system" clarified and the Quinault Tribe's ignored petition to protect their forest from illegal cutting by outside timber companies demonstrated how the "theory of wardship has proven a tragic farce."[60]

At this juncture, Deloria brought his historical analysis in *Broken Treaties* to the more recent disputes over the violation of treaties in the Pacific Northwest. Citing article 3 of the 1854 Treaty of Medicine Creek, which the United States signed with "delegates of the Nisqually, Puyallup, Steilacoom, Squawskin, S'Homamish, Stehchass, T' Peek-sin, Squi-aitl, and Sa-heh-wamish tribes and bands of Indians, occupying the lands lying round the head of Puget's Sound and the adjacent inlets,"[61] Deloria affirmed the tribes' right to fish in all their customary places. As such, no action was required of Congress. Nevertheless, as Deloria expressed the tribes' exasperation: "The major difficulty Indians face is getting the United States to respect these articles which require only the good faith of the United States."[62] Unfortunately, as made clear by the numerous treaty disputes, be they at Puget Sound, the Indian Claims Commission, or elsewhere, the United States had been negligent at, not only displaying any good faith, but also at respecting tribes as being higher than states. Instead, the United States insisted on asserting for itself the role of guardian over the rights and resources of people it claims in a condescending political fiction are "dependent" on it.[63] Sadly, it has been within this legal environment that duly ratified treaties, complete with self-operating articles like the Medicine Creek one cited above, had been either ignored or flagrantly violated as "federal and state governments" nit-picked "about the interpretation of the articles" or pretended that "the mere passage of time and changing of conditions is sufficient to invalidate them."[64]

With the sovereign status of tribes weighing in the balance, Deloria concluded his analysis of the doctrine of plenary power by arguing that tribes' relation to the Constitution was clearly defined by *Cherokee Nation* and *Native American Church*, which was to say that tribes were each an "international protectorate," complete with the powers of self-governance that placed them "higher than states." It was because the federal government, namely Congress, had unilaterally chosen to ignore its own Supreme Court's decisions that the chaotic situation that confronted tribes had been allowed to develop, as of the early 1970s, into a nationwide crisis. In light of which, Deloria proposed a "strict construction of the constitutional relationship between Indian tribes and the United States" for the purpose of unburdening tribes of the "many inconsistent and onerous interpretations of the [federal-Indian] relationship" that hindered "tribal progress" at effectively utilizing their assets. "Considering the many lawsuits," Deloria added, "that have been filed against the United States for its inept management of Indian assets, the determination of a distinct status of the tribes as advocated by the development of the concept of an international protectorate should be considered."[65] At this point, Deloria sought to define tribal self-determination beyond the limits demarcated by U.S. federal Indian law and policy, instead reaching for an international scope to Indigenous nationhood.

While *Lone Wolf* may appear to have settled the question of Indian tribal political status, namely that they were in fact wards whose treaties could be unilaterally abrogated whenever Congress saw fit, the 1924 Indian Citizenship Act and the 1934 Indian Reorganization Act (IRA) subsequently complicated the picture. At the same time, then, that Congress may seek to absolve itself of its treaty promises, it was obliged to respect the rights and privileges that Indians maintained as citizens. Moreover, as members of Indigenous nations, the Indian Citizenship Act stated: "the granting of such citizenship shall not in any manner impair or otherwise affect the right of any Indian to tribal or other property."[66] In turn, the IRA not only ended the terrorism of land allotment but also reinvigorated Indigenous peoples' sense of nationhood. However cautious one ought to be about idealizing Commissioner John Collier's epic change in Indian affairs, there was no denying the fact that the wording of this legislation unequivocally stated: "Any Indian tribe, or tribes, residing on the same reservation, shall have the right to organize for its common welfare."[67]

For many Indigenous nations, their common welfare depended on protecting the land and resources promised to them in their treaties — and, in many cases, executive orders — with the United States. Securing hunting and fishing rights, a natural resource, was another recurring and important topic in innumerable treaties, not just the ones that became a lightning rod of conflict and controversy in the Pacific Northwest during the early 1960s. Nonetheless, what Deloria said about the Pacific Northwest was relevant to other regions in which tribes battled local non-Indians over their ratified treaty rights to traditional sources of sustenance.[68] Paralleling the conflicting worldviews mentioned above, Deloria pointed out in *Custer*: "Today hunting and fishing are an important source of food for poverty-stricken Indian peoples, but they are merely a *sport* for white men in the western Pacific states."[69] Consequently, since Indigenous people were concerned about feeding themselves, as opposed to making a profit, as occurred in the sporting industry, their needs were regarded as wasteful and a threat to "conservation."[70] This type of attitude goes all the way back to American agitation for Indian lands during the 1820s in the Southeast, when Cherokees were accused by Georgians during the 1820s of wasting the natural resources of the region by trying to limit the land to a few Indians, namely the Cherokee who wandered the vast stretches of their "wilderness" for the purpose of chasing deer. Such aggressive and vindictive stereotyping is what led to the 1830 Indian Removal Act and the precedent it set for federal Indian policy. Indeed, this will be how Deloria characterizes termination policy in chapter 4.

Given that treaties were written by the Americans and ratified by Congress, one might think that Indigenous nations would have an easy time at convincing the federal government, not to mention the American people, of its obligations. Unfortunately, because of America's borderline personality disorder, the treaty relations that Indigenous nations had striven to maintain had been anything but reliable. While the United States made numerous treaties for the purpose of acquiring allies against the British, promising tribes the sun and the moon, they just as anxiously took actions to betray their much-needed allies as soon as the danger had passed.[71] Other treaties were promulgated under similar conditions, complete with equally outrageous violations. Consequently, whenever Indigenous nations bring up their treaty concerns, they are confronted with the same response: "In many instances, when the tribes have attempted to bring their case before the public, it has turned a deaf ear, claiming that the treaties are some historical fancy dreamed up by the Indian to justify his irresponsibility."[72]

As an example of American duplicity, Deloria referred his reader to the Choctaw Nation whose treaty relations with the United States culminated in 1825, when "articles of a convention made between John C. Calhoun, Secretary of War, being specially authorized therefor by the President of the United States [John Quincy Adams], and the undersigned Chiefs and Head Men of the Choctaw Nation of Indians, duly authorized and empowered by said Nation" were signed by both parties, agreeing to specific provisions regarding Choctaw lands. Of particular interest was article 7: "It is further agreed . . . that the Congress of the United States shall not exercise the power of apportioning the lands, for the benefit of each family, or individual, of the Choctaw Nation, and of bringing them under the laws of the United States, *but with the consent of the Choctaw Nation*" [emphasis added].[73] Nonetheless, as the Choctaw were pressured against their will into accepting lands in Oklahoma, individual tribal members had the option of staying in Mississippi. However, as the Choctaw Nation recounts on its web page: "the price of doing this was the loss of Choctaw identity and the acceptance of United States and Mississippi citizenship." Unsurprisingly, most Choctaw reluctantly chose to relocate, embarking on a very difficult and often fatal trek to their new lands in southeastern Oklahoma. As for those that stayed in their traditional homeland:

> So many of those who remained were cheated out of their land by corrupt officials of the state and local governments that in 1842 the Federal government was once again forced to intercede. This time in a slightly less unfriendly way. Choctaw who had . . . lost their land

were reimbursed, but only if they relocated to their new land in Indian Territory, now known as Oklahoma. As a result of this fresh round of removal only 3000 Choctaw remained in Mississippi.[74]

In addition to their nation being rent asunder by an inhumane removal policy, the Choctaw continued to endure further hardships at the hands of federal bureaucrats. As of 1969, when *Custer* appeared on bookshelves: "the Choctaws and other people of the other 'Civilized' Tribes are among the poorest people of America."[75] Of course, poverty remained a prevalent problem across the reservation system throughout the United States, including American Indian communities living off reservation.[76] In which case, the Choctaws were emblematic of Deloria's account of United States–Indian treaty relations, which were exacerbated by the termination policy that dominated the 1950s and 1960s. Indeed, the congressional action that initiated termination, HCR 108, which led to multiple termination acts, in addition to P.L. 280, was a prominent example of how statutes undermined treaty rights and agreements.[77] As Deloria observed: "Although a treaty would promise one thing, subsequent legislation, designed to expand the treaty provisions, often changed the agreements between tribe and federal government completely."[78] Prucha, as may be recalled, challenged Deloria on this particular point in *American Indian Treaties*. Needless to say, as far as Deloria was concerned, American treaty breaches and the violation of human rights they precipitated was a recurrent theme of federal Indian policy, which was often done with the color of law.

Further illustrating Deloria's argument that treaties were often broken through statutes and resolutions passed unilaterally by Congress, a number of other instances were mentioned in *Custer*, beginning with a joint resolution passed on April 16, 1800, regarding "copper lands adjacent to Lake Superior."[79] The objective of the resolution was to authorize the president to appoint an agent in charge of determining the terms on which the "Indian title" to the land could be "extinguished."[80] In the 1826 treaty with the Chippewa that followed, signed by Lewis Cass and Thomas L. McKenney, on behalf of the United States, and eighty-five signatories representing a dozen communities, which was "done at the Fond du Lac of lake Superior, in the territory of Michigan,"[81] article 3 granted to the United States the "right to search for, and carry away, any metals or minerals from any part of their country."[82] While the article goes on to acknowledge the continued Indian title to the land, the treaty did not provide for any compensation, be it purchasing or royalty payments, for the coveted mineral wealth.[83] In fact, the Chippewa were not informed at all of how much copper meant to the American economy. Deloria did not hesitate to call this an act of fraud, which was not only repeated throughout Indian affairs, but was perpetrated under the obnoxious assumption that the proponents of federal Indian policy had a paternal obligation to the betterment of their Indian "wards," complete with disposing their resources and handling their affairs with little, if any, consent from the tribes.[84]

In turn, the 1834 Indian Trade and Intercourse Act was largely focused on the federal licensing and regulation of traders conducting business with Indian tribes for the explicit purpose of preserving "peace on the frontiers."[85] Complementing the Indian trade act, Congress passed "An Act to provide for the organization of the department of Indian affairs," which established, "That there shall be a superintendency of Indian affairs for all the Indian country not within the bounds of any state or territory west of the Mississippi river." In addition to the various duties of the superintendents, namely supervising the bureau employees under their respective charge, section 7 further enacted:

> That the limits of each agency and sub-agency shall be established by the Secretary of War, either by tribes or by geographical boundaries. And it shall be the general duty of Indian agents and sub-agents to manage and superintend the intercourse with the Indians within their respective agencies, agreeably to law; to obey all legal instructions given to them by the Secretary of War, the commissioner of Indian affairs, and to carry into effect such regulations as may prescribed by the President.[86]

Ultimately, the bureau that would be transferred to the Department of Interior in 1849 became, in 1834, a fully articulated and comprehensive bureaucracy exhibiting "immense power . . . over the lives and property of the Indian people."[87] Thus, the colonization of Indigenous nations had reached a climactic period in its history, establishing hegemonic control over tribes for decades to come.

By 1887 Indian affairs had become, at least in the eyes of the federal government, a completely domestic issue. Congress had terminated treaty making nearly two decades earlier (1871)[88] and had since turned its attention to Indians as a social engineering problem, in which the objective was to "raise the Indian into civilization." Based on a notion, corroborated by social scientists and historians, from Lewis Henry Morgan to Karl Marx, that all humans were on the same ladder of development—an ascent from illiterate primitivism to modern western civilization—the 1887 General Allotment Act postulated that the so-called Indian problem could be resolved by compelling Indians into the next stage of their "natural development." More specifically, the statute—titled "An act to provide for the allotment of lands in severalty to Indians on the various reservations, and to extend the protection of the laws of the United States and the Territories over the Indians, and for other purposes"—stated in its preamble:

> *Be it enacted by the Senate and House of Representatives of the United States of America in Congress assembled,* That in all cases where any tribe or band of Indians has been, or shall hereafter be, located upon any reservation created for their use, either by treaty stipulation or by virtue of an act of Congress or executive order setting apart the same for their use, the President of the United States be, and he hereby is, authorized, whenever in his opinion any reservation or any part thereof of such Indians is advantageous for agricultural and grazing purposes, to cause said reservation, or any part thereof, to be surveyed, or resurveyed if necessary, and to allot the lands in said reservation in severalty to any Indian located thereon[emphasis in original].[89]

The target of this statute was the roughly ninety million acres still under collective tribal control, as validated by custom, treaty, executive orders, and previous statutes. As the allotments proceeded, according to the guidelines articulated in the statute's provisions, the aggregate lands held by the tribes began to shrink, generating "surplus lands" that were placed on the open market, which were quickly acquired by non-Indian purchasers. As for the allotted land, a patent was issued to the Indian head of family that placed the allotment in the trust of the United States for twenty-five years. At the end of the trust period, assuming the allottee was deemed, according to the 1906 Burke Act, which amended the 1887 statute, competent and had made sufficient agriculturally oriented improvements to the land, said allottee presumably possessed the land in fee simple title.[90] Moreover, the allotment process purported to lead Indian families into becoming fit for American civilization, i.e., citizenship. Unfortunately, not to mention outrageously, as Deloria was quick to point out, "nothing was done to encourage [Indians] to acquire the [necessary agricultural] skills and consequently much land was immediately leased to non-Indians who swarmed into the former reservation areas." In the end, "by 1934, Indians had lost nearly 90 million acres through land sales, many of them fraudulent."[91]

Endorsed by an array of notables in the Indian rights movement of the latter nineteenth century, including Sen. Henry L. Dawes (R-MA),[92] who sponsored the bill, and a number of Christian progressive leaders, the most noteworthy among whom was Episcopalian bishop William H. Hare,[93] the 1887 Dawes Act (as the Allotment Act was otherwise known) was one of the biggest land swindles in the history of the world. While there was certainly much more that can be added to this centuries-long travesty, the point that Indian nations have undergone a massive amount of government malfeasance, corporate greed, and religious hypocrisy, which informed their status today had been made. Indeed, with respect to the nadir reached at the end of the nineteenth century, Deloria commented:

> Gone apparently was any concern to fulfill the articles of hundreds of treaties guaranteeing the tribes free and undisturbed use of their remaining lands. Some of the treaties had been assured by the missionaries [like Bishop Hare]. The Indians had not, however, been given lifetime guarantees.[94]

As a way of underscoring the deliberately dishonest and inhumane way in which the United States, in particular Congress, treated tribes since violating the terms of the 1794 Pickering Treaty, Deloria pointed out that the only positive highlight in Indian affairs did not occur until 150 years later when the 1934 Indian Reorganization Act was passed. While it did not retain all of the radical reforms that its main proponent John Collier wanted, it did unequivocally end land allotment, enabling tribes to instead recover land either through purchase or having unsold "surplus" lands restored. Equally important was the opportunity to "organize for its [the tribes'] common welfare" by means of establishing for each a "constitution and bylaws."[95] Although, Deloria, along with a number of other critics, pinpointed a range of flaws and limitations throughout this groundbreaking statute, during the climactic years of the Indian protest movement, the 1934 IRA was touted as a seminal change in federal Indian policy. With that in mind, compared to other congressional initiatives, Deloria acknowledged: "Overall the IRA was a comprehensive piece of legislation which went far beyond previous efforts to develop tribal initiative and responsibility."[96] If nothing else, the 1934 IRA was the first major legislation that did not ostensibly seek to alienate Indians from their land.

As for how the 1934 IRA set the stage for the 1973 Wounded Knee conflict recounted in *Broken Treaties*, after going over the now familiar highlights of late nineteenth-century Indian affairs, complete with the ravages of the 1887 Allotment Act, Deloria evoked the name of Hubert Work, a former physician and secretary of interior, who organized the Committee of One Hundred, which ushered in a long sought-after period of Indian Bureau reform. What resulted was a book-length report titled *The Problem of Indian Administration*, which soon became popularized as the 1928 Meriam Report, in honor of Lewis Meriam, who led the research that included nearly a hundred tribes in nearly two dozen states. Unfortunately, as Deloria noted: "Most of the recommendations were disregarded when President Hoover timidly appointed Charles Rhoads to supervise the suggested reforms," who did little to nothing, which was a disappointment exacerbated by the devastation of the Great Depression.[97] Nonetheless, the scene had been set for a new era in Indian affairs.[98] It was at this point, that Deloria highlighted Rhoads's successor, John Collier, a sociologist who earlier distinguished himself when he spearheaded the American Indian Defense Association to combat the infamous 1922 Bursum Bill, which would have legalized an array of land seizures committed by white settlers against multiple Pueblo communities. Ultimately, the "Bursum Bill was defeated, and in its place the [1924] Pueblo Lands Act was passed. This statute reversed the procedure for proving title to lands; white men had to prove how they had obtained their titles, not the Indians."[99] Indeed, Collier continued to excel as an advocate for Indian rights, from land disputes to religious freedom, along with promoting the suggested reforms outlined in the Meriam Report. In fact, one of Collier's pre-1934 accomplishments was getting the Senate Indian Committee to leave its perch in Washington DC and see for themselves the reservations over which they had so much influence.

> On many reservations the Indians' stories shocked even the most hardened Senator. The abstractly phrased suggestions of the Meriam Report began to take on flesh as the committee saw instance after instance of deprivation in their investigation of allotments, competency commissions, and arbitrary actions of the government.[100]

If, then, the original fifty-page bill introduced to Congress had passed as is, the way Collier wanted it, it would have nearly restored tribes to their original status as independent sovereign nations. In addition to providing for self-governing organizations, the drafted version of the bill even validated and supported the teaching of traditional Indian culture as part of the tribal school curriculum, not to mention a much-needed Court of Indian Affairs. For all of its idealism, though, Deloria did see one major flaw, namely "the provision that there would be no more inheritance of lands by individual Indians." While the provision was stipulated for the purpose of consolidating fractionated lands, which was (and still is) a major obstacle to tribal economic development, its effect on Indian communities was one of resistance, particularly in Oklahoma, which, despite being exempted from the bill, nonetheless criticized the provision as depriving "them of their rights to property."[101] As for the Court of Indian Claims, if it had been endorsed by Congress, "The court would have eliminated the perennial problems of the tribes' having to litigate their treaty rights in state courts with appeal to the federal court system."[102]

For the federal government, not to mention the society it represented — which had long regarded Indians as children in need of its civilized guidance—Collier's revolutionary approach to tribal self-governance was too much for many in Congress. Even Christian missionaries were opposed to Collier's alleged revival of "paganism," which they feared would undo their years of work at controlling Indian minds. "Incorporated in the Indian Reorganization Act was a provision allowing the practice of native religions on an equal basis with the Christian religions that had been superimposed on the different tribes half a century before when the respective reservations were allotted to the various missionary societies."[103] Reaction from others, including tribal leaders and BIA employees, was mixed, depending on what they had at stake in the status quo. While many whites involved in Indian affairs were anxious to hand over governance issues to tribes, they were nonetheless apprehensive about the consequences of the Indian-preference hiring in the proposed legislation. "The Indian Bureau had been the exclusive domain of non-Indians for nearly a century. With the exception of a handful of well-educated Indians such as Carlos Montezuma, an Apache, and Charles Eastman, a Sioux, both doctors, few Indians had been employed in government service."[104] In the case of tribal leaders, while they were excited at the prospect of recovering and consolidating the tribes' land bases, they balked at that part of the bill that forestalled further individual land inheritances, in particular those who were anticipating title to lucrative pieces of real estate. Undaunted, Collier, true to his visionary principles, took it upon himself to break free of the tradition of unilateral decision making: "He decided to consult the Indian people on the legislation, and called a series of Indian congresses around the nation."[105]

Similar to the experiences of the senators on the Senate Committee on Indian Affairs, whom Collier convinced to tour Indian Country, the congresses were a concrete lesson in United States–Indian relations. As examples of the deeply entrenched attitudes toward any Indian initiative sponsored by the federal government, even one purporting to be dramatically different from its predecessors, Deloria referred to the opposition to Collier's plan displayed at the Northern Plains congress in Rapid City, South Dakota, on March 2, 1934, and from the Navajo in the Southwest, later that same year. Whereas the Sioux were concerned by a tribal government "dominated by mixed bloods who had already sold their lands and simply hung around the agencies looking for a handout," the Navajos were still reeling from the desolation their nation endured in the aftermath of Collier's sheep stock reduction, which presumably was to preserve the environment from overgrazing, but which instead had a profoundly negative impact on the Navajo economy. By the time his bill was ready for consideration, Collier's plans were "gutted." Gone was the Court of Indian Claims, as was the ban on individual land inheritances. Moreover, the state and territory, Oklahoma and Alaska, with the largest number of communities were "ineligible for the legislation."[106] Nevertheless, the 1934 Wheeler-Howard Act, as the Indian Reorganization Act was also known, was passed into law on June 18.

Tribes were compelled to accept or reject the proposition, articulated in section 16 for creating a constitutionally based tribal government within a one-year period. The confusion that ensued was due to the murky legal status that had been burdening tribes since the Marshall Trilogy. A mere decade after being catapulted into becoming U.S. citizens, these same Indians were now being challenged to conceive of something that had never existed before, namely a constitution-based tribal government. More to the point, uncertainty arose when tribes, which had for countless generations maintained Indigenous governance customs based on kinship relations, had to somehow adopt a social contract type of organization grounded on a hierarchical distribution of power. That and the fact that many tribes had muddled enrollment rosters, if they had any at all, added to the hesitation about how to even carry out the vote, which was a predicament that the BIA worsened when it arbitrarily decided that those who refrained from voting would nonetheless count as positive votes for accepting the measure. To put things simply, "There was no rhyme nor reason to the sequence of the law as written."[107]

So, then, why did Deloria have such admiration for what Collier achieved? As was often the case when evaluating the impact of federal Indian law, one has to look for the silver lining. More to the point, the 1934 IRA revived the notion that tribes have a right to self-governance, which had been obfuscated under years of assimilation policy. Furthermore, the act stopped the land-allotment process—a point that deserves reiteration—even if it did little to resolve ongoing land disputes. "Not only was allotment stopped but the constant necessity of petitioning the Secretary of the Interior to extend the period of trust was remedied by making all lands of IRA tribes, as those who accepted the Act came to be called, indefinite trust lands until changed by Congressional directive."[108] Also important was the fact that the BIA, under Collier's supervision, was supportive of maintaining traditional tribal values, be it in the form of sacred ritual or governing principles, which was a meaningful step away from the previous efforts at demonizing tribal culture in the name of white Christian civilization. "More important, perhaps, for the long-term effect on Indians was the provision legalizing Indian religions on the reservations."[109] Having said that, Deloria was still forced to acknowledge the anemic response from the bureau, which did not show much interest, particularly after Collier was gone, at fulfilling its obligations to tribes. Also, when it came to the Democratic Congress that voted for the legislation, even "Senator [Burton K.] Wheeler [D-MT] had rejected it by 1937 and sought its repeal," which was a development that would turn into a crisis once the Republicans became the majority party in 1947.[110] Wheeler, it should be noted, was one of the principal sponsors of the 1934 IRA—along with Rep. Edgard Howard (D-NE)—that he introduced into the Senate as chair of the Senate Indian Affairs Committee.

In retrospect, Collier's legacy in the struggle for tribal self-determination was seen less in the legislation that passed and more in the bill that did not. More exactly, Deloria argued that Collier's original bill, which was an expression of the Indian commissioner's belief in "ancient Indian values and beliefs," anticipated the Trail of Broken Treaties' "Twenty-Point Position Paper," which was a clear indication to Deloria that the BIA was capable of the kind of reform that Indian protest leaders sought a generation later. Of particular interest to Deloria in this regard was Collier's proposition of a Court of Indian Claims, which, as conceived, addressed the source of much of the conflict between tribes and the federal government, namely treaty disputes over land claims. As for the powers invested in tribes, Deloria responded to the IRA's critics, particularly among Indian activists, who asserted that the statute entailed a lessening of aboriginal sovereignty in exchange for a tribal constitution and government, by pointing out section 16, which affirmed that tribes shall continue to possess powers accorded them through existing law, in addition to which a tribal constitution enabled a given tribe to acquire further powers, namely: "To employ legal counsel, the choice of counsel and fixing of fees to be subject to the approval of the Secretary of the Interior; to prevent the sale, disposition, lease, or encumbrance of tribal lands, interests in lands, or other tribal assets without the consent of the tribe; and to negotiate with the Federal, State, and local Governments." Of course, section 16 was also the same section that directed the secretary of the interior to consult with tribes about the "appropriation estimates" that the Department of the Interior presented to Congress, which included "federal projects" pertinent to tribes.[111]

Although, as Deloria pointed out, the consultation provision was not adequately fulfilled, the principle of self-governance had an effect on subsequent law and policy. As a sign of changing times, Deloria referred once again to the *Toledo* case, in which the Supreme Court determined that Jemez Pueblo had the sovereign power to "forbade Protestant missionaries" from entering the Pueblo. As an example of the exercise of aboriginal sovereignty, coupled with the court's affirmation of this right, Deloria saw this as an endorsement of such rights among all tribes. Even when the federal trust relation was under serious assault during the years 1954 to 1961, "the policy of the government had been supportive of tribal sovereignty and self-government." At the same time, while it was critical that the federal government acknowledged its own laws, such as the IRA, it was not up to either Congress or the Bureau of Indian Affairs to take full advantage of the law with respect to revitalizing Indigenous governance. At this point, tribes had to take charge of their own destiny. Foregoing the opportunity for nation building based on innovative adaptations of traditional customs and values into modern tribal life was an issue with the obsolete attitudes of certain tribal leaders, whose concepts of nationhood were handicapped by hanging on to the past. As Deloria summarized the situation:

> That the fullblood Indians would be unable to take advantage of the provisions of the act was probably a foregone conclusion. Too many of them sought to return to the days of Fort Laramie, forgetting that in

the intervening decades the world had changed. *If they believed, with Collier, that customs could be preserved, they should also have realized that new customs had to be devised so that the tribes could survive their encounter with the modern world* [emphasis added].[112]

Indeed, the objective of Deloria's discourse on the Indian Reorganization Act was that it was still as relevant in 1974 as it was in 1934, in particular as a statement of the validity of tribal self-governance, which was now ripe for reform along the lines that Collier drew up in his original draft. On the one hand, Deloria's assertion that Indian affairs was ripe for Collier-like reform was an affirmation that tribal self-determination was an idea whose time had arrived. On the other hand, because of the effects of termination on the Indian collective psyche, it also felt like the federal attitude toward Indians was jarringly returned to pre-Collier years when Indians were systematically treated like indigents. Such are the unpredictable currents of Indian affairs. With regard to the latter, when Helen L. Peterson (Cheyenne/Lakota) took a historical look at assessing the current state of Indian affairs in a 1957 article for the *Annals of the American Academy of Political and Social Science*, she observed: "In 1950, approximately fifteen years after the passage of the [1934] IRA, a general reversal of philosophy, harking back to the days of the [1887] General Allotment Act, began to emerge in the policies and procedures of the Indian Bureau. This is clearly seen in recent efforts to reorient federal responsibility in several ways."[113]

The United States, alas, has never been a nation in which Indians could expect to be treated equally under the law, nor allowed the freedom to live and worship as they pleased, let alone prosper according to their traditional values. On the contrary, despite the 1924 Indian Citizenship Act and the 1934 Indian Reorganization Act, the political status of tribes has been perpetually caught in a federal system that has schizophrenically regarded tribes as simultaneously "wards" and "domestic dependent nations." Consequently, tribes have been constantly either ignored or categorically blocked from pursuing their rights and claims to a duly processed settlement. Was it any surprise that America was abruptly confronted, as of 1969, with droves of angry Indians? Given the United States' megalomaniacal foreign policy, which rationalized its intervention into Southeast Asia, not to mention being appalled that any other nation—namely, the Soviet Union—would presume to challenge it for superpower status, it was not shocking that the United States perceived the Indian protest movement as an offence to American hegemony, rather than as a political crisis for which it was responsible to see settled peacefully and justly. How America mistreated Indians has always been an indication of the values at work in its treatment of others, be it domestically or internationally.[114] In light of which, Vietnam was simply the latest chapter in America's history of imperialistic ambitions:

> The Indian wars of the past should rightly be regarded as the first foreign wars of American history. As the United States marched across this continent, it was creating an empire by wars of foreign conquest just as England and France were doing in India and Africa. Certainly the war with Mexico was imperialistic, no more or less than the wars against the Sioux, Apache, Utes, and Yakimas. In every case the goal was identical: land.[115]

Suffice it to say, America has a lot of blood on its hands. With this in mind, if the United States was at all interested in redeeming itself, then it needed to start honoring its commitments, beginning with the hundreds of treaties its own Senate ratified as the law of the land. Additionally, Deloria proposed, Indian land could be restored by transferring control from federal agencies within reservation boundaries, as well as adjacent lands in the public domain.[116] In turn, dozens of unrecognized tribes, many of which were in areas east of the Mississippi, should be recognized by statute, complete with permitting them access to the rights and resources of the 1934 IRA.[117] With regard to land claims, the United States should have considered building upon the principle established with the 1946 Indian Claims Commission.[118] "Perhaps the last reform made by the New Deal philosophy was the Indian Claims Commission. . . . Since the pre–Civil War era Indian tribes had not been given standing to sue the government for violation of treaties and agreements. If a tribe desired to go to court . . . it had to seek Congressional authorization."[119] A mere twelve years after the IRA, Karl E. Mundt (R-SD)[120] stated: "If any Indian tribe can prove that it has been unfairly and dishonorably dealt with by the United States it is entitled to recover. This ought to be an example for all the world to follow in its treatment of minorities."[121] Unfortunately, the Indian Claims Commission, similar to the Indian Reorganization Act, was hampered by sectarian politics and the intractable prejudice against tribal rights and sovereignty. Yet, Deloria touted it as a first step—once endorsed by Congress, which it had the power to reaffirm—that needed to be rehabilitated in the next generation, the 1970s, of Indian affairs. Ultimately, as Deloria emphatically argued:

> Cultural and economic imperialism must be relinquished. A new sense of moral values must be inculcated into the American blood stream. American society and the policies of the government must realistically face the moral problems created by the roughshod treatment of various segments of that society. The poverty program[122] only begins to speak of this necessity, the Employment Act of 1946[123] only hinted in this direction. It is now time to jump fully into the problem and solve it once and for all.[124]

Deloria's passionate call for a moral equivalent to war—resolving the problems generated by racism, inequality, and poverty—was a stark counterpoint to the chapter in federal Indian law and policy that followed, which generated the most distressing period in Indian history since the infamous Trail of Tears: termination. As for Deloria's contribution to the discourse on tribal self-determination, his critique of federal Indian law and policy initiated in *Custer* and *Broken Treaties* was more than an enumeration of injustices perpetrated by the United States in its relations with tribes, it demonstrated that what tribes were demanding for themselves, namely to be regarded as sovereign nations, was not only possible within the federal system, but also based on historical precedent, as endorsed by a bevy of statutes and case law. In the end, the claim that tribes are sovereign powers within the definition of the U.S. Constitution and international law was not a pipe dream but an accurate and legal definition of tribes, which, if the federal government was sincere about assisting in its trust obligations, it would be wise to recognize if it does not want its negligence to spark a belligerent response. In that sense, the termination policy that defined nearly two decades of the post–World War II era was a lesson in how not to manage Indian affairs.

CHAPTER 4

For the Good of the Indian

Termination Policy and the Pillaging of Indian Country

While for many, comparing what happened to Indians during the 1950s and 1960s under the federal government's termination policy to what happened to Jewish populations under the Nazi "Final Solution" is hyperbole at best, not to mention inappropriate. For others, in light of Hannah Arendt's 1961 reports on the Eichmann trial in Israel, what one can argue that these two historical moments had in common was what Arendt labeled "the banality of evil." Although Arendt used the phrase only once in her controversial book, *Eichmann in Jerusalem*, when she described the Nazi henchman's execution by hanging, the infamous phrase nonetheless evoked the state-run and efficiently managed Holocaust. Earlier, in chapter 1 of the present work, Tom Holm referenced the analysis of state-managed power articulated by Max Weber, author of the 1905 classic *The Protestant Ethic and the Spirit of Capitalism*, in his essay on Deloria's critique of Indian leadership. More specifically, Holm cited Weber's concept of "legitimate authority," which was a form of "domination." Holm characterized this as "bureaucrats, who place an emphasis on management rather than on the abilities to solve problems." Whereas Holm contrasted this type of leadership with the kinship- and consensus-based authority of tribal communities, in the context of federal Indian policy Weber's category of power management is useful at describing the way in which state-run agencies, such as the BIA, under the aegis of Congress, could inflict harm on Indians without acknowledging any wrongdoing. Policymakers, namely Congress and the president, were cut-off from the Indian lives they impacted through a vast bureaucracy, which reduced Indian lives to statistics, graphs, and budgets. "This system," as Holm renounced, "has led to political divisiveness, governmental impotency, and social and cultural strife in several Native communities."[1] In the case of termination, the policy wreaked havoc for tens of thousands of Indians, and left a palpable and pervasive sense of dread around Indian Country as the February-March 1965 issue of the *NCAI Sentinel* stated in an editorial titled "Now Is the Time":

> Deep down there is a real sense of sadness when the names Klamath, Menominee, and Seneca come to mind, for these things could not have happened if the tribes throughout the country had presented a unified front from start to finish. What names will bring tears to our eyes in 1975? Mescalero? Yakima? Red Lake? Nez Perce?[2]

Deloria's analysis in "The Disastrous Policy of Termination" in *Custer Died for Your Sins* stands apart from the previous discourse on laws and treaties for two important reasons. First, from the perspective of the late 1960s, termination was directly influencing current affairs, as opposed to being a distant historical event like the 1887 Dawes Act. Second, as a current trend in Indian affairs, it went a long way at explaining the emergence of the Indian protest movement, which saw the occupation of Alcatraz Island on November 20, 1969. Deloria also thought tribal leaders' 1966 confrontation at Santa Fe, New Mexico, with Secretary Stewart Udall over his proposed omnibus bill (H.R. 10560) was a major highlight of the Indian protest movement. Otherwise known as the Indian Resources Development Act of 1967, the proposed ninety-seven page bill "to authorize the Interior Dept. to provide the best economic use of Indian-owned land and financial resources; to promote the development of industrial, commercial, and agricultural enterprises on or near the reservations; and to encourage Indian ownership and management of their corporate endeavors."[3] All of which to be done unilaterally without proper consultation with tribal leaders. In some ways, it was accurate to say that Deloria regarded the 1966 confrontation to be as impactful as the 1969 Alcatraz occupation in spite of not grabbing any headlines. Certainly there was evidence that the confrontation over the omnibus bill set a political precedent that Deloria believed ought to be reused as a strategy. In a note to John Belindo (Navajo/Kiowa), Deloria's successor as NCAI executive director, Deloria stated:

> About two years ago Philleo [Nash] and I discussed the possibility of NCAI issuing reports on various bills. He suggested that when we got ready to move particularly on the Omnibus Bill [H.R. 10560] that we simply write a report and submit it to the committee with a short letter that since this topic is of general interest to Indians and the committee members the NCAI is taking the initiative and is using this method to inform the committee of the issues it feels are involved. . . . It would apply only to bills of overriding import, [P.L.] 280, fishing, Omnibus, taxation, loans.[4]

The confrontation in Santa Fe marked a turning point in NCAI history, which was influenced by Deloria's leadership and his desire that the organization be more assertive at making its demands known to the BIA and Congress.

As for Deloria's focus, he premised his exposition of HCR 108 and P.L. 280, both of which were passed in 1953, on the observation that one need not look to the nineteenth century in order to see American atrocities against Indians. According to Deloria: "during the past twenty years [since the end of World War II] federal medical services have been denied various tribes, resulting in tremendous increase in disease."[5] Deloria, unfortunately, did not provide his reader any details, be it the reason for the denials or the diseases that were spreading. Curiously, Deloria also omitted mentioning his earliest congressional testimony on record, which was a letter—cited in the chapter 1—dated February 10, 1965, to Rep. Winfield K. Denton (D-IN), chairman, Subcommittee of the Committee on Appropriations of the Department of the Interior and Related Agencies on the topic of Indian health care.

> While our membership is impressed with the accomplishments of the Division [of Indian Health] has achieved to date, which has resulted in

an improved level of health of the Indian people, it is equally impressed with the fact our people still suffer from many illnesses and diseases which set them apart from the general population of the Nation.

We believe the attached resolution reflects the great concern on the part of tribal leadership of this country with regard to the low health status of American Indians. We believe that the request for additional appropriations contained in the resolution is reasonable since it is based upon already existing recommendations made by several national health organizations who are knowledgeable in this field.[6]

Indeed, in Deloria's estimation, the treatment of Indians had not improved much since the time Lord Jeffrey Amherst distributed smallpox-infested blankets to Indians during Pontiac's eighteenth-century Rebellion. As for omitting his letter to Congressman Denton from his commentary in *Custer*, one can only speculate. What was obvious was the contrasting tones of the two examples. Whereas the letter to the congressman was expressed in measured tones, clearly for the purpose of getting more appropriations for Indian health needs, the reference to Amherst's sociopathic attempt to exterminate Indians in *Custer* was for the purpose of generating outrage in his readers about an ongoing crisis in Indian health care.

With regard to modern Indian health care, on August 5, 1954, Congress transferred the management of Indian hospitals and health service from the Bureau of Indian Affairs to the Public Health Service as part of its downsizing plan for Indian affairs. As a result, the newly established Indian Health Service (IHS) claimed ten years later that it had made substantial progress at improving the overall health status of Indians. The new agency's critics, nonetheless, decried the lack of adequate access to treatment and facilities, such as those who testified at the above-cited 1960 hearing. Both perspectives were true, though they were divided in their point of view. The IHS, more specifically, based its claims with an eye to justifying continued support and appropriations. Tribal community advocates, on the other hand, were trying to increase access to health care, particularly in urban centers.[7] Deloria, as indicated by his statement to Congressman Denton, was on the side of those whose IHS access was impeded by ongoing federal Indian policy.[8]

Termination, however, was more than cases of medical mismanagement, it was also about an assault on tribal self-governance—the federal support of which was established in the 1934 IRA—and the sinister way in which members of Congress exploited the positive results of New Deal programs for their own anti–New Deal political objectives.[9] "No government can function without revenue," D'Arcy McNickle warned his *Indians at Work* readers in 1938. "So long as tribal funds remain tied up in the United States Treasury, the tribes will have to look elsewhere for the funds necessary to operate on."[10] However, 1953 was the year in which the federal government attempted to solve the "Indian problem" by unilaterally absolving itself of its trust responsibilities to tribes. Consistent with previous policy initiatives, termination was enacted with the insincere assumption that its dictates were for the good of the Indian community. Indeed, on August 1, 1953, HCR 108 was passed, in which both chambers of Congress proclaimed that it was now their intent "to end [Indians'] status as wards of the United States," in addition to which they would be granted "all of the rights and prerogatives pertaining to American citizenship."[11]

> "Freeing" the Indians, in the campaign slogans of the early 1950s simply meant that these longstanding protections would be denied to the tribes in violation of the United States' pledged honor that it would never leave them at the mercy of private citizens and state courts. . . .
> [HCR 108] passed both Houses of Congress without a dissenting vote as obscure resolutions are wont to do. The following year [1954] Indians learned to their sorrow exactly what the resolution meant.[12]

HCR 108 was nothing if not condescending toward tribes, who had been self-governing since before the American republic was founded, as corroborated in the treaties that Deloria highlighted in his discourses on federal Indian law and policy. Furthermore, all Indians already had their rights as U.S. citizens recognized in 1924. In which case, if Congress wanted to unburden tribes of its belittling attitude of regarding them as "wards," then it would have been more productive—not to mention lawful—if Congress had passed a concurrent resolution to honor its treaty promises, executive orders, and other agreements, thereby building upon the principles set forth in the 1946 Indian Claims Commission. Instead, as Deloria observed in *Custer*: "Congress always wants to do away with paternalism [which is the obverse of wardship]. So it has a policy [e.g., termination] designed to do away with Indians. If there are no Indians, there cannot be any paternalism."[13]

As for HCR 108, if Congress had actually ended its mistreatment of Indians as dependent wards in need of white American supervision, that would have been a meaningful development in Indian affairs. Unfortunately, a few days after passing HCR 108, Congress imposed the restrictions of P.L. 280. On August 15, 1953, more specifically, Congress amended the United States Code to extend state jurisdiction over crimes committed within Indian Country, such that the laws and penalties governing the state justice system would apply in the same way and to the same extent as the rest of the state. In other words, in the states listed in P.L. 280—Minnesota, California, Wisconsin, Nebraska, Oregon—tribes lost their sovereign right to police and prosecute criminal offenders within reservation boundaries, which, of course, was in addition to what all tribes had lost in the aftermath of the 1885 Major Crimes Act, which was premised on the racist assumption that Indians could not be trusted to police themselves.[14] P.L. 280 simply extended that prejudice into the modern era.

Looking more closely at how Deloria portrayed termination, he analyzed the deprivation of service mentioned above in terms of Congress's age-old obsession with acquiring more Indian land.[15] In a very brisk account of termination's historical background, Deloria presented a policy trajectory that went from the 1928 Meriam Report,[16] which documented the deplorable conditions in the reservation system, to Indian Commissioner John Collier's legendary effort at getting the 1934 IRA passed. Thwarting Collier's ambitious reforms, as Deloria observed, were opponents to the Indian New Deal who were at work behind the closed chamber doors of Congress. More to the point, the Senate Interior Committee—which previously endorsed the Meriam Report and Indian Reorganization Act, but now had different members with different motives—periodically renewed its original 1928 resolution to continue investigating conditions on the reservations.[17] Ostensibly to assess progress made since 1934, successive reports on the status of Indian tribes formed the basis for rethinking not only federal Indian policy, but also congressional appropriations for Indian affairs, which is to say budget cuts. By 1943 the Senate Interior Committee was determined that "the Indian Bureau should be abolished," which was a proposition that did not initially get very far because of the disruptions of World War II. Although Deloria did not provide evidence in *Custer* for the exact reasons why Congress proposed the abolition of the Indian Bureau, nonetheless in the historical record there was an ongoing criticism from anti–New Deal senators, in which Collier was obliged during an official hearing to not only justify his office's expenditures on Indian programs, but also convince committee members that Indians were doing their part to support the war effort. Paralleling actions in the Senate committee, the House Interior Committee issued its own evaluation of the Indian Office in a subcommittee report chaired by Rep. Karl E. Mundt.[18] The House committee subsequently reported: "the Wheeler-Howard Act [the alternate name of the IRA] was not accomplishing its task of bringing the Indian people up to the level of their white neighbors."[19] Tribal leaders, of course, were not asked for their assessment of their progress under the provisions of the 1934 IRA, let alone their ideas for new programs or policy initiatives.

In 1947 the Republican-controlled Congress seized the opportunity to divest in the New Deal, including the programs created from the IRA. More to the point, Deloria referred to a Senate Civil Service Committee hearing, in which the assistant commissioner of the Office of Indian Affairs, William Zimmerman Jr., provided epoch-changing testimony that articulated the basis for what became HCR 108. As for Zimmerman's testimony, he was called in as Collier's acting successor by Sen. William Langer (R-ND)[20] for the purpose of suggesting "certain procedures by which the personnel and expenses of the Indian Office might be reduced." The justification for this hearing was articulated in Senate Resolution 41 (1947), which Senator Langer submitted to the Senate that led to gathering testimony from various federal officials, in which they accounted for their agencies' budgets.[21] Required to accommodate the committee's agenda, Zimmerman focused on curtailing, even eliminating, services rendered, such as education, health, roads, and irrigation. Furthermore, Zimmerman stated before segueing into the data: "It would also be possible to reduce the number of Indians who are entitled to this service." Toward that end, Zimmerman proposed "three groups of tribes" at three levels of progress that could become fully self-sufficient. The most significant of which were those tribes, in the first group, that were then ready or nearly ready (within ten years) for the termination of their status as federal wards. The second group was those tribes that would be ready for termination in about ten years' time. While the third group was those tribes that needed an "indefinite" amount of time before they were ready for termination.[22] Contingent upon tribal consent, not to mention state governments willingness to take on what had historically been a federal responsibility, Zimmerman laid out a plan for completely reconfiguring Indian affairs. Along with listing tribes making up the three groups, Zimmerman drew up three separate bills for "the Klamath, Osage, and Menominee Tribes," each of which, according to the recorded testimony, "has substantial assets, each of them has a small degree of tribal control, and each of them has indicated that it wants to assume more control, if not full control, of its tribal assets and its tribal operations."[23]

Before continuing with Deloria's analysis of Zimmerman's termination plans, it is important to acknowledge what Deloria had left out of in his portrayal of the above Senate hearing, namely the testimony of tribal leaders. Testifying before the same committee as Zimmerman were representatives of the Mission Indian Federation of California,[24] specifically, Adam Castillo (Cahuilla), president; Purl Willis, counselor; and, Avery M. Blount, attorney.[25] As each took turns disparaging the Indian Bureau, noteworthy were President Castillo's remarks. In response to committee chairman Langer's question, "You want to tell this committee, do you, what you think about abolishing the Indian Bureau?" Castillo stated:

Well, there is no need of Indian Bureau in California. This Congress been spending lot of money, giving it to Indian Bureau, and that money has been fighting us all these years. It has not done any good. Our Indian citizens are self-supporting. Indian children go to day schools, I mean the public schools. We pay the school taxes, pay the sales taxes.[26]

While Castillo was neither the first nor the last American Indian to pro-
claim that the Indian Bureau was an unnecessary burden on Indian lives
and sovereignty, it was unlikely that Castillo was seeking an irreversible
cessation to the federal government's trust obligations to tribes.[27] In
other words, Indian Bureau and trust relationship are not synonymous
terms, they are mutually exclusive. As to why Deloria did not include the
above testimony in his analysis in *Custer*, one can only conjecture. For
starters, did Deloria even see the above item in the published hearings,
which ran a good 350 pages? While one of Deloria's distinctions was his
encyclopedic knowledge of Indian law and policy, this did not preclude
him from overlooking key items in the documents he cited to corroborate his argument. In other words, as tempting as it is to interpret the
omission of Castillo's remarks as either an example or counterexample
to Deloria's concept of tribal self-determination, without evidence that
Deloria read but deliberately omitted Castillo's testimony, all one knows
for certain is that it was not mentioned in *Custer* when it should have
been, given the significance of the topic.

With regard to what Zimmerman had in mind for the Klamath, Osage,
and Menominee, the three separate bills, noted above, proposed to turn
these tribes into corporations, the sustainability of which was dependent
on the revenue-producing natural resources available at each location,
such as timber and mineral wealth.[28] Tribal members, in turn, would
become shareholders in these enterprises.[29] Given how the historical
record has confirmed the indisputably destructive results of termination,
it would be easy to denounce, even demonize Zimmerman's proposals.
However, when one reckons with the way in which bills submitted to
Congress often bear little resemblance to the statutes they become,
it was not surprising that the same thing happened to Zimmerman's
well-laid plans.

> Every plan put forward by Zimmerman required that the tax immu-
> nity remain on Indian lands until the tribal enterprise was financially
> secure in its new method of operation. Plans also included provisions
> for approval by a clear majority of the adult members of the tribes
> before they were to go into effect, and some proposals were not to

be initiated by the bureau but had to come from the tribal governing body at its own request.

The suggestions were basically sound. They incorporated plans that had been discussed in the past between the bureau and the tribes. If carried out according to the original design, the program would have created a maximum of self-government and a minimum of risk until the tribes had confidence and experience in the program.[30]

In the hands of Langer and the Senate Interior Committee, however, what could have substantially enhanced tribal sovereignty became instead more about repealing the Wheeler-Howard Act.[31] Toward that objective, the committee argued for reducing the federal budget under the pretense that the war and the Great Depression were over. Consequently, because Zimmerman's plan scarcely generated any savings, Congress proceeded with further investigations into the status of its Indian wards. Thus, "three years after the Senate hearings the House Interior Committee began a massive study of Indian affairs."[32] More accurately, on June 24, 1952—little more than five years after Zimmerman's testimony—Rep. James J. Delaney (D-NY) introduced H. Res. 698, titled "Authorizing Interior and Insular Affairs Committee to conduct investigation of Indian Affairs Bureau."[33] The resulting report was submitted to the Committee of the Whole House on December 15, 1952. From cover to cover, the report was a hefty 1,814 pages divided into dozens of chapters, subsections, and addenda, including "Names of tribes, bands, or groups of Indians now qualified for full management of their own affairs" and "Legislative proposals designed to promote the earliest practicable termination of all Federal supervision and control over Indians." As was typical, the study and its recommendations were largely conducted without any input from tribal leaders.

As for Deloria's reference to the 1952 Department of the Interior report in *Custer*, he quoted at length two passages. First, from chapter 3, "What are the requirements of scientific procedure in studying Indian tribes," in which the House Interior Committee stated as its methodology: "In applying scientific procedure to Indian affairs it would be appropriate to mention the 'certain principles of elementary logical thought' which were enumerated by René Descartes (1596–1650) in his famous Discourse on Method." The report goes on to quote, as does Deloria, Descartes's method of radical doubt, which begins with never accepting "anything for true which I did not clearly know to be such." Deloria, of course, was nonplussed. Insofar as the House Interior Committee wished to take a scientific approach to assessing how tribes had fared since the passage of the 1934 IRA, it was nothing short of incomprehensible as to why they chose a seventeenth-century book on logical thinking, as opposed to the contemporary research methods developed by an array of distinguished scholars in the social sciences, be they in anthropology, sociology, or political science. In any case, the absurdity did not end there. The second component that Deloria observed in the report was an arcane reference to the Domesday Survey. In chapter 7 of the committee report, titled "The Domesday Survey of England in 1086 As a Model," it stated: "The economic and social survey made by William the Conqueror of his domains in England, some 20 years after the Norman Conquest, was one of the most remarkable feats ever accomplished in the history of governments."[34] It was as if Congress was shamelessly mocking tribes, as it flaunted its plenary power, reducing Indian affairs to a tragic farce. One can sense Deloria's anger as he wrote: "With this contemptuous announcement of royal power of Congressional committees, the stage was set for the disastrous era of the Eighty-third and ensuing congresses and the termination period in Indian Affairs."[35]

Enter, then, Dillon S. Myer, stage right. Myer, the former director of the War Relocation Authority, who oversaw the unconstitutional internment of Japanese-American citizens during World War II,[36] was nominated to become commissioner of Indian affairs on April 17, 1950.[37] Despite some animosity toward his appointment—including from Crow Nation leader Robert Yellowtail[38] (who advocated for an Indian appointed as commissioner) and Rep. George H. Bender (R-OH) (who, in 1951 was concerned with Myer's performance)[39]—Myer maintained strong support from senators and representatives who appreciated his enthusiastic backing of their policy agenda. Symptomatic of the mostly Republican attitude toward the BIA, Rep. George B. Schwabe (R-OK) was recorded as saying: "The Bureau of Indian Affairs has been a stench in the nostrils of this Government for many years."[40] In response, on August 5, 1952, again in pursuant to H. Res. 698 (passed July 1, 1952), Commissioner Myer dispatched a memorandum at the behest of a House Interior sub-committee charged with gathering the information, which became the basis for implementing the "withdrawal program." In spite of whatever opposition from tribal leaders that the Indian Bureau may have encountered, the objectives of the withdrawal program were regarded as policy, such that agency personnel were directed to obtain to the best of their ability the cooperation of tribes. As Myer stated in an effort to motivate the rank and file:

> I look to the area and agency personnel, as the representatives of the Bureau of Indian Affairs, to assume primary responsibility for instituting and carrying on cooperative withdrawal programing work at field levels. It is in the field that we have the basic sources of necessary information and the means of enlisting Indian support and participation. In your work with Indian groups I want you to use every opportunity to place before the Indian tribal membership the need for and advantages to be derived from cooperative withdrawal programing effort. Tribal leaders should be encouraged to obtain maximum membership participation in this work.[41]

Recognizing that Myer's direction to his staff to "work with Indian groups" was little more than a hypocritical regard for tribal rights and sovereignty, Deloria excoriated Myer, stating vehemently: "The policy from Commissioner to field clerk was to get rid of Indians as quickly as possible, treaties or no. When the termination hearings were later held, the bureau had much to say. It gave every possible excuse to get rid of the particular tribe which was under consideration by the committee."[42] Exit Dillon Myer; enter Arthur Watkins and the termination bills.

During the summer of 1953, as Sen. Arthur Watkins (R-UT)[43] and Rep. E. Y. Berry (R-SD)[44] worked in tandem, HCR 108 was passed on August 1, 1953. Watkins, in particular, was a zealot for termination. As Deloria portrayed his political verve: "Watkins' idea [in contradistinction to Zimmerman's more measured proposal] was to get rid of as many tribes as possible before the 1956 elections. He feared that if the Great Golfer

[President Dwight D. Eisenhower] were not re-elected the movement would be stopped by a President who might pay attention to what was happening in the world around him."[45] In the meantime, Watkins's name appeared on multiple bills terminating federal services rendered to dozens of tribes. Among his noteworthy accomplishments was the transfer of Indian Health to the Public Health Service, which brings us back to where we began.[46]

As for the accusation that termination was nothing more than a government land grab, Deloria illustrated his point with references to the Paiutes, Klamath, Kansas Potawatomi, Alabama-Coushattas, Flatheads, Turtle Mountain Chippewas, and Menominees, summarizing the political and economic impact that HCR 108 had on these communities. In each case, Watkins, as chair of the Subcommittee on Indian Affairs, which was charged by the Senate Interior Committee to implement termination, ruled over tribes with a draconian passion. Deloria characterized the subcommittee's work during from 1954 to 1968 as being nothing less than government-sanctioned coercion. In fact, one can say that the method employed echoed the land-exchange treaties during the Indian Removal Era:

> The basic approach of the Senate [sub]committee never varied for fourteen years. Unbearable pressures, lies, promises, and threats of termination were made whenever a tribe won funds from the United States [through the Indian Claims Commission] because of past swindles by the federal government. Whenever a tribe needed special legislation to develop its resources [even though it was in concert with HCR 108], termination was often the price asked for the attention of the [sub]committee. And if a tribe compromised with the Senate [sub]committee it was on the road to termination. Quarter was asked but none given.[47]

Unsurprisingly, an equal amount of fear erupted across Indian Country during the latter 1950s as happened during the 1830s. While the termination of supposedly self-sustaining tribes like the Klamath and Menominee was expected, because Watkins dispensed with Zimmerman's original tiered groupings of tribes, this meant that smaller, less economically sustainable tribes like the Paiutes in Watkins's home state of Utah were vulnerable to termination. Promising the Paiute recognition of their "tribal marriages,"[48] Watkins instead, in documents labeled "Liberation of Utah Indians,"[49] simply terminated their tribal services without any mention of marriages, tribal or otherwise.[50] "The Paiutes had been too poor to come to Washington for the hearings," as Deloria lamented, "and when they found out what Watkins had done it was too late."[51] Perhaps more than anything, the realization that smaller tribes, meaning ones that did not have the resources to defend themselves, were unpredictably prone to termination generated an "absolute terror" that "spread through Indian country."[52] To which the federal government responded with bureaucratic indifference.

Distinct among the victims of termination were the Menominee of Wisconsin, who were on Zimmerman's 1947 list of tribes that were "ready now," not to mention being on the list of ten tribes in HCR 108. Despite being one of the few tribes "paying for all its own services," the Menominee had the audacity to win a settlement against the United States in 1951 for the sum of $8.5 million, which made national headlines.[53] However, when the enabling legislation made its way to the House of Representatives, authorizing the distribution of per capita payments of $1,500 per tribal member, "Watkins attached a provision to the bill in the Senate, requiring the tribe to submit to termination in order to get the money."[54] When the Menominee, who did have the resources to make it to Washington in 1960 to defend themselves, submitted a request for an extension on their termination date, they met with Sen. Frank Church (D-ID),[55] who was now the chair of the Senate Subcommittee on Indian Affairs.[56] Senator Church, at a subcommittee hearing in which Menominee representatives attended, questioned H. Rex Lee, associate commissioner, Bureau of Indian Affairs. Lee was called to explain "how the Menominee termination had come about."[57]

Deloria quoted the dialog between Church and Lee at length, which was regarded sarcastically as "enlightening." What one learned from the exchange was the fact that the Menominee never put the matter of accepting termination (in order to acquire their duly awarded funds) to a referendum. As Lee explained to Church: "As I recall there was no referendum. The tribal delegates can correct me on this. They had a group that was negotiating with the conferees here in Washington and they stood up in the committees and agreed to this termination, I think, on the basis that the termination was coming regardless because of the resolution requiring termination."[58] Menominee tribal attorney, Glenn A. Wilkinson, then interjected that what in fact influenced the Menominee decision to accept termination was a meeting they had had with Senator Watkins. As Wilkinson recalled, Watkins told the 174 Menominee attending a meeting of their general council that "they could not have a per capita payment unless they accepted termination."[59] In spite of recognizing the impoverished conditions in which the Menominee endured, Watkins did not have any qualms about misleading them. He was even recorded has having felt quite good about his visit to Wisconsin, referring to the occasion as a "very interesting experience."[60]

Presumably, according to logic that only make sense to a politician, Menominee economic sustainability was contingent on accessing their settlement money, which was "over ten million dollars in the federal treasury," including the $8.5 million settlement noted above.[61] The total dollars would provide investment capital that the Menominee would manage as they took control over their own forest and timber. Unfortunately, the Menominee had already designated the funds, which was mandated by statute, for per capita distribution to Menominee tribal members. Consequently, as Deloria observed: "the termination plan was based upon money that no longer existed."[62] One can sense in Deloria's sarcasm as he wondered what happened to Congress's plan to employ Descartes methodology? Obviously, congressional logic worked far differently than Cartesian logic.

As for the State of Wisconsin, it was adamantly opposed to termination for the simple reason that they were worried about the fallout when the Menominee eventually depleted their timber supply. Referring back to the 1954 joint hearing before the House and Senate Subcommittees on Indian Affairs, Harry Harder, commissioner, Wisconsin Tax Commission, spoke on behalf of state interests, in which he stated: "we may have a substantial welfare problem."[63] In spite of the potential social-service crisis, Watkins maintained the opinion that state agencies were better positioned to manage Indian affairs than the federal government. Wilkinson responded with a reminder of Zimmerman's proposal that terminated tribes be accorded a fifty-year tax exemption. Having long dispensed with Zimmerman's liberal accommodations, Watkins reacted tersely, asserting that referring to the 1947 testimony "was not going to make a lot of difference one way or another."[64] To put it succinctly, as Menominee chairman Jerome Grignon explained in a 1960 hearing before the House Subcommittee on Indian Affairs, "the Government was going out of the Indian business."[65] As often happens when a discreditable violation of tribal rights is imminent and options for redress are exhausted, the only thing left in a tribe's arsenal was an appeal to conscience. Toward that end, Deloria noted that Grignon's predecessor Antoine "Tony" Waupochick, chairman, Menominee Advisory Council—who met with Watkins at the Menominee General Council meeting mentioned above—made an ethical appeal to the committee in 1954: "History records that the Menominees have been loyal to this Government and have stood by their bargains when they have relinquished land to the United States. We think that your action should be governed by a desire to see that history will record that Congress was loyal to the Menominee people."[66] But as typically results when tribal leaders invoke the moral high ground, their words fell on deaf ears, hence the urgent need six years later for the 1960 hearing on amending the Menominee Termination Act.

Deloria's analysis of Menominee travails concluded with an account of the financial consequences of termination, which were enormous. On this point, Grignon made the distressing observation: "I believe if we are to terminate December 31 [1960, assuming the extension was granted] with our economy so low where we cannot afford this county which is the cheapest for us to take, we will go until our money runs out."[67] It did not matter for the Menominee that the American presidential administration and Congress had switched from one party to the other. Termination was still policy. Consequently, what one did not see at the 1960 hearing was anyone other than the Menominee arguing that termination was a huge mistake. In addition to fallible logic, Congress was also an entity without a moral compass, as Deloria observed with palpable disgust: "These same Senators [such as Watkins and Church] who cold-bloodedly created a pocket of poverty in Wisconsin would later vote for the War on Poverty with good conscience."[68] The implication was that the same senators who supposedly cared so much for the poor under the auspices of the Economic Opportunity Act (1964) did nothing to stop Congress from deliberately impoverishing the Menominee Tribe.

As occurs in many instances in Deloria's critiques of federal Indian policy, there were points when the author of *Custer* could not help but be astounded by the obvious and wasteful displays of government absurdities. Deloria indulged in such a moment when he transitioned into the astronomical cost of Menominee termination to the state and federal government, which was evidence of the untenable objective that the Senate Subcommittee on Indian Affairs had for its policy initiative, which was cutting the federal budget and saving money.[69] In addition to the millions spent on keeping Menominee County solvent, Deloria expounded on the humanitarian crisis that termination created:

> Clearly, with some $5 million of special federal aid, over $1 million in state aid, and a rapidly sinking economy combined with increasing health and education problems and skyrocketing tuberculosis rate, termination has not been a success for the Menominees. It has been a rationally planned and officially blessed disaster of the United States Congress.[70]

As for pending disasters, Deloria made clear that termination was yet to be relegated to the past, as he alerted his reader to a pending termination bill regarding the Confederated Tribes of Colville Indians, which was perpetrated by Watkins's ideological successor, James H. Gamble, who, as it turned out, was neither a senator nor representative, but a "staff member." Despite working on behalf of Sen. Henry "Scoop" Jackson (D-WA),[71] who, as of 1963, was the chair of the Senate Committee on Interior and Insular Affairs, Gamble was regarded as the impetus for keeping termination an active option for the Senate Subcommittee on Indian Affairs, which, as noted above, was chaired by Senator Church. Deloria even went so far as to characterize Jackson as Gamble's "front man."[72] As for the accuracy of Deloria's accusation, what was indisputable was the fact that Gamble's name was all over the hearings to terminate the Colville Reservation.[73]

Similar to the Menominee, when the Colville succeeded in their claim for the restoration of land that had been previously opened for homesteading, the political cost of getting the land reinstated as part of their reservation was accepting the terms of termination. The Colville were not permitted any alternative.[74] What troubled Deloria most about the Colville situation, even more than the fact that termination was still policy, was the realization that whereas before the face of termination was represented by senators and representatives, it now took the form of someone working in the background, a congressional aide.[75] Either way, termination would be equally devastating for the Colville reservation as it was for the Menominee. As a result, the Colville termination case prompted the "major tribes of the nation" to wage "a furious battle" against this proposed legislation, in light of which, "the House Interior Committee has been sympathetic to Indian pleas and has to date not passed the bill." Indeed, the Colville termination hearing would be another instance, albeit eight years earlier than the Menominee hearing, in which Deloria went before Congress to try and protect another tribe from federal devastation.[76] Of course, not passing a bill was less impactful than renouncing termination categorically as policy.[77]

Indeed, the specter of termination was very much on Deloria's mind when he authored a December 7, 1969, *New York Times* editorial in which he criticized Nixon's secretary of interior, Walter Hickel, for having described the federal government as "'overprotective' of Indian rights."[78] The Seneca, like the Menominee and the Colville, were expected to accept termination in exchange for the compensation they rightfully deserved for the flooding of their lands.[79] Deloria reminded his reader that the Seneca were the same tribe that signed the 1794 Pickering Treaty and whose rights were violated when the Kinzua Dam was built in violation of that ratified agreement. Demanding, then, that the Seneca accept termination was not only adding insult to injury, but was also "truly ironic": "the only federal assistance the Seneca received in recent years was a staff man assigned by the Bureau of Indian Affairs to assist them in problems caused the tribe by the building of Kinzua Dam." Similar to the Menominee and Colville cases, the federal government stood to gain very little beyond a host of problems and expenses as a result of

Seneca termination. Yet, Congress was intransigent about changing policy, despite vocal opposition from tribal leaders, intertribal councils, and the National Congress of American Indians.[80] In a 1965 editorial titled "Justice and 'Just Compensation'—The American Way of Land Acquisition," which was a scorching condemnation of the federal privilege of eminent domain and how it has been applied to Indians lands, it stated with respect to the Seneca and the Kinzua Dam:

> Certainly no one can look at the Seneca settlement and feel that justice was done for the Seneca people. Not when the Pennsylvania Railroad got $20 million for a right of way while an entire nation of Indian people was hopelessly uprooted and in order to get their money, which was an inadequate settlement to begin with, must present to Congress within 3 weeks a plan to completely abrogate their remaining rights under the 1794 [Pickering] Treaty which was nullified by a gross violation of that Treaty by the United States government.[81]

What developed, nevertheless, from the activism against termination was a realization that Indians, for all that they had been asked to sacrifice in the name of "settling the continent," not to mention all that they had been asked to cede—sometimes with their consent (treaties), more often without (statutes)—they were still orphans in the storm. Did the Indians have any allies? Tribes were regularly relied upon as America's allies, but on whom did the tribes rely on during a crisis? Historically, men of the cloth were the ones, like Samuel Worcester or Bishop Henry B. Whipple, to stand up on behalf of tribes and demand a more charitable policy toward America's first inhabitants. More recently, of course, there was activist and reformist John Collier. As for the post-1953 generation, perhaps because of what Collier's reorganization agenda did to their stranglehold on reservation communities, the churches seemed to have moved on. At best, Indians and their concerns about termination were given lip service; at worst, they were deliberately overlooked for the civil rights movement. On this point, Deloria recounted his father's experience: "My father was fired from his post with the Episcopal Church for trying to get the church involved with the termination issue in the 1950's."[82]

In the final analysis, the Menominee, Seneca, and Colville were victims of an ideological battle between the two dominant and non-Indigenous political parties vying for power over the nation's wealth and resources. Indians may occasionally be courted as allies, but they were inevitably exploited as means to political ends, be it seizing title to the land, occupying territory, expropriating natural resources, or cutting federal budgets. "In practice," as Deloria affirmed, "termination is used as a weapon against the Indian people in a modern war of conquest." America has never been great—at least, not in the sense of being a nation of justice and democratic principles. Rather the few exploit the land and use their power to make the masses compete for a much smaller share of the wealth. Furthermore, because of the inequities of American society, certain segments of the population, be they immigrants, people of color, or religious minorities, are denied the rights and resources they need to succeed:

> When the Kennedys [John and Robert] and [Martin Luther] King were assassinated people wailed and moaned over the "sick" society. Most people took the assassinations as a symptom of a deep inner rot that had suddenly set in. They needn't have been shocked. America has been sick for some time. It got sick when the first Indian treaty was broken. It has never recovered.[83]

Renewing his appeal for a moral equivalent to war, Deloria made an urgent appeal to his readers that it was not too late to recover from its soul sickness and redeem itself. Americans, most importantly, needed to decide if they were going to continue condoning a Congress that abused its power at the expense of Indian people? Did Americans believe in the principles they espoused such as freedom and democracy, only when they wanted to scorn other nations, such as the Soviet Union, or did they protect these principles at home, especially for the politically vulnerable? At some point, as the biblical wisdom goes, America will have to reap what it has sown. In which case, Deloria warned: "America is running up a great [moral] debt. It may someday see the wholesale despoliation of its land and people by a foreign nation."[84] Deloria went on to make clear that America's redemption must begin with revising the gross inaccuracies that have pervaded its portrayals of American Indians, be it in its congressional studies or its social science books. More to the point, as long as America holds on to seeing Indians as primitive folk, godless heathens, and childlike wards, it will inevitably make the same mistakes again, thereby compelling history to repeat itself, letting the people decide when they have had enough. Termination policy compelled Indians to organize in a variety of ways, from the NCAI to Alcatraz Island, to tell the federal government that they had have enough. Instead, tribal demands in response to terminating the trust relation had been a growing exigency that tribes be respected as sovereign nations. But what was the relative health of tribes, even after more than thirty years of IRA-based self-governance?

As of the time that the 1973 Wounded Knee confrontation was grabbing national headlines, there were two instances in which Deloria characterized tribal governments as possessing powers comparable to student governance groups, which was his way of making the point that the self-governance initiated by the 1934 IRA had run its course and was in desperate need of improvement as a vehicle for tribal sovereignty. First, somewhat cynically in a *Los Angeles Times* editorial, Deloria stated: "Our tribal governments have all the self-governing powers of student governments in a large high school. Everything they do is subject to the approval of the Washington DC bureaucracy—thousands of miles from the problem."[85] Second, in a more scholarly context, Deloria stated in a special issue of the *North American Review*:

> In those days [during the Depression, when the 1934 Indian Reorganization Act was passed] tribal income was exceedingly small; federal programs, even with the expansive nature of the New Deal, were miniscule, and none provided for direct funding of administrative costs to the tribes themselves. Thus the governments of the reservations resembled student governments in the large colleges rather than municipal governments with the ability to expand and contract according to the conditions that existed.[86]

With respect to the ambitious agenda of independence that Deloria promoted in *Broken Treaties*, its prelude appeared in the late summer 1973 issue of *Akwesasne Notes*, in which Deloria outlined a post–Wounded

Knee plan. More specifically, Deloria reiterated the need to modernize the now dated 1934 IRA-based tribal governments that proved inadequate at handling the economic growth that tribes had since seen, in which "many tribes are now million dollar a year corporations." In the spirit of growing self-determination, Deloria stated: "Many of the decisions that are now made by bureaucrats should be made by Indian people through [the] referendum process." Furthermore, in light of increased tribal revenues, "our tribes need to have their tax status clarified." Also, in terms of social justice, tribes "need to be told exactly what their responsibilities are with respect to the 1968 Civil Rights Act," which Deloria saw as a threat to tribal government. Speaking of the legal system, Deloria argued for establishing an Indian treaty court, mentioned earlier, which obliged state governments to bring their grievances against tribes into a system specifically designed to handle such disputes. In light of recent conflicts in the Pacific Northwest and the Great Lakes between tribes and local white communities, in which state agencies recurrently sided with the whites in violation of treaties, an Indian treaty court would preclude tribes from being harassed by state agencies:

> [An Indian treaty court] would mean an end to harassment of our fishermen and hunters because few game departments would want to take frivolous cases into federal court located some distance from their state capitols, and in a court that had expertise in Indian treaties. It is one thing to get the local JP [justice of the peace] to say that a treaty is no longer good. It is another to convince a competent judge with a background in treaty law to nullify a treaty.

In Deloria's editorial what were ultimately the most important matters that had to be addressed were twofold. One, tribes needed to reconcile the factionalism that had torn communities like Pine Ridge apart over the previous decade. The Indian protest movement had forced traditionals and progressives alike to confront the federally stipulated limitations on their self-governance and their ability to meet the needs of their own people. Second, speaking of the needs of the people, Indians, of whatever political persuasion, needed to do more than complain about the federal government's treatment of tribes:

There has been little effort on our part to bring the questions we have to the attention of the government in a systematic manner. Sure, we have all complained about various practices, but we have not given a thorough explanation of what alternatives we believe are open to us. Thus if we wait to see what the government will do about the treaties, we shall be in Hell when it freezes over.[87]

In light of the above predicament, in *Broken Treaties* Deloria argued that tribes needed to pursue their land claims against the federal government, preferably in an Indian Court of Claims, in which the objective of the 1946 Indian Claims Commission of litigating land disputes could be resolved in terms of land restoration to tribes. Secondly, tribes should set a legal agenda in which they reinterpret Indian case law in light of the international relations arena in which Indian–United States relations began, as documented in the treaty-making record and Marshall's *Cherokee Nation* (1831) and *Worcester* (1832) opinions. Thirdly, it would behoove tribes to reinitiate the treaty-making process, not only because tribes are independent sovereign nations (in spite of what Prucha might have thought), but also because it would clarify the political alliances that the original treaties established between tribes and the United States.[88] Most importantly, Deloria was adamant that it was Indians who had to think their way out of their own dilemmas. As he admonished his readers in the aftermath of the 1973 Wounded Knee conflict:

We have had over three years of symbolic protest now and we have very little to show for it. It's time we stopped dramatizing things and got to work solving problems. It's time we read our treaties instead of accusing the government of breaking them and letting it go at that. It's time we accepted the responsibility for governing ourselves instead of asking the BIA to "give" us self-determination.[89]

Deloria's discourse on tribal self-determination was a tour de force of political thinking in which American statutes and case law limiting tribal sovereignty were deconstructed and the affirmation of tribes possessing a status higher than states was revealed and that much more was possible when tribes dispensed with the handicap of believing themselves wards of the BIA. It may have taken the threat of termination to wake up Indians to their rights and powers as nations, but the realization has nonetheless obliged all facets of the American Indian community, from tribal chairmen to urban Indian college students, to stop and take inventory of their grievances with and their demands from the federal system. As archaic as treaty-making may sound, as it evoked a bygone era of powdered wigs and peace pipes, the pursuit of a sovereign-to-sovereign relationship with the United States was nothing short of revolutionary. Not since Collier advocated on behalf of the tribal right to self-governance has Indian-white relations seen such a dramatic change in ideas and values. Granted, tribes could not achieve the kind of decolonization that other colonized people have attained in other parts of the world, such as Asia and Africa, but the idea of decolonization and self-determination nevertheless as articulated within the parameters of federal Indian law and policy could still substantially change the system from within—making Indian autonomy more of a reality. The question that faced Indians at this point was, how to think like nations and not minorities.

CHAPTER 5

Not Your Minority

Tribalism during the Civil Rights Era

Charles A. Eastman was once asked, according to his own account in *The Indian To-Day*, why the American Indian community had not produced a "Booker Washington," the highly regarded Black activist-intellectual, author of *Up From Slavery* (1901), cofounder of the Tuskegee Normal and Industrial Institute, and the National Association for the Advancement of Colored People (NAACP). References to Carlos Montezuma as a comparable figure notwithstanding, Eastman's response largely consisted of pointing out that Indians came from dozens of different tribal groups, many of which were historic rivals, for whom political unity was a fairly recent idea.[1] Indeed, even calling themselves "American Indian," as in the Society for American Indians, signified a seismic change in the thinking among Indigenous peoples. Whereas the whites who invaded Indian lands had always seen the continent's first inhabitants as being of one race, the Indigenous nations of many lands, languages, and customs saw themselves as discrete groups bounded by kinship relations and a common dialect, each one distinct from the other. Such tribal relations, generations after Eastman, persisted as Indians struggled anew during Deloria's time to find common cause through such organizations as the National Congress of American Indians (founded in 1945), the National Indian Youth Council (founded in 1961), and American Indian Movement (founded in 1968).

As for American Indians during the civil rights era, Deloria stated in his conclusion to the 1971 edition of Jennings C. Wise's *The Red Man in the New World Drama*, which he revised for the Macmillan Company:

> The important aspect of the story of the red man is his stubborn refusal to give up his tribal identity and become simply another American citizen. While the years have shown a partial assimilation of other groups, only the red man has stood firm, resisting all efforts to merge him with the groups that surround him.

Ultimately, Deloria argued, regardless of tribe, location, or historical epoch, "there is something uniquely different about Indian people that sets them apart from other Americans."[2] As for the relationship between Indian activism and the Black civil rights movement, Deloria discussed the often tenuous connection between the two communities. In *Custer*'s "The Red and the Black," Deloria attempted to explain why the two movements never united as much as one may have expected, given the common source their grievances, namely the systemic racism of American government and society. In fact, while there were significant exceptions in the Indian protest movement who did participate, for example, in the 1968 Poor People's Campaign, such as Hank Adams, the legal differences between Blacks and Indians, which were first introduced in "Indians Today, the Real and the Unreal," created a political gap that was even more significant than the cultural one. Nonetheless, this did not preclude Indians from communicating and learning from the Black protest movement. When Deloria revisited the topic of Indian-Black relations in *We Talk, You Listen*, specifically in the chapters titled "Another Look at Black Power" and "The Forman Manifesto," he took a more generous view of the influence of Black nationalism on how the Indian protest movement adapted the former's direct-action tactics and rhetoric to the cause of Indian nationhood.

As noted, the first instance in which Deloria brought up the divergent histories of Blacks and Indians was in *Custer,* chapter 1. At that juncture, Deloria underscored that, whereas whites were often adamant about denying the Black community any access, let alone equal access, to the rights and privileges of American citizenship, the white attitude toward

Indians was completely opposite: "Law after law was passed requiring him [the Indian] to conform to white institutions."[3] With respect, then, to the 1960s civil rights movement, Deloria saw the situation in terms of the ways in which Blacks and Indians had been designated differently under the law, which was informing the contemporary debate on "race relations." As Deloria emphasized in *We Talk, You Listen*, race relations in America was by definition Black-and-white relations. More specifically, Deloria critiqued the notion of "Others" as a sociological category into which Indians were often placed, which was largely due to the general ignorance in American society regarding Indian tribes. Indians did not fit the more dominant Black-white paradigm of race relations. Denise Bates, for example, documented the frustrations that the Houmas and the Choctaws of Mobile and Washington Counties, Alabama, more commonly referred to as the MOWA Choctaws, encountered when attempting to affirm their identities as Indian:

> Although the specific experiences of the Houmas and MOWA Choctaws are unique, the impact of being racially "othered" shaped remarkably similar experiences in both communities. They were identified as "Indians" in some contexts, while in other situations they were deemed "so-called Indians," "hybrids," "mongrels," "Sabines," or "Cajuns."

The Houma and MOWA Choctaw situation was not only a consequence of the perceived racial ambiguity of the populations in question, but also the intransigence of state governments (Louisiana and Alabama) that were locked into a biracial system, which was not legally structured to recognize Indian communities, in particular ones that "were not federally recognized and spent many decades keeping to themselves."[4] As for the larger issues facing tribes in a biracial mindset, even other "minority" groups showed a tendency to treat Indians either as a form of "Black" or else as an "unknown" quantity. What was in order, Deloria argued, was the need for the recognition of multilateral relations between varying and unique ethnic and racial groups:

> Intergroup relations is thus an extremely complex field in which all groups are related to each other according to their experiences of

each other, exclusive of their relationships with other groups. There is an Indian-black relationship and an Indian-white relationship that remains hidden and unexamined if one is simply to lump Indians into the white-black vocabulary and thought-world by saying AND INDIANS TOO.[5]

Insofar as *We Talk, You Listen* was Deloria's second effort at influencing the discourse on tribalism, picking up on themes introduced in *Custer*, it is worth observing that this volume was a departure from the experience-driven commentary and satire that readers acclaimed in his inaugural book. Perhaps as a result of the start of his academic career at Western Washington University, where he joined the ethnic studies department, *We Talk, You Listen* was more theoretical in tone, complete with a conscientious attempt at placing the Indian protest movement in a much broader cultural and political context, as evident in the references to Black Power and Marshall McLuhan's notion of the "media is the message." In light of which, it may also be worth acknowledging that Deloria's second major work appeared in the shadows of Dee Brown's *Bury My Heart at Wounded Knee* and Angie Debo's *A History of the Indians of the United States*. Because of *Custer* and the Indian protest movement it symbolized, Indians were entering mainstream American society—at least to the extent that more Americans than before were aware that tribal nations were part of the modern world, along with the Black community and the Viet Cong. As such, *We Talk, You Listen* was Deloria's effort to build a bridge between the rise of Indian nationalism with the dialog on race in America.

Conceivably because Deloria ventured too far out of his areas of expertise, when *We Talk, You Listen* was reviewed, readers were largely underwhelmed. Jean K. Boek, for example, in her 1975 review for *American Anthropologist* was frustrated with the way in which Deloria "hops from one topic to the next" without providing his reader much information on each of the topics covered, such as omitting the names of the "five powerful government agencies" that had "fought with the Lummi tribe" of Washington state over the previous five years.[6] With regard to Deloria's argument that the best hope for redressing the social, political, and environmental crises that had been afflicting the United States was through adopting a tribal perspective on developing solutions, critics tended to portray Deloria's philosophy of tribalism as at best idealistic. Lawrence C. Kelly, in his 1971 review for *Arizona and the West*, concluded: "To comment that Deloria's blueprint for encouraging the emergence of neo-tribalism is neither very clear . . . nor very practical would be to miss his point that there is really no other acceptable alternative for survival."[7] As for the social and political crises that have been burdening American society, Merle Wells summarized in his 1972 review his reaction to Deloria's proposition that America take a more multilateral and ethnically diverse approach to problem-solving:

> Trying to offer guidance rather than to seek advice from the Indians, white leaders have developed a society that offends the Indians, Negroes, and Chicanos, and that fails to appeal to many Anglos as well—especially those of the younger generation. Over the centuries, Indian leaders—including Vine Deloria [Jr.]—have been ready to offer their answers to many urgent problems, and now they want the whites to listen to them.[8]

Speaking of compelling whites to listen, ethnic studies, as the intersection of law, politics, history, and race, potentially can play a role in articulating the issues and objectives of each group. Toward that end, Deloria referenced the "Kerner report," which was the product of the Kerner Commission, headed by Gov. Otto Kerner Jr. (D-OH). The eleven-member commission was appointed by President Johnson and tasked with understanding the causes of the "race riots" that had torn apart American urban centers since 1965.[9] Officially named the National Advisory Commission on Civil Disorders, the "Riot Report" was read into the Congressional Record on March 1, 1968. According to Sen. Walter F. Mondale (D-MN), who had read a *Washington Post* article about the report by William Chapman: "The riots are not caused by conspirators, but arise from an 'explosive mixture' of pervasive discrimination, poverty, and Negro concentration in the slums. 'White racism' is basically responsible for that mixture, the Commission said."[10] Indeed, the intensity of the Black-white racial divide was so traumatic that at one time, American political commentators saw the country as literally splitting into two distinctive nations, "one black, one white—separate but unequal."[11]

With respect to how American Indians fit into this dreadful situation, Victor H. Palmieri summed it up in his 1968 article about the implications the "Riot Report" had for the City of Los Angeles, California: "The deep and ominous split that is taking place within the country has several critical dimensions. The first has to do with the way in which the minority population—particularly the Negro population, but including also Spanish-surname Americans and *other ethnic minorities*—is becoming more and more concentrated within the central core areas of our major metropolitan regions [emphasis added]." While Deloria did acknowledge that the Indian protest movement was influenced by the Black civil rights movement, most importantly in terms of utilizing direct-action tactics that enabled Black activists to get their message heard, in terms of the political dimensions of the two movements, Deloria was consistent about the substantial differences between Indian tribes as nations and the Black community as individuals.

Because the 1964 Pacific Northwest fish-ins, which inaugurated the Indian protest movement, were based on an ongoing treaty-rights dispute between the State of Washington and local tribes (such as the Puyallup), the controversy was less about race relations and more about the legality of the treaties signed in the 1850s. Consequently, to have the Indian protest movement glossed over with the phrase "other ethnic minorities" was nothing less than frustrating. No, America cannot resolve a treaty dispute between tribes and Washington state with what is appropriate for Black-white relations in Los Angeles. As Deloria stated rather wryly in *We Talk, You Listen*: "One could conclude that there are not really any Indians in American society, but that it has been infiltrated by OTHERS."[12] Deloria's comment signified the cultural divide that existed between Blacks and Indians, and how each was misunderstood by whites. Referring once again to the Southern Indian Movement, Bates cited anthropologist J. Anthony Paredes, who observed "during the civil rights movement 'new fault lines became evident in the racial system of the South [and] many Indians sought even more to distance themselves from any identification with blacks.'" As Bates explained: "Indians disassociated themselves from the black civil rights movement as a matter of protecting themselves from the racial violence that became commonplace during the period."[13]

Diversifying ethnic studies, then, as Deloria argued in *We Talk, You Listen* entailed diversifying the curriculum, which encountered heated debates over the value of such changes as well as bringing into light the inadequacies of how race and ethnicity were currently handled at all levels of American education. What was evident, nevertheless, was that America's white-centric master narrative was no longer valid. As such, what many in America regarded as its society shattering into pieces was really a sign that America was growing and diversifying as a nation. As of 1970, more and more groups had found their voices, which was a theme that Deloria would examine more closely in *The Metaphysics of Modern Existence* (1979) in chapter 12, "Our Transforming Institutions." In the meantime, in *We Talk, You Listen*, Deloria argued that Indian-Black relations needed to be taken more seriously, especially between Blacks and Indians. In Deloria's opinion, the Black Power movement could benefit from including "others," namely Indians, in their discussion of race relations. As it was, race relations was stuck on a Black-white-only note, which was being endlessly repeated. What Indians had to offer were new ideas on "tribalism," which was a departure from the integrationist discourse that was otherwise prevalent. With the latter objective in mind, Deloria identified the intersection between the Indian and Black communities in the "Forman Manifesto," which was a profound declaration of nationhood. Also known as the "Black Manifesto," Gladys L. Knight summarized its legacy:

> The Black Manifesto, which was created in 1969 [by James Forman, Student Nonviolent Coordinating Committee], includes a demand for monetary reparations; a summary of the violence, crimes, and other oppressive acts that justify redress; and an outline of how the reparations ought to be spent for the creation of numerous black self-help programs, businesses, and institutions. . . . The Black Manifesto reflected the radical switch from nonviolence to Black Power in the mid-1960s. The Black Power movement ushered in a new era of black assertiveness and militancy.[14]

The ongoing polarization of American society, however, into Black/white, rich/poor, urban/rural, Republican/Democrat, have/have not spheres precluded those concerned from ever solving the country's social problems. On the contrary, as these problems intensified, Americans felt driven into disorganized groups. This was most apparent in urban centers, like Los Angeles. American society, be it church, school, or government was run by too many out-of-touch old men, who were vehemently resistant to change. Tribes, on the other hand, were commonly run by young people, but ones who were held accountable by their elders—entailing more of a balance between young and old. Yet, it was the youth movement, as Deloria surmised that may potentially reap great change in American society. However, before that could happen, America needed to rethink how it thought about social organization. More to the point, America needed to do more from the bottom up, including "others" from the start.[15]

Before going on to take a closer look at the political history of Black and Indian relations, in *Custer* Deloria shared an example of how the civil rights–oriented thinking in mainstream churches and seminaries dominated the awkward relations between churches and tribes: "The most common attitude Indians have faced has been the unthoughtful Johnny-come-lately liberal who equates certain goals with dark skin." In other words, for this type of mindset, all nonwhite minorities were essentially alike. Furthermore, echoing his diatribe against anthropologists and other "experts," Deloria pointed out: "Foremost in this category have been younger social workers and clergymen entering the field directly out of college or seminary. For the most part they have been book-fed and lack experience in life." Similar, then, to ethnographers who relied on their own theories for explaining the Indian world they observed, social workers and clergymen on the reservations "depend primarily on labels and categories of academic import rather than on any direct experience." Heaven forbid they should ever acknowledge any ignorance about Indians.[16]

It is worth pointing out that Deloria revisited the above issues in "The Theological Dimension of the Indian Protest Movement" (1973) and "The Churches and Cultural Change" (1974). In the case of the former, it appeared in *The Christian Century*, which had long been an important resource for Protestant denominations around the English-speaking world. Deloria's short piece appeared alongside an article by Jean Caffey Lyles about a workers' strike in El Paso, Texas, and, more interestingly, a politically charged essay on the topic of "Executive privilege and judicial prerogatives" by J. Claude Evans, which was about the recent Watergate scandal. With respect to the misunderstanding of what motivated Indians to protest in the first place, Deloria stated: "Failing to understand the Indians' relationship to the land, non-Indians saw Alcatraz as nothing more than a symbolic defiance of the federal government—in which nearly everyone had lost faith anyway. Thus they responded to the Indian protest by allowing Indians to have their day in the media sun."[17] In the case of "The Churches and Cultural Change," Deloria was more emphatic about how far churches and tribes had grown apart since the era when the Board of Indian Commissioners influenced federal Indian policy, stating with respect to the current state of church-Indian relations: "Not a single Christian church has a consistent policy concerning its role among American Indians."[18]

As for being regarded as "a subcategory of black" among mainstream churches, Deloria and others tried pointing to the linguistic diversity among tribes as a substantive difference between the Black and Indian communities, only to be rebutted by the assertion that "blacks also have a language problem." Deloria retorted that it was because of each tribe's language needs that there was a drive for bilingual education on the reservations, among which the Navajo language–based school at Rough Rock was historically important. Deloria, moreover, reminded his reader of the way in which whites conceived Blacks and Indians as two types of animals, draft and wild, meaning a difference of less than human and all of a kind. However, that fundamental attitude, "the apelike draft animal and the wild free-running antelope," from the perspective of American law and politics, was also the ineluctable source of Blacks and Indians' divergent places in the federal system and in American society.[19]

At this juncture, it is worth asking whether or not Deloria knew anything about Black American culture and history? Nowhere in *Custer* or his other writings did Deloria demonstrate any connection, be it political or intellectual, with the Black community, except indirectly. In fact, given his earlier role as NCAI executive director, Deloria may have been more influenced by the race issues affecting southern tribes than by Black civil rights leaders. Furthermore, Deloria, like so many other Indians, dwelled in a cultural and political realm that was largely bereft of any contact with the Black community. Perhaps urban Indians were encountering a different experience, but Deloria was not an urban Indian. Having said that, what was at issue in "The Red and the Black" was the fact that Deloria did not acknowledge his ignorance about the Black community, let alone the racism that existed within the Indian community toward Blacks in general. In a rare acknowledgement of any problems with Indian-Black relations, Deloria observed: "The sparsity of their numbers"—meaning Indians participating in the 1963 March on Washington DC—"was a true measure of the importance which Indians placed on the civil rights movement. The absence of any tribal delegations disappointed the liberals, but was an accurate gauge of Indian feelings. Sad to say, much of the early resistance of Indians to the civil rights movement was simply inherited racial attitudes which Indians had learned from whites."[20] For what it may mean, Deloria carefully avoided these issues—including not acknowledging that among the sparse attendees of the 1963 march was Clyde Warrior (Ponca), whom he otherwise respected—choosing instead to say little more than that there was tension between the two communities, as exemplified with his "We Shall Overrun" anecdote, recalled below, which was a reference to a rather tense situation recounted in the Indian humor chapter of *Custer*. More specifically, Deloria brought up the surprise that many non-Indians expressed when they learned that Indians generally were not a part of the civil rights movement.[21] As Deloria elaborated, whereas Blacks wanted equal rights as part of American society, Indians wanted their treaty rights upheld as part of their status as sovereign nations, which was of course a political status that other groups, including Blacks, did not share. In respect to which, in the real world of race relations, misunderstandings between groups with very little communication, such as Indians and Blacks, were always prone to occurring, straining relations:

In 1966, beside the Custer [Died for Your Sins] cards, we put out a card which read "We Shall Overrun," which, at least to us, harked to the scenes in Western movies where a small group of Indians mysteriously grows as it is outlined along the rim of a canyon until it appears as if several thousand warriors have sprung from the initial group of a dozen.

When we showed the card to various blacks in the Civil Rights movement, they didn't know how to take it and several times there was a tense situation until the card was explained.[22]

Typical of Deloria's storytelling, he did not state where he was in 1966, what was going on, or who he meant by "us," let alone who the "various blacks" were with whom he and the unnamed others shared their "We Shall Overrun" slogan. Rather than expand on Black and Indian relations, though, Deloria opted to turn his attention to the teasing that occurred between tribal groups, complete with another selection of mostly Sioux-centric anecdotes.[23]

With regard to the unfortunate "inherited racial attitudes" toward Blacks, Sherry L. Smith documented a rather explosive exchange between Deloria and Lucius Walker, executive director of the Interreligious Foundation for Community Organizing (IFCO), in which Deloria did all of the exploding. During 1969, Walker actively sought affiliation with American Indian activists, which was actually in response to inquiries from members of the National Indian Youth Council—of which Clyde Warrior was a member—who were interested in building an alliance. More specifically, Walker invited Deloria and others, including Mel Thom, to an "Indian-American Task Force" meeting in Chicago. While several Indian invitees accepted the invitation, Deloria adamantly declined. Deloria simply could not see what good such an alliance would do for Indians. If Walker wanted to understand the Indian situation better, Deloria argued, rather than invite a few Indian leaders to Chicago, he should go to New York and learn from tribal community members there, such as at Onondaga, what issues they were facing and how they were organizing to defend their sovereignty. Obviously wary of allowing the Indian protest movement to be subsumed into Walker's IFCO, Deloria contended rather abrasively: "I have always fought against white paternalism. . . . But I am not about to substitute white paternalism for black paternalism and fight the old fight of the last decade over again." When Walker resent his invitation, complete with an explanation that the IFCO wanted to promote Indian self-determination through the formation of a "Native American advisory committee," Deloria grew much more combative against what he must have regarded as an attempt to coopt Indian leadership into the Black political movement: "How Unfortunate That Indians Spontaneously Came Together, Set Up a Representative Board and Then Applied to Join 'IFCO.' And how DOUBLY unfortunate that IFCO voted to accept them!!! . . . Seriously, man. You spades do your thing and us savages will do ours." As evidence that Deloria perceived what the IFCO was doing with respect to the NIYC, under the pretense of alliance building was an act of cooptation, Deloria warned Walker that, given the opportunity to meet on an "hombre-hombre basis," he would not be "a friendly Indian companion like Tonto and Mel Thom." Presumably to emphasize that his intelligence had been insulted, Deloria added: "I will not ask you to eat dog soup if you don't serve me watermelon. In the meantime, try and be a credit to your race."[24] While Deloria's choice of words was indisputably offensive, it was unclear where the source of his antagonism arose. Did he really regard Walker as presumptuous or was he angrier at Thom and the other allegedly coopted Indians? At the same time Deloria could show admiration for the Black nationalist movement, such as its intellectuals' capacity to frame the discussion on race and justice. Deloria, alas, could be equally myopic with respect to seeing the multiple points of intersection between the two movements.

Speaking of intersections between Blacks and Indians, while mixed Black-and-Indian people have been a part of Indigenous communities for as long as there has been a United States, the presence of Black Indians in the discourse on American Indians nevertheless has never been a prominent topic until recently. When Jack Forbes (Powhatan-Lenape-Saponi) published *Africans and Native Americans: The Language of Race and the Evolution of Red-Black Peoples* in 1988, the situation for Black-Indian studies changed appreciably, and one started seeing more scholarship on the topic. At the time of *Custer* and *We Talk, You Listen*, unfortunately, it was still the case that the discussion about Indian race relations, especially the controversy of "blood quantum," was almost exclusively limited to Indian-white issues. In terms of the interrelation between Indians, Blacks, and whites, Eva Marie Garroutte observed in *Real Indians: Identity and the Survival of Native America*:

> Far from being held to a one-drop rule, Indians are generally required— both by law and by popular opinion—to establish rather *high* blood quanta in order for their claims to racial identity to be accepted as meaningful, the individual's own opinion notwithstanding. Although people must only have the slightest trace of "black blood" to be *forced* into the category of "African Americans," modern American Indians must (1) formally produce (2) strong evidence of (3) often rather substantial amounts of "Indian blood" to be *allowed* entry into the corresponding racial category. The regnant biological definitions applied to Indians are simply quite different than those that have applied (and continue to apply) to blacks. Modern Americans, as . . . Jack Forbes . . . puts the matter, "are *always finding 'blacks'* (even if they look rather un-African), and . . . *are always losing 'Indians.'*"[25]

Perhaps showing some awareness of his limitations, Deloria proceeded in *Custer* with the legal distinctions between Blacks and Indians, beginning with the unkept promises that white political leaders made to each. In the case of Indians, they were told that the source of their conflict with whites was due to "cultural" differences, which could supposedly be resolved through access to white institutions, namely religion, education, and agriculture. However, the price was Indian land and resources, which tribe after tribe relinquished, only to see a paltry return on their investment. While federal Indian policy had possessed a "civilizing" component since the Washington administration, the kind of pressure that Deloria referred to in his remarks was characteristic of the enforced assimilation efforts that began during the Andrew Jackson era, in which tribes such as Cherokee Nation were coerced into abandoning their traditional ways. Elias Boudinot (Cherokee), for example, founder of the *Cherokee Phoenix* newspaper, famously implored in his 1826 "An Address to the Whites" that Cherokees be allowed to remain on their ancestral lands in light of the fact that as a nation the Cherokee had accomplished so much in their own efforts at adopting settler customs and institutions, from agrarian enterprises to the number of Christians they counted among themselves.[26]

In the case of Blacks, as Deloria understood their legal status, white Americans promised them equality in the form of the 1964 Civil Rights Act, not to mention the Thirteenth, Fourteenth, and Fifteenth Amendments, all of which were hampered by decisions made by white leaders, who persisted in denying Blacks their lawful rights, such as the infamous Jim Crow laws. "Can one blame the black athletes at the recent [1968] Olympic Games for their rebellion against the role cast for them by white society?" Deloria asked his reader. "Should they be considered as specially trained athletic animals suitable only for hauling away tons of gold medals for the United States every four years while equality remains as distant as it ever was?"[27] Deloria, of course, was referring to the silent but profound protest for Black rights enacted by Tommie Smith and John Carlos, American Olympic runners, at the 1968 Summer Olympics in Mexico City.[28]

With respect to the lessons drawn from these parallel histories, Deloria asserted that Indians' discordant relations with whites had nothing to do with their lack of the white man's ways and everything to do with the white man's desire for Indian land and resources. "The black must understand," Deloria asserted, on the other hand, "that whites are determined to keep him out of their society," regardless of civil rights laws. For Indians, however, they needed to focus on radically reforming policies, statutes, and case law, not trying to become more white. For Blacks, Deloria suggested, they needed to change the racist attitudes that whites have historically maintained toward them, which had for too long been endemic within white American society.[29]

> He [the white man] must examine his past. He must face the problems he has created within himself and within others. The white man must no longer project his fears and insecurities onto other groups, races, and countries. Before the white man can relate to others he must forego the pleasure of defining them. The white man must learn to stop viewing history as a plot against himself.[30]

Moreover, with his white reader still in mind, Deloria segued into a summation of European history, which was based on conquest, colonization, feudalism, and sectarian strife. The purpose of this discourse was to demonstrate the historical process that European settlers brought with them to the Western Hemisphere, which their descendants Americanized as they built an empire on the backs of Black slaves and stolen Indian lands.

The Catholic Church, in particular, as a political power was rent asunder by the Protestant Reformation and Counter-Reformation, which was a sectarian conflict that drove Protestant and Catholic nations into finding new nations to conquer. In the case of the Protestant settlers that occupied North America, in addition to their vehemently anti-Catholic creed, they brought traditions of "self-centered individuals" and a feudalistic relation to the land. Influential to Deloria's interpretation of European history and the subsequent colonization of North America was Jennings C. Wise's politico-legal study of American Indian history, about which Deloria observed with great interest: "In large part he [Wise] viewed the history of the American Indian as a part of a world drama of conflicting religions," namely Catholic and Protestant, replete with the destruction of droves of Indigenous sacred ways as collateral damage.[31] Deloria then further observed about the Protestant founding of the American colonies: "Whereas feudalism conceived man as a function of land, the early colonists reversed the situation in their efforts to create 'new' versions of their motherlands." The settlers were now the landlords and the Indians and Blacks were to be the vassals. As for that "City on the Hill":

> The early colonists did not flee religious persecution so much as they wished to perpetuate religious persecution under circumstances more favorable to them. They wanted to be the persecutors. The rigorous theocracies which quickly originated in New England certainly belie the myth that the first settlers wanted only religious freedom. Nothing was more destructive of man than the early settlements on this continent.[32]

In Deloria's estimation, European and American oppression of Indians and Blacks was not only due to replicating the oppression that the settlers had supposedly fled, but it was also the consequence of an alien people striving to impose itself on land that was not meant for them. In other words, Deloria's Indigenous criticism of Euro-American colonialism was premised on the principle that the colonists were violating a basic precept among Indigenous peoples, namely that to each nation was *given* a homeland. Contrary to the biblical interpretation that colonists gave to their deliberate occupation of Indian lands, Indian creation stories were accounts of how tribes were bestowed their homelands. As such, the land belonged to a given people in a sense comparable to how one belonged to their family—the relationship was a form of kinship, as opposed to property. Hence, it was commonplace in Indigenous thinking that a tribe could no more sell their ancestral land than one could sell their mother. Forcibly occupying the land, then, as many settlers did, was tantamount to kidnapping. In turn, selling the land was akin to human trafficking. Remember the elder Chief Joseph's dying words to his son, which Deloria recalled in *God Is Red*:

> You must stop your ears whenever you are asked to sign a treaty selling your home. A few more years and the white men will be all around you. They have their eyes on this land. My son, never forget my dying words. This country holds your father's body. Never sell the bones of your father and your mother.[33]

However, because of the coercion wrought by *Johnson v. M'Intosh* (1823), the Indian Removal Act (1830), and the General Allotment Act (1887), Indian lands were legally seized in the name of progress and American Manifest Destiny. Yet, it is another truism of history that colonial empires eventually fall. In the case of the American empire, it was predestined to fall because it had forced itself onto a place where it did not belong—either in the legal or ontological sense of the term. As for the historic evidence for the fall occurring, in all likelihood Deloria had in mind as he wrote *Custer* the global rebellions against the old European colonial order that were current from Africa to Southeast Asia, including the relatively recent expulsion of Britain and France from India and Indochina, respectively.[34]

Interestingly, instead of arguing for the kind of popular rebellion that was part of the global decolonization movement, in which people's armies struggled against colonial powers, Deloria envisioned a scenario in which the Indians' colonial overseers played a role in their liberation.

More to the point, evincing his Christian seminarian background once more, Deloria made explicit reference to the founding of the State of Israel in 1948. Taking what might be called an Indian perspective on biblical narrative, Deloria stated prophetically: "The Holy Land, having been periodically conquered and beaten into submission by a multitude of invaders, today remains the land which God gave to Abraham and his descendants. So will America return to the red man."[35] Indeed, Deloria's Judeo-Christian vision of a re-Indianized America was given an even more emphatic treatment in *Behind the Trail of Broken Treaties*.

More specifically, Deloria referred to the support that the United States gave to the nascent Israeli nation in 1947—which included allied support, most importantly that of Great Britain—in its founding. In fact, Britain was acknowledged as having convinced the United Nations "to create separate, independent states for Jews and Arabs." What Deloria thought this had to do with American Indian sovereignty and the struggle for self-determination was twofold. First, Deloria referred to Israel in a chapter titled "The Size and Status of Nations," in which he argued that, when compared to other small nations, tribal nations were comparable in terms of land mass, population, economic viability, and educational levels to many of their peers in the global community. Israel, then, was the ultimate example of a small, struggling nation, which turned into a formidable power in large part because of the substantial support it received from the international community, namely Britain and the United States. In light of which, the second aspect to Deloria's American Indian-Israel connection was summed up with this recognition:

> The role of the United States in the birth of Israel must not be ignored, because if the US can recognize the historic claim of a specific people to land in the Middle East, there is no reason in fact or logic for it to continue to ignore the claim of the native Americans to territorial sovereignty over a small portion of their historic land.[36]

In an obvious omission of the Palestinian claim to this same homeland, not only in *Broken Treaties* but also *Custer*, Deloria referred to the "Hebrew-Jewish conception of the Homeland," seemingly oblivious to the fact that the descendants of Abraham were not just Jewish and Christian, but also

Muslim. In light of this, one can argue that there were clearly points at which even Deloria was unaware of his own colonized thinking. As for how Deloria explained his fascination with the Hebraic tradition as an analog to the American Indian:

> The only people in the modern world comparable to the Hebrews that I could see were the Indian tribes. Like the Hebrews they had been shunted aside by more powerful people and made to taste the bitter dregs of an alien culture. Yet like the four-hundred-year sojourn in Egypt, Indians had managed to maintain their culture and basic social life.[37]

In the meantime, with respect to his foretelling of an Indigenous future for America, Deloria explained the nature of the American colonization of Indian lands as an act of sheer political power. "Land," Deloria asserted in *Custer*, "has been the basis on which racial relations have been defined ever since the first settlers got off the boat." The growth of the American republic had been built on the legalized expropriation of Indian land, which was then exploited through the economic institution of slavery. Justice, if such was possible, was contingent on the restoration of Indian lands, and, per the "FormanManifesto," compensation to Blacks, as signified by the proposition "forty acres and a mule." At the same time, the terms of justice for Indians and Blacks was anything but synonymous. On this point, Sharon Holland examined the divergent lives of Blacks and Indians in her analysis of Nettie Jones's *Mischief Makers,* a 1991 novel about an Afro-Native family living in Michigan during the 1920s. More specifically, the story focuses on Raphael de Baptiste, the daughter of a physician at a hospital for Negroes, who has green eyes and peachy skin. As such, Raphael marries a Chippewa, who thinks she is white. Consequently, Raphael learns firsthand about her husband's Chippewa heritage, including the occupation of Indian land, treaties, and the imposition of the reservation system. As for how Indians compare to Blacks in American society, Holland quotes Raphael as asserting:

> "The Indians got their forty acres and more. The poor Negroes didn't get their forty acres or the mule they were promised. Haven't gotten

it 'til this day. None of the homesteaders that settled around here on the land they were practically given were Negroes either." *She was surprised at the bitterness in her voice* [emphasis added].[38]

In the case of Indian land claims, Deloria acknowledged the work done through the Indian Claims Commission, which was an anomaly similar to the 1934 IRA, that arose amidst a concerted effort at terminating federal trust relation to tribes. Not only did Americans presume they had a superior right to Indian land, based on their religion and civilization, but also when it came to the restoration of Indian land—or even the remuneration for land, as occurred in the Indian Claims Commission—there was an assumption on the part of Congress that this should occur only insofar as Indians had assimilated into American society. This was not much different than the criteria for being regarded "competent" by the competency panels created by the 1906 Burke Act. Deloria then directed his reader to the creation of the Court of Claims in 1854, "in which the United States would voluntarily submit itself to suit on its contractual obligations." With respect to the Indians' access to this court:

> The Indian treaties and treaties with foreign nations were, of course, the foremost contracts outstanding against the United States, and tribes began to file suits in the Court of Claims to get some redress. The situation looked optimistic, but when the tribal cases got near judgment, Congress recognized the danger of allowing the court to handle the many breaches of treaty obligations and decided to restrict the jurisdiction of the court to exclude any claims deriving from treaties.[39]

In the case of the 1946 Indian Claims Commission, which operated until 1978, while the intent of the commission was much more progressive than its 1854 predecessor, it was nonetheless handicapped by the fact that it was "halfway between a court and a true commission." The commission's jurisdiction therefore was unclear, including whether or not it could hear cases that were turned away by the Court of Claims. Nonetheless, it ultimately enabled tribes to bring dozens of suits before it, which resulted in monetary settlements. While far from the land restoration that tribes undeniably deserved, Deloria nonetheless felt obliged to acknowledge the commission's accomplishments: "The present payments from claims cases received by tribes does not settle treaty obligations, but is more in the nature of compensating tribes for the real-estate contract aspect of their treaties."[40] Unsurprisingly, many of the tribes represented in these claims, most notably the Sioux reservations such as Pine Ridge, "demanded that the [1868 Fort Laramie] treaty be honored and the stolen lands returned."[41] As of the early 1970s, as the Indian protest movement quickly moved toward a conflict at Wounded Knee, the attitude shown toward the Indian Claims Commission was one in which bringing suit against the United States for monetary compensation was far from enough. While it was true that empowering tribes to bring their grievances before a congressional committee was once a progressive step for Indian rights, it was only a first step in the struggle toward full recognition of tribal sovereignty, which was premised on the expectation that the United States live up to its own legal principles, of which treaties were subject, and provide restitution for its contractual and political obligations to the Indigenous nations it named as "friends," which was to say allies, in its treaties with them. (Parenthetically, it may be worth observing that it was in part the 1946 Indian Claims Commission that informed Deloria's adulation of Britain and America's 1948 founding of the State of Israel.)

As for Black reparations, Deloria analyzed its social and religious dimensions in *We Talk, You Listen*, specifically in the concluding chapter titled "The Forman Manifesto." Deloria gave a critical historical analysis of James Forman's 1969 document, which demanded substantial reparations, including land and programming support, from churches and synagogues in compensation for slavery and segregation. The foregoing was based on the premise that churches benefitted financially from the exploitation of Black assets, not to mention the laws keeping Blacks from equal access to resources and opportunities. Church leaders, unfortunately, balked at supporting Forman outright. They were willing, however, to tacitly and indirectly support him, but only in a way that did not alienate white parishioners. Deloria saw this as proof of the churches' complicity in the exploitation, in addition to the disenfranchisement and the expropriation of nonwhite properties, above all, that of Indians. The modern church was a farce when it came to its supposed support of social issues and causes. It was still, by and large, the same church community that justified the evils of westward expansion.

With respect to making churches relevant to today's society, many church leaders opted for the superficial accoutrements of street clothes and pop music as part of their Sunday services. The last thing that mainstream white Americans wanted was for a religious figure from the nonwhite world to rise in prominence, replete with the power to jolt people, especially nonwhites, from their complacency with the system. For an indication of how much whites feared such a prophet, one needed to only look at the assassinations of King and Malcom X, along with the animosity they expressed toward the ethnic power movements. In reaction, white politicians' calls for law and order, and the political repression that that entailed, were hawked as the answer to America's social strife. However, America was in desperate need of replenishing its soul, a soul that, alas, it had lost long before when it broke its first treaty and endorsed slavery in its constitution. The power movements, the looming environmental crisis were signs in Deloria's eyes that America was in need of a religious movement for its own times. It was just waiting for its sage to arrive.[42] More urgently, Deloria believed that the arrival of these apocalyptic times was precipitated by the crises that were distressing all aspects of American society. In Deloria's assessment, America was in need of tribalism, meaning a more holistic approach to problem-solving:

> American society is undergoing a total replacement of its philosophical concepts. Words are being emptied of old meanings and new values are coming in to fill the vacuum. Racial antagonisms, inflation, ecological destruction, and power groups are all symptoms of the emergence of a new world view of man and his society. Today thought patterns are shifting from the traditional emphasis on the solitary individual to as yet unrelated definitions of man as a member of a specific group.[43]

With regard to the subaltern groups suffering under the American system, especially tribes, it was imperative that they remember their tribal ways. Tribalism, as Deloria envisioned it, meant nothing if Indian and Black communities could not sustain themselves economically. Land and the opportunity for prosperity were required. Critical, then, to reaching one's goal of liberation was being able to clearly articulate those objectives, lest the ambiguities devolved into conflict between all those concerned.[44] As a first step, respect for each other's uniqueness as peoples was more important than equality. In Deloria's opinion, equality was too often defined as sameness, which meant that nonwhites should aspire at becoming more like their white American peers. Frustratingly, when the principles of equality were applied to the Black community's demand for equal access under the law, "everybody began to climb the walls in despair" when, in spite of the 1964 Civil Rights Act, equality did not turn out as intended.[45] What this signaled to Deloria was that assimilating Indians into the mainstream's definition of equality entailed surrendering those things, such as political sovereignty and cultural differences, that made them Indian. Indians, Deloria concluded, had already been pressured enough toward assimilation. It was time to set a contrarian agenda.

So, then, why did Indians refrain from joining the 1968 Poor People's Campaign organized by Martin Luther King Jr.? Not all did, of course, but the event certainly does not loom large in American Indian history, especially when compared to Alcatraz or Wounded Knee. At the same time, those who did, such as Hank Adams, were not without a meaningful connection to Deloria's personal and professional lives. In the case of Adams, he stated on behalf of Survival of the American Indian Society in a project proposal to the Episcopal Church: "We were one of the most active elements of the Poor People's Campaign in Washington, DC."[46] With respect to which, one naturally wonders why Deloria, who was otherwise in an intellectually symbiotic relation with Adams, departed so dramatically on the topic of Indian-Black relations and the Poor People's Campaign. In a personal account that included a retelling of tribal leaders' confrontation with Interior Secretary Stewart Udall in Santa Fe during which tribes became more aware of their political power as they overturned Udall's unilateral plans for reforming Indian affairs, Deloria affirmed that tribal self-determination became the priority for reshaping federal-Indian relations. In other words, the drive for self-determination that Collier had sparked in the hearts and minds of tribal leaders with the 1934 IRA had now blossomed into a movement driven by tribal leaders against the Department of Interior for more political autonomy. Indeed, as reported in the NCAI *Sentinel Bulletin*:

> The Santa Fe meeting of the NCAI was on the whole successful and despite the denials of certain officials of the Bureau of Indian Affairs that there never was any intention of taking tribal OEO [Office of Economic Opportunity] funds and programs over, we believe that had the tribes not met at Santa Fe to voice their opinions that the proposed switch of funds would have occurred. . . . One cannot help but recognize in the events of Santa Fe, however, a real turning point in the relations of tribes, the NCAI, and non-Indian Interest [*sic*] groups. . . . The Santa Fe meeting had 62 tribes coming together as a single voice to say to the country, "It is time we had a say in our own future."[47]

On that basis, Deloria wondered in *Custer*, did Indians see a comparable ambition among their counterparts in the Black community, and was that one of the objectives of the Poor People's Campaign? At one time, it appeared that the Black Power movement had realized the necessity of nationhood, such as Stokely Carmichael's notion of Black nationalism. More specifically, Carmichael signified that the Black community recognized the value of "peoplehood." "Peoplehood," moreover, "is impossible without cultural independence, which in turn is impossible without a land base." In light of the emphasis on peoplehood, which ultimately meant community self-empowerment, "the concept of self-determination suddenly [became] valid."[48] However, when the Poor People's Campaign was organized, it was premised on the notion that all poor communities were one in their poverty. Because of this preconception, the possibility of Indians joining with their counterparts in the Black community became less feasible.

> Indians had understood when Carmichael talked about racial and national integrity and the need for fine distinctions to be made between white and black. But when [Martin Luther King Jr.] began to indiscriminately lump together as one all minority communities on the basis of

their economic status, Indians became extremely suspicious. The real issue for Indians—tribal existence within the homeland reservation— appeared to have been completely ignored. So where Indians could possibly have come into the continuing social movement of the 1960's, the Poor People's Campaign was too radical a departure from Indian thinking for the tribes to bridge.[49]

What Deloria may have thought about Hank Adams attendance was left unspoken in his writings. Instead, referring his reader once again to his ongoing conflict with church leaders, Deloria recalled an incident in 1963, "when the Civil Rights drive was at its peak, many of us who occupied positions of influence in Indian Affairs [*sic*] were severely chastised by the more militant churchmen for not having participated in the March on Washington." The reference was to the organized march for civil rights and racial equality, which culminated with Martin Luther King Jr.'s seminal "I have a dream" speech. In fact, the unnamed militant churchman in question even went so far as to forewarn Deloria: "unless Indians *got with it* there would be no place for us in America's future" [emphasis in original].[50] One may argue that this anecdote was as much an explanation as anything else in the historical record for why Deloria did not take up the civil rights cause as an Indian cause. If Indians were perceived as not having a future unless they "got with it," then Deloria's response was, "Oh, really?"

At the same time, while Deloria was clear about his reasons for foregoing identifying the Indian protest movement—insofar as the NCAI represented that aspect of it defined by reforming federal Indian policy—with the civil rights movement, this did not preclude Deloria from partaking in the discussion on civil rights in America, provided that he could do so as a representative of his own opinions about Indigenous nations. An unexpected example of Deloria's tacit amenability to non-Indian causes was an invitation to join the National Committee for Free Elections in Sunflower County (Mississippi). In a letter dated July 1, 1966, and signed by Martin Luther King Jr., Harry Belafonte, Fannie Lou Hamer, Paul Moore Jr., and John de J. Pemberton Jr., the invitation to the join the committee on free elections stated that Deloria was invited because "your name has long been associated with principles of justice, democracy, and equality. Only if people like yourself join us can we hope to rally the broad-based nationwide support it will take to open up a county whose pattern of voting rights discrimination is among the most pronounced and best documented in the country." When read in context, the reasons that King, et al., gave for inviting Deloria were obviously the generic appeal of a form letter (none of Deloria's distinctions were mentioned); nonetheless, perhaps Deloria thought that he could in some way expand the civil rights movement to include tribes. In any case, Deloria responded to the invitation on July 13, 1966: "I am afraid that I would not be able to devote much time to this cause but I would be most happy to be listed as a member of this committee because I feel that this cause has much merit." Deloria concluded by making certain that his membership would be as an individual and not in his official capacity as NCAI executive director.[51]

By 1968 all of America was in disarray and on the eve of a presidential election, with two starkly opposed choices —Nixon and Humphrey— America's future was indeed in the balance. In the aftermath, however, of the 1968 Poor People's Campaign, tribes began hunkering down, intending to weather the storm that was brewing around the federal government, including an uncertain future for Indian affairs. Would termination policy intensify even as tribes saw benefits from the War on Poverty programs? As an indication of where tribal leadership was headed, Deloria mentioned two tell-tale examples. First, "Tribal leaders became concerned about ongoing economic development which would be aimed at eventual economic independence for their tribes, rather than accepting every grant they could squeeze out of government agencies." Johnson's War on Poverty and the Community Development Corporation programs were becoming less of a federal priority, leaving tribes faced with a more libertarian future. Second, because the goals of the Poor People's Campaign were too generalized to include tribal concerns, the NCAI—which may have been who Deloria had most in mind when he referred to Indian resistance to the Black civil rights movement—embarked instead on "a systematic national program aimed at upgrading tribal financial independence," which may be regarded as a significant step toward the notion of Indian self-determination that Congress sanctioned in 1975.[52] With regard to the NCAI's response to the Poor People's Campaign, Hazel W. Hertzberg noted:

> The National Congress of American Indians refused to endorse the Poor People's March. In a statement that expressed sympathy with the organizers' ultimate goals and aims, the NCAI asserted that the Poor People had no clear legislative goals and that in the absence of these, with the potentialities of violence inherent in the situation, and with considerable division on the matter within its own membership, the NCAI could not offer its endorsement.[53]

What Hertzberg did not mention was that at this moment in NCAI history it became infamous for promoting the notion that "Indians Don't Demonstrate," which presumably also characterized the NCAI during Deloria's tenure as executive director.[54] In fact, in a 1966 issue of the *NCAI Sentinel Bulletin,* readers were admonished to return to their clan, meaning kinship, orientation when it came to organizing the ongoing struggle for tribal self-determination, stating: "Indians are not like other groups and if we adopt their [Black Power?] ideology and method of operation we shall surely lose. We should not have the bitterness of the other groups even though we have suffered terrible treatment through the years."[55] Deloria then explained the tribal withdrawal from mainstream politics in terms of his observations of Clyde Warrior, who died July 1968 under unfortunate circumstances, "some say of alcohol, most say of a broken heart." More to the point, Deloria perceived the movement toward economic development and financial independence, complete with tribes investing in the stock market, as consistent with an agenda that Warrior had advocated earlier. In fact, in addition to attending the 1963 March on Washington—which Deloria, as noted, did not acknowledge—Warrior, as was acknowledged, supported Barry Goldwater's 1964 presidential campaign when most other Indians were on the Johnson-Humphrey bandwagon. Warrior's rationale was twofold. At one level, Warrior foresaw that when the 1964 Civil Rights Act, as indicated above, did not lead to the kind of equality, i.e., sameness, that the Civil Rights movement demanded for Blacks, it would result in "inter-group disaster." "Warrior," Deloria affirmed, "had been right." At another level, insofar as Goldwater promised to maintain the status quo, Warrior saw that as an opportunity for tribes to consolidate their "gains at a time when the Indian people had great need to consolidate." In which case, Warrior's objective for tribes was "mutual respect" between them, whites, and other groups, complete with tribal "economic and political independence."[56] What becomes clear at this point in Deloria's discourse on tribal self-determination was that it was a combination of a radical critique of federal Indian law and policy, Christian doctrine, and the social sciences, in addition to a tribal-centric agenda of nation building within the federal system. The latter was based on the principle of according tribes more political power over their own affairs, complete with lifting the racist barriers to that power, such as the impositions of P.L. 280, not to mention congressional plenary power.

Given that most Indians, as Deloria perceived them, did not want to be compelled to change their cultures further in order to access mainstream American society, they were naturally reluctant to join the 1968 Poor People's Campaign. Certainly, from the point of view of the former NCAI executive director, this was the case. Furthermore, as Deloria portrayed the Indian community's reaction to the "civil disorders" that Johnson's National Advisory Commission's reported on, they were blatantly resistant to joining arms with the Black Power movement once racial relations hit critical mass, as exemplified by the 1965 Watts Riots.[57] From the vantage point of tribes, as Deloria understood them from his NCAI infused perspective, they were confused by what they saw and what it meant to the struggles for their rights. Whereas many Indians, such as Warrior and the NIYC, were motivated to protect and preserve tribes' sense of peoplehood, complete with their political status as sovereign nations, they were not sure what their counterparts in the Civil Rights movement wanted more, cultural uniqueness, i.e., Black nationalism, or acceptance as part of mainstream American society. As far as many Indians were concerned, Deloria in particular, "the [whites] had no culture other than one of continual exploitation." For Indians, any rights or compensation gained through the American political system, such as the Indian Claims Commission, entailed that tribes surrender either land (mostly land), parts of their culture, or, most recently, the federal trust relation. Insofar then, as the Civil Rights movement was about gaining full access to American society as fully enfranchised citizens, tribes were going to refrain from participating.

> There is, therefore, basically no way in which the ideology of the Civil Rights movement could reach Indian communities in a communicative sense. Outside of black power nothing that the Civil Rights people could have said would have indicated their meaning or opened lines of interaction by which the Indian people would have understood what the movement was all about.
>
> The sight of blacks carrying TV sets through riot-torn streets completely turned off those Indian people who were trying to understand Civil Rights. America, rioters seemed to be saying, is a color TV and this is what we want from her.[58]

In essence, accepting the civil rights agenda as an objective for the Indian community meant accepting the principles on which HCR 108 were based.

As Deloria reflected in *Custer* on the Watts riots (which he alluded to, but does not name) and, maybe, the assassination of Malcolm X[59] (which he did not mention at all), he stopped to express how the Black Power movement looked from an Indian perspective, which he saw divided between admiring its accomplishments at becoming a major force in America, complete with influencing national politics, and denouncing its ambition to become part of mainstream American society. As Deloria further argued in *We Talk, You Listen*:

> Once we have rejected this melting pot, we can arrive at new definitions of social problems. In recognizing the integrity of the group [i.e., the tribe] we can understand the necessity for negotiations between groups. Thus, the self-interest which each group has, and which the respective groups present in their own terms, can be correctly communicated to society as a whole. Perhaps on this basis we can finally arrive at a society of laws and justice.[60]

In light of the above, when King (and later, Ralph Abernathy) and the Southern Christian Leadership Conference organized the Poor People's

Campaign in late 1967, Indians were obviously skeptical about partaking, though with notable exceptions. In addition to Tillie Walker, who was a part of Deloria's United Scholarship days, Robert Dumont and Mel Thom were major figures in the American Indian community who made a conscious decision to march in the Poor People's Campaign. Unsurprisingly, Thom, as Warrior's NIYC ally, was also a critic of Deloria's leadership on this issue: "At one point, in 1967, Thom, frustrated with the slow pace of change in Indian Country, accused the National Council [sic] of American Indians (NCAI), and its president [sic] Vine Deloria Jr., of being sell-outs to the white power structure after NCAI passed a resolution opposing NIYC's militant protests."[61]

In Deloria's assessment of events, Indian participation in the 1968 Poor People's Campaign, which was modest but visible, left many American Indians concerned that what Americans saw in the event's symbolism was Indians' implicit desire to become a part of white middle-class America. While Deloria did not discuss what became of the Poor People's Campaign plans in the aftermath of Martin Luther King Jr.'s assassination on April 4, 1968, let alone what it meant to Indian people, he did underscore the political divide between tribal leaders, such as himself, and young militants.[62] More specifically, Deloria observed the developments that led to the Occupation of Alcatraz (1969–71), the Trail of Broken Treaties caravan (1972), and the climactic confrontation between Indian militants and tribal government "goons" at Wounded Knee (1973), which were motivated as much by the political and generational divisions within the American Indian community as they were by the issues driving all Indians into conflict with the federal government. With respect to his flawed portrayal of Indian-Black relations, Deloria, for all of his insight into the Indian psyche represented by the NCAI, was too quick to dismiss Warrior, Thom, and Adams's interest in exploring the political and intellectual common ground between the Black and Indian power movements. In the final analysis, Deloria was limited by these major shortcomings: his own lack of experience with the Black community, the influence of a conservative NCAI membership, and the generation gap that existed between him and urban Indians.

Emblematic of the troubles confronting the people at Pine Ridge was its infamous chairman, Richard "Dickie" Wilson. While, on the one hand, Wilson was the duly elected leader of the Pine Ridge tribal government, which was based on its 1936 constitution (one of the products of Collier's 1934 IRA); on the other hand, Wilson represented all that was wrong with Indian affairs. As Deloria observed in *Broken Treaties*, Wilson was ushered into office largely by those "who were dependent upon the government and tribal jobs at Pine Ridge," as opposed to "the country people," who lived in places like Oglala, "one of the most remote and traditional communities on the reservation." Insofar, then, as the American Indian Movement appealed to young activists and older traditionals, Wilson's response to AIM when they showed up to demand justice for Raymond Yellow Thunder—who was murdered in the border town of Gordon, Nebraska—was anything but welcoming. Indeed, the fateful encounter between AIM and Wilson occurred in the aftermath of the Trail of Broken Treaties caravan to Washington DC.

> When the Trail of Broken Treaties caravan occupied the Bureau of Indian Affairs building in Washington, [Richard] Wilson went to his council almost immediately and received support for a resolution banning the activities of the American Indian Movement on the reservation. He made it clear that there would be no victory dances held by AIM at Pine Ridge when they returned.[63]

Apparently, in spite of the 1968 Indian Civil Rights Act, which extended U.S. constitutional protections of civil liberties onto tribes, including the First Amendment protection for freedom of speech, Wilson and his council did not have any qualms about suppressing AIM members right to peaceably assemble for the sake of their cause. Since militant leaders were perceived as willing to overturn the political order between tribes and the federal government, which the militants justified on the basis that "dangerous times" laid "ahead for reservation people," tribal councils at various reservations responded by creating an "atmosphere within which issues [could] be brought forward for solution." Self-determination, as the will of the people, and not just of tribal government, had become a movement.[64] In which case, the situation that developed between 1966 and

1973 was one in which tribes had successfully fended off Udall's omnibus bill and its top-down approach to problem solving, had seen some gains from OEO project grants, but failed to see the value of the Indian protest movement, in particular the militantism that had emerged among the urban Indian population. Instead, as Deloria observed in *Custer*, tribal leadership was hunkering down, turning their attention to economic development and pursuing financial independence, as opposed to, say, endorsing the Trail of Broken Treaties "Twenty-Point Position Paper." Consequently, if radical change was going to happen, it would have to happen from outside of the federal system, which proved frustrating to Deloria, who thought that neither the complacency of tribal leaders nor the radicalism of activists was sufficient by themselves to reap long-term positive change. Both major segments of the Indian community needed to band together. In the meantime: "Indian people all over have begun to question the nature of their situation. They are asking what their specific rights and benefits are and what the Poor People's March could possibly do to improve their situation."[65]

At this response, many Indians realized that their political issues stemmed from their legal relations with the United States, not from their cultural differences, i.e., lack of assimilation. As for Indian-Black relations, as Deloria defined it, whereas Indians and Blacks could not find a point at which they could effectively unify their movements, in the case of Indians and whites, because of the political power that the latter possessed, there was a presumption that Indians wanted whatever whites were willing to offer them. In response, Deloria expressed incredulity toward those who wanted to "*help Indians*," in particular certain "leading Democratic Senators," whom he regarded as having an ulterior motive, specifically "a quiet move against the Indian land base." Think again about the Kinzua Dam. What Deloria appeared to be saying here was that, insofar as there were cultural differences between Indians and whites, which revealed that whites were ignorant about Indian cultural values, it stood to reason that their idea of helping was premised on the misguided, not to mention discredited, notion that Indians wanted to assimilate into American society. After all, it was not all that long before when the Menominee, and other tribes, were dealing with an Eighty-sixth

Congress that blindly imposed the requirements of termination on them. In which case, what was the agenda for moving forward?

> Indian tribes need the basic gift of the white to the Negro — readjustment of tribal rights to protect person and property from exploitation by the federal government and private persons. *Treaties need to be reaffirmed as the law of the land. Guarantees of free and undisturbed use of the reservation lands need to be enforced. Congressional pressure to destroy the Indian tribes and communities needs to be lifted* [emphasis added].[66]

At the continued risk of overstepping his right to speak, Deloria ventured back into making additional suggestions to the Black Power movement. Perhaps without realizing it, Deloria was assuming that the "Black plight" was as transparent as the "Indian plight." Be that as it may, in Deloria's determination, what "the black" needed more than "legal rights" was the "freedom to develop himself though experimentation," in which freedom began with the elimination of the "prejudicial practices in law enforcement," i.e., police harassment. The Watts Riots, after all, began with a white policeman pulling over a young black male for a suspected DUI, which turned into a scuffle involving the black male's mother, who lived nearby, which then escalated into a major confrontation between local residents and the Los Angeles Police Department.[67] Deloria noted: "During the riots after the assassination of Martin Luther King, those cities where militant black nationalists were strongest were the quietest because the young blacks kept order in spite of the white police."[68] What the exact connection was between "the black quest for cultural development" and black nationalists keeping predominately Black neighborhoods quiet during times of riot remained unclarified. Perhaps the implication was that Black communities were capable of self-governance. Instead, Deloria went on to advocate for separatism on the basis that "white culture" destroys other cultures because of its "abstractness." Separatism, on the other hand, as Deloria argued, was a means to equality between communities and an opportunity for the Black community in particular to come to an "understanding of themselves as a people."[69] In other words, instead of taking an adversarial approach to political reform, a more decentralized concept of society was in order. An anti–law-and-order agenda was emerging.

In "Another Look at Black Power," Deloria reflected, in *We Talk, You Listen,* a year after *Custer,* more deeply on the phenomenon of Black nationalism as a form of tribalism. Integration, similar to assimilation, was based on the notion that one's race, ethnicity, and other distinctions as a person were to be considered as "handicaps." The Black Power movement rejected this assumption, which inspired comparable power movements, Chicano, Red, and so on, to do the same, which one can say Deloria did in *Custer.* In the case of the Black Power movement, Deloria demonstrated an interest in the 1967 book, *Black Power: The Politics of Liberation in America* by Stokely Carmichael (now known as Kwame Ture) and Charles V. Hamilton. Of particular interest to Deloria was Ture and Hamilton's analysis of the problem of the cooptation of Black leadership, which the two coauthors covered in a chapter titled "The Myths of Coalitions." More specifically, Ture and Hamilton began their critical analysis by questioning the premises on which coalitions between Blacks and whites were based: "There is a strongly held view in this society that the best—indeed, perhaps the only—way for black people to win their political and economic rights is by forming coalitions with liberal, labor, church and other kinds of sympathetic organizations, including the 'liberal left' wing of the Democratic Party." With respect to liberal churches, Deloria mentioned multiple times in his discourse on Christianity that white church leaders prided themselves on their support of the Black civil rights movement, typically at the expense of understanding the needs of tribes. Yet, whereas one might think that such overt endorsements of Black civil rights cause from white churches added to the strength of the Black Power movement, Ture and Hamilton begged to differ. As they observed with alarm: "All too frequently, coalitions involving black people have been only at the leadership level; dictated by terms set by others; and for objectives not calculated to bring major improvement in the lives of the black masses."[70] For Deloria, instances of the latter could be seen in the National Tribal Chairmen's Association and, more importantly, the National Council on Indian Opportunity.

As Deloria understood this, the only function of coalitions, as described in *Black Power*, was to affirm the beliefs and values of whites. Perhaps it was because of the influence of Ture and Hamilton's criticisms that Deloria had some misgivings about the National Council on Indian Opportunity. Illogically, though, Deloria then renewed his critique of the Poor People's Campaign, an example of the type of coalition-building criticized above, as an inherently flawed effort. Illogically, for the simple reason that the Poor People's Campaign was not a white-run organization, although, as observed above, he did accuse Lucius Walker of "black paternalism." Regardless, Deloria argued that basing the campaign on poverty exposed it to the fractioning of disparate ethnicities and the problem of representation. Indians and Chicanos, who brought to the table the traditions of tribalism and "La raza," in Deloria's assessment of power movement accomplishments, made the mistake of regarding the Black Power movement as something new. Nationhood and independence, on the contrary, had long been a part of Indigenous and Mexican history. Because these communities relented on making a substantial contribution to the dialog on community, they were susceptible to the demagoguery of the few who wanted attention and who thought that scaring people was more important than communicating with them. In other words, ethnic nationalism became synonymous with the violent overthrow of American society. Whites reacted as one would expect—fearfully. With such lessons in mind, Deloria admonished his reader, in particular those who participated in any of the power movements—perhaps with an eye on Mel Thom and Hank Adams, that they should rethink the philosophy of self-determination.

So, then, where did Deloria lead the discussion in *We Talk, You Listen*? For starters, he advocated for renouncing the American melting-pot myth as racist propaganda, which, of course, was a proposition that was hardly unique to American Indians,[71] in addition to developing intergroup dialog based on the recognition of groups as political entities, not merely as individuals who happened to be from different minority groups. Moreover, Deloria asserted that whites had to stop assuming that all nonwhites were alike and that their fundamental humanness meant that they would all assimilate into the American mainstream at some point. With regard to government and its agencies, they needed to be reorganized with particular attention paid to which bureaucracy was serving which community, in addition to staffing that agency with people from that group—something that should extend to local offices and services, e.g., schools and police. The War on Poverty was an example, in Deloria's assessment, of leadership cooptation among Indians. Unfortunately, in spite of his earlier admiration, it became just another white-run bureaucracy, instead of a means for facilitating tribal leadership on issues and problems, let alone learning how the Indians saw these. The BIA, after all, as of 1970, still ran programs and services on behalf of tribes, which had been the case since 1849—though conditions improved substantially in the aftermath of the 1934 IRA. Nevertheless, Indian affairs during this era was a perfect example of what happens when tribes were not allowed to govern themselves but were instead subjected to the ignorance and prejudices of outsiders. The 1934 IRA at least allowed for this situation to begin turning around. Congress, however, attempted to overturn the progress that tribes made by terminating its trust obligations during the 1950s. P.L. 280, in this regard, turned the reservations where it was applied into a jurisdictional no-man's land. As tribes were regaining their rights—remember Deloria's comments about *Talton* (1896) and *Sandoval* (1913)—they also realized the importance of solidifying their power as a distinct group, free of federal intervention.[72]

With respect to Indian-Black relations, if Deloria ever sought feedback from Black intellectuals and activists on his ideas and opinions, he did not mention it in either *Custer* or *We Talk, You Listen*. For a community dealing with a history of slavery, Jim Crow laws, and "separate but equal," one can imagine what might have been the response to the proposition of separatism. What Deloria surely would have had to explain was that when he said "separatism," he was more specifically referring to the legally separate sphere in which Indians existed with respect to the federal system, which was created by the anomaly, as Prucha would say, of treaties, then further defined by subsequent statutes and case law. Such legal separatism was what Indians were currently exploiting for the purpose of reasserting their nationhood status.[73] Such a legal space, which coincided with the literal space of the reservation, enabled Indians to reaffirm their cultural sovereignty, which was a space that the Black community, in Deloria's estimation, did not possess.

> The black needs time to develop his roots, to create his sacred places, to understand the mystery of himself and his history, to understand his own purpose. These things the Indian has and is able to maintain through his tribal life. The Indian now needs to create techniques to provide the economic strength needed to guarantee the survival of what he has.[74]

In an effort to justify the proposition of tribalism maintaining its distance from the social sciences, Deloria initiated an opprobrium of so-called white culture's capacity for conceptualizing things scientifically, including race, in which endemic "problems" were addressed by the "white man's social machine," which appeared to be a reference to the phenomenon of social engineering that emerged during the Progressive Era, from 1880s to the 1920s, when Indians were the target of the Indian Bureau's civilization experiments on the reservation, such as the imposition of boarding schools. Deloria's point was that the white man's social machine had yet to solve anything, least of all "the Indian problem" or "the Negro problem."[75] At the risk of hasty generalization, Deloria's portrayal of white culture elicited an emotional truth that many Indians recognized as part of their own experiences, even as it simultaneously alienated his white reader. Consequently, Deloria's remarks may come across as reactionary, as an impetuous rejection of western modernity for a romanticized tribalism. At the same time, a more generous interpretation of Deloria's negative portrayal of American civilization, or white culture, might recognize his prescience at realizing that self-determination required more than simply taking over the reins of power, especially if one wanted to overcome the problem of self-colonization.

Because of the homogenizing effects of the American social machine, which was premised on a melting-pot mentality, the institution of welfare, as the embodiment of government largesse, was seen less in terms of how it met the needs of a diverse range of needy Americans—be they rural whites, urban Blacks, reservation Indians, or immigrant communities—and more in terms of where utilizing any form of welfare (unemployment, food stamps, Medicaid) situated one with respect to the American middle class. More to the point, how one thought about welfare was typically determined by how one regarded its relative value to the economy. Conservatives scorned welfare as wasteful spending that was nothing more than a "free ride" for "lazy" people, while liberals regarded it as "a basic right to life," which was a fundamental obligation of government. What both sides were arguing about, according to Deloria, was the extent to which welfare recipients deviated from the ideal man, who was "defined as white, Anglo-Saxon Protestant, healthy, ambitious, earnest, and honest, a man whom the Lord smiles upon by increasing the fruits of his labor."[76] In a sense, the debate over welfare was exemplary of how America's political leaders, its government, comprehended social issues, including race relations. Welfare was a synecdoche for nonwhite populations, irrespective of cultural or political differences. In the case of Indian affairs, one needed to only look at the racialized assumption that Indians got everything for free, as opposed to the federal government fulfilling its trust obligations to tribes. A parallel but ultimately different political history explained the stereotypes of the Black community.

With the foregoing in mind, one has to stop and wonder whether or not the two-party system had anything to offer nonwhite, nonaffluent communities beyond condescending attitudes. "Republicans represent the best of the white economics," which meant the Puritan myth of forging one's destiny on the frontier, where one either survived or perished. Such religious like mythology informed the more contemporary myth of the unregulated entrepreneur going from a single store front to corporate empire based solely on hard work and opportunity. "Nixon's election was the last gasp of this quasi-religious nineteenth-century, Horatio Alger, WASP ethic." As for the Democrats, they were characterized concomitantly as the party of "deviants," meaning those who did not meet the criteria of the white Anglo-Saxon Protestant male, outlined above, and of "special interests." As for "minority groups," including Indians, they had recurrently turned to the Democrats as the party of the poor and of the working class. As for the Republicans, they did not even acknowledge the poor as a concern of government, let alone Indians.[77] As, Deloria characterized the American political divide in *God Is Red*, he referred to liberals and conservatives in these terms:

> Traditionally we have been taught to define differences neither by ancestral backgrounds nor cultural attitudes but by political persuasions. Conservative and liberal, terms initially that described political philosophies, have thus taken on the aspect of being able to stand for cultural attitudes of fairly distinct content. Liberals appear to have more sympathy for humanity, while conservatives worship corporate freedom and self-help doctrines underscoring individual responsibility.[78]

Such distinctions, though, as Deloria explained in "Thinking in Time and Space," were nonetheless based on a linear time-based paradigm of history, which ultimately marginalized the nonlinear space-focused perspective on values and relationships that defined the tribal experience.

When it came to the Kennedy myth, as an example of the Democratic appeal to the poor and working class, Deloria reminded his reader that it was President Kennedy who deliberately broke the 1794 Pickering Treaty in addition to maintaining the termination policy that the previous Republican administration had instituted. "Few members of the Indian community," Deloria pointed out, "realize or will admit how little the Kennedys really did for Indians." One only had to look at the legislative history. Jack's brother Bobby was little better. Nevertheless, in the heady days of the 1968 presidential campaign, the hagiography that emerged around the Kennedy name after the elder brother's assassination metamorphosed into an unshakeable belief among the Kennedy faithful that "the New Frontier" would be resurrected and Indians would somehow benefit. As Deloria observed this phenomenon with respect to Indians:

> Indian people loved the idea of Robert Kennedy replacing Jack. For them it was an affirmation of the great war chief from the great family leading his people in his brother's place. Robert Kennedy became as great a hero as the most famous Indian war chiefs precisely because of his ruthlessness. Indians saw him as a warrior, the white Crazy Horse. He somehow validated obscure undefined feelings of Indian people which they had been unwilling to admit to themselves. Spiritually, he was an Indian.[79]

When the younger Kennedy gave a speech before the NCAI on September 13, 1963, just over a year before Deloria was appointed as executive director, what some may have noticed was the fact that he premised his remarks on a recalcitrant assumption on the part of federal leaders, namely that what Indians really wanted was to be assimilated into American society. "It is a tragic irony," as Kennedy began his speech, "that the American Indian has for so long been denied a full share of freedom—full citizenship in the greatest free country in the world."[80] For Deloria, such remarks must have set the tone for what the Kennedy idealism was really about, which was compelling Indians, not to mention other nonwhites, to join that "city upon a hill," whether or not that was what they wanted to do. The ultimate irony of this adoration of the Kennedy mystique was the fact that it was Nixon who ended termination and proclaimed self-determination as federal Indian policy.

In turn, as an example of how Indians were misunderstood by their counterparts in the Black community, Deloria shared the following anecdote: "Time and again blacks have told me how lucky they were not to have been placed on reservations after the Civil War. I don't think they were lucky at all. I think it was absolute disaster that blacks were not given reservations."[81] Of course, the reservation system was contingent on tribal land cessions to the United States, in which the remaining tracts of land, the reservations, were placed under the authoritarian control of an Indian agent. Reservations really only became a political asset in the aftermath of the 1934 IRA, when tribes were permitted the opportunity to form governments, thus initiating the drive to greater self-governance. Implicit in the way Deloria recalled these encounters between Blacks and Indians was his supposition that separatism, which was to say tribalism, ought to be an objective for the Black community as much as it was for tribes. At least as of 1968, Deloria was of the opinion that tribes had a political advantage when dealing with the federal government on the basis of the reservations, which since 1934 were run by constitutional tribal governments, in addition to being recognized as a legitimate part of the federal system. Although the Black community clearly had prominent leaders, their influence on the federal government was dependent on "newspaper coverage," in addition to their representing communities that were racially segregated parts of mainstream society. The above situation was categorially different from tribes, which were independent political entities, however colonized they might be. As such, without a land base of a federally recognized form of self-government, the Black community was precluded from engaging the world around them as a "corporate body"; whereas, the 1934 IRA actually gave tribes the right to incorporate for the purpose of acquiring land and government loans.[82] What Deloria might have said about the gains that the Black community made in the ensuing decades, which saw the emergence of a Black Congressional Caucus, in addition to a tradition of Black mayors, governors, and, most importantly, a Black president, one can only conjecture. Not only did Deloria not live to see the election of Barack Obama as the forty-fourth president of the United States in 2008, but also, except for elaborating on his observations of Indian-Black relations in his subsequent book, *We Talk, You Listen* (1970), Deloria never felt obliged to reexamine what he covered in "The Red and the Black" again, let alone updating his analysis to match current affairs. In fact, the term tribalism disappeared from Deloria's lexicon in subsequent works, namely *God Is Red* and *Broken Treaties*.

As Deloria concluded his remarks in *Custer* on the topic of Indian-Black relations, he emphasized that what Indians and Blacks both needed was a time for seclusion, specifically for the purpose of reflecting on who they were and what they wanted to become. Such objectives necessitated being free from the political and social pressure to assimilate into white middle-class society. Because Indians had been accorded reservations, tribes were equipped with homelands into which they could withdraw during times of upheaval. Other communities, for better or worse, were obliged to confront the hostility of a white-centric nation that regarded cultural diversity and the political rights it demanded as an affront to the "Founding Fathers," if not in fact treason. Accordingly, there were those who felt justified in resorting to lethal violence in the name of their ideological principles, be it white power, America first, and the like. "Already the cracks are showing," Deloria asserted. "The berserk sniper characterizes the dilemma of the white man. Government by selective assassination is already well established as the true elective process."[83]

Add to this the problem of police brutality and tribal termination, among so many other crises, and one gets a clearer picture of an America unable to live up to its democratic principles for all.

In the final analysis, the political chaos that assailed America as of the 1968 presidential campaign, and as documented in the "Riot Report," was the result of an American ideal, the white Protestant city on the hill, that could no longer maintain itself as a realistic objective for all Americans. The Brotherhood of Man was dead. It remained dead. And America had killed it. Indeed, in *God Is Red*, Deloria portrayed the civil rights movement as the last time that the idea of Christian brotherhood motivated the masses. Perhaps, the demise of this ideal of brotherhood was the reason why Deloria abandoned what may be regarded as the Indian counterpart, namely tribalism. At the same time, tribalism as a political philosophy signified in general the historic end to such over-arching ideas, as evident by the fragmentation of the civil rights movement, and its struggle for social justice, into an array of power movements, in which various subaltern groups became politically aware of themselves.

> The Civil Rights movement was probably the last full-scale effort to realize the avowed goals of the Christian religion. For better than a century, the American political system had proclaimed the brotherhood of man as seen politically in the concepts of equality of opportunity and justice equally administered under the law.[84]

In 1974 Deloria explored in "Non-Violence in American Society" the idea of nonviolence that underpinned the above concept of social movement and why it failed to achieve its goals, namely the peaceable restitution of justice and equality to all citizens, regardless of race, ethnicity, or class. What was underestimated, though, was the inherent inertia of social dynamics to fundamental change. More to the point, while the astounding results of sit-ins and protest marches, complete with the reprehensible response from local police, generated a hitherto unseen galvanization of public consciousness, the basic decency that nonviolent activists depended on in their fellow Americans for change moved slowly, when it moved at all.

By the time of the Poor People's March [in 1968], the issues were so profound and so much more complicated than the simplicity of integration that the inertial social mass could no longer understand the complexity of tangential issues which the leaders of social change could clearly see. Television became a demon creating instant leadership and raising issues of emotional intensity which had no structural place in the process of defining the meaning of human existence.[85]

As more people became more aware of their history and how they had been cheated by the American system, the more they rightfully demanded the proverbial seat at the table, complete with the rights and privileges that that entailed. Whereas the forces of white privilege once kept non-whites oppressed through law-and-order tactics, such strategies were losing their capacity to enforce control over people's hearts and minds. Police brutality was now seen for what it was, which was brutality, not governance. What would become of race relations in America was anyone's guess in 1968. However, what was predictable was the demise of the Puritan myth and the WASP ideal. While white mythology remained strong among large segments of the white community—as evident in Nixon's 1972 landslide reelection, which was possible because of the "silent majority"—its power to intimidate nonwhites into rejecting their own histories and cultures weakened substantially.[86] As for the future of Indian relations, Deloria argued that that would depend on other groups accepting what he called tribalism as an indispensable part of the Indian community. "Indians," Deloria stated unequivocally, "will not work within an ideological basis which is foreign to them." Perhaps, then, if the discussion in the Black community returned to Black nationalism, there would then be a basis on which Blacks and Indians could unite. "If such is possible within the black community," Deloria concluded, "it may be possible to bring the problems of minority groups into a more realistic focus and possible solution in the years ahead."[87] In the end, insofar as Deloria thought that tribalism was a viable alternative for ethnic groups to adopt as a way of disrupting an inappropriate melting-pot approach to social justice in which ethnic and racial differences disappear into a homogeneous concept of American citizenship, and instead affirm their distinct political, cultural, religious identities, complete with demanding that these be respected under the law, then what Deloria meant by tribalism needed to be clarified. More to the point, it needed to be explained how tribalism could be adopted by, not only non-Indian groups, but also urban Indians and modern reservations that were completely enmeshed in contemporary social, political, economic, and mass-media networks. In other words, tribalism needed to be liberated from the generic super Indian concocted by anthropologists.

CHAPTER 6

Here Come the Anthros!

A Tribal Critique of the Social Sciences

When *Custer Died for Your Sins* hit libraries and bookstores from coast to coast in 1969, as pointed out elsewhere, American Indian authors—especially those writing in genres other than fiction and poetry—were few and far between. In which case, the discourse on America's "First People" was dominated by historians that focused on the nineteenth century and the closing of "the frontier," dime store novelists enthralled with the white mythology of "cowboys and Indians," and, of course, anthropologists who were preoccupied with premodern Indian cultures, either as objects they were striving to salvage for their journals and museums or as living laboratories where they could observe a "primitive people" vanishing under the wave of progress that overtook their lands by white settlers.[1] Very few, if any, of these mavens of the Indian showed any interest in current Indian affairs, let alone the struggle for treaty rights and Indian policy reform that many on the reservations were engaged with, while white men did little more than fantasize about a world that never was. In light of this situation, it was no wonder that whenever the rare Indian writer broke through the buckskin curtain and published a work on actual Indian lives from an Indian perspective, that Indian writer was typically motivated by the desire to set the proverbial record straight. For example, Delaware historian Richard C. Adams (1864–1921) stated in *A Delaware Indian Legend and the Story of Their Troubles* (1899): "Full justice has never been done the Indian in the American histories, and I should like to write one as it should be written from the Indian's own point of view."[2] Then, in his 1900 work, *The Indian Problem; From the Indian's Standpoint*, Andrew J. Blackbird (Odawa) proclaimed: "Many white people think that what we are called savage nations do not know anything of their former history, but we all have records and traditions of events in very ancient times."[3] Then, in 1916, as Charles A. Eastman (Dakota) reflected on his life work in *From the Deep Woods to Civilization*, he famously surmised about his purpose:

> My chief object has been, not to entertain, but to present the American Indian in his true character before Americans. The barbarous and atrocious character commonly attributed to him has dated from the transition period, when the strong drink, powerful temptations, and commercialism of the white man led to deep demoralization. Really it was a campaign of education on the Indian and his true place in American history.[4]

It was from out of this Indigenous intellectual tradition that Deloria set out in *Custer* to "discuss the other side—the unrealities that face *us* as Indian people," and to instead acknowledge that tribes are "reordering their priorities to account for the obvious discrepancies between their goals and the goals whites have defined for them."[5] Toward that end, one of Deloria's most significant targets was the Indian cultures portrayed through the lens of social-science theories that had been promulgated for decades by an array of anthropologists working as ethnographers, archeologists, and evolutionary biologists, all of whom have presumed to possess the final authority on the Indigenous peoples of these lands.

Probably one of the most poignant examples of the social-science attitude toward Indigenous peoples was shared in the pages of *God Is Red*, which Grosset and Dunlap published in 1973. Prior to this seminal publication, in a letter to Hank Adams, Deloria obliquely referred to the third installment of his Red Power Tetralogy as something that would be his "most startling book."[6] As an intellectual event, *God is Red* overlapped with the bloody confrontation at Wounded Knee, not to mention the ongoing Watergate scandal and the American troop withdrawal from Vietnam. Moreover, *God Is Red* appeared at a time when America's status in the global community had reached its nadir. Indeed, one could say that the Viet Cong had brought the United States to its knees and forced it into peace talks, much in the way that Red Cloud and the Lakota had done back in 1868. Unlike the nineteenth century when the United States was a super power in ascendance, the United States of the early 1970s was a global force in decline. And along with that political fall went its social, scientific, and religious traditions, the prominence of which were then in a state of flux. When Robert E. Fleming reviewed *God Is Red* for the *Rocky Mountain Review of Language and Literature* in 1976, he began with the statement: "For the reader who belongs to the mainstream of American culture"—which is to say white and likely conservative—"*God Is Red* will be an experience both provocative and provoking—provocative because Deloria raises questions not often raised in America until very recently, provoking because of the book's rare mixture of keen insights and telling satirical thrusts."[7] As for one of these mainstream American readers, William M. Newman devoted every word of his review in *Sociological Analysis* to express his disdain for Deloria's work, even stooping to casting aspersions on his character:

> Deloria, a lawyer, does show a respectable grasp of the theological issues he addresses. But the book is far short of a scholarly treatment of its subject. In the context of the contemporary Indian movement, this book [*God Is Red*] is at best an illustration of how religion can be used to legitimate almost any social cause. At worst, it is an example of how leaders of such movements attempt to cash in on a good thing.[8]

No doubt Newman felt that all he had done was dish back to Deloria the kind of sarcasm that Deloria had shown his nemeses. How Deloria responded to this criticism is not in the historical record. As for Deloria's ongoing battle with the tenets of Western social science, in the case of *God Is Red*, Fleming did pick up on the significance of the recurring cases of grave desecration and the condescending attitudes that Indians regularly faced from museum officials and archeologists. However, on this point, Fleming was critical of the way in which Deloria assembled his examples: "At times Deloria seems to fail to discriminate between major and minor abuses. For example, he lumps together some terrible examples of grave desecration by whites and a dispute with the Field Museum of Chicago, which was amicably settled."[9]

In reference, to the archeologists' stranglehold on human origins in North America, Deloria took a swipe at the presumptuousness characteristic to this type of research when he expressed indignation with an excavation that was "sponsored by the Twin Cities Institute for Talented Youth." Recounted in a chapter titled "America Loves Indians . . . And All That," Deloria recalled an episode that occurred in June 1971 in Welch, Minnesota, where forty-five students excavated "artifacts" over a five-week period. Unsurprisingly, the local Indigenous communities took umbrage. Among the outraged was Clyde Bellecourt (White Earth Ojibwe) and other members of the American Indian Movement, who took it upon themselves to put this blatant display of disrespect to a stop by seizing excavation tools, burning research notes, then reburying everything and everyone who had been wrongfully disinterred. Equally unsurprising was the extent to which the student archeologists felt that they were the true victims:

> Les Peterson, a Minnesota Historical Society member who had headed the dig, said "five weeks of work down the drain," indicating that the moral question of disturbing the dead had somehow eluded him. The students also failed to comprehend the problem. One student who has been planning a career in archaeology said that the incident made her lose respect for Indians. Another student was in tears as she tried to explain how carefully the students had been with the materials they had uncovered. "We were trying to preserve their culture, not destroy it," a third student remarked.

Such attitudes continued when reports of the altercation appeared in local newspapers. Hardly any non-Indians on either side of the debate demonstrated any understanding for "the Indian objections to disturbing the dead."[10] The living, unfortunately, have not been treated much better, such as occurred in Glenwood, Iowa, and at Chicago's Field Museum. More than raising the salient ethical issues of exhuming Indian remains and artifacts without so much as a consultation with tribal members,

Deloria wanted to make a philosophical point about the appropriation of Indigenous history into the colonial narrative in which the rise and fall of nations ends with the arrival of Western civilization as the natural outcome.

In the case of the Iowa excavation, in June of the same year of the aforementioned Minnesota incident, road workers uncovered the remains of more than two dozen people, one of whom possessed "several hundred glass beads, some brass finger rings, and metal earrings." The cemetery was estimated to be at least a century old, based on the testimony of a local resident whose grandmother was buried there in 1867. As for the deceased bearing the beads and jewelry, those remains were immediately designated as belonging to an "Indian girl" and, consequently, treated differently from the others. Whereas the "other bodies were reverently taken to the Glenwood Cemetery and reburied," the presumed Indian girl was taken into custody by the Iowa state archaeologist, Marshall McKusick.

Intervening and demanding that the remains be returned for proper reburial was a Yankton Sioux woman, Maria Pearson, who was also known as Running Moccasins. Her advocacy work would later play a role in the passage of the Native American Graves Protection and Repatriation Act (NAGPRA) (1990). In 1971, however, without the benefit of NAGPRA, Running Moccasins was left with her own resolve at attaining respect for the unknown person being treated like a museum artifact rather than a deceased human being. The response to McKusick's demands reeked of scientific and bureaucratic indifference: "I don't want that woman to think in any way that if she raises a fuss, I'll give her a couple of boxes of bones." After Running Moccasins attempted to contact Gov. Robert D. Ray's Office, McKusick defended his actions by referring to the Code of Iowa[11] and asserting that it would take a court order to force him "to release the remains to the tribe to which the girl belonged."[12]

Then, at three Susquehannock villages near Harrisburg, Pennsylvania, another egregious case arose in which the scientific method clashed with Indian human rights. Conducted under the auspices of the William Penn Memorial Museum, the needless exposure of four graves, two of which belonged to children, was deemed by Ira F. Smith III to be "an overwhelming success." As Smith explained his elation:

The West Branch Project [as the dig was named] was not only a great success from the scientific standpoint . . . but, perhaps more important, from the human interest it generated. We received a tremendous amount of genuine interest, enthusiasm, and even volunteer participation from local residents. All too often, people fail to comprehend what we are trying to do in these field explorations, and seem to resent our presence in their locality.[13]

One can only suppose that the reason for this particular excavation was to learn, in archeological terms, the historical fate of the Susquehannock people who once dwelled along the banks of the Susquehanna River. At a superficial level, wanting to learn the history of a people and their community is commendable. In fact, one can argue that there ought to be an obligation for anyone to know the history of the place in which they lived and called home. In which case, when it came to the Susquehannock village being unearthed, the individuals "researching" this historic community should have known and informed others that the Susquehannock were also known as the Conestoga, who were the victims of a 1763 massacre perpetrated by "the Paxton Boys," which was a purported militia ostensibly protecting settler homesteads from Indian aggression, but which was instead a racism-driven vigilante mob on the prowl for unsuspecting targets.[14] What this meant was that the disinterred remains that Smith and his collaborators took great excitement in uncovering were the descendants, maybe even the survivors, of that heinous assault. Of equal concern was the conspicuous absence of any attempt on the part of researchers to develop any kind of relationship with the Indigenous peoples of the region, let alone showing any interest or respect for tribally based histories of the place and people that the archeologists appropriated in the name of science.

As an indication, though, of how Indian-white relations could be more agreeable, even when dealing with culturally sensitive remains and artifacts, Deloria turned his reader's attention from state archeologists to a prestige museum. During a Field Museum–sponsored dig, after finding the remains of what were identified as seventeenth-century Miami Indians, Matthew War Bonnet led a delegation of Indian activists to confront museum curator Donald Collier. What the Indian group wanted was "that the bones be given to [them] for ceremonial reburial in a Winnebago burial ground in Wisconsin," which the museum accommodated, apparently in an effort to avoid a public incident. At the same time, similar to the Iowa case above, the Field Museum was more concerned about setting what it considered an unacceptable precedent for Indian-museum relations:

> The museum, in a hasty effort to recoup some semblance of respectability, paid for the evening ceremonial fire, hired a medicine man to perform the ceremonies, and provided gifts to be given at the ceremonies. The museum wryly noted that, despite providing financial support for the Indian ceremonies, it did not want to be considered a "soft touch," thus indicating that its overture was more of a "bribe" than a gift.[15]

On the one hand, the Field Museum case was confirmation that Indians could make some progress and achieve some success on the issue of repatriation. On the other, the condescending attitude that the Field expressed toward the Indian activists was evidence of how deeply entrenched the assumption of cultural and scientific superiority was among museum leaders. Deloria concluded his catalog of archeological desecrations with a brief anecdote regarding the pilfering of Nez Percés graves near Clarkston, Washington, in which skulls were severed from bodies and sold on the black market.[16]

What happened during the summer of 1971, then, was the start of a rise in collective consciousness, in which Indians realized that they did not have to accept the authority of non-Indigenous archeological experts as final. Instead, they asserted their own authority over how their ancestors' mortal remains and the cultural patrimony that was buried with them were to be regarded ethically, culturally, and historically. Toward that objective, Deloria added to the discourse on self-determination the religious necessity of reclaiming ancestral remains. Spurned by an array of consciousness-raising events, more Indians became aware of their right to criticize the ghoulish objectification of their ancestors as scientific artifacts covered by non-Indian property law.

Deloria's caricature of anthropology in *Custer* was so well-known among Indians and anthropologists alike, it seems redundant to go over his critique of this most American of social sciences here. Yet, one cannot appreciate Deloria's aspiration for a fully realized tribal form of self-determination without looking at his criticisms of anthropology. Similar to the law and policy discourse on "the Indian problem" in *Custer* and *Broken Treaties*, which were contingent on the Doctrine of Discovery, treaties, and the expropriation of Indian lands, complete with the oppression of tribal sovereignty, so, too, was the anthropological discourse on Indian communities premised on colonization. As Deloria famously introduced his reader to this unique facet of Indian lives: "Every summer when school is out a veritable stream of immigrants heads into Indian country. Indeed the Oregon Trail was never so heavily populated as are Route 66 and Highway 18 in the summer time."[17] What Deloria was describing was, of course, an invasion.

As such, Deloria's critique not only initiated an examination of anthropological theories and methodologies, but also sparked two important movements—one political, one academic. More to the point, Deloria inaugurated a discussion on the importance of making one's research relevant to the community studied, in addition to acknowledging each tribal community's right to evaluate the appropriateness of the research being conducted on their land and people. The latter eventually led to the establishment of tribal institutional review boards (IRBs). As for the academic movement, the critique of anthropology inspired a burgeoning field, namely American Indian/Native American studies to contemplate what made their developing discipline distinct from their counterparts in cultural anthropology. As Bea Medicine stated in her 1970 paper "Anthropologists and American Indian Studies Programs": "The majority of Native American Studies Programs deal with student populations of an inter-tribal character. This is yielding a 'contrived culture' with roots in a variety of experiences and cultural backgrounds." Then, with a reference to *We Talk, You Listen*, Medicine added: "The examination of 'experience relevant to the group' that Vine Deloria [Jr.] suggests has potential in redirecting curriculum."[18] For Deloria, the priority should be placed on American Indians driving the discourse on their contemporary lives and nations, not on an antiseptic notion of culture, let alone a romanticized past.

Despite the comic overtones, the invasion of anthropologists—even if they only stayed for the summer before returning to their institutions of higher learning—had a profound impact on tribal existence. More to the point, in addition to being an intrusion into people's privacy, as non-Indian field researchers asked about a community's religious beliefs and kinship relations, it was also another instance of expropriation. Legendary among the cases in which anthropologists have embedded themselves within the community, not only mining its secrets, but also dominating the discourse on its culture and history, was Zuni Pueblo, which straddled the New Mexico–Arizona border. Ever since Frank Hamilton Cushing invited himself into Zuni Village during the late nineteenth century, complete with disclosing its religious secrets in a series of popular works, this otherwise remote community has been subjected to the experiments of anthropological field work, including the infamous transgressions of Matilda Coxe Stevenson.[19] In this case, how Indians perceived themselves, as expressed in their oral traditions and material culture, was ultimately subsumed into the analyses and theories of anthropologists. As Deloria stated in *God Is Red*: "The tragedy of America's Indians—that is, the Indians that America loves and loves to read about—is that they no longer exist, except in the pages of books."[20] Distinct within this American literary tradition was Joseph K. Dixon's *The Vanishing Race: The Last Great Indian Council (1913)*, which stood shoulder to shoulder with the visual pageantry of Edward S. Curtis at establishing the Indian's noble past as a timeless paean to the fading Red Man.[21] Parenthetically, it should be noted that there were anthropologists whom Deloria admired, beginning with his paternal aunt Ella Deloria and his close friend Robert K. Thomas (Cherokee), not to mention the high praise expressed for the work of Fr. Peter Powell and his not-to-be-overlooked work with Raymond DeMallie. "If I were asked," Deloria once said, "to make a list of the useful anthropologists, it would be very short."[22] At the same time, Deloria's appreciation did sometimes stray into the controversial—begging the question as to what Deloria meant by "useful"—be it his references to Frank Waters's *Book of the Hopi* or his unexpected veneration of John

C. Neidhardt's *Black Elk Speaks*.[23] With this in mind, Deloria's critical lens highlighted the social transgressions inherent in the anthro-Indian relationship, which informed federal Indian policy.

Speaking of anthropologists, Robert K. "Bob" Thomas, noted above as an exception to Deloria's general disdain for anthropology, had a substantial influence on Deloria, which went back to their first meeting in 1963 when the yet undistinguished future author of *Custer* had interviewed for a position with the United Scholarship Service. From there, Thomas was a part of each stage of Deloria's growth as a national Indian leader, activist, and attorney turned professor. As an Indigenous intellectual in his own right, Thomas was remembered for his nuanced and experience-driven work on Southeastern Indian communities. While Thomas did not publish as much as many of his admirers would have liked—there was an obvious absence of any monograph—one could not question the capaciousness of his knowledge or the wisdom of his insights into the cultural-historical-political spectrum of Indigenous communities inhabiting enclaves from the Appalachians to the Ozarks. In his memorial essay on his dearly remembered colleague at the University of Arizona's American Indian Studies department, Deloria recounted feeling astounded at watching Thomas teach a class on the Five Civilized Tribes, during which several long minutes were spent on drawing an elaborate map:

> Finally, he [Thomas] stepped back, adjusted the mountains in Arkansas, and began to talk. Using geography he described the various kinds of lands in the region, what plants were dominant, and how the land forced people to live in certain ways. Then he went into the social structure of each of the Five Tribes, outlining how they settled each area, how property descended, how the Muskogees were able to connect towns in their confederacy, and how the relations between the Choctaws and Chickasaws on the one hand and the Muskogees and Seminoles on the other had to take certain structures in relation to the lands. He then gave an exhaustive analysis of what being full blood or mixed blood in terms of tribal traditions really meant, arguing that simple classification by these labels would not explain the political configurations brought on by the removal policy.

Thomas's lecture consisted of little more than a chalk drawing on a blackboard and good old fashion storytelling, yet in Deloria's final appraisal: "It was a tour de force that one can wait a lifetime to experience."[24]

In a departure from his method of analyzing the laws, policies, and treaties, which began with the Delaware and the Iroquois, Deloria instead took an ahistorical approach to his assessment of anthropology. Rather than taking his reader back to the start of anthropology's history in Indian Country—beginning with Thomas Jefferson's *Notes on the State of Virginia* (1781) and moving through a litany of amateurs until the 1890s, when Columbia University established the first anthropology department—Deloria referred to anthropology's origins as lost in the mist of time. From the Indian perspective, it was as if anthropologists have always been there. As Deloria drolly remarked: "Indians are . . . certain that Columbus brought anthropologists on his ships when he came to the New World. How else could he have made so many wrong deductions about where he was?"[25] Deloria then deliberately stereotypes the typical anthropologist, who stands out like a sore thumb in any Indian community, a ridiculous "creature" characterized as making "OBSERVATIONS." These observations, gleaned from the anthropologist's periodic visits to the reservation, were then published as books and peer-reviewed papers that espoused the latest theory explaining "the Indian problem," be it that Indians were "BICULTURAL," "FOLK," "BETWEEN TWO WORLDS," and the like. With regard to these concepts, which were more than just parodies, Deloria likely had the works of Steven Polgar, Malcolm McFee, Robert Redfield, and Ruth Benedict in mind. One can only speculate, however, as to whom Deloria really had in mind. For what becomes apparent as one delves further into *Custer*'s chapter 4, "Anthropologists and Other Friends," was an absence of proper names. Deloria preferred to make indirect references to the targets of his critiques. As for the anthropological enterprise, the work was divided between "PURE RESEARCH" and "APPLIED RESEARCH." Nevertheless, while the research techniques may have differed, what both types of anthropologists had in common was the fact that "he ALREADY KNOWS what he was going to find."[26]

When James E. Officer, professor of anthropology at the University of Arizona and former associate commissioner of Indian affairs, reviewed

Custer for a 1970 issue of *Arizona and the West,* he thought of Deloria's book as being more about how non-Indians perceived Indians than it was about Indians. Furthermore, in reaction to the satirizing of anthropology, Officer mused:

> Many of Deloria's comments are laced with sarcasm and a Twain-like flair for burlesque. Some of these passages are very funny, even to an uptight anthropologist. His caricature of the summer invasion of the reservations by anthropology graduate students provides a devastating opportunity for many of us to see ourselves as others see (or have seen) us. Still, Deloria's humor, which often creeps unexpectedly into otherwise serious passages, may leave the reader uncertain as to whether the author means what he is saying or is only "funning."[27]

Historic among the reactions to Deloria's assault on the integrity of the anthropological profession was, as mentioned in the chapter 1, a 1970 meeting sponsored by the Bureau of Indian Affairs, which ran concurrently with the annual meeting of the American Anthropological Association. Titled "Anthropology and the American Indian," the assembled panels were held in San Diego, California. Then, at the 1989 annual AAA meeting in Washington DC, there was a panel dedicated to the twentieth anniversary of Deloria's influential critique.[28] Even many years later, what often gets overlooked was the point to Deloria's excoriation, which was the negative effect that social-science observations and theories had on federal Indian policy. Philleo Nash made a sincere effort in 1970 at disclaiming any connection between anthropology and federal Indian policy. Others at both meetings simply ignored the accusation policy was being affected. Nonetheless, *Custer* was much more than its satirical portrayal of anthropologists: "The massive volume of useless knowledge produced by anthropologists attempting to capture real Indians in a network of theories has contributed substantially to the invisibility of Indian people today."[29] Unfortunately, as Deloria summarized the anthropological enterprise, the obsessive focus on traditional culture had generated "a mythical super-Indian," compared to which Indians living on the reservation paled in comparison.[30] This mythical Indian, more importantly, influenced government opinion in Washington

DC, where "bureaucrats and Congressmen are outraged to discover that this 'berry-picking food gatherer' has not entered the mainstream of American society." Indeed, this was the attitude that ushered in termination.[31] Prior to 1953, in particular during the era of the Indian agent, Congress and the Indian Bureau were regularly concerned with the "Returned Student Problem," which was the evident lack of success at assimilating Indian students at the boarding schools, which they were forced to attend. More specifically, the nature of the so-called problem was the number of students who became "blanket Indians," meaning those boarding-school students who dispensed with their education and resorted to their traditional ways, including speaking their Indigenous languages. During a 1919 hearing before the House Committee on Indian Affairs, in a session titled "The Condition of Various Tribes of Indians," Rep. John Reber (R-PA) referred to "blanket Indians" numerous times in the context of discussing a survey authorized by Congress to study the "returned student problem." Reber was especially disturbed by the level of recidivism that occurred among students who had been exposed to the "civilizing" effects of education.[32]

While for many Indian readers Deloria's portrayal of anthropology's vapid research resonated with a deep emotional truth, his hasty generalizations were not only infuriating to social scientists, but also, like any stereotype, easily rebutted with real-world fact and example. Prominent among these examples was the advocacy work on behalf of the Native American Church conducted by James Mooney and Omer Stewart. In fact, Mooney and Stewart were part of a long lineage of social scientists that studied and defended church members against state-sanctioned persecution, not to mention church groups, temperance societies, and the Indian Bureau, which was a struggle recounted to great effect in Thomas C. Maroukis's 2010 book, *The Peyote Road: Religious Freedom and the Native American Church.* As stated above, Deloria was aware of anthropological work that even by his own standards was exemplary. So, why the ad hominin screed? At the heart of Deloria's rant against the institution of anthropology, in which anthropologists must compete for funding—which entailed meeting non-Indian funding criteria—was the way in which Indians were left out of the analysis of their cultures and histories. In other words, anthropological studies were the epitome of the alleged transparency of the Indian plight, as described in *Custer's* chapter on "Indians Today, the Real and Unreal." Indians need not be consulted at all, remember? In spite of the appearance of the occasional Indian anthropologist, including the likes of Robert K. Thomas, Bea Medicine, and Alfonso Ortiz, not to mention historically important figures like Francis La Flesche and Ella Deloria, anthropology was still largely made-up of non-Indian researchers writing about Indians. Even when one took into consideration that every anthropologist conducting field work relied upon "informants" from the community under study, these contributors generally did not have authorial control over how their testimony was used and analyzed.[33]

As evidence of anthropology's colonial influence over Indians, Deloria mentioned cases in which Indians who "have come to parrot the ideas of anthropologists because it appears that the anthropologists know everything about Indian communities."[34] Without naming anyone, Deloria implied that what has passed for "Indian thinking" over the previous decade, meaning since the mid-1950s, had been little more than a recycling of anthropological ideas. Perhaps Deloria had McNickle in mind? Maybe even Thomas? As for who and what Deloria was criticizing, an important hint was given when one read: "Since 1955 there have been a number of workshops conducted in Indian country as a device for training 'young Indian leaders.'" On July 6, 1956, Sen. James E. Murray (D-MT) submitted Senate Concurrent Resolution 85, which proposed establishing an "American Indian point 4 program," to be administered by the Bureau of Indian Affairs for the purpose of "raising the standard of living" among American Indians.[35] The objective of the resolution was to implement in the reservation system an economic-development program similar to the one that the Truman administration had implemented in its Third World interests, which federal officials regarded as having had success.[36] How this related to Deloria's examination of anthropology's role in Indian affairs was that, according to Dorothy R. Parker, D'Arcy McNickle played a significant part in the organization of the BIA's "point 4" program, which included a series of leadership workshops. "Point 4" was a reference to the name that foreign-policy pundits gave to the nation building initiatives pursued under Truman's secretary of state Dean Acheson, which focused on American aid in the so-called Third World. During the mid 1950s, McNickle consulted with Ruth Bronson about a point 4 program for Indian Country. Bronson, who served in the guidance office of the BIA's Office of Education, worked with McNickle along with a number of other persons dedicated to Indian affairs, including anthropologist Sol Tax of the University of Chicago. Tax was well known for developing action anthropology, which purportedly focused on issue-related research that addressed the social and political needs of a given community. Together, McNickle and Bronson wanted to create something that offered "training in the knowledge and skills [that young Indian people] would need for leadership roles in their tribal communities."[37]

As for Deloria's assessment of these workshops—the spirit of which metamorphosed into the VISTA (Volunteers in Service to America) program of the Johnson years—in spite of the fact that McNickle was against termination and resigned from the BIA in protest, the workshops' good intentions of preparing young Indians for the inevitability of termination apparently did nothing to soften Deloria's appraisal of their effectiveness. More specifically, the point 4 workshops did little more than inculcate young Indians with the same out-of-touch scholarly theories—which Deloria observed had devolved into mere "slogans"—that had ossified into an orthodoxy among the anthropologists perpetuating these notions. Based on the premise that Indians and whites live in two very different and irreconcilable worlds, anthropologists claimed, as Deloria summarized: "Indians are between two cultures, Indians are bicultural, Indians have lost their identity, and Indians are warriors." Consequently, as these precepts were repeated, not only in the academic literature, but also in the workshops that Deloria belittled, the young Indians supposedly being trained to become leaders wound up losing one of the key attributes of leadership—the ability to think critically and originally. On the contrary, as Deloria decried: "These insights . . . have come to occupy a key block in the development of young Indian people. For these slogans have come to be excuses for Indian failures. They are crutches by which young Indians have avoided the arduous task of thinking out the implications of the status of Indian people in the modern world."[38] Indeed, in a 1966 editorial titled "Which Way Indians?" the NCAI asserted: "It will only be when we understand how we fit into the national picture as modern people that we will be able to get away from the perennial question of 'Two cultures' that anthropologists love to throw at us."[39]

In anticipation of *Custer*'s reflections on Indian-Black relations, and the division this created between NCAI and NIYC members, the workshop Indians were disparaged for being no more than "unwitting missionaries" of "anthropological doctrines." In fact, as Paul R. McKenzie observed in his political biography of Clyde Warrior: "[Deloria] remembered listening to Mel Thom and Herb Blatchford testifying before the secretary of interior in 1963 and recalled feeling 'a bit betrayed that Thom and Blatchford did not have ideas of their own—but merely recycled the concepts they had learned from Bob Thomas at the Workshop.'" Such an opinion, however, may have been a part of what Hank Adams referred to as Deloria's revisionist history. More to the point, the relationship between Warrior and Deloria, according to McKenzie-Jones, was one in which Deloria was perceptive about Warrior's capacity for inspiring through his "verbal militancy" an intellectual paradigm shift in the way that Indians advocated for themselves: "Vine Deloria, Jr., later described Warrior [in a 1998 essay dedicated to the memory of Robert K. Thomas] as having had 'a way of presenting his points crudely and effectively so that people would not forget,' and his rhetoric marked an important shift in the methodology of American Indian protest."[40] While those who knew Warrior may not deny the validity of Deloria's appraisal, there were those who were of the opinion that Warrior's absence from Deloria's discourse on the Indian protest movement was the result of a rather personal revisionist history. As McKenzie-Jones further observed: "Despite Warrior being one of the most influential figures in Indian affairs at the time of [*Custer*'s] writing, the only reference Deloria made to Warrior's activism was to retell one of his jokes."

Hank Adams later accused Deloria of "undergoing some revision" in his memories of Warrior. Warrior, who died long before Deloria forged a career as one of the most formidable American Indian intellectuals and critics of federal Indian policy in the twentieth century, preferred to simply include Deloria as one of the many Indians he saw as failing to fight enough for Indians, as he railed against the "finks" in the NCAI.[41]

Perhaps as an indication that Deloria was not unaware of what Warrior and Adams thought of him, foibles and all, Deloria stated in the afterword to *Custer*: "When one writes a book, or at least tries to write a book, a great deal of one's soul is surrendered and placed in print for all to see. Thus, to quote my old friend Clyde Warrior, 'I've sold out.' At least in many ways."[42] With regard, then, to Deloria's workshop comment, Warrior and Thom's alleged collusion "was actually quite a feat for two of the driving forces behind the NIYC, as neither had at that point attended the workshops as students (Thom did several months later), and Deloria himself had yet to meet Thomas either."[43] Whatever the truth of the matter, by contrast, in Deloria's estimation, Black activists were regarded as intellectually more dynamic, which some Indians had striven to emulate, but with meager results, such as parodying "some black slogans" while having "created none of their own." With conspicuous envy, Deloria portrayed the Black civil rights movement as one that was created by young Black people who "pushed the whole society to consider the implications of discrimination which in turn created racial nationalism." Can young Indians create anything comparable and in their own voices? Deloria answered with a resounding yes— "tribalism."[44] Rather than define his concept, which he saved for a later part of *Custer*, namely "Indians and Modern Society," which was followed by *We Talk, You Listen*, Deloria pointed out that the thinking about tribalism had been impeded by the inherent limitations of the "Indians-are-a-folk-people" mentality, which precluded Indians from imagining themselves as an active part of the modern world. On the contrary, the focus was on Indians belonging to small, discreet rural populations in which "folk art," such as baskets and pottery, was created, time moved slowly, and the people deliberately remained aloof from the world around them—much like the Mexican villages that Oscar Lewis observed in his 1951 book, *Life in a Mexican Village: Tepotzlán Restudied*.[45] As such, Deloria acknowledged that thinking about tribalism was absent in some circles, such as the workshops above, but not in others. One just had to look to a different generation, in particular one that was "supposedly brainwashed by government schools and derided as 'puppets' of the Bureau of Indian Affairs," but whose experiences lent them the capacity to be themselves as Indians within a larger context.[46]

Once again without mentioning any names, Deloria launched into a tribute to the Apache tribes of Mescalero, San Carlos, White Mountain, and Jicarilla. Perhaps the source of Deloria's adulation were the two Apache presidents of the NCAI during his 1964–67 tenure, specifically Clarence Wesley (San Carlos) and Wendell Chino (Mescalero). Whatever the source, these tribes, in spite of a dearth of college graduates—in addition to largely foregoing the workshop circuit—had managed to maintain an impressive level of political and economic independence.

> Apaches could not care less about the anthropological dilemmas that worry other tribes. Instead they continue to work on the massive plans for development which they themselves have created. Tribal identity is assumed, not defined, by the reservation people.[47]

What Deloria regarded as workshop Indians, on the other hand, stood as a cautionary tale against letting non-Indian academic theories do your thinking about tribalism for you, especially when these theories precluded you from ever imagining, let alone strategizing, your tribe's response to alarming developments in federal Indian policy. Just as Deloria indicted anthropologists for their absence from the struggle against termination, so too would these workshop Indians be ill-prepared for fight for Indian rights and tribal self-determination.

In Deloria's estimation, the workshop Indians were too young and inexperienced to confront the problems facing tribal communities, such as the health-care issues raised earlier, and come up with viable solutions. As for the anthropological theories that were imparted to young Indians at these workshops, they tended to answer the questions that they raised, thereby preempting critical thinking. For example, one workshop focused on Indians as living "BETWEEN TWO WORLDS," meaning the folk-urban divide. Indians caught in this irresolvable situation often "DRANK," or so the workshop students were taught, which led to the deduction that real Indians drank as part of their identity. These young people, obviously, did not realize that they were perpetuating one of the most heinous stereotypes inflicted upon them and their communities, namely the scourge of the "drunken Indian."[48] In the case of the leadership workshops, the theory that living between two worlds leads to drinking explained the problem satisfactorily, such that it validated the workshop Indians' drinking habits as part of their Indian experience. "Lumping together," however, as Deloria observed, "the variety of tribal problems and seeking the demonic principle at work which is destroying Indian people may be intellectually satisfying. But it does not change the real situation."[49] On this point, Nancy O. Lurie took Deloria to task:

> I do not agree with Vine Deloria Jr.'s syllogism that young Indians were sold the notion by anthropologists that Indians live in two worlds; people who live in two worlds drink; therefore, to be real Indians they must drink. But, like Deloria, I, too, have "lost some good friends who DRANK too much." Some took their lives before managing to drink themselves to death. And, like Deloria, my grief evokes anger and bitterness that they died as they did and that others are likely to go the same route so long as we pursue policies that continue to deprive Indians of lands, water rights, and other natural resources or so long as we offer them the opportunity to achieve decent living standards only if they measure up to our particular philosophical standards.[50]

Regardless of what Lurie may have thought, Deloria repeatedly showed very little patience for any type of research on Indians that was not focused on redressing problems. With regard to Deloria's disbelief toward the workshop theory about Indian drinking, he remarked in the introduction to *We Talk, You Listen* likely with Lurie in mind:

> Last summer [1969], a noted female anthropologist presented a scholarly paper to the effect that Indians drink to gain an identity. Anyone who has ever seen Indians would laugh at the absurdity of this idea. It is unquestionably the other way. Indians first ask what your name is, then what your tribe is. After these preliminaries you are sometimes asked to have a drink. Drinking is only the confirmation of a

friendship already established by the fact that you belong to a specific tribe. If we acted the way anthropologists describe us, we would get lousy stinking drunk, THEN DECIDE WHAT TRIBE WE WANTED TO BELONG TO, and finally choose a surname for ourselves.[51]

While Deloria did not identify the anthropologist in question, he did make his disdain for what he considered ill-informed theory quite clear. On this point, James Mackay, a lecturer on comparative literatures, who has written about American Indians in the European imagination, observed:

> The fury of those capital letters must be understood in the context of a book published just one year after the founding . . . of the first Native American Studies Program at the University of California, Berkeley. In other words, there was yet no effective power base within the academy from which Indians could challenge mistaken perceptions and academic abuses. The published anthropological account would have, for most outsiders, greater force than the insiders' lived experience.[52]

Speaking of the Indian lived experience, where one finds chronic alcoholism, one frequently finds endemic poverty. Poverty was another major problem confronting tribes that was in need of focused research for the purpose of tribal economic development. Rather than bemoan the alleged decline in traditional culture, making whole communities feel humiliated for the consequences of state-sponsored racism, Deloria argued that energy should be spent on understanding the political causes of tribal poverty along with developing the necessary policies and resources to alleviate the situation. The Gila River Indian Community and the Pyramid Lake Paiute, for example, were desperately poor in large part because the natural resources that once sustained them had been appropriated in the name of progress. Consequently, "straddling worlds is irrelevant to straddling small pieces of land and trying to earn a living." Virtually every tribe was in a similar circumstance, specifically dealing with colonially induced poverty and natural-resource issues, which coincided with the oppression of pre-reservation customs and values. As for the fate of Indigenous customs, traditional dances—which Deloria highlighted—had typically been "transposed into church gatherings, participation in the county fair, and tribal celebrations," such as "fairs and rodeos."[53] Insofar that the decline of traditional culture was the direct result of federal Indian law and policy, it was nothing short of offensive to criticize tribes for not being more like their ancestors as if the status of such customs was due to the current generation simply being "lazier" than their predecessors.

As an example of the way in which far-fetched theories interfered with realistic solutions to Indian poverty, Deloria recalled an anecdote in which a proposal was made during the "summer of 1968" to "solve the desperate credit needs of reservation communities." The proposed plan was based on the assumption that "Indian reservations have a great deal of HOARDED wealth," which, if the Indians could be coaxed into investing in "reservation banks, mutual funds, and small businesses," it would go a long way at addressing the anemic economic growth in Indian communities.[54] As for where this rumored wealth came from in the first place—Deloria's story was dated twenty years prior to the Indian Gaming Regulatory Act (1988)—one can only speculate. A likely source was the total sum of monies that the Indian Claims Commission had awarded tribes since 1946. Because Deloria often provided his reader only the barest of hints as to what and whom he was referring, it is impossible to make more than a superficial analysis of the anecdote's place in the critique of anthropology. Be that as it may, Deloria implied that the historical fiction of hoarded wealth, as a concoction of anthropologists, was another instance of the social sciences failing the Indian community.

As a counterexample to the myth of Indian wealth, Deloria referred to his service on the "[Citizens'] Board of Inquiry into Hunger and Malnutrition in the United States," which was organized by the Citizens' Crusade against Poverty (CCAP). The CCAP was a nongovernmental "coalition of labor unions, businesses, churches and synagogues, charitable foundations, advocacy groups, and grassroots organizations." Under CCAP's auspices a survey was conducted from July 1967 to April 1968, the results of which were published as *Hunger, USA: A Report.*[55] With respect to hunger and malnutrition among Indians, not to mention other impoverished communities, Deloria recalled feeling "shaken at what we found."[56] As often happens with the urgent issues covered in

Custer, there were congressional hearings about the accumulated data and testimony assembled in *Hunger, USA*. Although Deloria did not testify, members of the board of inquiry that worked on the report did attend on May 23, 29 and June 12, 14, 1968, which included multiple references to tribal communities, such as Navajo Nation, the Havasupai Tribe, and the Standing Rock Sioux Reservation. No hoarding of wealth here, but plenty of undernourished children. In a report from the U.S. secretary of health, education, and welfare, senators learned of a health crisis:

> A variety of studies in a number of States show the relationship of poverty to anemia in children and pregnant women. There is also evidence of poor nutrition among migrants and the aged, among Alaskan Eskimos and Indians. Among the American Indian population, particularly the most recent information from the Division of Indian Health shows disturbing evidence of clinical malnutrition in hospital admissions of young children.[57]

To assume, then, that such populations possessed unutilized sources of wealth was not only misguided but also potentially dangerous. After making a plea for the speedy end to the hoarded-wealth proposal, Deloria moved on, after a satirical diversion in which he evoked a stream of Indian "investors" making their way to Pine Ridge with bags of rare coins, to another preposterous notion, this time regarding the Oglala.

After touting the military prowess of Red Cloud and Crazy Horse, Deloria pointed out that the Oglala made an admirable adjustment to reservation life, adapting their land to the ranching business, a factor he brings up again in *Broken Treaties*, complete with an account of how the U.S. Army devastated Lakota ranching during World War I. "By World War I," Deloria recounted, "many of the Sioux families had developed prosperous ranches. Then the Government stepped in, sold the Indians' cattle for wartime needs, and after the war leased the grazing land to whites, creating wealthy white ranchers and destitute Indian landlords."[58] As westward expansion across the Northern Plains ensued, populations migrated and tribal boundaries shifted, complete with non-Oglala moving into the area, both whites and non-Lakota Indians. Furthermore, as the population grew, while Indian land was reduced through allotment and appropriation, which had a negative impact on the tribal economy, a situation developed in which the reservation could not support its primary Oglala Indian residents. Meanwhile, white settlers prospered on land that was once part of the reservation.

Outsiders to Pine Ridge wondered about the reservation's lack of progress. The problem of white settler occupation was overlooked for an Indian-centered explanation. Why were the Oglala destitute? Obviously, as Deloria sarcastically noted, it had nothing to do with the BIA leasing Indian land to whites. The answer must therefore be *cultural*. According to one unnamed researcher, an observable difference existed between those tribal members with cattle compared to those without, which was illustrated with an array of charts and graphs.[59] Such mundane truths as the class distinctions that occurred with economic development, however, did not get at the heart of a tribal people. The Oglala required an especially Indian explanation, or so some researchers presumed. With that in mind, "one day a famous anthropologist advanced the thesis that the Oglala were WARRIORS WITHOUT WEAPONS." Deloria did not identify the anthropologist except for the slogan that he popularized. Gordon Macgregor, of course, was the unnamed proponent of this particular concept.

In his classic 1946 study of the transition the "Pine Ridge Sioux" made into the reservation system, Macgregor referred to the same historic land loss that Deloria outlined above. However, Macgregor postulated a different interpretation of the Lakota community under BIA administrative control than the one warranted by the facts. In chapter 1 "Warriors on the Reservation" Macgregor's readers learned: "The Dakota came onto the reservation not as a vanquished people but rather as eagles driven by a winter storm to accept captivity and food until they could fly away again."[60] As flattering as this romanticized image may have seemed, the evoking of eagle and warrior imagery did little to assist the Pine Ridge Reservation at addressing the political and economic issues it faced as a result of an uncooperative South Dakota state government and a federal government growing more interested in terminating its trust responsibilities than in honoring its treaties with the Great Sioux Nation. What happened instead, according to Deloria, was that a bevy of additional studies were generated, all of them based on Macgregor's thesis that the Sioux were repressed warriors. "Why expect," Deloria sardonically asked, "an Oglala to become a small businessman when he was only waiting for that wagon train to come around the bend?"[61] As for how Deloria portrayed the post–World War II generation, he saw what may be described as a combination of reawakened political and cultural sovereignty induced by the 1934 IRA and dramatic exposure to a wider, more complicated world—none of which was adequately addressed in Macgregor's work:

> After the war Indian veterans straggled back to the reservations and tried to pick up their lives. It was very difficult for them to resume a life of poverty after having seen the affluent outside world. Some spent a few days with the old folks and then left again for the big cities. Over the years they have emerged as leaders of the urban Indian movement. Many of their children are the nationalists of today who are adamant about keeping the reservations they have visited only on vacations. Other veterans stayed on the reservations and entered tribal politics.[62]

Macgregor's influence on subsequent studies was, of course, immaterial here. Enumerating the works that bore the weaponless-warrior mark would be an exercise in futility. Deloria's more urgent point was neither about reforming anthropology nor about romanticizing Sioux history. It was about how a non-Indian researcher sets an agenda to meet his own needs as a non-Indian interested in Indians—in this case, a desire to find some evidence of the nineteenth-century Plains Indian warrior—the fulfillment of which led to the obfuscation of Indian reality as Indians saw it.

> I lived eighteen years on that [the Pine Ridge] reservation and know many of the problems it suffers. How, I ask, can the Oglala Sioux make any headway in education when their lack of education is ascribed to a desire to go to war? Would not perhaps an incredibly low per capita income, virtually non-existent housing, extremely inadequate roads, and domination by white farmers and ranchers make some difference?

Deloria continued with this point with an oblique reminder of his work on the Citizen's Board of Inquiry: "If the little Sioux boy or girl had no breakfast, had to walk miles to a small school, and had no decent clothes and place to study in a one-room log cabin, should the level of education be comparable to New Trier High School?"[63] Part of the dilemma, as Deloria and others explained, was the deeply entrenched assumption that "traditional" was unequivocally tied to the historical past while "modern" inevitably meant an irreversible break with that same past. In which case, if one determined that a given community required a return to its storied past in order to ameliorate its collective malaise, then one was—based on the above assumption about tradition and modern—precluding that community from participating in so-called modern society. In the absence of Indian self-determination, studies based on theses like the one advocated in Macgregor's work brought many non-Indian researchers to a common conclusion: "Indians must be re-defined in terms that white men will accept, even if that means re-Indianizing them according to a white man's idea of what they were like in the past and should logically become in the future."[64] The role of history and tradition, of course, became a critical issue for Indian activists as well. However, there was a difference between romanticizing the past as opposed to revitalizing languages and customs for the benefit of future generations. In light of which, in the context of self-determination, Deloria argued for a notion of tradition that was adaptable to the world in which Indians actually lived, which, for better and for worse, was shaped by modern non-Indian technology and ideas.

Ever since Lewis Henry Morgan theorized in *Ancient Society* (1877) that every human community was on the same ladder of social evolution, in which the pinnacle was occupied by those nations possessing notions of private property, democracies, and, most importantly, modern technology, researchers have subjected Indigenous peoples around the globe to this ethnocentric, not to mention racist, scale of development. In an essay for a special issue of the *North American Review* titled "The Indian Problem, 1823–1973," Deloria summarized the social Darwinism that drove federal Indian policy—not to mention the social science of the day—during the late nineteenth century, which culminated with the 1887 Allotment Act:

The predominant—one might say overriding—concern of the influential whites of a century ago was somehow to place the savage tribes on the evolutionary rail road track to civilization. Without examining the popular folklore of social evolutionary theories, whites assumed that nations of men followed inexorable rules of development. Arriving at national consciousness in a hunting state, the embryo-nation was supposed to pass eventually to an agricultural state and then gradually evolve into a modern urban society. This process was believed to be part of God's divine plan, and American history was perverted to explain the process.[65]

As for social scientists, researchers may not be collecting Indian skulls, as did Aleš Hrdlička, but the anthropologists heading to places like Pine Ridge in the aftermath of World War II were clearly still beholden to a version of human history that was firmly lodged in the nineteenth century. Whereas Richard Pratt, founder of the Carlisle Indian School, wanted to "kill the Indian and save the man," anthropologists like Macgregor wanted to "save the Indian and kill his future." Having said that, what difference did it make if anthropologists or, for that matter, any type of researcher waxed poetic about a tribe's past glories against the U.S. cavalry or its spiritual relationship with nature? When one's community was not on the receiving end of spurious theories about, say, a supposed warrior essence, then such work may appear to be irrelevant, even harmless. Yet, when one considered that the vast body of anthropological reports were written for the Bureau of American Ethnology, which was run under the auspices of the Smithsonian Institution, then the extent to which anthropological research impacted Indian affairs starts to become more apparent. Hazel W. Hertzberg, in her seminal 1971 study of the Society of American Indians, mentioned the participation of anthropologists multiple times in the formulation of pre-1934 federal Indian policy. For example, the Committee of One Hundred had an abundance of anthropologists. Secretary of Interior Henry W. Work tasked the committee in 1923 with reviewing and advising on recent Indian policy, setting the stage for the 1928 Meriam Report, about which Hertzeberg wrote: "One of the more interesting aspects of the committee's composition was the strong representation of anthropologists, a factor both indicating and foreshadowing the increasing importance of anthropology in the formulation of Indian policy."[66] This clearly contradicted an assertion that Philleo Nash had made a year earlier at the 1970 AAA meeting dedicated to *Custer's* critique of anthropology, noted in chapter 1, in which Nash argued that the influence of anthropologists was negligible. It was true that the American government has long had a love-hate relationship with its own learned experts, as their work was used or ignored for various political purposes; nonetheless, as an institution, the science of anthropology has long had the most substantial form of political endorsement—an appropriation as an agency of the federal system, in this case the Smithsonian Institution and its Bureau of American Ethnology.

As for Deloria's critique in *Custer*, he went on an extended opprobrium against the arrogance with which anthropological theories were assumed by their non-Indian proponents to explain Indian lives, politics, and cultures. To add emphasis to his point about the wastefulness of anthropological research, Deloria recounted an anthropologist who boasted about having spent "close to ten million dollars" studying a small tribe. As usual, neither the anthropologist nor the tribe are named. What was more important than naming names, though, to Deloria's outrage was the amount of money spent. "Imagine," Deloria exclaimed, "what that amount of money would have meant to that group of people had it been invested in buildings and businesses."[67] The pedantic response, of course, would be to explain that there were restrictions on how funding can be spent, whether it was from a government grant or an independent foundation. Nonetheless, insofar as any institution reflected the values of the society that sustained it, then the point to Deloria's outcry was that more value was being placed on studying Indians than on helping them.

Based on Deloria's evaluation, anthropological reports were not much different than the numerous studies that Congress authorized about the status of American Indians. Social-science studies, like government programs, were typically done without any input, let alone direct control, from the tribes they were supposedly intended to help. In the absence of the Indian voice, all that appeared in studies and reports were the opinions of non-Indian experts, who largely spoke to one another in the language of their academic or political communities. Accordingly, their status as experts, signified by PhDs and tenured professorships, automatically rendered their estimation more sacrosanct than the Indians for whom their work was created. Under those conditions, if an expert concluded that Indians were hoarding wealth or were despondent warriors, then those were the only conclusions that mattered. Any dissenting opinion from Indian people was summarily dismissed out of hand, such as happened to the Menominee during their termination hearing when they were the only ones saying that termination was a bad idea. Then again, referring to Harrington's work in *The Other America*, Deloria observed that this was what happens to poor communities in general.[68]

With respect to anthropologists as members of the academic community who were obliged to fulfill the expectations of tenure and promotion, complete with pressure to acquire grants and produce publications, Deloria's response was clear—that was no excuse at all. Indeed, Deloria also maintained this attitude toward American Indian faculty, too, many of whom he accused of having become complicit with the values and objectives of their respective academic institutions. More pointedly, Deloria bemoaned the state of things among the "Indian professoriate": "All indications are that the function of this group is not to be useful to Indian communities with skills gained in higher education but simply to console each other that they have such a hard time climbing the academic ladder. Presumably these are the intellectuals who will lead Indians in the next generation."[69] Looking back once again on recent events in Indian-white relations, Deloria voiced his frustration:

> The implications of the anthropologist, if not for all America, should be clear for the Indian. Compilation of useless knowledge "for knowledge's sake" should be utterly rejected by the Indian people. We should not be objects of observation for those who do nothing to help us. During the crucial days of 1954, when the Senate was pushing for termination of all Indian rights, not one single scholar, anthropologist, sociologist, historian, or economist came forward to support the tribes against the detrimental policy.[70]

Deloria vehemently repeated this accusation of political and ethical indifference on the part of anthropology's absence in the struggle against termination during his comments at the 1970 AAA meeting, even scolding luminary Margaret Mead for her presumptions about the humanitarianism of the social sciences. As Deloria reflected on the situation in the late 1960s, other groups certainly were in need of similar changes to the research agendas that dominated America's universities and research institutes, such as African Americans and poor whites. Remember, as implied in James Mackay's comments earlier, *Custer* appeared at a time when there was no such thing, in the case of Indians, as American Indian studies, Indian professors, Indian scholars, Indian journals, or tribal colleges. Although these changes were imminent, they encountered an academic world in which policies and resources did not yet exist to accommodate their needs. The struggle for positive change was just getting underway. In the meantime, the question on Deloria's mind was, will non-Indian academics rise up against America's violation of Indian rights as they were doing against the Vietnam War? If not, then Deloria suggested that tribes follow the example set by Roger Jourdain, chairman, Red Lake Ojibwe, who "casually had the anthropologists escorted from his reservation."[71]

In an effort to resolve the serious predicament in which tribes found themselves with respect to researchers, anthropologists above all, Deloria made some suggestions for policies that tribes should consider adopting. *Custer* was an Indian manifesto, as the reader should recall. In which case, it should come as no surprise that the chapter on anthropologists ultimately led to *what tribes can do for themselves*, as opposed to waiting for the non-Indian academic community to change itself. Toward that end, Deloria stated with tribal leaders clearly in mind:

> I would advocate a policy to be adopted by Indian tribes which would soon clarify the respective roles of anthropologists and tribes. *Each anthro desiring to study a tribe should be made to apply to the tribal council for permission to do his study.* He would be given such permission only if he raised as a contribution to the tribal budget an amount of money equal to the amount he proposed to spend in his study. Anthropologists would thus become productive members of Indian society instead of ideological vultures [emphasis added].[72]

In light of the anecdote about Jourdain, the skepticism about the value of anthropological research was clearly a visible concern among tribes. In fact, when ideas like the one above was shared among members of the anthropological community, "it curled no small number of anthropological hairdos. Irrational shrieks of 'academic freedom' rose like rockets from launching pads."[73] As a policy statement, Deloria's proposition was years ahead of its time, anticipating the creation of tribal IRBs, which universities now required their researchers to accommodate, in addition to their own IRBs, whenever research involved a tribal community on Indian land. As for the revenue sharing that was a major part of Deloria's proposal, while it has become commonplace for researchers to articulate how their work will benefit the tribe they are studying, the kind of matching-funds obligation outlined above has not become a normal part of researcher-tribal relations. Tribal consent, however, was the more important issue. On this matter, Deloria warned that unless anthropologists and other researchers learned the difference between freedom and license, they would face a time when tribe after tribe became fed-up with their presumptuousness and simply slammed the door shut on any research whatsoever. This, of course, happened when Havasupai blood samples were mishandled, in which the privacy and human rights of several tribal members were violated because an Arizona State University researcher allowed sensitive genetic data to be shared indiscriminately in contradiction to what she promised participants.[74]

Deloria closed his critique of anthropology with a critical review of Peter Farb's *Man's Rise to Civilization as Shown by the Indians of North America from Primeval Times to the Coming of the Industrial State*, which appeared in early 1968. The book is now considered dated, however, when it was published it created a sensation. In fact, Farb's work was endorsed by Stewart Udall, whose name has been invoked multiple times in the foregoing discourse. Perhaps with that accolade in mind, Deloria warned his readers that Farb's book may very well generate a tidal wave of influence—similar to MacGregor's—which, when it turned into government programs, would likely wreak havoc in Indian affairs. So, what was Farb's book about that was of concern to Deloria? On the one hand, the book was premised on the ethnocentric social evolutionary paradigm criticized above, which placed so-called civilization, meaning Western nations, on the top rung of the evolutionary ladder. On the other, insofar as Farb was regarded as an important voice for conservation, the recognition from Udall was problematic.

> Udall has allowed Pyramid Lake in Nevada to languish some eight years with a mere pittance of water although it is the finest natural water resource in the state. And although he has repeatedly promised the Pyramid Lake Paiute tribe water for the lake. In many people's minds the best way to eradicate a species is to authorize Udall to conserve it.[75]

As Deloria analyzed Farb's thesis, it was based on the preposterous assumption that the so-called Indian rise into civilization was instigated by the comprehensive effort of non-Indian settlers to commit genocide. In other words, Farb was making the case for colonialism. Furthermore, Farb was seen as claiming that Indians "weren't really conservationists," after all. This notion that Indians were just as harmful, if not more so, to their environment than their white European counterparts would form the basis of Paul S. Martin's 1973 "Pleistocene Extinction" theory—sometimes called the "Pleistocene Overkill"—which claimed that "paleo-Indians" hunted megafauna to extinction as they spread across the Western Hemisphere after the last Ice Age.[76] Based on such preconceptions, Deloria warned, the implication for the future of federal Indian policy was dire, a sign of which was Udall's omnibus bill (H.R. 10560), otherwise called the "Indian Resources Development Act."[77]

As for Farb's portrayal of Indian culture as it changed over time, Deloria pointed out that he liked using words such as "test tubes" and "living laboratories," as if each type of tribal group were also a type of experiment, shuddering at the implications this characterization had for the implementation of "pilot projects" in Indian communities. Whether or not this was a fair analysis of Farb's thesis was open to some debate. Farb only used the phrase "living laboratory" twice and "test tube" once in his book, each instance of which should be read in context. Suffice it say, without digressing too far into a close reading of Farb's text, Deloria was perturbed by the use of such language at all, however many times a given phrase was used.[78] In terms of what the repercussions might be should the assertion that Indians were not the conservationists of a romanticized past ever inform federal Indian policy, the potential was that Congress may disregard Indian opinions about how best to manage their lands and natural resources in favor of their own scientific and business values.

"Like the missionaries," as Deloria brought his tirade against anthropology to a close, "anthropologists have become intolerably certain that they represent the ultimate truth." Having laid siege on the anthropological mission in Indian Country, Deloria did not hesitate in his conclusion to acknowledge the likelihood—maybe the better word is inevitability—of a robust confutation of all that he said thus far. Deloria seemed almost welcoming of the outrage he expected. "If nothing else," Deloria mused, "this book [*Custer*] should make enough people take sides either defending it, which will be that valiant few, or condemning it, which will be spearheaded by my friends in the anthropology classes into whose hitherto exclusive domain I have intruded and hopefully given a new sense of conflict to Indian Affairs [*sic*]."[79]

Not long after Stan Steiner's foundational 1968 portrayal of Deloria as an NCAI advocate for tribal rights and values, in 1973 the *Indian Historian* published the proceedings of a symposium titled *Anthropology and the American Indian*. Summarized in chapter 1, this historically important, but little regarded event, was held during the American Anthropological Association's annual meeting in San Diego, California on November 20, 1970. As was typical of this type of publication, *Anthropology and the American Indian: A Symposium* included introductions from the symposium's organizer, James Officer, as well as the panel discussions that occurred following each of the six papers presented by Nancy O. Lurie, Philleo Nash, Omer C. Stewart, Margaret Mead, Bea Medicine, and Alfonso Ortiz. At the end of the panels, Deloria was given the opportunity to respond. The impetus for this gathering of anthropological luminaries was, of course, Deloria's remarks in chapter 4 of *Custer*. As Officer and Francis McKinley collectively noted in their preface: "Indian author Vine Deloria Jr., dropped a bomb on the anthropological fraternity of the United States in 1969 when he included a chapter in his best selling [sic] book, *Custer Died for Your Sins* (Macmillan), blaming these social scientists, along with government officials and missionaries, for many of the problems of American Indians today."[80] As one might expect, the non-Indian anthropologists were anxious to present on the exceptions to Deloria's claim that anthropology was not only disrespectful of Indian communities but also exploitive and self-serving. They challenged Deloria in particular on his accusation that anthros virtually gave nothing back to these communities for their knowledge or services rendered. Lurie, for example, began the morning session defending the virtues of action anthropology:

> The trouble with action anthropology is that while anthropology, distinguished as pure and applied, is being roundly criticized these days by Indian people, action anthropology can and does respond to Indian people on their terms but it gets no credit, or even notice, because its very unobtrusiveness is a measure of its effectiveness.[81]

Philleo Nash then argued in his presentation that, in spite of Deloria's claim that anthropologists had negatively influenced federal Indian policy, there was in fact no credible evidence of this occurring during John Collier's tenure as commissioner of Indian affairs.[82] Omer C. Stewart then defended the anthropologist as expert witness and as Indian ally in his paper on peyote and the Native American Church, in which the legendary work of James Mooney was highlighted. Stewart also pointed out anthropological work that he thought was very helpful to tribes in their cases before the Indian Claims Commission, albeit tepidly. As Stewart admitted: "Although anthropologists did not participate in the hearings preceding the passage of the Indian Claims Commission Act of 1946, their services have been important in the hearings since January 1952."[83]

As for the relationship between anthropologists and the Indians with whom they collaborated, Margaret Mead, the most distinguished scholar present, was emphatic about the respect that she and her colleagues had shown Indian community members. More specifically, even though Mead confessed that she had very little experience working with American Indians, she could nevertheless speak knowledgably about the community of

"Americanists," in which she developed her skills as a social scientist. More specifically, Mead described herself as "a student of Franz Boas and Pliny Earle Goddard," in addition to having "worked with Clark Wissler and Ruth Benedict and Ruth Bunzel." Mead then proceeded to share various anecdotes purporting to emphasize the humane treatment that anthropologists had shown Indian communities, from Boas referring to the Kwakiutl as "my dear friends" to her confrontation with the National Institute of Mental Health on behalf of the American Museum of Natural History, in which she asserted that they "had no *subjects*" in the human testing sense of the term because they, the social scientists at the museum, "do not treat human beings as subjects; we treat them as informants, which means colleagues and collaborators, and we work with their understanding and permission."[84] In the spirit of collegiality, Mead even took up the habit of referring to these colleagues as "Indian intellectuals," which remained her preferred epithet for the remainder of her presentation.

Before Deloria stepped up to the lectern to share his feedback on these vigorous defenses of the social sciences, two American Indian anthropologists, Bea Medicine and Alfonso Ortiz, made their presentations. In the case of Medicine, she focused her analysis on the emergence of "Native American Studies Programs" at major universities, which were serving a student population that, as of 1970, was actively examining and questioning the college experience. While Native American studies, along with ethnic studies and Third World studies, harbingered great changes in the academic community, the role of anthropology, as a product of the colonial past, remained in doubt. "A workable approach to Native American Studies," Medicine averred with a nod to Deloria, "is effective only in an intellectual milieu which views North American Indian cultures as dynamic, pluralistic and enduring."[85] Lastly, Ortiz admitted in his presentation that he "initially went into anthropology because it was the one field in which [he] could read about and deal with Indians all of the time and still make a living."[86] At the same time, Ortiz recounted the multiple instances in which he encountered the presumptuousness of white researchers, as well as their cultural naïveté. For Ortiz, consequently, the issues that he had seen in the anthropological profession created a crisis of faith:

Anthropology is a science born of imperialistic and colonial powers and that, at best, all too many of its practitioners still approach their tribal and peasant subjects with a neo-colonialist attitude. Those of us who do not come from the kind of cultural background which fosters this attitude can reject categorically in our own work the neo-colonialist underpinnings and trappings, but we are still too few to reorient the whole field. This is truly a festering sore, and it will not just go away of its own accord.[87]

When Deloria at last presented his comments, he did not, as one might expect, hold anything back—let alone temper his criticism of anthropology. In particular, the merits of Mooney's advocacy of the Native American Church notwithstanding, anthropology had done a very poor job at supporting tribes in their ongoing disputes with the federal government. As Deloria asked rhetorically, "During the termination period, if we were really intellectual colleagues and compadres, I say *where* were you *when*?" [emphasis in original]. [88] Instead of assisting tribes in their struggle against what was the most serious assault against their rights as sovereign nations since the 1830 Indian Removal Act, anthropologists were more concerned with protecting their status as "experts" on Indian cultures. Needless to say, the panel discussions were quite lively, however they were too varied and numerous to summarize here. In sum, the symposium did much to bring the American Indian appraisal of anthropological research into perspective, along with demonstrating that Deloria's chapter on anthropology in *Custer* created a shockwave that was felt for decades to come.[89]

In the end, it did not matter if one can successfully argue that not all anthropologists were like the ones singled out for criticism in *Custer*. It was not enough to redeem a profession whose existence thrived on the scholarly exploitation of Indians by making excuses about tenure and promotion. As the political awareness of tribes continued to grow, Deloria advised anthropologists "to get down from their thrones of authority and PURE research and begin helping Indian tribes instead of preying on them. For the wheel of Karma grinds slowly but it does grind finely. And it makes a complete circle."[90]

CHAPTER 7

"Merciless Indian Savages"

Christianity, Churches, and the Soul of the Indian

In his *Philosophical Dictionary*, Voltaire said of "The Ecclesiastical Ministry," which was a reference to the Catholic Church as a political institution
in France: "The institution of religion exists only to keep mankind in
order, and to make men merit the goodness of God by their virtue.
Everything in a religion which does not tend toward this goal must be
considered alien or dangerous."[1] While Voltaire, for personal and practical
reasons, never openly declared himself an atheist, he was nonetheless
infamous for his satirical musings on the inherent flaws of otherwise
lofty institutions—above all, the Church and the hypocritical tendencies
of priest, bishops, and even monarchs—that purported to embody and
defend the virtues of the state. As the reader may recall from chapter
1 of the present volume, Stan Steiner, in *The New Indians*, referred to
Deloria as "the Rousseau" of his generation. Such a sobriquet was valid
to the extent that one was talking about Deloria as a source of political
liberation from an oppressive system such as the federal government's
termination policy that was imposed upon Indian lives. However, when
one took Deloria's sarcastic wit and scandalous insights into the mach-
inations of government and the white men who served in Congress and
the Bureau of Indian Affairs—along with a host of other targets of his
rhetoric—into consideration, then it was also valid to call Deloria the
Voltaire of the Indian protest movement.

In his 1969 afterword to *Custer* Deloria explained his decision to ultimately forsake the life of the clergy, a decision that was based as much, if
not more, on his family experience than on his philosophical differences
with the Christian tradition.

I often considered the ministry when I was younger. But as I watched
the frustrations of my father [an Episcopal missionary and, later,
archdeacon] within the Episcopal Church I decided that church life
was totally irrelevant to Indian needs. Time after time my father would
advance a plan by which the church could be made stronger in South
Dakota. Each time, white church administrators vetoed the plan, primarily because it was a plan that had been advanced by an Indian.[2]

Then, in his 1972 essay, "It Is a Good Day to Die," Deloria further accounted
for why he left his seminary training unsatisfied with the Christian worldview. At the root of Deloria's discontent was the realization that Christian
beliefs about the world, God, and man were disconnected from the actual
lives in which Christian followers lived, which was more nuanced than
the credos he was learning as a novice minister, something he regarded
eventually as less of a calling and more of a "vocation." Equally troubling was his recognition that the vocation of the priesthood was not
only separated from the "brutal problems" of ordinary people, but it
was also a class apart from those to whom it was supposed to minister:

The posture of the seminary as repository of ancient and self-evident
truths only increases one's sense of belonging to an elite which has
been mysteriously ordained to promulgate the ground rules of the
game of life, occasionally calling the fouls, but generally winking
at minor transgressions confident that they are being recorded up
above anyway.[3]

As an institution, the church was to maintain a kind of spiritual status
quo, reaffirming its truths without ever questioning or exploring the relationship between its concepts and the lives of the people who accepted
its tenets as their faith. As for the "pastor, priest, or minister," he "reveals
himself as a fund-raising agent of the establishment and not a prophetic
figure of the ages." Whether or not Deloria's seminary training included

any regard for the American Indian congregants with whom he would have worked like his father and grandfather before him, he did not say. In all likelihood, such cultural diversity was utterly absent from the 1950s curriculum. Nonetheless, Deloria recalled his seminary experience in positive terms, far from the caustic critique he would soon subject the Christian tradition to in his writings: "My years at Augustana were very happy. The Lutherans welcomed me with great warmth. I was allowed to take any courses I wanted in any sequence I wanted . . . soaking up whatever theological doctrines caught my fancy."[4] As for how Deloria felt about the legal tradition, another pillar of western civilization, in light of his seminary experience:

> Having entered seminary thinking that religion was real and discovering upon graduation that it had little or nothing to do with life in the manner in which life presented itself, I rather naively entered law school determined to find a constant from which new vistas of humanity could be constructed.[5]

Deloria, of course, as mentioned before, went into law school because of what he observed during his three years as NCAI executive director, which was the overarching role that the law, especially Indian law, played in shaping the issues that tribes faced in their often-contentious relationship with the federal government. In light of which, Deloria went to law school with the same intention that he went into seminary, which was to make a difference in the communities that depended upon these institutions for giving their struggles meaning, along with the possibility of a redress. As for how law school compared to seminary, Deloria stated: "Graduation from law school returned the same message as had graduation from seminary. Law was even less related to life than theology."[6] It was nonetheless out of these parallel experiences, seminary and law school, that Deloria embarked on his critique of religion and its nefarious relationship with the state.

Because of the extent to which *Custer's* chapter on "Anthropologists and Other Friends" overshadowed much of the rest of *Custer*, Deloria's comments about Christian missionaries has not received nearly as much attention in spite of the fact that Christians were frequently no happier about their treatment in Deloria's critique than were anthropologists. As for the references to the Christian impact in American Indian history, one typically turns to *God Is Red* more so than *Custer*. Consider the work of Robert Warrior, Jace Weaver, and James Treat referenced in chapter 1 for examples. With respect, though, to the argument initiated in *Custer*, "Missionaries and the Religious Vacuum" was essential to tribes reexamining "themselves in an effort to redefine a new social structure for their people." In many ways, the imposition of missionaries onto tribal communities—which became federal policy during the 1870s—was even more reprehensible than the invasion of anthropologists. Whereas anthropology presumed to colonize the scholarly discourse on Indian cultures and histories, missionaries, as representatives of the Christian religion (in its various denominations), sought to dominate Indians' spiritual lives both as an outwardly visible institution on the reservation (churches, camp meetings, ministers and priests), and as an interior perception of themselves as sinful and in need of salvation. According to many oral traditions, Indians did not even know about sin and the Devil until they were introduced by European settlers.

As was commonplace in Deloria's analyses, he moved quickly in *Custer* from examples of Indian humor regarding the historic arrival of Christianity in Indian communities to claiming that the spread of Christianity across North America went hand in hand with the appropriation of Indian land. He then segued into the fundamental differences between Christianity and the Indian Way, a discourse that he expanded in *God Is Red*. As usual, Deloria's exegesis was short on details (there was scarcely even a hint of source material) and long on rhetoric ("Missionaries and the Religious Vacuum" was basically an opprobrium rejecting Christianity). Nevertheless, the objective of Deloria's approach was to express the generations of frustration, fear, and hope that tribes had felt as they were pressured into adopting the colonizer's new religion. Indeed, Indians were compelled to confront a bevy of religious concepts that were often antithetical to the premises on which Indigenous beliefs and customs were maintained, beginning with the assumption that any religion could be universal, as opposed to unique gifts from the Creator to particular peoples. Or that one can convert as a discreet religious experience into the religion of another, rather than being born and raised into the ways of one's relatives. Or that arguing about "God" was as important as defending one's hunting grounds. Or that there was a place of "eternal damnation," which was radically different from the land of the dead, where one's ancestors dwelled.

Similar to *Custer*'s treatment of anthropology, what began as a recounting of historic wrongs became a set of proposed reforms of and suggested rebellions against the religious status quo. More to the point, the purpose of Deloria's critique of Christian missionaries was to criticize the limitations of the Western concept of religion with respect to the First Amendment and its inability to accommodate the religious rights of groups that did not fit the Judeo-Christian text-based—not to mention church- and temple-based—form of worship. Creed and action, doctrine and custom, Chosen People and Indigenous People were some of the antinomies that Deloria raised in order to make the point that Christianity and the Indian Way were substantially different, and that when Christianity, in complicity with the federal government, repressed tribal traditions, it shattered the foundations of a people's collective sense of self. In order for tribes to reconstruct their pre-Christian sense of peoplehood, they needed, among other things, access to and respect for sacred places, including the right to worship in their customary ways, which may have required, for example, exemption from wildlife and environmental laws.[7] Certainly, the struggle for religious freedom that the Native American Church pursued throughout most of the twentieth century included seeking exemptions from federal drug laws, which erroneously listed peyote as a narcotic.

Speaking of the environment, "Most mysterious," as Deloria explained the ineffable powers that many tribes worshipped ceremonially, "was the Indian reverence for the land. When told to settle down and become farmers, most Indians rebelled. For centuries they had lived off the land as hunters, taking and giving in their dances and ceremonies."[8] In Deloria's haste to denounce a federal policy that demanded—most explicitly in the 1887 General Allotment Act—that tribes give up their old ways for the ways of the yeoman Christian farmer, he engaged in one of the Plains-centric arguments of which Alfonso Ortiz took issue with in his review.

Referring his reader to the Crow Nation custom of regarding the land they were given, according to their Creation Story, as being "just right," Deloria ignored the fact that many tribes maintained agrarian cultures, such as the Gila and Salt River Pima and the Puebloan groups, including Hopi. In fact, across North America, many tribes developed agricultural and horticultural traditions, which was not to imply that agricultural tribes had it easier than their nonagrarian cousins. Nevertheless, Deloria should have considered diversifying his examples, by which he could have made the case that the federal government was guilty of environmental authoritarianism, as it wanted the land managed according to its laws and values, regardless of a given tribe's land traditions. As it was, Deloria, recalled the personal experience of having "watched Indian people look sadly over the miles of plowed ground of South Dakota, wishing that the land was returned to its primitive beauty, undefiled and giving to man and animal alike the life only land can give."[9] Meanwhile, down in Arizona, there were generations of Pima (Akimel O'odham) who looked at a dried-up Gila River, who also bemoaned what the Americans did to the land—and their Indigenous agrarian way of life.

As for the conflict of worldviews that erupted when whites invaded Indian lands in the name of their God and religion, Deloria described this as the difference between a time-based religion (Christianity) and their space-oriented converse (tribal customs and beliefs). In the central chapters of *God Is Red*, Deloria embarked on a theological and historical analysis of the Christian linear concept of Biblical history, its consequent detachment from place, and the havoc it wreaked on Indian lives as this religious concept intersected with the colonial ambitions of European and American settler nations. Aware of the global implications of his thesis, Deloria portrayed his work in a 1975 letter to Hank Adams, two years after the publication of *God Is Red*, as "going far afield with theology." More specifically, Deloria described the work he was doing that summer as "a planetary theology."[10] Indeed, one might interpret this as a reference to the application of Immanuel Velikovsky's thesis in *Worlds in Collision* that appeared in *God Is Red*, which would appear again in *The Metaphysics of Modern Existence* (1979), then more dramatically influence *Red Earth, White Lies* (1995). Picking up, then, where he left off in *Custer*, Deloria examined in *God Is Red* the implications of Christianity's time-based worldview, which was devoted to the biblical narrative going from Genesis to Revelations, in which God purportedly worked through historical events. The linear progression, moreover, from Creation to Revelations informed the western notion of destiny that, in time, justified the exploitation and colonization of the Western Hemisphere. As Robert Warrior condensed Deloria's critique of Christianity's time-based worldview:

> The basic problem with Christianity for Deloria, then, is its subsuming of place by a time-centered theology. In this it completed the movement away from what remained of space-centered theology in post-Exilic Judaism. Following the apocalyptic trends of their time, the followers of Jesus after his death developed a theology that "looks toward a spectacular end of the world as a time of judgment and thus an end of history." Rather than a god who acts in history with a specific group of people in a specific place, Christianity became one universal version of what had been at one time a religion tied to Palestine—its people and places.[11]

From the papal bulls establishing the Doctrine of Discovery, which was reinforced by the 1494 Treaty of Tordesillas, dividing the known world between Spain and Portugal, to the nineteenth-century American concept of Manifest Destiny that inspired droves of pioneers to settle on cheaply acquired homesteads, Europeans and their American descendants repeatedly claimed to see "the hand of God" in the forced occupation of Indian lands. However, from the vantage point of the early 1970s, in which the old colonial order was tearing at the seams, as so-called Third World nations successfully cast off their colonial shells, including Southeast Asia where American foreign policy ran into formidable opposition from the Viet Cong, it appeared to be apropos that one reexamined the tenets of the West's ethnocentric concept of linear time, not to mention its Christian master narrative. For in spite of what social scientists and philosophers of a by-gone age had argued, the world's nations and peoples were, in fact, not on the same uniform path from savagery to civilization in which "civilization" was unequivocally white and Euro-American. On the contrary, as Deloria observed, the world "is not a global village so much as a series of non-homogeneous pockets of identity." Moreover, these pockets of identity often sprouted "religious movements" that appeared to be "out-of-time" with respect to the Western calendar.[12] More important, these religious movements, such as those that occurred among American Indians in the aftermath of World War II and federal termination policy, entailed the reaffirmation of space, which was to say homeland.

As an example of the out-of-time phenomenon that motivated the Indian protest movement, Deloria recalled in *Broken Treaties* how the decision to organize the Trail of Broken Treaties caravan occurred during Sun Dance, which was part of the cultural revitalization that was happening at reservations around the country.[13] The revitalization was possible, as may be recalled, because of the 1934 Indian Reorganization Act. Furthermore, when space as a concrete location was reintroduced into how one of these nonhomogeneous pockets of identity, say at Rosebud Indian Reservation, conceived of itself, it disclosed the intrinsic limitations of a time-based concept of time's ability to explain events in incongruent locations in which these locations were also home to disparate (largely non-Christian) cultures. Whereas a tribal Creation Story explained a given people's relationship with a given place, complete with an account of how their ancestors were made and how they found their homeland, the Christian doctrines of sin and redemption only served to define people as fallen with respect to the Christ ideal. In which case, the Bible was reduced to a series of parables that illustrated a particular church's credo but did little to explain the nature of the world beyond how people had strayed from the moral dictates of their faith. As such, the Christian timeline, as defined by the books of the Bible, not only distanced itself from place, including the Holy Land, but also from history. In other words, insofar as history was a people's account of its origins in time and the succession of persons and events that had formed its identity, then the nations in which Christianity had spread, above all the Americas, were disconnected from the Christian narratives. As a result, one was not Christian because one was descended from the personages named in the Bible's two testaments, but because one had *converted* to Christianity, renouncing in turn whatever one was before, be it Indian, sinner, or heathen. As Deloria noted with regard to the Bible as a source of dogmatic tales: "Perhaps the best that can be said is that temporal theologians place great reliance upon the poetic imagination as the source of religious symbolism."[14] This was as opposed to oral traditions as narratives of a people's collective experience, complete with knowledge about the world in which these people actually dwelled—not a far-off kingdom seen only on a map or recounted in scripture.[15]

What emerged as a text-based religion spread beyond its original boundaries was that its followers tended to maintain a contradictory pair of assumptions about the veracity of its sacred stories, namely historical truth and metaphorical truth. More specifically, as Deloria observed in *God Is Red* in "The Concept of History": "The events of the Old Testament were seen as actual events of history in which a divine purpose was gradually unfolding." The assumption that the Old Testament was a, albeit divinely inspired, historical record was asserted to the exclusion of all other spiritual traditions, be they non-Western written traditions like the Rigveda or oral traditions like tribal Creation Stories, which were at best regarded as naïve tales and at worst heresies. In the case of "The Problem of Creation," the story told in the Book of Genesis was thereby accorded the status of historical truth, specifically miraculous events that happened at a particular point in time and which transpired in seven extraordinary days. In light of which, Genesis, complete with its story of Eden, Adam and Eve, the Serpent, and God's subsequent curse on man and woman, formed the basis of the Christian timeline in which God's "plan" was unfolding. Integral to this plan was the sinfulness of humans, which was instigated by a non-human creature, the Serpent, who dwelled in the untended wildness of Eden. Man's destiny, then, upon being cast out of Eden, was to toil, establishing dominion over the earth (including womankind), and atoning for his sins. The New Testament, of course, provided a path to salvation through Christ, the New Adam, who showed people how to free themselves from their post-Edenic burden. Christians, in turn, were charged with spreading "the Good News" to all nations. With respect, then, to the relation between Genesis and

Jesus and how much the story of Christ depended on the legitimacy of the Christian creation story:

> We have no need to question the historical existence of Jesus of Nazareth. . . . But we cannot project from the historical reality of Jesus as a man existing in Palestine during the time of Augustus and his successors to the historical existence of a man called Adam in a garden someplace in Asia Minor. Yet without the historical fact of the existence of Adam, we are powerless to explain the death of Jesus as a religious event of cosmic significance.[16]

Throughout *God Is Red*, in particular the chapters on space and time, creation, and history, Deloria interjected the varied ways in which tribal traditions regarded creation. Because they were oriented toward a given place, as opposed to an abstract concept of linear time, tribes maintained beliefs about humans, animals, spirits, and places that were in opposition with the Christian tradition. More specifically, the nonlinear tribal way of thinking about place, as the fundamental concept of one's relationship to Creation, was that one's relationship with that place became integral to understanding one's role in the scheme of Creation. For example, Creation Stories commonly evoked landmarks, such as mountains, rivers, and lakes, which defined, not only the traditional boundaries of a given tribe's homeland, but also where certain sacred beings lived, where extraordinary events happened (as recounted in oral tradition), where medicine can be gathered, and where one may commune with the spirits who live in these places. Consequently, a tribe maintained a respect relation with the sacred places around them, which included the animals and other natural phenomena, the customs of which were taught in the Creation Story and were continuously handed down through the generations. In a word, kinship became the guiding value—as opposed to a doctrine or credo—that shaped one's relation to the spaces of one's homeland. With these values in mind, Deloria observed: "The Indian is confronted with a bountiful earth in which all things experienced have a role to fill. The task of the tribal religion, if such a religion can be said to have a task, is to determine the proper relationship that the people of the tribe must have with other living things."[17] Thus, unlike Christianity, which saw the world around it as corrupt and in a constant state of decay, tribal spiritual customs saw the world as buoyant with life and overflowing with a steady cycle of birth and rejuvenation—the earth was a gift of plenty.

As for the missionary presence in tribal communities, Deloria added in *Custer* to the list of grievances regarding Christianity's relation to the Indian Way. First, there was how the Reformation created the distinction between church and state, consequently opening a moral divide between the two spheres of power, such that the ethics governing one (church) did not necessarily apply to the other (state). Moreover, within this binary scheme the state was beholden only to the laws of men (deliberately gender biased), such that the justification for the state's actions only required the legalizing power of the state's law givers. No higher appeal was necessary. On this premise, church leaders regularly endorsed state actions that were otherwise anathema to the credos of the churches. As an example, Deloria pointed to Cardinal Francis Spellman, who endorsed America's war in Vietnam, which was another instance of church leaders historically validating such morally questionable practices as "slavery, poverty, and treachery."[18] As long as churches maintained their power over people's lives—and their religion spread—there was always a biblical verse that justified the means used to achieve the desired end. Consequently, American church and state rolled over Indian Country, complicit in their desire to colonize Indian lands and peoples, yet traveling in separate ethical realms. As settlers and soldiers devastated successively wider regions, missionaries appeared in the upheaval seeking to save the victims and refugees of westward expansion. All the tribes wanted was to be left alone to maintain their ways, keeping the balance between themselves and their homelands:

> When the two religious movements came into conflict, the Christian religion was able to overcome tribal beliefs because of its ability to differentiate life into segments which were unrelated. When a world view is broken into its component disciplines, these disciplines become things unto themselves and life turns into an unrelated group of categories each with its own morality and ethics.[19]

There should be no mistake, then, as Deloria emphasized, the objective of missionaries, regardless of denomination, was to completely replace Indian traditions with "Christian values." Toward that end, missionaries consistently disparaged Indian beliefs and customs, especially those associated with medicine men, whose effectiveness as healers were dismissed as "works of the devil."[20] For example, the missionary who served the Gila River Pima–Maricopa Community, Charles Cook, not only demonized the work of the ma:kai, or medicine man, as "sorcery," but also blamed them for all the unrest in the region:

> There is but little doubt that if all the facts could be known, many of the murders of whites by the Apaches, and other tribes and wars and depredations in this territory, could be traced to the instigation of these medicine men. They are one of the most dangerous elements with which government, especially the Indian department, has to contend. They are ambitious, artful, and unscrupulous, and in this vicinity have done more to destroy the efforts of Indian agents to improve the condition of the Indian, both in school-work and their moral elevation, than all other undermining and checking influences combined. [21]

What mattered more than medicine was memorizing creeds such that salvation "became a matter of regurgitation." Armed with the trappings of modern Western civilization, from whisky to wagon wheels, missionaries descended upon tribes, weaning them from their former lives and, of course, from their land. Basically, the material goods were "bribes" for accepting the Christian religion. The Indian Way, in its various incarnations across a plethora of tribes, was not without a profound response to this religious onslaught. Sitting Bull, Tenskwatewa, Handsome Lake, and Wovoka, among others, emerged during times of great crisis, only to see their resistance movements die out. Yet, while they lasted they gave expression to the peoples' deep desire to restore the relationships between places and peoples that they once knew before the white man arrived. "When these great leaders died," as Deloria underscored the current state of affairs, "Indian religion went underground and became, like its white competitor, unrelated to the social and political life of the tribe."[22]

As recounted elsewhere, Deloria regarded the struggle embodied by the Indian protest movement and its assertion of Indigenous political and cultural rights as ultimately a religious struggle against the authoritarianism of Christian-influenced federal Indian policy, which was a colonial tradition going back before the founding of the American republic. In his 1972 missive to church leaders, titled "An Open Letter to the Heads of the Christian Churches in America," Deloria recounted the dogmatic set of beliefs that undergirded the twisted justification for the unlawful occupation of Indian lands called the Doctrine of Discovery. However, while Deloria later explained the Doctrine of Discovery in *Behind the Trail of Broken Treaties* as the product of papal bulls and Anglo-Saxon law, in the case of his letter to church leaders, the focus was more on doctrine as a set of beliefs, as opposed to policy. In which case, Deloria reminded his Christian audience that the principles used to sanction the colonization of the Western Hemisphere were supposedly based on the Christian beliefs about spreading the gospel to the heathenish peoples of the New World. Furthermore, insofar as the Doctrine of Discovery was still the law of the land, which was presumably upheld in case law and statutes, because of Congress's unwillingness to uphold its treaty and trust obligations, Deloria argued: "We have been placed beyond the remedies of the Constitution of the United States because of the Doctrine of Discovery has never been disclaimed either by the governments of the Christian nations of the world or by the leaders of the Christian churches of the world."[23] Consequently, Indigenous peoples were precluded from establishing a place in America's tradition of religious freedom, not to mention occluded from reconnecting to their sacred places. For tribal religions have been pushed aside by westward expansion and the spread of Christianity across the American continent, which relegated tribes to the past, where the so-called primitive ways of Indians must surrender to the alleged inevitability of progress and Christian civilization. At the same time, modern American civilization has long been criticized by Christian and Indian alike as having strayed from the Christian values it claimed for itself, often spreading as much misery, if not more, as it did opportunity. In this context, Indian suffering had less to do with whether or not they had accepted Jesus and more to do with the gross violations of its promises to Indian friends and allies who accepted the friendship and protection of the United States.

> If we have political institutions that do not serve us today it is because our religious institutions have not called those governments and the people who run them to a greater vision of humanity. Justice has become merely justification of man's condition and not a call for the integrity resulting from credibility or the expansion of man's vision of himself. . . . At what point can we as peoples of the creation look to Christianity to demand from the political structures of the world our dignity as human beings? At what point can we become men and not mere appendages of the Christian Doctrine of Discovery?[24]

With regard to a supposedly Christian civilization that would compensate tribes for their enormous losses, Deloria referred to the post–Civil War period when President Ulysses Grant inaugurated his 1869 Peace Policy, only a few months after winning the 1868 presidential election against Democratic candidate Horatio Seymour. The Peace Policy, in turn, was intended as an antidote to the corruption that had led to conflicts like the 1862 United States–Dakota War, which was the consequence of Indian agent corruption and the inhumane treatment of the Indian community whose welfare was put at serious risk. It is also worth noting that the 1864 Sand Creek Massacre and the Navajo Long Walk occurred during this epoch. Essential to Grant's policy initiative was the authorization of the Board of Indian Commissioners. Serving without remuneration, the board consisted of "ten persons, to be selected by him [the president] from men eminent for their intelligence and philanthropy," who assisted the secretary of the interior, Jacob D. Cox, who was succeeded by Columbus Delano, in carrying out the president's Indian policy. According to the authorization dated April 10, 1869, the policy from hereon was to "maintain the peace among and with the various tribes, bands, and parties of Indians, and to promote civilization among said Indians, bring them, where practicable, upon reservations, relieve their necessities, and encourage their efforts at self-support."[25] What Deloria did not acknowledge with respect to the implementation of this policy was that one of its proponents was Ely S. Parker, the first

American Indian appointed as commissioner of Indian affairs. Parker, a member of the Seneca Nation, had distinguished himself in the Union Army during the Civil War, in addition to being a critical resource for Lewis Henry Morgan's book on the Haudenosaunee. However, as the reader may recall, Parker forever left his mark on the history of federal Indian policy when he played a pivotal role in the unilateral end of treaty making in 1871.

As Deloria began his appraisal of contemporary Indian-Christian relations, it was clearly informed by this troubling history. First, as to the allocation of reservations to their sectarian overseers: "It always bothered me that these churches who would not share pulpits and regarded each other as children of the devil, should have so cold-bloodedly divided up the tribes as if they were choosing sides for touch football."[26] Second, the hagiographic accounts that missionaries relayed to their congregations and hierarchies about their successes in the name of Jesus prompted this reaction:

> It always amuses me to hear some white missionary glamorize the reception of Christianity by the Plains tribes. He will tell how "two or three were gathered together and gladly heard the word of God preached." The simple fact is that had the two or three not been talking about the white god they probably would have been shot down for fomenting an uprising.[27]

As for the atrocities committed against Indians in the name of Christ, Deloria argued in *God Is Red* that colonization and exploitation worked hand in hand, as settler nations sought validation for their conquests, while churches took advantage to gain new converts. In "The Aboriginal World and Christian History," Deloria explained Christian culpability for the occupation of Indian lands and the subsequent crimes against humanity that took place under the guise of (state-supported) religion. More specifically, Deloria recounted the early colonial religious and legal developments that formed the basis of the Doctrine of Discovery, which, as acknowledged above, was also recounted in his 1972 "Open Letter," and again in *Broken Treaties*, beginning with Pope Alexander VI's *Inter Caetera* bull, "which laid down the basic Christian attitude toward the New World," in which the "'barbarous nations be overthrown and brought to the faith itself.'"[28] From this inaugural proclamation arose three significant developments: the 1494 Treaty of Tordesillas, the debate between Las Casas and Sepulveda over Indian enslavement, and the "wars for control of the North American continent."[29] Indeed, by the time the United States stipulated the 1787 Northwest Ordinance, which was its "first articulation of the Christian attitude toward the native peoples and their rights," the cycle of discoveries, conquests, and colonization had been going on for centuries. Yet, it was far from over. In fact, America's war against "godless nations" continued well into the twentieth century, not to mention around the world, most recently in Vietnam. Reflecting on the depth of the devastation generated from when the first explorers claimed Indian land in the name of their religion, Deloria wrote:

> The responsibility of Christianity for this state of affairs must certainly be heavy. Without the initial Christian doctrines giving Europeans free reign over the rest of the world, much of the exploitation would not have occurred. It was only when people were able to combine Western greed with religious fanaticism that the type and extent of exploitation that history has recorded was made possible.[30]

Ultimately, Deloria was trying to impress upon his reader that the dominant presence that Christianity enjoyed in the 1960s and early 1970s reservation communities was largely the product of missionaries taking advantage of federal government coercion of Indians to accept the customs and values of American society. As brought up above, Indian spiritual customs were criminalized in the 1883 Court of Indian Offenses, which was authorized less than a week after General Sherman had declared an end to the Indian problem as a military concern. Under the auspice of Secretary of Interior Henry M. Teller, the Indian Bureau was directed to organize the suppression of Indian customs deemed detrimental to Indian progress. Quoting a letter, dated December 2, 1882, that Teller wrote to the commissioner of Indian affairs, Hiram Price, he stated:

> I desire to call your attention to what I regard as a great hindrance to the civilization of the Indians, viz the continuance of the old heathenish

dances, such as the sun-dance, scalp dance, &c. These dances, or feasts, as they are sometimes called, ought, in my judgment, to be discontinued, *and if the Indians now supported by the Government are not willing to discontinue them, the agents should be instructed to compel such discontinuance* [emphasis added].[31]

What was not apparent from Teller's missive was the fact that he was a strong opponent to the allotment policy that was gaining momentum as the next great development in Indian affairs. Teller, to his credit, recognized that the 1887 General Allotment Act was nothing more than an illicit land grab. In fact, Deloria emphatically acknowledged Teller's political courage in *Of Utmost Good Faith*, in which an 1881 speech from the then Colorado senator was included in a very short section titled "White Defenders of Indian Rights." Teller was elected to the Senate just prior to his appointment as secretary of Indian affairs. In Deloria's estimation, Teller put his political career, not to mention his safety, at risk when he condemned land allotment while representing a state that was as virulently racist against Indians as his. Not long before Teller's speech, Coloradans celebrated the Sand Creek Massacre in the streets of Denver, in light of which Deloria stated: "Teller had everything to lose by even acknowledging that Indians had any rights whatsoever." Nevertheless, "Teller ended his speech with a prophecy that Indians would curse the day when people wanted them to allot their lands." In contradistinction to the legion of hypocritical ministers preaching the virtues of the yeoman Christian farmer only to stand idly by as tribe after tribe was robbed blind of its lands, "Senator Teller of Colorado should receive his just due as a true friend of Indian people."[32]

In spite of the ostensible effort at treating Indians more humanely by shepherding tribes into civilization via allotment, however patronizing this attitude seems today, there was a growing undercurrent of hostility toward the Indian Way—it was dangerous. Only America's hatred of immigrants competed with the hostility that tribes faced during the latter nineteenth century. Not long after *Ex Parte Crow Dog* (1883) and the Major Crimes Act (1885), the Ghost Dance emerged, which was a nativist response to the oppressive conditions that were prevalent throughout the reservation system. Tribes from the Sierra Nevada to the Northern Plains took up the message and dance given to them by Wovoka, whose teachings portended the return of long-lost ancestors, the rejuvenation of tribal values, and clearing the land of white settlers. It was a peaceful movement, but the Indian Bureau running the reservations and the U.S. Army charged with keeping the peace on the frontier became increasingly anxious about its possible ramifications for their control, particularly when the Ghost Dance reached South Dakota. Many Americans, nearly a century later, however, who were becoming politically aware during the 1960s and 1970s did not learn what happened to the unarmed Indians rounded up by federal troops at Wounded Knee—an historical precursor to the 1968 My Lai Massacre—until Dee Brown published *Bury My Heart at Wounded Knee* (1971). Nevertheless, Deloria referred to America's genocidal actions on December 29, 1890 as an example of the ideological extremism to which the United States was willing to go in order to enforce its Indian policy. "Soon [after Wounded Knee]," Deloria wrote, "the only social activity permitted on reservations was the church service. Signs of any other activity would call for a cavalry troop storming in to rescue civilization from some non-existent threat."[33] For Deloria, the Wounded Knee Massacre was more than a date in a history, it was both community memory and family history.

> The most memorable event of my early childhood was visiting Wounded Knee where 200 Sioux, including women and children, were slaughtered in 1890 by troopers of the Seventh Cavalry in what is believed to have been a delayed act of vengeance for Custer's defeat. . . . The massacre was vividly etched in the minds of many of the older reservation people, but it was difficult to find anyone who wanted to talk about it.
>
> Many times, over the years, my father would point out survivors of the massacre, and people on the reservation always went out of their way to help them.[34]

With this historic tragedy in mind, Deloria wrote passionately in the days after the Second Wounded Knee in 1973 about the religious dimension of the Indian protest movement, including the Americans' broken covenant, the 1868 Fort Laramie Treaty, which underlay the conflict between the American Indian Movement and federal troops. Indeed, in his editorial for the *Los Angeles Times*, Deloria observed: "The specter of the original Wounded Knee Massacre of 350 Sioux Indians by US soldiers has hovered over the proceedings of the past month, filling the air with a terrible dread."[35] In another 1973 essay titled "The Theological Dimension of the Indian Protest Movement," Deloria argued that what was needed was a "truly native ideology—that is, the tribal ideology of the American Indian." In other words, the wave of the future, as Deloria saw it, would be tribalism. Insofar, then, as the Indian protest movement was part of the power movements that defined the 1960s and early 1970s, Red Power distinguished itself by exceeding the limitations of the civil rights movement's capacity to effect positive change based on all power movements' common interest in poverty, at least in those defined by ethnicity. As Deloria saw it, power movements were the political awakening of whole groups, such as tribes, which wanted their rights recognized, as opposed to individuals seeking admission into the privileged white middle class. For better and for worse, most Americans, including church and political leaders, could not see these movements for the paradigm shift that they embodied. Consequently, one of the shortcomings of the Indian protest movement was its inability to express its message of treaty rights, tribal rights, and land rights in a way that Americans could comprehend beyond the occupations and confrontations they were seeing in the mass media of the time. On the contrary, most Americans only saw angry Indians and not the law- and treaty-based reasons for why they were angry: "In their own minds, the Indians' escalation of their demands and the increasing violence of their protest recalled the days of Indian glory. To the white society, the protest was novel because of its intensity."[36] The Indians, of course, were looking for much more than novelty; they, on the contrary, wanted their nationhood recognized as documented in their treaties and being equal partners in the community of nations. Furthermore, tribes were not declaring their independence from the United States so much as they were reminding the United States that tribes were independent in the first place. As further explained in *Broken Treaties*:

Fundamentally, the Wounded Knee issue was a moral one involving the Fort Laramie Treaty of 1868, which forbids the taking of any Sioux land without the approval of three-fourths of the adult males of the tribe concerned. In effect the Indians were asking the United States why it refused to live up to its own laws. A hard question which allowed no quibbling. When it signed the treaty, the United States surely anticipated that whites would want the Black Hills some day [sic]. Therefore it could not pretend that events had now created a situation so desperate as to require overriding the promises made in the treaty. To have given an adequate answer at Wounded Knee, the federal government would have had to admit that it is and always has been made up of pathological liars. But by definition whites and Christians, the civilized peoples of the world, do not lie.[37]

The objective of Deloria's deliberately anti-Christian account of missionary history in Indian Country was to explain the extent to which reservation conditions, as of the Indian protest movement that was grabbing headlines, still bore the traces of these historic events. Invariably, though, explaining Indian history and life on the reservation was a never-ending process. As an example, Deloria recalled when, in 1964, "church officials from the East came out to reservations to bring the new message and to get Indians involved in the [Civil Rights] struggle." A particular, however unnamed, visitor from New York was regaled with a variety of standard hymns while on a South Dakota reservation, sung in the Dakota language. In reaction to what was basically an exhibition of Dakota Christian culture, which had persisted unchanged since the 1870s, the visiting New Yorker expressed outrage that the Dakota brethren were completely unaware of the civil strife surrounding them, from Mississippi to Los Angeles. Rather than feeling chagrined, though, the Dakota expressed disappointment with their detractor. The story paralleled another, first told by Charles Eastman in *The Soul of the Indian* (1911), then recounted in *God Is Red*, about a priest, a black robe, who visited the Dakota, where he shared his religion's beliefs about how the world and humans were created, including the story of Adam and Eve. The Dakota reciprocated with their story about the origin of corn, which, alas, elicited an angry and condemning reaction from the priest. Taken aback, the Indians reprimanded their needlessly rude visitor, saying: "'My Brother . . . it seems that you have not been well grounded in the rules of civility. You saw that we, who practice these rules, believed your stories; why, then, do you refuse to credit ours?'"[38] Sadly, the Dakota oral tradition has rarely been credited by their white Christian brothers, not at the time of first contact, not now: "Where, therefore, Christianity was accepted, it became so ingrained in the social life of the people that it often became impossible to change. And the tribes generally accepted what they felt was important and disregarded the rest."[39] What this implied about the absence of hymns that were pertinent to the civil rights movement was that the Dakota community in question did not regard this as their struggle, regardless of what that unnamed visitor from New York may have thought. In other words, in berating the Dakota congregation for being out of sync with current affairs in America, the New York visitor was showing how out of touch he was, as a representative of his church, with the spiritual lives of Indian people.

In Deloria's estimation, the encounter with the church official, the one from New York, must have been no different than the Protestant do-gooders who comprised the Board of Indian Commissioners. Filled with the pretentiousness that came with feeling culturally superior to one's charges, these ten persons and the Protestant churches that bene-fitted from their patronage, divided the reservations among themselves with the honor of thieves dividing the loot. Each church, in turn, did not hesitate to accept the opportunity to acquire exclusive influence over the reservations they were awarded in exchange for refraining from missionizing another church's territory. What mattered more, as previously recounted, was the assurance of territorial power. When reservation communities had largely accepted the prescribed forms of "civilization" that they were required to accommodate in order to persevere, there were still people coming onto the reservations with condescending attitudes, passing judgment on how fit they were for contemporary life. What Deloria saw in these churchmen was a tradition of hypocrisy, incompetence, and egotism seeking Indian Bureau approval of their missionary agendas. In addition to the sectarian squabbles that were the norm among the various Christian sects, when it came to their objectives for civilizing the Indians, it was a mish-mash of memorizing credos, mimicking ritual actions, and adopting the attire of citizenship:

> Churches struggled to make Indians cut their hair because they felt that wearing one's hair short was the civilized Christian thing to do. After the tribal elders had been fully sheared, they were ushered into church meeting, given pictures of Jesus and the Disciples, and told to follow these Holy Men. Looking down at the pictures, the ex-warriors were stunned to discover the Holy Dozen in shoulder-length hair![40]

Deloria's anecdote epitomized the arbitrariness with which Indians were unfairly pressured into accepting the values of American society. It also illustrated, from an "ex-warrior's" perspective, just how unaware the churchmen were with how far they had strayed from the examples of their own holy men. Indeed, calling America on its un-Christian behavior has long been a prominent theme among American Indian writers, such as Eastman, who famously scolded in *From the Deep Woods to Civilization*:

> From the time I accepted the Christ ideal it has grown upon me steadily, but I also see more and more plainly our modern divergence from that ideal. I confess I have wondered much that Christianity is not practised by the very people who vouch for that wonderful conception of exemplary living. It appears that they are anxious to pass on their religion to all races of men, but keep very little of it themselves.[41]

In *God Is Red*, in "Christianity and Contemporary American Culture," Deloria surveyed a variety of eccentric examples of Christian denominations, which began appearing across post-1945 America. Among these were the "Reverend Mr. Mike Crain," who "runs a Judo and Karate for Christ Camp" and "Dean Blakeney," who "apparently is further advanced [than Crain] in the Christian life, for besides karate he uses swords and curved Turkish Gurkha knives in his ministry." Then, as a demonstration of entrepreneurship in modern American religious culture, there was "The Cathedral of Tomorrow," an innovator in the church as conglomerate movement, and, in the spirit of Oral Roberts and Billy Graham, Deloria took great amusement in "Explo 72," which was held at the Cotton Bowl in Dallas, Texas, during which legendary Cowboys quarterback Roger Staubach was "the hit of the event." Staubach was most remembered for "comparing life to a football game with salvation as the goal line and the Christian as being in good field position" because of his faith.[42] The purpose of Deloria's display of absurdities in the name of Jesus—there were several more not mentioned above—was to exhibit the ways in which American cultural values, especially its individualism, innovative spirit, and hucksterism, have resulted in a cacophony of gospel traditions.[43] Equally important was the extent to which American Christianity was completely removed from its historical origins, be it the European churches from which it was derived or its Middle Eastern homeland. For, indeed, if American churches were the epitome of the Christian spirit that went from Paul the Apostle to the Plymouth Pilgrims, then that religious spirit has been overwhelmed by modern American materialism and commercialization.

> The old certainties have become stumbling blocks and the question is not whether one can make Christianity relevant in the modern world. The question is whether the modern world can have any valid religious experiences or knowledge whatsoever. The traditional assumption that Christianity represented the highest form of evolved religion can no longer be considered valid. Nor can the contention that it is the revealed truth of God, perhaps the only revealed truth.[44]

As congregations grew in number and the custom of Sunday church attendance became the norm under the watchful eyes of Indian agents, who sent in ebullient reports to the commissioner of Indian affairs about "their Indians'" admirable progress into civilization, church officials gloated about their denominations' successes at gaining new followers. Outpacing the Catholic Church, whose global presence was disconcerting to their Protestant competitors, was a primary concern among missionaries. For example, Rev. Thomas C. Moffett, New York, in "The First Americans—The Indians," proclaimed: "Christianizing America includes as a primary obligation winning the native race, the Red Men, from nature worship and pagan superstitions to the faith of the Gospel."[45] "By 1930," Deloria noted, "the majority of the Indian people had a tradition of three generations of church life behind them."[46] As of the time of the Indian protest movement, it was not uncommon for Indian children to have grown up thinking that the church of their parents and grandparents had always been there, complete with their pre-Christian Indigenous ways being but a faint memory, a relic of the past. Moreover, in lieu of the old ways, as tribal community leaders became church leaders—even becoming lay ministers through places like the Cook School for Christian Leadership—many "people hoped and expected that the mission status of Indian churches would soon be ended and they would receive full parish and congregational equality." Unfortunately, just as Indians were regarded by the BIA as incapable of governing themselves politically, so too did church hierarchies assume the same ineptitude with respect to Indian church leadership. What, after all, would the white missionary do if Indians ever reached a point where they did not need him?[47]

Subsequently, as the Depression gave way to the prosperity of the post–World War II years, succeeding generations of missionaries went out to the reservations, prepared to "save" the Indian all over again. Like the New Yorker above, who chastised the Indian congregation for being behind the times, so too did previous missionaries belittle the spiritual progress of their Indian flocks. Typical of how little the missionary attitude had changed since the Board of Indian Commissioners divvied-up the reservations, Deloria recalled a frustrating encounter with a missionary to Choctaw Nation, who was having great difficulty at getting Choctaw Sunday school children to learn "the seven steps to salvation." "Apparently," Deloria observed, "the Lord would ask all people to recite the seven steps on Judgment Day." Upon further discussion, the missionary confided that the source of her frustration was undoing what a Baptist missionary had previously taught them, which she felt left "them terribly confused." In response to this, her "first task had been to correct all the heretical theology the Baptists had taught them. She said that she wouldn't dream of leaving and letting some other church come in after her and again confuse the children. On such incisive insights is Christian mission to the Indians founded."[48]

Similar to their anthropological counterparts, Christian missionaries were guilty of holding hard to an out-of-date nineteenth-century stereotype of Indians as lost children in need of a white shepherd leading them to redemption. Just as Macgregor and other anthros thought that the Indians at Pine Ridge were depressed warriors without weapons or war path, the missionaries saw Indian destitution as evidence of their need to become Christian soldiers and follow the path of Jesus. Long after the dissolution of the Board of Indian Commissioners in 1933,[49] did the missionaries accomplish their goals of bringing Indians sufficiently into the Christian fold, such that they could relinquish control of their churches to the Indians themselves? In answer to this question, Deloria recalled a Presbyterian missionary conference on Long Island, where a missionary gave an account of his work among the Shinnecock:

> I asked him [when he opened the floor to questions] how long the Presbyterians intended to conduct mission activities among a tribe that had lived as Christians for over three hundred and fifty years. His answer to my question was representative of Christian attitudes toward Indian people today: "Until the job is done."[50]

Apparently, Indians will forever be in need of salvation in the eyes of non-Indian missionaries like the one serving the Shinnecock.

With respect to *Custer*, after expressing his profound disappointment with the missionary attitude toward Indians, Deloria began discussing the resurgence of traditional ways among tribes everywhere. In defiance of the dominant non-Indian narrative that referred to the 1890 Massacre at Wounded Knee as the terminal point of the "Indian wars"—the massacre is still officially regarded as a "battle"[51]—and the "closing of the frontier," tribes have not only retained meaningful and even substantial vestiges of their Indigenous customs but also, along with Indians' political awakening, they were seeking to revitalize their old ways. The Sun Dance, once targeted for elimination by the Indian Bureau, was reappearing at the Pine Ridge and Rosebud Reservations. In addition, the Medicine Lodge was seeing a renewal of interest among the Ojibwe and Ho-Chunk.[52] And the Native American Church, once reviled by Christian leaders as a drug-crazed cult, was witnessing a surge in its presence among tribes. "It appears," in Deloria's assessment, "to be the religion of the future among the Indian people. At first a southwestern-based religion, it has spread since the last world war into a great number of northern tribes. Eventually it will replace Christianity among the Indian people."[53]

The revitalization of traditional ceremonies like the Sun Dance are still underway as of this writing while the vestiges of Christianity persevere. As for the Native American Church, although its presence in Indian Country is substantial, it is still far from claiming the status, as Deloria thought he foresaw, of being *the* Indian religion. Indeed, the relative health of Indigenous sacred customs is in large part due to the resiliency of tribes that endured roughly fifty years of oppression, from 1883 when the Court of Indian Offenses criminalized the Sun Dance and other practices deemed morally corrupting by the Indian Bureau to the eventual decriminalizing of Indian traditional religion under the auspices of commissioner John Collier, whose legacy was the 1934 Indian Reorganization Act. Furthermore, as Deloria argued throughout his writings on religion, the more compelling reason why traditions like the Sun Dance survived in the first place was because of their religious value to a community whose spiritual needs have been little met by Christianity.

> Tribal religions are making a strong comeback on most reservations. Only in the past few years have the Oglala Sioux and Rosebud Sioux revived their ancient Sioux Sun Dance. And this revival is not simply a re-enactment for tourists. The dance is done in the most reverent manner and with the old custom of piercing the dancers' breasts.[54]

During the epoch in which the Sun Dance was scorned by Indian agents the ceremony was forced underground, hidden behind religious and patriotic exhibitions that met with the approval of church and federal authorities. The fact that it was then, as of the 1960s, being practiced out in the open, without any concern for either churches or BIA, was a significant development in the reaffirmation of the Sioux's cultural sovereignty. As Deloria remembered the slow but meaningful reawakening of his community's cultural identity that began during his childhood:

> My earliest memories are of trips along dusty roads to Kyle, a small settlement in the heart of the reservation, to attend the dances. Ancient

men, veterans of battles even then considered footnotes to the settlement of the West brought their costumes out of hiding and walked about the grounds gathering honors they had earned half a century before. They danced as if the intervening 50 years had been a lost weekend from which they had fully recovered. I remember best Dewey Beard, then in his late 80's and a survivor of the Little Big Horn. Even at that late date Dewey was hesitant to speak of the battle for fear of reprisal. There was no doubt, as one watched the people's expressions, that the Sioux had survived their greatest ordeal and were ready to face whatever the future might bring.[55]

Yet, in spite of how much encouragement Deloria saw in the revitalization of Indigenous sacred practices, Indians had suffered under oppressive conditions for generations, and the pressures of modern American society were still all around them. With that in mind, Deloria stated in *God Is Red*: "The fundamental question facing tribal religions is whether the old days can be relived—whether, in fact the very presence of an Indian community in the modern electronic world does not require a massive task of relating traditional religious values and beliefs to the phenomena presenting themselves."[56]

In *God Is Red*, in "Tribal Religions and Contemporary American Culture," Deloria invoked a scenario in which the repatriation of sacred bundles was necessary for a hypothetical tribe's religion, presumably Plains, to be renewed before the last elder possessing the appropriate ceremonial knowledge passed away.[57] Deloria then posed the rhetorical questions: "Do we storm the museum? Will the whites understand why we need the sacred bundles back?"[58] Deloria asked these questions at a time when the 1978 American Indian Religious Freedom Act—which was a joint resolution and not a statute—and the 1990 Native American Graves Protection and Repatriation Act were still years away. Think of the activist work that Running Moccasins did, as recounted above in chapter 6. With that in mind, when it came to answering Deloria's question about the feasibility of revitalizing the old ways in modern times, one of the first things that tribes had to ask themselves was, how much religious freedom was currently available to them? In addition to First Amendment protection to believe in whatever religion an individual may choose, tribes had been spared BIA persecution since, as documented earlier, Collier spearheaded the passage of the 1934 IRA. Yet, what about the privacy rights that Deloria raised in *Custer* with his criticisms of anthropology, including the tribes' right to review the proposed research on their cultures? What about the tribes' access to sacred places on nonreservation land, such as national parks? What about treaty-based rights to hunt in their customary places, which may include hunting for birds and animals, such as eagles, which are now considered endangered according to federal wildlife laws, but which were vital to certain ceremonial traditions? And, what about the countless sacred items that were removed, typically under duress, from tribal communities into public and private collections? How did one protect the religious customs of a land-based tribe under religious freedom laws that were designed for time-based, not to mention text-based, churches?

Focusing on the above questions, Deloria embarked on an historical analysis of the trends and movements that shaped the early 1970s effort among tribes to renew their religious traditions. In so doing, Deloria was conscientious about acknowledging the positive role that missionaries had played in the defense of tribal communities against the onslaught of colonization, such as Samuel Worcester, who was the antithesis of John Chivington, the perpetrator of the 1864 Sand Creek Massacre.[59] Occasionally, Deloria took time to recognize the good work that individual, certainly exceptional, Christians did on behalf of Indian communities. Then, there was the hybridization of Christianity and Indian religion seen in the Ghost Dance, along with the Native American Church, both of which emerged out of a reservation system from the 1880s to 1920s that was tightly controlled by the Indian Bureau's missionizing policy. To put it succinctly, the conflict between Christianity and Indian religions was, on the one hand, a battle for America's soul; while, on the other hand, it forged a new identity for tribes seeking ways to endure as tribal peoples. "For several decades," Deloria observed with respect to the status of the post-1945 generation, "the tribal religions held their own in competition with the efforts of the Christian missionaries." Nevertheless, the generation that survived mission and boarding schools was undergoing an existential crisis as they slowly realized that the American civilization that they were taught was superior to their own was showing its inadequacies at meeting the needs of tribal people, especially its spiritual and health needs. For example, "Often through healing ceremonies performed by the holy men of the tribe, sicknesses were cured that urban white doctors could not cure." As a result of such personal experiences, "In the last several years[prior to *God Is Red*] tribal religions have seen a renewal of interest that astounds many people," Indian and non-Indian alike.[60] Moreover, in Deloria's opinion, it was because of the intensity of this spirit of renewal—which arose during a time of great distress, as Congress instigated its termination policy—that motivated an entire generation to rise up against the forces of destruction. Deloria then invoked a discourse of resistance that he repeated in his preface to *Broken Treaties*, namely his account of the confrontation at Wounded Knee in 1973, about which he offered this observation:

> Perhaps the most important aspect of the Wounded Knee protest was the fact that the holy men of the tribe and the traditional chiefs all supported the AIM activists and younger people on the issues that were being raised. Some were fearful of the violence that threatened their lives, but the strong ceremonial life and the presence of medicine men in the Wounded Knee compound defused a great deal of the criticism that would have been forthcoming from members of the other Indian tribes.[61]

The resurgence of traditional religions was also producing personages who became the faces and voices for this deliberate turn toward the old ways. Deloria highlighted, in particular, Hopi elder Thomas Banyacya, who, along with Tuscarora elder, Wallace "Mad Bear" Anderson, took their message of "peace and purity" on a 1967 tour of reservation communities.[62] Banyacya's teachings were considered the more significant of the two for two reasons. One, Banyacya's message was based on Hopi prophecies, which were a foretelling based on a pre-colonial oral tradition. Second, because the prophecies were about more than just the Hopi, and included the global community, complete with important implications for international affairs.

In the late fifties a Hopi delegation went to the United Nations to deliver a message of peace, as Hopi prophecies had required them to do. Legends said that should the Hopi delegation be refused entrance—as they were—the series of events foretelling the end of the world would begin. Banyaca's [sic] message to other Indian people is to orient them as to the number of prophecies now fulfilled.[63]

For whites, the Hopi prophecies were no more credible than those of Nostradamus. Such an attitude was hardly surprising, especially among Americans, considering that they seemed to believe that their rich and powerful nation was capable of withstanding anything, even the Armageddon foretold in their own Book of Revelations. As for Deloria, he respected Banyacya's teachings whose essence he seemingly regarded as untainted by the corruption of modern life. In fact, the gist of Banyacya's message, particularly to Hopi, was to form a religious resistance to modern American life by re-embracing the Hopi Way.[64] While it was unclear if Banyacya ever recommended Frank Waters's *Book of the Hopi* (1963) to either his Indian or non-Indian audiences, Deloria did not hesitate to make the recommendation in *Custer*. The volume was a reminder "that Indian gods still roam these lands."[65] Indeed, the Hopis' ancient connection to their homeland gave them their prophecies, which was a power that Christianity cannot duplicate because it was alien to this continent. Furthermore, because of the uniqueness of each traditional way, their return constituted a spiritual movement that Christians, not to mention policy makers, may condemn or disdain, but it cannot be ignored: "If and when native religion combines with political activism among the small tribes in western Washington, they are going to become extremely active in the coming Indian religious revival that many tribes expect in the next decade."[66] Such were the times in which Deloria wrote *Custer*: traditional religion was on the ascent, the Native American Church was poised to become the dominant faith in Indian Country, Christianity was on the wane, and prophecies filled the air.

As for where this left the Christian future in Indian Country, as of the early 1970s, Deloria saw the situation as dim for church leaders. So far, they had responded with pathetic attempts an Indianizing their liturgical practices, complete with setting up tipis and trying to convince Indian parishioners that "the Sun Dance and the Holy Communion are really the same thing."[67] When Eastman made the same comparison in *The Soul of the Indian* (1911), he did so with the intention of demonstrating for his white readers that those who had denounced the Sun Dance as intrinsically evil were mistaken about its alleged savagery.[68] On the contrary, he explained, the Indians who practiced this annual custom were engaging in ritual actions that were as meaningful and spiritually sophisticated as anything in the Christian tradition. *Custer* and *God Is Red*, to the contrary, replete with their criticisms of Christianity as a colonial institution marked a seismic change in the order of things. More specifically, Deloria asserted that Indians no longer had to justify their customs and beliefs by convincing whites that they were as "civilized" as their Christian counterparts. At the same time, Deloria acknowledged the deep roots that Baptism had among Oklahoma's Five Civilized Tribes, in particular among the Creeks. The explanation for this exception lay in the way that the Creeks, Cherokees, Choctaws, Chickasaws, and Seminoles were at the opposite end of the spectrum from the situation that Deloria saw among the Shinnecock, mentioned earlier. "This strength," Deloria elaborated, "is due primarily to the large number of native clergy among the tribes. The Creeks particularly seem to have taken the Christian doctrines and made them their own. Native preachers exert tremendous influence among the Creeks and Cherokees. If Christianity is to have an Indian base of survival, it will be among the Creeks."[69]

At this juncture, one might expect Deloria to categorically reject Christianity as a viable option for Indian self-determination. Counterintuitively, Deloria proceeded with making suggestions for reforming church praxis vis-à-vis tribal communities. More exactly, like Martin Luther, Deloria proffered a set of theses for the radical reformation of Christianity, which he viewed as having been corrupted from too much power over Indian people's lives. At the top of the list was the restoration of lands that had been appropriated on reservations for the exclusive use of the churches assigned to these communities, particularly where congregations were practically nonexistent. Furthermore, where churches remained, recruitment of Indian ministers was essential to their viability in their respective communities.[70] Toward this end, churches needed to recognize that Indians were as capable of ministering to their flocks, be they Indian or white, at the same level of competence as their white peers. In fact, when it came to Indian congregations, the cultural knowledge that an Indian minister possessed, especially if he was from the community he was serving, was invaluable at making church doctrine relevant to the lives of the people attending Sunday service. Add to that the possibility of preaching in an Indigenous language, complete with a native choir. As for what the Christian community can do other than apologize for historic wrongs was take responsibility for reforming—and redeeming—its current relations with American Indians.

> Christians must disclaim the use of history as a weapon of conquest today. In doing so they must support the fight of the aboriginal peoples wherever it exists. They must demand a new status for native peoples around the planet. They must demand protection of natives and of their lands, cultures, and religions. They must honestly face the problems of the Western societies and consider what real alternatives now exist for those societies to survive in a world that is growing smaller—a world that must contain a great number of smaller groups whose existence is guaranteed and whose rights are not to be trampled underfoot.[71]

Standing in the way of these developments, Deloria observed, were the simple and unfounded prejudices of church officials who doubted that translating their precious credos into an Indigenous language would sufficiently convey the proper message.[72] A missionary once, as Deloria shared another enlightening anecdote, asked a Navajo who translated a sermon for an unnamed church for the Navajo word for faith. "Quickly," Deloria related, "the Navajo replied with the desired word." To which the missionary reacted with, "'that's all very nice. Now what does that word mean?' 'Faith,' said the Navajo smiling." The missionary, of course, remained skeptical.[73] As a result of this kind of race-based doubt, church after church on one reservation after another languished for lack of interest and competent leadership.

> Much mission work is done by white clergymen who are not capable enough to run white parishes. In most cases, the Indian field is their

last stop before leaving the ministry altogether. They are hauled from pillar to post by frantic church officials desperately trying to shore up the sagging fortunes of their mission fields. A great deal of money is spent covering up disasters created by these white misfits. When they cause too much controversy in one place they are transferred to another and turned loose again. More money is spent on them than on recruitment and training of Indian people for church work.[74]

Worsening the situation was the unequal compensation for Indian ministers in comparison to their white colleagues, which overall was pretty meager to begin with. On top of this was the indignity of always being given the worst assignments, worsened with no opportunity for personal advancement—a predicament that cut across denominations. Deloria referred to this state of affairs as "blatant racial discrimination." "It is a marvel," Deloria admitted, "that so many Indian people still want to do work for the churches." Perhaps, rather than take Indian devotion for granted, the churches should recognize and respect their Indian followers.[75] With respect to Deloria's personal experience watching Indian clergy like his father suffer the belittling disregard that churches had for their Indian brethren, he observed in his account for why he abandoned his religious career:

> Over the years I observed that Indian clergy were shunted aside when it came time for promotions. Indians could spend an entire lifetime in the Episcopal Church and never achieve any advancement. Whites, on the other hand, were often made superintendents of missions within a couple of years after they had graduated from seminary.[76]

Between a faltering church, then, and resurgent tribal traditions what lay on the road ahead for Indigenous nations? What Deloria saw were communities that, whatever they felt in their hearts about Jesus, no longer had faith in their non-Indian missionary shepherds. As of the mid 1960s, the mainstream churches were preoccupied with civil rights rather than the fight against termination. Similar to social scientists, the churchmen had been as silent as anthropologists when it came to the struggle for Indian rights. In fact, Deloria pointed out in *Custer* that

"Indian people receive little if any help from their friends." Furthermore, as recalled above, Deloria bemoaned the churches' absence during the fight against federal termination policy: "The attitude of the churches is not new. My father [Vine Deloria Sr.] was fired from his post with the Episcopal Church for trying to get the church involved with the termination issue in the 1950's."[77] Indian people were now awaiting "a religious leader to rise from among the people and lead them to total religious independence."[78] Therein lay their salvation from the deleterious effects of colonialism. But what exactly did this mean, a prophet, a pan-Indian leader? Previous efforts at leading tribes to their liberation faltered and faded from the landscape, from Pontiac to Wovoka. Only the Native American Church, inspired by John Wilson's vision, had endured into present times. However, if this was the source from which Deloria saw this future spiritual leader rising, he did not say one way or the other.

In a personal anecdote, Deloria recounted that a woman on the Wind River Cheyenne reservation who owned a telephone, which she freely allowed numerous friends and relatives to use. Consequently, the woman's bill ran as high as one hundred dollars a month. Nevertheless, the woman kept sharing her phone. The local Catholic priest however saw this so-called sharing as a complete waste. His reasoning was that, should the woman be more careful with her phone service, she and the others could donate their money to the church. As for how the Indians reacted to the priest's criticism, according to Deloria, they regarded "the missionary's form of sharing as a sophisticated attempt to bribe the Great Spirit." What Deloria did not make clear in *Custer*, but clarified elsewhere, was what a rare luxury a telephone was on the reservation:

> During the Depression there were about five telephones in Martin, [South Dakota]. If there was a call for you, the man at the hardware store had to come down to your house and get you to answer it. A couple of years after the war [World War II] a complete dial system was installed that extended to most of the smaller communities on the reservation. Families that had been hundreds of miles from any form of communication were now only minutes away from a telephone.[79]

After pointing out that Protestants were no better than their Catholic counterparts when it came to giving exclusively to their church, as opposed to sharing generously with each other, especially the poorest among them, Deloria made a statement about the need for an Indian religious movement based on Indigenous values:

> Sharing, the great Indian tradition, can be the basis of a new thrust in religious development. Religion is not synonymous with a large organizational structure in Indian eyes. Spontaneous communal activity is more important. Thus any religious movement of the future would be wise to model itself on existing Indian behavioral patterns. This would mean returning religion to the Indian people.[80]

As an example of Deloria's notion of tribalism, the emphasis on communal sharing, which is most typically kinship based, was also a marker for how tribalism differed philosophically from the Christian concept of the brotherhood of man, which was based on an abstract concept of humanity. Furthermore, given that Deloria was celebrating Indigenous sharing traditions as much as he was criticizing Christian leaders' ethnocentrism, the above remarks about the basis for a religious development appeared to be meant to encompass both the Indian Way and Christianity. It was unclear, though, if Deloria was maintaining as radical a distinction between Indian and Christian at this point as he was earlier when he was more clearly contrasting the two based on their time and space traditions. The confusion likely arose from the fact that within any reservation community, it was commonplace to see families and individuals participating in both their Indigenous ways and a Christian church. Insofar, moreover, as Deloria thought that the Native American Church would become the dominant religion among Indians, he may have had this in mind as the source of a possible Indian religious movement.[81]

With regard to the divergent worldviews signified by the terms "sharing" and "giving," Deloria made two salient observations about "group identities" in *God Is Red*. More specifically, Deloria observed that the names that tribes had for themselves, regardless of the language, meant some variation of "The People." As such, a "substantial number of tribal names indicate the fundamental belief that the tribe is a chosen people distinct from other peoples of mankind."[82] Interestingly, it was this tribal proclivity to name themselves as "the people," "the human beings," and the like that distinguished Indians in the minds of anthropologists, such as Robert Redfield, as a "folk people." More specifically, Robert K. Thomas understood Redfield's "folk urban continuum" in a way that challenged or, at least, corrected Deloria's account of traditional tribal names:

> Most American Indians who still have a closed, bounded tribal outlook refer to themselves as "people," not "The People," as many anthropologists have translated this term. They mean simply "persons." Other tribes are referred to by specific names, but the name for their own society and the name we could best translate in English as "human being" is the same.[83]

While Thomas made clear that tribes generally did not evoke what one might call a biblical inflection to the names for themselves, they were nonetheless provincial in their regard to other persons. As Thomas elaborated, still making reference to Redfield: "They [American Indian tribes] conceived of those outside their group as a different order of being, almost a different species."[84] As descendants of common ancestors, tribal groups typically cohered around a kinship system, which maintained exogamy at the same time it preserved a sense of identity. Churches, on the other hand, were banded around a set of beliefs but were otherwise made up of individuals who may or may not be related. Because tribes were kinship based, sharing emerged as a prominent value. Sharing, moreover, was a form of respect for one's kin, be they blood relatives, friends, or visitors. Indeed, as Deloria pointed out in a reference to Mingo Chief Logan, Indian hospitality toward their colonial neighbors not only characterized the tribal approach to Indian-White relations, but also demonstrated that Indians were often more Christian in their treatment of others, including strangers, than were the professed Christians.[85]

Returning again to the future of Christianity in Indian Country, Deloria proposed that the mainstream denominations take an ecumenical approach to reforming their relationship with tribes. More specifically, Deloria recommended creating "a national Indian Christian Church," which would be "wholly in the hands of Indian people." The objective of such a reformation was threefold. First, the denominational competition that had long fractionated Indian communities into sectarian camps should be eliminated. Second, existing resources should be consolidated into a single organization with a specific focus on making itself completely relevant to how Indians live today. Third, insofar as there were without a doubt Indians who wanted to remain Christian, then they ought to be accorded the dignity of religious self-determination in the form of having leadership roles within their churches. In terms of his proposal's feasibility, Deloria admitted: "Such a proposal is too comprehensive for most denominations to accept at the present time. The primary fear of turning over the sacred white religion to a group of pagans would probably outrage most denominations, too few of whom realize how ridiculous denominational competition really is."[86]

Yet, as the Indian protest movement continued to influence young people, which included rediscovering their Indigenous ways, the Christian churches appeared to be unfortunately locked in their attitudes and had not shown any concern for their decreasing significance in Indian Country. As may be recalled, mainstream churches were more focused on the civil rights movements than on the political turmoil of Indian-white relations. Meanwhile, as "Indian nationalism continues to rise, bumper stickers like 'God is Red' will take on new meanings. Originally put at the height of Altizer's 'God is Dead'[87] theological pronouncements, the slogan characterizes the trend in Indian religion today." In a sense, Indians were picking up where Red Cloud and Wovoka left off, defending their communities' spiritual well-being by striving to cast out the harmful effects of "civilization." How would proponents of "the white man's religion" respond to this situation? Would they respond at all or had churches become too decrepit as institutions to react accordingly? As Deloria posed these dilemmas, he revealed to his reader where his heart was at: "I personally would like to see Indians return to their old religions wherever possible. For me at least, Christianity has been a sham to cover over the white man's shortcomings. Yet I spent four years in a seminary finding out for myself where Christianity had fallen short."[88] Deloria's personal revelation echoed a call to consciousness issued in the *NCAI Sentinel Bulletin* a mere two years earlier, in which was proclaimed:

We must return to the traditional Indian values and regain those virtues which made our ancestors great. . . . We have survived every pressure which has been brought to bear for 400 years and we still find within ourselves the strength to last another 400 if we make the decision to live in the best traditions of our people. We are still a people, each tribe, and we must remain together sharing whatever comes our way and as a people we shall survive and the last person to stand on the American continent will be an "Indian."[89]

As for Deloria's discourse on tribal self-determination, between his critique of federal Indian law and policy, his analysis of Indian-Black relations, his deconstruction of anthropology, and his assailing of Christianity, the principles on which Indian sovereignty rests have become clear. Self-determination was less about enabling Indians to access the rights and privileges of American citizenship and more about the inherent right of Indigenous nations to affirm their own laws and customs as the basis of their political, cultural, and spiritual existence. As such, they should be respected as independent nations, as documented in treaties, statutes, and case law, complete with the power to bring their grievances for redress before an impartial venue, be it a court or commission in which Indian affairs are handled exclusively, complete with the right to appeal. Rather than as a minority group, Indians should be regarded as a unique political group (composed of as many nations as are recognized and unrecognized), which, in addition to possessing dual citizenship (tribal and U.S.), maintain differing cultural traditions that the tribes have the right to preserve, and for which they ought to be able to expect the federal government to facilitate as a proclaimed friend and ally to Indigenous nations. As for what Deloria thought Indians should do to advance their self-determination, aside from political reform, such as was proposed in the Trail of Broken Treaties "Twenty-Point Position Paper," they needed to foment the movement among their nations for cultural revitalization. Perhaps such an environment would generate the kind of spiritual leadership that Deloria said was needed. For without the spiritual dimension, Indigenous nations were little more than the "political anomalies" that Prucha observed in his work on Indian treaties.

CHAPTER 8

The Scandal of Indian Affairs

Policy, Reservations, and the Future of Indian Freedom

In many ways, one cannot appreciate the epochal change initiated by President Nixon's 1970 proclamation that federal Indian policy would henceforth be based on developing tribal self-determination without taking into account how this impacted the tribes' historic relationship with the Bureau of Indian Affairs. Since 1849 when the Indian Bureau was placed in the newly created Department of Interior, all of the policy initiatives affecting tribes within the reservation system were mediated by this subagency of Interior. Indeed, when it came to issues regarding the political status of tribes, the extent to which they were regarded as wards as opposed to nations was often measured by the level of interference the BIA maintained in tribal internal affairs. As the agency responsible for carrying out the federal government's trust relationship, in the context of Deloria's portrayal of federal policy history, the BIA had gone from the authoritarian era of the Indian agent (1870s–1920s) to the radical reforms of the John Collier era of tribal governments (1930s–1940s), which were followed by the effort at stripping these tribal governments of federal support, instigated by termination (1950s–1960s) that culminated in the 1966 rebellion against Stewart Udall's omnibus bill and the subsequent drive for tribal self-determination, financial independence, and the return to treaty making. Having said that, it is remarkable that the latter chapters of *Custer*, which covered the BIA, tribal leadership,

248

and the future of Indian affairs have largely been ignored in the annals of American Indian/Native American studies. This omission was surprising for the simple reason that since the 1970s there has been an increase in the number of federally recognized tribes, which was facilitated by the BIA issuing a set of regulations for applying for recognition in 1978. Furthermore, the percentage of the American Indian population living in off-reservation areas has also increased. As such, while for some, Deloria's commentary on recognition and urbanization have become dated, perhaps even irrelevant, for those interested in Deloria's influence on the idea of tribal self-determination as a historical movement, these chapters are indispensable to understanding the origin of this idea, which, since the 1975 Indian Self-Determination and Education Assistance Act, has defined Indian affairs.

During the years 1934 to 1973, the Bureau of Indian Affairs, in spite of the Indian-preference hiring initiated by the 1934 Indian Reorganization Act, scarcely increased its number of Indian employees, which, as David E. Wilkins and Heidi Kiiwetinepinesiik Stark noted, "rose from 34 percent in 1934 to 57 percent in 1973." Unsurprisingly, as the BIA workforce became more Indian, however incrementally, there was resistance from those who saw this as a threat to the status quo. In fact, it took the Supreme Court to affirm, in *Morton v. Mancari* (1974), the legality of this federally mandated hiring practice, which was intended to rectify the BIA's historic mistreatment of tribes. Nevertheless, as Wilkins and Stark noted: "The majority of the positions held by Indians were in the lower ranks, and few Indians held supervisory positions."[1] Such was the BIA that Deloria observed as he wrote his Red Power Tetralogy. Even more dominant than the Christian churches in Indian Country has been the Bureau of Indian Affairs. Beholden only to the laws of white men in Washington DC, the BIA is a secular force that has been guided only by the policies stipulated by non-Indian political leaders serving the interests of a colonial nation, the United States of America. Within the BIA's sphere of influence, Indians have long been regarded as "the Indian problem." As Indian-rights proponents advocated for Indian Bureau reform, policies changed from, as iterated above, civilizing the Indian to making him a citizen to liberating him from federal support to the then-current, as of 1969, struggle for self-determination.[2] Through it all, tribes have had to withstand various efforts at assimilating them into the American mainstream while insisting that federal entities, from Congress to the BIA, fulfill their trust obligations. "Many services," such as health care, which was brought up in Deloria's analysis of termination, "are set out in early treaties and statutes by which Indians bargained and received these rights to services in return for enormous land cessions."[3]

After summarizing the history of the BIA from its inception in the War Department (1824) to its transfer to the Department of the Interior (1849), in which the president set policy and the secretary of the interior in turn delegated responsibility for Indian affairs to a commissioner (later to become an assistant secretary),[4] which, in *Custer*'s time, oversaw a field of operation that was divided "into ten area offices which are scattered throughout the country. Each area office provides supervision for a number of tribes in the different states." As a bureaucracy, whose role among tribes has been shaped by "the whims of Congress, churches, and pressure groups," its effectiveness left much to be desired. After roughly fifteen years of termination policy (1954–69), Deloria had this to say about the quality of the BIA as a government service to Indians:

> The area office in Minneapolis serves tribes in Minnesota, Wisconsin, and Michigan. In fact, that area office ignores the Michigan Indians, persecutes the little Indian settlement at Tama, Iowa, and muddles around in Wisconsin and Minnesota. The last Interior official to visit Michigan came in a covered wagon shortly before [General] Custer organized his famous Michigan regiment. It is unfortunate for the Michigan tribes that he was too late to join the outfit.[5]

Deloria proceeded with enumerating cases of BIA ineptitude. Noteworthy was the fact that the cases mentioned were not historic, but contemporary, the purpose of which was to outline the current state of affairs in tribal-BIA relations. Toward that end, Deloria informed his reader about an elementary school in Tama, Iowa, that was closed without consulting the tribe. Tribal land consolidations enacted under the auspices of the Aberdeen, South Dakota, office were invalidated during the 1950s. After the Rosebud Sioux had been successful in their land consolidation efforts, the Aberdeen office "suddenly discovered that the process they had been using . . . was not legal." The discovery, however, did not prevent the Aberdeen office from advising the Pine Ridge Reservation to use the same invalid process. Over at the Billings, Montana office, in spite of provisions available through the 1934 IRA, they were at a loss as to what to do with the landless Indians there who were descendants of Chippewa chief Little Shell's band. "They have been lingering ever since." For some reason, Oklahoma had two area agencies, Muskogee and Anadarko, whereas whole regions elsewhere were served by only one office. Then, there was Albuquerque, New Mexico, where once upon a time the area office provided services to the Tiguas in El Paso, Texas until, for undisclosed reasons, they stopped. "It took half a century for the Tiguas," as Deloria told his reader, "to get their status as Indians back, and then they had to become a state serviced tribe, not a federal tribe."[6] As for Phoenix, Arizona, the area office was the epitome of the BIA's strategic thinking. For example, as Deloria explained with characteristic sarcasm, the "tribes of Utah and Nevada are some thousand miles from Phoenix, which makes it easy for them to run down to the area office to check on things."[7]

In a sense, Deloria had made his point about the detached inefficiency of the BIA after the first pair of examples. So, why continue with further examples, including ones yet to be mentioned, namely Sacramento, California; Portland, Oregon; Juneau, Alaska; and Washington DC? Juneau, by the way, was the only exception to an otherwise dismal list of failed area offices.[8] The most obvious reason, other than venting his frustration in a paroxysm of sarcasm, Deloria wanted to present a wide pattern of mismanagement, including a bevy of unresolved issues, missing forms, and an apathetic response to the needs of tribes. In other words, Deloria was substantiating two things. One, the BIA was still a bloated and ineffective bureaucracy, perhaps not much different from the one criticized in the 1928 Meriam Report. Second, by means of the BIA, Deloria was making the case that the federal government did not care about upholding its trust responsibilities to tribes, at least, not beyond a nominal effort. Remember, Deloria had just made the earlier point that BIA services were in return for the enormous land cessions that tribes made to the United States. In other words, the BIA that the federal government's termination policy created was a shambles.

Taking into consideration that most Americans, including most Indians, did not know how the system of Indian affairs operated, Deloria outlined in *Custer* the eye-opening process of decision making that occurred between the commissioner of Indian affairs, the area offices, and the tribes, complete with an option that tribes can go to the national office and appeal their case directly to the commissioner. "Perhaps," as Deloria made a mild concession to area office usefulness, "the best service provided by the area offices is keeping records." Otherwise, excepting those instances when an area office chose not to fulfill an obligation, thereby compelling a tribe to go to the commissioner, once a decision was made on a tribe's issue, it then went to the area office for distribution to local, i.e., reservation, agencies. "The agency personnel," as was further explained, "then interpret the decision according to their local policies, which usually makes the tribe mad enough to go back to see the Commissioner." And so on. Then, in an unexpected acknowledgement of efficiency, Deloria stated: "The process described above is the area office at its worst. In fact, most area offices operate quite smoothly and are in touch with tribes continuously. But one unpleasant incident can ruin the reputation of an area office quicker than one would imagine."[9] People remember you for your mistakes, not your accomplishments. Yet, it was how one rectified one's mistakes that was a true test of both character and competency.

At the same time, one of the larger problems that area offices faced, which automatically became a problem for both local agencies and tribes was, "the lack of funds to carry out their assigned tasks."[10] According to Deloria's assessment, the situation at hand was due to more than just federal indifference. It was also a matter of how effectively tribes utilized their connections to their senators and representatives. The more adept a tribe or tribes were at lobbying Congress, the more resources they were likely to see appropriated for them. Deloria illustrated his point by referring his reader to the tribes in Michigan.[11] "The tribes of that state do not demand programs from their Senators and Congressmen and so do not receive consideration."[12] At this point, Deloria began drawing his focus, once more, on the decision-making process and how it started to break down, leaving the tribes' concerns unattended. More specifically, Deloria brought up the dearth of partnerships between area offices and tribes with respect to acquiring federal support. Consequently, in the absence of collaboration, area offices "lose sight of the reservations' needs and plan programs according to the funds they have available." On this basis, Deloria made his first substantial recommendation for reform: "If area offices would work more closely with Indian people to support tribal programs, they would soon find the tribes out seeking more funds for programs."[13] It was at this level that Deloria began thinking about the practicality of reforming the management of federal support to tribes, which became tribal self-determination.

Given that tribes were sovereign nations with a unique relationship to the federal government, partnering with their area office could make a substantial difference in tribes' ability to cover their needs. More exactly, whether a tribe was dealing with a local, state, or federal agency, that "tribe is able to exercise [via its BIA area office] its fundamental sovereignty at all levels of government," which was due to the tribes' status within the federal system as higher than states. This contrasted sharply with non-Indians, whose local social-service agency became less important the further up the governmental hierarchy they took their citizens' issues, eventually becoming a proverbial number. "Thus," when tribes put their unique status to work for them, "tribes have become eligible for a great variety of programs by qualifying as local sponsoring bodies and then using their federal status in Washington, DC as a competitive edge over other applicants for funding." Indeed, as Deloria readily acknowledged, the Economic Development Administration "has been the most responsive to tribal programs."[14] As Wilkins and Stark observed with regard to the 1956 Vocational Training Act and the 1961 Area Redevelopment Act: "Such laws were some of the first cases where Congress and the executive branch made tribes eligible for federal assistance on a basis similar to that of other governments. This precedent would be greatly expanded when Lyndon B. Johnson became president."[15]

In one sense, the BIA, as a political entity, was subjected to the same kind of scorn and suspicion that the rest of the federal government faced, as it was regularly faulted for social and economic woes, regardless of the actual source of the problem. "America," in general, Deloria claimed, including its Indian citizens, "has been brainwashed to define government programs as paternalistic per se." Especially prone to this accusation were programs designed for the public good or social justice, such as the BIA, which were regularly regarded as a waste of taxpayers' money. In other words, the moment a program was identified as benefitting a minority or special interest group, it was automatically denounced as a boondoggle. Deloria pointed out as counterexamples, the Federal Deposit Insurance Corporation (FDIC) and the Social Security Administration—which were also New Deal creations, like the 1934 Indian Reorganization Act (which enacted major reforms in the BIA)—and which were retained as vital to the general needs of the American people. Perceived as a special interest, the "BIA is therefore tagged as paternalistic because people *feel* that its services are holding Indians back [emphasis added]."[16]

Complicating the situation for tribes, as Deloria explained, was the bureaucracy in which the BIA was embedded. As noted above, whereas the secretary of interior was a cabinet-level appointment, the commissioner of Indian affairs was not. Consequently, Indian affairs was a sub-agency of Interior's operations, whose policy was set by the president. Like most bureaucratic systems, each level of the administration was obliged to meet the expectations set for it by the next level above it. So, in the case of the BIA, the local agency was held accountable by the area office, which was held accountable by the national office, and so on to the secretary of interior and the president of the United States. The latter two were in turn under the legislative and regulatory control of Congress, both houses of which maintained a committee on Indian affairs that, during the 1950s and '60s, were actually subcommittees of the Senate and House Committees on Interior and Insular Affairs. What all of this meant for tribes was that their interests were typically hamstrung by overarching policies, above all within the Department of the Interior, which may not have been in the tribes' interests. In other words, it was unlikely that tribes could expect the BIA to respond to tribal issues if what they were demanding contradicted Interior policy. For example, tribes asserted that termination was a mistake. "When tribes are unhappy," as Deloria explained, "they traditionally contact their representatives for redress. When people become concerned about how Indians are being treated, they write their representatives in Congress demanding an answer. All of these pressures fall upon the few members of the two Interior committees."[17] Remember Senators Watkins and Church from an earlier chapter? It was because of this predicament that tribes had begun agitating for more self-determination and less federal inertia.

Belittling the system's conservatism and its lack of agility at handling problems as they arose, Deloria described a cycle of complaints going without remedy from senatorial committee to department secretary to field officers who wound up doing nothing for the tribes. In a classic example of the bureaucratic shuffle, Deloria recalled a tribe—unnamed, as usual—who contacted him for help at finding out if their "attorney contract had been approved."[18] Upon calling the Phoenix area office, Deloria was catapulted into a game of pass the buck, being told by one office that the responsibility lay with another office, who sent him back to where he started. Eventually the tribe learned that its contract had been approved. In fact, copies of the contract were at both the Phoenix and Washington DC offices. However, "rather than admit they [the BIA officers] were behind on their correspondence, both offices pushed the problem to and fro in an effort to absolve themselves from the blame, if any."[19]

In another example, this time highlighting how policy preceded people, Deloria recounted seeking qualified Indian students for a prestigious scholarship that would enable them to benefit from the secondary-school placement program from the United Scholarship Service (USS). Upon finding students who met the qualifications, Deloria ran into opposition from BIA-employed teachers. Because the program entailed taking these students out of their schools, the BIA teachers were concerned about the consequences to themselves. More specifically, the BIA-run schools were expected to "produce certain marks and standards," otherwise they "would fall below that of other bureau schools." In fact, the BIA teachers were allegedly reluctant to even inform their students about the USS program in the first place.[20] This predicament was further complicated by attitudes from those that one might have expected to be more supportive:

I insisted that all the students who entered the program be able to qualify for scholarships as students and not simply as Indians. I was pretty sure we could beat the white man at his own educational game, which seemed to me the only way to gain his respect. I was soon to find that this was a dangerous attitude to have. The very people who were supporting the program—non-Indians in the national church establishments—accused me of trying to form a colonialist "elite" by insisting that only kids with strong test scores and academic patterns be sent east to school. They wanted to continue the ancient pattern of soft-hearted paternalism toward Indians. I didn't feel we should cry our way into the schools; that sympathy would destroy the students we were trying to help.[21]

In another scholarship anecdote, Deloria recounted inquiring at a BIA area office, along with USS colleague and friend, Tillie Walker (Three Affiliated Tribes), about the scholarship money available to eligible Indian students. Not only did this office have approximately $17,000 on hand, but also it was expecting additional scholarship money that would double that amount. What shocked Deloria was learning that the area office in question was not planning to spend any of it. When Deloria asked why, he was informed that in a world divided between Democrats (who encouraged spending) and Republicans (who frowned upon it), his office had to plan ahead. More to the point, although the BIA was currently under a Democratic administration (Johnson), it would one day be under Republican control. "They might, he told us, examine the books of that area office and discover that he had spent to the limit every year he had the money." Obviously the official with whom Deloria spoke saw the writing on the political wall and anticipated having to answer to Republican politicians, which, of course, was what happened when Nixon defeated Humphrey. Nonetheless, it was the Indian students who paid the highest price for this case of realpolitik.[22] So, what could tribes expect from such a morally ossified institution when it came to defending their rights from, say, state or corporate infractions?

Bureau officials are very reluctant to defend tribal rights. Time and again tribes have come more than part way in pushing for a vital issue only to have the bureau fall back in fear at the last moment. Classic in this field has been the failure of the bureau to defend the fishing rights of the Northwest tribes. Although it is federal law that the bureau is responsible for defending Indian treaty rights as trustee, the bureau dodged the fishing rights issue for years. Finally, when Robert Bennett (Oneida) became Commissioner he took the bull by the horns and got the bureau to intervene. But the attitude of local bureau personnel, western Washington people told me, was to compromise Indian rights as much as possible.[23]

Deloria then returned to the theme of termination, which had defined Indian affairs throughout much of the 1960s and had induced an irrational response from the BIA to the uproar that tribes generated over their legal rights. On the one hand, the BIA demanded termination as the inevitable price for any gains that tribes made on their claims and grievances. On the other hand, the BIA adamantly resisted any tribally produced suggestions for streamlining BIA operations. What Deloria described, more specifically, was a situation in which tribes were manipulated by BIA officials who goaded them into action and inaction without any account of their specific place in the BIA's agenda. "No one knows until the dirt is turned," whether or not their plans for a new hospital, school, or roads had been approved. As for any tribal initiatives at self-governance, the shadow of termination loomed large. In other words, at a time when tribes were called upon to exercise extreme self-reliance, the BIA wanted to maintain bureaucratic control as much as possible over tribal affairs. "No Indian is so foolish as to believe that it can't happen again. So the tribe generally gives in and follows the bureau line. The risk of total destruction of the Indian community [is] too great to treat lightly."[24] Deloria then noted that as executive director of the National Congress of American Indians, these threats of termination came up regularly, which the NCAI resisted on tribes' behalf. Ironically, the situation fomented the absurd accusation that the NCAI was implicitly advocating for termination by acting in contradiction to the BIA.[25]

As of the late 1960s tribes still relied on the BIA for social services, which was what bureau officials took full advantage of in their sparring with tribal leaders over issues. In response, Deloria made another recommendation for reform, specifically, "with proper training and development of community facilities many tribes could become self-sufficient and federal services and supervision would become nominal."[26] Unfortunately, because the BIA was focused on termination, there was very little done to facilitate tribal efforts at developing their own services and infrastructure. William Zimmerman's 1947 three-tiered organization of tribes under federal supervision, in which tribes not ready for termination would be supported toward that objective, was now completely forgotten. The United States wanted to abandon the Indian reservations—including all those tribes with treaties stating that the United States would always be their friend and protector. As things were, according to *Custer*, there was a copious lack of enthusiasm for tribal nation building. Instead, tribes had to deal with an uneven array of budget items. For example, "an area office may have a surplus in education funds and a deficit in funds for roads or law and order."[27]

Referring to a familiar pattern in American politics, in which budget sums were pointed out as self-evident displays of largesse—as though the amount itself was a clear indication that enough had been done—Deloria recounted how Sen. Clinton Anderson (D-NM) claimed in 1968 that "nearly a half billion dollars a year" had been expended on tribes, so he did not believe that these communities were neglected, at all. What Anderson did not take into account, though he should have known, was the way in which the budget was divided up into particular items that precluded area offices from spending the resources other than as directed, not to mention the fact that any new programs were impossible because of a lack of any surplus funds. In other words, Congress funded the status quo and nothing more. In the case, then, of Navajo Nation's need for more school construction during the early 1960s, because the BIA was slow in responding to requests for funding allocations, Navajo children were sent to schools outside of the reservation, such as Chemewa, Oregon, and Stewart, Nevada; as a result, Indian students closer to those locations were prevented from entering those schools. "The Navajo situation has begun to ease now," thanks to Philleo Nash's intervention, "but the dropout rate of the other tribes who had to send their children to public and parochial schools increased during that period so that nationally the

Indian education picture is about the same as it was years ago."[28] With respect to efforts at innovation among tribal leaders, Deloria pointed out a series of 1966 meetings that Nash's successor, Robert Bennett, had at the behest of Secretary of Interior Udall to "determine the needs of the tribes." This was of course in response to the historic confrontation in Santa Fe between Udall and tribal leaders. At the session held in Minneapolis, a plan was proposed to turn welfare payments into a work program, which "couldn't be adopted under the present laws." Moreover, when the idea was discussed, "various 'liberal'-minded people said that it would be demeaning for people to have to work for welfare." Apparently, the notion that Indians could be workers, as opposed to welfare recipients, was too radical for some people to comprehend.[29] Furthermore, insofar as Americans were ideologically divided between liberals and conservatives who regularly opposed each other on a range of issues, such as welfare, the work-program plan may have had too much of a conservative flavor, which the liberal-minded people could not stomach.

Given the system of the times, a more viable alternative for tribes was "the Public Health Service, the Office of Economic Opportunity, the Labor Department, the Federal Housing Authority, and the Economic Development Administration." The advantage with these was that, rather than working with a fixed budget, each of these agencies operated on grants management. What this meant was that tribes could develop their own programs; apply for a grant; and, if one were awarded, acquire funds for a specific need in the community. In anticipation of the grants and contracts established under the 1975 Indian Self-Determination Act (amended in 1988), Deloria argued that the agencies enumerated above were much more adept at responding to the needs of tribes. At the same time, the progress created by these grant opportunities was still hidden from public perceptions, including elected officials, who still bemoaned poverty on the reservation. Unfortunately, they were unable to appreciate how much had changed for the better over the previous twenty years. Considering that the reservations that they saw were established in the 1870s, under Grant's Peace Policy—when the system consisted of little more than poorly funded detention camps, which received no major investments until after the 1934 IRA, when a credit system was installed—the tribes had done admirably well. They had performed commendably, indeed, in spite of having expended a lot of energy on defending themselves against the termination efforts of the 1950s and early 1960s. Only as the 1960s drew to a close, "after nearly a century of neglect, funds began to become available for capital improvements such as tribal buildings, community halls, roads, and housing. The past few years have been the first time there has been money available for development of the reservations."[30]

As an example of the endemic stereotype of Indian poverty and how it clouded non-Indian perception of tribal self-reliance and innovation, on October 25, 1966, Bob Kohl hosted a radio show on KBUN on the topic of welfare, which included interviews and observations about the Red Lake Ojibwe Reservation. While the portrayal of Ojibwe poverty was purported to be fair, displaying different cases of economic need, such as a wheelchair-bound elderly widow, a mother of five young children, and another mother of "nearly a dozen," the evaluation of their character ranged from pitiable to deplorable. Ultimately, the broadcasters argued for welfare reform on behalf of the largely non-Indian taxpayer, as opposed to the Indians dealing with the consequences of generations of federal Indian policy. "Perhaps," Kohl opined with reference to an alleged case of extreme degeneracy, "that is where the welfare laws could be re-written . . . to help only those who are salvageable . . . only those who will make some effort to help themselves . . . only those who have some chance of being educated and reaching a productive stage of adulthood." As for those who did not meet these criteria, Kohl suggested that they ought to be left to the consequences of their allegedly self-destructive behavior.[31] Unsurprisingly, members of the Red Lake community took great umbrage with how they were portrayed, even filing a complaint with the Federal Communications Commission.[32] When asked for comment about the incident, Red Lake chairman Roger Jourdain stated: "It is more than disappointing . . . when broadcasts are resorting to the name calling of Indians, ignoring the good efforts of the possible faults of a few." Because of the racial bias of the KBUN producers, what was ignored entirely was the progress that Red Lake had made addressing its own issues. On this point, the *Red Lake News* reported:

Red Lake Reservation's income has risen sharply in recent years, and the payroll of the Fishery, Sawmill, Fence Plant, School, Hospital, Government Offices, and Community Action Program is over $2 million annually, most of which goes to Bemidji merchants and businesses as there are few retail and service facilities on the reservation.

In the end, Jourdain called on Red Lake's friends and neighbors in Bemidji to speak out against the disparaging commentary to which the Indians had been unfairly subjected, reminding both Indian and non-Indians of the productive relationship that the two communities had worked hard at forging. However, if in fact the Indians—and the revenue they brought into Bemidji—were not appreciated, then the people of Red Lake would be more than happy to take their business elsewhere.[33]

As was often the case, the only thing that stood between tribes and a good idea was a politician. Stewart Udall once again appeared in Deloria's account of Indian affairs. However, this time the secretary of interior was more amenable to tribal ambitions. In 1966 the same year as Udall's infamous omnibus bill, tribes wanted to build upon the OEO grants, to which Udall responded with a "contract method" comparable to the OEO programs. Tribes seized on this proposal as the wave of the future and, against all odds, it was initiated in 1968 at the Salt River Pima–Maricopa Indian Community in Arizona. "To date," in spite of the short amount of time in which the Salt River program had been in operation, Deloria was ready to affirm that it "has proved successful and plans are being made to expand the idea to other tribes."[34] While Deloria once again left it to his reader to figure out the specific project to which he referred, the most likely "Salt River project" was based on the 1968 appeal that Salt River Pima–Maricopa Indian Community president Carlos Filmore made to the Senate Special Subcommittee on Indian Education to run their own schools.[35]

The groundwork, however modestly pursued, such as at Salt River, was being laid for an emergent era of Indian self-determination. Toward this end, Deloria made five proposals in *Custer* for immediate BIA reform, which went a long way toward facilitating tribal interests in running their own programs and achieving more self-governance. Expressing a principle that had been guiding the rest of *Custer*, Deloria stated: "It would be foolish to outline the basic problems of the bureau without offering alternative ideas by which it could be made more responsive."[36] On that note, Deloria's proposals were:

Programming by size of tribe;
Discretionary funds;
Tribal employment would be civil service;
Reorganization of the Bureau of Indian Affairs;
Disposition of federal responsibility to Indians.

The first proposition was self-explanatory. Deloria suggested not lumping all the tribes together as if they were identical. On the contrary, features like population, land base, and resources should be taken into consideration. Larger tribes, in particular, should be supported at taking more control over their own programs. Smaller tribes ought to be accorded the opportunity to develop revenue through cost-plus contracts, consolidate land with loan-grant funds, thereby developing "basic community strength." The second proposition was the basis of true self-determination. More specifically, Deloria proposed allowing tribes to set their own budget agenda, as opposed to BIA officials and politicians in the Beltway. In essence, Deloria suggested what became known as "638 contracts." A critical addition to the proposed tribal contracting system was enabling the jobs created to become civil-service positions, complete with retaining the civil-service grades. Such an allowance would enable tribes to recruit the most qualified members of the BIA's local and area office personnel into its own programs. As the BIA was downsized among tribes, however, the bureau as a whole would require reorganization. Toward that end, Deloria recommended, as his fourth proposition, moving the BIA to the Economic Development Administration, where it could serve as "a fact-finding agency matching tribal projects with available programs in government and opportunities available in the private business sector." Lastly, with an eye to maintaining the trust relationship between the U.S. government and tribes, Deloria asserted that, even after the previous four proposals had been implemented, tribes should categorically qualify for grants from all federal agencies.

Furthermore, tribal land should remain tax exempt with "the income derived from them" used "to provide social and community services to reservation residents."[37]

At this point, Deloria acknowledged the ambivalent role of the BIA in Indian affairs. On the one hand, it was a necessary bulwark against the dissolution of tribes into the mainstream, which was what would occur if the forces of termination got their way. On the other hand, it was a government sham covering up the federal government's inexcusable negligence of its trust responsibilities in the name of intransigent policies and red tape. As for "giving the Indians 'more responsibility,'" such talk from the BIA meant little more than letting tribes take the fall for BIA mismanagement. In which case, rather than talking of taking responsibility like a parent for a teenager, the talk should be about tribes' inherent sovereignty and the nation-to-nation relationship that ought to define Indian affairs. "Treaties," after all, as Deloria reminded his reader, yet again, "recognize this basic fact of legal existence. Tribes agreed to go to the reservations provided they could have their basic community rights of self-government."[38]

Historically, as the federal bureaucracy for administering Indian affairs grew, so too did the divide between tribal sovereignty, which became a thing of the historical past, and the reservation system, which became the domain of both the churches and their civilizing efforts and local Indian agents who reported back to the national office. Only Collier realized that the attempt at making Indians into whites had been a failure. He was also the only one to realize that they were already Indian, so needed neither Indian agent nor anthropologist. What Collier achieved then with the 1934 IRA was to articulate the political status of tribes, enabling them to form their own constitutions and governments, complete with planning their own development. At least, those were the principles embedded in the statute. With Congress's own legislation in view, Deloria challenged congressional leaders to support the IRA's implications for tribal self-governance:

Congressional policy should recognize the basic right to tribal sovereignty. Such sovereignty should include all promises contained in treaties and should recognize the eligibility of tribal governments for all federal programs which are opened to counties and cities. In this way the onus of having failed the Indian people would not be placed on Interior or Congress. Tribes would be free to develop or not, according to the desires of the people in the tribe.[39]

In the absence of a clear recognition of tribal sovereignty, many believed that tribal governments were no more than puppet regimes whose strings were pulled by the BIA. Under these conditions, meaningful progress at rectifying the very real problems on the reservation was hampered with doubt and suspicion that a secret agenda was being pursued, much like South American or Middle Eastern dictatorships in alliance with the United States. If Congress and the executive branch openly supported tribal sovereignty and self-determination, it would go a long way at ameliorating the distrust and acrimony that plagued 1960s and 1970s Indian affairs. Until then, the BIA was little more than "the scapegoat for the collective sins of both red and white." Deloria concluded his analysis with the hope that the "culture" of apathy infecting Indian affairs could change when all those concerned realized that the "technique" of administering Indian affairs could change for the better—*if they wanted it.*

Complementing Deloria's critical analysis of the Bureau of Indian Affairs was his reflections on the problems of Indian leadership. The connection was based on the fact that tribal leaders had to govern their communities within a political environment that included the BIA and the federal system that it represented. Deloria was aware that one could not enact a regime change from a BIA-run system to one of more tribal self-governance without taking into consideration the challenges that awaited Indian leaders once they were on their own. Throughout Deloria's writings, readers were introduced to a variety of Indian leaders, from respected and historic figures like Roger Jourdain to the utterly reviled like Dickie Wilson. Then, of course, there was the phenomenon during the rise of the Indian protest movement of a number of young leaders, such as Clyde Warrior, Richard Oakes, and Russell Means, to name a few, who inspired a generation that rapidly became more aware of its Indianness. In *Custer*, in "The Problem of Indian Leadership," Deloria issued a rallying cry to meet the new decade head-on. More specifically, Deloria proclaimed that tribes would be called upon to present their issues, stipulate their resolutions, and make no apologies for their status as sovereign nations. With that agenda in mind, Deloria recounted the historic ascent of tribal leaders during the late nineteenth century, when Sitting Bull, Chief Joseph, Dull Knife, and others were feared and celebrated by Americans, from the open frontier to the halls of power in Washington DC. Only after succumbing to the forces of westward expansion, when tribes were corralled onto reservations, did Indians see their presence in the American conscience diminish. Otherwise, Indians were as important to Americans during the 1870s to the early 1890s as was the Black community during the 1950s and 1960s. For Deloria's Indian readers, this historical perspective was important to recognize as leaders of the Indian protest movement, not to mention tribal leaders, assessed their struggle for self-determination in comparison to their counterparts in the Black Power movement. As things stood in the late 1960s, Black leaders, such as "Martin Luther King [Jr.], James Farmer, Bayard Rustin, Whitney Young, John Lewis, and others"[40] were familiar to many Americans. These leaders were frequently in the national news, and they were immediately identified with the campaign for civil rights and racial equality. While the struggle for civil rights became increasingly murky and complicated after 1965, nonetheless, civil rights and the Black Power movement were indisputably prominent parts of America's political dialog.[41]

Perhaps as a precaution against Indian leaders uncritically trying to mimic what they saw Black leaders doing on behalf of their cause, Deloria reminded his reader of two things. One, when the legendary warrior chiefs named above were a conspicuous part of American "domestic" policy concerns, they were representing tribal nations, not a "minority group." Second, when Indians looked around to see if any of them were as renowned as, say, King or Farmer, they should remember that, when they found no one of this stature, they should note that their nations had been emerging out of the repressive conditions of the reservation system. "After the war chiefs," Deloria observed, "had been killed or rendered harmless, Indians seemed to drift into a timeless mist. There appeared to be no leaders with which the general public could identify." Consequently, as the warrior chiefs faded into myth, the reality of the reservation was dominated by the Christian missionaries, in which even a personage as formidable as Gall had given in to the proselytization that was all around him.[42]

In spite of the popularity of Jim Thorpe and Will Rogers, whose distinctions were based on their success at adapting to white-American institutions, namely sport and humor, their accomplishments did little to inform the American general public about conditions on the reservations, let alone Indian Bureau malfeasance, or the struggle for treaty rights. On the contrary, whereas a previous generation was grievously concerned with tribes that were resisting American domination—such as the Lakota under Red Cloud—the Progressive Era saw the emergence of the dime-novel Indian tale. The Indian wars from thereon were reimagined as pabulum for mass consumption, sanitized of the violence and suffering that Indian people endured as part of America's "God mandated" quest to settle the land. Enter Tonto. Just as the German philosopher G. W. F. Hegel thought that Napoleon Bonaparte was "the world spirit on horseback," ushering in a new European era as he rode into the Prussian capital after the 1806 Battle of Jena, so too did Deloria see Tonto ushering in a new era for Indians as the Lone Ranger's "loyal companion" rode into American living rooms everywhere.

> Tonto was everything that the white man has always wanted the Indian to be. He was a little slower, a little dumber, had much less vocabulary, and rode a darker horse. Somehow Tonto was always *there*. Like the Negro butler and the Oriental gardener, Tonto represented a silent subservient subspecies of Anglo-Saxon whose duty was to do the bidding of the all-wise white hero.[43]

Tonto, as such, cast a long shadow over Americans' limited knowledge and understanding of Indians. In addition to figures like Gall, Sitting Bull, and Chief Joseph being relegated to the pages of history books, no one emerged to take the places of Thorpe and Rogers. Pop-culture myth and local stereotypes distorted what Americans learned of historical figures, such as Squanto, Keokuk, and Washakie.[44] Meanwhile, more white Americans claimed some form of Indian descent. Echoing Robert K. Thomas's essay on pan-Indianism, Deloria observed: "The Sioux warbonnet, pride of the Plains Indians, became the universal symbol of Indianism." Consequently, actual Indian leaders, be they tribal government officials, community leaders, or representatives of newly formed organizations like the National Congress of American Indians were hidden behind a veil of half-truths and mass market images. "Contemporary Indian leadership," as Deloria portrayed the frustrations of tribes, "was suppressed by tales of the folk heroes of the past. Attempts to communicate contemporary problems were brushed aside in favor of the convenient and comfortable pigeonhole into which Indians had been placed." During the 1940s and 1950s, as the reader may recall from the law and policy chapters above, tribes were persistently confronted with a Congress that had largely made up its mind about what was best for Indian affairs. Thus, it was under these conditions that the post-1945 generation of Indian leaders organized and struggled to obtain acknowledgement from the federal government and general public alike.

Just as Carlos Montezuma once proclaimed that the Indian's biggest battle was against racial prejudice, Deloria asserted that Indians must now confront the equally profound problem of mass-media stereotypes. For the most part, in *We Talk, You Listen*, in the chapter titled "Stereotyping," Deloria presented an extension of *Custer*'s discourse on Indian "transparency." However, in *Custer*'s sequel, Deloria focused more exclusively on the Hollywood movie tradition of stereotyping, particularly in World War II movies, in which, for example, a platoon was made up of various ethnic types, including Indians, whose languages were a "secret weapon."[45] Although specific actors were named, such as "John Wayne, Randolph Scott, Sonny Tufts, [and] Tyrone Power," specific movies and directors were not. Television was also alluded to (e.g., *The Untouchables*) but was not a prominent part of this discussion in spite of Deloria's interest in the work of Marshall McLuhan.[46] Eventually, Deloria segued into documentaries, which, in spite of purportedly portraying real life, nevertheless, romanticized Indian poverty.[47] Adding to the distortion of

Indian lives was the "cameo" approach to movie making, in which token minorities popped up in otherwise white American-centric movies.[48]

The discourse on movies subsequently morphed into a critique of ethnic studies, which was also guilty, in Deloria's opinion, of distorting ethnic histories. At this point, the reader may recall that as of 1970 when *We Talk, You Listen* appeared, Deloria was beginning his academic career in ethnic studies at Western Washington University. In light of which, the role of academia takes on more importance in the struggle for tribal self-determination. With that said, similar to their Hollywood counterparts, ethnic studies proponents created histories that were for the sake of making minorities, including Indians, more accessible, not to mention acceptable, to mainstream Americans. Ethnic studies, as Deloria understood the field, was naïve in its idealism.[49] Complementing that tendency was the random insertion of nonwhite faces into the symbolism of the dominant culture, such as portraying Jesus as Indian or Mexican. Deloria argued in the end that each ethnic group, including tribes, needed to affirm their own uniqueness in America as opposed to validating the master narrative of Manifest Destiny. This was important for comprehending how events, such as the California Gold Rush, affected different peoples differently, be they, in the case of the Gold Rush, white, Indian, Mexican, or Chinese.

Toward the aforementioned objective, Deloria set an example of ethnic-based American history when he contributed a history lesson disguised as an editorial to the *New York Times*, titled "Grandfathers of Our Country," which paid overdue homage to the role that the Iroquois Confederacy played in the political origins of the United States. As recounted, the Iroquois both sided with the British during the 1754 French and Indian War and, perhaps more significantly, provided Benjamin Franklin an idea for organizing the colonies into a workable union. With respect to this, Deloria asserted: "If George Washington is the father of this country because he defeated the English, then logic impels one to conclude that the men of the Iroquois are the grandfathers of this country."[50] Derived from the proposition that the founding of the American republic was multiethnic was the thesis that the principles laid out in the Constitution meant something different to different groups. More important, from the vantage point of tribes, it was therefore time to reject the right-of-conquest interpretation of the Constitution.[51]

Thus initiating an anti–Manifest Destiny interpretation of historic Indian leadership, Deloria recalled how Indian confederacies, such as the Haudenosaunee, were founded throughout the eastern United States. However, as Indian communities and confederacies east of the Mississippi were dissolved by westward expansion, improvised alliances for the purpose of resisting the settler invasion began to appear, such as the alliance forged by Tecumseh.[52] As westward settlements continued, tribes relied on their historic relations with other tribes with whom they shared hunting grounds in order to fend off the non-Indigenous aggressors invading their lands. All of which was to no avail as tribes did not maintain the kind of large populations that white settlements did nor a standing military. Consequently, alliances divided, tribes splintered, and the agricultural-mining-railroad-military-industrial complex occupied more and more Indian lands: "In separate groups the tribes were easily defeated and confined to reservations through a series of so-called peace treaties. In fact, treaties were ultimatums dictated by historical reality. While the tribes could have fought on, absolute extinction would have been their fate."[53] All of this was old news for anyone familiar with Indian history, but a startling revelation for the innumerable *Times* readers who likely were unacquainted with the Indian role in American history. Because of the impact that colonization had on tribes' land masses (diminishing them substantially) and populations (fragmenting them when they were not succumbing to war and disease), Deloria was obliged to remind his readers, furthering his anti–Manifest Destiny agenda, that *even a colonized nation was still a nation*. Furthermore, these nations, whatever their apparent shortcomings, nonetheless possessed both rights and sovereign powers. As Deloria later explained the objectives of contemporary Indigenous nations in *Broken Treaties*:

> Indians are not seeking a type of independence which would create a totally isolated community with no ties to the United States whatsoever. On the contrary, the movement of today seeks to establish clear and uncontroverted lines of political authority and responsibility for

both the tribal governments and the United States so as to prevent the types of errors and maladministration which presently mark the Indian scene.[54]

In terms of the leadership that arose out of this dilemma, an unfortunate development was the "treaty chief," a tragic example of coopted leadership, which was an individual of convenience, meaning someone willing to treat with the settlers regardless of their actual authority to do so. The tragedy was that tribes often found themselves asked to leave land that they did not agree to leave, without authorizing anyone to sign away their claims, which of course mattered little to the Americans coveting their land. As far as the Americans were concerned, anyone signing the treaties that they wrote for them was the only recognized authority of a given tribe. The so-called treaty chief was in dramatic contradistinction to the kind of leadership that emerged organically among persons who distinguished themselves according to the communal values that bonded a given tribe together as a people, which is to say a kinship system that was aware of itself as a unique group.[55]

> Most tribes had never defined power in authoritarian terms. A man consistently successful at war or hunting was likely to attract a following in direct proportion to his continuing successes. Eventually the men with the greatest followings composed an informal council which made important decisions for the group. Anyone was free to follow or not, depending upon their own best judgment. The people only followed a course of action if they were convinced it was the best for them. This was as close as most tribes ever got to a formal government.[56]

Aside from the obvious bias for highlighting the Plains Indian governance tradition as exemplary of the Indian way of leadership, Deloria was also guilty of a conspicuous gender bias, which needs to be acknowledged before proceeding. Among tribal traditions women have long had a prominent part in the governance of their communities. Only if one relied solely on the patriarchal studies of tribal communities, such as were created by explorers, missionaries, and Indian Bureau officials, will one be ignorant of women's customary roles and statuses in a range of tribal groups. Unfortunately, Deloria was a product of his times, in which the gender biases that had been a part of the American civilization effort among tribes had rooted itself in the Indian psyche. Consequently, one of the major shortcomings in Deloria's otherwise expansive achievements as a scholar and activist was the profound absence of women appearing in the topics he covered, including their omission from his portrayals of traditional tribal culture. This was in spite of the fact that, in addition to prominent women within the Sioux community, such as Zitkala-Sa and Helen Peterson, Deloria was surely exposed to the influence of his aunt, Ella Deloria. Fortunately, the work of Beatrice Medicine and Paula Gunn Allen would initiate a more inclusive and equitable discourse on American Indian cultures and societies.[57]

Interestingly, Deloria claimed that the "basic Indian political pattern has endured despite efforts by the federal government to change it." Aside from the negative impact of American Christian patriarchal policies on tribes under the duress of the reservation system, which pushed women and the LGBT community into the furthest margins of Indian societ-ies,[58] not to mention driving much of non-Christian traditional culture underground, there was the transformative power that the 1934 Indian Reorganization Act and its provision for forming tribal governments had on the tribes that adopted constitutions. In other words, there was progress that occurred with respect to tribal sovereignty as a legal con-cept, while tribal cultural sovereignty remained in a state of suppression. Although Collier stopped the BIA'S persecution of tribal customs, the revitalization of these customs would take more than legislative action. As for the political gains, many Indians regarded their tribal governments as illegitimate, as noted, which put into question Deloria's assertion that "leadership patterns have not changed at all."[59] As a statement on behalf of Indigenous endurance, perhaps there was some truth to that remark, but as a statement about the health of the governance traditions in the reservation system, that was another matter. Some clarification as to what Deloria meant was explained in an application to the Council on Indian Affairs Joint Leadership Project, in a section titled "Indian Leadership as Seen within the Non-Indian Society": "Through the IRA leadership positions were created in the Bureau of Indian Affairs and in tribal government where a certain expression of native leadership patterns could once again operate. Many capable young Indian people soon entered the field of 'Indian Affairs' [sic] as workers in government and tribal administration."[60]

Premising his ideas on a measurably growing presence of Indians in leadership positions from tribal councils to the ranks of the BIA, Deloria seemingly believed that these institutions would slowly change under Indian influence. Thus, Deloria remained focused on the historic custom he brought up previously, namely of individuals accruing a following based on their distinctions as hunter, warrior, and the like. As for modern distinctions within the IRA template, Deloria enumerated in *Custer* leaders who had become powerful figures in their tribes, such as Frank Ducheneaux (Cheyenne River Sioux), Joe Garry (Coeur D'Alene), Marvin Mull (San Carlos Apache), Roger Jourdain (Red Lake Ojibwe), and James Jackson (Quinault), who were in contradistinction to the ones in communities that regularly deposed their leaders from office, which Deloria did not bother to illustrate with examples.[61] In both cases, however, staying in office typically "depends upon the ability to gain concessions from governmental agencies." In addition, when it came to the pursuit of tribal unity:

> Some chairmen use state and national organizations as sounding boards for militant speeches that hopefully prove to reservation people that they are not afraid to fight for Indian rights. Other chairmen withdraw from national and state inter-tribal organizations when they are elected to demonstrate that by their power alone the tribe is protected from its enemies.[62]

Without examples—Deloria did not bother illustrating why he pointed the above five leaders as exemplary—it was unclear if the two tendencies were exclusive. Whereas intertribal organizations were mentioned in the second tendency, they were not mentioned in the first, which begged the question, was Deloria referring to non-Indian organizations? Perhaps both are implied. What was clear was the arduous challenge of maintaining a semblance of sovereignty in a federal system that remained dubious about recognizing tribal sovereignty.

Exacerbating the diminished status of tribal sovereignty, induced by HCR 108, was the equally diminished stature of so-called tribal leadership, which was a predicament that Deloria underscored in a 1973 editorial for *Akwesasne Notes*:

> When Indians think back to Chief Joseph, Crazy Horse, Dull Knife, Cochise, and other leaders that the tribes have had and then compare them with the present incumbents who are afraid to mention anything unpleasant to the federal government, they can tell how far the Indian people have fallen. At the least, the capable tribal chairmen of today must realize that as long as the National Tribal Chairmen's Association is allowed to exist and as long as its officers are handmaidens to the director of the NCIO [National Council on Indian Opportunity], for so long will tribal governments and tribal officials be regarded as the clowns of Indian Affairs [*sic*] and not the leaders.[63]

While tribes have long known how to manage their internal affairs, as well as intertribal relations, many of which extended back into the times recounted in oral histories, the challenge for Indian leaders was representing tribal interests on a national stage that was built by settler-colonial powers, complete with their rules for how discussions may proceed, such as occurred at congressional hearings or national conferences. Until tribal leaders learned how to operate within such non-Indigenous venues, they would leave themselves vulnerable to interlopers from the non-Indian community seeking to install themselves as spokesmen for the Indians. Indian communities, however, were not without reason for feeling optimistic. In an application to the Council on Indian Affairs Joint Leadership Project, the status of contemporary Indian leadership opportunities was summarized:

> Since 1960 there has been a remarkable change in leadership opportunities. With the creation of the United Scholarship Service that year Indian young people were given the chance to administer and develop programs for their people within the private sector. . . . Policy making

and advanced planning by Indians and for Indians with economic support from the non-Indian community was made possible. And with this development there was also allowed to Indian people the possibility of returning to the people on the reservations at regular intervals so that leadership could be won through service as in the manner most familiar to Indians. In 1965 the OEO provided additional funding so that many capable young Indians could occupy leadership roles on reservations through Community Action Programs. In every case, public and private sufficient funding was provided so that Indian young people could work in a program long enough to win respect through their work and did not become either masters or puppets of the society at large.[64]

In the tradition of white-organized Indian conferences, Oliver La Farge stood prominently among his peers. "Of all the white saviors," Deloria wrote, "Oliver La Farge was perhaps the best known and most skillful manipulator of Indian people." While La Farge's work has largely been forgotten, during the 1930s through the 1950s, when anthropologists dominated the discourse on Indian culture, the author of *Laughing Boy* (1929) was a highly regarded popularizer of contemporary anthropological theories. However, Deloria scorned La Farge less for his quaint fictional portrayals of Indian lives and more for his ineffective role as president of the Association on American Indian Affairs (AAIA). More to the point, aside from only mingling with "Uncle Tomahawks," while tribes were fighting heroically against the federal government during the onslaught of termination, La Farge did little more than avail himself of the title "defender of the lowly childlike Indian."[65] In other words, he spoke to journalists who provided him some publicity but did not do the yeoman work of speaking before Congress. In reference to which, the NCAI stated in a 1966 editorial: "To wistfully look to the Oliver La Farges for counsel is sheer folly today as events are moving too fast in American history to have Indians take a back seat in decision-making in favor of a 'wise all-knowing' white friend."[66] The AAIA is of course credited with having played a supporting role in the founding of the National Congress of American Indians. However, as Deloria might have said, there was good reason why one never sees the AAIA mentioned in the annals of Indian protest history. However, when the AAIA set its mind to it, the organization emerged as a major force in the struggle for change. For example, because of the work of Felix Cohen, the AAIA played a pivotal role in the advocacy of the 1934 IRA, even bringing suits against the states of New Mexico and Arizona for not providing Indians with welfare benefits under the Social Security Act.[67]

In essence, La Farge symbolized everything that was inherently wrong with the "white man's burden" attitude toward Indian affairs. More specifically, Deloria regarded La Farge as exhibiting a condescending disregard for Indian leadership, even going so far as to steal the idea that Indian leaders had for starting their own version of the Point 4 Development Program—outlined above in chapter 6, which D'Arcy McNickle was credited with a founding role—and publicly claiming it as his own. Furthermore, because of his status as a renowned academic, La Farge frequently interjected himself as spokesman for the Indian through his connections to the "public relations media in the East," which occluded Indian leaders from being perceived as competent at speaking on their own behalf. For better and for worse, as Deloria recounted, La Farge's status eventually faded and a new generation appeared, which consisted of a "more sophisticated type of white man," who was less impressed with La Farge's claims to expertise and more interested in finding "successful Indians" who represented their generation as potential leaders.

> In the 1960's the government has also seen a new type of employee in the Bureau of Indian Affairs. This is a fairly well educated person, fairly liberal in thought and deeply appreciative of Indian social values who is able to encourage Indian people to make decisions for themselves. Quite often outstanding social scientists have influenced, though their writings or class work, these non-Indian people to the extent that they become quite nationalistic on behalf of Indians and have an historical perspective which enables them to help Indian people view their problems in new ways.[68]

Interestingly, the kind of "successful Indians" described in *Custer* were considered "successful" because of their capacity to adapt themselves into white society. Was Deloria therefore admitting a self-realization about why he was invited to partake in this generational transition? It was a bit unclear. On one hand, Deloria said of the "last generation" of Indian leaders, they "made their reputations by demonstrating their ability to be non-Indian," even comparing them to the Indians performing for Buffalo Bill. On the other hand, Deloria said of his own generation, complete with youthful sarcasm and latent rebellion: "Many of us were dragged from conference to conference to hear nearly identical speeches by model Indians of the day." The speeches—or *the* speech—in question consisted of an Indian version of the rags-to-riches narrative, in which assimilating into white society was part of the notion of success that was validated by these so-called leaders. "I am now a success. I am accepted by the best people and eat in the fanciest hotels."[69] With respect to Deloria's role during this generation of aspiring Indian leaders, there was a personal account in his 1970 editorial for the *New York Times*:

> In the mid-nineteen-sixties, the whole generation that had grown up after World War II and had left the reservations during the fifties to get an education was returning to Indian life as "educated Indians." But we soon knew better. Tribal societies had existed for centuries without going outside themselves for education and information. Yet many of us thought that we would be able to improve the traditional tribal methods. We were wrong.
>
> For three years we ran around the conference circuit attending numerous meetings called to "solve" the Indian problems. We listened to and spoke with anthropologists, historians, sociologists, psychologists, economists, educators and missionaries. We worked with many Government agencies and with every conceivable doctrine, idea and program ever created. At the end of this happy round of consultations the reservation people were still plodding along on their own time schedule, doing the things they considered important. They continued to solve their problems their way in spite of the advice given them by "Indian experts."[70]

Deloria's ridicule of so called "Indian experts" who gave in to the temptations of status and celebrityship were not limited to the "Uncle

Tomahawks" scorned above. In his 1974 account of the Trail of Broken Treaties caravan, Deloria recalled the inexcusable lapse of responsibility exhibited by several individuals who were in charge of going ahead to Washington DC for the purpose of arranging accommodations for the multitude that was on its way.

> The bulk of the demonstrators went immediately to the Bureau of Indian Affairs, [after their arrival on November 3, 1972] where they gathered in the auditorium to await word from their leaders as to the housing arrangements for their stay in the city. Some of the [unnamed] leaders, who had been in Washington for several weeks before the arrival of the caravan, had been delegated to arrange housing for the caravan people. But those responsible for housing had wasted their time enhancing their images as glamorous Indian leaders, and had done little to secure rooms for the people coming to town.[71]

Maintaining an aloof perspective on his anecdotal history of post–World War II Indian leadership, Deloria noted that the "successful Indian" example rarely led to equally successful imitators. Instead, what appeared was the phenomenon of the "professional rebel," who distinguished himself through his recitations of how the whites had wronged the Indian throughout the nineteenth century à la *A Century of Dishonor*. Commonplace was a devastating narrative on the evils of colonialism that typically concluded with the whites redeeming themselves, presumably under the auspices of the 1934 IRA. The moral of the story was that the whites had made a complete "about-face" and that they were trying "to atone for the past." If atonement ever occurred, it was lost on Deloria and his peers. What was also missing was any mention of how the United States treated other nonwhite groups, let alone any comparison between Indians and others for how they were regarded differently under the law. Indians were simply different, albeit vaguely. What was more important was that the non-Indian organizers of these conferences wanted to be seen as essential to the future well-being of the Indians over whom they asserted their "expertise." Think again of La Farge. The role that Indians were expected to play was to make the whites feel like they had in fact atoned for their sins.[72] As an example of white redemption, Deloria refers to the "All-American Platoon" theory of diversity, which was mentioned above in the context of Hollywood movie history. "Under this theory," Deloria stated, "members of the respective racial minority groups had an important role in the great events of American history." In the case of Indians, westward expansion was still the stuff of Hollywood-style legend, which "takes a basic 'manifest destiny' white interpretation of history" and embellished it with "a few feathers, woolly heads, and sombreros."[73] Such are the absurdities when others recount your history for you.

When stereotyping gave way to self-determination, however, the discourse on American history diversified into an array of historical narratives: "Self-awareness of each group must define a series of histories about the American experience." The implications of group self-awareness included reframing the basis of American law, from the individual to the group, which was what Deloria strove to do in the "Laws and Treaties" chapter of *Custer*, then again in the major doctrines chapters of *Broken Treaties*: "We can survive as a society if we reject the conquest-oriented interpretation of the Constitution," in which nonwhite communities were expected to surrender to the dominance of white American civilization and assimilate as individual citizens. "While some Indian nationalists," Deloria argued, "want the whole country back, a guarantee of adequate protection of existing treaty rights would provide a meaningful compromise."[74]

At this juncture, the problem of Indian leadership appeared to be a problem of non-Indian leadership over Indian affairs. As the federal government changed from Republican conservative to Democratic liberal, the attitude of non-Indian leadership toward Indians changed, but the top-down approach to problem solving did not, as evidenced by the 1966 confrontation with Udall, not to mention the reluctance of the Nixon administration to acknowledge the demands of the Trail of Broken Treaties "Twenty-Point Position Paper." As indicated at previous points, Deloria was no fan of the War on Poverty, which he regarded as poorly conceived and premised on racial stereotypes. With respect to the issue of leadership, Deloria portrayed the War on Poverty as instigating a wave of ineffectual conferences, complete with a host of proposals, for resolving poverty and all of its attendant issues on the reservations.[75]

"Universities," in particular, "that hadn't known that Indians existed outside of the textbooks charged into the forefront of social responsibility." Presumably, the proposals sent into Washington DC represented "grass roots" initiatives, which may have meant local but not necessarily tribal. As usual, Deloria did not provide his reader any clear examples of what he was criticizing beyond his parody of how "conferences" about Indian poverty were run. With respect to Indian participation, Deloria made a point about the elusiveness of tribal unity, which was largely the product of the inconsistent perceptions of Indian people. For example, Deloria recounted: "One educator constantly blasted me because NCAI didn't represent *all* the Indians. Then one day a fellow bureaucrat received a buffeting by urban Negroes and this same educator asked me to send a telegram of support because NCAI 'represented all the Indian community.'" In light of such self-contradicting propositions, the Indians who contributed to the dialog on Indian affairs ultimately represented a spectrum that was complete with its own contradictions. As Deloria summarized a typical slate of speakers: "The first Indian will announce that he lives in a one-room shack. He will be rebutted by an Indian educator who has lost his identity between two cultures. Another will agree about the two cultures and will immediately be refuted by an old timer fighting for his treaty rights who is simultaneously challenged because he doesn't speak for all the Indians."[76]

With respect to the grass-roots component, since Deloria did not provide any details to his critique, one was left to speculate about who was organizing these conferences, how they were funded, and what proposals they were discussing. Sometimes, rather than clarifying his criticisms, Deloria all too often lapsed into riddles. For example, when Deloria ridiculed the failed attempts at forging tribal unity at the aforementioned unnamed conferences, he explained the poor results in terms of two opposed statements: "The white society is not satisfied with anything less than the efficiency of an Irish political machine. The Indian society expects little articulation, but infallible and successful exploits. And there is no attempt by either white or Indian to distinguish between the two." Apparently, the characterization of "the white society" was based on Tammany Hall, a reference that was inconsistent with what was portrayed above regarding the War on Poverty. If the characterization was justified, it was not made clear enough in Deloria's criticisms of the Indian poverty conferences. In any case, the Irish stereotyping of Tammany Hall was intended to contrast with a generic observation about Indian leadership, which Deloria characterized in terms of its non-teamwork, anti-political-machine traits: "Assignment of personnel to component jobs within an action plan leaves Indians cold. Rather, they expect leaders to charge ahead and complete the task. If anyone wants to assist in the job, so much the better. But there is no sense of urgency or need for efficiency in anything that is undertaken."[77] The latter was also in opposition to traditional Indian leaders who acquired a following through exemplary behavior. If Deloria was summarizing observations he made during his tenure as NCAI executive director, it was not made obvious, let alone if he was including his own leadership experience into his analysis.

Aside from the fact that it was uncertain what facet of Indian leadership he was referring to in his comment—traditional leaders, such as the much-revered Sitting Bull or modern tribal government leaders—Deloria also did not indicate if he was including Indian leaders like LaDonna Harris (Comanche) in his observations about the War on Poverty in Indian Country. According to Harris, when she recounted the founding of Oklahomans for Indian Opportunity, the precursor for Americans for Indian Opportunity: "The association began in my living room. We became the first statewide Indian organization, got a great board put together, but couldn't be funded directly because we weren't a reservation group. So, we had to use our university contacts and get the University of Utah to fund our program in Oklahoma."[78] Except for the NCAI, Deloria did not disclose any of the organizations, conferences, or leaders he was analyzing. Did Deloria assume that the targets of his caustic remarks were well-known enough to his late 1960s reader? Surely, there were likely many readers who had a good sense of who Deloria had in mind. Or was Deloria being politically astute and utilizing generalizations in order to avoid singling out key figures, like Harris, with whom he may have wanted to preserve a working relationship? Since he was an experienced political leader, this proposition is probable. At the same time

Deloria was inveighing against national church bodies, he was working for groups like United Scholarship Service, which was directly supported by the Board for Home Missions of the United Church of Christ. Given the analysis earlier, it was likely that Deloria was summarizing his observations of NCAI and AAIA meetings, along with grassroots organizations like Oklahomans for Indian Opportunity, not to mention, maybe, the meetings that occurred with Udall over his omnibus bill. Whatever the sources of the observations, with respect to Indian leadership as a unique tradition, Deloria brought up the "War Chief complex" as something that was endemic to the American Indian community.[79]

The origin of the War Chief complex, as Deloria described it, derived from the age-old Plains Indian tradition of leadership through distinguished behavior, namely the accomplished warrior, hunter, or statesman. A tribe's success or failure was often seen as hinging on a leader's exploits. As a result, leadership acquired a "quasi-religious vocation." As such, historical figures such as Red Cloud, Sitting Bull, Crazy Horse, Roman Nose, Chief Joseph, and Geronimo became mythologized—not mere men but immortals in the Indian imagination. Added to this was the mythology of the Indian messiah, as exemplified by Wovoka.

> In the Ghost Dance days, messiahship came to dominate Indian thought patterns and all expectations were tinged with this other-worldly hope of salvation. Every Indian leader of today must face the question of whether or not he is a great figure of the past reincarnated to lead his people to victory, for legends die hard among our people.
>
> One in a leadership role is therefore constantly bothered by undefined doubts as to his ultimate role in his people's historical journey. He is inevitably drawn to compare himself in a mystical sense with Crazy Horse, Joseph, Geronimo, and others.[80]

While the identification of the proposed complex was credible, at the same time its gender bias may be reason enough to advocate for more female leadership among American Indian groups, be it in tribal government or Indian-advocacy organizations. Also, the complex as defined begged the question, did this occur among leaders of tribes who did not have a popular and well-known figure like Crazy Horse? On a personal note, I have yet to see anyone in the Gila River Pima-Maricopa Indian Community compare himself in "a mystical sense" with, say, Chief Antonio Azul or Ira Hayes. And if anyone dared to compare himself to Crazy Horse or Geronimo, he would likely be asked if he was enrolled with the right tribe. In any case, the downside to success in the American Indian community, as Deloria experienced firsthand, was the steady increase of responsibilities, including minor ones. As Deloria recalled his own career as an Indian leader: "At my first convention of the NCAI there was very little for me to do because I was so new that no one had any confidence in me. A couple of years later I was fairly run to death doing minor errands because people had come to depend on me for a great many things."[81] A year later, Deloria elaborated on his NCAI experience in an editorial for the *New York Times*: "Every conceivable problem that could occur in an Indian society was suddenly thrust at me from 315 different directions. I discovered that I was one of the people who were supposed to solve the problems."[82] Whether or not Deloria compared himself to any storied ancestors, he did not say, instead he settled for making the point that the bane of Indian leadership was that the more one succeeds, the more others will burden that person, doing less and less for themselves. Unsurprisingly, national Indian leaders were fleeting, as workloads and fragile alliances—which were exacerbated by tribal rivalries and personal jealousies—took their toll.

> We had put together a very effective [NCAI] team the previous year, working hard to develop the organization and increase its ability to bring the tribes together. I had assumed that we would all be elected again because of our success in reconstituting the organization. To my chagrin I discovered that the tribes were systematically dissolving and reforming our team simply because they wanted to have an exciting election and feared that we would be re-elected without any real fight. They wanted action.[83]

In a nutshell, the future of Indian leadership at the height of the Indian protest movement was indeterminate, at least as Deloria characterized his generation as a young NCAI director. Dissent and jealousy were commonplace, as was the fickleness of followers who may suddenly abandon an otherwise successful leader "without so much as a backward glance." Under such conditions, it did take someone with exceptional charisma to break through the wall of resistance in order to effect change. Such sage advice was important if tribal leaders, both present and future, were going to effectively take on the responsibilities of more tribal self-governance. Most importantly, tribes and their peers in groups like the NCAI needed to resolve the burn-out issue in addition to being better prepared for long-range planning.

While Deloria was able earlier to enumerate some examples of strong leaders among individual tribes, such leaders at the national level were wanting. Clyde Warrior, alas, came and went too quickly; at the time Deloria wrote *Custer,* Russell Means and Dennis Banks had yet to appear on the horizon. When Means and Banks did appear in *Broken Treaties,* they did so within the context of the 1973 confrontation at Wounded Knee, which was focused less on leadership and more on the failings of federal Indian policy. As things stood in *Custer,* "it would be highly unlikely that an Indian meeting," which relied on consensus and the humbling of its would-be war chiefs, "would or could develop a Poor People's Campaign or a March on Washington." Direct action, after all, meant foregoing the benefits of indirect alternatives. The Hualapai Tribe, to the contrary, "reversed its stand completely on the Marble Canyon Dam, finally supporting it, and no one thought a thing about it. [Ralph] Abernathy would not have dared make such a turnabout after his campaign began in Washington; the Hualapai could have changed every year and pulled it off."[84] As for Means and Banks as national leaders, Deloria—perhaps, once again, revealing his tribal bias—thought that Means may have been the charismatic national leader that Indians had been awaiting. In the epilogue to their 1996 history of the Indian protest movement, Paul Chaat Smith (Comanche) and Robert Allen Warrior quoted Deloria's observations of a speech Means gave in the aftermath of the American Indian Movement's protest on behalf of Raymond Yellow Thunder:

As I was listening to Russell Means I continually looked around the room to see the faces of the people as he spoke. Almost every face shone with a new pride. . . . I came away from Mean's speech with the feeling that Russell is a terribly important man to our tribe. He may be the greatest Lakota of this century and his ability to light the eyes that have been dimmed so long is probably more important for us than anything that anyone else can do. I think it is the pride in living that many Indians have lost and in the manner of clarity of Russell Means's speech many Indian people found that pride and also found a strength they did not know they had possessed.[85]

So, where does this leave us? Deloria asserted that supporting the NCAI was the best option for the future of Indian affairs, certainly as opposed to groups like the AAIA. For all of its flaws, which Deloria displayed with brutal honesty, the NCAI was important, not only because it stood as a national organization, but more importantly it was an Indian-run organization—emblematic of the Indians' ability to handle their own affairs. In the 1965 convention issue of the NCAI *Sentinel Bulletin*, it was proclaimed:

> The year is 1965. Not 1944 or 1955. We need new faces and new ideas. We are witnessing fantastic changes in this country. There have been more major programs in this year than in the previous twenty years. The role of the NCAI is changing in the same manner. . . . In addition, Indian tribes must begin to face the current social movement [toward greater individual freedom]. . . . We need people who will face the difficult task of asking themselves—what do we want [as tribes]? How can we get it?, and how can I help other Indians and tribes achieve what they want?[86]

At the same time, the Achilles heel of Indian politics was the tribes' tendency to forego national approaches to local problems. In a 1968 memo to his successor as NCAI executive director, John Belindo (Navajo/Kiowa), about compiling an NCAI database to "codify Tribal Statutes," Deloria noted: "NCAI is an organization of tribes but has never interfered with the internal operations of a tribe. To begin such a program would raise the most vociferous hue and cry imaginable. Picture, if you will, explaining to Robert Jim why NCAI has to have all of the Yakima

Tribal Code on computers."[87] In spite of the success at Frank's Landing at turning a local fishing-rights issue into a national cause, through the intervention of the NIYC and Hank Adams, both of which organized the fish-ins, nonetheless, it would be several years away before the tribes in Washington state benefitted from the 1974 Boldt Decision. In which case, from a tribal leadership perspective, the Indian protest movement had yet to produce any tangible results beyond energizing Indian college students and garnering media attention. Whereas a local violation of civil rights, such as refusing to serve certain customers because of their race sparked national outrage complete with action taken by national organizations that strived to pressure change at the federal level, in the case of tribes, what happened locally tended to stay local, with no recourse to national organizations. Consequently, rather than achieving a positive resolution, tribes were usually bogged down in the federal system. At most, they may "wait to take advantage of the tide of legislation and gain a few crumbs when the goods are divided." However, as Deloria warned:

> Unless Indians can adapt their tactics to place more emphasis on exploiting the local situation they will remain an unknown factor in American life. Always, it seems, issues detach themselves from the local situation and nebulously float off into the paragraphs of the perennial Task Force reports done by Interior and related agencies every few years.[88]

In addition to direct action, or at least an Indian version of direct action, Deloria strongly recommended that Indian groups and their leaders learn how to "externalize" themselves to non-Indians. In other words, it was not enough for Indians to understand themselves, relying on unwritten and even unspoken understandings between group members to achieve incremental gains. They must acquire the skills necessary to communicate their ideas and issues to others. They must be more clear and resolute, as the Trail of Broken Treaties caravan was when it created its "Twenty-Point Position Paper." What Deloria observed to the contrary were national meetings that functioned like pow wows in the sense that they brought people from different tribes together for the purpose of socializing. While renewing relations should not be disparaged, when it came to redressing problems that may be common to a number of tribes, was commiserating enough by itself? Should not the comradery lead to a more substantial outcome? "Indians have always rejected unity as a weapon, though a number of younger Indians want unity precisely for that reason."[89] Hearing the call to battle arising from a younger generation, Deloria concluded his argument with a proclamation:

> As Indians we will never have the efficient organization that gains great concessions from society in the marketplace. We will never have a powerful lobby or be a smashing political force. But we will have the intangible unity which has carried us through four centuries of persecution and we will survive. We will survive because we are a people unified by our humanity; not a pressure group unified for conquest. And from our greater strength we shall wear down the white man and finally outlast him. But above all, and this is our strongest affirmation, we SHALL ENDURE as a people.[90]

While it was safe to say that most Indians agreed without hesitation that they would endure as a people, it was unclear what Deloria was claiming were the implications of such endurance. In addition to the historic observation that tribes have survived centuries of colonial abuse, there was the added expectation that as of the current generation, there was an irreversible move toward Indian-led organizations like the NCAI taking over Indian affairs. The mediation of non-Indian groups, be it the Indian Rights Organization of Eastman's generation or the AAIA of McNickle's, had become a thing of the past. However, Deloria's conclusion, quoted in full above, evoked a "we shall overcome" — or maybe it was "we shall overrun" — sense of realization. Did this mean that Deloria identified something in his critique of Indian leadership that inspired this proclamation? If so, it was difficult to say what that was exactly. While the NCAI may have looked like the American Indian community's best option for unity, according to Deloria's own analysis, it was often weakened by tribes' reluctance to utilize it as a force for change. A hint of what Deloria envisioned, however, was expressed in his March 1970 *New York Times* editorial about Alcatraz:

In 1965 I had a long conversation with an old Papago [Tohono O'odham]. I was trying to get the tribe to pay its dues to the National Congress of American Indians and I had asked him to speak to the tribal council for me. He said that he would but that the Papagos didn't really need the NCAI. They were like, he told me, the old mountain in the distance. The Spanish had come and dominated them for 300 years and then left. The Mexicans had come and ruled them for a century, but they also left. "The Americans," he said, "had been here only about 80 years. They, too, will vanish, but the Papagos and the mountain will always be here.[91]

In the final analysis, Deloria was unclear about what lessons he wanted his reader to draw from his various examples of Indian leadership and organization, in addition to providing very little in terms of concrete recommendations. In which case, perhaps Deloria's anecdotes were a collection of cautionary tales, alerting would-be leaders about the pitfalls and limitations of tribes and tribal organizations as political forces, lest they succumb to burnout, bickering, and the warrior chief syndrome.

As for the Indian protest movement, in *We Talk, You Listen*, Deloria took up the problem facing all social movements seeking substantial changes in the political order, namely turning their community's local issues into political topics that were part of the national dialog on social justice. More specifically, in "Tactics or Strategy?" Deloria essayed on how Indians had been reprimanded by their white peers for not adopting tactics regarded as "successful" by other groups, be it Black activists or anti–Vietnam War protests. Direct action, however, e.g., anti–Vietnam War street action, was limited as became clear when Nixon responded by extending the war into Cambodia, which was preceded by a massive prowar endorsement during the 1972 election from the "silent majority." In light of this conundrum, Deloria evaluated Martin Luther King Jr.'s peaceful civil rights movement, which got legislation passed, specifically the 1964 Civil Rights Act, but did not change the hearts and minds of those opposed to the movement. King, in Deloria's estimation, had to keep creating symbolic events, which were based on perpetual crisis.

To the extent, then, that the countercultural phenomena—be it opposing the Vietnam War, the struggle for civil rights, or questioning the
American Way—affected ethnic groups, including American Indians,
ethnic studies could, in Deloria's opinion, play a role in the rethinking
of the symbols pertinent to these groups, such as marches, occupations,
sit-ins and fish-ins. However, ethnic studies needed to do more than con-
centrate on past wrongs and injustices. Each ethnic group had to think
about how it saw itself in the here and now. Tribes, in this regard, had
always been adept at taking a comprehensive approach to their advocacy, nimbly switching from one objective to another, as opportunities
for change and improvement availed themselves, such as the Havasupai
mentioned above. The objective, in the case of tribes, was to nimbly
keep pressure on the BIA.

> When a problem is defined as a lack of education, Indian people have
> balanced it off with demands for programs for housing and economic
> development. Waiting until education began to loosen up, they con-
> centrated on economic development, hunting and fishing, or law and
> order problems, so that wherever a breakthrough occurred, they were
> ready to explore whatever progress could be made.[92]

Sometimes, though, tribes' experiments with non-Indian movements
failed. Even the NCAI was blind to the needs of tribes because of its
perspective on national issues as opposed to local ones, which was the
converse of the issue raised above in which tribes did not see their
localized issues as part of national politics. The goal of tribes, in this
context, was to obtain as much power for themselves over their own
affairs as possible, freeing themselves from federal control, while retaining federal protection of lands and services, i.e., the trust relationship.
From a tribal perspective, then, intergroup relations—be it intertribal
or interracial—needed to be done with recognition of cultural or group
uniqueness, not in terms of generalities (so-called color-blindness). With
that in mind, Deloria counseled that one needed to be more aware of
how the political system worked. More to the point, as Deloria looked
back in *We Talk, You Listen* from the vantage point of 1970, what had
happened most regularly had been efforts at overloading the system. For

example, King determined that "Southern cities could not possibly jail everyone who marched," so he orchestrated marches that overloaded the jails. Similarly, the "People's Park" protest at Berkeley, which amassed some twenty-five thousand participants, overwhelmed the city's ability to respond, as evidenced by the havoc and casualties that ensued. However, tactics for upsetting the system meant little if there was no plan for fundamental change, which is to say, dramatically reforming the system in question.

> There are an incredible number of tactics which could be used to bring about a radical change in present structures. Use of them depends upon how clearly those people advocating change want a change and understand the nature of the system they are facing. This means strategy by which moral and ethical questions can be raised so that they will convey a maximum of issue-education while making maximal use of the weaknesses of the system. In that way the good things within a system would be made better and a real type of guerilla warfare, though on a more sophisticated level, could be waged with deadly effectiveness.[93]

With respect to the major event in the Indian protest movement as of 1970, the occupation of Alcatraz Island by the Indians of All Tribes, while Deloria did not mention this in *We Talk, You Listen*, he did analyze this seminal episode in *Broken Treaties*, in which Deloria commented on Richard Oakes, "the charismatic [St. Regis] Mohawk" who led the successful landing and occupation of this well-known federal site. While Oakes and his fellow activists did issue statements to the press, complete with enumerating their plans for the island facility, it was debatable that these were promoted with any comprehension of the federal system they were protesting.

> He [Oakes] attributed his fame to the invasion phase of the movement and failed to recognize the necessity of prolonged negotiations in completing the transfer of title to the lands which the activists wanted. Thus Oakes made plans for additional invasions of federal property in northern California and at key places around the country. Other

Indians followed Oakes's lead, and soon the only issue was landing on pieces of surplus federal property, not securing them in Indian hands through legislation or litigation.[94]

Inspired by the spectacular feat of the Indians of All Tribes, dozens of occupations and demonstrations took place around the country, which continued into the late 1970s, which may have been effective at garnering media attention, but were short on producing long-term political reform.[95] With the latter in focus, Deloria suggested a legal strategy, when, with reference to America's responsibility for the devastations wreaked at the Sand Creek and Wounded Knee massacres, he stated: "Instead of taking over abandoned islands to which there is a tenuous claim, Indian militants could be proclaiming the admitted liability of the United States from every rooftop."[96]

With respect to Deloria's appraisal of Oakes's legacy, it was reflective of his rather uneven relationship with the purported radicals of the Indian protest movement, which has been documented at various points throughout this volume. In his memoir account of the Alcatraz occupation, Adam Fortunate Eagle (Red Lake Ojibwe) (in collaboration with Tim Findley), shared some of Deloria's experiences trying to work with the Indians occupying Alcatraz Island, in which the occupiers' perception of Deloria was less than salubrious: "You know, I'd get halfway up the hill there, and somebody would say, 'what are you doing here?' Well, the Bay Area Indians asked me to come out. . . . But that didn't impress them. It was like anyone who didn't swim ashore was really suspect."[97] Paul Chaat Smith and Robert Allen Warrior later elaborated on Deloria's tenuous relation with the Alcatraz occupiers:

In April [1970], Vine Deloria Jr. . . . visited San Francisco. He had visited the island in the early days of the takeover, and was impressed with the energy and boldness of Alcatraz but felt the activists' inexperience severely limited their effectiveness. During his April visit, he told reporters that "only ten Indians in the country are qualified to negotiate with the federal government." His obvious sense that none of them were affiliated with Indians of All Tribes was not lost on island residents.[98]

At the same time, to be fair, Deloria scolded older and more experienced tribal leaders for not intervening on behalf of their younger counterparts, specifically in terms of availing themselves as resources whose knowledge and experience could have abetted the activists' cause. Indeed, what Deloria regarded as lost opportunities for seasoned tribal leaders on the reservations to unite in common cause with the Indian youth movement was an issue that Deloria raised in a 1971 commentary:

> By late 1970 the tribal leaders were cringing in fear that the activists would totally control Indian affairs. . . . But it was the tribal leaders' own fault that the activists had parlayed Alcatraz into a national phenomenon. For decades the NCAI and other national groups had cast aside young people and urban Indians in favor of local reservation citizens.[99]

According to Chaat Smith and Warrior, what Deloria proposed was building a coalition between the older and younger Indian organizations that were shaping the discourse on Indian rights at this time. More specifically, at the 1971 annual convention, "Deloria proposed that the NCAI work in coalition with three other organizations: the National Indian Youth Council (NIYC), the National Tribal Chairman's Association (NTCA), and AIM."[100] The practicality of this proposed alliance, however farfetched and idealistic as it appeared, was summarized in a press release for the American Indian Press Association.

> NCAI would focus on lobbying Congress. NTCA would deal with the Bureau on issues affecting the reservations. NIYC would "organize Indian youth and get them into the various programs available to Indian people. The other organizations will not have to have youth programs with NIYC around. They can concentrate on doing their jobs without having to stop and develop other programs that do not relate to what they are doing." As for AIM, they would provide "the activist punch that any solid movement needs. At times the bureaucracy needs a swift kick in the you-guessed-it. AIM can provide this and NTCA and NCAI will not have to forsake their jobs to do it."[101]

In Deloria's estimation, the kind of coalition he proposed was not only a practical and efficient use of available resources, but could also provide a viable foundation for establishing an Indian-organized approach to creating a new relationship in Indian affairs between urban and reservation. In the end, the problem of Indian leadership was about organizing a spectrum of groups—governmental, activist, and intellectual—into a coalition of Indian political forces that were reflective of the Indian populations various needs, be it legislative, political, communal, or motivational.

CHAPTER 9

Twentieth-Century Tribes

Nonlinear People in a Linear World

In "Indians and Modern Society," chapter 10 of *Custer,* Deloria reached the penultimate stage of his analysis of the Indian condition in post–World War II America. Basically, the argument was that the ironic result of America's growth as a global economic power was the supplanting of puritan rugged individualism with the emergence of corporate tribalism. However, the corporation was not limited to the wealthy white elite. On the contrary, returning to his initial admiration of the War on Poverty programs, Deloria heralded the Community Development Corporation (CDC), which was a creation of the Community Self-Determination Act (1969), as a form of tribalism. More specifically, Deloria stated: "If the CDC was brand new for blacks it had a mighty familiar ring to the Indian people. The tribal council, as set up under the Indian Reorganization Act, had precisely the same powers, functions, and intents. Indians have been using the tribal council as organized under IRA for nearly a generation. As Indians viewed the 'new' CDC, the blacks were finally ready to tribalize. One young Indian waggishly suggested that if they made up enrollments they might call them blacklists."[1] In the case of tribes, ever since the 1934 IRA provided for the incorporation of tribes as businesses capable of enacting their economic development, tribes had been taking advantage, to varying degrees of success, of partaking in the larger American economy. Tribal corporate identity in the federal system was as important, if not more so, than their concomitant identity as individual citizens as accorded by the 1924 Indian Citizenship Act.

As a sign of the times in which he wrote, Deloria referenced William H. Whyte Jr.'s *The Organization Man* (1956), which argued that the collectivism of corporate life was replacing Americans' reverence for rugged individualism.[2] It was within the rise of what Eisenhower called the "military industrial complex" and what C. Wright Mills labeled the "power elite" that post-1945 Indian affairs developed into the termination of the federal trust relation with tribes. Ironically, the federal government was attempting to coerce tribes into individualism, leaving their tribal corporate identity behind, presumably for whatever non-Indian corporate identity awaited them in the urban job market. As for the business world, which was run exclusively by whites, Deloria saw the rise of not just the corporation but also the conglomerate as evidence of America's imminent tribalization. "The corporation," Deloria asserted, "provided everything that a man might need if he were to maintain an affluent life over and above that of non-corporate man and befitting a person of vast educational achievement."[3] Insofar as there was no evidence of sarcasm in Deloria's observations, one was obliged to take his thesis that corporate culture was the modern American version of tribalism at face value. At the same time, what was undeniably real was the consequences of the modern technology-driven economy on the average person's quality of life. How the American system was responding to the needs of its citizens, i.e., workforce, was indicative, in Deloria's opinion, of a need for a tribal approach to social problems:

> Non-Indian society is gradually being forced to come to grips with social problems which its competitiveness has created for it and its proposed solutions are merely re-castings of traditional Indian social values although Indian people have not been able to communicate these values to the society at large. Last June [1965] Attorney General Katzenbach advocated "substitute parents" to combat juvenile delinquency—a variation of the Indian kinship system. Recently there has been talk of re-imbursement by the state of people injured by criminals at large—another facet of Indian society. Leisure time and

the guaranteed annual income are also being discussed and these are variations of Indian social organization. The "welfare state" providing everything from birth to death is merely [an] objectification of the "undifferentiated" Indian society where life is a whole and not a series of unrelated functions.[4]

Supposedly, what Deloria was presenting was how the rise of post–World War II America looked from an Indian perspective. "Rarely does anyone ask an Indian what he thinks about the modern world."[5] Unfortunately, given Deloria's ongoing gender bias—the corporate world, not to mention Deloria's conception of tribes, appeared to be made up solely of men—and his uncritical acceptance of capitalism as a given rendered his observations as naïve, as opposed to prophetic. Ever since settlers began their invasion of Indian lands at the end of the American Revolution, they had repeatedly adopted various components of Indigenous cultures into their own way of doing things, all the while maintaining their fundamental belief in an intolerant God and the Gospel of Wealth.[6] Having said that, Deloria was hardly the first one to cast a hopeful eye at American progress, seeing signs of an Indigenous reawakening. Charles Eastman, author of *The Soul of the Indian (1911)*, occasionally lapsed into this kind of fantasy, seeing the emergence of outdoor organizations like the Boy Scouts and Campfire Girls, along with the establishment of the National Park System, as indications that Americans were becoming "more Indian." Furthermore, Deloria's remarks about corporations—in addition to hippies, which is covered below—was part of a distinctive tradition in American Indian thought. On this premise, Deloria made an interesting comparison between conglomerations and Indian alliances:

The corporation became comparable to the great Indian coalitions such as the Iroquois and the Creek confederacies which stretched for thousands of square miles and in which a member was entirely safe and at home. And like the Indian tribes, success was measured against those outside the corporations, by prestige and honors. Where eagle feathers measured an Indian's successes, thickness of carpets measured executive success.[7]

What was not yet apparent was what all of this meant for Indian tribes, as opposed to corporate tribes? Delaying any answer, Deloria persevered with his analysis of post–World War II American life. With respect to his observations about corporations, another aspect to America's growing tribalization was the corporate mentality that it instilled in its members, which Deloria likened to the kinship relations that actual tribes maintained that obliged them to think of the group's well-being. Insofar as the corporation provided its members a salary, complete with rewards for exceptional performance, provisions for health insurance and retirement, not to mention a corporate identity, in Deloria's assessment, the corporation was a tribe-like entity. The question was, would corporations and the modern Americans who work for them, openly acknowledge their tribalization and build upon this?[8] Because Americans were taught by social scientists and others to regard tribes as prehistoric and the corporation as contemporary, acknowledging their tribalization would not come easily. In the meantime, as the corporation became more tribal, the American family became less familial.

The alleged decline of the American community as one in which a certain social ideal was determined to be in distress, namely the notion of America as the Christian "City upon a Hill." More to the point, the source of this ideal was believed to be in America's mythical past, where once upon a time there was social stability and neighbors knew one another. It was a place, moreover, where the "American Dream" came true. America's fallen virtue, however, had long been a prominent concern among sociologists, political scientists, and other pundits who basically regarded America's white hegemony as the norm and its disruption due to global affairs and civil unrest as evidence of American civilization's undoing.[9] Such melancholy for the American Dream only made sense, of course, to the extent that one's community was privileged enough, which is to say white enough, to had taken the ideal for granted in the first place. As the civil rights movement and the concomitant power movements demonstrated, there was a difference between bowling alone when one's affluent economic existence precluded one from developing friendships, as opposed to bowling alone because one was, say, racially segregated. Segregation, of course, also impacted gender, sexual orientation, political, religious, and even age-group differences (most of which, as noted, Deloria does not even mention).

With racial segregation in mind, Deloria observed in *We Talk, You Listen* the pervasive effect of electronic media, not only on affluent white communities, but also their less affluent, nonwhite counterparts. The communication gap, as Deloria understood it, was also a generation gap, and a gap between communities, all of which was driven by changes in communication technology. To illustrate his point, Deloria invoked a narrative that began with hard-working immigrant parents who handed down their work ethic to their children, only to see their value of hard work come under question during the Great Depression. The economic upheaval that was the 1930s generated a fear for the future. Enter the Radio Age, in which millions of Americans were soothed by President Roosevelt's message that they had nothing to fear but fear itself. Such idealism, though, after World War II, was fractured by the Television Age, in which people were exposed to a wider world, including a vast nonwhite world, in which the rags-to-riches narrative was not equally applied to everyone. Another social crisis ensued. Young people, such as Deloria, were having their world shaped in a completely different way than the previous generation. The world as it was then experienced did not match the world that they were taught to believe was really real. Consequently, the symbols of the old era were emptied of meaning. In their place emerged a selfish subjectivism and cultural relativism. Fortunately, at the same time mass media was fracturing the symbols of the old order, the new media was connecting people and groups in ways that were not possible before. A new mythology was developing. In fact, it needed to develop to explain the new world that people were living in now. Indians were part of this dynamic: the Indian myths with which white Americans once lived comfortably were being confronted with the Indian reality that entered their television screens. Meanwhile, back on the reservation, what one saw was a step behind the rest of America. Yet, these communities, too, were undergoing irreversible change: "Families [on Pine Ridge] that had been hundreds of miles from any form of communication were now only minutes away from telephone." Furthermore, as Deloria reminisced:

Roads were built connecting the major communities of the Pine Ridge country. No longer did it take hours to go from one place to another. With these kinds of roads everyone had to have a car. The team and wagon vanished, except for those families who lived at various "camps" in inaccessible canyons pretty much as their ancestors had. (Today, even they have adopted the automobile for traveling long distances in search of work.)[10]

With an eye to how tribalism, as a creation of Indigenous cultures, could play a role in assisting Americans at adjusting to their growing tribal existence, Deloria continued enumerating the social issues currently facing them. As a consequence of corporate culture, the American nuclear family was spending less time together as a unit and more time apart pursuing individual activities. More specifically, family members were spending their time away from home "participating" in "clubs," be it the Boy Scouts, a country club, or the local PTA. A club, which was an organization dedicated to a particular interest, was another form of tribalism, albeit writ small. Interestingly, Deloria's illustrated his point with a reference to *Playboy*—the same magazine that had recently published his chapter on anthropologists—which during the 1960s, and well into the 1980s—also ran clubs in a number of cities:

> The best example in intellectual circles of a tribal phenomenon is the magazine. *Playboy* early on capitalized on tribal existence, although exemplified in the hutch instead of the tipi, and turned a magazine into a way of life. If ever there was a tribal cult oozing with contemporary mythology and tribal rites it is the Playboy club. Identity is the last concern of the Playboy, yet it is what his tribe offers him—and with a key.[11]

Whereas Eastman's generation saw the rise of fraternal lodges, such as the Teepee Order and the Improved Order of Red Men, Deloria witnessed the allure of the Playboy Club.[12] Clearly, Deloria was not a feminist, nor was he even the slightest bit aware of the second-wave feminist movement that was underway during the 1960s.[13] In fact, by the time Deloria published *Custer*, Betty Friedan, author of *The Feminine Mystique* (1963), had founded the National Organization of Women (1966) and introduced the Equal Rights Amendment into the U.S. Senate (S. J. Res. 61). As for Playboy, Gloria Steinem had published her exposé on working as a Playboy bunny in *Show Magazine* (May 1 and June 1, 1963). Nevertheless, Deloria's comments about the Playboy phenomenon quickly gave way to his firsthand observations about the appearance of hippies in Indian Country during the "summer of 1966," which Deloria recounted from his days as executive director of the NCAI:

> I used to sit in my office and suddenly find it invaded by a number of strange beings in gaudy costumes who would inform me of their blood-intellectual relationship with Indians. . . . Yet many hippies whom I met had some basic humanistic beliefs not unlike those of Indian people. Concern for the person and abhorrence for confining rules, regulations, and traditions seemed to characterize the early hippie movement. When the hippies began to call for a gathering of the tribes, to create free stores, to share goods, and to gather all of the lost into communities, it appeared as if they were on the threshold of tribal existence.[14]

Unfortunately, in spite of their alleged interest in Indians, hippies remained adamantly adverse toward sustaining any form of "customs," which they regarded as stifling. In that sense, they were the obverse of the corporate tribe described above, which remained decidedly oblivious to the tribalism, complete with customs it was creating. Eventually, corporate culture degenerated into the 1980s "Greed is good" Gordon Gekko type, replete with selfishness, materialism, and hostile takeovers. Meanwhile, hippie culture simply burned out, to be replaced by a more self-indulgent 1970s "Me Generation." Consequently, the youth movement or the "counter culture" that Theodore Roszak wrote about in his 1969 book, *The Making of a Counter Culture: Reflections on the Technocratic Society and Its Youthful Opposition*, was overcome by the cynicism of Generation X. Neither type of almost-a-tribe ever reached an awareness that tribes had known since time immemorial about the intrinsic relation between land, kinship, and custom. As Deloria lamented in *Custer*: "Only a few hippies made an effort to develop a land base. A few communes are beginning to spring up around the country. But most of the flowers, unfortunately, have yet to be planted."[15]

At this point, Deloria brought his reader to an assessment of the United Fund as an example of corporate success in the name of philanthropy and social service. Obviously, the social and political upheaval of the 1960s was going to have to be grounded in something more stable. More specifically, as an organization the United Fund succeeded in making itself indispensable as a mediating power between donors and recipients, much like other economic institutions, e.g., banks, in the management of financial wealth, namely loans and investments. With respect to the relation between the United Fund and tribes, Deloria observed with an eye to how tribes could further adapt their self-determination to the modern economy: "As tribal corporations meet the challenges of modern life, there will be less use for United Fund agencies and their revenues programs will decline."[16] Tribes, as of *Custer*, largely relied on the fund-raising endeavors of non-Indian institutions like the United Fund for their philanthropic needs, which changed during the 1970s, as Indian-founded nonprofits began to grow.[17] As things were, circa 1969, tribes were subjected to non-Indian definitions of being "in need." How Indians faired in United Fund campaigns was an indication of which way the winds were blowing with respect to non-Indian attitudes toward Indians. In light of which, Deloria's point seemed to be twofold: one, tribes ought to initiate a collective enterprise by forming their own united fund, in which they were the mediators between donors and recipients; and, two, the first option would largely be contingent upon tribes' ability to become more financially independent, which was to say more self-determining as a tribal corporate body. The suggestion here seemed to be for pursuing a nonprofit model for developing tribal self-determination, one in which resources were amassed for the purpose of serving the public interest, which was to say tribal members.

Speaking of the public tribal interest, Deloria broached the urgent topic of the 1968 Indian Civil Rights Act, which was regarded as a serious impingement on traditional Indian customary law, as the federal statute compelled tribes to curtail their justice system to fit within the limits of a non-Indian Bill of Rights. The absurdity of this presumption on the part of Congress, which passed H.R. 2516, was that in the opinion of many, including Deloria, Indian customary laws were more humane than their non-Indian counterparts. Unlike "law and order" politicians who espoused a punitive approach to lawmaking, complete with high-levels of incarceration, many tribes maintained a restitutive concept of justice, which was concerned more with the victim and the community.[18] However, because of accusations against tribal governments of abuse and corruption, Congress took it upon itself to limit their powers, in particular in its court system, by stipulating through legislation that they should abide by the American code of individual rights. Unsurprisingly, tribes were seeking to amend the Indian Civil Rights Act, to which Deloria counseled: "Although the Bill of Rights is not popular with some tribes, the Pueblos in particular, I do not believe that it should be amended. With the strengthening of tribal courts Indian tribes now have a golden opportunity to create an Indian common law comparable to the early English common law."[19] Deloria expressed such ideas during his 1965 testimony before the Senate Subcommittee on Constitutional Rights, during which he stated: "I think that if the tribes had funds and that if we could set up training for our tribal judges so they could understand judicial procedure, that we could begin to build a judicial system of a correct balance of law and custom."[20] Such common law was possible, Deloria explained, if tribal judges wrote lengthy opinions "incorporating tribal customs and beliefs with state and federal codes and thus redirecting tribal ordinances toward a new goal."[21] With regard to the 1968 Indian Civil Rights Act, Deloria later summarized its historical imposition onto tribal jurisdiction in *Broken Treaties*:

> Until 1968, when Congress extended the Bill of Rights to cover the relationships between tribal governments and tribal members, Indian tribes were not affected by the constitutional protections when dealing with their own affairs. Even today, the 1968 Civil Rights Act is under constant challenge by tribes attempting to define how the Bill of Rights affect tribal sovereignty.[22]

Such ambitious objectives as developing an Indian case-law tradition were surely within the realm of possibility. However, they not only required persons who were willing to initiate new customs within the limitations of existing law, but also a class of innovators educated in the ways of both tribal and nontribal jurisprudence. In which case, Deloria became more vocal in his hope for the upcoming generation of college-educated Indians at leading a new era of tribal self-determination in all of its manifestations. "Ideologically," Deloria announced with enthusiasm, "the young Indians are refusing to accept white values as eternal truths." Indeed, one can say that *Custer* had been one long rejection of "white values" regarding Indians and Indian affairs, which he continued in *We Talk, You Listen, God Is Red,* and *Broken Treaties.* Was Deloria's "Indian manifesto" therefore calling for a revolution? In a manner of speaking. More specifically, he was calling for a revolution in Indian thinking, asking Indians of all ages to stand up and speak out on behalf of their own future. Toward that objective, Deloria suggested, referring back to his suggestion of a nonprofit approach to nation building, that tribes take the initiative of forming their own "housing authorities, development corporations, and training program supervisors, continuing to do business according to Indian ways."[23]

Providing for the good of all, such as food and shelter, as well as valuing people for what they had accomplished on behalf of the people were two Indian values that Deloria highlighted as examples of "Indian ways." Recall the Sioux woman earlier who kept sharing her telephone, regardless of the expense. America by contrast was a country whose leadership was based on "image" at the expense of issues.[24] In this regard, Deloria excoriated both Nixon and the Kennedys for exploiting image over substance. In a grant application to the Council on Indian Affairs, the profound differences between Indian and non-Indian, namely Protestant, leadership traditions were articulated:

> Competition, in the traditional Protestant sense has been unknown. Prestige and honor have not been lacking in Indian society however. But the mere acquisition of wealth or the attempt to create an "image" has not been accepted as an ultimate basis for either social or personal value. Within this type of social structure humility and politeness

were highly respected and honors earned became a matter of social concensus [*sic*] rather than achievement awards.

In the end, leadership depended "upon the willingness of the people to follow."[25] With respect to issues, one of the most important for tribes was land use, which Indians wanted to preserve for their children and grandchildren, while whites wanted it to utilize for maximum and immediate financial gain. On this point, Deloria wrote:

> Some tribes have zoned their reservations so that the land is used primarily for the benefit of reservation people. Gradually planners in the white society will come to recognize the necessity of reserving land for specific use rather than allow helter-skelter development to continue unchecked.[26]

While Deloria was in one respect in tune with the emerging environmental movement, in another one can say that he underestimated the intransigence of those who derived money and power from the exploitation of the natural world. Then, again, rather than confront the ambitions of energy and mining corporations, such as Peabody Coal, which was wreaking havoc in the Southwest, Deloria abruptly switched from pointing out the radical difference between how Indians and whites regarded the land to affirming that "minority groups" ought to "emphasize what they share with the white society, not what keeps them apart." Perhaps Deloria became aware that he was creating an unbridgeable chasm between Indians and whites and wanted to redirect his discourse lest he lose the opportunity to promote any hope for political reform. In any case, in light of *Custer*'s analysis of Indian-Black relations, it was clear that Deloria did not think of Indians as a "minority group" but rather as sovereign nations. It was also clear from every other chapter in *Custer*, not to mention *God Is Red*, that Deloria saw a huge cultural divide between whites and Indians. So, where was Deloria going with this recommendation, which was contrary to the "burn it down" declaration that many readers may have expected from him? Reminding his reader that he was not a radical militant, Deloria took the opportunity to criticize the Black Power movement, which turned into an admonishment for Indians against absolute statements and ultimatums: "Black may be beautiful but such a slogan hardly contributes to the understanding of non-blacks." With respect to the Indian protest movement, Deloria asserted that Indians did not need a comparable slogan, such as "Red is beautiful." Insofar as the exclamation of "Red Power" was an emotional outlet, such a need was already fulfilled by means of the pow wow.

As for building bridges between Indians and whites, Deloria explained the difference between nationalism and militancy with respect to the American Indian community. In a nutshell, the majority of Indians were nationalists in the sense that their primary concern was the well-being of their tribe, regardless of their relationship with the non-Indian world. However, not all Indians were militants. Militancy signified a proclivity for impulsive responses to developments in white society and government. While nationalists may at times resort to "violence and demonstrations," in Deloria's opinion, the militants engaged in such actions for the sole purpose of drawing attention to their cause as opposed to being a part of creating an overall strategy for "undermining the ideological and philosophical positions of the establishment and capturing its programs for their own use." Since the occupation of Alcatraz Island had yet to happen, as Deloria published these words in *Custer*, it was left to speculation as to whom and what Deloria was referring. Potentially, as Deloria took another swipe at the Black community, he had in mind the Southern Christian Leadership Conference (SCLC),[27] which he regarded as exhibiting the consequences of militancy for militancy's own sake. More to the point, the SCLC embodied the proposition that militancy will "inevitably lead on to more militancy": "This is apparent in the dilemma in which the SCLC found itself after the 1966 Civil Rights Bill. Demonstrations had proved successful and so SCLC found itself led on and on down that path, never satisfied. Even after King's death, when SCLC could have changed its goals and techniques, it continued to the disaster of Resurrection City."[28] Such a situation in which perpetual crises defined a political movement would preclude that movement from achieving its goals, assuming it had any beyond confrontation.

In concluding his thoughts on these matters, Deloria proclaimed a bright and prosperous future for tribes, who would reap a hitherto unimaginable effect on American society and politics, insofar as they learned as a community to "articulate values they wish to transmit to the rest of society." Because the apparent poverty of tribes made them look small and insignificant, certainly when compared to the dominant nation that colonized them, "the rest of society" had yet to hear what Indians had to say for themselves. "But in many ways," Deloria proclaimed, "the veil is lifting and a brighter future is being seen. Night is giving way to day. The Indian will soon stand tall and strong once more." Although Deloria's concluding proclamation of hope and resurgence was "in many ways" incongruent with his analysis of modern society; nonetheless, as history proved, he was right about the rise of the Indian voice in America, which inspired the pages of *Broken Treaties*, complete with its argument that tribes were still independent sovereign nations. Indeed, tribal nationhood had endured even the lowest ebb of federal Indian policy, which presumed to dictate to tribes what their rights were under Congress's plenary powers.

> Instead of vanishing . . . the American Indian has redoubled his efforts to bring the tribe back together. With this movement [toward greater self-determination] has come a realization that the tribe must stand before history and reclaim its political and cultural identity and independence. Not all tribes lost their sense of independence.[29]

And those that did were getting it back.

CHAPTER 10

The Good Red Road Ahead

Self-Determination

One of the two motivating factors that led Deloria to pursue a law degree after serving as the NCAI executive director was his work with small tribes, such as those at Pyramid Lake, Yakima, and Havasupai, which were hidden behind the more dominant nations, whose names, such as Navajo, Apache, and Sioux, stand more prominently in the American imagination. Deloria learned, to his utter dismay, "that these tribes were without legal counsel, had no idea what their rights were, and had no way to find out such information." Given the economic status and remoteness of most tribes throughout, say, in the Four Corners area, it was easy to understand how they were left out of the global village that had come to define the media-drenched First World nations. More to the point, Deloria observed that what worked for larger nations, such as the success stories that benefitted from the 1934 Indian Reorganization Act, was not nearly as effective for tribes that had far fewer resources, be it land or people. In light of which, Deloria surmised that a more viable approach to reforming Indian affairs was to focus on the smaller tribes first, then apply what was learned to larger groups:

> I believe that the solution to many problems affecting Indian people can only come through intensive work with such small tribes. They are basically one community unit, whereas larger tribes may consist

of a number of small communities. If a course of action can be shown to work with a small tribe, chances of its succeeding with a larger tribe are much greater.[1]

Even when the language of tribal self-governance was cleansed of colonial influences—such as the adoption of nation over reservation, sovereign over ward, traditional names over foreign names, and so on— at some point that empowered, self-governing tribe would still have to reckon with the forces and influence of the United States. Consequently, the question was, under what terms would that encounter take place? The whole point of Deloria's writings was to change the political and intellectual landscape on behalf of American Indians who were otherwise obliged to live and struggle alongside the non-Indian worlds populating their lands. Of particular concern had been the language, ideas, and theories governing Indian affairs, which had undergone a plethora of permutations since the first treaty was signed between the Delaware and the fledgling American republic in 1778. The trajectory of that law and policy discourse, complete with the Indian responses, was covered in *Custer* and *Broken Treaties*, all of which was analyzed in the preceding chapters, including the proposal that treaty making be reinstated. Insofar, then, as Indigenous nations were enmeshed within the federal system, those same Indigenous nations had been motivated to make a vigorous response to the claims placed upon their land and political rights. What Deloria accomplished toward this objective, as we segue into the concluding chapter of his epic discourse on tribal self-determination, was articulating tribal grievances against the injustices of federal Indian law and policy, specifically the gross malfeasance on the part of the president and Congress, across multiple administrations and Congresses, in their trust responsibilities to tribes. Furthermore, through the political agenda explained in *Custer, We Talk, You Listen, God Is Red,* and *Broken Treaties,* Deloria developed a clear political path to tribal independence, in terms of tribal political, cultural, and economic sovereignty.

Toward the above objectives, according to Deloria, March 1966 marked the beginning of the "modern era of Indian emergence." More specifically, this was when Tom Diamond came to the National Congress of American

Indians meeting in El Paso, Texas, to ask for the organization's support. Deloria recounted how the Tiguas of Ysleta del Sur Pueblo were forced into exile when retreating Spanish forces, which had been pushed out by Popé's Rebellion in 1680, wound up in present day, Juarez, Mexico. At which point, once they no longer served the Spanish, the Tigua survivors were given land that was eventually engulfed by the modern city of El Paso. The point of Deloria's historical anecdote was to illustrate how a once forgotten tribe was reasserting its existence, complete with seeking federal recognition. In Deloria's estimation, the Tiguas signified a trend that will have huge implications for the future of Indian affairs. In the case of the Tiguas, they once had federal recognition but were then bureaucratically forgotten by the Bureau of Indian Affairs. Fortunately, because of Diamond's advocacy and NCAI assistance, President Johnson signed "into law a bill that officially recognized the Tiguas as an Indian tribe." That act of recognition sent a wave of realization throughout Indian Country, namely:

> Discovery of the Tiguas rocked Indian people in several respects. Indians had been brainwashed into accepting the demise of their tribe as God's natural plan for Indians. Yet the Tiguas plainly demonstrated that Indian tribal society had the strength and internal unity to maintain itself indefinitely within an alien culture.[2]

With respect to the Tigua, their case occurred at time when termination was official policy. It also, of course, occurred the same year as the fateful confrontation with Stewart Udall in Santa Fe. Indian Country, as Indians and non-Indians alike realized, was more populated and extended much farther geographically than previously thought. The drive for federal recognition was underway as the NCAI contacted several other groups that had been overlooked federally and historically.[3] Symbolic of the reemergence of unrecognized tribes was the appointment of Lacy Maynor of North Carolina's Lumbee Nation to the "First Citizens for Humphrey-Muskie, a coalition of Indian people supporting the Democratic ticket in 1968." Maynor distinguished himself locally and nationally when he led a group of Lumbees into an unsuspecting Ku Klux Klan meeting and "sent them packing."[4] Not since the days of Sitting Bull was a more cathartic rejection of white hegemony seen in Indian Country.

Deloria noted that it was not only organizations like the NCAI that had acknowledged the importance of reemergent tribes. So, too, had anthropologists, who, during the 1960s were attempting to overtake the discourse on hitherto unknown groups with theories about "pan-Indianism." Pan-Indianism, it should be pointed out, as a social science theory was different from its application as a political movement. Whereas organizations like the NCAI and the Society for American Indians before it were pan-Indian in the sense that representatives of numerous tribes formed political alliances to address their common interests, e.g., treaty rights, social scientists spoke of cultural traits that signified an essential Indianness that they thought was universal across tribal groups.[5] The assumption among anthropologists with regard to liminal tribal groups, such as the Tiguas or Lumbees, was that their identity was a composite of more prominent cultural groups. Alleged evidence for this phenomenon was derived from one of two scenarios: one, a historic group was adopted into a larger group; two, a marginal group appropriated the traits and customs of other groups. Either of the two scenarios placed a given group's identity as a unique tribe under doubt, potentially precluding them from federal recognition. "Pan-Indianism implies that a man forgets his tribal background and fervently merges with other Indians to form 'Indianism.' Rubbish."[6] In his 1971 review of Hazel W. Hertzberg's *The Search for an American Indian Identity: Modern Pan-Indian Movements*, which appeared the same year, Deloria commented on the book's subtitle and its implications for the reemergence of unrecognized tribes:

> One must complain slightly about the use of the phrase "Pan-Indian." The author herself freely admits that Indians do not use this phrase, most abhor it. Why, then, use it? Scholarly works are not done in a vacuum these days. Many Indians will read the book and be puzzled by the technical use of Pan-Indianism and will not see in the struggles of the Society of American Indians the same problems, successes, and failures that they have experienced. The mere use of Pan-Indian, originating as it does within anthropological circles, makes the past seem

more past then [*sic*] it really is. In fact it makes that particular past the province of scholars and not of Indians. And that development only perpetuates the tension already existing between scholars and Indians.[7]

Robert K. Thomas, on the other hand, provided a more nuanced analysis of pan-Indianism in his 1972 essay.[8] In one regard, Thomas was skeptical about applying the concept to his understanding of the communities with whom he had worked, which he regarded as maintaining discreet identities as opposed to anything that was an amalgamation of other cultures, be it the Sac and Fox of Oklahoma or the Sioux at Pine Ridge. In another regard, Thomas observed pan-Indianism occurring at the political level of social organization, which was the result of intertribal relations, including intermarriage, that expressed itself in what may be described as "a new identity."[9] Unsurprisingly, the kind of acculturation that informed the intertribal relations that Thomas observed, which was a product of twentieth-century social and political movements, influenced organizations like the National Congress of American Indians. Thomas portrayed this as "in flavor Pan-Plains," complete with "'Indian Dances' nearly every night" at its "conventions."[10]

If Deloria read Thomas's essay on pan-Indianism, then what he may have noticed, aside from the Plains-centric definition of pan-Indianism, was the fact that Thomas's historical analysis did not apply to all tribal groups in all regions. The Southwest, which extended into northern Mexico, was conspicuously missing from consideration. Deloria's contention, as it was with the tribes seeking recognition, was that the reason the Tiguas and others had endured into the twentieth century in the first place was because of the strength of community they maintained against pressures to assimilate, be it into another tribe or mainstream American society. For many Indians, becoming politically conscious during the latter 1960s, the reemergence of hidden tribes testified to the strength of tribal identities. In the case of Southeastern tribes, they had even formed "an inter-tribal council to work specifically on their problems."[11] Perhaps inspired by the Southern Indian movement, Deloria stated: "As federal policies change and become clarified, there is little doubt that the southeastern United States will experience a great Indian revival, bringing the focus in Indian Affairs [sic] to philosophy [i.e., tribalism] rather than program considerations."[12] "As a result," Denise Bates observed:

> Southern Indian leaders and activists became heavily involved in intertribal coalitions and alliances, previously unorganized groups developed tribal governments, tribes embarked on new economic ventures, and petitions for federal recognition were submitted by the dozens by groups hailing from the South.[13]

Augmenting the reemergence of nonrecognized tribes was the growing presence, not to mention influence, of urban Indian coalitions. Intertribal for practical reasons, urban Indians, even those that commuted home regularly, were beginning to appreciate the need for organizing as a distinct facet of the American Indian community. In terms of what happened in twentieth-century urban areas in, say, southern California, John A. Price, contributed an article titled "The Migration and Adaptation of American Indians to Los Angeles." More specifically, Price paid special attention to those relocatees who participated in "the post-1955 . . . Employment Assistance ('Relocation') Program," which was a byproduct of HCR 108. Focusing more on economic forces, as opposed to cultural ones like intermarriage, Price observed in the data he gathered a different portrait of the pan-Indian community living in Los Angeles metropolitan area, beginning with the fact that it "has the largest population of American Indians in the United States." As for the post-1955 relocatees, they tended to (in comparison to those who did not participate in the federal government's relocation program):

> (1) be younger (median age, 25 years); (2) have resided in Los Angeles a shorter time (median, just less than two years); (3) have a lower income (median, $4,000); (4) live in the central Los Angeles area more often (59 per cent); (5) associate with other Indians more often; *(6) speak an Indian language more often (86 per cent) and better (84 per cent of those who speak an Indian language speak it "quite well")*; and (7) more often would return to their reservation if they could get a job at their current rate of pay (56 per cent) [emphasis added].[14]

While it may be the case that reservations, complete with tribal governments, were the primary conduit between Indians and the federal government, it was urban Indian communities that composed the largest segment of the overall Indian population. Nevertheless, at the same time that Deloria regarded urban Indians as "the cutting edge of the new Indian nationalism," they were the target of ongoing suspicion from their nonurban counterparts.[15] In fact, sometimes the friction between urban and reservation Indians was as intense as the one between Indians and border-town whites. Deloria shared as an example a meeting of urban Indians in Seattle, which was disrupted when members of the "Colville reservation" intervened because they were worried that the meeting would result in the urban Indians selling out the reservation, such as occurred during "the late 1950's." Back then, "off-reservation Colvilles were organized by a white man for the specific purpose of selling the large Colville reservation."[16] The urban-reservation divide, as has been well-documented, was not limited to the Colville. It had a tragic effect on the outcome of the 1972 Trail of Broken Treaties caravan, which led to the violent confrontation at Wounded Knee, where there were fatal encounters between pro– and anti–American Indian Movement forces.

In *Behind the Trail of Broken Treaties*, in "The Emergence of Indian Activism," Deloria pointed out instances in which the urban Indian population was a major impetus for the Indian protest movement, which was the result of the effect that other power movements had on Indians as of the mid 1960s. Moreover, although Deloria mentioned a pointed meeting between urban Indian activists and Indian Commissioner Robert Bennett, "which happened in Minneapolis in the fall of 1966," he nevertheless asserted that the primary "center of action was the urban areas of the West Coast," which, of course, was the site of Alcatraz Island. Consequently, "The government's immediate response to the invasion of Alcatraz was to channel more funds from the Office of Economic Opportunity to Indian groups in urban areas. Arrangements were made to fund an umbrella organization in the San Francisco Bay area as an alternative to funding the group on Alcatraz. In this way the [Nixon] administration hoped to defuse the impact which the occupation was having on Indians across the nation." As of 1972, though, as Deloria segued into his narrative on the occupation of the Bureau of Indian Affairs building in Washington DC, the "ceremonials of the Plains tribes were filled to overflowing with Indians, many of them urban activists who had come to join in the revitalization of Indian cultures." Perhaps what Indians across the country were finally realizing was that what was much stronger than the white man's artificial distinctions of urban and reservation were the kinship ties that bound them as tribal people. After all it was not the tribes that created the reservation system, nor was it the tribes that built the urban centers that now occupied their ancestral lands. In which case, accepting these colonial divisions of their peoples only served to sever the ancient ties that were at the root of the identities that they were now working toward reaffirming through ceremony and political activism. Unsurprisingly, as Deloria further observed, federal officials attempted to misrepresent the unified Indian community that marched into Washington just before the 1972 presidential election: "The government would later interpret the Trail of Broken Treaties as primarily an urban movement, even though its members represented nearly every tribe, age group, political persuasion, and ideology in Indian country."[17]

While misunderstandings between urban and reservation Indians may have continued, what was irrefutable was the fact that the urban-Indian population had taken great strides at affirming its presence in the cities where American Indian centers and other institutions had been created, such as "Chicago and Minneapolis," which "represent the most comprehensive development of urban Indianism"—a phenomenon that was not only politically significant but also multitribal, as opposed to pan-Indian (in the social-science sense of the term). Although Deloria did not mention the 1961 Chicago Indian Conference, he did note that the "cities are beginning to furnish the catalytic agents for total national organization." In fact, urban Indians' organizational powers were even compelling the federal government to respond in a meaningful way. In light of various "demonstrations against Bureau of Indian Affairs offices . . . in three cities," a National Council on Indian Opportunity was convened in April 1968 at the behest of President Johnson, which his vice president, Hubert Humphrey, oversaw. More specifically, the council consisted of six members, all of whom, according to the executive order, "have to be American Indians." In consideration of which, the six inaugural members that Johnson appointed were Wendell Chino (Mescalero Apache), LaDonna Harris (Comanche), William Hensley (Inupiak), Roger Jourdain (Red Lake Ojibwe), Raymond Nakai (Navajo), and Cato Valandra (Rosebud Sioux).[18] What all of this meant was that the future of Indian affairs was being set by off-reservation Indians whose political awareness was sparked by termination, relocation, grassroots activism, national organizations, media coverage, American Indian centers, and the times in which all Indians were living, in which America was a nation in social and political upheaval.

> Chicago has seen the rise of Indian nationalism by younger people. In addition to the established centers and clubs, young people have started to move the urban Indian structure toward a more militant stance in regard to urban programs available through the mayor's office. Denver has recently seen the organization of another Indian club that is avowedly more militant with regard to programs being administered by the city. Omaha has a group of younger Indians which threatens to begin to move city Indians toward community involvement.[19]

What the developments outlined above meant for Indian affairs was that the old paradigm of BIA–tribal council relations needed to be drastically revised in response to the emergence of influential but nongovernmental groups, such as those organized in urban, as opposed to reservation, centers. The status quo of BIA-approved developments, complete with pitting tribes against each other, was now poised for reform. In addition to the rise of urban Indian centers, there was now interagency competition for Indian projects as a result of the War on Poverty.

> Urban Indians have a great advantage over our reservation people. They have no restrictions on the way they raise or spend money. The bureau has no means by which it can influence decisions made by urban Indian centers. Thus, if it is to influence urban Indians at all, it must be by offering them something. Urban Indians have nothing to

lose and everything to gain, so initial success breeds deeper thought and more comprehensive planning for the next go-round.[20]

Taken together, urban Indians and reemerging tribes, stood to radically redefine the scope and demographics of the American Indian community. What Deloria was anticipating, more specifically, was the formation of the American Indian Movement, which had been, as of the time of *Custer*, only recently founded in the Little Earth neighborhood of Minneapolis, next door to the University of Minnesota, where the first department of American Indian studies was established in June 1969. Indeed, the Twin Cities and Minnesota held a special place in the history of the Indian protest movement, which was equaled only by what happened in the San Francisco Bay area. According to Frank C. Miller, Minnesota regarded itself as more enlightened than most states with respect to the civil rights movement and minority groups. Hubert Humphrey, for example, "had been made an honorary member of the Red Lake Band of Chippewa Indians when he was United States Senator from Minnesota." Also, future Carter vice president, Walter Mondale, assumed the "role of being one of the leading spokesmen for the needs of Minnesota Indians" once Humphrey became Johnson's vice president. As for the Indians in Minnesota, Miller recalled:

> The Indians themselves were becoming more involved in the political and social life of the state; individuals were emerging in key roles, in both public agencies and community organizations. In the Twin Cities the number of Indian organizations proliferated as migration [into the Twin Cities] accelerated, and the Urban Indian Federation was formed to facilitate communication among them. One of the most visible groups was the American Indian Movement (AIM), the first militant Indian organization in the region and one of the first in the nation.[21]

Also on the horizon was the formation of BIA guidelines in 1978 for the formal process of acquiring federal recognition.[22] In the meantime, the growing political activism among urban Indians implied a yet to be appreciated impact of urban Indian voters, who had already demonstrated a likelihood of voting in higher percentages than their reservation kinfolk.[23] The potential, as Deloria saw things, was for these concerned urban Indians to compel candidates for local and national offices to address Indian-affairs issues in a way that they had not been obliged to do before—at least, not since their state was a territory. At the same time, lest Deloria got too carried away with his enthusiasm, he tempered his idealism with this observation:

> Tragically, Indian Affairs [*sic*] within the Bureau of Indian Affairs is today exclusively oriented toward individual reservations. Little concern is shown for program development on a regional, state, or inter-area office basis. Thus the BIA is extremely vulnerable to unexpected pressures from regional groups which combine urban concentrations or urban centers and reservations.[24]

If Deloria had an example in mind of such "unexpected pressures," he did not say. Instead, Deloria expressed concern for "reservation entanglements and the black power movement." Because of the paranoia created by nearly two decades of termination politics, tribal leaders on the reservation were constantly on the defensive, always wary of any new proposals. Compounding the problem was the reservation mindset of Indian Country, which precluded any consideration for urban Indians, not to mention non-federally recognized groups. In fact, urban Indians regularly thought only in terms of the reservation and completely forgot their own needs as off-reservation communities. Consequently, when it came to the kind of policy reform that Deloria was nudging at with his previous remarks, the level of comprehensiveness achieved was contingent upon how inclusive one was when referring to the American Indian community. There was the federal definition of Indian and Indian Country, then there was the more complex reality of Indian lives in the late twentieth century. Part of the problem was in not being able—at least during *Custer*'s era—to get an accurate count of urban Indians. "Programs designed to provide employment on certain reservations may be woefully out of touch with the nomadic tendencies of the people of that reservation to move back and forth."[25] More specifically, Deloria was proposing an urban relocation program that respected and supported the ties that American Indians wanted to maintain with their respective reservations, as opposed to the federal government's program, which was premised on the eventual termination of federal support.[26]

What Deloria suggested, making reference to the Sioux City Indian Center,[27] was the coordination of reservation and urban Indian populations in terms of the regions in which they lived and worked. An Indian center had the capacity to "coordinate employment, housing, education, and organization of Indian people" in given areas, even ones encompassed by multiple states. Focusing on the region, as opposed to merely an individual reservation, could enable policymakers to think in terms of all aspects of a tribe's population, not just those limited to reservation boundaries. "Combining urban and reservation goals must, therefore, be led by urban people who are much more aware of opportunities for specific developments. If urban Indians can take the time and trouble to plan for the future, they will gain a strong influence over Indian Affairs [sic] locally and eventually nationally."[28] As of 1969, the economic malaise of urban Indian populations was handled with at best mixed results by a network of federal and state agencies. More specifically, during a congressional hearing held in 1967, titled "Effect of Federal programs on rural America," the House Subcommittee on Rural Development took into account testimony on Indian reservations, in which was noted:

> In recognition of the need for vigorous action the Manpower Administration, in cooperation with the Bureau of Indian Affairs, sponsored a National Conference on Manpower Programs for Indians held recently in Kansas City, Missouri. The conference brought together some 200 Indian tribal leaders from 25 States, forming the largest intertribal gathering in the history of this Nation. Representatives from government agencies, interested organizations, and the business community also attended.
>
> As one immediate result of the conference, approximately 200 new positions have been allocated to State agencies for the extension of the Human Resources Development services to reservations and communities with significant Indian populations. These services include outreach, referral to other agencies for supportive services,

various opportunities for training, intensive job development, and a job information and reporting program. Implementation of other recommendations is proceeding with the advice of the conference leaders.[29]

With respect to the militancy of urban Indians, Deloria expressed some consternation over the adoption of Black Power–type slogans and activities among those, such as Mel Thom, who participated in the Poor People's Campaign, complete with the emergence of "red power movements." As Deloria observed: "In Omaha and Chicago, Oakland and Los Angeles, young Indians are talking like black militants and beginning to ape their ideas and techniques." Whether or not the reference to aping was intended as a racial slur, deliberate or otherwise, was open to debate. As to the political point that Deloria was trying to make, he saw the situation as one in which "bureaucrats," presumably the BIA, were telling Indian militants that "'Indians don't act like that'" with regard to their Black Power–style of militancy; while Indian militants, taking umbrage with the bureaucrats' attitude, became even more militant. However, the potential problem that Deloria saw in prioritizing militancy for its own sake was that it occluded non-Indians, be they Bureau of Indian Affairs officials or the general public, from learning, let alone understanding—and thereby reforming—anything about Indian issues. "Indians who copy blacks simply because they are attracted by the chance to make their names household words are embarking on a disastrous course of action."[30] As an example, Deloria referred to the "threats" that Ralph Abernathy made during the Poor People's Campaign "if his demands were not met," only to see him turn out to be a paper tiger. "Abernathy could no more have produced on his threats than he could have reached the far side of the moon."[31]

Drawing attention to oneself meant nothing if one or one's group did not have a firm basis of respect and influence within one's community. Before one can expect decision-making authority over vital issues, protesters must take the time to consolidate the powers they did possess, which, in the case of Indian affairs, necessitated knowing about the powers that tribes and their urban Indian relatives possessed within the federal system. As Deloria counseled would-be militants:

Indians must first understand the position they occupy in urban and national affairs. Then they must become aware of the weak points where leverage and power can be combined to provide a means of pivoting the power structure that confronts them. Only then can they apply their power to the situation and contemplate significant results.[32]

Deloria developed this advice further, as observed earlier, in *We Talk, You Listen* regarding the communication gap as also being a generation gap in which the latest technology actively divided younger generations from their elders as well as marginalized how young people agitating for change were perceived by their older peers, who were often the ones in power. Then, in *Broken Treaties*, there were Deloria's observations of the limitations of direct action, such as the occupation of Alcatraz Island, led by Richard Oakes, not to mention the droves of young people that poured into Washington DC as part of the Trail of Broken Treaties caravan, which failed to get its "Twenty-Point Position Paper" taken seriously. With respect to Deloria's criticism of activism as the primary source of political change, he made an interesting statement during the Menominee Restoration Act hearings held during May and June 1973 to Washington representative Lloyd Meeds, the chair of the Subcommittee on Indian Affairs:

I would like to make one concluding statement which is a lot of us have advocated coming to Congress, presenting our case, rather than going on the activist trail, and going through all the trauma that has been on [the news?]. We very badly need an action by Congress, such as the restoration of [the] Menominee, to show the activists that you can work through the system.

Every day, I face a lot of people in the American Indian Movement, and other movements, and [they] say what have you been able to do going through the system[?] You haven't gotten anything done. You had your chance, and so we're taking over.

We have got to have this particular bill, and we have to have immediate restoration of [the] Menominees. Now, we can go out and talk to people and show them that the thing [the system?] does work. And without that, you are leaving the whole middle ground of Indian affairs virtually defenseless, because we can't point any place and say that it [the system] does work. You see, passing this bill will give us the ammunition to bring the Indian community together and present other legislation. I think that would be more helpful.[33]

Even when the system did work, Deloria still warned his reader against expecting the United States to be a civilized nation. It was not. It was founded in violence, which it had fetishized into a love of war. "Unconditional surrender" was its mantra, and the "body count" was its mark of success. Love was not the answer, not if it meant compromise. Deloria substantiated his point by excoriating America and its long and terrible history of militarism, which was a form of militancy taken to the extremes of total war. In spite of its claim at being "first in peace," America had been much more proficient at being "first in war," certainly from an Indian perspective, whether one was talking about George Washington, who inspired the credo, or the American republic he helped found—a nation that did not waste any time at ruthlessly invading Indian lands. Like the adolescent nation it was—a mere 193 years old when *Custer* appeared—it was overly sensitive about its image, alienating "everyone who does not immediately love it," replete with making petulant and impulsive threats to the global order. America, for all of its might, was in need of parental guidance. With that in mind, perhaps as the first inhabitants of this land, Deloria thought that Indian people could play an important role in shaping a more mature future for America: "This country could easily be influenced by any group with a more comprehensive philosophy of man if that group worked in a non-violent, non-controversial manner."[34]

Indeed, as America ever so slowly aged as a nation, it would need the seasoned and ancient teachings of American Indians, be it about the environment or human relations. In the ongoing battle for America's future, as Deloria saw things from the vantage point of *We Talk, You Listen*, the political and social turmoil that generated from the civil rights movement, the anti–Vietnam War movement, along with the rising counterculture, which instigated an array of power movements including Red Power, had brought American society to a crossroads. At this juncture were two paths: "the castle or the tipi," which was to say, "neofeudalism" or "neotribalism." Insofar, then, as Deloria had observed the youth movement as being the wave of the future, not the least of which was the youthfully driven struggle for tribal self-determination, he proclaimed: "American society is unconsciously going Indian." The question, however, was in what way could this tendency be nurtured into a paradigm shift away from the rugged individualist-based system that colonized the country to a more tribally oriented way of doing things?

> The best method of communicating Indian values is to find points at which issues appear to be related. Because tribal society is integrated toward a center and non-Indian society is oriented toward linear development, the process might be compared to describing a circle surrounded with tangent lines. The points at which the lines touch the circumference of the circle are the issues and ideas that can be shared by Indians and other groups. There are a great many points at which tangents occur, and they may be considered as windows through which Indians and non-Indians can glimpse each other. Once this structural device is used and understood, non-Indians, using a tribal point of view, can better understand themselves and their relationship to Indian people.[35]

Deloria used this method to great effect in *God Is Red*, in which he strived at communicating Indian religious values by examining the points at which the linear time-based traditions of Christianity touched the circumference of the nonlinear customs and beliefs of Indian peoples. At the same time, Deloria wrote *God Is Red* with a critical awareness of the limited effect that Indians have had on how others think about the environment and society: "The peculiar tragedy of the Indian movement is that it has never been able to influence the intellectual concepts and values by which white Americans view the world."[36] Obviously, Deloria kept having to rethink his assumption that Americans were on the brink of adopting tribalism as an organic result of their relationship to this continent. Clearly, they needed more meaningful guidance.

Changing how people think, what Deloria called "ideological leverage," was a more potent force for change than violent tactics. It was not just that violence begot violence, but also it produced an obsession with expecting others to challenge one's status in an endless game of King of the Hill. Ever since the American colonies fought for their liberation from their monarchal oppressor during the late eighteenth century, Americans have been living in constant fear of three possibilities: one, a British resurgence in North America, in which the United States was recolonized; two, a slave rebellion that threw the American economy into upheaval, not to mention the social unrest; and, three, a pan-Indian alliance of tribes on a scale that could push the settler colonials back into the ocean.[37] While the British eventually diminished as a threat, the United States spent decades dealing with the ramifications of its Indian policy, in addition to going through a civil war, which in large part was an armed dispute over the future of slavery in America. And now, during the 1960s, the United States was engaged in a potentially catastrophic arms race with the Soviet Union, in addition to seeing communist rebellions everywhere, as nonwhite militant groups and nations struggled against American imperialism and the vestiges of European empires. As asserted earlier, with respect to the United States, one was dealing with a people that saw the world as one big conspiracy against it. In response to which, Deloria advised:

> It would be fairly easy, however, with a sufficient number of articulate young Indians and well-organized community support, to greatly influence the thinking of the nation within a few years. The white man only asks the opportunity to chase the almighty dollar. Whoever can take the burden of thinking from him is worshipped and praised beyond belief. Thus did Americans immortalize John Kennedy who did little to solve America's problems but seemed as if he thought about them a great deal.[38]

Without the benefits of white privilege, though, it was unclear how these "articulate young Indians" could attain the respect, however superficially placed, of an American society that currently regarded Indians as relics of the past. Did Deloria think that American Indian/ Native American studies or ethnic studies would be a platform? Or did he envision more Indians in law schools? Perhaps attention-getting acts of militancy would help? After all, one of the reasons that *Custer* garnered nationwide interest was due to the rising profile of militant groups, which lent Deloria's articulations about Indian affairs its sense of urgency. Obviously, Deloria did not know at the time he was writing *Custer* that it would become a best seller, let alone one of the most important books in American Indian intellectual history. Nonetheless, it was fair to say that in light of recent events, be it the Pacific Northwest fish-ins or the confrontation with Interior Secretary Udall, Deloria was aware that a major impetus for writing this book in the first place, along with *We Talk, You Listen, God Is Red*, and *Broken Treaties*, was thanks to Indian activism.

In any case, Deloria segued into a comparison of Johnson as the antithesis of Kennedy, which he based on the observation that Johnson was vastly underappreciated for his leadership on domestic issues, such as civil rights and poverty, even though he clearly thought and did much more than his predecessor. The point of this comparison was that one could follow Johnson's path and focus on legislation and programs that addressed the important issues of the community.[39] Or one could put on airs of sophistication, complete with creating one's own Camelot myth. Could one have it both ways? Whichever way one chose, Deloria cautioned, if one did so to the exclusion of participating in the realm of ideas and opinions, what Deloria referred to as "ideology," then one was leaving it to others to interpret one's actions according to their own biases and uninformed assumptions.

> *So it is vitally important that the Indian people pick the intellectual arena as the one in which to wage war.* Past events have shown that the Indian people have always been fooled about the intentions of the white man. Always we have discussed irrelevant issues while he has taken the land. *Never have we taken the time to examine the premises upon which he operates so that we could manipulate him as he has us* [emphasis added].[40]

The Indigenous mind is the Indigenous community's most potent weapon against colonialism. So, then, what kind of ideas ought Indian intellectuals invest their efforts? In Deloria's opinion, a "redefinition of Indian Affairs [*sic*]" entailed a redefinition of the Department of Interior's mission and the scope of its jurisdiction. More specifically, Interior and its Bureau of Indian Affairs needed to widen its service areas to include off-reservation Indians, not just those living on trust land. In turn, it needed to make policy based on whole regions, not just on individual reservations. In *Broken Treaties*, Deloria, as noted, highlighted some of the more thought-provoking proposals presented in the "Twenty-Point Position Paper," among which was a proposal for abolishing the BIA as an obsolete government agency, to be replaced by a new structure under a proposed "Indian Community Reconstruction Act":

> [Such an act] should . . . provide for an alternative structure of government for sustaining and revitalizing the Indian-federal relationship between the President and the Congress of the United States, respectively, and the respective Indian Nations and Indian people at last consistent with constitutional criteria, national treaty commitments, and Indian sovereignty, and provide for transformation and transition into the new system as rapidly as possible prior to abolition of the BIA.[41]

With respect to the Indian brain trust, Deloria expressed concern in *Custer* for tribes that did not possess the resources to hire "influential lawyers from big law firms" to represent them, leaving them exposed to the whims of Congress. Fortunately, the Native American Rights Fund was soon founded in 1970, which became the primary source for legal representation in the ongoing struggle for self-determination.[42] As for the likeliness of these kinds of changes happening, Deloria acknowledged with Machiavellian acuity: "It is doubtful if Interior will initiate change. The department is ridden with career men who have spent their lives defending the traditional way of doing business." Yet, even the most stalwart of institutions was vulnerable to at least incremental change. With regard to Indian affairs, that opportunity had availed itself in the form of the National Council on Indian Opportunity, in spite of its shortcomings.[43]

> The most useful thing Interior and its component bureaus could do in the immediate future is to begin contracting with tribes and Indian centers to provide a comprehensive national program for development and training. A tribe or number of tribes could combine with an urban center to provide a reservation-city program of training and

employment placement. In this way people could be trained in a city to take over specific jobs existing on the reservation and reservation people could be given pre-urban orientation before they left the reservation. In either case an Indian agency, the tribe or urban center, would be aware that they were receiving training and could expect employment, housing, and services when their training was finished.[44]

As things stood, the federal trust relationship obliged the federal government, not just Interior or the BIA, to be responsible for all Indians, regardless of where they lived. Consequently, all of the issues between Indians and the federal government were the result of the federal government's failure at fulfilling its trust responsibilities in an adequate and comprehensive manner. In the name of reducing the federal budget, which included, as the reader may recall, multiple hearings about BIA expenditures, Indian affairs had been left wanting, or rather begging, and now Indians were growing more aware of their rights and how the federal system had oppressed them. In which case, Interior was confronted with a choice: either listen to the Indian leaders on the National Council on Indian Opportunity or wait for a more militant response from groups who were tired of feeling ignored. However, as long as persons like Udall were put in charge of Interior, whose disdain for Indians became legendary, the status of Indian-U.S. relations could only grow more tense. "A new Secretary [sic] could begin programs on a national scale that would give tribes almost total control of reservation programs. Expanding the scope of services would mean less decision-making in government and more by Indians. The natural movement in Indian Affairs [sic] now exerting itself could fill the vacuum that exists in bureau programs." Interestingly, Deloria realized that what his recommendations amounted to was the assumption of tribal control over the relocation program that was integral to federal termination policy. The difference, though, aside from Indian control, was the development of a meaningful collaboration between reservation and urban groups, in which the mutual well-being of both communities was addressed by persons familiar with both.[45]

As for national Indian organizations, Deloria was unequivocal, the days of the non-Indian-run entities, such as the Indian Rights Organization and the Association on American Indian Affairs, were quickly coming to an end, in spite of ongoing fundraising and the perpetuation of nominal Indian programs. In their stead were the Indian-organized movements springing from around the country, mostly from urban centers, which were the future. "Urban Indians, under the new American Indians United, will swiftly move into the lead position in Indian Affairs [sic], determining the trends and issues which will attract both urban and reservation Indians alike."[46] According to Hazel W. Hertzberg, Deloria played an active role in the organization of programs for uniting urban and reservation populations:

> In an attempt to bring together urban Indian groups whose major organization vehicles were the urban Indian centers, the Council on Indian Affairs asked Vine Deloria, Jr., to head a committee for an Urban Indian Consultation Conference financed largely by church groups. At the conference held in Seattle, Washington, in January 1968, the participants were more interested in social services for urban Indians than in political action. A few urged affiliation with the NCAI, but this suggestion received little support. The delegates from the Indian centers thereupon met separately, and elected an ad hoc committee whose chairman was Jesse Sixkiller (Cherokee) to form a federation of urban Indian groups. In October 1968 American Indians United was founded in Chicago with Sixkiller as chairman in a convention attended by representatives from Indian centers in 14 states. The role of the group was declared to be to support and serve Indian centers, providing technical assistance in programming and fundraising, economic development, and cultural expression. One of the first tasks the organization set forth was the development of good relations with the NCAI. However, this attempt to unite off-reservation Indians in a national body and to form an alliance between urban and reservation Indians, despite its brave beginnings, did not come to fruition.[47]

According to Deloria, two years after his initial enthusiasm, American Indians United "could find no common ground among the urban Indians other than their disenfranchisement from programs enjoyed by reservation Indians."[48] American Indians United, thus, became another example of the struggle of Indian leadership to unite Indians on a national level.

In addition to having access to all of the resources available to anyone living in a metropolitan area, such as libraries, universities, and media resources, because of their growing population, off-reservation Indian groups could potentially surpass tribal governments in the sheer number of people working on important issues. Tribal governments, of course, mandated by tribal constitutions, which had been approved by the secretary of interior, still had the advantage of being governing entities, complete with relations to the federal government that were better defined than their urban counterparts. Still, insofar as people power meant anything, the strength of the urban Indian population was its size and the dedication of its members to seeking social justice for all Indians. Speaking of which, Deloria indicated an awareness of what eventually became the Native American Rights Fund, when he observed: "Individual Indians are now examining the method used by [the] ACLU [American Civil Liberties Union] in building its branch offices. [The] ACLU underwrites the creation of field offices and returns a percentage of income raised by a field office to the local branch. Eventually the local branch builds a sufficient income to operate its own programs."[49]

Statewide Indian organizations would be essential, not only for pooling resources for the benefit of member tribes, but also as a way of bridging the divide between urban and reservation communities. As the urban Indian population grew and the reservations' shrunk, intertribal alliances would play a vital role in preserving an overall sense of peoplehood, as tribes must necessarily adjust to the changing dynamics generated by relocation, commuting, and modern communications. In other words, the reservations that the federal government created for Indians during the nineteenth century would have to be radically reimagined for the latter half of the twentieth century and beyond. Self-determination, in a word, was the wave of the Indian future. "Once freed from the confining definitions of rights and privileges of the past, Indians will embark on a series of community development projects that are based upon new concepts of tribalism." On this basis, Deloria foresaw a time when traditional reservation-based service programs gave way to "the private sector of life." Thus, there would be a point when Congress ought to "extend the eligibility for funding to non-federal Indians in the next decade."[50]

Deloria brought *Custer* to its conclusion with a prediction that "tribalism" would form into a national, if not international, movement, encompassing not only tribal groups but others seeking to establish their sense of peoplehood as an antidote to the fragmentation and alienation of modern life.[51] In the case of American Indians, Deloria anticipated an effort at recolonizing former Indian lands, either by migrating back from urban areas into existing communities on the reservation or through the acquisition of new lands, which would form the foundation of extending the tribal domain. Deloria mentioned an Ojibwa group in Canada that moved off its reserve and developed land they had purchased for the purpose of creating "a corporation for community development," in which their economy was based on contracting "for pulp wood from some of the papermills [*sic*] in the area." Such endeavors required both an understanding of modern economics and the strengths that a tribal group possessed.[52] On these premises, the corporation as a type of tribal group, as Deloria examined this above, would have to be employed and subjected to further revision in order to accommodate tribal values, especially sustainability and group welfare, as opposed to maximum profit and personal benefits. Whether or not Deloria thought that even a small corporation run by a tribe could withstand the influences of modern capitalism and its emphasis on growth, he did not say, preferring to remain idealistic in his aspirations for a more tribalized future. In the spirit, then, of what he was calling "recolonization," Deloria stated:

> Tribes already have corporation charters under the Indian Reorganization Act. Some urban centers have incorporated as non-profit organizations. The next logical step is a corporation for development purposes in which both reservation and non-reservation people participate. These corporations would be formed to explore ideas of development outside either reservation boundaries or urban centers.

The objective was for tribes to benefit from generating their own revenue, which would supplant their dependency on federal support. Presumably, tribal values would preclude the kind of alienation that was endemic to producing goods and services in a money-based economy. The concept of money was something that did not get spoken about very much, either in discourses on colonization or in propositions for tribal economic reform, even though it was one of the most significant items that European and American settlers brought with them into Indian Country. Deloria, perhaps for pragmatic reasons, seemed to be taking money and capitalism as a given, the effects of which he was hopeful would be ameliorated by tribal-centric programs and developments. In any case, Deloria was emphatic that the future for Indians did not consist of the anthropological expectation that they would vanish, nor did they need Christian salvation from their Indigenous spiritual ways, but instead the future consisted of initiatives that would allow them to "retribalize, recolonize, and recustomize" their communities and values for a vibrant reemergence. "Now that Indian people have realized that their problems are legal and not cultural, legal solutions will be found through political action, and Indian people will not only be free to revitalize old customs, but also to experiment with new social forms."[53] Toward this end, one important option was to build upon the network of nonprofits already serving the Indian community:

> There currently exists an informal network of relationships in the private sector of the society as seen in the relationships of the members of the Council on Indian Affairs. The United Scholarship Service, sponsored by the Episcopal Church, The United Church of Christ, and the National Indian Youth Council, provides for college and secondary school students. The American Indian Development, Inc. conducts the summer workshop for Indian college students to give them further background in contemporary social thought and concentrated course in current Indian issues. Arrow, Inc. provides leadership training sessions for tribal business managers, councilmen, and other officials who might not necessarily have [a] college background but who are largely responsible for [the] development of tribal programs. The American Friends Service Committee and the National Congress of American Indians have been pursuing various types of intern programs which will enable young Indians to gain valuable experience both in Washington, DC and on the different reservations. The National Council of Churches has been very active in attempting to help non-Federal

Indians to rebuild their communities through private programs. The American Indian Historical Society has been very active in getting textbooks corrected to show the true story of the Indian people.[54]

In the end, the federal government must give up on its effort at detribalizing Indian communities by prioritizing its expenditures on its futile relocation program. The bonds of the tribe were much stronger than the misguided and biased attempts at assimilating Indians into mainstream society. History had proven that tribal identities are resilient. Even in the aftermath of massive migrations into urban centers, Indians' sense of peoplehood had endured amidst an array of modern conveniences and inconveniences. Now, ironically, Indians were striving to revitalize their nations, prevailing over federal, anthropological, and even theological expectations that they disappear into the wreckage of forgotten peoples. Working against this tide, Deloria warned, would only lead to a violent reaction:

> The more support that can be given to retribalizing of the people, the better the chances are to avoid violence. Paradoxically, a greater sense of urgency in retribalization will tend to curb possible violence. Nationalism must be the ally of future policies. New policies must not be directed at breaking tribal ties because they will break upon the rock of the tribe.[55]

Having said that, Deloria concluded with caution, namely for unanticipated developments in other sectors of American society, such as the Black Power movement, which had influenced Indian affairs before and may do so again. What Deloria was anticipating exactly, he did not say. Though he may have sensed the growing tension in the Red Power movement as its demands for change grew increasingly emphatic, a situation that later erupted at Wounded Knee. The implication was that the blood that was shed at Wounded Knee might have been avoided if the reforms Deloria outlined, such as the Trail of Broken Treaties' "Twenty-Point Position Paper," had become policy thereby dissipating the anger and frustration that erupted in 1973. Instead, as of *Custer*, Deloria pointed out that during the 1968 election season both Democratic and Republicans spouted calls for "law and order," which most understood as code for repressing the Black community, but which also had implications for other groups that had organized for social justice, including American Indians. If that occurred, Deloria speculated, it would inevitably affect how Indian issues were perceived by both the federal government and the general public, which typically viewed race relations through the lens of "Black-and-white," entailing that all "minority groups" would have to endure similar repercussions. In the case of the Trail of Broken Treaties caravan's occupation and subsequent ransacking of the BIA building in Washington DC, Deloria observed: "[White Americans] have been brought up to visualize the Indian/white relationship in terms of the First Thanksgiving and Tonto loyally following the Lone Ranger around, and so when the first news of property damage surfaces, they get angry at the senseless destruction of property."[56] That anger, of course, turned into intransigence on the part of federal officials who refused to take seriously the proposals outlined in the Trail of Broken Treaties' "Twenty-Point Position Paper," which led to the oppressive military tactics employed against AIM radicals that went out to Pine Ridge to support the people enduring the injustices of Tribal Chairman Dickie Wilson.

Looking back, it is easy to surmise that, as disappointed as Deloria must have been with the results of the 1972 Trail of Broken Treaties and the subsequent 1973 confrontation at Wounded Knee, it was nonetheless easy to understand how he was unlikely unsurprised by how things turned out. As of 1971, when Deloria began his academic career as a lecturer at Western Washington University, he expressed both great hope and great despair in his two most significant publications at that transitional year. In *Of Utmost Good Faith*, Deloria enthused about the dramatic developments in Indian Country for which Indians could take full credit:

> There are presently in excess of 7,000 Indian students in college and graduate school. Industries are booming on many reservations. Indian people are assuming command of their own affairs at a very rapid rate. Militants are raising issues that would have been unthinkable just five years ago. Churches are setting up committees of Indian churchmen

who will soon completely take over the mission fields. The level of Indian people now in government service is continually rising. The last two Commissioners of Indian Affairs [sic] have been Indians. Most of the important posts dealing with Indian Affairs [sic] are now filled with Indian people. Clearly the situation never looked so bright.[57]

On the other hand, while Deloria's belief in the wherewithal and resiliency of Indian people has always been sincere and unflagging, his faith in the federal system and the white men who ran things was less than encouraging. Reflecting on Jennings C. Wise's history of America's epic betrayal of tribes in *The Red Man in the New World Drama*, which culminated with a chapter on the rise of Indian activism, Deloria commented on the future of Indian affairs:

> Many Indians believe that for the first time the federal government is listening to the voices of Indians. This is not true. . . . The government always listened to Indians but it rarely did what they wanted it to do. This principle will probably hold true for the future. The government will continue to do what it thinks is best for Indians and somehow the Indians will absorb whatever program is devised for them and remain in much the same state as they formerly were.[58]

Taken together, race relations, the media, and the Indian protest movement, the struggle for self-determination was about to enter a new era in which an equally new way of thinking would be required: "But hopefully, enough Indian people will take the time to reflect on their situation, on the things going on around them both in the cities and on the reservations, and will choose the proper points of leverage by which Indian renewal can be fully realized."[59] In the end, what Deloria foresaw was the emergence of a new generation of intellectuals, writers, teachers, and community organizers that would shape the discourse on American Indian sovereignty, self-determination, nation building, language and cultural revitalization, repatriation, and decolonization for the decades ahead.

In March 1970, as first recounted in chapter 1, Deloria participated in the First Convocation of American Indian Scholars, which was coordinated by the American Indian Historical Society and held at Princeton University. In addition to Deloria, presenters included Rupert Costo (Cahuilla), Alfonso Ortiz (San Juan Pueblo), N. Scott Momaday (Kiowa), Jeanette Henry (Cherokee), Samuel Billison (Navajo), W. Roger Buffalohead (Ponca), Fritz Scholder (Luiseño), Lionel deMontigny (Chippewa), Robert Bennett (Oneida), and Bea Medicine (Standing Rock Sioux).[60] The event marked a milestone, which saw Deloria appear in the program twice: first, on the 1968 Indian Civil Rights Act and, second, on the "urban Indian scene." In the case of the 1968 Indian Civil Rights Act, Deloria argued that tribes ought to challenge the constitutionality of the statute based on the legal confusion of how tribes were regarded in the Constitution and case law, which was in terms of tribes being corporate entities, and how tribes were identified in the statute under dispute, which enumerated tribes as conglomerates of individuals. As for urban Indians, Deloria moderated a panel that consisted of Herb Blatchford (Navajo), Rosemary Christensen (Chippewa), Mary Byler (Cherokee), Bud Mason (Arikara-Mandan), and Jesse Green (Nez Percé). In spite of the dolorous future that Deloria foresaw with regard to Indian affairs, he took great encouragement from the community of Indian scholars that gathered for the purpose of sharing knowledge and ideas about the Indian community from a spectrum of Indian perspectives—all of whom were learned, insightful, and dedicated to creating greater self-determination for their nations. The convocation was indeed a milestone in modern American Indian history:

> It was the first time that so many Indians had gathered to consider the intellectual and theoretical implications of having a national Indian community. The conference served notice to Indian and non-Indian alike that the obscurity in which Indian people had spent the twentieth century had passed and a new day of intellectual respectability had dawned.[61]

Beyond this gathering, a new and exciting generation of Indian writers and thinkers emerged, of which Deloria was prominent. Indeed, from *Custer* and *We Talk, You Listen*, in which the premises of tribal self-determination were set politically, culturally, and spiritually, through

God Is Red, which redefined the concept of religion from a nonlinear, place-oriented perspective, to *Behind the Trail of Broken Treaties*, which reinterpreted federal Indian doctrines from the perspective of tribal nationhood, Deloria set the intellectual agenda for a reinvigorated struggle for tribalism, which was to say self-determination based on Indigenous values and customs.

As of 2018, when these final pages were written, there are dozens of degree programs, certificates, and concentrations across the United States dedicated to the study, teaching, and advocating for the rights of American Indians as members of sovereign Indigenous nations.[62] Commonplace in the curricula offered are courses surveying the history of federal Indian law and policy, in which the critique that Deloria launched in the pages of *Custer* and *Broken Treaties* is still informing the discourse on tribal self-determination. Equally important has been the steady increase in the numbers of American Indian and Alaska Native students earning college and graduate degrees.[63] An increase in the Indian student population, naturally, has been complemented with an increase in the number of American Indians and Alaska Natives serving as educators at all levels, from K-12 teachers to tenured professors and university administrators. Many of these academics are members of some of the organizations that have developed in the years since 1970, such as the National Indian Education Association (founded 1970) and the American Indian Higher Education Consortium (founded 1973), both of which were inspired by the first convocation of American Indian scholars mentioned above. Also, while it is far beyond the scope of this book to do justice, the number of significant books, articles, and studies produced by American Indian/Alaska Native researchers and scholars has grown exponentially over the decades since the height of the Indian protest movement. With respect to Deloria's pervasive presence and influence in the contemporary discourse on Indian affairs, a basic search for references to *Custer Died for Your Sins* turned up over three thousand results, and over two thousand for *God Is Red*.

As for what became of the trajectories that Deloria launched with his seminal tetralogy, what his book publications indicated was a move away from articulating the legal definition of tribal sovereignty and self-determination toward exploring their application to the issues stemming from tribal self-governance in the aftermath of the 1975 Indian Self-Determination and Education Assistance Act. Of particular note was *American Indians, American Justice* (1983), which took on the monumental but necessary task of explicating the inherent jurisdictional powers and federally imposed limits to tribal governance and the justice system. Most importantly, when trying to understand tribes' relationship with the federal system was the maze of laws, from the 1885 Major Crimes Act and P. L. 280 (1953), to the holdings of *Oliphant v. Suquamish Indian Tribe* (1978), which defined the rules for bringing a criminal case to trial. Deloria and Clifford Lytle's critical analysis concluded with an assessment of Indian civil liberties, religious freedom, and the right to basic governmental services. Also noteworthy, and again coauthored with Lytle, was *The Nations Within: The Past and Future of American Indian Sovereignty* (1984), which took a closer look at the legislative and political history of the 1934 Indian Reorganization Act, its role in fomenting the Indian protest movement, the subsequent call for greater tribal self-determination, and the case for revitalizing the original bill, in which tribes would be fully restored to their pre-reservation political status as independent sovereign nations, with which the United States ratified hundreds of treaties.

The more significant developments in Deloria's post–Red Power scholarship was the philosophical work that he continued, in which the critique of the western Christian intellectual tradition initiated in *Custer*'s chapter on missionaries and in the time, space, and history chapters of *God Is Red*—what Deloria referred to as his "global theology"—was directed into an analysis of the concepts driving modern American science and society. Most noteworthy was *The Metaphysics of Modern Existence* (1979), in which Deloria examined a western civilization that was undergoing major upheavals in its thinking about the nature of reality, which went from Newtonian physics to the chaos of quantum mechanics, which in turn affected western thinkers' notions about human history that led to an initial critique of evolutionary theory, arguing instead for a nonlinear approach to understanding humanity. The latter reached critical mass in *Red Earth, White Lies: Native Americans and the Myth of Scientific Fact*

(1995), which was a comprehensive assault on the premises of early human societies in the Western Hemisphere, as postulated in the annals of archeology, which presumed the absoluteness of human evolution, the unilateral population of North and South America that arrived by the Bering Land Bridge, and the consequent annihilation of Pleistocene megafauna by roving bands of paleo-Indians. To the contrary, Deloria argued vigorously for examining early human history in North America through the lens of Indigenous oral traditions, in which Creation Stories demonstrated much knowledge about the natural history of the lands recounted in these ancient narratives that was too often overlooked in the name of science.

Clearly there is much yet to be done at analyzing and critiquing Deloria's work on American Indian cultures, histories, and politics, and the influence that he continues to have on the discourse on Indian affairs. Even in an era like today, which is driven more by issues of intersectionality, transnationalism, not to mention gender, feminism, and decolonization, Deloria's critique of federal Indian law and policy and his notion of tribal self-determination are still fundamental to understanding the political status of tribes within the American political system. At the same time, similar to other seminal figures in intellectual history, be they prominent thinkers like Darwin and Freud or marginal innovators like Immanuel Velikovsky, Deloria's works are as prone to criticism as they are influential. With that in mind, this critical reflection on Deloria's Red Power legacy concludes with the hope that the ideas, issues, and criticisms raised in the preceding chapters will initiate a growing body of scholarship focusing on Deloria as a writer, thinker, activist, learned elder, and Indigenous person. Based on the foregoing chapters of this volume, there is more work to be done regarding Indian-Black relations, how they overlap and diverge as races, communities, and political "problems"; then, of course, there are the issues that arose regarding Deloria's admiration for Israel, both theologically and politically, as an analogue for the American Indian experience; also, a Native feminist critique of Deloria's work is in order, beginning with the gender bias in his portrayal of traditional Indian cultures and the absence of women in his recounting of the Indian protest movement; lastly, there is the question of Deloria's relation to his contemporaries in the global decolonization movement, which arose in the so-called Third World, and his aloofness to Marxist theory. Insofar as Deloria has probably had the greatest influence on the intellectual agenda defining American Indian/Native American studies, such critical analysis will be essential to furthering the discourse on sovereignty, particularly as this becomes more global in scope, not to mention as tribes continue to incrementally acquire more powers of self-governance in spite of the recurring setbacks inflicted by Congress and the courts. In the spirit, then, of George Tinker's eulogy for his friend, "Coyote Old Man," may Deloria's influence go on for the next one hundred years—indeed, may it continue for the next seven generations.

NOTES

PROLOGUE

1. Steiner, *The New Indians*, 26, 94–95, 124–25, 140.
2. Wilkinson, *Blood Struggle*, 108.
3. Dee Brown, "Behind the Trail of Broken Treaties," *New York Times*, November 24, 1974.
4. Edward Abbey, "Custer Died for Your Sins," *New York Times*, November 9, 1969.
5. John Leonard, "Red Powerlessness," *New York Times*, November 18, 1969. Two days later, Leonard would preface his review of Ulf Hannerz's *Inquiries into Ghetto Cultures and Community* with a reference to Deloria's criticism of anthropology. See John Leonard, "Burn, Culture, Burn," *New York Times*, November 20, 1969.
6. Deloria, "Custer Died for Your Sins," 131–32, 172–75. Also included was an article by Sen. Frank Church, "The Global Crunch." For the table of contents, see magawiki, "1969–08 Playboy Magazine Contents," http://magawiki.com/1064 /playboy-magazine/1969-08/. For a personal account of Deloria's *Playboy* article and the popularity of *Custer Died for Your Sins*, see Utley, *Custer and Me*, 117–18.
7. Deloria, "The War between the Redskins and the Feds," *New York Times Magazine*, 47, 82–98, 102. With regard to the use of "Redskins" in the latter headline, the term does not appear anywhere in the text of Deloria's op-ed piece, suggesting the likelihood that it was the creation of a *New York Times* editor. See also Vine Deloria Jr., "This Country Was a Lot Better Off When the Indians Were Running It," *New York Times*, March 8, 1970. Additional editorials coincided with Deloria's subsequent book publications, which are cited at the appropriate points throughout the discourse at hand.

8. For episode details, see tv.com, The Merv Griffin Show. Multiple sources claim that Deloria also appeared on *The Dick Cavett Show* sometime in 1971. However, there is no archival evidence that this took place (see tv.com, "The Dick Cavett Show"; and dickcavettshow.com). In an email to the archivist at the dickcavettshow.com web page inquiring about the alleged episode details, Cal Vornberger, director of digital media, Daphne Productions, replied: "We have no evidence he [Deloria] was ever on The Dick Cavett Show" (June 6, 2016). For resources claiming that Deloria appeared on *The Dick Cavett Show*, see De Leon, *Leaders from the 1960s*, 72; Tahmahkera, *Tribal Television*, 182n82; and, Adams, "A Vine Deloria Jr. Collaboration." None of the latter three cited sources provides any detail, such as air date, other guests' names, or photos that would corroborate this claim, which suggests the possibility that claimants are misremembering *The Merv Griffin Show* as *The Dick Cavett Show*. However, in Deloria's *God Is Red*, the legendary talk show host is mentioned twice: first, when Kahn-Tineta Horn is named as a "confidant of Dick Cavett"; second, and more substantially, in reference to Cavett's 1972 on air interview with *Black Elk Speaks* transcriber, John Neihardt. See Deloria, *God Is Red* (1973), 11, 35. Lastly, in the thirtieth-anniversary edition of *God Is Red*, Deloria mentions that members of the Indians of All Tribes, who earned national notoriety when they occupied Alcatraz Island during the fall of 1969, "appeared on the Merv Griffin talk show." Curiously, in this same edition, Deloria does in fact make his own claim to having been on Dick Cavett's program, during which he stated that he showed photos of a police raid on a Tacoma Indian camp, where they were protesting on behalf of Nisquallie and Puyallup fishing rights, which resulted "in great public outcry against the actions of the police." See Deloria, *God Is Red* (2003), 6, 9. One resource that does corroborate the appearance on Merv Griffin is Fortunate Eagle's *Heart of the Rock*, in which the author states: "Vine offered to help [the Indians occupying Alcatraz] with a package that would trade the submarginal land of Alcatraz for something more valuable. The Indians on the island said no. Instead he was asked to do an interview about the Rock with Merv Griffin" (161). Further corroborating the Merv Griffin connection is a 1997 book chapter by Deloria, "Alcatraz, Activism, and Accommodation," in which the following anecdote is relayed: "In January 1970, hoping to highlight a land and treaty issue, I invited Merv Griffin to come out to Alcatraz and do part of a show from there" (48). See Deloria, "Alcatraz, Activism, and Accommodation," 45–51. With respect to Dick Cavett, Deloria did write to Cavett on August 1, 1972, in which Deloria points out: "I was a guest on your show about two years ago. I showed some pictures of the brutality of the Tacoma police beating up the Indian fishermen." For more, see Vine Deloria Papers.

9. Buffalohead, "Custer Died for Your Sins," 553–54.

10. Ortiz, "Custer Died for Your Sins," 953–55.

11. See Prucha, *American Indian Treaties*.

12. See Lurie, "The Voice of the American Indian," 478–500. See also Steiner, *The New Indians*.

13. See Shirley Hill Witt, "Nationalistic Trends," 51–74. See also Shreve, *Red Power Rising*.

14. See Chrisman, "The Fish-in Protests."

15. See Brook, "What Tribe? Whose Island?," 51–56. See also Heath, "No Rock Is an Island," 397–99. *Custer*'s role as the voice of the Indian protest movement, which coincided with the occupation of Alcatraz, is acknowledged in Edward Lazarus's book on Lakota–U.S. relations and the Black Hills. See Lazarus, *Black Hills, White Justice*, 292–93.

16. Vine Deloria Jr., "This Country Was a Lot Better Off When the Indians Were Running It," *New York Times*, March 8, 1970, 32.

17. For more about Ishi and his historically important role in the development of American anthropology, see Kroeber and Kroeber, *Ishi in Three Centuries*.

18. During Deloria's tenure as NCAI executive director, Josephy's critically acclaimed book was highlighted in the *NCAI Sentinel Bulletin* for its recognition of Indians, not as savage opponents to white civilization, but as "patriots" to their own nations: "In *The Patriot Chiefs*, we find a real acknowledgement of the fact that Indian tribes were and are nations and that Indian heroes are as much heroes as are patriots of other nations and lands," "Justice and 'Just Compensation.'"

19. Deloria cites Josephy's *The Indian Heritage of America* twice regarding the Iroquois Confederacy's critical role in the formation of the American republic in "Grandfathers of Our Country," *New York Times*, February 22, 1971.

20. In a summer 1965 issue of the *NCAI Sentinel Bulletin*, the National Council of Churches was noted for its Commission on Race and Religion, in which it was apparent that the council was up on the civil rights movement, but behind the curve when it came to the Indian protest movement: "[the National Council of Churches] has let it be known that they would like first hand [*sic*] information on Indian problems and attitudes in this field. In an hour presentation, NCAI reminded them of the idea of the 'chosen people' that we see in the Old Testament," "Justice and 'Just Compensation.'"

21. Deloria, *Custer Died for Your Sins*, 148.

22. Two examples of the slogan "Custer died for your sins" turning up as a political statement are reported in two articles in the *New York Times*, published in 1966 and 1968. See Alvin M. Josephy Jr., "Soldiers and Indians," *New York Times*, July 3, 1966; and Judy Klemesrud, "The American Indian: Part of the City, And Yet . . ." *New York Times*, September 18, 1968. In Josephy's article, he recounts when Robert L. Bennett (Oneida) was appointed as the first commissioner of

Indian affairs of American Indian descent since Ely Parker (Seneca). According to Josephy: "[Bennett] handed to many of the persons invited to witness the occasion a printed card reading, 'Custer died for your sins!'" In the Klemesrud article, which is about American Indian women living and working in New York City, the organizations for American Indians they have founded, and the issues they face, the status of the growing protest movement was described in guarded terms: "So far the militant movement has not caught on strongly among Indian youngsters, although there are a few who show up at peace demonstrations and protest marches carrying signs such as 'Red Power' and 'Custer Died for Your Sins.' But, generally, Indians have not been strongly opposed to the war in Vietnam."

23. Deloria would critique the theological meaning of covenant, focusing on Christianity's disappointing relation to Indians; see Deloria, "A Violated Covenant," 5–8.

24. Deloria, *Custer Died for Your Sins,* 2.

25. Deloria, *Custer Died for Your Sins,* 268.

26. In spite of the common identification between Deloria and Red Power, when one looks closely at his writings during this era (1964–74) one can see a clear preference for the descriptive phrase "Indian Protest Movement" over "Red Power." Curiously, Deloria is credited with having coined the phrase "Red Power" while giving a speech at the 1966 annual meeting of the National Congress of American Indians. See Wilkins, *American Indian Politics,* 229. However, according to McKenzie-Jones in *Clyde Warrior,* "'Red Power' first appeared as a slogan in November 1966 when [Clyde] Warrior, [Mel] Thom, Della Warrior, and two more [National Indian Youth Council] members drove a car, against NCAI wishes, adorned with 'Red Power, National Indian Youth Council' on one side and 'Custer Died for Your Sins' on the other, in the NCAI annual convention parade in Oklahoma City. The incident marked a dramatic shift in relations between the NIYC and NCAI. Hank Adams remembered it creating a "'big scandal for the NCAI,' with organizers, including Vine Deloria Jr., demanding, 'How did that 'Red Power' banner make it into the parade?'" 72. As for how the NCAI reported its annual meeting, in its 1966 convention issue, the organization declared their event "a Most Successful Meeting." Furthermore, "Records were set for attendance at a convention, for Tribal and individual memberships, and for the number of official Tribal delegations at a convention," "22nd Annual Convention in November."

27. See Talayesva, *Sun Chief.* Talayesva's book is a classic in the field of American Indian autobiography, specifically the "as told to" form of personal narrative, in which the narrator recites their life-history to a non-Indian researcher, typically an anthropologist, and most often with an accompanying translator. In this case, Leo W. Simmons was the Yale-trained anthropologist who recorded Talayesva's story.

28. See Dyk, *Left Handed.* Another as-told-to life story, recorded by Walter Dyk, another Yale-trained social scientist, specializing in linguistics.

29. Deloria, *God Is Red,* (2003), 26. For an analysis of this anecdote, see Martínez, "Neither Chief nor Medicine Man, 36–37. Also, Deloria told the cited story in the original 1973 edition of *God Is Red.* However, it was unclear that Deloria was referring to his own experience. See Deloria, *God Is Red* (1973), 41–42.

30. Velikovsky's work, in fact, would have a direct influence on Deloria's thinking about the relationship between Indigenous oral tradition and the formation of the earth and solar system. See Deloria, *God Is Red* (1973), 139–51. Much later, paralleling Velikovsky's influence, will be the work of Dorothy B. Vitaliano regarding the concept of geomythology. See Vitaliano, "The Impact of Geologic Events," 5–30. See also Deloria, *Red Earth, White Lies,* 161–86.

31. Although Deloria demonstrates his knowledge of Harrington's book on poverty in *Custer Died for Your Sins,* then more clearly exhibited in *We Talk, You Listen,* Deloria refrains from acknowledging that Harrington's critique of poverty and capitalism was rooted in Marxist theory. Indeed, in spite of the dominance of Marxist theory in much of the discourse on contemporary global affairs, Deloria deliberately turns a blind eye to its insights into the relation between class struggle, the distribution of wealth, and colonialism that was driving a major trend in Third World intellectual circles, most notably Frantz Fanon's *The Wretched of the Earth,* which Grove Press published in an English translation in 1963. On the contrary, it would be twenty years before Deloria made his one and only attempt at discussing the intersections between Marxism and American Indians. See, Deloria, "Circling the Same Old Rock," 113–36. Regardless of the supposed topic of "alienation," Deloria makes it clear that he is more comfortable with at most quasi-Marxist theorists like Herbert Marcuse, preferring instead social critics like Marshall McLuhan, theologians like Teilhard de Chardin, and post-Marxists like Jean-François Revel.

32. Whereas contemporary theorists will refer to settler-colonialism to signify the stage of colonialism developed by the nations that succeeded their European predecessors, such as Canada, Mexico, and the United States, during the time that *Custer Died for Your Sins* appeared, Deloria was influenced by the analysis of the classic and internal models of colonialism articulated by Robert K. Thomas. See Thomas, "Colonialism: Classic and Internal."

33. Letter from Vine Deloria Jr. to Hank Adams, June 22, 1970. Vine Deloria Papers.

1. TRIBAL SELF-DETERMINATION

1. Deloria, *Custer Died for Your Sins,* 277. The main reason that Deloria's afterword has been forgotten is for the simple reason that most readers, since 1988, when the University of Oklahoma Press published its edition of *Custer,* read a version of the book in which the afterword was omitted.

2. Menominee Restoration Act.

3. ICMN Staff, "Salute to Vine Deloria Jr."

4. American Anthropological Association, *Anthropology and the American Indian.*

5. Biolsi and Zimmerman, *Indians and Anthropologists.*

6. Deloria, *Custer Died for Your Sins,* 269.

7. Vine Deloria Jr., "This Country Was a Lot Better Off When the Indians Were Running It," *New York Times,* March 8, 1970.

8. Deloria would also recount his family history in his preface to Ella Deloria's *Speaking of Indians.*

9. Treat, introduction, 6.

10. "Vine Deloria Sr, Episcopal Executive, 88," *New York Times,* March 8, 1990. http://www.nytimes.com/1990/03/08/obituaries/vine-deloria-sr-episcopal -executive-88.html.

11. Founded in 1902, the Missionary Education Movement sprung from the Young People's Missionary Movement, which was inspired by the work of the YMCA (Young Men's Christian Association). Eventually, in 1950, "the Movement became a part of the National Council of Churches with its activities being assumed by the Joint Commission on Missionary Education of the Division of Christian Education." Among its more important accomplishments was the establishment of the Friendship Press, which began publishing books and other material in 1926, including Ella Deloria's *Speaking of Indians.* See Presbyterian Historical Society, the National Archives of the PC(USA), "Guide to the Missionary Education Movement of the United States."

12. Vine Deloria Jr., "This Country Was a Lot Better Off When the Indians Were Running It," *New York Times,* March 8, 1970, 48.

13. Deloria, introduction, xii, xvii.

14. Vine Deloria Jr., "This Country Was a Lot Better Off When the Indians Were Running It," *New York Times,* March 8, 1970, 50.

15. In spite of how he criticized mainstream Christian churches, Deloria was not beyond remaining conversant with members of the church community. In a letter dated March 12, 1968, Clifton H. Johnson wrote to Deloria on behalf of the United Church Board for Homeland Ministries, stating: "Your presentation at the 1966 Institute made a very favorable impression on my colleagues and the Planning Committee has directed me to ask you to speak again this year." Vine Deloria Papers.

16. In a letter dated November 23, 1964, to Cato Valandra (Rosebud Sioux), Deloria explained his decision to leave the United Scholarship Service: "I have had to resign from The United Scholarship Service as of November 18, 1964 to be effective December 31, 1964 to devoted [sic] full time to the NCAI corporation. I will probably finish my responsibilities for the Secondary School Program

and be making some trips on behalf of NCAI membership in early December."
Vine Deloria Papers.

17. Deloria, *Custer Died for Your Sins,* 270–71. In a rather caustic letter from Dolly Akers, area vice president, Wolf Point, Montana, dated December 26, 1964, it was indicated that Deloria's ascension into the position of NCAI executive director was anything but a clear case of consensus: "Mr. Deloria in your December 3, 1964 letter you deplore the failure of the October meeting in Denver and the abbreviated meeting in Washington in November to come to any *conclusions.* Therefore, you and I agree on one point, namely *no* firm *conclusions* of business were arrived at in either of said meetings. . . . Mr. Norman Hollow, Fort Peck delegate, traveled back to Montana with President [Walter] Wetzel and myself. The three of us deplored the lack of unity that plagued our meeting" [emphasis in original]. Nevertheless, as of October 1964, Deloria began his duties as NCAI executive director, regardless of the uncertainty of the NCAI executive council, of which Akers was a member. In a letter to Allen Aleck, chairman, Pyramid Lake Paiute Tribe, dated December 1, 1964, Deloria mentioned that "Mr. Melvin Thom" had encouraged him to contact Aleck, then outlined his plans for the organization, which included a weekly newsletter "on legislation, programs in education, employment, health, and whatever else tribes and Indian individuals can take advantage of, and programs and opportunity of non-government agencies." Vine Deloria Papers.

18. Letter from Imelda N. Schreiner to Roger Jourdain, September 2, 1964. Vine Deloria Papers.

19. Wise, *The Red Man in the New World Drama,* 375.

20. McKenzie-Jones, *Clyde Warrior,* 107–8. Documentation of Deloria's NIYC membership was corroborated in a letter dated December 16, 1964, from Deloria to Imelda Schreiner, office secretary, NCAI, in which a list of membership dues paid to the NCAI was enumerated. Among those listed were Deloria, Clyde Warrior, Mel Thom, and Ed Johnson, all four of whom had asterisks next to their names. Deloria noted to Schreiner: "The names marked (*) are National Indian Youth Council Members and are paying $5.00 membership as their part." Vine Deloria Papers.

21. Vine Deloria Jr., "This Country Was a Lot Better Off When the Indians Were Running It," *New York Times,* March 8, 1970.

22. National Congress of American Indians, *NCAI Governance.*

23. "Now Is the Time."

24. Deloria, *Custer Died for Your Sins,* 271. Membership and fundraising was a frequent concern for Deloria, as documented in a travel report, dated September 30, 1966, in which the following itinerary was outlined: "Travel expenses for trips to San Carlos, White Mountain, Farmington, NM [,] Reno, Nevada, Hopi,

Kaibab Paiute, All Pueblo Council to discuss with tribes current programs of OEO, EDA and the Offices of Education, tribal membership and support for the NCAI and NCAI FUND programs." Vine Deloria Papers.

25. Deloria, *Custer Died for Your Sins,* 271. According to the February–March 1965 issue of the NCAI *Sentinel Bulletin, in an editorial titled "Now Is the Time":* "At the moment tribal membership, paid up and in good standing is at 13. Individual memberships for Indians stand at 35, and non-Indian at 13."

26. Deloria, *Custer Died for Your Sins,* 272. In a letter to the executive director of the Field Foundation, Leslie Dunbar, dated October 21, 1966, Vine Deloria Jr. admitted: "Tribal memberships continue to come in and we will apparently have a good year[,] although as late as September I was pretty worried about the membership." Vine Deloria Papers.

27. Steiner, *The New Indians,* x–xi, 26.

28. Department of the Interior and Related Agencies Appropriations for 1966, Part 2.

29. Colville Termination. 89th Cong 1 (1965). Deloria added a brief update to one of the chapters he contributed to his revised edition of Wise's *The Red Man in the New World Drama,* stating in part: "The Colville tribe faces continual pressures from the Senate Interior Indian subcommittee [*sic*] to accept the termination bill during every Congress" (369). For the complete update, see Wise, *The Red Man in the New World Drama,* 369–70.

30. To Provide for Guaranty and Insurance of Loans to Indians and Indian Organizations. House. 89th Cong. 1 (1965).

31. To Amend the Law Establishing the Indian Revolving Loan Fund. Senate. 89th Cong. 1 (1965).

32. Constitutional Rights of the American Indian. See also memorandum, Vine Deloria Jr. to John Belindo, August 22, 1968. Vine Deloria Papers. For a more recent analysis of this issue, see Washburn, "American Indians, Crime, and the Law," 709–77.

33. Examination of the War on Poverty Part 3.

34. 0501 Cong. Rec. 11274.

35. Vine Deloria Jr., "This Country Was a Lot Better Off When the Indians Were Running It," *New York Times*, March 8, 1970.

36. Wise, *The Red Man in the New World Drama,* 374.

37. Wise, *The Red Man in the New World Drama,* 391.

38. McKenzie-Jones, *Clyde Warrior,* 107.

39. Letter from Vine Deloria Jr. to Hank Adams, June 22, 1970. Vine Deloria Papers.

40. Letter from Vine Deloria Jr. to Leslie Dunbar, December 3, 1967. Vine Deloria Papers.

41. Indianz.com, "Vine Deloria Jr., Giant in Indian Country, Dies at 72." For the *New York Times* obituary, see Kirk Johnson, "Vine Deloria Jr., Champion of Indian

Rights, Dies at 72," *New York Times*, November 15, 2005, http://www.nytimes.com /2005/11/15/us/vine-deloria-jr-champion-of-indian-rights-dies-at-72.html. For the *Washington Post* obituary, see Teresa Wiltz, "The Indian Who Overturned the Stereotypes," *Washington Post*, November 16, 2005, http://www.washingtonpost .com/wp-dyn/content/article/2005/11/15/ar2005111501722.html.

42. Elizabeth Cook-Lynn, "Comments for Vine Deloria Jr.," 149–50.

43. Wilkins, "Vine Deloria Jr. and Indigenous Americans," 152, 153.

44. Wilkins, "Vine Deloria Jr. and Indigenous Americans," 154. For more on the concept of "exilic intellectual," see Said, *Representations of the Intellectual,* 47–64.

45. Tinker, "Walking in the Shadow of Greatness," 167.

46. Tinker, "Walking in the Shadow of Greatness," 170.

47. Warrior, *Tribal Secrets,* 93.

48. Warrior, *Tribal Secrets*, xvi.

49. Weaver, *That the People Might Live,* 127.

50. See Native American Graves Protection and Repatriation Act.

51. Deloria, *Red Earth, White Lies*, Deloria's comprehensive critique of evolution, the Bering Land Bridge theory, and the Pleistocene Overkill, appeared in 1995, which put it just beyond the scope of Biolsi and Zimmerman's volume. Anyone who has edited an anthology understands that coordinating the work of multiple authors is time consuming and the project typically does not easily avail itself to relatively late developments in their subject area very readily.

52. Biolsi and Zimmerman, "Introduction: What's Changed, What Hasn't," 4.

53. The infamous "Is God Dead?" issue of *Time Magazine* appeared several years earlier on April 8, 1966.

54. Treat, introduction, 12.

55. Grounds, Tinker, and Wilkins, preface, viii.

56. Morris, "Vine Deloria Jr.," 98–99.

57. Corbett, "When God Became Red," 190.

58. Corbett, "When God Became Red," 191.

59. Churchill, "Contours of Enlightenment," 245–72.

60. Talamantez, "Transforming American Conceptions," 274–75.

61. For Deloria and Lytle's analysis of tribal constitutional governments, see Deloria and Lytle, *The Nations Within,* 28–37.

62. Holm, "Decolonizing Native American Leaders," 48.

63. Holm, "Decolonizing Native American Leaders," 50.

64. Wilkins, "Forging a Political, Educational, and Cultural Agenda," 158.

65. Lawrence, *Radicals in Their Own Time,* 246–47.

66. Hoxie, *This Indian Country,* 351–52.

67. Hoxie, *This Indian Country,* 351–52.

68. Equally caustic remarks would later be aimed at Deloria's 1995 book *Red Earth, White Lies,* which ridiculed much of contemporary archeology. In fact, whereas the criticism of anthropology in *Custer* may have left room for dialog, the argument in *Red Earth, White Lies,* which rejected the Bering Land Bridge theory and the Pleistocene Overkill outright, appears to have left very little room for discussion.

69. Warrior, *Tribal Secrets,* xv.

70. It must be noted straightaway that Deloria published two additional books during the time frame of the present study (1964–74), specifically a revised edition of Jennings C. Wise's *The Red Man in the New World Drama* (1970) and the edited volume *Of Utmost Good Faith* (1971). While these two items are not without their place in Deloria's intellectual development during this time and will be cited at the appropriate points in the ensuing analysis; these works only have a peripheral role in the construction of Deloria's major discourse on tribal self-determination, meaning that they are regarded as a part of Deloria's enduring legacy as an Indigenous political thinker.

71. Jorgensen, "Indians and the Metropolis," 67.

72. Jean K. Boek, "We Talk, You Listen," 109.

2. COYOTE OLD MAN TELLS A STORY

1. The problem of Indian stereotypes is not just a political issue, but also a health issue, which was recognized not long after *Custer Died for Your Sins'* appearance. For how this matter was seen to relate to the psychological counseling of Indian youth, see Spang, "Understanding the Indian," 97–102. Spang was an assistant professor of education and director of the Indian Studies Program at the University of Montana, Missoula. Spang's article is one of the earliest in a specialty focused on the psychological effects of derogatory racial stereotypes on young people. For more recent research, see Fryberg, et al., "Of Warrior Chiefs and Indian Princesses." 208–18.

2. Roemer, "Custer Died for Your Sins,"273.

3. Deloria, *Custer Died for Your Sins,* 2.

4. The discourse on popular images and stereotypes that Deloria inaugurated in *Custer* regarding American Indians has become a subgenre in American Indian/Native American studies. See, for example, Berkhofer, *The White Man's Indian*; Mihesuah, *American Indians*; Smith, *Everything You Know*; and Treuer, *Everything You Wanted to Know about Indians.*

5. Pocahontas, the Powhatan "princess," is a close second, as evident in Brown, Meyers, and Chappel, *Pocahontas' Descendants.*

6. Eva Marie Garroutte would discuss the phenomenon of ethnic fraud, including the "Cherokee princess" tradition, in chapter 4 of *Real Indians,* titled "If You're Indian and You Know It (but Others Don't): Self-Identification."

7. Bates, "Reshaping Southern Identity and Politics," 141.
8. Bates, "Reshaping Southern Identity and Politics," 141. For the original article, see Ray, *The New Encyclopedia of Southern Culture*, 6:39.
9. Tiya Miles, for example, recounts the fascinating life of an Afro-Cherokee woman known only as "Nancy," who found herself caught up in the racialized politics of late eighteenth, early nineteenth century Tennessee and Virginia, as white American settlers begin building their new nation on slavery and the unlawful occupation of Indian land. See Miles, "The Narrative of Nancy," 59–80.
10. Numerous studies have been produced on the topic of human origins in North America, which span a variety of fields, including theology, history, paleontology, and genetics, much of which has been antithetical to American Indian oral traditions. For Deloria's critique of the Western scientific tradition, which he regarded as racially biased against American Indian–knowledge traditions, see Deloria, *Red Earth, White Lies*. Then, for a contrarian view on North American human origins, see Crawford, *The Origins of Native Americans*.
11. Deloria, *Custer Died for Your Sins*, 5–6.
12. The phrase "Indian problem" began appearing regularly in 1867 during the Grant administration, thus becoming a part of the vernacular in federal Indian affairs.
13. "Council on Indian Affairs Joint Leadership Project," undated. Vine Deloria Papers. Although there is no author credited for this grant application, the writing style and the ideas expressed throughout are similar to the enumeration of differences between Indian cultures and American society and politics that Deloria regularly highlighted in *Custer Died for Your Sins,* such as the chapter on Christian missionaries, and the time, space, and history chapters of *God Is Red* (1973).
14. See Apess, *Eulogy on King Philip,* 53–55.
15. See Winnemucca Hopkins, *Life among the Piutes,* 76–136.
16. See Eastman, *From the Deep Woods to Civilization,* 92–135.
17. Deloria, *Custer Died for Your Sins,* 8. For more on the boarding-school era, see Adams, *Education for Extinction.* For more about the Board of Indian Commissioners and the missionization of the reservation system, see Fritz, *The Movement for Indian Assimilation.*
18. For a historical examination of the bureaucratic half-truths perpetuated by the Office of Indian Affairs, see Rockwell, *Indian Affairs and the Administrative State.*
19. Two of the most important studies analyzing the relationship between Indian Bureau corruption and federal Indian policy were Fritz, *The Movement for Indian Assimilation* (1963) and Hoxie, *A Final Promise* (2001).
20. The most notorious example of this alleged progressive tradition was the Lake Mohonk Conference, which from 1883 to 1916 published annual reports documenting their efforts at civilizing the Indian. See Report of the Annual Lake Mohonk Conference.

21. Deloria, *Custer Died for Your Sins,* 10.
22. For an anecdote of Indian children wearing donated clothing, see Eastman, *From the Deep Woods to Civilization,* 21.
23. For a historical analysis of Indian Bureau corruption during Grant's Peace Policy, see Prucha, *The Great Father,* 152–210.
24. See Parker, "The Legal Status of the American Indian," 198–202. For a historical analysis of the struggle for American Indian citizenship, see Hertzberg, *The Search for an American Indian Identity.* Until 1924, when the Indian Citizenship Act was passed, conferring citizenship status on all Indians born within the territorial limits of the United States, the legal status of American Indians was a constant and pressing problem for Indian individuals who did not know what rights and laws applied to them. For example, Seneca intellectual and founding member of the Society of American Indians, Arthur C. Parker, addressed this issue in his 1914 article "The Legal Status of the American Indian," in which he sought to clarify the Indian's path to citizenship that was established by the 1887 General Allotment Act, but muddied by the 1906 Burke Act.
25. Deloria, *Custer Died for Your Sins,* 12. For a political analysis of modern tribal governments, their structures and powers, see O'Brien, *American Indian Tribal Governments.*
26. The phrase "Indian problem," a notion the U.S. government inherited from their British predecessors, is seen throughout countless official documents, primarily those generated by the Indian Bureau with respect to the reservation system. For two very different viewpoints on this matter, see Blackbird, *The Indian Problem* and Leupp, *The Indian and His Problem.*
27. Deloria, *Custer Died for Your Sins,* 15. Michael Harrington would acknowledge his oversight in a subsequent edition of *The Other America,* stating: "And I should add one minority I quite wrongly omitted from my original [1969] analysis: the American Indian" (196). Also, Harrington would recount his personal experience with the Rosebud Indian Reservation in section 12 of chapter 9, "Poverties," which was in his 1984 book, *The New American Poverty,* 219–24.
28. Deloria, *Custer Died for Your Sins,* 13, 14.
29. Deloria, *Custer Died for Your Sins,* 15.
30. Wells, "An Indian Manifesto,"163.
31. Ortiz, "Custer Died for Your Sins," 954. Seemingly in anticipation of Ortiz's criticism, a professor of education at the University of Chicago makes passing reference to *Custer* in an essay about the Rough Rock School in Navajo Nation. See Erickson, "Custer Did Die for Our Sins!," 76–93.
32. Deloria, *Custer Died for Your Sins,* 15–16.
33. Deloria, *Custer Died for Your Sins,* 16.
34. Deloria, "On Wounded Knee 1973," 38.

35. 4 Stat. 411. See also 4 Stat. 729. For a historical analysis of the creation of Indian Territory, see Satz, *American Indian Policy*.

36. For more on the historical development of the OCCO, see Wahrhaftig, "Institution Building." 132–47.

37. For more, see Johansen, "Survival of American Indians Association," 241–44.

38. A Project Proposal to the General Convention Special Program. Vine Deloria Papers.

39. Deloria, *Custer Died for Your Sins,* 18–19. The phenomenon of urban Indians and their role in the Indian Protest Movement was also addressed by a panel of experts at the First Convocation of American Indian Scholars. See, Deloria, "The Urban Scene and the American Indian," 333–55.

40. Deloria, *Custer Died for Your Sins,* 25.

41. For more on Pueblo Indian nation building, see Sando, *Pueblo Nations*. Then, for a more updated article on Pueblo economic development, see Pinel, "Culture and Cash," 9–39.

42. For more on Mescalero Apache resistance to American colonialism, including the tribe's twentieth-century political and economic development, see Sonnichsen, *The Mescalero Apaches*. Then, for an updated report on Western American Indian economic development, see Browne and Nolan, "Western Indian Reservation Tourism Development," 360–76.

43. Deloria, *Custer Died for Your Sins,* 21–22. For more about Minnesota Ojibwe history, including the tribes' reactions to developments in federal Indian policy, including termination, see Treuer, *Ojibwe in Minnesota*. The relationship between education, migration, poverty, job opportunities, and unemployment is a complex issue, which can easily be oversimplified with phrases like "brain drain." One recent study of the complexities of this phenomenon is *The Impact of Occupational Dislocation: The American Indian Labor Force at the Close of the Twentieth Century* (1999) by Patricia Kasari.

44. Insofar as Deloria is referring to political leaders aside from the infamous Dick Wilson, for more about Pine Ridge Reservation history, see Reinhart, *Ruling Pine Ridge*.

45. Deloria, *Custer Died for Your Sins,* 22–24. For more on the legal and political history of treaty rights in the Pacific Northwest, see Cesare Marino, "History of Western Washington," 175–78.

46. 384 F. Supp. 312.

47. Deloria, *Custer Died for Your Sins,* 27. While his presence in history books is scant, Alex Chasing Hawk does show up in the Congressional record. See Joint Hearing: Hearing before the Committee on Interior and Insular Affairs House, 83rd Cong. 2 (1954); Problems, Plans, and Programs of the Cheyenne River Reservation, South Dakota. House, 86th Cong. 1 (1959); Indian Heirship Land

Problem. Part 3. Senate, 88th Cong. 1 (1963); Indian Claims Commission Act Amendments. Senate, 90th Cong 1 (1967).

48. As often happens in Deloria's writings, beginning with *Custer*, anecdotes are shared without a corroborating citation. In the case of the Alex Chasing Hawk story, the only reference in the Congressional record is of Rep. Robert W. Kastenmeier (D-WI) retelling Chasing Hawk's story as something that is now well-known because of "Vine Deloria's book" (37096). For the latter instance in its original context, see the Congressional Record, C.R.-1969–1204. Contained therein, Representative Kastenmeier reads into the Congressional Record a speech titled "The American Indian in Today's World," which was delivered by Rep. Donald M. Fraser (D-MN) before the 13th Annual Minnesota AFL-CIO Institute on Human Relations on November 2, 1969. For a brief biography of Kastenmeier, see "Kastenmeier, Robert William, (1924–2015)." For a brief biography of Fraser, see "Fraser, Donald McKay, (1924–)."

49. Sitting Bull is reported to have said "Please tell them [the whites] I want none of their gold or silver, none of their goods, but that I desire to come back and live upon my lands; for there is plenty of game and grass, and we can live well if they will only let us alone." For more, see State Historical Society of North Dakota, *Collections of the State Historical Society.*

3. THE LAW OF THE LAND

1. Deloria, *Of Utmost Good Faith*, 1.
2. McNickle, "Four Years of Indian Reorganization," 270.
3. Lyndon B. Johnson, "Text of Message by President Johnson to Congress on the State of the Union," *New York Times*, January 11, 1967.
4. In all likelihood, Deloria was referring to Nixon's ongoing criticism of the Soviet Union during the 1968 presidential campaign regarding Johnson's pursuit of a nonproliferation treaty to control the arms race, in addition to the spread of communism in Eastern Europe and Southeast Asia. For example, see R. W. Apple Jr., "Nixon Promises Arms Superiority over the Soviet," *New York Times*, October 25, 1968.
5. In his opinion, Justice Stanley F. Reed matter-of-factly and infamously stated on behalf of the majority: "Every American schoolboy knows that the savage tribes of this continent were deprived of their ancestral ranges by force and that, even when the Indians ceded millions of acres by treaty in return for blankets, food, and trinkets, it was not a sale, but the conquerors' will that deprived them of their land," Tee-Hit-ton Indians v. United States.
6. Prucha, *American Indian Treaties,* 18.
7. Deloria, "The Subject Nobody Knows," 144. In a grant narrative likely written by Deloria for the Council on Indian Affairs there was a section recounting the

treaty-making tradition, in which some initial confusion took place as the custom was established: "Early attempts at treaty signing caused untold confusion in the minds of the non-Indian because there seemed to be no central authority figure to which all members of the tribe owed obedience." Council on Indian Affairs Joint Leadership Project, undated. Vine Deloria Papers.

8. Deloria, *Custer Died for Your Sins*, 29.

9. Deloria's portrayal of Cabot's alleged "discovery" of America is given without so much as a hint about the source material. For Cabot's own account of his presumed discovery, see Eliot, "John Cabot's Discovery of North America (1497)," 47–50.

10. In a little-cited book that Deloria revised and edited, *The Red Man in the New World Drama,* author Jennings C. Wise titled his chapter on the Indian Removal Era "Adams and Jackson: The Rape of the Eastern Tribes" (210–22). Colonization of Indigenous people as a specifically gendered oppression of women and the feminine also became a topic of analysis in Paula Gunn Allen's *The Sacred Hoop* (1986). Colonization as a form of rape with respect to women and the feminine has more recently been addressed in Andrea Smith's *Conquest* (2005) and Sarah Deer's *The Beginning and End of Rape* (2015). These works are important on their own merits; however, their value is increased when one considers that Deloria had disappointingly little to say about women and gender.

11. Deloria, *Custer Died for Your Sins,* 30.

12. For more about the American treaty-making tradition, see Prucha, *American Indian Treaties.*

13. Kickingbird and Ragsdale are given credit for chapters 5 and 10, "The Doctrine of Discovery" and "Litigating Indian Claims." Deloria, however, was still given final authorial credit based on the fact that he was listed as the sole author of *Behind the Trail of Broken Treaties* and that the analyses are consistent with how these topics were presented in other writings, including *Custer Died for Your Sins.* Ragsdale, it should also be noted, contributed an essay to *American Indian Policy in the Twentieth Century*, which Deloria edited and contributed an introduction. See, in the aforementioned volume, Fred L. Ragsdale Jr., "The Deception of Geography," 63–82.

14. Fairbanks, "Review: Behind the Trail of Broken Treaties," 171.

15. Hoxie, *This Indian Country,* 351–52.

16. Deloria, "On Wounded Knee 1973," 38.

17. For the role of the right of aboriginal occupancy and the extinguishment of Indian title through treaties, see Prucha, *American Indian Treaties*, 226–34.

18. Deloria, *Behind the Trail of Broken Treaties,* 96–97.

19. For more on the Georgia-Cherokee controversy, see Prucha, *American Indian Treaties*, 156–61.

20. Deloria, *Behind the Trail of Broken Treaties*, 106.

21. Prucha, *American Indian Treaties*, 182.
22. Holden v. Joy.
23. United States v. Shoshone Tribe of Indians.
24. Deloria, *Behind the Trail of Broken Treaties*, 108.
25. Deloria, *Behind the Trail of Broken Treaties*, 109.
26. Deloria, *Behind the Trail of Broken Treaties*, 111.
27. Deloria, *Custer Died for Your Sins*, 31.
28. Cherokee Nation v. State of Georgia.
29. Prucha focused a subsection of chapter 2 of *American Indian Treaties* on the negotiation of the Hopewell Treaty, in which he saw the 1785 Cherokee treaty as a prelude to the United States regarding Indian treaties as domestic policy, as opposed to international affairs. See Prucha, *American Indian Treaties*, 59–66.
30. Kappler, "Treaty with the Cherokee, 1785."
31. Johnson & Graham's Lessee v. McIntosh.
32. 25 U.S. Code § 1–4307.
33. Deloria, *Custer Died for Your Sins*, 31.
34. Kappler, "Treaty with the Six Nations, 1794."
35. For example, see Sleeper-Smith, *Rethinking the Fur Trade*; and Dolin, *Fur, Fortune, and Empire*.
36. Deloria, *Custer Died for Your Sins*, 33.
37. Deloria, *Custer Died for Your Sins*, 33. For the original 1778 treaty, please see Kappler, "Treaty with the Six Nations, 1794." For an analysis of the 1778 Treaty with the Delaware as the inauguration of the tradition of federal recognition, see Quinn, "Federal Acknowledgment of American Indian Tribes," 331–64.
38. Deloria, *Custer Died for Your Sins*, 34. For an analysis of the 1785 Hopewell Treaty's role in Indian affairs, see Breutti, "The Cherokee Cases," 33–34.
39. ;adjfdlkjfd;lkjfd;ljfdljfdla;jadl;jdl.
40. Deloria, *Behind the Trail of Broken Treaties*, 118–19.
41. Deloria, *Custer Died for Your Sins*, 35.
42. Deloria, *Custer Died for Your Sins*, 36. See Kappler, Treaty with the Wyandot, Etc., 1789, articles 2 and 3; Kappler, Treaty with the Kaskaskia, 1803, article 1; Kappler, Treaty with the Sauk and Foxes, 1804, article 4; Kappler, Treaty with the Wea, 1818, article 2.
43. Deloria, *Custer Died for Your Sins*, 37. For a critical and historical analysis of tribal jurisdiction, see Luna-Firebaugh, *Tribal Policing*.
44. Kappler, "Treaty with the Kiowa and Comanche, 1867."
45. John Fletcher Lacey (R-IA). Committee of the Whole House. House Committee on Indian Affairs. Opening for Settlement Certain Lands in Oklahoma (57 H. R. 16280). Washington, DC: Government Printing Office.

46. Deloria, *Custer Died for Your Sins,* 37. See also Lone Wolf v. Hitchcock. For an historical analysis of the Kiowa leader, his cause, and the precedent-setting Supreme Court case, see Clark, *Lone Wolf v. Hitchcock.*

47. Deloria, *Behind the Trail of Broken Treaties,* viii.

48. For more on this troubling history, see McCool, "Indian Voting," 105–34; and Laughlin McDonald, *American Indians and the Fight for Equal Voting Rights.*

49. Deloria, *Of Utmost Good Faith,* 129.

50. Deloria, *Behind the Trail of Broken Treaties,* 147.

51. Deloria, *Of Utmost Good Faith,* 132.

52. Talton v. Mayes.

53. Deloria, *Behind the Trail of Broken Treaties,* 150–51.

54. Deloria, *Behind the Trail of Broken Treaties,* 151.

55. Deloria, *Of Utmost Good Faith,* 170.

56. Deloria, *Behind the Trail of Broken Treaties,* 153. See also Native American Church v. Navajo Tribal Council. For the Jemez Pueblo case, see Toledo v. Pueblo De Jemez.

57. According to Fred L. Ragsdale Jr., contemporary Indian law began in 1959 with Williams v. Lee, 358 U.S. 217 (1959), which affirmed the sovereignty of the tribal court system, as opposed to the state court, over civil cases involving non-Indian defendants. See Ragsdale, "The Deception of Geography," 63–82.

58. Deloria, *Behind the Trail of Broken Treaties,* 154. See also Colliflower v. Garland.

59. Deloria, *Behind the Trail of Broken Treaties,* 154.

60. Deloria, *Behind the Trail of Broken Treaties,* 154–55.

61. See Kappler, "Treaty with the Nisqualli, Puyallup, etc., 1854."

62. Deloria, *Behind the Trail of Broken Treaties,* 158.

63. It was this theme of "good faith" that motivated Deloria to organize an anthology of the pertinent government documents at the basis of Indian-white relations from the beginning of the American republic, which served as a companion volume to *Custer* and *Broken Treaties.* See Deloria, *Of Utmost Good Faith.*

64. Deloria, *Behind the Trail of Broken Treaties,* 158–59. For a more recent study of the treaties signed in the Pacific Northwest, see Harmon, *The Power of Promises.*

65. Deloria, *Behind the Trail of Broken Treaties,* 159–60.

66. *U.S. Statutes at Large,* 43:253. The adjoining proviso states: "Tribal rights not affected."

67. See section 16 of *U.S. Statutes at Large,* 48:984–88. For Deloria's analysis of the 1934 Indian Reorganization Act, see Deloria and Lytle, *The Nations Within.* See also Deloria, *The Indian Reorganization Act.*

68. For an overview, see Rosier, "Native American Treaty Rights," 31–60.

69. Deloria, *Custer Died for Your Sins,* 40. For a more comprehensive look at Deloria's account of Pacific Northwest tribal history and politics, see Deloria, *Indians of the Pacific Northwest.*

70. Deloria, *Custer Died for Your Sins,* 40–41.

71. For an example of how the United States treated its Indian allies, see Glatthaar and Martin, *Forgotten Allies.*

72. Deloria, *Custer Died for Your Sins,* 41.

73. Kappler, "Treaty with the Choctaw, 1825." See also Deloria, *Behind the Trail of Broken Treaties,* 130–31.

74. Choctaw Nation of Oklahoma. History: Removal.

75. Deloria, *Custer Died for Your Sins,* 43.

76. For a summary analysis of this topic, see Trosper, "American Indian Poverty on Reservations," 172–95.

77. Although a concurrent resolution does not have the force of law, as would P.L. 280, it does clearly signify the direction in which the legislative powers of Congress would be jointly focused, as was notoriously exemplified by the dozens of tribes whose federal support was subsequently terminated. For the definition of concurrent resolution, see U.S. Senate, "Legislation, Laws, and Acts." For HCR 108, see 67 Stat. B132, Statutes at Large, 83rd Cong. 1 (1953), *and for* P.L. 280, see P.L. 83-280; 67 Stat. 588, Statutes at Large, 83rd Cong. 1 (1953)

78. Deloria, *Custer Died for Your Sins,* 43.

79. Deloria, *Custer Died for Your Sins,* 44.

80. Sixth Congress, Session 1, Resolutions, V, April 16, 1800. The presumption of this resolution to extinguish the Indian title to the lands in question derive from a "right of discovery" that would be articulated and attain the status of legal precedent in Johnson & Graham's Lessee v. McIntosh.

81. Kappler, "Treaty with the Chippewa, 1826."

82. Kappler, "Treaty with the Chippewa, 1826."

83. Deloria, *Custer Died for Your Sins,* 44–45. What Deloria does not mention, as it is beyond the scope of his topic, is the fact that the Chippewa signatories participated in the treaty making under a cloud of suspicion and acrimony generated by an alleged capital crime against American citizens near Lake Pepin. In a "supplementary article," it states: "As the Chippewas who committed the murder upon four American citizens, in June, 1824, upon the shores of Lake Pepin, are not present at this council, but are far in the interior of the country, so that they cannot be apprehended and delivered to the proper authority before the commencement of the next Summer; and, as the Commissioners have been specially instructed to demand the surrender of these persons, and to state to the Chippewa tribe the consequence of suffering such a flagitious outrage to go unpunished, it is agreed, that the persons guilty of the beforementioned murder shall be brought in, either to the Sault St. Marie, or Green Bay, as early next summer as practicable, and surrendered to the proper authority; and that, in the mean time, all further measures on the part

of the United States, in relation to this subject, shall be suspended" (Kappler, "Treaty with the Chippewa, 1826.").

84. Deloria, *Custer Died for Your Sins,* 45–46. For a historical and political analysis of this episode in Chippewa history, see Wrone, "The Economic Impact of the 1837 and 1842 Chippewa Treaties," 329–40.

85. 4 Stat. 729.

86. 4 Stat. 735. Deloria does not provide his reader for what he calls a "companion act," the above trade and intercourse statute.

87. Deloria, *Custer Died for Your Sins,* 46. Deloria mistakenly refers to the Department of Interior as part of the federal government in 1834. While the Indian Bureau, complete with a commissioner of Indian affairs, was established at this time, the DOI was not created until March 3, 1849, when it was called the "Home Department," see 9 Stat. 395. Section 5 of the 1849 statute specifically provides for the secretary of the Home Department to have supervisory authority over the commissioner of Indian affairs, including the various superintendencies enumerated in the 1834 act organizing the Department of Indian Affairs. For more about this historic transfer, see Fixico, *Bureau of Indian Affairs,* 26–28.

88. 16 Stat. 544. See also Prucha, *American Indian Treaties,* 289–310.

89. 24 Stat. 388.

90. 24 Stat. 388. See, section 5. The president had the power to extend the trust period as needed, meaning that fee-simple title and citizenship were far from guaranteed. Also, when section 6 of the General Allotment Act was amended on May 8, 1906, it gave the secretary of interior to power to determine is an Indian allottee is competent enough to manage his own affairs before a fee-simple patent is awarded (34 Stat. 182).

91. Deloria, *Custer Died for Your Sins,* 46–47.

92. For a brief biography of Dawes, see "Dawes, Henry Laurens, (1816–1903)."

93. For a personal account of Hare's work among the Indians, see Howe, *The Life and Labors of Bishop Hare.*

94. Deloria, *Custer Died for Your Sins,* 47–48.

95. 48 Stat. 984. For more about the formation of tribal governments, see section 16. For more about Deloria's analysis of the legislative and political history of the 1934 Indian Reorganization Act, see Deloria and Lytle, *The Nations Within.*

96. Deloria, *Custer Died for Your Sins,* 48.

97. Deloria, *Behind the Trail of Broken Treaties,* 192.

98. Interestingly, one thing the Meriam Report does not bring up as an option for reforming Indian affairs is tribal self-governance. D'Arcy McNickle made this observation in his 1949 book *They Came Here First,* in which he stated: "The fact that almost no mention is made of tribal self-government in the Meriam Report

(of 1928), and that it contains no recommendations on this subject, illustrates how completely Indian social organization has been forgotten" (242).

99. Deloria, *Behind the Trail of Broken Treaties*, 193. See also To Quiet Title to Lands within Pueblo Indian Land Grants in New Mexico.

100. Deloria, *Behind the Trail of Broken Treaties*, 193–94. See also Survey of Conditions of the Indians in the United States.

101. Deloria, *Behind the Trail of Broken Treaties*, 194–96. For the bill that was introduced into the Senate on May 18, 1934, see 73 S. 3645. The problem of Indian land heirship returned again as a major problem, the proposed solution to which tribes resisted again when Sen. Franck Church introduced S 1049 (1964), which, according to the NCAI, "would cause Indian-held trust lands to be shifted through forced sale into non-Indian hands." For more on the NCAI's concerns, see "Johnson Promises Help for Indians."

102. Deloria, *Behind the Trail of Broken Treaties*, 196.

103. Wise, *The Red Man in the New World Drama*, 359.

104. Wise, *The Red Man in the New World Drama*, 359.

105. Deloria, *Behind the Trail of Broken Treaties*, 196–98.

106. Deloria, *Behind the Trail of Broken Treaties*, 198–99.

107. Deloria, *Behind the Trail of Broken Treaties*, 199–201.

108. Wise, *The Red Man in the New World Drama*, 358.

109. Wise, *The Red Man in the New World Drama*, 358.

110. Deloria, *Behind the Trail of Broken Treaties*, 202. What the Republican majority Congress did to the Indian New Deal, beginning in 1947, was hardly a surprise to those who watched Indian affairs closely. D'Arcy McNickle observed as early as 1938 that "There is a tendency in Congress to reduce the funds allotted for Indian Reorganization purposes, in its theory that, now that, so many of the tribes are organized, the need for future work is diminishing." See McNickle, "Four Years of Indian Organization," 4–11.

111. Deloria, *Behind the Trail of Broken Treaties*, 203–4. See also S. 3645.

112. Deloria, *Behind the Trail of Broken Treaties*, 206.

113. Peterson, "American Indian Political Participation," 295.

114. For a historical analysis of how an ongoing fear of pan-Indian alliances shaped the identity of the American republic, see Owens, *Red Dreams, White Nightmares*.

115. Deloria, *Custer Died for Your Sins,* 51.

116. For a history of Indian land claims, including what occurred after *Custer's* 1969 publication, see Royster, "Indian Land Claims," 28–37.

117. Deloria revisited the issue of federal recognition in a sequel to *Custer Died for Your Sins*; see *A Better Day for Indians,* 17–21. Then, on December 15, 1977 Sen. James Abourezk (D-SD), whose role in the 1973 confrontation at Wounded Knee Deloria would cover in *Behind the Trail of Broken Treaties*, introduced S.

2375, which proposed establishing administrative criteria for acknowledging "the existence of Certain Indian tribes." The bill went before the Senate Select Committee on Indian Affairs, April 18, 1978, where it then went to the Bureau of Indian Affairs, which published acknowledgement criteria in the Federal Register, September 25, 1978; these were then codified as 25 CFR 54, which, when the Register was recodified in 1994, became 25 CFR Part 83.

118. 60 Stat 1049. See section 2 for an enumeration of the classes of claims that may be brought to the commission for adjudication.

119. Wise, *The Red Man in the New World Drama,* 361.

120. For a short biography of Karl E. Mundt, see "Mundt, Karl Earl, (1900–1974)."

121. Cited in Deloria, *Custer Died for Your Sins,* 52. For Mundt's complete comments, see Representative Mundt, "Indian Claims Commission Bill."

122. Deloria is referring to an array of laws and policies initiated during the Lyndon B. Johnson administration, which became more popularly known as the "War on Poverty." For more on poverty in the United States, see Harrington, *The Other America.* See also 78 Stat. 508; Bureau of Indian Affairs PL 88–452 and Select Subcommittee on Poverty, "War on Poverty."

123. 15 U.S. Code § 1021.

124. Deloria, *Custer Died for Your Sins,* 53.

4. FOR THE GOOD OF THE INDIAN

1. Holm, "Decolonizing Native American Leaders," 48. For more on "legitimate authority," see Weber, "Bureaucracy and Legitimate Authority," 17–23.

2. "Now Is the Time," 1.

3. Indian Resources Development Act of 1967.

4. Letter from Vine Deloria Jr. to John Belindo, December 1, 1967. Vine Deloria Papers.

5. Deloria, *Custer Died for Your Sins,* 54.

6. Department of the Interior and Related Agencies Appropriations for 1966, Part 2. According to the editorial, "Now Is the Time," in the *NCAI Sentinel Bulletin,* the letter cited was the result of a resolution that the NCAI executive board passed. The resolution, titled "N.C.A.I. Supports Indian Health Budget," stated: "Now, therefore be it further resolved, that the Executive Director of the National Congress of American Indians submit this resolution to the House and Senate Sub-committees on Appropriations for the Department of Interior and Related Agencies who will soon consider the Division of Indian Health's appropriation request for the 1966 fiscal year."

7. 68 Stat. 674. See also Office of Indian Affairs, Department of Interior, PL 83–568. For a summary of improvements made in Indian health status since the 1955 Transfer Act, see chapter 3, "Strengthening the Structure, 1962–1968," in Rife

and Dellapenna, *Caring and Curing.* For a summary of the issue with health-care access for members of federally recognized tribes during the Termination era, see Indian Health Care Improvement. Hearing before the Committee on Indian Affairs.

8. In a statement published in the *NCAI Sentinel*, titled "NCAI Supports Indian Health Budget," the progress that the IHS has made since 1955 is acknowledged, along with the challenges that laid ahead. In addition to enumerating the numbers of hospitals, health centers, and physicians, IHS has also established "three training programs for practical nurses, two for dental assistants, and one for sanitary aids." However, "Indian birth rates are about twice that of the total population. Newly reported tuberculosis has dropped 54%, but is still 6 times the all races figure. Infant death rate has declined 40%, but is still 70% higher than all races. TB, gastroenteric and other infectious diseases are still 3 times higher than all races figure," 2.

9. For an analysis of termination as a political response to New Deal reforms, see Philip, "Termination: A Legacy of the Indian New Deal," 165–80.

10. McNickle, "Four Years of Indian Organization," 11.

11. 67 Stat. B132.

12. Wise, *The Red Man in the New World Drama,* 365.

13. Deloria, *Custer Died for Your Sins,* 14.

14. 67 Stat. 588. See also 18 U.S. Code § 1162. The states effected are California, Minnesota (excepting Red Lake), Nebraska, Oregon (excepting Warm Springs), and Wisconsin (excepting Menominee).

15. Deloria, *Custer Died for Your Sins,* 54–55.

16. Brookings Institution, *The Problem of Indian Administration.*

17. For the original Senate resolution commissioning the Meriam Report, see 1928 S. Res.; 70 S. Res. 79.

18. Deloria, *Custer Died for Your Sins,* 55. For an example of the level of scrutiny that BIA expenditures were subjected, see Subcommittee on Interior Department Appropriations, Interior Department Appropriation Bill for 1943.

19. Deloria, *Custer Died for Your Sins,* 55. For the 1943 Senate Interior Committee report, see Subcommittee on Interior Department Appropriations, Interior Department Appropriation Bill for 1944. In a supplemental statement to Collier's justifications of Indian Bureau expenditures, in response to Representative Mundt's criticism of wasteful spending, it is claimed: "Indians now practically self-supporting: It should be stated here that most of the Indians manage to procure their livelihood without any aid from the Federal Government" (6).

20. For a short biography, see "Langer, William, (1886–1959)."

21. 1947 S. Res.; 80 S. Res. 41.

22. Committee on Civil Service, Part 3, 80th Cong. 1 (1947).

23. Committee on Civil Service, Part 3, 80th Cong. 1 (1947).
24. The Mission Indian Federation (MIF), as it is now known, has a storied tradition of battling the Bureau of Indian Affairs on behalf of California's Indigenous nations, including Indian Commissioner Collier. As the MIF summarizes its historic role on its web page: "The Mission Indian Federation (MIF) was Southern California's most popular and long-lived grass-roots political organization. Between 1919 and 1965, its membership wrestled with some of the most difficult political and legal questions of the 20th century. The MIF asserted rights to internal sovereignty, rejecting the Bureau of Indian Affairs (BIA) paternalism. The MIF's clashes with the federal government's BIA employees in the Mission Indian Agency (MIA) continually had its members in court, but occasionally confrontations turned violent. In 1934, Commissioner of Indian Affairs John Collier described the MIF's aspirations toward sovereignty saying the organization 'resisted the work of the Indian service in the spirit of ousting a foreign power from the native soil or beating off an invasion of a foreign power.' Drawing its membership from reservation and non-reservation California Indians of southern California, the MIF could best be described as a quasi-governmental, pan-Indian organization purporting to represent the collective will of Southern California's reservation people." See The Mission Indian Federation, "General Description."
25. For more Adam Castillo and the Mission Indian Federation, see Hertzberg, "Indian Rights Movements, 1887–1973," 311; and, Bauer, "California," 290.
26. Committee on Civil Service, Part 3, 80th Cong. 1 (1947). For the impact of termination on the California Indian community, see Daly, "Fractured Relations at Home," 427–39.
27. With respect to the objective of abolishing the Indian Bureau, no one stands more prominently than Yavapai activist-intellectual Carlos Montezuma (c 1866–1923). For more about Montezuma's life and work, see Iverson, *Carlos Montezuma*; and Speroff, *Carlos Montezuma, M.D.* In addition, what should be noted in the anti-Indian Bureau tradition is that terminating the BIA was on the agenda for the organizers of the Trail of Broken Treaties. See Adams, et al., "Trail of Broken Treaties 20-Point Position Paper," 345-57.
28. It is worth noting two things about the proposition of tribes incorporating and developing the natural resources available on a given reservation. First, the 1934 Indian Reorganization Act, section 17, enables tribes to incorporate: "Such charter may convey to the incorporated tribe the power to purchase, take by gift, or bequest, or otherwise, own, hold, manage, operate, and dispose of property of every description, real and personal, including the power to purchase restricted lands and to issue in exchange therefore issues in corporate property, and such further powers as may be incidental to the conduct of corporate business, not inconsistent with law, but no authority shall be granted to sell,

mortgage, or lease for a period exceeding ten years any of the land included in the limits of the reservation" (48. Stat. 984). Second, prior to the 1934 IRA, Oneida activist-intellectual Laura Cornelius Kellogg proposed developing the "Industrial Organization for the Indian" (1912), in addition to an early proposal for tribal self-determination called the "Lolomi Program" (1920).

29. Committee on Civil Service, Part 3, 80th Cong. 1 (1947).

30. Deloria, *Custer Died for Your Sins,* 58–59.

31. See 79 S. 797; 80 S. 797; and 78 S. 1218.

32. Deloria, *Custer Died for Your Sins,* 59.

33. 82 H. Res. 698. For a brief biography of Delaney, see "Delaney, James Joseph, (1901–1987)."

34. 11582 H. rp. 2503.

35. Deloria, *Custer Died for Your Sins,* 61.

36. For more about the Japanese American experience under Myer, see Hirabashi, *A Principled Stand*; and Bannai, *Enduring Conviction.*

37. 81 S. 6406. During the Committee on Interior and Insular Affairs meeting, the committee chairman, Sen. Joseph C. O'Mahoney (D-WY) is recorded as stating: "There were no objections [to Myer's nomination] filed with the committee, except Bob Yellow Tail appeared before the committee and urged the appointment of an Indian. Of course it would be beyond our jurisdiction [as nominations are made by the president]." For a brief biography of Senator O'Mahoney, see "O'Mahoney, Joseph Christopher, (1884–1962)."

38. For more about Robert Yellowtail, see Edmunds, "Robert Yellowtail," 55–77.

39. During a meeting of the committee, Representative Bender is recorded as stating: "I asked the question of one of my colleagues here as to who the Administrator of this [Indian] Bureau was and I was informed that it was a gentleman by the name of Dillon Myer. And I said, I can now understand why you are having difficulty with the administration of that Bureau; why you are dissatisfied. Is he not the same gentleman who handled the Japanese detention camps, and did not the military policy testify that they had more trouble with him than they had with all the Japanese combined? Is this not the same Dillon Myer who bungled the housing business? Is he not the same gentleman who was in charge of this Inter-American relations program and made a mess of that?" For the full record of this meeting, see C.R.-1951-0425. For a brief biography of Representative Bender, see Biographical Directory of the United States Congress, "Bender, George Harrison, (1896–1961)."

40. 81 S. 6406. For a brief biography of Representative Schwabe, see "Schwabe, George Blaine, (1886–1952)."

41. 11582 H. rp. 2503. Deloria would retell the story of Myer and termination in *American Indians, American Justice* (1983) in the context of giving readers an

historical overview of Indian affairs policies, which have shaped contemporary tribal governments and their relationship with the federal system. See Deloria and Lytle, *American Indians, American Justice,* 15–21.

42. Deloria, *Custer Died for Your Sins,* 61.

43. For a brief biography of Senator Watkins, see "Watkins, Arthur Vivian, (1886–1973)." Watkins is also the author of *Enough Rope.*

44. For a brief biography of Representative Berry, see "Berry, Ellis Yarnal, (1902–1999)."

45. Deloria, *Custer Died for Your Sins,* 62.

46. Holden v. Joy, H.R. 303, S. 132 H. rp. 2503; and S. 2780. The report accompanying H.R. 303 states: "This proposed legislation is in line with the policy of the Congress and the Department of the Interior to terminate duplicating and overlapping functions provided by the Indian Bureau for Indians by transferring responsibility for such functions to other governmental agencies wherever feasible, and the enactment by the Congress of legislation having as its purpose to repeal laws which set Indians apart from other citizens."

47. Deloria, *Custer Died for Your Sins,* 62–63.

48. Termination of Federal Supervision of Certain Tribes of Indians. See therein George C. Morris, Letter to Arthur V. Watkins, February 12, 1954. Morris summarizes therein an "outline of points" discussed at Watkins's meeting with "the Utah Indians at Salt Lake City," in which is included among the five enumerated items: "3 Ratification of marriages, divorces, and adoptions performed by Indian custom up to date of act" (51).

49. S. 2670. For the tribes targeted by this bill, see Sec 2(a): " 'Tribe' means any of the following tribes or bands of Indians located in the State of Utah: Shivwits, Kanosh, Koosharem, and the Indian Peaks Bands of the Paiute Indian Tribe, Skull Valley Band of the Shoshone Indian Tribe, and the Washakie Band of the Northwestern Band of Shoshone Indians." Each of these tribes was appraised as "not competent to manage their own affairs." Such was the estimation of the Uintah and Ouray Agency of the Bureau of Indian Affairs, which was sent a questionnaire in pursuance of H. Res. 89 regarding the tribes under its charge. Among other criteria, each agency was asked to make an "appraisal of competency" with respect to a tribe's ability to conduct its own affairs. See 11747 H. rp. 2680.

50. 68 Stat. 1099. With respect to the Paiutes alleged consent to termination, a transcript of a meeting of the House Interior and Insular Affairs Committee is included, which was chaired by Rep. A. L. Miller (R-NE). On record at this hearing is Rep. E. Y. Berry, who testified: "Now down to the question of consent. Senator Watkins held several meetings out there [in Utah]. Apparently all the Indians at the time, all of the various six tribes, approved it. Some, however,

were noncommittal, because it is apparent that two of the tribes named the Washakie Band of Shoshone Indians and the Skull Valley Band of Shoshone Indians, comprising less than 200 altogether. These two tribes apparently do not wish to come under the provisions of this bill, and it was the thought of the subcommittee [on Indian Affairs] that they should be taken out since they have asked to be taken out." For a brief biography of Representative Miller, see "Miller, Arthur Lewis, (1892–1967)."

51. Deloria, *Custer Died for Your Sins,* 63.
52. Deloria, *Custer Died for Your Sins,* 65.
53. "Wisconsin Tribesmen Get $8,500,000 As Truman Signs Bill to Pay Up Claim," *New York Times,* November 3, 1951. For a summary of the 1951 Menominee petition to the Indian Claims Commission, see Menominee Indian Tribe of Wisconsin v. Thompson. Contained therein is a subsection titled "Facts Subject To Judicial Note," in which the "proceedings before the Indian Claims Commission in 1951" are summarized. Before taking their grievance to the ICC, the Menominee took their case to the United States Court of Claims; see Menominee Tribe of Indians v. United States.
54. Deloria, *Custer Died for Your Sins,* 65–66. See also Examination of the War on Poverty Part 3, and Office of Indian Affairs, Department of Interior. Contained therein is a statement in the preamble proclaiming: "That the purpose of this Act is to provide for the orderly termination of Federal supervision over the property and members of the Menominee Indian Tribe of Wisconsin"; in addition, section 7 states: "The tribe shall formulate and submit to the Secretary a plan or plans for the future control of the property and service functions now conducted by or under the supervision of the United States, including, but not limited to, services in the fields of health, education, welfare, credit, roads, and law and order. The Secretary is authorized to provide such reasonable assistance as may be requested by officials of the tribe in the formulation of the plan or plans heretofore referred to, including necessary consultations with representatives of Federal departments and agencies, officials of the State of Wisconsin and political subdivisions thereof, and members of the tribe. Provided, That the responsibility of the United States to furnish all such supervision and services to the tribe and to the members thereof, because of their status as Indians, shall cease on December 1, 1958, or on such earlier date as may be agreed upon by the tribe and the Secretary."
55. For a brief biography of Senator Church, see "Church, Frank Forrester, (1924–1984)."
56. In spite of playing a role in the termination of the Menominee, Senator Church, along with Sen. Leonard B. Jordan (R-ID), would be applauded in the *NCAI Sentinel Bulletin* (10, no. 3 [Spring 1965]) for their work establishing the Nez

Perce National Historical Park. "We are happy," the NCAI stated in its editorial, "that the Senators from Idaho are taking the lead in showing us all what American history really means," 2.2.

57. Deloria, *Custer Died for Your Sins,* 66.

58. Deloria, *Custer Died for Your Sins,* 67.

59. Deloria, *Custer Died for Your Sins,* 67. For summary of the Menominee claims against the United States, see Menominee Tribe of Wisconsin v. The United States. Contained therein is "History of the Termination Act," in which it is stated: "On June 20, 1953, Senator Arthur Watkins of Utah . . . visited the Menominee reservation and spoke at a meeting of the Menominee General Council. He made it clear that the $1500 per capita distribution would be denied unless the Tribe agreed to the termination of federal supervision. The Tribe was left with the impression that termination was inevitable. After Senator Watkins's speech, the Menominee men and women present at the General Council meeting voted 169 to 5 (in a standing vote) to accept the principle of termination. No plans for or consequences of termination were discussed, and the Indians believed that termination could be reversed if it was proven undesirable."

60. Deloria, *Custer Died for Your Sins,* 67–68. For a complete transcript of the Subcommittee on Indian Affairs 1960 hearings on Menominee termination, see 1960 Amendments to the Menominee Indian Termination Act of 1954. For a transcript of the meeting between Senator Watkins and Menominee Chairman Waupochick, see Termination of Federal Supervision of Menominee Indians. For a transcript of another meeting between Watkins and Waupochick, which is quoted in *Custer* (68), in which Watkins describes the soon-to-be-terminated Menominee reservation as similar to "the refugee camps of the Near East," see Termination of Federal Supervision over Certain Tribes of Indians. Part 6.

61. For a summary of Menominee financial resources, see Peroff, *Menominee Drums,* 44.

62. Deloria, *Custer Died for Your Sins,* 68.

63. Deloria, *Custer Died for Your Sins,* 68. For a transcript of Harder's testimony, see Termination of Federal Supervision over Certain Tribes of Indians. Part 6, (Testimony of Harry Harder).

64. Op cited in Deloria, *Custer Died for Your Sins,* 68–69.

65. For another account of the Menominee meeting with Senator Watkins, in which Jerome Grignon, chairman, Menominee Advisory Council, is meeting before the House Subcommittee on Indian Affairs, see To Amend the Menominee Termination Act.

66. Deloria, *Custer Died for Your Sins,* 69.

67. Deloria, *Custer Died for Your Sins,* 69. See also To Amend the Menominee Termination Act, (Testimony of Jerome Grignon).

68. Deloria, *Custer Died for Your Sins,* 70.

69. For more about the overall costs of Menominee termination, see Peroff, *Menominee Drums,* 78–127.
70. Deloria, *Custer Died for Your Sins,* 71–72. Much has happened, of course, since 1960 —even from the vantage point of *Custer,* which appeared in the late 1960s. With regard to the War on Poverty, Deloria gave an expansive analysis of these programs and their effect on tribes in *We Talk, You Listen.* A few years later, in 1973, Deloria testified before Congress on behalf of the Menominee, arguing for the tribe's restoration to federally recognized status. See Menominee Restoration Act.
71. For a brief biography, see "Jackson, Henry Martin (Scoop), (1912–1983)."
72. Deloria, *Custer Died for Your Sins,* 72. For an example of how Gamble's role was regarded in the discourse on Indian self-determination, see Castile, *To Show Heart,* 59.
73. Colville Indian Legislation, 88th Cong. 1 (1963).
74. Deloria, *Custer Died for Your Sins,* 72–73. See also 84 H.R. 7190; Office of Indian Affairs, PL 84–772; and 70 Stat. 626. For the connection between the statute for Colville land restoration and termination, see Colville Termination, 90th Cong. 2 (1968).
75. Gamble would be officially commended for his work as a Senate staffer. See "James H. Gamble Retires," Congressional Record, C.R.-1973–1011. For a portrayal of the way in which Gamble and his successor, Forrest Gerard, shaped federal Indian policy, see Trahant, *The Last Great Battle of the Indian Wars.*
76. Colville Termination, 89th Cong. 1 (1965).
77. Deloria, *Custer Died for Your Sins,* 73. For a full account of Colville's historic struggle against termination, see Arnold, *Bartering with the Bones of Their Dead.* Eventually, on July 8, 1970, President Richard M. Nixon presented his "Special Message to the Congress on Indian Affairs," in which he stated: "Federal termination errs in one direction, Federal paternalism errs in the other. Only by clearly rejecting both of these extremes can we achieve a policy which truly serves the best interests of the Indian people. Self-determination among the Indian people can and must be encouraged without the threat of eventual termination. For a transcript of the complete statement, see The American Presidency Project, "Richard Nixon." For an insightful analysis of Nixon's Indian policy and his historically important relationship with the American Indian community and the Indian protest movement, see Forbes, *Native Americans and Nixon.*
78. Vine Deloria Jr., "The War Between the Redskins and the Feds," *New York Times,* December 7, 1969.
79. Holden v. Joy. See also C.R. 1967-0912. Contained in the latter is a reference to Bill S. 2390, titled "Withdrawal of Federal Supervision Over the Property and Affairs of the Seneca Nation" (25123).

80. Deloria, *Custer Died for Your Sins,* 74–75.

81. "Justice and 'Just Compensation.'" The contentious issue of rights of way through Indian land was something that was a regular part of the NCAI's advocacy work on behalf of tribes, as evident in a memo from Deloria to John Belindo, dated December 4, 1967, in which Deloria noted: "the Secretary of the Interior has the power to issue rules and regulations for rights of way over tribal land according to the law passed February 5, 1948 (62 Stat. 17, H.R. 3322—Public Law 707, 80th Congress)." "Rights of Way Over Tribal Lands in Re Electric Power Reliability Act of 1967." Vine Deloria Papers.

82. Deloria, *Custer Died for Your Sins,* 75. Deloria would recount this story again, see Deloria, *Singing for a Spirit,* 83. For more about Vine Deloria Sr., see Philip J. Deloria, "Vine V. Deloria Sr. / Dakota," 79–96. As for the kind of missionary, like Worcester or Hare, or, for that matter, Samuel Pond or Bernard Haile, in the previously cited application to the Council on Indian Affairs Joint Leadership Project, there was this observation about the demise of such a committed individual to an ironically more secular type of missionary: "The 1930's and 1940's saw the demise of this type of person and except in families where this has become a tradition, has almost completely vanished. They have been replaced by a professional . . . missionary applying modern methods of efficiency and techniques to their work. Today missionaries have 'days off', are motivators, and are rarely on the inside of reservation life." Vine Deloria Papers. In 2008, Syd Beane (Flandreau Santee Sioux Tribe) wrote and coproduced *Native Nations: Standing Together for Civil Rights,* which was a documentary about the National Indian Lutheran Board and its historic ties to the American Indian Movement.

83. Deloria, *Custer Died for Your Sins,* 76.

84. Deloria, *Custer Died for Your Sins,* 77.

85. Vine Deloria Jr., "Bury Our Hopes at Wounded Knee," *Los Angeles Times,* April 1, 1973.

86. Deloria, "Indian Affairs 1973: Hebrews 13:8," 111.

87. Deloria, "Beyond Wounded Knee," 8.

88. Deloria, *Behind the Trail of Broken Treaties,* 207–63.

89. Deloria, "Beyond Wounded Knee," 8.

5. NOT YOUR MINORITY

1. Eastman, *The Indian To-Day,* 130–33. For more about this legendary figure, see Washington, *Up From Slavery;* and Smock, *Booker T. Washington.* It is worth noting that in *Up From Slavery,* Washington engaged in his own study of Black-Indian relations in chapter 6 "Black Race and Red Race," which was referenced in Smock's book.

2. Wise, *The Red Man in the New World Drama,* 399.

3. Deloria, *Custer Died for Your Sins,* 8.
4. Bates, "Reshaping Southern Identity and Politics,"129. In an undated pamphlet about the history St. Paul's Mission of Amherst, Virginia, in a section titled "About the Community," the residents are identified as an unrecognized southern Indian community: "The people are Indian-mixed of Cherokee descent. They came to the area during the early days when the government placed most Indians on reservations. It is believed that a small group of them came into these mountains and remained hidden for a long time. They are not reservation Indians in the true sense of the word. But however, they have always stayed in an area inside a 25 mile perimeter, the nearest town from the church is Amherst, 5 miles away. There are at the present time, about 250 of them over the 25 miles of road, over which the pastor travels to minister to them. A large yellow school bus is used to bring the parishioners to church and return home." St. Paul's Mission, undated. Vine Deloria Papers.
5. Deloria, *We Talk, You Listen,* 88. In an early articulation of the notion of tribalism that Deloria developed in *We Talk, You Listen,* Deloria argued in a letter to Leslie Dunbar, executive director of the Field Foundation: "I believe we must find a new interpretation of the reservations in terms of the fast changing economic patterns of today. In this respect I feel that if the Indian relationship with the federal government can be broadened so that Negro and Spanish local groups can develop a direct relationship with Washington that many problems could be solved. Among them the Hunger and Malnutrition areas which the committee has been investigating." Letter from Vine Deloria Jr. to Leslie Dunbar, December 3, 1967. Vine Deloria Papers. The committee alluded to in Deloria's letter to Dunbar was likely the Citizens' Board of Inquiry into Hunger and Malnutrition in the United States, which published *Hunger, USA: A Report.*
6. Boek, "We Talk, You Listen,"109.
7. Kelly, "We Talk, You Listen,"196.
8. Wells, "We Talk, You Listen," 172.
9. Lyndon Baines Johnson, Executive Order No 11365.
10. 114 Cong. Rec. 4834.
11. Victor H. Palmieri, "Los Angeles and the 'Riot Report'," *Los Angeles Times,* May 26, 1968.
12. Deloria, *We Talk, You Listen,* 86. The intersection between the "Riot Report" did occur at the level of Federal Indian affairs. See National American Indian and Alaska Natives Policy Resolution; Employment and Manpower Problems in the Cities.
13. Bates, "Reshaping Southern Identity and Politics," 131. In an undated pamphlet about the history of St. Paul's Mission of Amherst, Virginia, in a section titled "About the Community," the reluctance to be connected to the Black community

is observed as a distinguishing characteristic of the Amherst Cherokee community: "During the years of the mission school, there were only 7 grades and in one room with one teacher. The only public school open to the Indian people, was the Negro segregated school, and the Indians refused to be identified with the Negro." St Paul's Mission, undated. Vine Deloria Papers.

14. Knight, "Black Manifesto," 40–41.
15. Deloria, *We Talk, You Listen,* 85–99.
16. Deloria, *Custer Died for Your Sins,* 170.
17. Deloria, "The Theological Dimension," 912.
18. Deloria, "The Churches and Cultural Change," 56. In spite of Treat's comprehensive bibliography, he did not provide an entry for this particular article. Hence, other than the year (1974), it was undocumented as to where this piece originally appeared in print.
19. Deloria, *Custer Died for Your Sins,* 171–72. For more, see Reyes and Halcón, "Early Bilingual Programs, 1960s," 236–37. Kevin Noble Maillard does a brilliant job at analyzing the legally different ways in which Black and Indian adoptions are handled in "Parental Ratification: Legal Manifestations of Cultural Authenticity in Cross-Racial Adoption," 107–40.
20. Deloria, *Behind the Trail of Broken Treaties,* 25.
21. An important exception was the American Indians and Friends association founded by Robert Burnette (Rosebud Sioux), who was Deloria's immediate predecessor as NCAI executive director. With respect to the latter, Deloria bemoaned in a letter to John Belindo, et al., dated November 30, 1967: "Recently I have had a number of calls inquiring about this or that 'national' Indian organization. Additionally, because there are so many 'organizations' people like Robert Burnette are able to pass themselves off as leaders of legitimate organizations and are involving Indians in peace marches, various 'kinds' of 'Civil Rights' activities and any number of 'projects.'" Vine Deloria Papers.
22. Deloria, *Custer Died for Your Sins,* 161–63. There are at least two instances in which this episode of awkward cross-cultural satire is mentioned. First, Lincoln, *Indi'n Humor,* 26. Lincoln refers more specifically to the phrase "We shall overrun" being taken up as a chant during the 1970s among members of the American Indian Movement. Second, Smith, *Hippies, Indians and the Fight for Red Power,* 154. Smith shares the "We shall overrun" anecdote in the context of the often-tense relations between Indian leaders and the founding director of the Interreligious Foundation for Community Organization, Lucius Walker Jr. With respect to the Black community, the "We shall overrun" phrase did in fact become a part of the civil rights and Black Power lexicon. See, for example, Williams, *We Shall Overcome to We Shall Overrun* and Litwack, "'Fight the Power!,'" 10.

23. Deloria, *Custer Died for Your Sins,* 163–64. As of the time this chapter was written during the summer of 2016, the Black Lives Matter movement had become a nationwide political phenomenon, which generated a parallel Native Lives Matter movement, in addition to a discussion about what Indian people can learn from Black Lives Matter. See Vondall-Rieke, "How 'Black Lives Matter' Can Help Indians" and Native Lives Matter on Facebook.

24. Smith, *Hippies, Indians, and the Fight for Red Power,* 153–54.

25. Garroutte, *Real Indians,* 47–48.

26. Boudinot, "Address to the Whites," 41–49. For more, see Satz, *American Indian Policy in the Jacksonian Era.*

27. Deloria, *Custer Died for Your Sins,* 173–74.

28. For the story, see "2 Accept Medals Wearing Black Gloves," *New York Times,* October 17, 1968. Curiously, Deloria did not take the opportunity to mention the global distinction earned by Billy Mills (Lakota), when he won the gold medal for the ten-thousand-meter run at the 1964 Tokyo Olympics.

29. Deloria, *Custer Died for Your Sins,* 174.

30. Deloria, *Custer Died for Your Sins,* 174–75.

31. Wise, *The Red Man in the New World Drama,* ix.

32. Deloria, *Custer Died for Yours Sins,* 176–77. For more about the rise of Puritanism and its settlement in North America, see Bremer, *The Puritan Experiment.* For more about Puritan and Indian relations, see Vaughan, *New England Frontier.*

33. Deloria, *God Is Red* (1973), 175.

34. For an overview of this epoch, see Springhall, *Decolonization Since 1945.* For an analysis of the colonized mind and the radical political agenda necessary to overcome the effects of colonialism, see Fanon, *The Wretched of the Earth.* It is unclear if Deloria was aware of Fanon's work. Deloria, as noted, tended to shy away from work that was explicitly Marxist in orientation.

35. Deloria, *Custer Died for Your Sins,* 177–78.

36. Deloria, *Behind the Trail of Broken Treaties,* 184–85.

37. Deloria, *Custer Died for Your Sins,* 270.

38. Holland, "'If You Know I Have a History,'" 340.

39. Deloria, *Behind the Trail of Broken Treaties,* 210.

40. Deloria, *Behind the Trail of Broken Treaties,* 227.

41. Deloria, *Behind the Trail of Broken Treaties,* 227.

42. Deloria, *We Talk, You Listen,* 198–210.

43. Deloria, *We Talk, You Listen,* 15.

44. Deloria, *Custer Died for Your Sins,* 178–79.

45. Deloria, *Custer Died for Your Sins,* 179. For the statutory text, see P.L. 88-352 and 78 Stat. 241.

46. A Project Proposal to the General Convention Special Program, Executive Council, Episcopal Church. Vine Deloria Papers. As for whom was meant by "we" in the quoted statement, according to the section titled "Membership & Board of Directors," the members listed were: "President Don Matheson (Puyallup); Treasurer Edith McCloud (Walla Walla); Secretary Suzette Bridges (Puyallup-Nisqually); Projects Director Hank Adams (Assiniboine-Sioux); Billy Frank (Nisqually); Roxanne Allen (Quinault); Joe Louie (Nooksack); Ione Knox (Duwamish); Frank Allen (Stillaguamish); Ginger Saylor (Skokomish); Charles Boome (Skagit); Pauline Matheson (Coeur D'Alene); U.S. Army sergeant Richard Sohappy (Yakima); and Semu Huaute (Chumash)."

47. Editorial, NCAI Sentinel Bulletin 11, no. 2 (Spring, 1966).

48. Deloria, Custer Died for Your Sins, 180. For more about the role that Stokely Carmichael and others played in the rise of Black nationalism, see Pinkney, Red, Black, and Green.

49. Deloria, Custer Died for Your Sins, 182–83.

50. Deloria, Custer Died for Your Sins, 179. For how the event was covered in the news media, see, for example, E. W. Kenworthy, "200,000 March for Civil Rights Orderly Washington Rally; President Sees Gain for Negro; Action Asked Now 10 Leaders of Protest Urge Laws to End Racial Inequity Children Clap and Sing Says Nation Can Be Proud Leaders of Rally Urge Action 'Now' Ask Laws against Inequity—Picnic Air Prevails as Crowds Clap and Sing Dream of Brotherhood," New York Times, August 29, 1963.

51. Letter from Martin Luther King Jr., et al, to Vine Deloria Jr., July 1, 1966. Vine Deloria Papers; Letter from Vine Deloria Jr. to Martin Luther King Jr., July 13, 1966. Vine Deloria Papers.

52. Deloria, Custer Died for Your Sins, 183–84.

53. Hertzberg, "Indian Rights Movement, 1887–1973," 318. Unfortunately, Hertzberg did not provide a citation for the NCAI statement. As for the prioritization on tribal self-determination, the issue was quickly becoming a matter of federal Indian policy, when "President Nixon [sic]" addressed American Indians "through the National Congress of American Indians, on September 27, 1968, during his campaign for election," stating: "'Termination of tribal recognition will not be a policy objective, and in no case will it be imposed without Indian consent,'" Josephy, Nagel, and Johnson, Red Power, 81. For more, see pages 78–92. Nixon was mistakenly referred to as "President" at the time he issued his statement, when in fact he was a former vice president for Dwight D. Eisenhower. Nixon would not win the presidential election until November 5, 1968, then sworn into office the following January.

54. For more on this observation of the NCAI during the Indian protest movement, see Smith and Warrior, Like a Hurricane, 37.

55. "Back to the Clan."
56. Deloria, *Custer Died for Your Sins*, 184–85. For more about Warrior's life, death, and legacy, see McKenzie-Jones, *Clyde Warrior*. For more about Warrior within the context of the Red Power movement, see Smith and Warrior, *Like a Hurricane*.
57. The Watts riots in Los Angeles transpired over the better part of a week during August 1965. For more on when events became national news, see Peter Bart, "New Negro Riots Erupt on Coast; 3 Reported Shot; Police Seal Off 20 Blocks— Strife Called Worst in Los Angeles History," *New York Times*, August 13, 1965.
58. Deloria, *Custer Died for Your Sins*, 185–86.
59. For more, see Douglas Robinson, "Rights Leaders Decry 'Violence'; Wilkins and Others Shocked by Murder of Malcolm," *New York Times*, February 22, 1965. Other stories about Malcolm X's assassination were published in the same edition.
60. Deloria, *We Talk, You Listen*, 106.
61. For more, see Johansen, "Thom, Mel," 246–47. See also Shreve, *Red Power Rising*.
62. For a summary of the Poor People's Campaign, see "Poor People's Campaign (December 4, 1967—June 19, 1968)." For more, see Lawrence Van Gelder, "Dismay in Nation; Negroes Urge Others to Carry on Spirit of Nonviolence," *New York Times*, April 5, 1968.
63. Deloria, *Behind the Trail of Broken Treaties*, 70–71.
64. Deloria, *Custer Died for Your Sins*, 186–87. As is typical throughout *Custer*, Deloria refrains from identifying the individuals to whom he is referring, be they tribal council members or militant leaders.
65. Deloria, *Custer Died for Your Sins*, 187.
66. Deloria, *Custer Died for Your Sins*, 187–88.
67. For more on the incident that ignited the protest and rioting, see Peter Bart, "New Negro Riots Erupt On Coast; 3 Reported Shot; Police Seal Off 20 Blocks— Strife Called Worst in Los Angeles History," *New York Times*, August 13, 1965. For a historical analysis, see Horne, *Fire This Time*.
68. Deloria, *Custer Died for Your Sins*, 188.
69. Deloria, *Custer Died for Your Sins*, 188.
70. Ture and Hamilton, *Black Power*, 59–60.
71. Deloria criticized the melting pot myth in Collier "'White Society Is Breaking Down Around Us,'" 202–4, 269.
72. Deloria, *We Talk, You Listen*, 100–113.
73. Kevin K. Washburn observed while commenting on Duren v. Missouri (1979): "discrimination, or at least separatism, is a positive normative principle in Indian law, not a negative one, and not one in favor of Indians as a race but in favor of tribes as distinct political organizations that have a right to continue to exist

and exercise self-governance and self-determination" (758). See Washburn, "American Indians, Crime, and the Law," 709–77.

74. Deloria, *Custer Died for Your Sins,* 188.

75. Deloria, *Custer Died for Yours Sins,* 189.

76. Deloria, *Custer Died for Your Sins,* 189–90.

77. As of the 2016 presidential campaign, it is evident that the poor are not fairing any better now than they did during the 1960s. See, for example, Binyamin Applebaum, "The Millions of Americans Donald Trump and Hillary Clinton Barely Mention: The Poor," *New York Times,* August 11, 2016.

78. Deloria, *God Is Red* (1973), 75.

79. Deloria, *Custer Died for Your Sins,* 192–93. For an example of how the Kennedy myth lives on in Indian Country, see Reynolds, "Remembering Robert F. Kennedy." For a video of Kennedy speaking before the NCAI, see State Historical Society of North Dakota, "Robert F. Kennedy at National Congress of American Indians Meeting." A transcription of Kennedy's remarks, See Kennedy, "Remarks." For a reflection on the fiftieth anniversary of Kennedy's NCAI appearance, see Gipp, "Robert F. Kennedy's Legacy with First Americans."

80. Kennedy, "Remarks." Ironically, one of Deloria's closest friends and intellectual peer, Hank Adams, began a memoir essay about the author of *Custer Died for Your Sins* by invoking a connection with Kennedy: "Robert Kennedy's Day of Affirmation speech to the apartheid youth of South Africa in 1966 presents a best frame for knowing the visionary adult life and career of Vine Deloria Jr." For more, see Adams, "A Vine Deloria Jr. Collaboration." As for what Deloria may have thought about Edward "Ted" Kennedy, readers were left to speculate. However, in spite of the youngest Kennedy brother's absence from Deloria's analyses of federal Indian affairs, the senator from Massachusetts was definitely impressed with the author of *Custer Died for Your Sins,* as documented in the Congressional Record, in which Kennedy cited both Buffy Sainte-Marie and Deloria during his lengthy comments advocating for a proposed amendment to the Employment and Training Opportunities Act of 1970, in which the argument for major reforms in federal Indian policy, as presented in *Custer* were summarized by the senator. 116 Cong. Rec. 19927–19929.

81. Deloria, *Custer Died for Your Sins,* 194.

82. Deloria, *Custer Died for Your Sins,* 194. For a legal definition of "federally recognized tribe," see Bureau of Indian Affairs, "Frequently Asked Questions," "What is a federally recognized tribe?."

83. Deloria, *Custer Died for Your Sins,* 194. In their article on American Indian bilingual education and the importance of premising political reform on cultural diversity, K. Tsianina Lomawaima and Teresa L. McCarty observe that the difference in federal Indian policy between Indigenous customs that are acceptable

and unacceptable correspond to whether they are considered to be either "safe" (e.g., basket-making) or "dangerous" (e.g., the Sun Dance). See, Lomawaima and McCarty, "When Tribal Sovereignty Challenges Democracy, 279–305.

84. Deloria, *God Is Red* (1973), 60.
85. Deloria, "Non-Violence in American Society," 46. Essay originally appeared in *Katallagete* 5, no. 2 (Winter, 1974).
86. It may be worth noting that Deloria did his part to get out the Indian vote during the 1972 election. In a statement titled "Indian Power, Indian Votes," Deloria informed his reader: "In the 1968 Presidential election the margin of victory was slightly more than 500 thousand votes. That is the approximate voting strength of the Indian people in this country. "We DO Have The Power To Make The Difference Between The Winner And The Loser In The 1972 Election."
87. Deloria, *Custer Died for Your Sins,* 196.

6. HERE COME THE ANTHROS!

1. In a 1965 editorial in which Alvin M. Josephy Jr.'s *The Patriot Chiefs* was singled out for praise, the author, who may have been Deloria, observed that "the frontier" was an intrinsic part of the American myth, which it preserves as a part of its identity, complete with teepee-dwelling tribes, despite the disappearance of the frontier under the concrete layers of its progress: "America seems to be haunted by that frontier . . . While there is still the myth of the frontier, America does not have to face the reality of its present situation," *NCAI Sentinel Bulletin* 10, no. 3 (Spring 1965).
2. Richard C. Adams, "A Delaware Indian Legend and The Story of Their Troubles," 138.
3. Andrew J. Blackbird, "The Indian Problem; From the Indian's Standpoint," 147.
4. Eastman, *From the Deep Woods to Civilization,* 187.
5. Deloria, *Custer Died for Your Sins,* 2.
6. Letter from Vine Deloria Jr. to Henry Adams, June 17, 1972. Vine Deloria Papers.
7. Fleming, "God Is Red by Vine Deloria Jr.," 123.
8. Newman, "God Is Red by Vine Deloria Jr.," 153.
9. Fleming, "God Is Red by Vine Deloria Jr.," 124.
10. Deloria, *God Is Red* (1973), 30–31. Leslie D. "Les" Peterson was an archeologist for the Minnesota Historical Society, whose work included, in collaboration with Scott F. Anfinson, "Minnesota's Highway Archaeological Programs," *Minnesota Archaeologist* 38, no 2 (May 1979): n.p.
11. Similar to the Federal Code, the Code of Iowa is the codification of bills passed into law by the Iowa State Legislature. For the 1971 Code referred to in Deloria's account of the Maria Pearson story, see The Iowa Legislature, "Iowa Code Archive."
12. Deloria, *God Is Red* (1973), 32–33. Marshall McKusick was an accomplished archeologist who, in addition to being the Iowa State Archeologist, was also a

professor of sociology and anthropology at the University of Iowa. McKusick was also the author of *Men of Ancient Iowa as Revealed by Archaeological Discoveries* (1964) and, much later, *The Davenport Conspiracy Revisited* (1991). For more, see the University of Iowa Libraries, Special Collections and University Archives, "Marshall B. McKusick Papers." For more about Maria Pearson's life serving the American Indian community, and her distinctions in the repatriation movement, see Ames Historical Society, "Maria Pearson."

13. Deloria, *God Is Red* (1973), 33–34. The William Penn Memorial Museum is now the State Museum of Pennsylvania, which still boasts about its archeological collection, including Susquehannock artifacts: http://www.statemuseumpa.org /archc.html.

14. For more on this tragic episode in Indian-White relations, see Brubaker, *Massacre of the Conestogas*, and Kenny, *Peaceable Kingdom Lost*. For more on the archeological record, see Kinsey, "Eastern Pennsylvania Prehistory," 69–108.

15. Deloria, *God Is Red* (1973), 34–35.

16. Deloria, *God Is Red* (1973), 35.

17. Deloria, *Custer Died for Your Sins,* 78. In terms of the influence that Deloria's critique had on the field of anthropology, Elizabeth S. Grobsmith recollected: "Although the book's [*Custer*] message was powerful and had a tremendous impact on those of us in graduate schools in the late 1960s and early 1970s, Deloria did not totally succeed in keeping us away; in fact, social scientists flocked to reservations to document the phenomenon of the new pan-Indianism. He did, however, impose a test on us—a new standard, which those of us who would persevere had to meet. *Custer Died for Your Sins* became our primer for how not to behave, conjuring up the ultimate image of the tiresome meddler we dreaded and desperately hoped to avoid. It made us defensive, in the true sense of the term: we continually had to defend and justify our existence and practice self-reflection and introspection" (36–37). For Grobsmith's complete essay and her evaluation of *Custer*'s role in the development of anthropology, see "Growing Up On Deloria," 35–49. With respect to anthropology becoming more self-reflective, Kathleen J. Fitzgerald identifies the work of Murray L. Wax and Rosalie H. Wax as significant in this regard. See Fitzgerald, introduction, 25–26. For Murray L. Wax's response to *Custer*'s effect on anthropology, see Wax, "Educating an Anthro," 50–60. Little more than a nostalgic memory today, Route 66 once reigned supreme in many travelers' cross-country plans. Before Eisenhower's interstate highway system took over the country, Route 66 guided motorists from Chicago to Los Angeles, taking them along northern New Mexico and Arizona, where Puebloan, Navajo, and Hopi communities could—and still can—be found. For more, see American Indian Alaska Native Tourism Association, "American Indians & Route 66." See also Kelly, *Father of*

Route 66. While the tribal nations along Highway 18 are as well-known as their Southwestern counterparts, such as the Lakota, Cheyenne, and Pawnee, this stretch of the American road system—connecting Wisconsin, Iowa, South Dakota, and Wyoming—has a much more modest place in the American imagination.

18. Medicine, "Anthropologists and American Indian Studies Programs," 85. For more about the amalgamated American Indian communities emerging during the Termination Era, see Thomas, "Pan-Indianism," 75–83.

19. For more about the history of anthropology in Zuni, see Pandey, "Anthropologists at Zuni," 321–37. For more about Matilda Coxe Stevenson, see Miller, *Matilda Coxe Stevenson.* Marilyn Bentz (Gros Ventre), whose own work as anthropologist has focused on the Quinault Reservation, addressed the privacy and ethical issues raised by *Custer* in "Beyond Ethics: Science, Friendship, and Privacy," *Indians and Anthropologists,* 120–32.

20. Deloria, *God Is Red* (1973), 49.

21. See Dixon and Wanamaker, *The Vanishing Race.*

22. Deloria, *Custer Died for Your Sins,* 275. See Vine Deloria Jr.'s introduction to Ella Deloria's *Speaking of Indians.* See Deloria, "Bob Thomas as Colleague," 27–38. Deloria acknowledges the significance of Powell's monumental *Sweet Medicine,* volumes 1 and 2 in the first edition of *God Is Red* (1973), then more expansively in the thirtieth anniversary edition (2003). In addition, Deloria reviewed *Sweet Medicine* for the *New York Times* on April 26, 1970, saying of Powell's research: "It was a significant choice, for this two-volume set is certainly one of the most important works they [the University of Oklahoma Press] have published in their series [Civilization of the American Indian]." In a collaboration that should not be overlooked, Deloria and DeMallie coedited the monumental *Documents of American Indian Diplomacy.*

23. Deloria admired Waters complete body of work, both fiction and nonfiction, as a novelist, historian, and essayist. See Deloria, *Frank Waters: Man and Mystic.* See Vine Deloria Jr., introduction, *Black Elk Speaks.*

24. Deloria, "Bob Thomas as Colleague," 35. For more on the friendship and intellectual comradery between Deloria and Thomas, see Cobb, *Native Activism in Cold War America.*

25. Deloria, *Custer Died for Your Sins,* 79.

26. Deloria, *Custer Died for Your Sins,* 80. See, for example, Polgar, "Biculturation of Mesquakie Teenage Boys," 217–35; also, McFee, "The 150% Man, a Product of Blackfeet Acculturation," 1096–107. See, for example, Redfield, *The Folk Culture of the Yucatan*; Redfield, "The Folk Society"; Redfield, *A Village That Chose Progress: Chan Kom.* See also Benedict, *Patterns of Culture.*

27. Officer, "Custer Died for Your Sins," 293.

28. These papers and the discussion were released as a book. See Officer, *Anthropology and the American Indian*. Panelists and discussants included Nancy O. Lurie, Philleo Nash, Omer C. Stewart, Margaret Mead, Bea Medicine, and Alfonso Ortiz. These papers were also collected into a book, which were edited into an anthology, as opposed to a transcription of presentations and audience responses, which was the format of *Anthropology and the American Indian*. See Biolsi and Zimmerman, *Indians and Anthropologists*. Contributors included, in addition to the editors, Mary Bentz, Elizabeth S. Grobsmith, Herbert T. Hoover, Cecil King, Gail Landsman, Randall H. McGuire, Murray L. Wax, and Peter Whiteley. Also, Biolsi and Zimmerman's anthology includes a robust conclusion from Deloria, "Anthros, Indians, and Planetary Reality."
29. Deloria, *Custer Died for Your Sins,* 81.
30. Deloria, *Custer Died for Your Sins,* 81–82.
31. Deloria, *Custer Died for Your Sins,* 82.
32. See Indians of the U.S. Vol. 1. For a brief biography of Reber, see "Reber, John, (1858–1931)." Also, the Senate report authorized in pursuant to H. Res. 698, in which the Domesday Survey was lauded as an exemplary method of investigation, the results of which preceded HCR 108, refers to numerous works of anthropology in its 1952 portrayal of tribes. See 119582 H. rp. 2503.
33. Thirty years after *Custer* appeared, Linda Tuhiwai Smith wrote eloquently and insightfully about the relationship that persisted between research as an imperial enterprise and Indigenous peoples as objects of a colonial discourse on history, culture, and the effects of conquest. Although Smith focuses primarily on her own Maori experience, *Decolonizing Methodologies: Research and Indigenous Peoples*, has long been regarded as a seminal critique of academic research among many Indigenous communities, including American Indians.
34. Deloria, *Custer Died for Your Sins,* 82.
35. S. Con. Res. 85.
36. John Collier's successor, William Zimmerman Jr., recounted this development in a 1957 article on the Bureau of Indian Affairs. See Zimmerman, "The Role of the Bureau of Indian Affairs."
37. Parker, *Singing an Indian Song,* 180–82. Sol Tax (1907–1995), professor of anthropology, University of Chicago, is credited with the development of "action anthropology," in addition to playing a role in the 1961 American Indian Chicago Conference.
38. Deloria, *Custer Died for Your Sins,* 83.
39. "Which Way Indians?"
40. McKenzie-Jones, *Clyde Warrior,* 87.
41. McKenzie-Jones, *Clyde Warrior,* 109–10. At one time, at least, Deloria was quite interested in getting Mel Thom's feedback on developing the NCAI's political

agenda. In a letter dated December 1, 1964 to Stannard Frank, chairman, Walker River Paiute Tribe, Deloria prefaced his address to Frank with this disclosure: "Mr. Melvin Thom of your tribal council has been in contact with me for most of this last fall concerning the new administration of the National Congress of American Indians which began in Denver in October when I accepted the position of Executive Director. . . . I have suggested to Mel that he talk with everyone in Nevada about what they would want the National Congress to do for them. I do not plan on presenting a program until I heard what the tribes, especially the small tribes would like. Too often NCAI has not kept in touch with the tribes and so have lost their support. I would appreciate it if you would send the Washington office your council minutes and any suggestions you might have for making the National Congress work for you." Vine Deloria Papers.

42. Deloria, *Custer Died for Your Sins*, 268.

43. McKenzie-Jones, *Clyde Warrior*, 110.

44. Deloria, *Custer Died for Your Sins*, 83.

45. One folk community that Deloria worked with in his capacity as NCAI executive director was the Amherst Cherokee community of Amherst, Virginia. In a pamphlet describing this enclave, in a section titled "About the Community," it stated: "Like other isolated communities, they have a culture of their own. . . . They no longer dance in the fashion of their fathers and now thoroughly enjoy a western type dance, with some variations of their own. . . . Their speech is peculiar to the area and although it is English, they are sometimes difficult to understand until you become better acquainted with them through associations." St Paul's Mission, undated. Vine Deloria Papers.

46. Deloria, *Custer Died for Your Sins*, 83–84.

47. Deloria, *Custer Died for Your Sins*, 84.

48. In the years since Deloria broached this difficult topic in *Custer*, Beatrice Medicine has done much to create an Indian approach to the understanding of alcoholism, complete with treatment plans based on tribal values, such as her book, *Drinking and Sobriety among the Lakota Sioux*.

49. Deloria, *Custer Died for Your Sins*, 85–86.

50. Lurie, "The World's Oldest On-Going Protest," 331–32.

51. Deloria, *We Talk, You Listen*, 10–11. Nancy O. Lurie, stated,: "My hypothesis is that Indian drinking is an established means of asserting and validating Indianness and will be either a managed and culturally patterned recreational activity or else not engaged in at all in direct proportion to the availability of other effective means of validating Indianness." For this and more, see Lurie, "The World's Oldest On-Going Protest," 311–32. Also, in a footnote to the above statement, Lurie directly rebutted Deloria's characterization of her work in *We Talk, You Listen*, which was quoted in full, to which she responded: "Deloria goes on to

demonstrate the absurdity of such an idea, and I fully agree that it is absurd because I never made such an assertion. In fact, I wrote my paper to combat the idea he attributes to me. Let me explain my position by an analogy. I have no doubt whatsoever about my identity. I am completely secure on this score. But I, like anyone else, often have to validate my identity to do what I want to do; for example, I must produce a driver's license to cash a check. Indian people when among other Indians, as Deloria notes, often cite tribal identity to validate their claims as Indians among strange Indians. There are other times when people may accept that I am who I say I am but may make assumptions that I consider unwarranted and undesirable in defining what kind of a person I am. As a woman and an academic among other things, I engage in all kinds of symbolic behavior in dress and manner that I usually do not even think about but rely on as devices my culture provides to communicate things about myself which will be clearly understood." Lurie, "The World's Oldest On-Going Protest," 315n8.

52. Mackay, "Ethics and Axes," 44.

53. Deloria, *Custer Died for Your Sins,* 86–87. In spite of the implied criticism of D'Arcy McNickle earlier with regard to point 4 program inspired workshops, McNickle eloquently recreated the transposition of traditional culture into contemporary contexts in his classic novel, *The Surrounded.* Post-1945 studies of Sioux (Lakota/Dakota/Nakota) culture, prior to *Custer Died for Your Sins,* ran the gamut from Gordon Macgregor to Royal B. Hassrick. See Macgregor, *Warriors without Weapons* and Hassrick, *The Sioux.* Of particular interest to Deloria might have been a paper that Macgregor published about anthropology's government-service record. See Macgregor, "Anthropology in Government," 421–33. For recent studies of these two tribes, see DeJong, *Stealing the Gila*; and Knack and Stewart, *As Long as the River Shall Run.*

54. Deloria, *Custer Died for Your Sins,* 87–88. The myth of Indian wealth goes back to when European settlers first coveted Indian land, recurring periodically whenever tribes possessed anything that non-Indians wanted to extort, be it oil or casino revenue. For more, see Harmon, *Rich Indians.*

55. Cobb, "Citizens' Crusade against Poverty," 174–75. See also Citizens' Board of Inquiry into Hunger and Malnutrition in the United States, *Hunger, usa.*

56. Deloria, *Custer Died for Your Sins,* 88.

57. Citizens' Board of Inquiry into Hunger and Malnutrition in the United States, *Hunger, usa.*

58. Vine Deloria Jr., "This Country Was a Lot Better Off When the Indians Were Running It," *New York Times,* March 8, 1970.

59. Two examples of Indian cattle-ranching studies in the Northern Plains are Keller, "Sioux Boys and Girls Learn Cattle Handling," 540–42; and Malan and Schusky, *The Dakota Indian Community.*

60. Macgregor, *Warriors without Weapons,* 22.
61. Deloria, *Custer Died for Your Sins,* 90–91.
62. Vine Deloria Jr., "This Country Was a Lot Better Off When the Indians Were Running It," *New York Times,* March 8, 1970.
63. Deloria, *Custer Died for Your Sins,* 91. New Trier High School is a public four-year institution with two campuses located, respectively, in Northfield and Winnetka, Illinois. See New Trier High School: http://www.newtrier.k12.il.us.
64. Deloria, *Custer Died for Your Sins,* 92.
65. Deloria, "Indian Affairs 1973: Hebrews 13:8," 108.
66. Hertzberg, *The Search for an American Indian Identity,* 202.
67. In his March 8, 1970, editorial for the *New York Times,* Deloria mentioned an instance in which Health, Education, and Welfare gave $10 million "to non-Indians to study Indians. Not a single dollar went to an Indian scholar or researcher to present the point of view of Indian people." Vine Deloria Jr., "This Country Was a Lot Better Off When the Indians Were Running It," *New York Times,* March 8, 1970.
68. Deloria, *Custer Died for Yours Sins,* 94.
69. Deloria, "Intellectual Self-Determination and Sovereignty," 27. In a sense, Deloria echoed the complaint uttered by Carlos Montezuma in his 1915 speech, "Let My People Go," in which he scolded the Society of American Indians for doing little more than socializing and passing resolutions.
70. Deloria, *Custer Died for Your Sins,* 94. Anthropologists were complicit in asserting the alleged extinction of the Puyallup Tribe during two high-profile court cases involving Indian activists who were a part of the struggle for fishing rights in the Pacific Northwest. For the cases in question, see Department of Game v. Puyallup Tribe Inc.; and, Puyallup Tribe v. Department of Game. For historical analysis, see Bradley G. Shreve, "'From Time Immemorial,'" 431–32.
71. Deloria, *Custer Died for Your Sins,* 95. Documentation on this particular anecdote is lacking. However, what has been corroborated is the Red Lake Ojibwe attitude toward anthropology. For more, including references to Roger Jourdain's role in Red Lake politics, see Wub-e-ke-niew, *We Have the Right to Exist* This volume is also available online: http://www.maquah.net/We_Have_The_Right_To_Exist /WeHaveTheRight_00cover.html. Also, for Jourdain's historic role in Red Lake and Minnesota history, see Chuck Haga, "Roger Jourdain, Longtime Tribal Chairman, Dies," *Star Tribune,* November 19, 2007. http://www.startribune .com/roger-jourdain-longtime-tribal-chairman-dies/11610226/.
72. Deloria, *Custer Died for Your Sins,* 95.
73. Deloria, *Custer Died for Your Sins,* 95.
74. For more on this case, see Katherine Drabiak-Syed, "Lessons from Havasupai Tribe v. Arizona State University Board of Regents," 175–225.

75. Deloria, *Custer Died for Your Sins,* 96–97. Representing the NCAI, Deloria traveled to the Pyramid Lake Paiute reservation to meet with their tribal council regarding their "water problem" on January 5–7, 1968, during a meeting of the Nevada Inter-Tribal Council, as documented in a travel statement addressed to John Belindo. Vine Deloria Papers.

76. See Martin, "The Discovery of America," 969–974. For a more recent critique of American Indians and the environment, see Krech, *The Ecological Indian: Myth and History.*

77. See "The New Indian Resources Bill," *Spokesman-Review,* May 29, 1967. For the proposed legislation, see Indian Resources Development Act of 1967. Deloria recounted the effort that the National Congress of American Indians and other tribal leaders made at defeating Udall's proposed legislation in *Behind the Trail of Broken Treaties,* 29–32.

78. For how the terms "living laboratory" and "test tube" are used, see Farb, *Man's Rise to Civilization,* 116, 293.

79. Deloria, *Custer Died for Your Sins,* 268–69. At one point, in the aftermath of Deloria's critique of North American paleontology, his defense of the oral tradition as a source equal to, if not greater than, its Western scientific counterparts drew the ire of the scientific community, which regarded Deloria's ideas to be as abhorrent as the biblical literalism espoused by some Christian fundamentalists. For example, see George Johnson, "Indian Tribes' Creationists Thwart Archeologists," *New York Times,* October 22, 1996.

80. Officer and McKinley, *Anthropology and the American Indian,* xi.

81. Lurie, "Action Anthropology and the American Indian," 4. In 1968, Nancy O. Lurie coedited with Stuart Levine an important volume, originally published by the *Midcontinent American Studies Journal* in 1965, on the rising Indian protest movement as understood through the lens of contemporary anthropological theory. See, Lurie and Levine *The American Indian Today.*

82. Philleo Nash, "Applied Anthropology," 23–31. One of the organizers of the 1970 AAA meeting, James E. Officer, published an article titled "The American Indian and Federal Policy."

83. Omer C. Stewart, "Anthropologists As Expert Witnesses for Indians," 39.

84. Margaret Mead, "The American Indian as a Significant Determinant," 68–69.

85. Medicine, "Anthropologists and American Indian Studies Programs," 83.

86. Ortiz, "An Indian Anthropologist's Perspective on Anthropology," 86.

87. Ortiz, "An Indian Anthropologist's Perspective on Anthropology," 89.

88. Deloria, "Some Criticisms and a Number of Suggestions," 95.

89. In fact, the AAA again organized panels at its annual meeting for the purpose of looking back on the quarter century that had passed since Deloria's critique struck like a lightning bolt. More specifically, as Thomas Biolsi and Larry J. Zimmerman

recounted: "At the eighty-eighth annual meeting . . . a group of scholars—mostly, but not all, anthropologists—convened in a session titled 'Custer Died for Your Sins: A Twenty Year Retrospective on Relations Between Anthropologists and American Indians.'" The purpose of the session, of course, as is explained below, was to assess what had changed since Deloria's caustic critique first appeared. Speaking of the 1990s, the nascent field of Deloria studies would not see any significant contribution until near the end of Deloria's life and career.

90. Deloria, *Custer Died for Your Sins,* 100.

7. "MERCILESS INDIAN SAVAGES"

1. Voltaire, "Philosophical Dictionary," 109–10.
2. Deloria, *Custer Died for Your Sins,* 269.
3. Deloria, "It Is a Good Day to Die," 85.
4. Deloria, *Custer Died for Your Sins,* 270.
5. Deloria, "It Is a Good Day to Die," 86.
6. Deloria, "It Is a Good Day to Die," 87.
7. For a legal analysis, see Coggins and Modrcin, "Native American Indians and Federal Wildlife Law," 375–423.
8. Deloria, *Custer Died for Your Sins,* 103.
9. Deloria, *Custer Died for Your Sins,* 103–4.
10. Letter from Vine Deloria Jr. to Henry Adams, June 1, 1975. Vine Deloria Papers. In the above referenced letter, Deloria informed Adams that he was scheduled the summer of 1975 to teach at the Pacific School of Religion, which was an ecumenical seminary located in Berkeley, California. The institution was affiliated with the United Church of Christ, the United Methodist Church, and the Disciples of Christ.
11. Warrior, *Tribal Secrets,* 72.
12. Deloria, *God Is Red* (1973), 78–79.
13. Deloria, *Behind the Trail of Broken Treaties,* 46.
14. Deloria, *God Is Red* (1973), 84.
15. Deloria eventually developed a more expansive account of oral tradition as a form of knowledge, in particular natural history, in chapter 2 of *Red Earth, White Lies,* titled "Science and the Oral Tradition."
16. Deloria, *God Is Red* (1973), 101.
17. Deloria, *God Is Red* (1973), 102.
18. Slavery, in particular, was an especially painful episode in American Christian history. While there were many who spoke up heroically against this heinous institution, there were still others who justified it based on scripture. For more about this historic controversy, see McKivigan and Snay, *Religion and the Antebellum Debate over Slavery.*

19. Deloria, *Custer Died for Your Sins,* 104–5.
20. One of the most important studies of the Christian assault on Indian spiritual traditions was George Tinker's *Missionary Conquest.*
21. Cook and Whittemore, *Among the Pimas,* 63–64.
22. Deloria, *Custer Died for Your Sins,* 105–6.
23. Deloria, "An Open Letter," 81.
24. Deloria, "An Open Letter," 82–83.
25. 16 Stat. 13. See section 4 for the specific authorization of the Board of Indian Commissioners.
26. Deloria, *Custer Died for Your Sins,* 106.
27. Deloria, *Custer Died for Your Sins,* 107. One example of the romanticizing of missionary work are "The Pima Mission at Sacaton, Arizona" by Helen O. Belknap, which was an eight-page pamphlet distributed at Presbyterian churches around the Gila River and Salt River Reservations. For more, see Brunner, *Churches of Distinction in Town and Country.*
28. Deloria, *God Is Red* (1973), 274.
29. Deloria, *God Is Red* (1973), 277–78.
30. Deloria, *God Is Red* (1973), 281.
31. Department of Interior: Annual report of Secretary of Interior. See also Office of Indian Affairs, Department of Interior, I20.12:In2/3.
32. Deloria, *Of Utmost Good Faith,* 260–61.
33. Deloria, *Custer Died for Your Sins,* 106–7.
34. Vine Deloria Jr., "This Country Was a Lot Better Off When the Indians Were Running It," *New York Times,* March 8, 1970.
35. Vine Deloria Jr., "An Indian's Reflections: Bury Our Hopes at Wounded Knee," *Los Angeles Times,* April 1, 1973. For an historical analysis of the varying estimates of the casualties incurred at the 1890 Wounded Knee Massacre, see Kerstetter, "Spin Doctors at Santee," 45–67.
36. Deloria, "The Theological Dimension," 33.
37. Deloria, "The Theological Dimension," 34.
38. Deloria, *God Is Red* (1973), 99.
39. Deloria, *Custer Died for Your Sins,* 108.
40. Deloria, *Custer Died for Your Sins,* 108–9. Numerous studies and personal accounts of the Indian boarding-school era have been published. With respect to the enforcement of the haircut requirement and other behavioral policies, see Trafzer, Keller, and Sisquoc, *Boarding School Blues.* See also the permanent exhibit at the Heard Museum, Phoenix Arizona, "Remembering Our Indian School Days: The Boarding School Experience". http://heard.org/exhibits/boardingschool/. One might compare the Christian demand that Indians cut their hair with the more recent demand that Taliban rulers imposed on men in Afghanistan during

the 1990s. See, for example, John F. Burns, "Islamic Rule Weighs Heavily for Afghans," *New York Times*, September 24, 1997.

41. Eastman, *From the Deep Woods to Civilization,* 193.

42. Deloria, *God Is Red* (1973), 228–30, 233.

43. For an impressive display of the religious diversity in America, see Rosten, *Religions of America.*

44. Deloria, *God Is Red* (1973), 244.

45. Mooffett, "The First Americans," 856.

46. Deloria, *Custer Died for Your Sins,* 109–10.

47. Deloria, *Custer Died for Your Sins,* 110.

48. Deloria, *Custer Died for Your Sins,* 111–12. For more about the intervention of Christianity into Choctaw Nation, see Kidwell, *Choctaws and Missionaries in Mississippi*; and Pesantubbee, "Beyond Domesticity," 387–409.

49. Fixico, *Bureau of Indian Affairs,*113.

50. Deloria, *Custer Died for Your Sins,* 112. For more on the historical background of Christian missionary work on the east end of Long Island, see Eells six-part series in the *Journal of the Department of History.*

51. See, for example, Utley, "Wounded Knee, Battle of (1890)," 837.

52. For more, see Arthur Amiotte, "The Lakota Sun Dance," *Sioux Indian Religion: Tradition and Innovation* (1987): 75–89. For more, see Bieder, *Native American Communities in Wisconsin.*

53. Deloria, *Custer Died for Your Sins,* 112–13. For more about the theology and history of the Native American Church, including an account of its historic spread from Oklahoma to all parts of North America, see Maroukis, *The Peyote Road.* For a contemporary examination of the Native American church, see Stewart, "The Native American Church and the Law."

54. Deloria, *Custer Died for Your Sins,* 112.

55. Vine Deloria Jr., "This Country Was a Lot Better Off When the Indians Were Running It," *New York Times*, March 8, 1970.

56. Deloria, *God Is Red* (1973), 247–48.

57. C. Timothy McKeown tells such a story about William Tallbull, a respected member of the Cheyenne Dog Society, in *In the Smaller Scope of Conscience.*

58. Deloria, *God Is Red* (1973), 248.

59. For a portrayal of Worcester's work among the Cherokee outside of his role in the Worcester v. Georgia (1832) case, see Satz, "Cherokee Traditionalism, Protestant Evangelism," 380–401. For a historical biography of the infamous perpetrator of the 1864 Sand Creek Massacre, see Convery, "John Chivington."

60. Deloria, *God Is Red* (1973), 252–53.

61. Deloria, *God Is Red* (1973), 257–58.

62. For a brief account of Banyacya's life and legacy, see Robert McG. Thomas Jr., "Thomas Banyacya, 89, Teller of Hopi Prophecy to World," *New York Times*, February 15, 1999. Then, for an interesting account of Banyacya's response to the accusation that the Hopi sacred being Masau'u was actually the "Christian Devil," see Tyler, *Pueblo Gods and Myths*, 47–48. For more about Wallace "Mad Bear" Anderson, see Johansen, "Anderson, Wallace 'Mad Bear' (Tuscarora) [1927]–1985," 24–25.

63. Deloria, *Custer Died for Your Sins*, 114. As noted in Banyacya's obituary, "Thomas Banyacya, 89, Teller Of Hopi Prophecy to World," *New York Times*, February 15, 1999: "On his fourth attempt, in 1992, he was allowed to make a brief speech at the General Assembly hall, but on a day when the General Assembly was in recess. Only a few delegates were present when he carefully sprinkled cornmeal on the podium and then delivered his message stressing the need for world leaders to listen to those still living in harmony with nature." For more about Banyacya's mission and its role in Hopi cultural revitalization, see Clemmer, "'Then Will You Rise,'" 31–73.

64. Because of the symbolic value of the number four in many American Indian spiritual traditions, the fact that Banyaca was finally permitted the opportunity to speak before the UN General Assembly on his fourth attempt evokes a magical quality, for lack of a better term, in the minds of many. However, on December 10, 1992, when Banyacya delivered his message, it was part of the UN's inauguration of the "International Year of the World's Indigenous People," in which representatives from multiple groups were represented, including Hopi Nation. See Brooklyn Rivera, et al., "Living History," 165.

65. Deloria, *Custer Died for Your Sins*, 114.

66. Deloria, *Custer Died for Your Sins*, 114–15.

67. Deloria, *Custer Died for Your Sins*, 112–13.

68. For more on Eastman's portrayal of the Sun Dance, see Eastman, *The Soul of the Indian*, 51–84. In regard to the history of Christianity among the Sioux, including developments during the Red Power era, see DeMaillie and Parks, "Part Two. Christianity and the Sioux," 91–157. More generally, Deloria is referring to the phenomenon of syncretism, which has long been an aspect of Christianity's spread among Indigenous peoples, especially among those tribes exposed to Catholicism. For more on this religious phenomenon, see Martin, *Indigenous Symbols*.

69. Deloria, *Custer Died for Your Sins*, 115. For insight into the role of Baptism in the wider discussion Creek (Mvskoke) national identity, see Moore, "The Mvskoke National Question," 163–90. For more on the relationship between Christianity and tribal religions, see Deloria, "Christianity and Indigenous Religion," 31–43.

70. As of the time this was written in 2016, the Cook School for Christian Leadership, mentioned above, located in Tempe, Arizona, has folded, while the larger organization, Cook Native American Ministries Foundation, is still in operation. For more about both, see Cook Native American Ministries Foundation: http://cooknam.org; and, Lawn Griffiths, "Tempe's Cook School for American Indians Closing," *East Valley Tribune*, April 28, 2008. http://www.eastvalleytribune.com/news/article_4dffcf5b-af98-545e-a52e-b106443e9d5d.html.

71. Deloria, *God Is Red* (1973), 284.

72. For more about the historical effort at translating the Bible into Indigenous North American languages, see Hodge, "Bible Translations."

73. Deloria, *Custer Died for Your Sins,* 116–17.

74. Deloria, *Custer Died for Your Sins,* 117–18. What Deloria appears to know about but does not discuss is the plethora of abuses committed by priests, nuns, ministers, not to mention lay people representing churches against their Indian flocks, particularly against children. With respect to resources, a multitude of living survivors, witnesses, and perpetrators have emerged through a variety of venues, from memoirs to conference panels to truth and reconciliation committees, which are too numerous to list here. For an example of the complicity between church, state, and school in the abuse of Indian children, see Giago, *Children Left Behind.*

75. Deloria, *Custer Died for Your Sins,* 118. For examples of the challenges facing churches in Indian Country, see Bowden, "Native American Presbyterians," 234–56. See also Treat, *Native and Christian.*

76. Deloria, *Custer Died for Your Sins,* 269.

77. Deloria, *Custer Died for Your Sins,* 75.

78. Deloria, *Custer Died for Your Sins,* 118–19.

79. Vine Deloria Jr., "This Country Was a Lot Better Off When the Indians Were Running It," *New York Times*, March 8, 1970.

80. Deloria, *Custer Died for Your Sins,* 122.

81. For a historical perspective on Indian religious movements, see Gregory Evans Dowd, *A Spirited Resistance: The North American Indian Struggle for Unity, 1745–1815* (1993); and Irwin, *Coming Down from Above.*

82. Deloria, *God Is Red* (1973), 217.

83. Thomas, "Pan-Indianism," 739.

84. Thomas, "Pan-Indianism," 739–40.

85. Deloria, *God Is Red* (1973), 218.

86. Deloria, *Custer Died for Your Sins,* 123. For a more ecumenical approach to Christian thinking among tribal communities, see Treat, *Native and Christian,* 157–205. Then, for a comparative approach to blending Indian and Christian spiritual beliefs, see Kidwell, Noley, and Tinker, *A Native American Theology.*

87. The reference is to Altizer, *The Gospel of Christian Atheism*.
88. Deloria, *Custer Died for Your Sins*, 124.
89. "Justice and 'Just Compensation.'"

8. THE SCANDAL OF INDIAN AFFAIRS

1. Wilkins and Stark, *American Indian Politics*, 105. See also Morton v. Mancari.
2. As of the turn of the current century, David E. Wilkins and Heidi Kiiwetinepinesiik Stark described a much less aggressive Bureau of Indian Affairs: "Today . . . its primary tasks are centered on fulfilling the federal government's trust responsibilities (at a minimum, protecting tribal lands, natural resources, and moneys) and implementing the related policies of Indian self-determination and Indian self-governance," Wilkins and Stark, *American Indian Politics, 105*.
3. Deloria, Deloria, *Custer Died for Your Sins*, 125. For an analysis of how treaty promises shape Indian affairs, including tribes' sense of sovereignty, see, for example, Harmon, *The Power of Promises*. For examples of how tribes portray their understanding of treaty promises, see "Menominee Treaties and Treaty Rights"; Columbia River Inter-Tribal Fish Commission; and, Why Treaties Matter.
4. William E. Hallett (Red Lake Ojibwe) was the last person appointed as commissioner of Indian affairs; he served under the Jimmy Carter administration, 1979–81.
5. Deloria, *Custer Died for Your Sins*, 126–27.
6. For more about the Tiguas' travails, see Jeffrey M. Schulze, "The Rediscovery of the Tiguas," 14–39.
7. Deloria, *Custer Died for Your Sins*, 127–28.
8. Deloria, *Custer Died for Your Sins*, 128–29.
9. Deloria, *Custer Died for Your Sins*, 129.
10. Underfunding is a perennial issue that remains even in the early twenty-first century. See The Harvard Project on American Indian Economic Development, *The State of the Native Nations*, 58–59.
11. For a list of the federally recognized tribes in Michigan, complete with links to the tribes' web-pages, see Michigan Department of Health & Human Services.
12. Deloria, *Custer Died for Your Sins*, 129–30.
13. Deloria, *Custer Died for Your Sins*, 130. The partnerships that Deloria recommended can take a variety of forms, one of which is the Tribal-Interior Budget Council. For more, see U.S. Department of the Interior, Indian Affairs, "Tribal-Interior Budget Council (TIBC)."
14. Deloria, *Custer Died for Your Sins*, 130–31. Although the Economic Development Administration had not been in operation for very long when Deloria wrote his comments about its effectiveness for tribes, his insight proved prescient as the number of Indian projects supported by its funding grew across the United

States. See U.S. Department of Commerce, Economic Development Administration, Indian Projects Funded by EDA. The latter resource consists of a series of lists, divided by states, enumerating project titles and dollar amounts allocated. This compilation of funded projects was then referenced during a hearing about Department of Interior appropriations the following year. For the discussion, see Department of the Interior and Related Agencies Appropriations for 1978, Part 4.

15. Wilkins and Stark, *American Indian Politics,* 236.

16. Deloria, *Custer Died for Your Sins,* 131–32. For more on the institutionalization of the FDIC, see Calomiris and White, "The Origins of Federal Deposit Insurance." For more about the political and economic role of Social Security, see Scheiber and Shoven, *The Real Deal.* During a 1983 interview with Tom Brokaw, James Watt, infamous secretary of the interior under President Reagan, stated that reservations were "a classic example of failed socialism." For the interview, see "Interior Secretary James Watt Says Reservations Are Failing."

17. Deloria, *Custer Died for Your Sins,* 132.

18. It was once in the U.S. Federal Code that any selection of counsel by a tribe had to be formally approved by the BIA. For example, see 25 CFR §15.8 (1949). As for the political issue arising from Interior's "approval power," Deloria and Lytle would analyze the implications for tribal sovereignty in chapter 6 "The Role of Attorneys, Advocates, and Legal Interest Groups in the Indian System of Law," *American Indians, American Justice.*

19. Deloria, *Custer Died for Your Sins,* 133.

20. Deloria, *Custer Died for Your Sins,* 133–34.

21. Vine Deloria Jr., "This Country Was a Lot Better Off When the Indians Were Running It," *New York Times*, March 8, 1970.

22. Deloria, *Custer Died for Your Sins,* 134–35. According to Hazel W. Hertzberg, the United Scholarship Service was closely allied with the National Indian Youth Council. The service, more specifically, "was started in 1960 by Elizabeth Clark Rosenthal, an anthropologist who was the daughter and granddaughter of missionaries to Indians, and Tillie Walker (Mandan-Hidatsa), a staff member of the American Friends Service Committee. Both were board members of the Indian Rights Association. The United Scholarship Service, whose original purpose was to assist Indian and Spanish-American students in college, was sponsored by the Board for Home Missions of the United Church of Christ, the National Council of the Episcopal Church, and the Association on American Indian Affairs, organizations that had long been interested in the education of Indian young people. Vine Deloria Jr. (Standing Rock Sioux), the son and grandson of Episcopal missionaries, became staff associate in charge of this work" (316). For more on this episode, see Hertzberg, "Indian Rights Movements, 1887–1973," 305–23. For an example of the work accomplished by the United

Scholarship Service, see United Scholarship Service, Inc., Denver, CO, Annual Report of the United Scholarship Service.

23. Deloria, *Custer Died for Your Sins,* 135. For an account of Robert Bennett's advocacy for Indian fishing rights, see Ruby and Brown, *Esther Ross,* 58–63. Robert L. Bennett was commissioner of Indian affairs during the Nixon administration, 1969–1972.

24. Deloria, *Custer Died for Your Sins,* 135–36.

25. According to the NCAI's web-page, the national pan-Indian organization was founded in response to the termination policy that arose during the post–World War II years. See National Congress of American Indians, "Mission & History." For more about the NCAI's role in the battle against termination, see Cowger, *The National Congress of American Indians*; and Clarkin, *Federal Indian Policy in the Kennedy and Johnson Administrations, 1961-1969.*

26. Deloria would bring up the need for this particular reform in the historical context of the 1934 Indian Reorganization Act. See Deloria and Lytle, *The Nations Within.*

27. Deloria, *Custer Died for Your Sins,* 136–37. For documentation and discussion of Interior appropriations for the Bureau of Indian Affairs just prior to the publication of *Custer,* see Department of the Interior and Related Agencies Appropriations for 1968. Part 1.

28. Deloria, *Custer Died for Your Sins,* 137–38. For a brief biography of Clinton Anderson, see "Anderson, Clinton Presba, (1895-1975)." For Philleo Nash's reflections on Navajo Nation and education, see Allen, "Whither Indian Education?," 99–108.

29. Deloria, *Custer Died for Your Sins,* 138. See also Deloria, *Behind the Trail of Broken Treaties*, 31–35. The stereotypical belief that Indians are living off of the government dole or that they get everything for free by virtue of simply being Indian is a prejudice that persists to this day. For example, see Chavers, *Racism in Indian Country,* 21–22; and, Native American Rights Fund, "Frequently Asked Questions." In 1966 after firing Philleo Nash for having sided with the tribes over a policy dispute, Interior Secretary Udall had a study of Indian affairs commissioned, which was conducted by "a secret Presidential Task Force." The resulting report allegedly proposed moving the BIA from Interior to Health, Education, and Welfare. It was because of the alarm that that rumor caused among tribal leaders that Health, Education, and Welfare secretary John Gardner found himself at the 1967 man power conference in Kansas City, Missouri. After completing his presentation, Gardner opened the floor to questions. He was asked about the protection of treaty rights, maintaining the current method of operations, as well as the organization of Indian Affairs. After thoroughly assuring tribal leaders that absolutely nothing would change about the BIA

after it was transferred to Health, Education, and Welfare, Gardner was asked to most obvious of questions: Why change anything then, if everything is going to stay the same? Deloria, *Custer Died for Your Sins,* 159–60.

30. Deloria, *Custer Died for Your Sins,* 138–39. For more on the federal initiative at economic development in Indian Country just prior to the publication of Custer, see To Provide for the Economic Development and Management of the Resources of Individual Indians and Indian Tribes. For more about the issues and controversies at adapting tribal economies into the norms of the wider American economy, see Miller, *Reservation "Capitalism."*

31. "Full Text of KBUN Red Lake Commentary," Red Lake News, Special Supplement. Vine Deloria Papers.

32. In his letter to the Federal Communications Commission, Red Lake chairman Roger A. Jourdain, in addition to expressing his deep disappointment with the KBUN broadcast, solicited legal advice, asking: "Does this broadcast violate any regulations, rules, or provisions of the Federal Communications Commission? If so, which ones? What remedy do we have? What can and will you do to help us?" The FCC's response to the complaint was not recorded. Vine Deloria Papers.

33. "Challenge KBUN for Insulting Red Lakers," Red Lake News 1, no. 12, October 28, 1966. Vine Deloria Papers. On October 26, 1966, ahead of the Red Lake News exposé, KBUN attempted to defend its report by pointing out that Red Lake was just one of several communities examined, only one of which was an Indian reservation, and that it subjected all of the participating communities equally to its evaluation of the state of welfare in the area in and around Bemidji. Unfortunately, the statement from KBUN went on to reiterate its demeaning remarks about the economically disadvantaged, exhibiting gross ignorance about the sources of poverty in the communities portrayed, let alone any knowledge about how reservations are legally, socially, and economically different from their non-Indian neighbors. Vine Deloria Papers.

34. Deloria, *Custer Died for Your Sins,* 139–40. In a travel expenses report, Deloria documented the work he did in his capacity as NCAI executive director, in which multiple items raised in *Custer* were mentioned: "January 22–February 3, 1967—Travel to Washington, DC for Council On Indian Affairs—January 23 & 24, meeting with Secretary Udall & Undersecretary Luce on Omnibus Bill & Pyramid Lake Water Rights, meetings with Dep't of Labor on Kansas City Conference, meetings with Lawyers & Auditors, BIA meetings on Omnibus Bill & reception with VP Humphrey." Travel Report, February 10, 1967. Vine Deloria Papers.

35. See Indian Education: Hearings before the Special Subcommittee on Indian Education. See also Kelly, "United States Indian Policies, 1900–1980."

36. Deloria, *Custer Died for Your Sins,* 140.

37. Deloria, *Custer Died for Your Sins,* 140–43.

38. Deloria, *Custer Died for Your Sins,* 144.

39. Deloria, *Custer Died for Your Sins,* 144–45.

40. These "others" include Stokely Carmichael, whom Deloria does acknowledge, and Malcolm X, whom Deloria continues to ignore.

41. Deloria, *Custer Died for Your Sins,* 197–98.

42. Deloria, *Custer Died for Your Sins,* 198–99.

43. Deloria, *Custer Died for Your Sins,* 200.

44. For more about Squanto, see Frank Shuffelton, "Indian Devils and Pilgrim Fathers," 108–16. For more about Keokuk, see Jackson, *Black Hawk*. For more about Washakie, see Hebard, *Washakie*.

45. One film that Deloria may have had in mind was *To Hell and Back* (1955), directed by Jesse Hibbs. It featured a character named "Private 'Chief' Swope," played by Tohono O'odham actor, Felix Noriego. For more on American Indians in World War Two movies, see Holm, *Code Talkers and Warriors*. See also Deloria, "For an All-American Platoon," 11–12.

46. It may be worth mentioning that in a commentary titled " 'F Troop' — The Indian On TV" for the *NCAI Sentinel Bulletin*, the popular television comedy was used for political satire, as the author suggested story ideas for the Indians and Cavalry sitcom that might have enlightened viewers to contemporary issues in Indian affairs. For more, see " 'F Troop' — The Indian On TV."

47. While Deloria only gives his reader the barest hint of the documentaries to which he refers in *We Talk, You Listen*, one possibility was *The Exiles* (1961), directed by Kent Mackenzie, which was a docudrama set in the Bunker Hill neighborhood of Los Angeles. It featured an all-Indian cast, nonactors, all of whom were a part of the relocation community of southern California. Among those featured was the author's mother, who went by her maiden name, Marilyn Lewis.

48. Exemplary of the token minority appearance in movies, not to mention much beloved, was NFL legend Jim Brown, whose film credits included *Rio Conchos* (1964), *The Dirty Dozen* (1967) and *100 Rifles* (1969).

49. See Vine Deloria Jr., "The Rise and Fall of Ethnic Studies," 153–57.

50. Vine Deloria Jr., "Grandfathers of Our Country," *New York Times,* February 22, 1971.

51. Deloria, *We Talk, You Listen,* 33–44.

52. For more on Tecumseh and his ill-fated resistance alliance, see Sugden, *Tecumseh*.

53. Deloria, *Custer Died for Your Sins,* 204.

54. Deloria, *Behind the Trail of Broken Treaties,* 162.

55. Another example of a spurious chief, equally infamous, if not more so, was "Chief Lawyer" of the Nez Percés, who signed an 1863 treaty with the United States without the consent of the people. For more, see Prucha, *American Indian Treaties,* 210–13.

56. Deloria, *Custer Died for Your Sins,* 205. With respect to treaty of "paper chiefs," Deloria, the likely author of a grant application to the Council on Indian Affairs Joint Leadership Project, stated in an historical narrative on treaty-making: "The practice of creating 'paper chiefs' was soon instituted by the non-Indian. This method of reaching agreements on the white man's terms and through his political TECHNIQUES turned out to be disastrous for both parties. Indians refused to acknowledge any authority except that which they had freely given individually and non-Indians refused to honor the chosen leadership of Indian people because it was constantly changing and in many cases was stubbornly anti-white because of the military and political conflicts between the two groups." Council on Indian Affairs Joint Leadership Project, undated. Vine Deloria Papers.

57. For more on the lives of Indigenous women as cultural, political, and spiritual leaders, see Allen, *The Sacred Hoop*; See also Ackerman and Klein, *Women and Power in Native North America.*

58. For more on the effects of colonialism on Indigenous gender and sexual identities, see Rifkin, *When Did Indians Become Straight?* and Rifkin, *Settler Common Sense.*

59. While tribes that adopted the provisions of the 1934 IRA did have some leeway to modify the constitutional model to fit their needs, the extent to which a given tribe could maintain its traditional governance customs within that paradigm has long been debated, and is something that Deloria and his co-author Lytle take up in *The Nations Within.* As for one possible example in which Indigenous governance customs and IRA-based nation building appeared to mesh effectively was at Hopi. At least, according to D'Arcy McNickle, who observed on behalf of Collier's BIA: "At Hopi, where nine separate villages (speaking two languages and several dialects) have come down through the centuries, each jealous of its own identity and its own sovereignty, what seemed impossible was attempted—and achieved. . . . Hopi did want organization, or, as it was put in the preamble of the constitution, it wanted a way of working together for peace and agreement between the villages and of preserving the good things of Hopi life, and to provide a way of organizing to deal with modern problems with the United States Government and with the world generally," McNickle, "Four Years of Indian Organization," 9.

60. Council on Indian Affairs Joint Leadership Project, undated. Vine Deloria Papers.

61. In his 1970 editorial for the *New York Times,* Deloria was honored to mention the names of persons doing commendable work on behalf of their communities, ones who never attract media attention, yet are doing things that will bring long-lasting benefits to the people they serve: "Robert Hunter, director of the Nevada Intertribal Council, had already begun to build a strong state organization of tribes and communities. In South Dakota, Gerald One Feather, Frank LaPointe

and Ray Briggs formed the American Indian Leadership Conference, which quickly welded the educated young Sioux in that state into a strong regional organization active in nearly every phase of Sioux life. Gerald is now running for the prestigious post of chairman of the Oglala Sioux, the largest Sioux tribe, numbering some 15,000 members. Ernie Stevens, an Oneida from Wisconsin, and Lee Cook, a Chippewa from Minnesota, developed a strong program for economic and community development in Arizona. Just recently Ernie has moved into the post of director of the California Intertribal Council, a statewide organization rep resenting some 130,000 California Indians in cities and on the scattered reservations of that state." See, Vine Deloria Jr., "This Country Was a Lot Better Off When the Indians Were Running It," *New York Times*, March 8, 1970.

62. Deloria, *Custer Died for Your Sins,* 207.

63. Deloria, "On Wounded Knee 1973," 38.

64. Council on Indian Affairs Joint Leadership Project, undated. Vine Deloria Papers.

65. Deloria, *Custer Died for Your Sins,* 207–8.

66. Editorial, *NCAI Sentinel Bulletin* 11, no. 2 (Spring, 1966).

67. For more about Felix Cohen and the AAIA, see Kelly, "United States Indian Policies, 1900–1980," 74–75. For more about the Social Security Act, see P.L. 74-271, 49 Stat. 620, 42 U.S. Code § 7. For more about the Association on American Indian Affairs, see https://www.indian-affairs.org. The AAIA would later facilitate the passing of the 1978 Indian Child Welfare Act.

68. Council on Indian Affairs Joint Leadership Project, undated. Vine Deloria Papers.

69. Deloria, *Custer Died for Your Sins,* 208–9.

70. Vine Deloria Jr., "This Country Was a Lot Better Off When the Indians Were Running It," *New York Times*, March 8, 1971.

71. Deloria, *Behind the Trail of Broken Treaties*, 54.

72. Deloria, *Custer Died for Your Sins,* 210–11.

73. Deloria, *We Talk, You Listen,* 39.

74. Deloria, *We Talk, You Listen,* 43. Deloria further articulated this idea in *Behind the Trail Broken Treaties* in the chapters on "The Size and Status of Nations," "Litigating Indian Claims" and "Reinstituting the Treaty Process."

75. One incredible example of the smoke and mirrors approach to the War on Poverty was a 1964 National Conference on Poverty, to which Deloria was invited to assist coordinating, specifically with recruiting Indian leadership participation. Robert Choate, who was renowned for his work on consumer protection and poverty issues during the Johnson administration, was the principle organizer of this region-wide event. The production, which was scheduled to be held at a Ramada Inn in Tucson, Arizona, was an elaborate one in which "The attendees will include perhaps 25–40 articulate, imaginative, dynamic spokemen [*sic*] for the problems of poverty as seen by those who regularly face it in the Southwest.

Strong representation by Mexican-Americans, Indians, and Negroes is hoped for—in that order. Women must be included." In addition to a "horseshoe table" on a "raised stage," the event would include "ethnic rooms . . . wherein the arts, cultures, and advantages of each ethnic group participating can be stressed. This will help lessen the negative aspects of the conference." Report No 1 on planning for the "National Conference on Poverty in the Southwest," November 20, 1964. Vine Deloria Papers.

76. Deloria, *Custer Died for Your Sins*, 212–13. While Deloria was a strong proponent of overturning the conquest model of interpreting the Constitution, as acknowledged above, for the purpose of supporting group self-awareness and group rights, at the same time, he was skeptical of the federal government's intentions with respect to the rules and limitations attached to its "subsidies" and "largess." More specifically, Deloria raised this issue in the chapter on "Our Transforming Institutions" in *The Metaphysics of Modern Existence*. Putting a price on freedom, if you will, created an implicit obligation on the part of the recipient, such as a government grantee, to demonstrate their gratitude—maybe even allegiance—to the government that provided a given program its funding. Citing the work of Charles Reich, in particular "The New Property" and *The Greening of America*, Deloria proposed "recognizing largess as a right and not a privilege. Such a transformation would involve acknowledging that the rights of a citizen extend beyond political participation or economic independence, that these rights also include food, shelter, health care, and education." Deloria, *The Metaphysics of Modern Existence*, 175.

77. Deloria, *Custer Died for Your Sins*, 214.

78. Harris, *LaDonna Harris*, 59. For a critical and historical examination of the Oklahomans for Indian Opportunity, see Cobb, "The War on Poverty in Mississippi and Oklahoma," 395–403.

79. Deloria, *Custer Died for Your Sins*, 214–15.

80. Deloria, *Custer Died for Your Sins*, 215–16.

81. Deloria, *Custer Died for Your Sins*, 216.

82. Vine Deloria Jr., "This Country Was a Lot Better Off When the Indians Were Running It," *New York Times*, March 8, 1970. As an indication of how much Deloria thought about the weight that he carried on his shoulders during his three years as NCAI executive director, Deloria confided in a letter to Leslie Dunbar, executive director of the Field Foundation, dated December 3, 1967: "I felt it was alright to go ahead with my plans for Law School. It got so in 1967 that I was being run all over the country and did not have time to investigate the real issues. I found myself repeating the same old things and felt that this was not facing the real problems of tribes and that we had begun marking time by going over and over the same problems without finding any solutions."

Dunbar's response, dated November 21, 1967, stated, in part: "The news that you were stepping aside as director came as a shock. You have, I believe, done a magnificent job and I have enjoyed working with you." Vine Deloria Papers.

83. Deloria, *Custer Died for Your Sins,* 217.

84. Deloria, *Custer Died for Your Sins,* 219. For more on the Hualapai Tribe, see Shepherd, *We Are an Indian Nation.*

85. Smith and Warrior, *Like a Hurricane,* 273.

86. "22nd Annual Convention in November."

87. Memorandum, From Vine Deloria Jr. to John Belindo, August 22, 1968. Vine Deloria Papers. While tribal codes may have been beyond the ability of the NCAI to acquire for its database, such was not the case with federal Indian law. In the same 1968 memorandum cited just above, Deloria pointed out in a section titled "Additional Considerations": "We are presently preparing a cross indexing of all cases reported in state or federal reporters on Indian Law. We presently have all case[s] from the founding of the Republic to 1908 on cards by topic, holding and tribe and ready for use in [a] cross-indexing system. . . . We have become to build up files and pertinent materials on the topic of taxation and sovereignty. These two legal concepts are at the basis of Indian rights of tax exemption and tribal self-government. Material is being arranged to show that Indian tribal self-government and tax exemption is a Right Prior to the Creation of the United States Government and Therefore Cannot Be Destroyed by Any Actions of the United States Government." Vine Deloria Papers. A peculiar consequence of the congressional assumption of plenary power was the uneven distribution of sovereign powers that Indigenous nations retained. With respect to this problem, Deloria, in *Custer,* pointed out the examples of taxation and hunting and fishing rights. The former was the source of another misunderstanding that was expressed as a popular stereotype, namely "the general public usually believes that Indians get away with millions of dollars of tax-free money." Such an assumption persisted well into the current century, forming the basis of state governments extorting tribes for their casino revenue. The ambiguity of tribal sovereignty became a storied source of friction and open conflict on the so-called frontier, which led to the 1832 Black Hawk War, as well as the crisis during the 1960s, when Pacific Northwest Coast tribes organized to assert their fishing rights. In each example, Indigenous nations were assaulted, often literally, with racially biased notions regarding their historical and political statuses. With regard to the alleged tax-free status of Indians, the truth was much more complex, or rather "nebulous," as Deloria worded it. While individual Indians paid the same taxes that other U.S. citizens paid, from sales tax to income tax, the lands comprising a given "reservation" were not taxed. Certainly, there was nothing in the treaty record that supported the practice of subjecting tribes to

taxation—not the land marked off for reservations, nor the goods and annuities promised as compensation for signing treaties. Although Article I, Section 8 of the U.S. Constitution gave Congress the power to "regulate Commerce with foreign Nations, and among the several States, and with the Indian Tribes," it did not necessarily give Congress the power to impose taxes on tribes. Commerce, of course, was the buying and selling of goods; whereas taxes were a compulsory contribution to state or federal revenue. In fact, it is worth noting at this juncture that the tax-exempt status of Indian lands was of vital interest when, in 1947, acting-commissioner of Indian affairs, William R. Zimmerman, drew up bills for the incorporation of the Klamath, Osage and Menominee, which was a prelude to the termination policy that defined the 1950s. From the beginning of the republic, the fledgling federal government sought to define its jurisdiction above that of the states with respect to Indian affairs, most prominently in the form of ordinances issued in 1786 and 1787 regulating trade relations between Indians and the American government. Then, most significantly, the Trade and Intercourse Acts of 1790 and 1802 more clearly defined the federal role in Indian-white relations. As for taxation, Indigenous people were not U.S. citizens, so they did not vote in American elections, nor did they have any representation in Congress (in spite of the occasional offer, noted above, to change that). Furthermore, Indigenous nations did not import any goods into the United States from abroad, nor did they own any property outside of their traditional lands or reservations. As for personal income, there was very little to speak of, not to mention the fact that the United States did not impose a permanent income tax on its own citizens until 1913 (38 Stat. 114; H.R. 3321; H.R. 3322). For most of the history of United States–Indian relations the United States was more interested in expropriating land from tribes rather than taxes. With regard to the contemporary status of Indian tax exemption, Deloria observed that the succeeding treaties generally provided for lands to be held "as Indian lands are held." From this practice tribes have felt that their lands were tax free and the federal government has upheld the taxation theory of the tribes, although with an added twist. Current federal theory indicates the federal government supports tax exemption on the basis of its trusteeship rather than on the basis of its long-standing treaty promises. The distinction between trusteeship and treaty promises was more than a matter of semantics. The irreconcilable choice of phrases signified conflicting worldviews, in which Indigenous peoples were regarded as either incompetent wards of the federal government or as competent and independent sovereign nations. See Deloria, *Custer Died for Your Sins*, 38–40. For more about Robert Jim, see Landry, "Today in Native History."

88. Deloria, *Custer Died for Your Sins*, 221.
89. Deloria, *Custer Died for Your Sins*, 223.

90. Deloria, *Custer Died for Your Sins,* 224.

91. Vine Deloria Jr., "This Country Was a Lot Better Off When the Indians Were Running It," *New York Times,* March 8, 1970.

92. Deloria, *We Talk, You Listen,* 58.

93. Deloria, *We Talk, You Listen,* 67.

94. Deloria, *Behind the Trail of Broken Treaties,* 39. *Akwesasne Notes* reported on the occupation of Alcatraz Island regularly, beginning with a front-page reprint of the *New York Times* story, "Alcatraz: Taken Back," in which the issue displayed a super-title that read "Silent too damn long."

95. Wilkins and Stark, *American Indian Politics,* 234–35.

96. Deloria, *Of Utmost Good Faith,* 1.

97. Fortunate Eagle, *Heart of the Rock,* 162.

98. Smith and Warrior, *Like a Hurricane,* 81–82.

99. Smith and Warrior, *Like a Hurricane,* 203.

100. Smith and Warrior, *Like a Hurricane,* 123. Deloria's interest in organizing Indian organizations went back to his tenure as NCAI executive director. In a letter to John Belindo and other NCAI leaders, dated November 30, 1967, Deloria proposed a national conference in which the leaders of various Indian political organizations would convene to discuss their mutual interests: "At this conference we could listen to all of the 'other' organizations and make a full presentation of the NCAI programs particularly our strategy of PL 280, Omnibus, and Heirship. In effect the conference would highlight for non-Indians in the east the fact that the NCAI was the major, if not only, Indian voice on a national scale. . . . If we don't get these diverse groups together there will be no way to prevent any one of them from cutting our throats with foundations, press and Congress. If we can bring them together and at least separate those who will and those who won't work with us, we can be in a much better position to determine what the actual situation is with regard to groups claiming to represent Indians." Vine Deloria Papers.

101. Smith and Warrior, *Like a Hurricane,* 125.

9. TWENTIETH-CENTURY TRIBES

1. Deloria, Deloria, *Custer Died for Your Sins,* 227.

2. For more, see Whyte, *The Organization Man.* For a parallel development in European philosophy, which Deloria could have known about, see Marcuse, *One-Dimensional Man.*

3. Deloria, *Custer Died for Your Sins,* 228.

4. Council on Indian Affairs Joint Leadership Project, undated. Vine Deloria Papers. The reference to Katzenbach's "substitute parents" proposition also appeared in Deloria's testimony during the Senate hearing on the Constitutional Rights

of the American Indian. See Constitutional Rights of the American Indian. Katzenbach's recommendation was also referenced in connection with Clyde Warrior in Stan Steiner's account of the Red Power movement. See Steiner, *The New Indians,*147.

5. Deloria, *Custer Died for Your Sins,* 225.

6. Much has been done on the clash and melding of Indigenous and non-Indigenous peoples and cultures. See, for example, White, *The Middle Ground*; Calloway, *New Worlds for All*; and Phillips, *Trading Identities.*

7. Deloria, *Custer Died for Your Sins,* 228–29. Because Japan was still in the throes of its World War II defeat and subsequent occupation by the United States, it would only be long after Deloria initiated his comments on American corporate culture in Custer that the Japanese economic miracle occurred. For more, see Vogel, *Japan as Number One.*

8. Deloria, *Custer Died for Your Sins,* 230.

9. Perhaps the most influential recent example of this political and intellectual tradition was *Bowling Alone: The Collapse and Revival of American Community* by Robert D. Putnam.

10. Vine Deloria Jr., "This Country Was a Lot Better Off When the Indians Were Running It," *New York Times*, March 8, 1970.

11. Deloria, *Custer Died for Your Sins,* 231.

12. For more on fraternal orders during the 1920s, see Hertzberg, *The Search for an American Indian Identity,* 213–38.

13. Interestingly, Deloria did appear in two women's periodicals at the time of *We Talk, You Listen,* namely "'White Society Is Breaking Down Around Us" in *Mademoiselle* and "American Indians Today," in *Soroptimist Magazine.*

14. Deloria, *Custer Died for Your Sins,* 232.

15. Deloria, *Custer Died for Your Sins,* 232–34. For more on the phenomenon of hippies and Indians, see Smith, *Hippies, Indians, and the Fight for Red Power.*

16. Deloria, *Custer Died for Your Sins,* 235.

17. For more about the United Fund as an economic force, see Pfeffer and Leong, "Resource Allocations in United Funds," 775–90.

18. For a recent example of restorative justice in American Indian communities, see McCaslin, *Justice as Healing.*

19. In a 1968 memorandum that Deloria wrote to John Belindo, the establishment of an "Indian common law" as described above was considered to be part of the necessary work that the NCAI must do in preparation for a dramatic decline in the American system: "The eventual aim of the NCAI should be to make the crumbling American society conform to Indian methods of life rather than having tribes conform to state and federal law." Memorandum, from Vine Deloria Jr. to John Belindo, August 22, 1968. Vine Deloria Papers.

20. Constitutional Rights of the American Indian.
21. Deloria, *Custer Died for Your Sins,* 238.
22. Deloria, *Behind the Trail of Broken Treaties,* 149.
23. Deloria, *Custer Died for Your Sins,* 239.
24. The classic examples of this genre were White, *The Making of the President, 1960* and McGinnis, *The Selling of the President, 1968.*
25. "Council on Indian Affairs Joint Leadership Project," undated. Vine Deloria Papers. In this document, the distinguishing traits of the above-cited Protestant leadership tradition was expounded upon: "In non-Indian society the Protestant Ethic has been one of the driving forces in creating, defining and holding leadership. To attain leadership positions one must not only compete with his fellows he must win over them. Economically this has meant the stockpiling of tremendous surplus wealth against society followed by conspicuous consumption and then philanthropy to complete the cycle of the demonstration of leadership on all levels. Riches have been the sole value of a person and consequently the values of the rich have been applauded as the values which enable one to become rich. Once having become rich one must then use his wealth to create a favorable image so that the position of power and prestige is not surrendered by default. Public image has taken the place of personal worth and consequently a schizophrenia has developed in the society in which private and public morality are often incompatable [*sic*] because of the necessity to do two contradictory things based upon attaining and then holding leadership and power."
26. Deloria, *Custer Died for Your Sins,* 240.
27. For a look back on Resurrection City and the 1968 Poor People's Campaign, see Damien Cave and Darcy Eveleigh, "In 1968, a 'Resurrection City' of Tents, Erected to Fight Poverty," *New York Times,* February 18, 2017; and, for a contemporary account, see Calvin Trillin, "Resurrection City," 71.
28. Deloria, *Custer Died for Your Sins,* 241.
29. Deloria, *Behind the Trail of Broken Treaties,* 250.

10. THE GOOD RED ROAD AHEAD

1. Deloria, *Custer Died for Your Sins,* 274. In a letter to Allen Aleck, chairman, Pyramid Lake Paiute Tribe, dated December 1, 1964, Deloria made an early argument for focusing on smaller tribes as a priority for developing NCAI policy: "A small tribe can generally describe its problems very quickly and can usually tell what it feels would be the first practical step in solving its problems. If NCAI is to have a good program it should not only have the backing of small tribes but also the latest information on the tribes." Vine Deloria Papers. During the summer of 1965, the *NCAI Sentinel Bulletin* announced that throughout September, the

NCAI executive director, Vine Deloria Jr., "visited the Omaha, Rosebud, Crow Creek Sioux, Standing Rock Sioux, Fort Peck Sioux and Assiniboine, Fort Belknap, and Crow Tribes[,] as well as the University of South Dakota Institute of Indian Studies." Among his findings, Deloria's field research documented the needs of these tribes: "It would be a very helpful thing for the tribes to have a continual consultant on economic development and perhaps education to work with them," "Justice and 'Just Compensation.'"

2. Deloria, *Custer Died for Your Sins,* 245. See also Relating to the Tiwa Indians of Texas: Hearing before the Subcommittee on Indian Affairs. The NCAI issued a rallying call to support unrecognized tribes in a 1967 editorial titled "Our Other Brothers," in which the NCAI asserted: "It is our duty . . . to recognize the brotherhood we share as America's first citizens. We should make every effort to build up our tribes and communities wherever they are. We should not let one single group of Indian people drift aimlessly in a fog of misinformation, lack of rights, or lack of recognition as Indians."

3. Deloria once even suggested that it was possible to establish completely new tribes, above and beyond recognizing historic groups, such as the Tiguas or Lumbees: "In an old case in the Court of Claims . . . there is a ruling that an Indian "Band" may consist of members of different tribes PROVIDED THAT all people belonging to the band acknowledge one man as a figure of authority. Using this holding it is entirely feasible to combine it with Sections 7, 16, and 17 of the IRA and CREATE NEW INDIAN TRIBES THROUGH A PROCESS OF COLONIZING UNUSED LAND IN THE WEST." Memorandum, From Vine Deloria Jr. to John Belindo, August 22, 1968. Vine Deloria Papers.

4. Deloria, *Custer Died for Your Sins,* 246. For more on the Lumbee and their confrontation with the Ku Klux Klan, see Dial, *The Only Land I Know,* 158–61.

5. Noteworthy in this anthropological tradition are Benedict, *Patterns of Culture* and Underhill, *Red Man's Religion.*

6. Deloria, *Custer Died for Your Sins,* 246.

7. Deloria, "The Rise and Fall of the First Indian Movement," 663.

8. Thomas published an earlier version of the essay "Pan-Indianism" in Lurie and Levine, *The American Indian Today,* which was the book edition of a special issue of the *Midcontinent American Studies Journal* 6, no. 2 (Fall 1965).

9. Thomas, "Pan-Indianism," 741–42.

10. Thomas, "Pan-Indianism," 742.

11. Deloria was likely referring to the United South and Eastern Tribes, which was established in 1969. Joe Dan Osceola (Seminole) served as the council's first president, 1969–70.

12. Deloria, *Custer Died for Your Sins,* 247. For more on the struggle to gain federal recognition among tribes in the Southeastern United States, see Hill, *Strangers in*

Their Own Land; Miller, *Claiming Tribal Identity*; Williams, *Southeastern Indians Since the Removal Era*; and Blu, *The Lumbee Problem*.

13. Bates, "Reshaping Southern Identity and Politics," 126.

14. Price, "The Migration and Adaptation of American Indians to Los Angeles," 728, 731, 732. Complementing Price's work was a piece on northern California by Joan Ablon, "Relocated American Indians in the San Francisco Bay Area."

15. Deloria, *Custer Died for Your Sins,* 248.

16. Deloria, *Custer Died for Your Sins,* 247.

17. Deloria, *Behind the Trail of Broken Treaties,* 32, 34, 38, 43, 47.

18. For the original announcement, see Lyndon B. Johnson, Unnumbered Executive Orders.

19. Deloria, *Custer Died for Your Sins,* 250.

20. Deloria, *Custer Died for Your Sins,* 251.

21. Miller, "Involvement in an Urban University," 312–40. There was only one instance in which the Urban Indian Federation is mentioned in the archival record, other than the above citation. See 117 Cong. Rec. 8208 (1971).

22. For the story of the founding of the Department of American Indian Studies at the University of Minnesota, Twin Cities Campus, see Brady, "The Nation's first Department of American Indian Studies."

23. For more on American Indian voting, see McCool, "Indian Voting," 105–34.

24. Deloria, *Custer Died for Your Sins,* 252.

25. Deloria, *Custer Died for Your Sins,* 253.

26. For an overview of the urban Indian phenomenon, see Weibel-Orlando, "Urban Communities," 308–16. See also Fixico, *The Urban Indian Experience*; and Martinez, Sage, and Ono, *Urban American Indians*.

27. For further historical insight into the relation between Sioux City, Iowa, and the American Indian community, see Impact of Federal Policies on Employment, Poverty, and Other Programs.

28. Deloria, *Custer Died for Your Sins,* 254.

29. Effect of Federal Programs on Rural America (Statement of Stanley H. Ruttenberg). See also in the above hearing, Clark S. Knowlton, "Some Present Trends and Prospects Among Indians of the Southwest." For contemporary efforts at serving the urban Indian population, see ICMN Staff, "From Reservations to Urban Centers.

30. Deloria, *Custer Died for Your Sins,* 254.

31. Deloria, *Custer Died for Your Sins,* 254–55.

32. Deloria, *Custer Died for Your Sins,* 255.

33. Menominee Restoration Act; Hearings before the Subcommittee on Indian Affairs. In a letter, dated November 30, 1967, to John Belindo, Wendell Chino, Helen Mitchell, Georgeann Robinson, and Cato Valandra, Deloria bemoaned

how underappreciated the efforts of the NCAI were among the Indian community it represented: "Over the past 3 years I have noticed that we are often foiled in our attempts to get our programs underway because there are so many 'other' Indian organizations at work that people get confused about the real issues in legislation and programs. Too many people claim that 'NCAI's not doing anything' when in fact we are spending 18–20 hours a day on legislation, fund raising, information and programs." Nearly a year later, on August 22, 1968, in a memorandum addressed to John Belindo, Deloria enumerated thirteen initiatives that the NCAI Fund had undertaken over the past year, including amicus curiae, consultations, and support work for tribes. The last was in addition to a variety of support briefs on behalf of multiple tribes. Vine Deloria Papers.

34. Deloria, *Custer Died for Your Sins,* 256.

35. Deloria, *We Talk, You Listen,* 12.

36. Deloria, *God Is Red* (1973), 38.

37. For a recent work on this topic, see Owens, *Red Dreams, White Nightmares.*

38. Deloria, *Custer Died for Your Sins,* 257.

39. It is worth remembering that when Deloria served as NCAI executive director, 1964–67, his tenure coincided with Johnson administration, which saw an easing of termination policy that was not evident during Kennedy's brief time in office. More important to Indian affairs was Johnson's War on Poverty, which had a huge impact on Indian Country, as the economic initiatives gave tribes a wedge against termination. See, for example, "President Johnson Tells 100 Indian White House Visitors of Attack on Poverty."

40. Deloria, *Custer Died for Your Sins,* 257.

41. American Indian Movement, Trail of Broken Treaties.

42. For a history of the Native American Rights Fund, see Native American Rights Fund, "History of the Native American Rights Fund."

43. For more on the National Council on Indian Opportunity, see Lacy, "The United States and American Indians,"83–104.

44. Deloria, *Custer Died for Your Sins,* 258–59.

45. Deloria, *Custer Died for Your Sins,* 260. For a contemporary approach to these issues, see the Urban Indian Coalition of Arizona (UICAZ), Phoenix Indian Center.

46. Deloria, *Custer Died for Your Sins,* 261.

47. Hertzberg, "Indian Rights Movement, 1887–1973," 318. Within this article, Hertzberg also gives an account of the origin of the Urban Indian Federation (313). For more on Jesse Sixkiller and how he was remembered, see Mary Schmich, "Remembering Jess Sixkiller, a Native American ex-Chicago cop slain in Phoenix," *Chicago Tribune,* October 3, 2015: http://www.chicagotribune.com/news/columnists/schmich/ct -jess-sixkiller-killed-mary-schmich-1004-20151002-column.html.

48. Wise, *The Red Man in the New World Drama,* 377.

49. Deloria, *Custer Died for Your Sins,* 262.
50. Deloria, *Custer Died for Your Sins,* 262–63. For a report on the federal programming available to non-federally recognized tribes, see U.S. Government Accountability Office, "Indian Issues," The site contains a pdf link to the sixty-nine-page report submitted to Rep. Dan Boren (D-OK) during April 2012.
51. For an example of this trend, see the International Indian Treaty Council, which was founded in 1974: http://www.iitc.org.
52. For a more recent study of tribal entrepreneurship and economic sustainability, see Davis, *Sustaining the Forest.*
53. Deloria, *Custer Died for Your Sins,* 265–66.
54. There is evidence that Deloria actively followed his own recommendation for organizing collaborative efforts between the organizations he named. In a note to the Fiscal and Administrative Committee, NCAI, Deloria summarized in a "travel report" dated December 1–14, 1966: "To attend meeting of the Board of Directors. United Scholarships Services, Inc. with regard to possible joint research project combining NCAI Fund, USS and Harvard School of Education for work in Indian Education, to Washington, DC December 3 for conference with R. Sargent Shriver, Director of Office of Economic Opportunity with regard to funding of Indian Community Action Projects for 1967, meeting with Community Relations Service, National Institute of Mental Health in regard to project in Alcoholism for NCAI Fund, meeting with Office of Education in regard to administration of Title 1 Funds and conference on possibility of transferring Indian Education to Health, Education and Welfare, a meeting with United States Employment Service in regard to NCAI cooperation with conference to be held in Kansas City, Kansas in February to assist tribes in working with government agencies, meeting with Department of Defense in regard to conferences between Defense Department contractors and tribes with industrial sites for possible relocations of industry on Indian reservations, conference with NCAI lawyers in regard to Burnette case in Denver court, conference with Leopold and Linowes, NCAI auditors in regard to 1966 audit, travel to Michigan for visit with Michigan tribes and meeting with State Indian Commissioners in regard to development plans for Michigan tribes, travel to Chicago, Illinois to meeting with University of South Dakota Indian Community Action Project for discussions on expanding services to Indian tribes of the plains [*sic*] and woodlands [*sic*], tarvel [*sic*] to Washington, DC for conference with Office of Economic Opportunity people, travel to New York City to contact Field Foundation about funding for 1967 and talks with Mr. Harold Oram about funding and fund raising for NCAI and NCAI Fund for 1967, return tyo [*sic*] Denver." Council on Indian Affairs Joint Leadership Project, undated. Vine Deloria Papers.
55. Deloria, *Custer Died for Your Sins,* 266.

56. Deloria, "On Wounded Knee 1973,"38.

57. Deloria, *Of Utmost Good Faith,* 5.

58. Wise, *The Red Man in the New World Drama,* 400.

59. Deloria, *Custer Died for Your Sins,* 267.

60. For more, see Costo, *Indian Voices.*

61. Wise, *The Red Man in the New World Drama,* 378.

62. For a list of colleges and universities serving the Native community, complete with links to their web-pages, see Nelson, *A Guide to Native American Studies Programs.*

63. For more about national trends in Indian education, see the National Center for Education Statistics, "National Indian Education Study."

BIBLIOGRAPHY

ARCHIVES/MANUSCRIPT

Labriola National American Indian Data Center and Distinctive Collections: University Archives and Greater Arizona Collection.

Vine Deloria Papers. Yale Collection of Western Americana, Beinecke Rare Book and Manuscript Library.

Government Documents (Unless otherwise noted, all documents were accessed on ProQuest Congressional).

> 0501 Cong. Rec. 11274 (Statement of Senator Lee Metcalf). Congressional Record, Senate, 90th Cong. 1 (1967).
>
> 4 Stat. 411, Statutes at Large, Public Laws, 21st Cong. (1830).
>
> 4 Stat. 729, Statutes at Large, Public Laws, 23rd Cong. (1834).
>
> 4 Stat. 735, Statutes at Large, Public Laws, 23rd Cong. (1834).
>
> 9 Stat. 395, Statutes at Large, Public Laws, 30th Cong. (1849).
>
> 15 U.S. Code § 1021, United States Code, Title 15: Commerce and Trade; Chapter 21: National Policy on Employment and Productivity, United States Code Service (2018).
>
> 16 Stat. 13, Statutes at Large, Public Laws, 41st Cong. (1869).
>
> 16 Stat. 544, Statutes at Large, Public Laws, 41st Cong. (1871).
>
> 18 U.S. Code § 1162, United States Code, Title 18: Crimes and Criminal Procedure; Part 1: Crimes; Chapter 53: Indians, United States Code Service (2018).
>
> 24 Stat. 388, Statutes at Large, Public Laws, 49th Cong. (1887).
>
> 25 U.S. Code § 1-4307. Permalink: http://uscode.house.gov/browse/prelim@title25&edition=prelim. Available at the Office of the Law Revision Council, United States Code.
>
> 34 Stat. 182, Statutes at Large, Public Laws, 59th Cong. (1906).

38 Stat. 114, Statutes at Large, Public Laws, 63rd Cong. 1 (1913).

42 U.S. Code § 7, United States Code, Title 42: The Public Health and Welfare; Chapter 7: Social Security (2018).

48 Stat. 984, Statutes at Large, Public Laws, 73rd Cong. (1934).

49 Stat. 620, Statutes at Large, Public Laws, 74th Cong. 1 (1935).

60 Stat. 1049, Statutes at Large, Public Laws, 79th Cong. (1946).

62 Stat. 17, Statutes at Large, Public Laws, 80th Cong. 2 (1948).

67 Stat. 588, Statutes at Large, Public Laws, 83rd Cong. (1953).

67 Stat. B132, Statutes at Large, Concurrent Resolutions, 83rd Cong. (1953).

68 Stat. 674, Statutes at Large, Public Laws, 83rd Cong. (1954).

68 Stat. 1099, Statutes at Large, Public Laws, 83rd Cong. 2 (1954).

70 Stat. 626, Statutes at Large, Public Laws, 84th Cong. (1956).

73 S. 3645, Senate, Amendment in the Senate, 73rd Cong. 2 (1934).

78 S. 1218, House and Senate Reports; Reports on Public Bill, Committee on Indian Affairs, Senate, 78th Cong. 2 (1944).

78 Stat. 241, Statutes at Large, Public Laws, 88th Cong. (1964).

78 Stat. 508, Statutes at Large, Public Laws, 88th Cong. (1964).

79 S. 797, Statutes at Large, Public Laws, 88th Cong. (1964).

80 S. 797, Introduced in Senate, US Senate, 80th Cong. 1 (1947).

81 S. 6406, Hearings Unpublished, Committee on Interior and Insular Affairs. Senate, 81st Cong. 2 (1950).

82 H. Res. 698, House and Senate Reports; Reports on Public Bill, Committee on Rules. House, 82nd Cong. 2 (1952).

84 H.R. 7190, Statutes at Large, Public Laws, 84th Cong. (1956).

114 Cong. Rec. 4834, Congressional Record, Senate, 90th Cong. 2 (1968).

116 Cong. Rec. 19927-19929, Congressional Record, House and Senate Proceedings, 92nd Cong. 2 (1970).

117 Cong. Rec. 8208, Congressional Record, Senate and House Proceedings, 92nd Cong. 1 (1971).

384 F. Supp. 312 (W. D. Wash. 1974), aff'd, 520 F.2d 676 (9th Cir. 1975). Permalink: http://caselaw.findlaw.com/us-9th-circuit/1498559.html. Available at FindLaw for Legal Professionals, "Cases and Codes."

11582 H. rp. 2503, House and Senate Reports, Investigation of Bureau of Indian Affairs, 82nd Cong. 2 (1952).

11747 H. rp. 2680, House Report, Maps, Map showing Indian reservations in the United States, 83rd Cong. 2 (1940).

Amendments to the Menominee Indian Termination Act of 1954: Hearings before the Subcommittee on Indian Affairs; Committee on Interior and Insular Affairs. Senate, 86th Cong. 2 (1960).

Cherokee Nation v. State of Georgia 30 U.S. 1 (1831). Permalink: https://supreme
.justia.com/cases/federal/us/30/1/case.html. Available at JUSTIA US
Supreme Court.

Colliflower v. Garland, 342 F. 2d 369 (CA9 1965). Permalink: https://supreme
.justia.com/cases/federal/us/436/49/case.html. Available at JUSTIA
US Supreme Court.

Colville Indian Legislation: Hearings before the Subcommittee on Indian
Affairs; Committee on Interior and Insular Affairs. Senate, 88th Cong.
1 (1963).

Colville Termination: Hearings before the Subcommittee on Indian Affairs;
Committee on Interior and Insular Affairs. House, 90th Cong. 2 (1968).

Colville Termination: Hearings before the Subcommittee on Indian Affairs
of the Committee on Interior and Insular Affairs, Senate. 89th Cong. 1
(1965) (Testimony of Vine Deloria Jr.).

Committee of the Whole House. House Committee on Indian Affairs. Opening
for Settlement Certain Lands in Oklahoma (57 H.R. 16280).

Committee on Civil Service. Senate. Officers and Employees of the Federal
Government. Part 3, 80th Cong.1 (1947) (Testimony of Adam Castillo).

Committee on Civil Service. Senate. Officers and Employees of the Federal
Government. Part 3, 80th Cong. 1 (1947) (Testimony of William Zimmerman Jr.).

Cong. Rec. 8208. Congressional Record, House and Senate Proceedings,
92nd Cong. 1 (1971).

Congressional Record, C.R.-1969-1204, House and Senate Proceedings, 91st
Cong. 1 (1969) (Testimony of Robert Kastenmeier).

Constitutional Rights of the American Indian: Hearings before the Subcommittee on Constitutional Rights; Committee on the Judiciary. Senate.
89th Cong. 1 (1965) (Testimony of Vine Deloria Jr.).

C.R.-1951-0425, Congressional Record, House and Senate Proceedings, 82nd
Cong. 1 (1951).

C.R.-1967-0912, Congressional Record, House and Senate Proceedings, 90th
Cong. 1 (1967).

C.R.-1973-1011, Congressional Record, House and Senate Proceedings, 93rd
Cong. 1 (1973).

Department of Game v. Puyallup Tribe Inc, 70 Wn.2d 245 (1967). Permalink:
https://law.justia.com/cases/washington/supreme-court/1967/38611
-1.html. Available at JUSTIA US Law.

Department of Interior: Annual Report of Secretary of Interior, 1883, H.exdoc.
#1/11, House and Senate Documents, 48th Cong. 1 (1883).

Department of the Interior and Related Agencies Appropriations for 1966: Hearings before the Subcommittee of the Committee on Appropriations, House, 89th Cong. 1 (1965) (Testimony of Vine Deloria Jr.).

Department of the Interior and Related Agencies Appropriations for 1966, Part 2: Hearings before the Subcommittee of the Committee on Appropriations; House of Representatives. 89th Cong. 1 (1965) (Testimony of Vine Deloria Jr.).

Department of the Interior and Related Agencies Appropriations for 1968. Part 1: Hearing before the Subcommittee on Department of Interior and Related Agencies Appropriations, Committee on Appropriations. House, 90th Cong. 1 (1968) (Testimony of Charles F. Luce).

Department of the Interior and Related Agencies Appropriations for 1978, Part 4: Hearing before the Subcommittee on Interior Appropriations, Committee on Appropriations. House; Committee on Appropriations. House, 95th Cong. 1 (1977).

Effect of Federal Programs on Rural America: Hearings before the Subcommittee on Rural Development; Committee on Agriculture. House, 90th Cong.1 (1967) (Testimony of Clark S. Knowlton).

Effect of Federal Programs on Rural America: Hearing before the Subcommittee on Rural Development; Committee on Agriculture. House, 90th Cong. 1 (1967) (Statement of Stanley H. Ruttenberg, Assistant Secretary of Labor).

Employment and Manpower Problems in the Cities: Implications of the Report of the National Advisory Commission on Civil Disorders: Hearings before the Joint Economic Committee. Congress of the United States, 90th Cong. 2 (1968).

Examination of the War on Poverty Part 3: Albuquerque, N. Mex.: Hearing before the Subcommittee on Employment, Manpower, and Poverty; Committee on Labor and Public Welfare. Senate. 90th Cong. 1 (1967) (Testimony of Vine Deloria Jr.).

Holden v. Joy, 84 U.S. 211 (1872), H.R. 1794, H.R. 2828, H.R. 303, S. 132 H. rp. 2503, House and Senate Reports, Committee on Interior and Insular Affairs. House, 82nd Cong. 2 (1952).

H.R. 3321, U.S. House of Representatives, 63rd Cong. 1 (1913).

H.R. 3322, U.S. House of Representatives, 80th Cong. 2 (1948).

Hunger and Malnutrition in US: Hearings before the Subcommittee on Employment, Manpower, and Poverty; Committee on Labor and Public Welfare. Senate, 90th Cong 2 (1968) (Testimony of the Secretary of Health, Education, and Welfare.)

Impact of Federal Policies on Employment, Poverty, and Other Programs, 1973, Part 3: Hearings before the Subcommittee on Employment, Poverty, and Migratory Labor, Committee on Labor and Public Welfare. Senate; Committee on Labor and Public Welfare. Senate. 93rd Cong 1 (1973).

Indian Claims Commission Act Amendments: Hearing before the Subcommittee on Indian Affairs; Committee on Interior and Insular Affairs. Senate, 90th Cong 1 (1967) (Testimony of Alex Chasing Hawk.)

Indian Education: Hearings before the Special Subcommittee on Indian Education of the Committee on Labor and Public Welfare, Senate, 90th Cong. 1 & 2 (1968) (Testimony of Carlos Filmore).

Indian Health Care Improvement. Hearing before the Committee on Indian Affairs, Senate, 110th Cong. 1 (2007) (Testimony of Terry L. Hunter).

Indian Heirship Land Problem, Part 3: Hearing before the Subcommittee on Indian Affairs; Committee on Interior and Insular Affairs. Senate, 88th Cong. 1 (1963) (Testimony of Alex Chasing Hawk).

Indian Resources Development Act of 1967: Hearings before the Subcommittee on Indian Affairs; Committee on Interior and Insular Affairs. House, 90th Cong. 1 (1967).

Indians of the U.S. Vol. 1: Hearings before the Committee on Indian Affairs. House, 66th Cong. 1 (1919) (Testimony of John Reber).

"James H. Gamble Retires," Congressional Record, C.R.-1973-1011, House and Senate Proceedings, 93rd Cong. 1 (1973).

Johnson and Graham's Lessee v. McIntosh, 21 U.S. 8 Wheat 543 (1823). Permalink: https://supreme.justia.com/cases/federal/us/21/543/case.html. Available at JUSTIA US Supreme Court.

Joint Hearing: Hearing before the Committee on Interior and Insular Affairs. Senate; Committee on Interior and Insular Affairs. House, 83rd Cong. 2 (1954) (Testimony of Alex Chasing Hawk).

Lone Wolf v. Hitchcock 187 U.S. 553 (1903). Permalink: https://supreme.justia.com/cases/federal/us/187/553/case.html. Available at JUSTIA US Supreme Court.

Lyndon Baines Johnson, Executive Order No 11365, "Establishing a National Advisory Commission on Civil Disorders," July 29, 1967. Permalink: http://www.presidency.ucsb.edu/ws/index.php?pid=106100. Available at The American Presidency Project, Lyndon B. Johnson.

Lyndon B. Johnson, Unnumbered Executive Orders, Directives, and Proclamations, National Council on Indian Opportunity. Announcement of Appointment of Members, April 30, 1968. Permalink: http://www.presidency.ucsb.edu/ws/?pid=76359. Available at The American Presidency Project, Lyndon B. Johnson.

Menominee Indian Tribe of Wisconsin v. Thompson, 922 F. Supp. 184 (W.D. Wis. 1996). Permalink: https://law.justia.com/cases/federal/district-courts /FSupp/922/184/1592476/. Available at JUSTIA US Law.

Menominee Restoration Act: Hearings before the Subcommittee on Indian Affairs, Committee on Interior and Insular Affairs. House; Committee on Interior and Insular Affairs. House. 93rd Cong. 1 (1973) (Testimony of Vine Deloria Jr.).

Menominee Restoration Act: Hearings before the Subcommittee on Indian Affairs of the Committee on Interior and Insular Affairs, House, 93rd Cong. 1 (1973) (Testimony of Vine Deloria Jr.).

Menominee Tribe of Indians v. United States, Nos. 44304, 44296, 44298, 44300, 44303, 44305, and 44306, 1951 W.L. 57 (Ct.Cl. July 13, 1951) (unpublished order) (ratifying and adopting settlement agreement between the parties). Permalink: https://supreme.justia.com/cases/federal/us/391/404/case .html. Available at JUSTIA US Supreme Court.

Menominee Tribe of Wisconsin v. The United States (1997). Permalink: https:// law.justia.com/cases/federal/appellate-courts/F3/161/449/612345/. Available at JUSTIA US Supreme Court.

Morton v. Mancari, 417 U.S. 535 (1974). Permalink: https://supreme.justia .com/cases/federal/us/417/535/case.html. Available at JUSTIA US Supreme Court.

National American Indian and Alaska Natives Policy Resolution: Hearings before the Subcommittee on Indian Affairs of the Committee on Interior and Insular Affairs. Senate, 90th Cong.2 (1968); Rights of Members of Indian Tribes: Hearing before the Subcommittee on Indian Affairs of the Committee on Interior and Insular Affairs. House, 90th Cong. 2 (1968).

Native American Church v. Navajo Tribal Council, 272 F 2d 131—Court of Appeals, 10th Circuit 1959. https://scholar.google.com/scholar_case?about =10992068009710952686&q=native+american+church+v.+navajo +tribal+council&hl=en&as_sdt=806&as_vis=1.

Native American Graves Protection and Repatriation Act (NAGPRA), Public Law 101-601, 25 U.S.C. 3001 et seq., 104 Stat. 3048.

Office of Indian Affairs, Department of Interior: Rules governing court of Indian offenses [on establishment of court at each Indian agency, with regulations on war dances, polygamy, medicine men, destruction of property, prostitution, and other forbidden activities], March 30, 1883, I20.12:In2/3: P.L. 83-399, P.L. 83-568, P.L. 84-772, P.L. 88-352, P.L. 88-452, Executive Branch Documents (1883).

P.L. 63-16, Public Laws, 63rd Cong. 1 (1913).

P.L. 74-271, Public Laws, 74th Cong. 1 (1935).

P.L. 83-280; 67 Stat. 588, Statutes at Large, 83rd Cong. 1 (1953).

P.L. 88-352, Public Laws, 88th Cong. 2 (1964).

P.L. 707, Public Laws, 80th Cong. 2 (1948).

Problems, Plans, and Programs of the Cheyenne River Reservation, South Dakota: Hearing before the Subcommittee on Indian Affairs; Committee on Interior and Insular Affairs. House, 86th Cong 1 (1959) (Testimony of Alex Chasing Hawk.)

Puyallup Tribe v. Department of Game, 391 U.S. 392 (1968). Permalink: https:// supreme.justia.com/cases/federal/us/391/392/. Available at JUSTIA US Supreme Court.

Relating to the Tiwa Indians of Texas: Hearing before the Subcommittee on Indian Affairs; Committee on Interior and Insular Affairs. House, 90th Cong. 1 (1967).

Representative Mundt, "Indian Claims Commission Bill," Appendix to the Congressional Record 1946-0730, House and Senate Proceedings, 79th Cong. 2 (July 30, 1946): A4923.

S. 1049, House and Senate Reports; Reports on Public Bill, Committee on Interior and Insular Affairs. Senate, 88th Cong. 1 (1963).

S. 2670, Introduced into Senate, 83rd. Cong. 2 (1954).

S. 2780, Introduced into Senate, 82nd. Cong. 2 (1954).

S. 3645, Introduced into Senate, 73rd Cong. 2nd Sess. (1934).

S. Con. Res. 85, Concurrent Resolution, Introduced into Senate, 84th Cong. 2 (1956).

Select Subcommittee on Poverty; Committee on Labor and Public Welfare. Senate. "War on Poverty, the Economic Opportunity Act of 1964. Compilation of Materials Relevant to S. 2642." 88th Cong. 2nd Sess. July 23, 1964.

Sixth Congress, Session 1, Resolutions, V, April 16, 1800, Statutes at Large, Public Resolutions, 6th Cong. (1800).

S. Res.; 70 S. Res. 79, Senate Resolution, Reported in Senate, 70th Cong. 1 (1928).

S. Res; 80 S. Res. 41, Senate Resolution, Reported in Senate, 80th Cong. 1 (1947).

Subcommittee on Interior Department Appropriations; Committee on Appropriations. House. Interior Department Appropriation Bill for 1943. Part 2: Bureau of Indian Affairs, 77th Cong. 2 (1943) (Testimony of John Collier, et al.).

Subcommittee on Interior Department Appropriations; Committee on Appropriations. House. Interior Department Appropriation Bill for 1944. Part 2: Bureau of Indian Affairs, 78th Cong. 1 (1943) (Testimony of John Collier).

Survey of Conditions of the Indians in the United States: Parts 1–28, 1928–
1932. Subcommittee on S. Res. 79; Committee on Indian Affairs. Senate.
Permalink: https://catalog.hathitrust.org/Record/000622054. Available
at Hathi Trust Digital Library.

Talton v. Mayes, 163 U.S. 376 (1896). Permalink: https://supreme.justia.com
/cases/federal/us/163/376/. Available at JUSTIA US Supreme Court.

Tee-Hit-ton Indians v. United States, 348 U.S. 272 (1955). Permalink: https://
supreme.justia.com/cases/federal/us/348/272/. Available at JUSTIA
US Supreme Court.

Termination of Federal Supervision of Certain Tribes of Indians. Hearings
before the Subcommittees of the Committees on Interior and Insular
Affairs. Joint. 83rd Cong. 2 (1954).

Termination of Federal Supervision of Menominee Indians: Hearing before
the Committee on Interior and Insular Affairs. Senate; Committee on
Interior and Insular Affairs. House, 83rd Cong. 2 (1954).

Termination of Federal Supervision over Certain Tribes of Indians. Part 6:
Menominee Indians, Wisconsin: Hearing before the Subcommittee on
Indian Affairs; Committee on Interior and Insular Affairs. Senate; Sub-
committee on Indian Affairs; Committee on Interior and Insular Affairs.
House, 83rd Cong. 2 (1954).

Termination of Federal Supervision over Certain Tribes of Indians. Part 6:
Menominee Indians, Wisconsin: Hearing before the Subcommittee on
Indian Affairs; Committee on Interior and Insular Affairs. Senate; Sub-
committee on Indian Affairs; Committee on Interior and Insular Affairs.
House, 83rd Cong. 2 (1954) (Testimony of Harry Harder).

To Amend the Law Establishing the Indian Revolving Loan Fund; To Provide
for Guaranty and Insurance of Loans to Indians and Indian Organizations: Hearings before Subcommittee on Indian Affairs; Committee on
Interior and Insular Affairs. Senate. 89th Cong.1 (1965) (Testimony of
Vine Deloria Jr.).

To Amend the Menominee Termination Act: Hearing before the Subcommittee on Indian Affairs; Committee on Interior and Insular Affairs. House,
86th Cong. 2 (1960).

To Amend the Menominee Termination Act: Hearing before the Subcommittee on Indian Affairs; Committee on Interior and Insular Affairs. House,
86th Cong. 2 (1960) (Testimony of Jerome Grignon).

To Provide for Guaranty and Insurance of Loans to Indians and Indian Organizations: Hearing before the Subcommittee on Indian Affairs; Committee
on Interior and Insular Affairs. House. 89th Cong.1 (1965) (Testimony
of Vine V. Deloria Jr.).

To Provide for the Economic Development and Management of the Resources of Individual Indians and Indian Tribes, and for Other Purposes: Hearing before the Subcommittee on Indian Affairs; Committee on Interior and Insular Affairs. Senate, 90th Cong. 1 (1967).

To Quiet Title to Lands within Pueblo Indian Land Grants in New Mexico, 43 Stat. 636 and P.L. 68-253, House and Senate Reports; Reports on Public Bill, Committee on Public Lands and Surveys. Senate, 68th Cong. 1 (1924).

United States v. Shoshone Tribe of Indians, 304 U.S. 111 (1938) Permalink: https://supreme.justia.com/cases/federal/us/304/111/.

U.S. Department of Commerce, Economic Development Administration, Indian Projects Funded by EDA, August 26, 1965 — September 30, 1977 (Washington, DC: Department of Commerce, Economic Development Administration, 1977).

U.S. Department of the Interior, Indian Affairs, "Tribal-Interior Budget Council (TIBC)." http://www.bia.gov/WhoWeAre/as-ia/ocfo/tbac/index.htm.

U.S. Statutes at Large, 43:253 Permalink: https://congressional-proquest-com .ezproxy1.lib.asu.edu/congressional/docview/t53.d54.00043-stat-0253 -100233?accountid=4485.

U.S. Statutes at Large, 48:984–88 Permalink: https://congressional-proquest -com.ezproxy1.lib.asu.edu/congressional/docview/t53.d54.00048-stat -0984-100576?accountid=4485.

PUBLISHED WORKS

Ablon, Joan. "Relocated American Indians in the San Francisco Bay Area." In *The Emergent Native Americans: A Reader in Culture Contact*, edited by Deward E. Walker Jr., 712–27. Boston: Little, Brown and Company, 1972.

Ackerman, Lillian A., and Laura F. Klein. *Women and Power in Native North America*. Norman: University of Oklahoma Press, 2000.

Adams, Hank, et al. "Trail of Broken Treaties 20-Point Position Paper." In *The American Indian Intellectual Tradition: An Anthology of Writings, 1772–1972*, edited by David Martínez, 345–57. Ithaca: Cornell University Press, 2011.

Adams, Jim. "A Vine Deloria Jr. Collaboration: The First Decade." *Indian Country Today*, January 12, 2005: http://indiancountrytodaymedianetwork.com/2005 /01/12/vine-deloria-jr-collaboration-first-decade-94374.

Adams, Richard C. "A Delaware Indian Legend and The Story of Their Troubles." In *The American Indian Intellectual Tradition: An Anthology of Writings, 1772– 1972*, edited by David Martínez, 138–46. Ithaca: Cornell University Press, 2011.

"All American Indian Days: A Sadness at Sheridan." *NCAI Sentinel Bulletin* 11, no. 3 (Summer 1966).

Allen, Paula Gunn. *The Sacred Hoop: Recovering the Feminine in American Indian Traditions*. Boston: Beacon Press, 1986.

Allen, Ray A. "Whither Indian Education? A Conversation with Philleo Nash." *School Review* 79, no. 1 (November 1970): 99–108.

Altizer, Thomas J. J. *The Gospel of Christian Atheism*. Philadelphia: Westminster, 1966.

American Anthropological Association. *Anthropology and the American Indian: A Symposium*. San Francisco: Indian Historian Press, 1973.

American Indian Alaska Native Tourism Association. "American Indians and Route 66." http://www.americanindiansandroute66.com/.

American Indian Movement. "Trail of Broken Treaties Twenty-Point Position Paper." http://www.aimovement.org/archives/index.html.

"American Indians Today." *Soroptimist Magazine*, December 1971.

The American Presidency Project. "Richard Nixon." http://www.presidency.ucsb.edu/ws/?pid=2573.

Ames Historical Society. "Maria Pearson." http://www.ameshistory.org/content/maria-pearson.

"Anderson, Clinton Presba, (1895–1975)." Biographical Directory of the United States Congress. http://bioguide.congress.gov/scripts/biodisplay.pl?index=a000186.

Anfinson, Scott F., and Leslie D. Peterson. "Minnesota's Highway Archaeological Programs." *The Minnesota Archaeologist* 38, no. 2 (May 1979): 86104.

Apess, William. *Eulogy on King Philip: As Pronounced at the Odeon, in Federal Street, Boston*. Boston: published by the author, 1836.

Arnold, Laurie. *Bartering with the Bones of Their Dead: The Colville Confederated Tribes and Termination*. Seattle: University of Washington Press, 2012.

Associated Press. "Wisconsin Tribesmen Get $8,500,000 As Truman Signs Bill to Pay Up Claim," *New York Times*, November 3, 1951, 7.

"Back to the Clan." *NCAI Sentinel Bulletin* 12, no. 1 (Winter 1966).

Bannai, Lorraine K. *Enduring Conviction: Fred Korematsu and His Quest for Justice*. Seattle: University of Washington Press, 2015.

Bates, Denise E. "Reshaping Southern Identity and Politics: Indian Activism during the Civil Rights Era." *New South* 9 (2016): 125–51.

Bauer, William J., Jr. "California." In *The Oxford Handbook of American Indian History*, edited by Frederick J. Hoxie, 275–300. New York: Oxford University Press, 2016.

"Bender, George Harrison, (1896–1961)." Biographical Directory of the United States Congress. http://bioguide.congress.gov/scripts/biodisplay.pl?index=b000356.

Benedict, Ruth. *Patterns of Culture*. Boston: Houghton Mifflin, 1959.

Bentz, Marilyn. "Beyond Ethics: Science, Friendship, and Privacy." In *Indians and Anthropologists: Vine Deloria Jr. and the Critique of Anthropology*, edited by Thomas Biolsi and Larry J. Zimmerman, 120–32. Tucson: University of Arizona Press, 1997,

Berhofer, Robert F. *The White Man's Indian: Images of the American Indian from Columbus to the Present.* New York: Vintage, 1979.

"Berry, Ellis Yarnal, (1902–1999)." Biographical Directory of the United States Congress. http://bioguide.congress.gov/scripts/biodisplay.pl?index=b000416.

Bieder, Robert E. *Native American Communities in Wisconsin, 1600–1960: A Study of Tradition and Change.* Madison: University of Wisconsin Press, 1995.

Biolsi, Thomas, and Larry J. Zimmerman, eds. *Indians and Anthropologists: Vine Deloria Jr. and the Critique of Anthropology.* Tucson: University of Arizona Press, 1997.

———, eds. "Introduction: What's Changed, What Hasn't." *Indians and Anthropologists: Vine Deloria Jr. and the Critique of Anthropology.* 3–24. Tucson: University of Arizona Press, 1997.

Blackbird, Andrew J. "The Indian Problem; From the Indian's Standpoint," In *The American Indian Intellectual Tradition: An Anthology of Writings, 1772–1972,* edited by David Martínez, 147–55. Ithaca: Cornell University Press, 2011.

———. *The Indian Problem: From the Indian's Standpoint.* Philadelphia: National Indian Association, 1900.

Blu, Karen I. *The Lumbee Problem: The Making of an American Indian People.* Lincoln: University of Nebraska, 2001.

Boek, Jean K. "We Talk, You Listen: New Tribes, New Turf by Vine Deloria." *American Anthropologist,* n.s., 77, no. 1 (March 1975): 109.

Boudinot, Elias. "Address to the Whites." In *The American Indian Intellectual Tradition: An Anthology of Writings from 1772 to 1972,* edited by David Martínez, 41–49. Ithaca: Cornell University Press, 2011.

Bowden, Henry Warner. "Native American Presbyterians: Assimilation, Leadership, and Future Challenges." In *The Diversity of Discipleship: Presbyterians and Twentieth-Century Christian Witness,* edited by Milton J. Coalter, et al., 234–56. Louisville KY: Westminster/John Knox Press, 1991.

Brady, Tim. "The Nation's First Department of American Indian Studies, at the University of Minnesota, Celebrates 40 Years of Existence." http://minnesota.imodules.com/s/resources/templates/login/index.aspx?sid=1118&gid=1&pgid=1000.

Bremer, Francis J. *The Puritan Experiment: New England Society from Bradford to Edwards.* Hanover NH: University Press of New England, 1995.

Breutti, Ronald A. "The Cherokee Cases: The Fight to Save the Supreme Court and the Cherokee Indians." *American Indian Law Review* 17, no. 1 (1992): 291–308.

Brook, Richard. "What Tribe? Whose Island?" *The North American Review* 255, no. 1 (Spring 1970): 51–56.

Brookings Institution. Institute for Government Research. *The Problem of Indian Administration.* Baltimore: Johns Hopkins Press, 1928.

Brown, Stuart E., Lorraine F. Meyers, and Eileen M. Chappel. *Pocahontas' Descendants: A Revision, Enlargement and Extension of the List as Set out by Wyndham Robertson in His Book Pocahontas and Her Descendants (1887)*. Baltimore: Genealogical Publishing Company, 1997.

Browne, Rita-Jean, and Mary Lee Nolan. "Western Indian Reservation Tourism Development," *Annals of Tourism Research* 16 (1989): 360–76.

Brubaker, Jack. *Massacre of the Conestogas: On the Trail of the Paxton Boys in Lancaster County (PA)*. Charleston SC: History Press, 2010.

Brunner, Edmund de Schweinitz, ed., *Churches of Distinction in Town and Country*. New York: George H. Doran Co., 1923.

Buffalohead, W. Roger. "Custer Died for Your Sins: An Indian Manifesto." *Pacific Historical Review* 39, no. 4 (November 1970): 553–54.

Bureau of Indian Affairs. "Frequently Asked Questions," "What is a federally recognized tribe?" http://www.bia.gov/faqs/.

Cabot, John. "John Cabot's Discovery of North America (1497)." In *American Historical Documents, 1000–1904*, edited by Charles W. Eliot, 47–50. New York: Cosimo, 1910.

Calloway, Colin G. *New Worlds for All: Indians, Europeans, and the Remaking of Early America*. Baltimore: Johns Hopkins University Press, 1997.

Calomiris, Charles W., and Eugene N. White, "The Origins of Federal Deposit Insurance." In *The Regulated Economy: A Historical Approach to Political Economy*, edited by Claudia Goldin and Gary D. Libecap. Chicago: University of Chicago Press, 1994.

Castile, George Pierre. *To Show Heart: Native American Self-Determination and Federal Indian Policy, 1960–1975*. Tucson: University of Arizona Press, 1998.

Chavers, Dean. *Racism in Indian Country*. New York: Peter Lang, 2009.

Choctaw Nation of Oklahoma. History: Removal. Choctawnation.com http://www.choctawnation.com/history/choctaw-nation-history/removal/removal/.

Chrisman, Gabriel. "The Fish-in Protests at Franks Landing," University of Washington Seattle Civil Rights and Labor History Project. http://depts.washington.edu/civilr/fish-ins.htm.

"Church, Frank Forrester, (1924–1984)." Biographical Directory of the United States Congress. http://bioguide.congress.gov/scripts/biodisplay.pl?index=c000388.

Churchill, Ward. "Contours of Enlightenment: Reflections on Science, Theology, Law, and the Alternative Vision of Vine Deloria, Jr." In *Native Voices: American Indian Identity and Resistance*, edited by Richard A. Grounds, George E. Tinker, and David E. Wilkins, 245–72. Lawrence: University Press of Kansas, 2003.

Citizens' Board of Inquiry into Hunger and Malnutrition in the United States. *Hunger, USA: A Report*. Boston: Beacon Press, 1968.

Clark, Blue. *Lone Wolf v. Hitchcock: Treaty Rights and Indian Law at the End of the Nineteenth Century*. Lincoln: University of Nebraska, 1994.

Clarkin, Thomas. *Federal Indian Policy in the Kennedy and Johnson Administrations, 1961–1969*. Albuquerque: University of New Mexico Press, 2001.

Clemmer, Richard O. "'Then Will You Rise and Strike My Head from My Neck': Hopi Prophecy and the Discourse of Empowerment." *American Indian Quarterly* 19, no. 1 (Winter 1995): 31–73.

Cobb, Daniel M. "Citizens' Crusade against Poverty (CCAP)." In *Poverty in the United States: An Encyclopedia of History, Politics, and Policy*, edited by Gwendolyn Mink and Alice O'Connor, 1:174–75. Santa Barbara: ABC-CLIO, 2004.

———. *Native Activism in Cold War America: The Struggle for Sovereignty*. Lawrence: University Press of Kansas, 2008.

———. "The War on Poverty in Mississippi and Oklahoma: Beyond Black and White." In *The War on Poverty: A New Grassroots History, 1964–1980*, edited by Annelise Orleck and Lisa Hasirjian, 395–403. Athens: University of Georgia Press, 2011.

Coggins, George Cameron, and William Modrcin. "Native American Indians and Federal Wildlife Law." *Stanford Law Review* 31, no. 3 (February 1979): 375–423.

Collier, Peter. "'White Society Is Breaking Down Around Us . . . Even Its Myths—Like the Melting Pot—Are Dead': An Interview with American Indian Writer Vine Deloria Jr." *Mademoiselle*, April 1971, 202–4, 269.

Columbia River Inter-Tribal Fish Commission. "Treaty: Promises Between Governments." http://www.critfc.org/member_tribes_overview/treaty-q-a/.

Convery, William J. "John Chivington." In *Soldiers West: Biographies from the Military Frontier*, edited by Durwood Ball and Paul Andrew Hutton, 149–73. Norman: University of Oklahoma Press, 2009.

Cook, Charles H., and Isaac T. Whittemore. *Among the Pimas: or, The mission to the Pima and Maricopa Indians*. Albany NY: printed for the Ladies' Union Mission School Association, 1893.

Cook-Lynn, Elizabeth. "Comments for Vine Deloria Jr. Upon His Early and Untimely Death, 2005." *Wicazo Sa Review* 21, no. 2 (Autumn 2006): 149–50.

Cook Native American Ministries Foundation. http://cooknam.org.

Corbett, Cecil. "When God Became Red." In *Native Voices: American Indian Identity and Resistance*, edited by Richard A. Grounds, George E. Tinker, and David E. Wilkins, 189–93. Lawrence: University Press of Kansas, 2003.

Costo, Rupert, ed. *Indian Voices: The First Convocation of American Indian Scholars*. San Francisco: The Indian Historian Press, 1970.

Cowger, Thomas W. *The National Congress of American Indians: The Founding Years*. Lincoln: University of Nebraska Press, 2001.

Crawford, Michael H. *The Origins of Native Americans: Evidence from Anthropological Genetics*. New York: Cambridge University Press, 1998.

Daly, Heather Ponchetti. "Fractured Relations at Home: The 1953 Termination Act's Effect on Tribal Relations throughout Southern California Indian Country." *American Indian Quarterly* 33, no. 4 (Fall 2009): 427–39.

Davis, Thomas. *Sustaining the Forest, the People, and the Spirit.* Albany: State University of New York Press, 2000.

"Dawes, Henry Laurens, (1816–1903)." Biographical Directory of the United States Congress. http://bioguide.congress.gov/scripts/biodisplay.pl?index=d000148.

DeJong, David H. *Stealing the Gila: The Pima Agricultural Economy and Water Deprivation, 1848–1921.* Tucson: University of Arizona Press, 2009.

"Delaney, James Joseph, (1901–1987). "Biographical Directory of the United States Congress. http://bioguide.congress.gov/scripts/biodisplay.pl?index=d000211.

De Leon, David, ed. *Leaders from the 1960s: A Biographical Sourcebook of American Activism.* Westport CT: Greenwood Press, 1994.

Deloria, Ella. *Speaking of Indians.* New York: Friendship Press, 1944.

Deloria, Philip J. "Vine V. Deloria Sr. / Dakota." In *The New Warriors: Native American Leaders Since 1900,* edited by R. David Edmunds, 79–96. Lincoln: University of Nebraska Press, 2001.

Deloria, Vine, Jr. "Alcatraz, Activism, and Accommodation." In *American Indian Activism: Alcatraz to the Longest Walk,* edited by Troy Johnson, Joane Nagel, and Duane Champagne, 45–51. Urbana: University of Illinois Press, 1997.

———. "Anthros, Indians, and Planetary Reality." In *Indians and Anthropologists: Vine Deloria Jr. and the Critique of Anthropology,* edited by Thomas Biolsi and Larry J. Zimmerman, 209–22. Tucson: University of Arizona Press, 1997.

———. *Behind the Trail of Broken Treaties: An Indian Declaration of Independence.* New York: Delacorte, 1974.

———. *A Better Day for Indians.* New York: Field Foundation, 1976.

———. "Beyond Wounded Knee." *Akwesasne Notes* 5, no. 4 (Late Summer 1973): 8.

———. "Bob Thomas as Colleague." In *A Good Cherokee, A Good Anthropologist: Papers in Honor of Robert K. Thomas,* edited by Steve Pavlik, 27–38. Los Angeles: American Indian Studies Center, UCLA, 1998.

———. "Christianity and Indigenous Religion: Friends or Enemies? A Native American Perspective." In *Creation and Culture: The Challenge of Indigenous Spirituality and Culture to Western Creation Thought,* edited by David G. Bourke, 31–43. New York: Lutheran World Ministries, 1987.

———. "The Churches and Cultural Change." In *For This Land: Writings on Religion in America,* edited by James Treat, 51–57. New York: Routledge, 1999.

———. "Circling the Same Old Rock." In *Marxism and Native Americans,* edited by Ward Churchill, 113–36. Boston: South End, 1983.

———. *Custer Died for Your Sins: An Indian Manifesto.* New York: Macmillan, 1969.

———. "Custer Died for Your Sins." *Playboy Magazine,* August 1969.

———. "For an All-American Platoon." *Journal of the Forum for Contemporary History* 2, no. 1 (December 1972–January 1973): 11–12.

———, ed. *Frank Waters: Man and Mystic.* Athens: Ohio University Press.

———. *God Is Red.* New York: Dell, 1973.

———. *God Is Red: A Native View of Religion.* Thirtieth anniversary edition. Golden CO: Fulcrum, 2003.

———. "Indian Affairs 1973: Hebrews 13:8." *North American Review.* Special Heritage Issue: The Indian Question, 1823–1973 258, no. 4 (Winter 1973): 108–12.

———, ed. *The Indian Reorganization Act: Congresses and Bills.* Norman: University of Oklahoma Press, 2002.

———. *Indians of the Pacific Northwest: From the Coming of the White Man to the Present Day.* New York: Doubleday, 1977.

———. "Intellectual Self-Determination and Sovereignty: Looking at the Windmills in Our Minds." *Wicazo Sa Review* 13, no. 1 (Spring 1998): 25–31.

———. Introduction to *Black Elk Speaks: Being the Life Story of a Holy Man of the Oglala Sioux* by John G. Neihardt, xi–xiv. Lincoln: University of Nebraska Press, 1979.

———. Introduction to *Speaking of Indians,* edited by Vine Deloria Jr., ix–xix. Lincoln: University of Nebraska Press, 1998.

———. "It Is a Good Day to Die." In *For This Land: Writings on Religion in America,* edited by James Treat, 84–91. New York: Routledge, 1999.

———. *The Metaphysics of Modern Existence.* New York: Harper & Row, 1979.

———. "Non-Violence in American Society." *In For This Land: Writings on Religion in America*, edited by James Treat, 1–18. New York: Routledge, 1999):

———. "Non-Violence in American Society." *Katallagete* 5, no. 2 (Winter 1974): 4–7.

———, ed. *Of Utmost Good Faith.* New York: Bantam, 1971.

———. "On Wounded Knee 1973." *Akwesasne Notes* 5, no. 2 (Early Spring 1973): 38.

———. "An Open Letter to the Heads of the Christian Churches in America." In *For This Land: Writings on Religion in America.* edited by James Treat, 77–83. New York: Routledge, 1999.

———. *Red Earth, White Lies: Native Americans and the Myth of Scientific Fact.* Golden CO: Fulcrum, 1997.

———. "The Rise and Fall of Ethnic Studies." In *In Search of a Future for Education: Readings in Foundations*, edited by Stephen C. Margaritis, 153–57. Columbus OH: Charles E. Merrill, 1973.

———. "The Rise and Fall of the First Indian Movement." *Historian* 33, no. 4 (August 1971): 656–64.

———. *Singing for a Spirit: A Portrait of the Dakota Sioux.* Santa Fe: Clear Light, 1999.

———. "Some Criticisms and a Number of Suggestions." In *Anthropology and the American Indian: A Symposium,* edited by Rupert Costo, 93–99. San Francisco: Indian Historian, 1973.

———. "The Subject Nobody Knows." *American Indian Quarterly* 19, no. 1 (Winter 1995): 143–47.

———. "The Theological Dimension of the Indian Protest Movement." In *For This Land: Writings on Religion in America*, edited by James Treat, 31–35. New York: Routledge, 1999.

———. "The Urban Scene and the American Indian." In *Indian Voices: The First Convocation of American Indian Scholars*, edited by Rupert Costo, 333–55. San Francisco: The Indian Historian Press, 1970.

———. "A Violated Covenant." *Event: Issues and Viewpoints for Laymen* 11, no. 6 (June 1971): 5–8.

——— "The War Between the Redskins and the Feds." *New York Times Magazine*, December 7, 1969.

———. *We Talk, You Listen: New Tribes, New Turf.* New York: Macmillan, 1970.

Deloria, Vine, Jr., and Clifford Lytle. *American Indians, American Justice.* Austin: University of Texas Press, 1983.

———. *The Nations Within: The Past and Future of Indian Sovereignty.* New York: Pantheon, 1984.

Deloria, Vine, Jr., and Raymond J. DeMallie, eds. *Documents of American Indian Diplomacy: Treaties, Agreements, and Conventions, 1775–1979*, 2 vols. Norman: University of Oklahoma Press, 1999.

DeMallie, Raymond J., and Douglas R. Parks, eds. "Part Two. Christianity and the Sioux," *Sioux Indian Religion: Tradition and Innovation*, 91–157. Norman: University of Oklahoma Press, 1987.

Dial, Adolph L. *The Only Land I Know: A History of the Lumbee Indians*. Syracuse: Syracuse University Press, 1996.

Dixon, Joseph K., and Rodman Wanamaker. *The Vanishing Race, The Last Great Indian Council, A Record in Picture and Story of the Last Great Indian Council, Participated In by Eminent Indian Chiefs from Nearly Every Indian Reservation in the United States, Together with the Story of Their Lives as told by Themselves—Their Speeches and Folklore Tales—Their Solemn Farewell and the Indian's Story of the Custer Fight. The Concept off Rodman Wanamaker.* New York: Doubleday Page, 1914.

Dolin, Eric Jay. *Fur, Fortune, and Empire: The Epic History of the Fur Trade in America.* New York: W. W. Norton, 2010.

Dowd, Gregory Evans. *A Spirited Resistance: The North American Indian Struggle for Unity, 1745–1815.* Baltimore: Johns Hopkins University Press, 1993.

Drabiak-Syed, Katherine. "Lessons from *Havasupai Tribe v. Arizona State University Board of Regents*: Recognizing Group, Cultural, and Dignitary Harms as Legitimate Risks Warranting Integration into Research Practice." *Journal of Health and Biomedical Law* 11 (2010): 175–225.

Dyk, Walter. *Left Handed, Left Handed, Son of Old Man Hat: A Navajo Autobiography*. Lincoln: University of Nebraska Press, 1938.

Eastman, Charles A., (Ohiyesa). *From the Deep Woods to Civilization: Chapters in the Autobiography of an Indian*. Boston: Little, Brown and Company, 1916.

——. *Indian Boyhood*. New York: Doubleday, Page & Company, 1902.

——. *The Indian To-Day: The Past and Future of the First American*. New York: Doubleday, Page & Company, 1915.

——. *The Soul of the Indian: An Interpretation*. Boston: Houghton Mifflin Company, 1911.

Editorial. *NCAI Sentinel Bulletin* 10, no. 3 (Spring 1965).

Editorial. *NCAI Sentinel Bulletin* 11, no. 2 (Spring 1966).

Edmunds, R. David, ed. "Robert Yellowtail," *The New Warriors: Native American Leaders Since 1900*, 55–77. Lincoln: University of Nebraska Press, 2001.

Eells, Earnest Edward. *Journal of the Department of History (The Presbyterian Historical Society) of the Presbyterian Church in the USA* 18, 19 nos. 1–4, 7–8 (1939, 1940).

Erickson, Donald A. "Custer Did Die for Our Sins!" *School Review* 79, no. 1 (November 1970): 76–93.

Fairbanks, Robert A. "Review: Behind the Trail of Broken Treaties: An Indian Declaration of Independence by Vine Deloria Jr." *American Indian Law Review* 2, no. 2 (Winter 1974): 169–72.

Fanon, Frantz. *The Wretched of the Earth*. Shelter Island NY: Black Cat, 1963.

Farb, Peter. *Man's Rise to Civilization: As Shown by the Indians of North America from Primeval Times to the Coming of the Industrial State*. New York: E. P. Dutton, 1968.

Fitzgerald, Kathleen J. Introduction. *Beyond White Ethnicity: Developing a Sociological Understanding of Native American Identity Reclamation*. 1–30. Plymouth, UK: Lexington Books, 2007).

Fixico, Donald L. *Bureau of Indian Affairs*. Santa Barbara: ABC-CLIO, 2012.

——. *The Urban Indian Experience in America*. Albuquerque: University of New Mexico, 2000.

Fleming, Robert E. "God Is Red by Vine Deloria, Jr." *Rocky Mountain Review of Language and Literature* 30, no. 2 (Spring 1976): 123–25.

Forbes, Jack D. *Native Americans and Nixon: Presidential Politics and Minority Self-Determination, 1969–1972*. Los Angeles: American Indian Studies Center, 1981.

Fortunate Eagle, Adam. *Heart of the Rock: The Indian Invasion of Alcatraz*. Norman: University of Oklahoma, 2002.

"Fraser, Donald McKay, (1924–)." Biographical Directory of the United States Congress. http://bioguide.congress.gov/scripts/biodisplay.pl?index=f000350.

Fritz, Henry E. *The Movement for Indian Assimilation, 1860–1890*. Philadelphia: University of Pennsylvania Press, 1963.

"'F Troop'—The Indian on TV." *NCAI Sentinel Bulletin* 10, no. 3 (Summer 1965).

Fryberg, Stephanie, Hazel Rose Marcus, Daphna Oyserman, and Joseph M. Stone, "Of Warrior Chiefs and Indian Princesses: The Psychological Consequences of American Indian Mascots." *Basic and Applied Social Psychology* 30, no. 3 (2008): 208–18.

Garroutte, Eva Marie. *Real Indians: Identity and the Survival of Native America*. Berkeley: University of California Press, 2003.

Giago, Tim. *Children Left Behind: The Dark Legacy of Indian Mission Boarding Schools*. Santa Fe: Clear Light Publishers, 2006.

Gipp, David M. "Robert F. Kennedy's Legacy with First Americans." *Tribal College Journal*, November 29, 2013. http://www.tribalcollegejournal.org/archives/27884.

Glatthaar, Joseph T., and James Kirby Martin. *Forgotten Allies: The Oneida Indians and the American Revolution*. New York: Hill & Wang, 2006.

Grobsmith, Elizabeth S. "Growing Up on Deloria: The Impact of His Work on a New Generation of Anthropologists." In *Indians and Anthropologists: Vine Deloria Jr. and the Critique of Anthropology*, edited by Thomas Biolsi and Larry J. Zimmerman, 35–49. Tucson: University of Arizona Press, 1997.

Grounds, Richard A., George E. Tinker, and David E. Wilkins, eds. Preface. In *Native Voices: American Indian Identity and Resistance*. Lawrence: University Press of Kansas, 2003.

Harmon, Alexandra, ed. *The Power of Promises: Rethinking Indian Treaties in the Pacific Northwest*. Seattle: University of Washington Press, 2008.

———. *Rich Indians: Native People and the Problem of Wealth in American History*. Chapel Hill: University of North Carolina Press, 2013.

Harrington, Michael. *The New American Poverty*. New York: Holt, Rinehart and Winton, 1984.

———. *The Other America: Poverty in the United States*. New York: Macmillan, 1962.

Harris, LaDonna. *LaDonna Harris: A Comanche Life*. Lincoln: University of Nebraska Press, 2000.

The Harvard Project on American Indian Economic Development. *The State of the Native Nations: Conditions under U.S. Policies of Self-Determination*. New York: Oxford University Press, 2007.

Hassrick, Royal. *The Sioux: Life and Customs of a Warrior Society*. Norman: University of Oklahoma Press, 1964.

The Heard Museum, Phoenix Arizona. "Remembering Our Indian School Days: The Boarding School Experience." http://heard.org/exhibits/boardingschool/.

Heath, G. Louis. "No Rock Is an Island," *Phi Delta Kappan* 52, no. 7 (March 1971): 397–99.

Hebard, Grace Raymond. *Washakie, Chief of the Shoshones*. Lincoln, NE: Bison Books, 1995.

Hertzberg, Hazel W. "Indian Rights Movements, 1887–1973." In *Handbook of North American Indians*. Vol. 4, *History of Indian-White Relations*, edited by Wilcomb E. Washburn, 305–23. Washington DC: Smithsonian Institution, 1988.

———. *The Search for an American Indian Identity: Modern Pan-Indian Movements*. Syracuse: Syracuse University Press, 1971.

Hill, S. Pony. *Strangers in Their Own Land: South Carolina's State Indian Tribes*. Palm Coast FL: Backintyme, 2009.

Hirabashi, Gordon K. *A Principled Stand: The Story of Hirabashi v. United States*. Seattle: University of Washington Press, 2013.

Hodge, Frederick Webb. "Bible Translations." In *Handbook of American Indians North of Mexico*, part 1, 143–45 Washington DC: G.P.O., 1912.

Holland, Sharon. "'If You Know I Have a History, You Will Respect Me': A Perspective on Afro-Native American Literature," *Callaloo*. Native America Literatures, 17, no. 1 (Winter 1994): 334–50.

Holm, Tom. *Code Talkers and Warriors: Native Americans and World War II*. New York: Chelsea House Publishers, 2007.

———. "Decolonizing Native American Leaders: Vine's Call for Traditional Leadership." In *Destroying Dogma: Vine Deloria Jr. and His Influence on American Society*, edited by Steve Pavlik and Daniel R. Wildcat, 13–46. Golden, Colo.: Fulcrum Publishing, 2006.

Hopkins, Sarah Winnemucca. *Life among the Piutes: Their Wrongs and Claims*. Boston: Cupples, Upham & Company, 1883.

Horne, Gerald. *Fire This Time: The Watts Uprising and the 1960s*. New York: Da Capo Press, 1995.

Howe, Mark Antony De Wolfe. *The Life and Labors of Bishop Hare: Apostle to the Sioux*. New York: Sturgis & Walton Co, 1914.

Hoxie, Frederick E. *A Final Promise: The Campaign to Assimilate the Indians, 1880–1920*. Lincoln: University of Nebraska Press, 2001.

———. *This Indian Country: American Indian Activists and the Place They Made*. New York: Penguin Books, 2012.

ICMN Staff. "From Reservations to Urban Centers, Indians Struggle to Escape Poverty, Fight to Create Positive Change," April 17, 2013. https://indiancountrymedianetwork.com/news/business/from-reservations-to-urban-centers-indians-struggle-to-escape-poverty-fight-to-create-positive-change/.

———. "Salute to Vine Deloria Jr.; American Indian Visionary," *Indian Country Media Network*, January 12, 2005. https://indiancountrymedianetwork.com/news/salute-to-vine-deloria-jr-american-indian-visionary/.

Indianz.com. "Vine Deloria Jr., Giant in Indian Country, Dies at 72," November 15, 2005. http://www.indianz.com/News/2005/011288.asp.

"Interior Secretary James Watt Says Reservations Are Failing." NBC Nightly News, New York NY: NBC Universal, 01/19/1983. NBC Learn. https://archives.nbclearn.com/portal/site/k-12/browse/?cuecard=36461.

The Iowa Legislature. "Iowa Code Archive." https://www.legis.iowa.gov/archives/code.

Irwin, Lee. *Coming Down from Above: Prophecy, Resistance, and Renewal in Native American Religions.* Norman: University of Oklahoma Press, 2008.

Iverson, Peter. *Carlos Montezuma and the Changing World of American Indians.* Albuquerque: University of New Mexico Press, 1982.

Jackson, Donald, ed. *Black Hawk: An Autobiography.* Urbana: University of Illinois Press, 1990.

"Jackson, Henry Martin (Scoop), (1912–1983)." Biographical Directory of the United States Congress. http://bioguide.congress.gov/scripts/biodisplay.pl?index =j000013.

Johansen, Bruce E., ed. "Survival of American Indians Association" *Encyclopedia of the American Indian Movement,* 241–44. Santa Barbara CA: Greenwood, 2013.

———, ed. "Thom, Mel." *Encyclopedia of the American Indian Movement,* 246–47. Santa Barbara CA: Greenwood, 2013.

Johansen, Bruce Elliott. "Anderson, Wallace 'Made Bear' (Tuscarora) [1927]–1985." In *Encyclopedia of the Haudenosaunee (Iroquois Confederacy),* edited by Bruce Elliott Johansen and Barbara Alice Mann, 24–25. Westport CT: Greenwood Press, 2000.

"Johnson Promises Help for Indians." *NCAI Sentinel Bulletin* 9, no. 1 (February–March 1964).

Jorgensen, Joseph G. "Indians and the Metropolis," In *The American Indian in Urban Society,* edited by Jack O. Waddell and O. Michael Watson, 66–113. Boston: Little, Brown & Company, 197.

Josephy, Alvin M., Jr., Joane Nagel, and Troy Johnson, eds. *Red Power: The American Indians' Fight for Freedom.* Lincoln: University of Nebraska Press, 1999.

"Justice and 'Just Compensation'—The American Way of Land Acquisition." *NCAI Sentinel Bulletin* 10, no. 3 (Summer 1965).

"Justice and 'Just Compensation'—The American Way of Land Acquisition." *NCAI Sentinel Bulletin* 11, no. 3 (Summer 1966).

Kappler, Charles J., ed. "Treaty with the Cherokee, 1785." *Indian Affairs: Laws and Treaties.* Vol. 2, Treaties. Washington DC: Government Printing Office, 1904. http://digital.library.okstate.edu/kappler/Vol2/treaties/che0008.htm#mn3.

———, ed. "Treaty with the Chippewa, 1826." *Indian Affairs: Laws and Treaties.* Vol. 2, Treaties, Washington DC: Government Printing Office, 1904. Okstate .edu. https://dc.library.okstate.edu/digital/collection/kapplers/id/26109/.

———, ed. "Treaty with the Choctaw, 1825." *Indian Affairs: Laws and Treaties.* Vol. 2, Treaties. Washington DC: Government Printing Office, 1904. Okstate.edu. http://digital.library.okstate.edu/kappler/vol2/treaties/cho0211.htm.

———, ed. "Treaty with the Kaskaskia, 1803." *Indian Affairs: Laws and Treaties.* Vol 2, Treaties. Washington DC: Government Printing Office, 1904. https://dc.library .okstate.edu/digital/collection/kapplers/id/25918/rec/1.

————, ed. "Treaty with the Kiowa and Comanche, 1867." *Indian Affairs: Laws and Treaties*. Vol 2, Treaties. Washington DC: Government Printing Office, 1904. http://digital.library.okstate.edu/kappler/Vol2/treaties/kio0977.htm.

————, ed. "Treaty with the Nisqualli, Puyallup, etc., 1854." *Indian Affairs: Laws and Treaties*. Vol. 2, Treaties. Washington DC: Government Printing Office, 1904. http://digital.library.okstate.edu/kappleR/Vol2/treaties/nis0661.htm#mn5.

————, ed. "Treaty with the Sauk and Foxes, 1804." *Indian Affairs: Laws and Treaties*. Vol 2, Treaties. Washington DC: Government Printing Office, 1904. https://dc .library.okstate.edu/digital/collection/kapplers/id/25925/rec/1.

————, ed. "Treaty with the Six Nations, 1794." *Indian Affairs: Laws and Treaties*. Vol. 2, Treaties. Washington DC: Government Printing Office, 1904. Okstate .edu. http://digital.library.okstate.edu/kappler/vol2/treaties/del0003.htm.

————, ed. "Treaty with the Six Nations, 1794." *Indian Affairs: Laws and Treaties*. Vol. 2, Treaties. Washington DC: Government Printing Office, 1904. Okstate .edu. http://digital.library.okstate.edu/kappler/Vol2/treaties/six0034.htm.

————, ed. "Treaty with the Wea, 1818." *Indian Affairs: Laws and Treaties*. Vol 2, Treaties. Washington DC: Government Printing Office, 1904. https://dc.library .okstate.edu/digital/collection/kapplers/id/26011/rec/1.

————, ed. "Treaty with the Wyandot, Etc., 1789." *Indian Affairs: Laws and Treaties*. Vol 2, Treaties. Washington DC: Government Printing Office, 1904. https://dc .library.okstate.edu/digital/collection/kapplers/id/25869/rec/1.

Kasari, Patricia. *The Impact of Occupational Dislocation: The American Indian Labor Force at the Close of the Twentieth Century*. New York: Garland Publishing, 1999.

"Kastenmeier, Robert William, (1924–2015)." Biographical Directory of the United States Congress. http://bioguide.congress.gov/scripts/biodisplay.pl?index =k000020.

Keller, Leslie M. "Sioux Boys and Girls Learn Cattle Handling." *Clearing House* 20, no. 9 (May 1946): 540–42.

Kelly, Lawrence C. "United States Indian Policies, 1900–1980." In *Handbook of North American Indians*. Vol. 4, *History of Indian-White Relations*, edited by William C. Sturtevant, 66–80. Washington DC: Smithsonian Institution, 1988.

————. "We Talk, You Listen by Vine Deloria." *Arizona and the West* 13, no. 2 (Summer 1971): 194–96.

Kelly, Susan Croce. *Father of Route 66: The Story of Cy Avery*. Norman: University of Oklahoma Press, 2014.

Kennedy, Robert F. "Remarks," September 13, 1963, The U.S. Department of Justice. https://www.justice.gov/sites/default/files/ag/legacy/2011/01/20/09 -13-1963.pdf.

Kenny, Kevin. *Peaceable Kingdom Lost: The Paxton Boys and the Destruction of William Penn's Holy Experiment*. New York: Oxford University Press, 2011.

Kerstetter, Todd. "Spin Doctors at Santee: Missionaries and the Dakota-Language Reporting of the Ghost Dance and Wounded Knee." *Western Historical Quarterly* 28, no. 1 (Spring 1997): 45–67.

Kidwell, Clara Sue. *Choctaws and Missionaries in Mississippi, 1818–1918*. Norman: University of Oklahoma Press, 1995.

Kidwell, Clara Sue, Homer Noley, and George E. Tinker, *A Native American Theology*. Maryknoll NY: Orbis Books, 2001.

Kinsey, W. Fred., III. "Eastern Pennsylvania Prehistory: A Review," *Pennsylvania History*, 50, no. 2 (April 1983): 69–108.

Knack, Martha C., and Omer C. Stewart. *As Long as the River Shall Run: An Ethnohistory of the Pyramid Lake Indian Reservation*. Reno: University of Nevada Press, 1999.

Knight, Gladys L. "Black Manifesto." In *Encyclopedia of American Race Riots*, edited by Walter Rucker and James Nathaniel Upton, 1:40–41. Westport CT: Greenwood Press, 2007.

Krech, Shephard, III. *The Ecological Indian: Myth and History*. New York: W. W. Norton, 2000.

Kroeber, Karl, and Clifton Kroeber, eds. *Ishi in Three Centuries*. Lincoln: University of Nebraska Press, 2003.

Lacy, Michael G. "The United States and American Indians: Political Relations." In *American Indian Policy in the Twentieth Century*, edited by Vine Deloria Jr., 83–104. Norman: University of Oklahoma Press, 1985.

Landry, Alysa. "Today in Native History: Forest Land Returned to Yakama Nation." *Indian Country Today*, May 20, 2017. https://indiancountrymedianetwork.com /history/sacred-places/today-native-history-forest-land-returned-yakama-nation/.

"Langer, William, (1886–1959)." Biographical Directory of the United States Congress. http://bioguide.congress.gov/scripts/biodisplay.pl?index=1000070.

Lawrence, Michael A. *Radicals in Their Own Time: Four Hundred Years of Struggle for Liberty and Equal Justice in America*. New York: Cambridge University Press, 2011.

Lazarus, Edward. *Black Hills, White Justice: The Sioux Nation versus the United States,1775 to the Present*. Lincoln: University of Nebraska Press, 1999.

Leupp, Francis E. *The Indian and His Problem*. New York: C. Scribner's Sons, 1910.

Lincoln, Kenneth. *Indi'n Humor: Bicultural Play in Native America*. New York: Oxford University Press, 1993.

Litwack, Leon F. "'Fight the Power!' The Legacy of the Civil Rights Movement." *Journal of Southern History* 75, no. 1 (February 2009): 10.

Lomawaima, K. Tsianina, and Teresa L. McCarty. "When Tribal Sovereignty Challenges Democracy: American Education and the Democratic Ideal." *American Educational Research Journal* 39, no. 2 (Summer 2002): 279–305.

Luna-Firebaugh, Eileen. *Tribal Policing: Asserting Sovereignty, Seeking Justice*. Tucson: University of Arizona Press, 2007.

Lurie, Nancy O. "Action Anthropology and the American Indian," In *Anthropology and the American Indian: A Symposium*, edited by Rupert Costo, 4–15. San Francisco: The Indian Historian, 1973.

———. "The Voice of the American Indian: Report on the American Indian Chicago Conference." *Current Anthropology* 2, no. 5 (December 1961): 478–500.

———. "The World's Oldest On-Going Protest Demonstration: North American Indian Drinking Patterns." *Pacific Historical Review* 40, no. 3 (August 1971): 311–32.

Lurie, Nancy O., and Stuart Levine, eds. *The American Indian Today* Baltimore: Penguin Books 1968.

Macgregor, Gordon. "Anthropology in Government: United States," *Yearbook of Anthropology* (1955): 421–33.

———. *Warriors without Weapons: A Study of the Society and Personality Development of the Pine Ridge Sioux*. Chicago: University of Chicago Press, 1946.

Mackay, James. "Ethics and Axes: Insider-Outsider Approaches to Native American Literature." In *The Native American Renaissance: Literary Imagination and Achievement*, edited by Alan R. Velie and A. Robert Lee, 39–57. Norman: University of Oklahoma Press, 2013.

Maillard, Kevin Noble. "Parental Ratification: Legal Manifestations of Cultural Authenticity in Cross-Racial Adoption." *American Indian Law Review* 28, no. 1 (2003/2004): 107–40.

Malan, Vernon Duane, and Ernest Lester Schusky. *The Dakota Indian Community: An Analysis of the Non-Ranching Population on the Pine Ridge Reservation*. Brookings SD: Rural Sociology Department, Agricultural Experiment Station, South Dakota State College, 1962.

Marcuse, Herbert. *One-Dimensional Man*. New York: Beacon Press, 1964.

Marino, Cesare. "History of Western Washington Since 1846." *Handbook of North American Indians*. Vol. 7, *Northwest Coast*, edited by *Wayne Suttles*, 175–78. Washington DC: Smithsonian Institution, 1990.

Maroukis, Thomas C. *The Peyote Road: Religious Freedom and the Native American Church*. Norman: University of Oklahoma Press, 2010.

Martin, Kathkeen J., ed. *Indigenous Symbols and Practices in the Catholic Church (Vitality of Indigenous Religions*. Farnham, UK: Ashgate Publishing, 2010.

Martin, Paul S. "The Discovery of America," *Science*, n.s. 179, no. 4077 (March 1973): 969–74.

Martínez, David, ed. *The American Indian Intellectual Tradition: An Anthology of Writings from 1772 to 1972*. Ithaca: Cornell University Press, 2011.

———. "Neither Chief Nor Medicine Man: The Role of the 'Intellectual' in the American Indian Community." *Studies in American Indian Literature* 26, no. 1 (Spring 2014): 29–53.

Martinez, Donna, Grace Sage, and Azusa Ono. *Urban American Indians: Reclaiming Native Space: Reclaiming Native Space*. Santa Barbara CA: ABC-CLIO, 2016.

McCaslin, Wanda D., ed. *Justice as Healing: Indigenous Ways*. Saint Paul MN: Living Justice Press, 2005.

McCool, Daniel. "Indian Voting," In *American Indian Policy in the Twentieth Century*, edited by Vine Deloria Jr. 105–34. Norman: University of Oklahoma, 1985.

McDonald, Laughlin. *American Indians and the Fight for Equal Voting Rights*. Norman: University of Oklahoma Press, 2010.

McFee, Malcolm. "The 150% Man, a Product of Blackfeet Acculturation." *American Anthropologist* 70, no. 6 (December 1968): 1096–107.

McGinnis, Joe. *The Selling of the President, 1968*. New York: Trident Press, 1969.

McKenzie-Jones, Paul R. *Clyde Warrior: Tradition, Community, and Red Power*. Norman: University of Oklahoma Press, 2015.

McKeown, C. Timothy. *In the Smaller Scope of Conscience: The Struggle for National Repatriation Legislation, 1986–1990*. Tucson: University of Arizona Press, 2012.

McKivigan, John, and Mitchell Snay, eds. *Religion and the Antebellum Debate over Slavery*. Athens: University of Georgia Press, 1998.

McNickle, D'Arcy. "Four Years of Indian Organization." *Indians at Work* 5, no. 11 (July 1938): 4–11.

———. "Four Years of Indian Reorganization," In *The American Indian Intellectual Tradition: An Anthology of Writings from 1772 to 1972*, edited by David Martínez, 269–75. Ithaca: Cornell University Press, 2011.

———. *They Came Here First*. Philadelphia: J. P. Lippincott, 1949.

Mead, Margaret. "The American Indian as a Significant Determinant of Anthropological Style." In *Anthropology and the American Indian: A Symposium*, edited by Rupert Costo, 68–74. San Francisco: The Indian Historian, 1973.

Medicine, Beatrice. "Anthropologists and American Indian Studies Programs." In *Anthropology and the American Indian: A Symposium*, edited by Rupert Costo, 75–84. San Francisco: The Indian Historian, 1973.

———. *Drinking and Sobriety among the Lakota Sioux*. New York: AltaMira Press, 2006.

"Menominee Treaties and Treaty Rights." https://www.mpm.edu/wirp/icw-108.html.

Michigan Department of Health and Human Services. "Federally Recognized Tribes in Michigan." http://www.michigan.gov/mdhhs/0,5885,7-339-73971_7209-216627-,00.html.

Mihesuah, Devon A. *American Indians: Stereotypes and Realities*. Atlanta: Clarity, 1996.

Miles, Tiya. "The Narrative of Nancy, a Cherokee Woman." *Frontiers: A Journal of Women Studies*. Intermarriage and North American Indians, 29, nos. 2/3, (2008): 59–80.

"Miller, Arthur Lewis, (1892–1967)." Biographical Directory of the United States Congress. http://bioguide.congress.gov/scripts/biodisplay.pl?index=m000715.

Miller, Darlis A. *Matilda Coxe Stevenson: Pioneering Anthropologist.* Norman: University of Oklahoma Press, 2007.

Miller, Frank C. "Involvement in an Urban University," In *The American Indian in Urban Society,* edited by Jack O. Waddell and O. Michael Watson, 312–42. Boston: Little, Brown and Company,1971.

Miller, Mark Edwin. *Claiming Tribal Identity: The Five Tribes and the Politics of Federal Acknowledgement.* Norman: University of Oklahoma, 2013.

Miller, Robert J. *Reservation "Capitalism": Economic Development in Indian Country.* Santa Barbara CA: Praeger, 2012.

The Mission Indian Federation. "General Description." http://www.juaneno.com /index.php/history/mif-articles.

Mooffett, Thomas C., Rev. "The First Americans—The Indians," *Missionary Review of the World* 42, no. 2 (July 1919): 856–59.

Moore, John H. "The Mvskoke National Question in Oklahoma." *Science and Society* 52, no. 2 (Summer 1988): 163–90.

Morris, Glenn T. "Vine Deloria, Jr., and the Development of a Decolonizing Critique of Indigenous Peoples and International Relations." In *Native Voices: American Indian Identity and Resistance,* edited by Richard A. Grounds, George E. Tinker, and David E. Wilkins, 97–154. Lawrence: University Press of Kansas, 2003.

"Mundt, Karl Earl, (1900–1974)." Biographical Directory of the United States Congress. http://bioguide.congress.gov/scripts/biodisplay.pl?index=m001078.

Nash, Philleo. "Applied Anthropology and the Concept of 'Guided Acculturation' in Indian Administration." In *Anthropology and the American Indian: A Symposium,* edited by Rupert Costo, 23–31. San Francisco: The Indian Historian, 1973.

National Center for Education Statistics. "National Indian Education Study." https:// nces.ed.gov/nationsreportcard/nies/.

National Congress of American Indians. "Mission and History." http://www.ncai .org/about-ncai/mission-history.

National Congress of American Indians, NCAI Governance, "Constitution, Bylaws and Rules of Order." http://www.ncai.org/about-ncai/ncai-governance/constitution -bylaws-rules-of-order.

Native American Church v. Navajo Tribal Council, 272 F 2d 131—Court of Appeals, 10th Circuit 1959. https://scholar.google.com/scholar_case?about=1099206 8009710952686&q=native+american+church+v.+navajo+tribal+council &hl=en&as_sdt=806&as_vis=1.

Native American Rights Fund. "Frequently Asked Questions." http://www.narf.org /frequently-asked-questions/.

Native American Rights Fund. "History of the Native American Rights Fund." http:// www.narf.org/about-us/history/.

Native Lives Matter on Facebook. https://www.facebook.com/artactivistanon/.

"NCAI Supports Indian Health Budget." *NCAI Sentinel Bulletin*10, no. 1 (February–March 1965): 2.

Nelson, Robert M., ed. *A Guide to Native American Studies Programs in the United States and Canada*. https://facultystaff.richmond.edu/~rnelson/asail/guide/guide.html.

Newman, William M. "God Is Red by Vine Deloria, Jr." *Sociological Analysis*. Symposium on Civilizational Complexes and Intercivilizational Encounters, 35, no. 2, (Summer 1974): 152–53.

New Trier High School. http://www.newtrier.k12.il.us.

"Now Is the Time." *NCAI Sentinel Bulletin* 10, no. 1 (February–March 1965): 1.

O'Brien, Sharon. *American Indian Tribal Governments*. Norman: University of Oklahoma Press, 1989.

Officer, James E. "The American Indian and Federal Policy." In *The American Indian in Urban Society*, edited by Jack O. Waddell and O. Michael Watson. 8–65. Boston: Little, Brown and Company, 1971.

———. "Custer Died for Your Sins: An Indian Manifesto by Vine Deloria." *Arizona and the West* 12, no. 3 (Autumn 1970): 292–94.

Officer, James E., and Francis McKinley. Preface to *Anthropology and the American Indian: A Symposium*. edited by Rupert Costo, xi–xvi. San Francisco: The Indian Historian, 1973.

"O'Mahoney, Joseph Christopher, (1884–1962)." Biographical Directory of the United States Congress. http://bioguide.congress.gov/scripts/biodisplay.pl?index=0000088.

Ortiz, Alfonso. "Custer Died for Your Sins: An Indian Manifesto," *American Anthropologist* 73, no. 4 (August 1971): 953–55.

———. "An Indian Anthropologist's Perspective on Anthropology." In *Anthropology and the American Indian: A Symposium*, edited by Rupert Costo, 85–92. San Francisco: The Indian Historian, 1973.

"Our Other Brothers," *NCAI Sentinel Bulletin* 12, no. 5 (Late Winter 1967).

Owens, Robert M. *Red Dreams, White Nightmares: Pan-Indian Alliances in the Anglo-American Mind, 1763-1815*. Norman: University of Oklahoma Press, 2015.

Pandey, Triloki Nath. "Anthropologists at Zuni." *Proceedings of the American Philosophical Society* 116, no. 4 (August 15, 1972): 321–37.

Parker, Arthur C. "The Legal Status of the American Indian." In *The American Indian Intellectual Tradition: An Anthology of Writings from 1772 to 1972*, edited by David Martínez, 198–202. Ithaca: Cornell University Press, 2011.

Parker, Dorothy R. *Singing an Indian Song: A Biography of D'Arcy McNickle*. Lincoln: University of Nebraska Press, 1992.

Pavlik, Steve and Daniel R. Wildcat. *Destroying Dogma: Vine Deloria Jr. and His Influence on American Society*. Golden CO: Fulcrum Publishing, 2006.

Peroff, Nicholas C. *Menominee Drums: Tribal Termination and Restoration, 1954–1974*. Norman: University of Oklahoma Press, 1982.

Pesantubbee, Michelene E. "Beyond Domesticity: Choctaw Women Negotiating the Tension between Choctaw Culture and Protestantism." *Journal of the American Academy of Religion* 67, no. 2 (June 1999): 387–409.

Peterson, Helen L. "American Indian Political Participation." In *The American Indian Intellectual Tradition: An Anthology of Writings from 1772 to 1972*, edited by David Martínez, 290–303. Ithaca: Cornell University Press, 2011.

Pfeffer, Jeffrey, and Anthony Leong. "Resource Allocations in United Funds: Examination of Power and Dependence." *Social Forces* 55, no. 3 (March 1977): 775–90.

Philip, Kenneth R. "Termination: A Legacy of the Indian New Deal." *Western Historical Quarterly* 14, no. 2 (April 1983): 165–80.

Phillips, Ruth B. *Trading Identities: The Souvenir in Native North American Art from the Northeast, 1700–1900*. Seattle: University of Washington Press, 1999.

Pinel, Sandra Lee. "Culture and Cash: How Two New Mexico Pueblos Combined Culture and Development," *Alternatives: Global, Local, Political*. The Political Economy of Development in Indigenous Communities, 32, no. 1 (January-March 2007): 9–39.

Pinkney, Alphonso. *Red, Black, and Green: Black Nationalism in the United States*. New York: Cambridge University Press, 1979.

Polgar, Steven. "Biculturation of Mesquakie Teenage Boys." *American Anthropologist* 62, no. 2 (April 1960): 217–35.

"Poor People's Campaign (December 4, 1967–June 19, 1968)." Blackpast.org, http://www.blackpast.org/aah/poor-peoples-campaign-december-4-1967-june-19-1968.

Powell, Peter J. *Sweet Medicine*. 2 vols. Norman: University of Oklahoma Press, 1969.

Presbyterian Historical Society, the National Archives of the PC(USA). "Guide to the Missionary Education Movement of the United States and Canada Records," section "Biographical Note/Administrative History": https://www.history.pcusa.org/collections/research-tools/guides-archival-collections/ncc-rg-20.

"President Johnson Tells 100 Indian White House Visitors of Attack on Poverty," *NCAI Sentinel Bulletin* 9, no. 1 (February-March 1964).

Price, John A. "The Migration and Adaptation of American Indians to Los Angeles." In *The Emergent Native Americans: A Reader in Culture Contact*, edited by Deward E. Walker Jr. 728–38. Boston: Little, Brown and Company, 1972.

Prucha, Francis Paul. *American Indian Treaties: The History of a Political Anomaly*. Berkeley: University of California, 1994.

———. *The Great Father: The United States Government and the American Indians*, abridged edition. Lincoln: University of Nebraska Press, 1984.

Putnam, Robert D. *Bowling Alone: The Collapse and Revival of American Community*. New York: Touchstone Books, 2001.

Quinn, William W., Jr. "Federal Acknowledgment of American Indian Tribes: The Historical Development of a Legal Concept," *American Journal of Legal History* 34, no. 4 (October 1990): 331–64.

Ragsdale, Fred L., Jr. "The Deception of Geography." In *American Indian Policy in the Twentieth Century*, edited by Vine Deloria Jr., 63–82. Norman: University of Oklahoma Press, 1992.

Ray, Celeste, ed. *The New Encyclopedia of Southern Culture: Ethnicity*. Chapel Hill: University of North Carolina Press, 2007.

"Reber, John, (1858–1931)." Biographical Directory of the United States Congress. http://bioguide.congress.gov/scripts/biodisplay.pl?index=r000102.

Redfield, Robert. "The Folk Society." *American Journal of Sociology* 52, no. 4 (1947): 293–308.

———. *The Folk Culture of the Yucatan*. Chicago: University of Chicago Press, 1941.

———. *A Village That Chose Progress: Chan Kom Revisited*. Chicago: University of Chicago Press, 1970.

Reich, Charles A. *The Greening of America*. New York: Random House, 1970.

———. "The New Property." *Yale Law Journal* 73, no. 5 (April 1964): 733–87.

Reinhart, Akim D. *Ruling Pine Ridge: Oglala Lakota Politics from the IRA to Wounded Knee*. Lubbock: Texas Tech University Press, 2007.

Report of the Annual Lake Mohonk Conference on the Indian and Other Dependent Peoples. HeinOnline. https://home.heinonline.org/titles/History-of-International-Law/Report-of-the-Annual-Lake-Mohonk-Conference-on-the-Indian-and-Other-Dependent-Peoples/?letter=R.

Reyes, Maria de la Luz, and John J. Halcón. "Early Bilingual Programs, 1960s." In *Encyclopedia of Bilingual Education*, edited by Josué M. González, 236–37. Los Angeles: Sage, (2008).

Reynolds, Jerry. "Remembering Robert F. Kennedy." *Indian Country Today*, May 23, 2008. http://indiancountrytodaymedianetwork.com/2008/05/23/remembering-robert-f-kennedy-79350.

Rife, James P., and Allan J. Dellapenna. *Caring and Curing: A History of the Indian Health Service*. Landover MD: PHS Commissioned Officers Foundation for the Advancement of Public Health, 2009.

Rifkin, Mark. *Settler Common Sense: Queerness and Everyday Colonialism in the American Renaissance*. Minneapolis: University of Minnesota Press, 2014.

———. *When Did Indians Become Straight?: Kinship, the History of Sexuality, and Native Sovereignty*. New York: Oxford University Press, 2011.

Rivera, Brooklyn. "Living History: Inauguration of the 'International Year of the World's Indigenous People'; December 10, 1992, General Assembly of the United Nations, Plenary, 82nd meeting and special ceremony," *Transnational Law and Contemporary Problems* 3, no. 1, (1993): 165–222.

Rockwell, Stephen J. *Indian Affairs and the Administrative State in the Nineteenth Century*. New York: Cambridge University Press, 2010.

Roemer, Kenneth M. "Custer Died for Your Sins: An Indian Manifesto by Vine Deloria." *American Quarterly* 22, no. 2, Part 2 (Summer 1970): 273.

Rosier, Paul C. "Native American Treaty Rights." In *Native American Issues*, 31–60. Greenwood CT: Greenwood Press, 2003.

Rosten, Leo, ed. *Religions of America: Ferment and Faith in an Age of Crisis*. New York: Simon & Schuster, 1975.

Royster, Judith. "Indian Land Claims." *Handbook of North American Indians*. Vol 2, *Indians in Contemporary Society*, edited by William C. Sturtevant, 28–37. Washington DC: Smithsonian Institution, 2008.

Ruby, Robert H., and John A. Brown. *Esther Ross, Stillaguamish Champion*. Norman: University of Oklahoma, 2001.

Said, Edward W. *Representations of the Intellectual*. New York: Random House, 1996.

Sando, Joe S. *Pueblo Nations: Eight Centuries of Pueblo Indian History*. Santa Fe: Clear Light Publishers, 1992.

Satz, Ronald N. *American Indian Policy in the Jacksonian Era*. Norman: University of Oklahoma Press, 2002.

——. "Cherokee Traditionalism, Protestant Evangelism, and the Trail of Tears, Part II." *Tennessee Historical Quarterly* 44, no. 4 (Winter 1985): 380–401.

Scheiber, Sylvester J., and John B. Shoven. *The Real Deal: The History and Future of Social Security*. New Haven: Yale University Press, 1999.

Schulze, Jeffrey M. "The Rediscovery of the Tiguas: Federal Recognition and Indianness in the Twentieth Century." *Southwestern Historical Quarterly* 105, no. 1 (July 2001): 14–39.

"Schwabe, George Blaine, (1886–1952)."Biographical Directory of the United States Congress. http://bioguide.congress.gov/scripts/biodisplay.pl?index=s000155.

Shepherd, Jeffrey P. *We Are an Indian Nation: A History of the Hualapai People*. Tucson: University of Arizona Press, 2010.

Shreve, Bradley G. "'From Time Immemorial': The Fish-In Movement and the Rise of Intertribal Activism," *Pacific Historical Review* 78, no. 3 (August 2009): 403–34.

——. *Red Power Rising: The National Indian Youth Council and the Origins of Native Activism*. Norman: University of Oklahoma Press, 2011.

Shuffelton, Frank. "Indian Devils and Pilgrim Fathers: Squanto, Hobomok, and the English Conception of Indian Religion." *New England Quarterly* 49, no. 1 (March 1976): 108–16.

Sleeper-Smith, Susan, ed. *Rethinking the Fur Trade: Cultures of Exchange in an Atlantic World*. Lincoln: University of Nebraska, 2009.

Smith, Linda Tuhiwai. *Decolonizing Methodologies: Research and Indigenous Peoples*. London: Zed Books, 1999.

Smith, Paul Chaat. *Everything You Know about Indians Is Wrong*. Minneapolis: University of Minnesota Press, 2009.

Smith, Paul Chaat, and Robert Allen Warrior. *Like a Hurricane: The Indian Movement from Alcatraz to Wounded Knee*. New York: New Press, 1996.

Smith, Sherry L. *Hippies, Indians and the Fight for Red Power*. New York: Oxford University Press, 2012.

Smock, Raymond W. *Booker T. Washington: Black Leadership in the Age of Jim Crow*. Chicago: Ivan R. Dee, 2009.

Sonnichsen, C. L. *The Mescalero Apaches*. Norman: University of Oklahoma Press, 1973.

Spang, Alonzo T. "Understanding the Indian." *Personnel and Guidance Journal* 50, no. 2 (October 1971): 97–102.

Speroff, Leon. *Carlos Montezuma, MD: A Yavapai American Hero—The Life and Times of an American Indian, 1866-1923*. Portland OR: Arnica Publishing, 2003.

Springhall, John. *Decolonization Since 1945: The Collapse of European Overseas Empires*. New York: Palgrave, 2001.

Standing Bear, Luther. *Land of the Spotted Eagle*. New York: Houghton Mifflin, 1933.

State Historical Society of North Dakota. *Collections of the State Historical Society of North Dakota*, Vol. 1. Bismarck ND: Tribune, State Printers and Binders, 1906.

———. "Robert F. Kennedy at National Congress of American Indians Meeting," YouTube: https://www.youtube.com/watch?v=r7ax18irurw.

State Museum of Pennsylvania (formerly the William Penn Memorial Museum). Susquehannock Artifacts. http://www.statemuseumpa.org/archc.html.

Steiner, Stan. *The New Indians*. New York: Harper & Row, 1968.

Stewart, Omer C. "Anthropologists as Expert Witnesses for Indians: Claims and Peyote Cases." In *Anthropology and the American Indian: A Symposium*. edited by Rupert Costo, 35–42. San Francisco: The Indian Historian, 1973.

———. "The Native American Church and the Law." In *The Emergent Native Americans: A Reader in Culture Contact*, edited by Deward E. Walker. Boston: Little Brown, 1972.

Sugden, John. *Tecumseh: A Life*. New York: Henry Holt, 1998.

Tahmahkera, Dustin. *Tribal Television: Viewing Native People in Sitcoms*. Chapel Hill: University of North Carolina Press, 2014.

Talamantez, Inés. "Transforming American Conceptions about Native America: Vine Deloria, Jr., Critic and Coyote," In *Native Voices: American Indian Identity and Resistance*, edited by Richard A. Grounds, George E. Tinker, and David E. Wilkins, 273–89. Lawrence: University Press of Kansas, 2003.

Talayesva, Don C. *Sun Chief: The Autobiography of a Hopi Indian*. New Haven: Yale University Press, 1942.

Thomas, Robert K. "Colonialism: Classic and Internal" (1969), *Selected Works of Robert K. Thomas*: https://works.bepress.com/robert_thomas/26/.

————. "Pan-Indianism," In *The Emergent Native Americans: A Reader in Culture Contact*, edited by Deward E. Walker Jr. 739–46. New York: Little, Brown and Company, 1972.

Tinker, George E. *Missionary Conquest: The Gospel and Native American Cultural Genocide.* Minneapolis, Fortress Press, 1993.

————. "Walking in the Shadow of Greatness: Vine Deloria Jr. in Retrospect." *Wicazo Sa Review* 21, no. 2 (Autumn 2006): 167–77.

Toledo v. Pueblo De Jemez, 119 F. Supp. 429 (DNM 1954): http://law.justia.com/cases /federal/district-courts/fsupp/119/429/2147686/.

Trafzer, Clifford E., Jean A. Keller, and Lorene Sisquoc, eds. *Boarding School Blues: Revisiting American Indian Educational Experiences*. Lincoln: University of Nebraska, 2006.

Trahant, Mark N. *The Last Great Battle of the Indian Wars: Henry M. Jackson, Forrest J. Gerard and the Campaign for the Self-Determination of America's Indian Tribes.* Ft. Hall ID: The Cedars Group, 2010.

Treat, James, ed. Introduction to *For This Land: Writings on Religion in America*, 1–18. New York: Routledge, 1999.

————, ed. *Native and Christian: Indigenous Voices on Religious Identity in the United States and Canada*. New York: Routledge, 1996.

————, ed. "Tradition and Community," In *Native and Christian: Indigenous Voices on Religious Identity in the United States and Canada*, 157–205. New York: Routledge, 1996.

Treuer, Anton. *Everything You Wanted to Know about Indians But Were Afraid to Ask.* St Paul: Borealis Books, 2012.

————. *Ojibwe in Minnesota.* St. Paul: Minnesota Historical Society Press, 2010.

Trillin, Calvin. "Resurrection City." *New Yorker*, June 15, 1968.

Trosper, Ronald L. "American Indian Poverty on Reservations." In *Changing Numbers, Changing Needs: American Indian Demography and Public Health*, edited by Gary D. Sandefur, Ronald R. Rindfuss, and Barney Cohen, 172–95. Washington, DC: National Academy Press, 1996.

Ture, Kwame (formerly Stokely Carmichael), and Charles V. Hamilton. *Black Power: Politics of Liberation in America*. New York: Random House, 1967.

tv.com. The Merv Griffin Show. "Season 7, Episode 106, January 14, 1970." http:// www.tv.com/shows/the-merv-griffin-show/january-14-1970-1557178/.

"22nd Annual Convention in November." *NCAI Sentinel Bulletin* 10, no. 4 (1965).

Tyler, Hamilton A. *Pueblo Gods and Myths.* Norman: University of Oklahoma Press, 1972.

Underhill, Ruth M. *Red Man's America: A History of Indians in the United States.* Chicago: University of Chicago Press, 1973.

————. *Red Man's Religion: Beliefs and Practices of the Indians North of Mexico.* Chicago: University of Chicago Press, 1965.

United Scholarship Service. Denver CO, Annual Report of the United Scholarship Service, Inc., 1969. http://eric.ed.gov/?id=ed043422.

United States Department of Justice. https://www.justice.gov/sites/default/files /ag/legacy/2011/01/20/09-13-1963.pdf.

University of Iowa Libraries. Special Collections and University Archives. "Marshall B. McKusick Papers." http://www.lib.uiowa.edu/scua/archives/guides/rg99 .0028.html.

Urban Indian Coalition of Arizona (UICAZ). Phoenix Indian Center. http:// phxindcenter.com/community-engagement/urban-indian-coalition/.

U.S. Government Accountability Office. "Indian Issues: Federal Funding for Non-Federally Recognized Tribes." http://www.gao.gov/products/GAO-12-348.

U.S. Senate. "Legislation, Laws, and Acts." https://www.senate.gov/legislative /common/briefing/leg_laws_acts.htm.

Utley, Robert M. *Custer and Me: A Historian's Memoir*. Norman: University of Oklahoma Press, 2004.

———. "Wounded Knee, Battle of (1890)." In *The Oxford Companion to American Military History*, edited by John Whiteclay Chambers II, 837. New York: Oxford University Press, 1999.

Vaughan, Alden T. *New England Frontier: Puritans and Indians, 1620–1675*. Norman: University of Oklahoma Press, 1994.

Vitaliano, Dorothy B. "The Impact of Geologic Events on History and Legend with Special Reference to Atlantis," *Journal of the Folklore Institute* 5, no. 1 (June 1968): 5–30.

Vogel, Ezra F. *Japan as Number One: Lessons for America*. New York: Harper Colophon, 1979.

Voltaire. "Philosophical Dictionary." *The Portable Voltaire*, edited by Ben Ray Redman. New York: Viking Press, 1968.

Vondall-Rieke, Monique. "How 'Black Lives Matter' Can Help Indians," *Indian Country Today Media Network*, May 13, 2015. http://indiancountrytodaymedianetwork .com/2015/05/13/how-black-lives-matter-can-help-indians.

Wahrhaftig, Albert L. "Institution Building among Oklahoma's Traditional Cherokees." In *Four Centuries of Southern Indians*, edited by Charles M. Hudson, 132–47. Athens: University of Georgia Press, 2007.

Wallace Adams, David. *Education for Extinction: American Indians and the Boarding School Experience, 1875–1928*. Lawrence: University Press of Kansas, 1995.

Warrior, Clyde. "Which One Are You? Five Types of Young Indians." *ABC: Americans Before Columbus* 2, no. 4 (December 1964): 1–3.

Warrior, Robert Allen. *Tribal Secrets: Recovering American Indian Intellectual Traditions*. Minneapolis: University of Minnesota Press, 1994.

Washburn, Kevin K. "American Indians, Crime, and the Law." *Michigan Law Review* 104, no. 4 (February 2006): 709–77.

Washington, Booker T. *Up from Slavery: An Autobiography of Booker T. Washington.* Garden City NY: Doubleday & Company, 1901.

"Watkins, Arthur Vivian, (1886–1973)." Biographical Directory of the United States Congress. http://bioguide.congress.gov/scripts/biodisplay.pl?index=w000190.

Watkins, Arthur Vivian. *Enough Rope: The Inside Story of the Censure of Senator Joe McCarthy by his Colleagues.* Englewood Cliffs NJ: Prentice-Hall, 1969.

Wax, Murray L. "Educating an Anthro: The Influence of Vine Deloria, Jr." In *Indians and Anthropologists: Vine Deloria Jr. and the Critique of Anthropology,* edited by Thomas Biolsi and Larry J. Zimmerman, 50–60. Tucson: University of Arizona Press, 1997.

Weaver, Jace. *That the People Might Live: Native American Literatures and Native American Community.* New York: Oxford University Press, 1997.

Weber, Max. "Bureaucracy and Legitimate Authority." In *The Sociology of Organizations: Classic, Contemporary, and Critical Readings,* edited by Michael J. Handel, 17–23. Thousand Oaks CA: Sage Publications, 2003.

"We DO Have the Power to Make the Difference between the Winner and the Loser in the 1972 Election." *NCAI Sentinel Bulletin* (Winter 1972).

Weibel-Orlando, Joan. "Urban Communities." In *Handbook of North American Indians,* Vol. 2, *Indians in Contemporary Society,* edited by William C. Sturtevent, 308–16. Washington DC: Smithsonian, 2008.

Wells, Merle. "We Talk, You Listen: New Tribes, New Turf by Vine Deloria." *Pacific Northwest Quarterly* 63, no. 4 (October 1972): 172.

Wells, Merle W. "An Indian Manifesto: An Essay Review." *Pacific Northwest Quarterly* 61, no. 3 (July 1970): 162–64.

"Which Way Indians?" *NCAI Sentinel Bulletin* 12, no. 1 (Winter 1966).

White, Richard. *The Middle Ground: Indians, Empires, and Republics in the Great Lakes Region, 1650–1815.* New York: Cambridge University Press, 1991.

White, Theodore H. *The Making of the President, 1960.* New York: Atheneum Publishers, 1961.

Whyte, William H., Jr. *The Organization Man.* New York: Simon & Schuster, 1956.

Why Treaties Matter. "US-American Indian Treaties in Minnesota." http://treatiesmatter.org/exhibit/welcome/u-s-american-indian-treaties-in-minnesota/.

Wilkins, David E. "Forging a Political, Educational, and Cultural Agenda for Indian Country: Common Sense Recommendations Gleaned from Deloria's Prose." In *Destroying Dogma: Vine Deloria Jr. and His Influence on American Society,* edited by Steve Pavlik and Daniel R. Wildcat. Golden CO: Fulcrum Publishing, 2006): 157–204.

——. "Vine Deloria Jr. and Indigenous Americans," *Wicazo Sa Review* 21, no. 2 (Autumn 2006): 151–55.

Wilkins, David E., and Heidi Kiiwetinepinesiik Stark. *American Indian Politics and the American Political System.* New York: Rowan & Littlefield, 2011.

Wilkinson, Charles. *Blood Struggle: The Rise of Modern Indian Nations.* New York: W. W. Norton, 2005.

Williams, Hettie V. *We Shall Overcome to We Shall Overrun: The Collapse of the Civil Rights Movement and the Black Power Revolt (1962–1968).* Lanham MD: University Press of America, 2009.

Williams, Walter L., ed. *Southeastern Indians Since the Removal Era.* Athens: University of Georgia, 1979.

Wise, Jennings C. *The Red Man in the New World Drama: The Great Classic of the Political and Legal History of the American Indian,* revised and edited and with an introduction by Vine Deloria Jr. New York: Macmillan Company, 1971.

Witt, Shirley Hill. "Nationalistic Trends among American Indians." *Midcontinent American Studies Journal.* The Indian Today, 6, no. 2 (Fall 1965): 51–74.

Wrone, David R. "The Economic Impact of the 1837 and 1842 Chippewa Treaties." *American Indian Quarterly* 17, no. 3 (Summer 1993): 329–40.

Wub-e-ke-niew. *We Have the Right to Exist: A Translation of Aboriginal Indigenous Thought: The First Book Ever Published from an Ahnishinahbæótjibway Perspective.* New York: Black Thistle Press, 1995). http://www.maquah.net/We_Have_The _Right_To_Exist/WeHaveTheRight_00cover.html.

Zimmerman, William, Jr. "The Role of the Bureau of Indian Affairs Since 1933." In *The Western American Indian: Case Studies,* edited by Richard N. Ellis, 152–64. Lincoln: University of Nebraska Press, 1972.

INDEX

VD = Vine Deloria Jr.

AAA (American Anthropological Association), 13–14, 186, 201, 206–9, 381n89
AAIA (Association on American Indian Affairs), 274–75
Abernathy, Ralph, 159–60, 283, 318
Abourezk, James, 358n117
academic institutions: American Indian/Native American studies, 4, 34, 37, 43, 182, 208, 315; ethnic studies, 136, 138, 268, 288; improvements in, 334; Indian faculty at, 202; IRBs of, 182, 204; lack of Indian scholars, 194; needed research agenda changes, 203. *See also* anthropology; education; social science
Acheson, Dean, 189
action anthropology, 189, 207, 377n37
Adams, Hank (Sioux-Assiniboine), 26, 61, 133, 153, 165, 190–91, 215, 285, 342n26, 373n80
Adams, John Quincy, 94

Adams, Richard C., 175–76
Africans and Native Americans (Forbes), 143
agriculture, 98, 214–15
AIM (American Indian Movement), 9, 35, 43, 132, 161, 178, 228, 238, 291–92, 315, 369n22
Akers, Dolly, 345n17
Akwesasne Notes, 73, 128–29, 273, 397n94
Alcatraz Island occupation (1969–71), 3, 9, 43, 140, 160, 286–87, 289–90, 312–13, 397n94
alcoholism (stereotype), 192–94, 378n48, 378n51
Aleck, Allen (Pyramid Lake Paiute), 345n17, 399n1
Alexander VI (pope), 224–25
"All-American Platoon" theory of diversity, 278
Allotment Act (1887), 87, 97–99, 147, 199–200, 214, 226, 357n90

439

American Anthropological Association
(AAA), 13–14, 186, 201, 206–9,
381n89
American Indian Higher Education
Consortium, 334
American Indian Movement (AIM), 9,
35, 43, 132, 161, 178, 228, 238, 291–
92, 315, 369n22
American Indian/Native American
studies, 4, 34, 37, 43, 182, 208, 315
American Indians, American Justice
(Deloria and Lytle), 36, 335
American Indians United, 326–27
American Indian Treaties (Prucha), 69, 95
Americans for Indian Opportunity, 280
Amherst, Lord Jeffrey, 111
Amherst (VA) Cherokee community,
378n45
"ancient astronaut" theory, 31
Ancient Society (Morgan), 199
Anderson, Clinton, 258
Anderson, Wallace "Mad Bear" (Tuscarora), 238
anthropology: action anthropology,
189, 207, 377n37; colonization in
theories of, 182, 183, 188–94, 209;
"drunken Indian" theories, 192–94;
exceptions to VD's criticisms of,
183–85; "hoarded wealth" theories,
195–96; impact of VD's critique on,
13–14, 36, 375n17; impact on federal
Indian policy, 186–87, 195–96,
200–202, 380n70; Indian scholars
in, 188, 202; and IRBs, 204; lack of
Indian participation, 187–88, 201–2;
and Native American studies, 208;
pan-Indianism theories of, 309–10;
paternalism of, 56; researcher-tribal
relations, 203–4, 207–8; responding
to VD's criticism, 31–33, 206–9;

and termination policy, 202–3;
and tribal names, 245; and tribal
privacy rights, 237; VD's ahistorical
approach to, 185; VD's generalizations regarding, 187; wastefulness
of, 201; "weaponless warriors"
theory, 197–99. *See also* archeology;
social science
"Anthropology and the American
Indian" (symposium), 186, 206–9
Apache tribes, 62, 192
Apess, William, 52
archeology: early human history in,
336; grave desecrations, 177–81;
presumed "Indian expert" knowledge of, 32, 51, 176; in *Red Earth,
White Lies,* 31, 348n68. *See also*
anthropology
Area Redevelopment Act (1961), 253
Arendt, Hannah, 108
Arizona State University, 204
assimilation, 51–54, 87, 133, 144–45, 150,
153, 162–63, 164, 170, 187, 276, 330
Association on American Indian Affairs
(AAIA), 274–75
Augustana College (Rock Island IL),
19, 211–12

Banks, Dennis, 283
Banyacya, Thomas (Hopi), 238–39,
385nn63–64
Baptist denomination, 240
Bates, Denise, 50, 134, 137–38, 311
Beard, Dewey, 236
Behind the Trail of Broken Treaties
(Deloria): on the Alcatraz occupa-
tion, 289–90; Doctrine of Discovery
analysis, 71, 72, 78, 222; on the
Indian Civil Rights Act, 301; Indian
protest movement portrayed in, 49,

130, 217, 312–15; on land appropriations, 196–97; on land claims, 130;
legal agenda proposed in, 130; on
limitations of direct action, 319;
plenary power analysis, 85–86, 92;
proposed reforms in, 324; in the
Red Power Tetralogy, 14; rejection
of white values in, 302; reviews of,
2, 35, 72–73; on self-determination,
130; significance of, 43; on treaty
violations, 91–93, 228–29; tribal-
federal relations, 54, 161; on tribal
sovereignty, 63–64, 75, 82, 107, 269–
70; urban Indians portrayed in, 61,
312–15; VD's Judeo-Christian vision
in, 148; on white subversives, 74; on
Wounded Knee protest, 130, 228–29
Belafonte, Harry, 155
Belindo, John (Navajo/Kiowa), 24, 110,
284, 397n100
Bellecourt, Clyde (White Earth
Ojibwe), 178
Bender, George H., 118, 362n39
Bennett, Robert (Oneida), 257, 259,
312, 333, 341n22, 389n23
Bentz, Marilyn, 32
Berry, E. Y., 119, 363n50
BIA (Bureau of Indian Affairs). *See*
Bureau of Indian Affairs (BIA)
Billison, Samuel (Navajo), 333
Biolsi, Thomas, 31–33, 381n89
Blackbird, Andrew J. (Odawa), 176
Black Power (Ture and Hamilton),
164–65
Black Power movement: connections
to Indian activism, 133, 135, 154;
impact of coalitions on, 164–65;
impact on urban Indians, 318;
Indian perspectives on, 159–60;
leadership of, 265; militancy of,

158, 163; nationalism in, 154, 164;
reparation demands of, 151–52; and
tribalism, 138, 164; VD's criticism
of, 158, 303–4; VD's proposals
for, 163–65. *See also* civil rights
movement
Black-white relations: and coalitions,
164–65; compared to Indian-white,
52, 145, 149–50; as dominant
paradigm, 134; intensity of divide,
136–37. *See also* civil rights
movement
Blakeney, Dean, 231
"blanket Indians," 187
Blatchford, Herb (Navajo), 190, 333
"blood quantum" controversy, 143–44
Blount, Avery M., 115
boarding schools, 167, 187
Board of Indian Commissioners, 223, 230
Boas, Franz, 208
Boek, Jean K., 44–45, 135
Boldt Decision (1974), 63, 285
Book of the Hopi (Waters), 239
Boudinot, Elias (Cherokee), 144–45
Brokaw, Tom, 388n16
Broken Treaties (Deloria). See *Behind
the Trail of Broken Treaties* (Deloria)
Bronson, Ruth, 189
Brown, Dee, 2, 49, 135, 227
Buffalohead, W. Roger (Ponca), 2, 4, 333
Bureau of American Ethnology,
200–201
Bureau of Indian Affairs (BIA):
ambivalent role of, 263; anthropo-
logical meeting sponsored by, 186;
budget challenges, 252–53, 258–59;
bureaucratic nature of, 53, 108–9,
250, 254–56; civilizing experiments
of, 167; under Collier, 103; Congress
proposing abolition of, 114; control

Bureau of Indian Affairs (*cont.*)
over reservations, 79, 166, 249;
creation of, 96, 357n87; criticisms of,
118–19, 250–52, 253–58; decision-
making processes in, 252–53; and
health care, 111; historical Christian
leadership in, 54; Indian-preference
hiring, 101; Indian workforce in, 249;
and the MIF, 361n24; missionizing
policy of, 237; organization of, 250,
252–53; placed in the Department of
Interior, 248; point 4 program, 188–
90; proposed departmental move,
389n29; reforms within, 99–100,
248, 249–50, 387n2; regulations for
tribal recognition, 249, 315, 359n117;
and the "returned student" problem,
187; social services provided by,
257–58; suppressing tribal customs,
225–27, 271; during termination,
257–58; Trail of Broken Treaties
occupation of, 72, 73, 86, 160, 161,
217, 277, 312, 313, 331; trust obligations, 90–91, 248, 250, 251–52,
256–57; unpredictability in, 105;
and urban Indians, 314–18; VD's
proposed reforms for, 253, 258, 261–
63, 316–18, 324–25; white supporters
of Indians in, 275. *See also* federal
Indian law and policy
Burke Act (1906), 87, 98
Burnett, Robert (Rosebud Sioux), 20,
369n21
Bursum Bill (1922), 99–100
Bury My Heart at Wounded Knee
(Brown), 49, 135, 227
Byler, Mary (Cherokee), 333

Calhoun, John C., 94
capitalism, 295, 329, 343n31

Carlos, John, 145
Carmichael, Stokely (Kwame Ture),
154, 164–65, 391n40
Cass, Lewis, 95
Castillo, Adam (Cahuilla), 115–16
Catholic Church, 146, 210, 232. *See also*
Christianity
Cavett, Dick, 340n8
CCAP (Citizens' Crusade against Pov-
erty), 195–96
CDC (Community Development Corpo-
ration) programs, 156, 293
Chaat Smith, Paul, 283–84, 290, 291
Chapman, William, 136
Chariots of the Gods (Däniken), 31
Chasing Hawk, Alex (Cheyenne River
Sioux), 64, 352n48
Cherokee Nation, 76, 79, 88–89, 144–45;
Amherst (VA) community, 378n45;
Cherokee descent claims, 50; *Chero-
kee Nation v. Georgia,* 22, 90, 92; and
the Hopewell Treaty, 79, 81, 354n29;
Worcester v. Georgia, 76, 79
Cherokee Nation v. Georgia, 22, 90, 92
Chief Joseph's People (Josephy), 4
Chino, Wendell (Mescalero Apache),
21, 192, 314
Chippewa tribe, 95–96, 356n83
Choate, Robert, 393n75
Choctaw Nation, 94–95
Christensen, Rosemary (Chippewa), 333
Christianity: among the Five Civilized
Tribes, 240; and the civil rights
movement, 172, 341n20, 382n18;
colonizing role of, 146, 215–17,
220, 222–23, 224–25; compared
to Indigenous beliefs, 213–14,
217–20; compared to tribalism,
244; creation story, 217, 218–19;
denominational competition, 246;

distinction between church and state, 220; eccentric denominations, 231–32; future of, 239–40, 245–47; hybridization of, 237; hypocrisy of, 230–31; impacted by American values, 232; impact on federal Indian policy, 222; and the Indian Bureau, 54; and the Indian protest movement, 341n20; and land seizures, 70–71; prejudices within, 241–42; scholarly reaction to VD's commentary on, 33–34; time-based linear worldview of, 30, 215, 218; VD's discontent with, 33, 211–12; VD's proposed reforms for, 42, 240–42, 245–46. *See also* churches; missionaries

Church, Frank, 121–22, 358n101, 364n56

churches: abuse within, 386n74; Black Power seeking reparations from, 151–52; in the civil rights movement, 164–65, 246; Indian leadership in, 233, 240–42; in the Indian protest movement, 126, 242–43; relations between tribes and, 139–40; role in governing reservations, 53; VD's discontent with, 211–12; VD's proposed reforms for, 240–42. *See also* Christianity

"The Churches and Cultural Change" (Deloria), 139, 140

Churchill, Ward, 34–35, 36, 42

Citizen's Board of Inquiry, 198–99

Citizens' Crusade against Poverty (CCAP), 195–96

citizenship, 86–88, 92–93, 98, 112, 133–34, 350n24

civilization (WASP ideal): missionaries' goal of, 221, 230; relation to Christian values, 222; rules of development, 200, 205; social engineering experiments, 167; through forced assimilation, 52–53

Civil Rights Act, 129, 145, 157–58, 287

civil rights movement: Christianity in, 172, 341n20, 382n18; fragmentation of, 172; impact of coalitions on, 164–65; impact of youth on, 191; impact on WASP ideal, 173; Indian participation in, 137–38, 141, 153–60; and the Indian protest movement, 133–34, 137–38, 142–43, 153–60, 228; leadership of, 265; March on Washington DC, 141, 155; militancy in, 304; objectives of, 145, 159–60; "People's Park" protest, 289; Poor People's Campaign, 58, 133, 153, 154–55, 157, 158, 159–60, 165, 318; race riots, 136–37, 158, 159, 163, 372n57; and racialized politics, 50; reparation demands of, 151–52; results of, 287; tactics of, 289; VD's tacit amenability to, 155–56. *See also* Black Power movement

Cohen, Felix, 275

Cohen, Roger, 74

Collier, Donald, 181

Collier, John, 67, 74, 92, 99–103, 105, 113, 114, 126, 235, 263, 361n24. *See also* Indian Reorganization Act (1934)

Colliflower v. Garland (1965), 90

colonialism: and anthropology, 205, 209; and appropriation of Indigenous history, 179; challenging mythology of, 15; role of Christianity in, 215–17; Thomas's analysis of, 343n32; violating indigenous homelands, 146–47

341n22; on decolonization, 147–48; on the hippie movement, 299–300; impact of activism on, 3–4; impact on anthropology, 31–33, 375n17; on Indian-Black relations, 133–34, 144–45, 162, 171; on Indian-white relations, 15, 93, 149, 303; on leadership, 283; on legal representation, 324; objective of, 5, 57–58; organization of, 6–7; on post-World War II economy, 293–96; publication of, 5–6, 26; reactions to, 11–12, 207; in the Red Power Tetralogy, 7–8, 14; rejection of white values in, 302; reviews of, 2–3, 36, 48, 57, 185–86; significance of, 11–12, 43; slogan behind, 4–5; stereotypes addressed in, 48–49; termination analyzed in, 109–11, 113–14, 117–18, 258; on treaty violations, 68, 70, 84, 95–96; on tribalism, 234–36, 328; on tribal leadership, 265–67, 272; uncited references in, 44; VD's methodology, 49; on white colonization, 145–49

Dakota Sioux, 229–30
Dakota Texts (Deloria), 17
dances, 59, 194–95, 217, 226–27, 234, 235, 237, 240
Däniken, Erich Von, 31
Darwinian evolutionary theory, 31
Dawes, Henry L., 98
Dawes Act (1887). *See* General Allotment Act (1887)
Debo, Angie, 135
decolonization, 64, 131, 147–48
Delaney, James J., 117
Delano, Columbus, 223
A Delaware Indian Legend (Adams), 175–76

Delaware Treaty (1778), 81–83
Deloria, Barbara (née Sloat Eastburn; VD's mother), 16, 17
Deloria, Ella (VD's aunt), 17–18, 183, 188, 344n11
Deloria, Philip Joseph "Tipi Sapa" (VD's grandfather), 16, 17
Deloria, Sam (VD's brother), 17
Deloria, Vine Victor, Jr. (VD; Standing Rock Sioux): abandoning religious career, 19, 211, 242; academic career, 8–9, 15, 26, 135, 268; appointed NCAI executive director, 19–20; aversion to "intellectual" label, 29; awards received by, 13; changing relationship to the church, 35, 344n15; colonized thinking of, 148–49; congressional appearances of, 9, 12, 22–25, 110–11, 301, 319–20, 397n4; as "Coyote Old Man," 29; criticisms of writing style, 56–57, 142, 213, 279, 280, 352n48, 353n9; death of, 27; development of political agenda, 3, 21–27, 45; family background, 16–19; gender bias of, 270–71, 281, 295, 353n10; humor of, 186; in law school, 8–9, 15, 21, 25, 26–27, 212, 306, 394n82; legacy of, 1–2, 11–16, 27–45, 47, 334, 336–37; methodology of, 46, 49–50; as NCAI executive director, 14, 19–22, 41, 212, 282, 299, 345n17, 345n24, 378n41, 378n45, 381n75, 390n34, 394n82, 397n100, 402n39; Plains-centric biases of, 57, 214–15, 270–71; racism of, 50, 140–43; resigning from NCAI, 25–26; scholarly treatment of, 1–3, 29–45; seminary training, 19, 211–12; TV appearances, 340n8

Deloria, Vine Victor, Jr. (VD), works: "The Churches and Cultural Change," 139, 140; *Documents of American Indian Diplomacy,* 376n22; extent of publications, 12; "It Is a Good Day to Die," 211; *The Metaphysics of Modern Existence,* 31, 138, 215, 335, 394n76; *The Nations Within,* 36, 38, 54, 335, 392n59; "Non-Violence in American Society," 172–73; *Red Earth, White Lies,* 31, 216, 335–36, 348n68; "The Theological Dimension of the Indian Protest Movement," 139–40; *Of Utmost Good Faith,* 66–67, 226, 331–32, 348n70, 355n63. See also *Behind the Trail of Broken Treaties* (Deloria); *Custer Died for Your Sins* (Deloria); *God Is Red* (Deloria); *We Talk, You Listen* (Deloria)

Deloria, Vine Victor, Sr. (VD's father), 16, 17, 211, 243

DeMallie, Raymond, 183, 376n22

Democratic Party, 168–69

deMontigny, Lionel (Chippewa), 333

Denton, Winfield K., 23, 110

Department of Interior: bureaucratic nature of, 254; creation of, 357n87; Indian Bureau placed in, 79, 248; and trust obligations, 91; VD's proposed reforms for, 323–25. *See also* Bureau of Indian Affairs (BIA)

Descartes, René, 118

Destroying Dogma (Pavlik and Wildcat), 37–40, 42

Diamond, Tom, 308

The Dick Cavett Show, 340n8

Dixon, Joseph K., 183

Doctrine of Discovery, 50, 68, 70–76, 216, 222–23, 224–25

documentaries, 267–68, 391n47

Documents of American Indian Diplomacy (Deloria and DeMallie), 376n22

Domesday Survey, 118

drinking (stereotype), 192–94, 378n48, 378n51

Dumont, Robert, 160

Dunbar, Leslie, 27, 346n26, 368n5

Eastman, Charles A. (Sioux), 16, 52, 57, 101, 132, 176, 229, 231, 240, 295

Economic Development Administration, 253, 259, 262, 387n14

Economic Opportunity Act (1964), 24–25, 124

economy: corporate tribalism, 293–96; impact on social issues, 294; tribal financial independence, 156–57, 162; and tribalism, 328–29; and tribal self-determination, 300

education: bilingual education, 140; boarding schools, 167, 187; and budget restrictions, 258–59; and ethnicity, 138; and nationbuilding, 62; USS programs, 255–56. *See also* academic institutions

Eichmann in Jerusalem (Arendt), 108

Eisenhower, Dwight D., 120, 294

Elk, John, 87

Elk v. Wilkins (1884), 87

ethnic studies, 136, 138, 268, 288

Evans, J. Claude, 140

"Explo 72," 232

Fairbanks, Robert A., 72–73

Farb, Peter, 204–6

Federal Housing Authority, 259

federal Indian law and policy: anthropology's impact on, 186–87, 200–202, 205–6; bureaucratic nature of, 108–9; Christianity influencing, 222; during the colonial era, 74–76; cultural oppression integral to, 59, 195; Doctrine of Discovery in, 68, 70–71; General Allotment Act (1887), 87, 97–99, 147, 199–200, 214, 226, 357n90; Grant's Peace Policy, 223–24; and health care, 110–11; hypocrisies underlying, 52–54, 66–67; "Indian problem" myth informing, 55; and the Kennedy myth, 169–70; land allotments, 97–99; legal separatism, 166–67; during the removal era, 76–77, 94–95; reservation system created by, 60; social Darwinism driving, 199–200; and tribal self-governance, 13, 88–90; and tribes' political status, 92–93, 105, 107; Udall's omnibus bill, 21, 109–10, 153–54, 205; and unrecognized tribes, 308–11; urban Indians in, 316–18; and voting rights, 86–88. *See also* Bureau of Indian Affairs (BIA); Indian Reorganization Act (1934); termination policy; treaties

fee simple title, 98, 357n90

The Feminine Mystique (Friedan), 298–99

Field Museum, 180–81

Filmore, Carlos, 261

films, 267–68

Findley, Tim, 290

First Convocation of American Indian Scholars, 332–33

fishing and hunting rights, 26, 61, 62–63, 91, 93, 257, 380n70, 395n87

fish-ins (Pacific Northwest), 3, 20, 137, 285

Five Civilized Tribes, 184, 240

Fleming, Robert E., 177–78

"folk urban continuum," 245

Forbes, Jack (Powhatan-Lenape-Saponi), 143, 144

Forman, James, 138, 151

"Forman Manifesto," 138, 151

Fort Belknap Indian Reservation, 90

For This Land (Treat), 33–34

Fort Laramie Treaty (1868), 4–5, 151, 228, 229

Fortunate Eagle, Adam (Red Lake Ojibwe), 290, 340n8

Frank, Stannard, 378n41

Franklin, Benjamin, 268

Fraser, Donald M., 352n48

Friedan, Betty, 298–99

Friendship Press, 344n11

From the Deep Woods to Civilization (Eastman), 52, 176, 231

Gamble, James H., 124, 366n75

Gardner, John, 389n29

Garland, Colliflower v. (1965), 90

Garroutte, Eva Marie, 144

Garry, Leona (Coeur d'Alene), 21

General Allotment Act (1887), 87, 97–99, 147, 199–200, 214, 226, 357n90

Georgia, Worcester v. (1832), 76, 79

Ghost Dance, 226–27, 237

Gila River Indian community, 194

Glenwood (IA) excavation, 179

God Is Red (Deloria): "ancient astronaut" theory in, 31; Christianity critiqued in, 215–17, 218–20, 231–32, 240; civil rights movement portrayed in, 172; on colonization and exploitation, 216, 224; Dick Cavett mentioned in, 340n8; on "group identities," 244–45; historical context, 176–77; on Indian-white relations, 303; on land-religion

Indian Removal Act (1830), 93, 120, 147
Indian Reorganization Act (1934):
articulating political status of tribes,
92–93, 263; background of, 99–100;
Collier's initial draft, 100–101, 103–
4; criticism of, 99, 100–102; ending
land allotments, 90, 92, 99, 102–3;
impacts of, 67, 99, 102–5, 217, 271;
Indian-preference hiring, 249; *The
Nations Within* analyzing, 335;
opposition to, 103–5, 114, 117; passage of, 102; tribal councils under,
293; on tribal culture, 74, 103, 217;
tribal governments under, 38, 54,
59, 99, 102, 271, 392n59; on tribes
incorporating, 171, 361n28
Indian Resources Development Act
(1967), 21, 109–10, 153–54, 205
Indians and Anthropologists (Biolsi and
Zimmerman), 14, 31–33
Indians at Work (magazine), 67, 112
Indian Self-Determination and Education Assistance Act (1975), 9, 74, 259
Indians of All Tribes, 3, 9, 340n8. *See
also* Alcatraz Island occupation
(1969–71)
The Indian To-Day (Eastman), 132
Indian Trade and Intercourse Act
(1834), 96
Indian-white relations: and assimilation, 51–54, 144–45, 150; building
bridges in, 303–4; and Christianity,
139–40; and Collier's Indian congresses, 101–2; cultural differences,
162–63; historical colonization,
145–49; impact of mass media on,
266–68; and "Indian experts," 50–
51; and indigenous organizations,
60–61; and the Kennedy myth,
169–70; and modern Indigenous

traditions, 62–63; and paternalism,
55–56, 64; role of tribal governments in, 59–60; stereotypes,
48–49, 54–55, 58–59, 61–62, 85;
tribal approach to, 153, 245. *See also*
anthropology; federal Indian law
and policy; treaty making
individualism, 293, 294, 298
institutional review boards (IRBs),
182, 204
Inter Caetera bull, 224–25
Interreligious Foundation for Community Organizing (IFCO), 142–43
IRA (Indian Reorganization Act). *See*
Indian Reorganization Act (1934)
IRBs (institutional review boards),
182, 204
Iroquois Confederacy, 70, 87, 88, 268–69
Israel, 148–49
"It Is a Good Day to Die" (Deloria), 211

Jackson, Andrew, 77, 144
Jackson, Henry "Scoop," 124
Jemez Pueblo, 89, 104
Johnson, Clifton H., 344n15
Johnson, Ed, 345n20
Johnson, Lyndon B., 68, 136, 156, 253,
308, 313, 323, 352n4, 402n39
Johnson, Thomas, 75–76
Johnson v. M'Intosh (1823), 74, 75–76, 147
Jones, Nettie, 149
Jordan, Leonard B., 364n56
Jorgensen, Joseph G., 44
Josephy, Alvin, Jr., 4, 341n18, 341n19,
341n22, 374n1
Jourdain, Roger (Red Lake Ojibwe),
20, 203, 260–61, 264, 272, 314,
390n32
justice system: in *American Indians,
American Justice,* 335; common law

cases, 63; Congress limiting powers of tribal, 301; in the Indian Civil Rights Act, 300–302; and Indian land title, 77; Indigenous status in, 86–90; in original IRA draft, 100; state jurisdiction over tribes, 113; VD's development proposals, 24. *See also* federal Indian law and policy

Kastenmeier, Robert W., 352n48
Katzenbach, Nicholas, 294, 397n4
KBUN radio broadcast, 260–61, 390nn32–33
Kellogg, Laura Cornelius, 362n28
Kelly, Lawrence C., 136
Kennedy, Edward "Ted," 14, 373n80
Kennedy, John F., 70, 127, 169, 302, 323
Kennedy, Robert "Bobby," 127, 169–70, 302, 373n80
Kerner, Otto, Jr., 136
Kerner Commission, 136–37
Kickingbird, Kirke, 72, 353n13
Killbuck, John (Delaware), 81
King, Cecil, 32
King, Martin Luther, Jr., 58, 127, 152, 153, 159–60, 287, 289
kinship systems: compared to American corporations, 296; and group identity, 245; and homeland, 147, 219; and justice systems, 24; leadership in, 270; and urban-reservation relations, 313
Kinzua Dam, 70, 85, 125–26, 162
Klemesrud, Judy, 341n22
Knight, Gladys L., 138
Kohl, Bob, 260

Labor Department, 259
Lacey, John Fletcher, 84–85
La Farge, Oliver, 274–75

La Flesche, Francis, 188
Lake Mohonk Conference, 349n20
Lakota Sioux tribes, 62, 196–99
land: allotment policy, 84–85, 90, 97–99, 102–3, 226; ceded in treaties, 83–84; colonial conceptions of, 146–49, 216; conflicting approaches to use, 303; in the Doctrine of Discovery, 68, 71–72; ending of allotment policy, 92–93, 99; General Allotment Act (1887), 87, 97–99, 147, 199–200, 214, 226, 357n90; Indian land claims, 130, 150–51; Indian rights to, 76–77, 84; Indigenous relationship with, 30, 71–72, 147, 214–15, 217, 219–20, 237; in the IRA, 100; in the IRA original draft, 101; Israeli homeland analogy, 148–49; land title during colonial era, 74–76, 78–80; land title during removal era, 76–77; problem of Indian land heirship, 358n101; proposed reforms targeting, 106–7; race relations based on, 149; religious prejudice in seizures of, 70–71; rights of way through, 367n81; seized through coercion, 94–95, 147; seized through treaty violations, 70; and sovereignty, 42; Supreme Court rulings, 85, 352n5; tax exemption, 263, 396n87; white settler appropriation of, 196–98. *See also* treaties
Landsman, Gail, 32
Langer, William, 114, 115, 117
Larson, Sidner (Gros Ventre), 28
Lauriers, Françoise des "Saswe" (VD's great-grandfather), 16–17
Lawrence, Michael A., 40–41

Meeds, Lloyd, 2, 12, 319–20

melting pot myth, 165

Menominee Restoration Act (1973), 9, 12, 319–20

Menominee Termination Act, 123, 364nn53–54

Menominee tribe, 121–24, 365n59

Meriam, Lewis, 99

Meriam Report (1928), 99–100, 113, 200–201, 357n98

The Merv Griffin Show, 340n8

The Metaphysics of Modern Existence (Deloria), 31, 138, 215, 335, 394n76

Metcalf, Lee, 23, 24

Miles, Tiya, 349n9

militancy: of American colonization, 320; among urban Indians, 314, 318–20; in the civil rights movement, 138, 163; difference between nationalism and, 304; problems with use of violence, 321–22; and tribal leadership, 161–62. *See also* American Indian Movement (AIM); Black Power movement

Miller, A. L., 363n50

Miller, Frank C., 315

Mills, Billy (Lakota), 370n28

Mills, C. Wright, 294

Minnesota, 315

M'Intosh, Johnson v. (1823), 74, 75–76, 147

M'Intosh, William, 75–76

Mischief Makers (Jones), 149–50

missionaries: denominational competition among, 224, 230, 232–33, 246; hypocrisy of, 230–31; modern missionaries, 367n82; negative impacts of, 213, 229–34; objectives of, 221; opposition to Collier's reforms, 101; paternalism of, 56; positive role of, 237; presumed "expert" knowledge

of, 51; stereotyping Indians, 234; VD's critique of, 212–13, 229–34

Missionary Education Movement, 18, 344n11

Mission Indian Federation (MIF), 361n24

Moffett, Thomas C., 232

Mohawk, John C. (Seneca), 13

Momaday, N. Scott (Kiowa), 333

Mondale, Walter F., 136, 315

Montezuma, Carlos (Yavapai), 101, 361n27, 380n69

Mooney, James, 187

Moore, Paul, Jr., 155

Morgan, George, 81–82

Morgan, Lewis Henry, 97, 199, 224

Morris, George C., 363n48

Morris, Glenn T., 34–35, 42

Morton v. Mancari (1974), 249

movies, 267–68, 391n45, 391n48

MOWA Choctaws, 134

Mundt, Karl E., 106–7, 114

Murray, James E., 188

Myer, Dillon S., 118–19, 362n37, 362n39

NAGPRA (Native American Graves Protection and Repatriation Act), 32, 179

Nakai, Raymond (Navajo), 314

Nash, Philleo, 110, 186, 201, 206, 207, 258, 389n29

National Committee for Free Elections in Sunflower County (MS), 155–56

National Congress of American Indians (NCAI): and American Indians United, 326; appointment of VD as executive director, 19–20; challenges faced by, 20, 21, 25–26, 284–86, 345n24; executive committee of, 21, 345n17; factionalism

Nixon, Richard, 9, 68, 72, 86, 156, 168, 170, 248, 287, 302, 352n4, 366n77, 371n53

NIYC (National Indian Youth Council). *See* National Indian Youth Council (NIYC)

"Non-Violence in American Society" (Deloria), 172–73

North American Review, 128, 199–200

Northwest Ordinance (1787), 225

NTCA (National Tribal Chairman's Association), 291–92

Oakes, Richard (St. Regis Mohawk), 264, 289–90

Obama, Barack, 171

Occom, Samson (Mohegan), 3

Office of Economic Opportunity (OEO), 24–25, 259, 261, 274

Officer, James E., 185–86, 206–7

Of Utmost Good Faith (Deloria), 66–67, 226, 331–32, 348n70, 355n63

Oglala Sioux, 196–99

Ojibwe nations, 62, 234, 260–61, 390nn32–33

Oklahomans for Indian Opportunity, 280

O'Mahoney, Joseph C., 362n37

omnibus bill (Udall's; H.R. 10560), 21, 109–10, 153–54, 205

The Organization Man (Whyte), 294

Ortiz, Alfonso (San Juan Pueblo), 2, 14, 44, 57, 188, 206, 208–9, 214, 333

Osceola, Joe Dan (Seminole), 400n11

The Other America (Harrington), 6, 55, 202, 350n27

Paiute tribes, 121, 194, 205, 363n50, 381n75

paleontology, 31, 381n79

Palmieri, Victor H., 137

pan-Indianism, 309–11

Paredes, J. Anthony, 137

Parker, Arthur C. (Seneca), 350n24

Parker, Dorothy R., 188

Parker, Ely S. (Seneca), 223–24

paternalism, 55, 56, 64, 96, 113, 254

The Patriot Chiefs (Josephy), 4, 341n18, 374n1

Pavlik, Steve, 37

Paxton Boys Massacre (1763), 180

Peace Policy (1869), 223–24, 259

Pearson, Maria "Running Moccasins" (Yankton Sioux), 179

Pemberton, John de J., Jr., 155

"People's Park" protest, 289

Peroff, Nicholas C., 37

Peterson, Leslie D. "Les," 178, 374n10

Peterson, Nancy L., 105

peyote, 89, 214

The Peyote Road (Maroukis), 187

Philosophical Dictionary (Voltaire), 210

Piankashaw tribe, 75–76

Pickering, Timothy, 80

Pickering Treaty (1794), 70, 80, 85, 125–26, 169

Pine Ridge Reservation, 161, 196–99, 234

Playboy magazine, 298–99

"Pleistocene Extinction" theory, 205

plenary power, 85–86, 92, 395n87

point 4 program (BIA), 188–93, 275

political activism: communication techniques, 285–86; complex nature of, 172–73; direct action, 287, 319–20; as final option, 86; impact on *Custer*, 2, 3–4; increases in, 20; and national organizations, 325–26; sparked by termination, 126–28; VD's impact on, 34. *See also* civil rights movement; Indian protest movement

Poor People's Campaign, 58, 133, 153, 154–55, 157, 158, 159–60, 165, 318

poverty: conferences addressing, 278–80, 393n75; Harrington's critique of, 343n31; Poor People's Campaign, 58, 133, 153, 154–55, 157, 158, 159–60, 165, 318; power movements' common interest in, 165, 228; in the reservation system, 95, 194–96, 390n33; romanticized in documentaries, 267–68; stereotypes of, 194–96, 260–61, 390n33; War on Poverty programs, 9, 63, 124, 156, 166, 278–80, 293, 314, 393n75, 402n39

Powell, Peter, 183, 376n22

power management category, 108

Pratt, Richard, 200

Price, Hiram, 225

Price, John A., 311

Progressive Era, 87, 167, 266

The Protestant Ethic and the Spirit of Capitalism (Weber), 108

protest movement. *See* Indian protest movement

Prucha, Francis Paul, 2, 69, 76–77, 81–82, 95, 354n29

Public Health Service, 111, 120, 259

Public Law 280, 55, 95, 110, 113, 166

Pueblo communities, 62, 89, 100

Pueblo Lands Act (1924), 100

Pyramid Lake Paiute tribe, 194, 205, 381n75

race relations: Black-white paradigm, 134–35, 138–39, 331; and "blood quantum," 143–44; Indians as "Others," 134; misunderstandings straining, 141–42; and the political divide, 168–69; role of science in,

167; VD's views of, 50; and weakening white mythology, 173. *See also* Black-white relations; Indian-Black relations; Indian-white relations

racism: faced by Indian clergy, 242; in Indian-Black relations, 141–43; riots caused by, 136–37; of VD, 50, 140–43; and welfare, 168

"radical doubt" method, 118

Radicals in Their Own Time (Lawrence), 40–41

Ragsdale, Fred, 72, 353n13, 355n57

Ray, Robert D., 179

Real Indians (Garroutte), 144

Reber, John, 187

Red Earth, White Lies (Deloria), 31, 216, 335–36, 348n68

Redfield, Robert, 245

Red Lake Ojibwes, 62, 260–61, 390nn32–33

The Red Man in the New World Drama (Wise), 20, 67, 133, 332

Red Power movement: and the AIM, 35; distinguishing features of, 228; growing tension in, 330; in *The New Indians*, 1, 22; and the NIYC, 35; tribalism's role in, 71; VD's role in, 342n26. *See also* Indian protest movement

Red Power Tetralogy: organization of, 46; political and historical context of, 14–16, 45–46; role *Custer* played in, 7–8; scholarly criticisms of, 44; significance of, 43; works comprising, 14–15; works following, 334–36. See also *Behind the Trail of Broken Treaties* (Deloria); *Custer Died for Your Sins* (Deloria); *God Is Red* (Deloria); *We Talk, You Listen* (Deloria)

Reed, Stanley F., 352n5

religion (Indigenous practices and beliefs): under the 1934 IRA, 101, 103, 235; compared to Christianity, 39, 71–72, 213–14, 217–20; creation stories, 147, 215, 217, 219; criminalization of, 225; decriminalizing of, 235; "God is Red" slogan, 246; hybridization of, 237; impact of colonization on, 222; Indian Bureau suppressing, 225–27; and the Indian protest movement, 227–29; land-based nonlinear worldview of, 30, 71–72, 214–15, 219–20; missionaries disparaging, 221; protections of rights, 237; and religious freedom, 236–37; religious persecution, 146; resurgence of, 234–39, 238–39, 246–47; value of sharing in, 243–45

religion (Western): and Euro-American colonization, 146–47; and the Indian protest movement, 39, 227–29; religious persecution, 146; scholarly reaction to VD's commentary on, 33–34; Voltaire's analysis of, 210. *See also* Christianity; missionaries

religious freedom, 222, 236–37

relocation programs, 311, 325, 330

Removal Era, 76–77, 94–95

Representations of the Intellectual (Said), 29

Republican Party, 168–69

reservations: bilingual education on, 140; creation of, 60; denominations competing over, 224, 230; development improvements, 259–61; economic development programs, 188–90; Ghost dance, 227; governance traditions, 271–73; governed by churches, 53; impact of assimilation on, 53–54; impact of disenfranchisement on, 87–88; impact of electronic media on, 297–98; impact of missionaries on, 229–34; Indian Bureau's civilization experiments on, 167; and land cessions, 170; private sector paternalism in, 56; relationship with urban Indians, 312, 313, 326–27; relations with anthropological researchers, 203–4; Senate committee tour of, 100; telephones on, 243–44. *See also* leadership (tribal); termination policy; tribes (Indigenous nations)

Rhoads, Charles, 99

Riding In, James (Pawnee), 28

"Riot Report" (National Advisory Commission on Civil Disorders), 136–37

riots, 136–37, 158, 159, 163, 372n57

Roemer, Kenneth M., 48

Rogers, Will, 266

Rosebud Reservation, 234

Rosenthal, Elizabeth Clark, 388n22

Roszak, Theodore, 299

Running Moccasins (Yankton Sioux), 179

sacred bundles, 236

Said, Edward, 29

Salt River Pima-Maricopa Indian Community, 261

Sanchez, Barbara Deloria (VD's sister), 17

Sand Creek Massacre (1864), 223, 226

Saswe (VD's great-grandfather), 16–17

Scholder, Fritz (Luiseño), 333

Schreiner, Imelda N., 20, 345n20

Schwabe, George B., 118–19

science, 335–36

The Search for an American Indian Identity (Hertzberg), 309–10

self-determination: based on tribalism, 35, 42, 158; Collier's legacy in,
103–4; as expression of sovereignty,
13; and federal support reform,
253; future of, 305, 327–30, 332–
34; group self-awareness, 278; as
a historical movement, 248–49;
impact of the 1934 IRA on, 67;
Israeli homeland analogy, 148–49;
Nixon's message on, 72, 366n77,
371n53; nonprofit model for, 300;
principles underlying, 199, 247;
proposed political path toward, 15,
306–7; in the protest movements,
153–54, 157, 161–62, 165; and
repatriation, 181; role of *Custer* in,
7; role of education in, 302; role of
tribal governments, 59–60; through
financial reform, 24, 262; through
religious reforms, 240–41; VD
initiating discourse on, 14–15; VD's
impact on, 130–31
self-governance: in the 1934 IRA,
102, 104–5, 392n59; bureaucracy
blocking, 257–58; in federal Indian
policy and law, 13, 88–90; growth
in, 63; impact of termination
policy on, 112; and the Meriam
Report, 357n98; needed congressional support for, 263–64; needed
improvements in, 128; in the original IRA draft, 101; of reservations,
170; sovereignty needed, 395n87.
See also governments (tribal);
self-determination
Senate: Civil Service Committee,
114–16; Committee on Interior
and Insular Affairs, 362n37; and
the "Indian problem," 55; Interior
Committee, 113–14, 120; and land

allotments, 97–99; role in Indian
affairs, 254; Subcommittee on
Constitutional Rights, 23–24, 301;
Subcommittee on Employment,
Manpower, and Poverty, 24; Sub-
committee on Indian Affairs, 23,
121, 122, 124. *See also* Congress
Seneca Nation, 70, 125–26
separatism, 163–64, 166–67, 170–71,
372n73
Shoshone Tribe, United States v. (1938), 77
Shriver, R. Sargent, 403n54
Simmons, Leo W., 342n27
Sioux Treaty (1868), 4–5, 151, 228, 229
Sitting Bull, 352n49
"638 contracts," 262
Sixkiller, Jesse (Cherokee), 326
slavery, 149, 382n18
Smith, Ira F., III, 179–80
Smith, Linda Tuhiwai, 377n33
Smith, Sherry L., 142
Smith, Tommie, 145
Smithsonian Institution, 200–201
social Darwinism, 199–200, 204–5
social science: attitudes toward Indigenous people in, 176–81; exceptions
to VD's generalizations, 187; impact
of VD's criticism on, 14, 32; impact
on federal Indian policy, 186–87;
Indian intellectual traditions in, 175–
76; lack of tribal input, 201–2; and
Native American studies, 208; pan-
Indianism theories of, 309–10; racial
conceptions, 167; social Darwinism
driving, 97, 199–200, 204–5. *See
also* anthropology; archeology
society (white American): decline of
white "American Dream" ideal,
296–97; electronic media's impact
on, 297–98; polarization of, 139;

tribalism as solution to, 152–53, 294–95, 298–300, 320–21
The Soul of the Indian (Eastman), 229, 240, 295
Southern Christian Leadership Conference (SCLC), 159–60, 304
Southern Indian Movement, 50, 137, 310–11
sovereignty: acknowledged in federal law, 104, 395n87; activism addressing, 25; cultural sovereignty, 167; diminished status of, 128, 273; impact of the 1934 IRA on, 67; independence implicit in, 63–64, 77–78; and the Indian Civil Rights Act, 301; Israeli homeland analogy, 148–49; needed congressional support for, 263–64; plenary power violating, 85–86; principles underlying, 247; relation to self-determination, 13; in treaty making, 3, 77–78, 83, 263
Spang, Alonzo T., 348n1
Speaking of Indians (Deloria), 17–18
Spellman, Francis, 220
Spotted Eagle, Faith (Yankton Sioux), 27
Stark, Heidi Kiiwetinepinesiik, 249, 253, 387n2
Staubach, Roger, 232
Steinem, Gloria, 299
Steiner, Stan, 1, 4, 6, 21–22, 206, 210
stereotypes: anthropology's mythical Indian, 186–87; belied by Indigenous peoples, 61–62; *Custer* as response to, 5; "drunken Indian" myth, 192–94; as a health issue, 348n1; held by missionaries, 234; of "hoarded wealth," 195–96, 379n54; impact of mass media on, 266–68, 297; impact on federal policy, 93, 168; of Indian poverty, 260–61; "Indian problem" myth, 48–49; in movies and film, 267–68; and "racial erasure," 54–55; regarding Indian cultures, 58–59; regarding trust obligations, 168, 389n29, 395n87; "vanishing Indian" myth, 55; VD's method of addressing, 49–50, 127–28

Stevens, Ernie (Oneida), 393n61
Stevenson, Matilda Coxe, 183
Stewart, Omer C., 13–14, 187, 206, 207
St. Paul's Mission (Amherst), 368n4
Sun Dance, 59, 217, 234, 235, 240
Supreme Court: affirming tribal independence, 88–90; allowing for habeas corpus, 90; on BIA hiring practices, 249; *Colliflower v. Garland,* 90; *Elk v. Wilkins,* 87; *Holden v. Joy,* 77; on Indian land rights, 74, 75–76, 77, 85, 147; *Johnson v. M'Intosh,* 74, 75–76, 147; *Morton v. Mancari,* 249; *Native American Church v. Navajo Tribal Council,* 89, 92; *Talton v. Mayes,* 88–89; *Tee-Hit-ton Indians v. United States,* 69, 352n5; *Toledo v. Pueblo De Jemez,* 104; on tribal sovereignty, 104; on tribes' political status, 76, 79, 89, 92; *Worcester v. Georgia,* 76, 79
Survival of American Indians Association (SAIA), 60–61
Susquehannock tribe, 179–80
Sweet Medicine (Powell), 376n22

Talamantez, Inés (Apache/Chicana), 34–35, 36, 42
Talayesva, Don C., 342n27
Talton, Bob (Cherokee), 88
Talton v. Mayes (1896), 88–89
Tax, Sol, 189, 377n37
taxation, 129, 395n87

treaty making: during the colonial era, 78–84; Congress ending, 77–78, 97, 224; early attempts at, 353n7; exploitation through, 69; and "paper chiefs," 392n56; proposals to reinstate, 72–73, 86, 130; during the removal era, 76–77; sovereignty inherent in, 67–68, 77–78, 80, 83, 263; tensions during, 356n83. *See also* federal Indian law and policy

Treaty of Medicine Creek (1854), 91

Treaty of Tordesillas (1494), 216, 225

tribalism: anthropology's impact on, 191–92; as basis of self-determination, 35, 42, 153–54; Black nationalism as form of, 154, 164; clarification of, 174; communal sharing in, 244–45; compared to Christianity, 244; in corporate culture, 293–96; criticized as idealistic, 136; and cultural revitalization, 42, 158–59; and the economy, 328–29; future of, 327–30; in the hippie movement, 299–300; importance to power movements, 71, 138, 163–65, 170–71, 228; of *Playboy* magazine, 298–99; as solution to social issues, 152–53, 159, 165–66, 173–74, 298–300, 321; VD abandoning, 171, 172; VD's notion of, 368n5

tribal religions. *See* religion (Indigenous practices and beliefs)

Tribal Secrets (Warrior), 29–30

tribes (Indigenous nations): as corporate entities, 71, 293, 361n28; distinctiveness of, 132; economic development, 156–57, 162, 192, 194, 293, 300, 328–29; federal recognition of, 249; Israeli homeland analogy, 148–49; legal status of, 333; misconceptions of, 61–62; modern traditions emerging in, 62–63; political status as dependent wards, 79–80, 85, 87–88, 91–92, 105, 115; political status as domestic dependent nations, 22, 76, 105; political status as higher than states, 89–90, 91–92, 253; political status as sovereign nations, 67–68, 72, 77–78, 80–84, 87–88, 107; political status during colonial era, 74–78, 80–84; political status under the IRA, 263; protection of rights, 237; relations between churches and, 139–40; relationship to land, 71–72; relations with anthropological researchers, 183, 203–4; relation to U.S. Constitution, 26, 71, 92; resilience of, 54, 59, 62, 305, 330; seeking federal recognition, 308–11, 400n3; in social science studies of, 201–2; traditional tribal names, 244–45; VD's vision for, 92, 328–30. *See also* termination policy; treaties

Ture, Kwame (Stokely Carmichael), 154, 164–65, 391n40

"Twenty-Point Position Paper," 72, 73, 86, 103, 324

Udall, Stewart, 21, 109–10, 153–54, 204–5, 259, 261, 389n29

United Fund, 300

United Nations, 148, 385nn63–64

United Scholarship Service (USS) program, 19, 255–56, 273, 281, 329, 344n16, 388n22

United States-Dakota War (1862), 223

United States v. Shoshone Tribe (1938), 77

universities. *See* academic institutions

**In the New Visions in Native American
and Indigenous Studies series**

To order or obtain more information on these or other University of Nebraska
Press titles, visit nebraskapress.unl.edu.